1982

Growing Up Free

Growing Up Free

Raising Your Child in the 80's

Letty Cottin Pogrebin

McGRAW-HILL BOOK COMPANY

New York   St. Louis   San Francisco

Mexico   Toronto   Hamburg

1 2 3 4 5 6 7 8 9   DODO   8 7 6 5 4 3 2 1 0

LIBRARY OF CONGRESS CATALOGING IN PUBLICATION DATA

Pogrebin, Letty Cottin.
Growing up Free.
Includes bibliographical references and index.
1. Children—Management.   2. Sex Role.
3. Sexism.   I. Title.
HQ772.P58   649'.1   80-13054
ISBN 0-07-050370-2

Book design by Roberta Rezk

To Esther Pogrebin
for raising her son to be the man he is

To Abigail, Robin, and David
for the fine people they are becoming and

To Bert
for always

Contents

Author's Note

There are several things to keep in mind while reading this book:

• The numbered footnotes occuring throughout the text will refer you to the *Notes* section beginning on page 549. Each note either provides the source of the reference—whether a book, article, individual, or research study—or furnishes a list of additional resources, a kind of bibliography for those wishing to pursue a particular subject further. However, because the notes contain no ancillary commentary, the casual reader need not interrupt the book's flow to turn to the *Notes* section unless a particular reference or subject area is of special interest.

• The use of the pronoun "he" to denote "a person" in the generic sense is one of my basic objections to common language usage. (See Chapter 24 for a full discussion of language as an exclusionary tool of male supremacy.) Nonsexist pronouns (you, they, she or he, his or hers) appear in my text in all cases except where direct quotes taken from other writers include the generic "he." When the writer's sentence structure does not allow for bracketed alteration (as in "When a child is alone, he [or she] may be frightened") without imposing great awkwardness upon the syntax, I have left the male pronoun as is.

• The book's mix of anecdote, theory, and research data is my conscious attempt to bridge the often arbitrary gap between "popular" and "academic" writing. I believe general readers need to know about new lines of academic inquiry that may affect their attitudes and behavior, and that nothing is "dull" unless language makes it so. Similarly, I think scholars and clinicians need to stay in touch with the sound and texture of "real life," and that personal experience and idiosyncratic individual solutions to child-rearing problems have the kind of overruling validity that the sound of a heartbeat has when the electrocardiograph shows nothing.

• Certain words must, of necessity, recur throughout this book—words such as "sexism," "patriarchy," "feminism," "masculinity" and "femininity" and "nonsexist childrearing." Rather than let these words glance off the brain because of years of media misuse and exhortive rhetoric, let me define at the outset what I mean when I use them:

Sexism is bias, prejudice, or discrimination based on gender. Whereas a racist has preconceptions about people of color (usually negative generalizations regarding their inferiority to whites), a sexist has preconceptions about female human beings—usually negative generalizations regarding their inferiority to male human beings. Because sexism, like racism, is a deeply entrenched, often unconscious cultural attitude, many of us are unaware that we may be classifying someone's temperament, capabilities, or interests according to stereotyped expectations of what women and men or girls and boys are like.

Patriarchy, strictly speaking, is a social organization headed by the father and recognizing the male line of descent. In the larger political sense—that is, wherever *power relationships* are involved—patriarchy is any system that runs on hierarchical principles with the "top man" invested with absolute power over those "under" him. Father is considered the "head of the house"; he "wears the pants in the family," meaning he is the final word on important matters, the keeper of the family funds, and the parent whose acknowledged paternity confers "legitimacy" upon a child. Father passes the family name, business, and/or social legacy on to the sons. This patriarchy, this sexual class system, is the model for all other exploitative relationships, all other systems that take for granted vast disparities of power and privilege.[1]

Patriarchal organization of more grandiose dimensions is still the rule in governments and corporations, school systems and meeting rooms all over this country.

In a nonsexist society, home community, or what have you,

people would eschew power relationships based solely on the accident of gender and would organize themselves according to more functional, human divisions of labor.

"Femininity" and *"masculinity"* do not exist for me. They are fictions invented to coerce us into sex role behavior. They have no objective meaning. Each person's definition of these words is different, and most definitions are ludicrous: is "femininity" long fingernails, a high-pitched voice, a demure look? Then who is "feminine"—Barbra Streisand or Lauren Bacall? What's "masculinity" if both John Wayne and Al Pacino are supposed to have it? Throughout this book, you will find those words in quotation marks as a reminder that they are a false construct and not factual description. Someone female is feminine and someone male is masculine and all else is propaganda.

Feminism is an ideological commitment to the legal, economic, and social equality of the sexes. It does not seek to replace male supremacy with female supremacy or patriarchy with matriarchy. Rather, a *feminist* is any person, female or male, who envisions and works toward equal rights, opportunity, and human dignity.

Nonsexist childrearing is a commitment by a parent or other caring adult to helping children be free of sex role constraints, free of patriarchal predesination, and free to discover the very best in themselves.

Author's Acknowledgments

In addition to my family, *Suzanne Levine* was always there, understanding, cheering me on, letting me off the hook, being the first reader of this manuscript not related by blood, and always contributing energy and insight and love.

Wendy Weil, my literary agent, who never gave up on me or this seemingly endless project, has remained the calm and admiring support every author dreams about.

My colleagues at *Ms.* magazine, especially *Pat Carbine, Joanne Edgar, Robin Morgan, Gloria Steinem,* and *Mary Thom*, motivated me, helped me, kept me laughing through the struggle, and believed in this book enough to let me leave them for two years—without guilt.

Evelyn Israel, my indefatigable research assistant, somehow managed to retrieve any journal from obscurity, and never complained about my bizarre means of communicating assignments to her: her expertise was enhanced by her feminism.

For putting her magical computer to work on my behalf, I thank *Cindi Carbine*, without whom the research on this book would have taken another eight years, and the Social Sciences Information Utilization Laboratory of the *University of Pittsburgh*, whose data banks Cindi used.

I am grateful to the *MacDowell Colony* in Peterborough, New Hampshire, for affording me the precious solitude of Watson studio during December 1979, for having bucolic woods and trails where one can walk and think, for having a staff dedicated to the needs of writers and artists, and for existing at all.

Others who deserve acknowledgment for their kindness and help are Dr. Gloria Freidman, Dr. Joseph Pleck, Dr. Robert Brannon, the late Dr. Marcia Guttentag, Dr. Judith Minton, my editor, Gladys Carr, and her associate editor, Gail Greene.

I
Motives and Myths

1
A Funny Thing Happened
on the Way to the Typewriter

I came to feminism at the beginning of the seventies in a series of blinding, never-turn-back flashes of perception. I suddenly saw all the sexism in my life and my world. I went the now-familiar route: self-questioning, discussions with my husband, a career change, women's organizations and demonstrations, and an intensive two or three years in a consciousness-raising group.

In 1971, however, three developments fortunately dovetailed to expand my view beyond myself. First, I began writing for the *Ladies' Home Journal,* a column on "The Working Woman," which required widespread research and interviews.

Secondly, in July 1971, I went to Washington, D.C., to join in the founding of the National Women's Political Caucus. And, thirdly, in the fall of 1971, I became a founding editor of *Ms.* magazine and was given my first assignment: an article on nonsexist childrearing.

The assignment was mine by default: I was the only one at the editorial meeting who had children. The others simply assumed that my husband and I had applied a feminist ideology to rearing our twin daughters, Abigail and Robin, who were six at the time, and our three-year-old son, David. But while Bert and I had altered our behavior within our marriage, argued endlessly about sex roles, and talked and read together to sort out the ramifications of feminism, we had not consciously passed any of it on to our children. Obviously, we had skipped a vital beat.

I hadn't given a thought to the next generation in my writing and activism, either; we grownups had enough trouble with our struggle for the Equal Rights Amendment and reproductive freedom, or against job discrimination and other economic inequities.

What the *Ms.* article assignment did for me was more than

add a new item to that list of concerns. It set off shock waves that changed my life and the lives of my children.

I began by asking myself the questions I would ultimately ask experts, other parents, and friends—questions that would goad me for the next eight years:

How can a parent counter the omnipresent sex bias in the culture-at-large? What is the difference between gender identity and sex-role identity? Can a child's developing sexuality possibly be affected by whether or not its father does the dishes or its mother drives a truck? How relevant to a child's self-image is the dynamic of the parents' marriage or of the single parent's attitude toward the opposite sex? Are the sexes really "opposite" or have we been brainwashed into believing in artificial sex dichotomies that serve the status quo?

What are the quantifiable differences between females and males (such as hormones and musculature), and how much do these differences predestine children? On the other hand, how many of those observed differences are the result of cultural conditioning? Is it moral for a parent to "tamper" with socially acceptable norms of female or male behavior? Will we risk our children's becoming social outcasts among their peers?

Is it enough merely to expose children to all options—in play, toys, hobbies, playmates, educational choices, dress, and behavioral style—regardless of what is considered "sex-appropriate"? Or must parents verbalize and propagandize to make a dent that society cannot knock right out of the child? Is it possible, or desirable, to spare our children the disappointments, exclusions, and identity crises that we have had to grapple with as adults? How *does* one help a child to grow up free, day by day, year by year, without imposing a new set of do's and don'ts to replace the "boys do" and "girls don't" doctrine of the past?

What is nonsexist childrearing and how does it work? Has anyone practiced it successfully? Can I?

Early in the research and writing of the *Ms.* article, I learned that there was no formal academic discipline or psychological subspecialty called "nonsexist childrearing." A few psychologists and educators were aware of the impact of the Women's Movement on families, but for the most part social scientists had limited themselves to narrow research investigations. I found, for example, longitudinal studies on the effect of father absence on young males, and dissertations on the aspirations of college women who had been raised by mothers who worked part-time, but no general Spock-type guidebooks for parents who might earnestly be trying to raise a free child in a sexist society.

Since research had turned up little that was populist and practicable, I turned to feminist mothers. "How are you translating your feminism into a new style of childrearing?" I asked.

Surprisingly, instead of success stories or how-to formulas, my interview subjects expressed frustration and pleaded for advice:

"I've been a working physicist throughout my daughter's life. With a mother like me, why does she think she can be a nurse but not a doctor?"

"What do you do when your husband pressures your son to defend himself 'like a man' and you know the kid is a sensitive, noncombatant little person?"

"I'm the clean-scrubbed blue jeans type and I've always felt good about my natural self. So how come my teenaged daughter is wearing gold lamé and blue eyeliner and saving up for a nose job?"

"When my son's friends ridicule him for playing with dolls, do I do more damage by supporting his choice, or should I buy him an Erector set?"

Hundreds of such questions were added to my own list. It occurred to me that if feminist mothers were actively seeking guidance and not finding it, traditional parents were certainly unlikely to stumble upon enlightenment.

I began to worry about all of our children. In the midst of this twentieth-century feminist revolution, I worried about new generations of human beings who were still being tracked: little "ladies," future housewives and mothers, polite and pretty sex objects in one line; little "gentlemen," tough and brave heroes, future soldiers and rulers in another line. Both ruts. Both lines marching relentlessly toward conformity; both impatient with wanderers, deviates, or explorers who might imagine a new path or venture to the "opposite" line. And I worried about young people in disrupted environments where poverty and neglect crush self-esteem, and where sex-linked ideals of the beauty queen and boxing champ may be the only routes of escape. I thought too about the children of well-meaning feminist parents who felt they were losing the battle against a powerful and stultifying culture. And finally, I thought about my own children, whom I was beginning to observe through a clearer lens.

In watching them, I saw myself.

One day, I brought home a miniature basketball hoop with a light, spongy ball. As I affixed the hoop to the closet door in my son's room, my husband stopped me.

"Why in the world are you putting that up in David's room?" Bert asked. "He's three years old and barely three feet tall. Besides, the girls are much better athletes."

We moved the basketball set to Robin and Abigail's room while I bemoaned all the sex-role connected decisions—such as basketball-equals-boy—that I must have been making since our children's births. That week alone, I remembered giving comb-and-mirror sets as Halloween party favors to girls, and matchbox cars to the boy guests. And not twenty minutes before the basketball hoop incident, I'd praised one of my daughters for her neatness and my son for his block structure.

Bert reported his sins: One day in the car with all three children, he'd found himself exclaiming, "Hey, David, look at that big crane!"—even though Robin and Abigail were also in the back seat gawking at the impressive machine.

Within a day or two, I heard one of my children refer to the hammer and screwdriver as "Daddy's tools," despite the fact that I am the fixer of the household at least as often as is Bert. And then I listened in awe as Robin described to her brother the line of succession in our family, which I had until then imagined to be sublimely nonhierarchical: "When Daddy isn't home, Mommy is in charge and when Mommy isn't home, the girls are in charge, and if nobody's here, David, you're in charge."

David's answer stunned me completely. "Oohh, no," he said in an absurdly confident baby voice. "When Daddy isn't home I'm in charge because then I'm the man of the house."

Where did he get *that?* Was it possible that the world had already initiated this toddler into the rights and rites of patriarchy? Had some invisible force reached into our house to devalue female human beings when I wasn't looking? Or had Bert and I transmitted the values on which we ourselves were weaned rather than those in which we believed?

Because I was the one whose consciousness was supposed to be the highest in the house, all these observations struck me like blows. I saw myself as a cliché—a feminist counterpart of the psychiatrist who purports to "cure" a vast clientele while rearing neurotic children of her own. Surely I was an inauthentic social reformer if I hadn't even managed to set things right in my own life with my own children.

Despite these bouts of self-flagellation, I went ahead and wrote the article on nonsexist childrearing, in which I emphasized concrete suggestions for role relaxation, and rethinking children's rooms, toys, books, and school curricula. But I knew I hadn't come to grips with all the "whys" and "what ifs" that muddled my brain. It would take a book to do the job right.

I began the research phase by devouring works on the psychology of children, books and studies on child development, sex role socialization, motherhood, fatherhood, the educational system, the origin and dynamics of family life, the politics of sex. I plowed through obscure journals to learn about cross-cultural comparisons of sex-role behavior, about hormones and genes, right and left brain hemispheres, homosexuality and heterosexuality, and conventional methods of measuring "masculinity" and "femininity."

Although not trained as a social scientist, I was determined to distill from each discipline, as well as from "ordinary" people, all that might be considered relevant to sex differences, sex role development, and nonsexist alternatives to conventional childrearing.

I attended seminars; interviewed professors and psychologists; enrolled in a teacher-training course on sexism in education; placed a classified ad soliciting personal anecdotes from parents and teachers across the nation; sat for hours observing in classrooms and day-care centers and playgrounds; and took notes on the conversations of children from two-year-olds to teenagers.

In order to anchor my thoughts in a larger context, I also "read into" the areas of economics, linguistics, children's legal rights, divorce, media, population, and philosophy. Every specialty seemed to have trivial and cosmic implications for my subject. For more than five years, I was hooked on research.

During those years as an "autodidact," I also tried to effect change. I worked with Marlo Thomas on *Free to Be, You and Me*, a record, book, and television special that brought nonsexist songs and stories into millions of homes and schools. As editor of the "Stories for Free Children" section of *Ms.* magazine, I kept abreast of new nonsexist books published for young readers. I tested thousands of playthings and games in order to write my annual review of "Toys for Free Children" to help guide parents in their holiday gift-giving.

As a consultant on a nonsexist day-care curriculum, as advisor on a film project on nontraditional occupations, as a speaker at several state teachers' conventions, and as a member of a commission charged with eliminating sex bias from the New York City public schools, I began to feel a growing confidence in my re-vision of childhood. I could see what was wrong and how it might be made right. I became more and more convinced that childhood must be changed. For the next three years, I put those convictions on paper in the words you are now reading.

Thus, from one magazine assignment grew an obsession— eight years of study, self-appraisal, and writing. This book does not have all the answers, but I think it asks most of the right questions. There are loose ends here that you will have to tie together to fit your needs and your children's. The radical will not find in this book any futuristic schemes for abolishing childhood or "the family," or for cultivating genderless offspring. Conversely, the traditionalist will quickly discover that I consider no childrearing expert or principle sacred if he, she or it tramples on the uniqueness of any girl or boy.

My bias is simply pro-child. My intention is to question everything we do with, to, for, and around children—our speaking habits, living styles, adult relationships, household chores, academic standards and our way of dealing with punishment, privilege, religion, television, sex, money, and love.

At this point in history, we cannot rear our children in a world free of sexism. But we can try our best to rear free children at the same time as we work to change the world.

Our children cannot wait for the revolution.

2
Girls and Boys:
What's the Difference?

The most important message of this book can be put in a single sentence:

Nonsexist childrearing is good for your child.

Behind all the whys, whats, and how-to's, there is that one simple glowing assertion. Moreover, nonsexist, role-free childrearing is also easier for *you.* As a way of approaching all the experiences and challenges of parenthood, this method above all is informed by common sense, logic, and love.

It doesn't tell a child "You must"; it says, "You may."

It doesn't enforce sameness (the "unisex" bugaboo); it recognizes, encourages, and respects differences—the thousands of individual differences that make your child unique.

Instead of dividing human experience in half, locking each child in the prison of either "masculine" or "feminine" correctness, and creating two separate definitions of human integrity, the nonsexist parent celebrates the *full* humanity of each girl or boy.

Very nice, you say. But it sounds too idealistic, too "feminist," maybe even dangerous. Who knows what would happen if we tampered with children's sexual identities. Besides, you and I were raised traditionally and give or take a few psychic struggles, we turned out all right. It's one thing to raise one's consciousness as an adult, but where children are concerned, don't we have to respect the *real* differences between the sexes; the "God-given" differences so basic to human life?

How can one dismiss the two distinct sexual essences that are distilled in every school of human thought: anthropology's hunter and childbearer, philosophy's masculine and feminine principles, religion's Man and Helpmeet, psychology's Oedipus Complex and

Penis Envy, not to mention such age-old sexual dichotomies as carnal/spiritual, Science/Mysticism, and Yin/Yang?

And what about the polarities that inspire art and passion? Soft/strong in the poet's sonnet, light/dark in the painter's portrait, subject/object in the lover's pursuit—each seems to borrow its aesthetic tension from the original attracting "opposites," male and female.

Whether or not such expressions are the cause or the effect of sex differences, do we really want to live without them? Maybe the French are right: *Vive la différence.* So why not leave well enough alone?

Because it isn't well enough or good enough. In fact, the cult of sex differences hurts both sexes. It creates a gender caste system with reasoning that leaps from

the two sexes are different,

to

the two sexes are opposites,

to

one sex is better than the other.

Differences and "opposites" seem to cry out for hierarchical evaluation, which is where the trouble starts. When Dr. Samuel Johnson was asked who is more intelligent, men or women, he replied, "Which man and which woman?" But that respect for human individuality has been rare through the centuries. Most people find it easier to generalize, to earmark group traits and make sure everyone acts accordingly.

By instructing a child to *act* like a girl or *act* like a boy, the cult of sex differences says "Conform," "Pretend," "Act"; it does not say "Be your best self." It makes children imposters within their own sex and strangers to their "opposites." It decrees a half-life for a girl and a half-life for a boy. In short, the cult of sex differences cheats children.

But outraged proclamations will not persuade those with a lingering trust in the "natural order of things." So let us consider the question of sex differences—which of them are indisputable, variable, debatable, or untrue; then perhaps we can reach agreement that sex differences matter for sex and not much else.[1]

BIOLOGICAL SEX DIFFERENCES

Children are taught to be "feminine" or "masculine," but they are born female or male.

For the first six weeks after conception, "Nature's first choice is to make Eve."[2] Unless a male hormonal mix changes its course, the embryo will develop into a female. All babies have the same sex hormones; only the proportions of the mixture differ. In a boy, androgens are predominant over estrogens, and in a girl, estrogens are predominant over androgens.

In order to be born male, an embryo must inherit "XY" sex chromosomes, an "X" from its mother and a "Y" from its father. After six weeks, the "XY" chromosomes send a message to the gonadal tissue to develop into testes, which manufacture the male hormonal mix, which differentiates the anatomical and reproductive structures of a male.

In order to be born female, an embryo must inherit "XX" sex chromosomes, one "X" each from its mother and its father. After twelve weeks (in the absence of a "Y") the "XX" chromosomes send a message to the embryo's gonadal tissues to develop into ovaries and to differentiate the female anatomical and reproductive structures.

Thus, sex difference #1: *A normal boy baby has a penis, scrotum and testicles, and a normal girl baby has a clitoris, vagina, ovaries, and uterus.*

In adolescence, a second burst of hormones goes to work on the organism. In a boy, testosterone influences the development of male body hair, a deepened voice, and the formation of semen. In a girl, estrogen and progesterone influence the development of breasts, female body hair, hip contours, and the onset of menstruation. The result, sex difference #2: *A normal male can impregnate and a normal female can gestate* (be pregnant) *and lactate* (breast-feed).

Evidence is accumulating that men have cycles of varying periods roughly comparable to the female menstrual cycle.[3] But, while males may suffer a mid-life crisis, only females experience menopause. So biological sex difference #3 appears later in life: *Around age fifty women lose the ability to bear and nurse children, while some men have been known to be capable of impregnation well into their seventies.*[4]

Assuming no genetic anomalies or surgical intervention, those three are the only true *vive la différence* factors. They permit all human beings to have sexual intercourse and make babies. They are the biological characteristics that make *all* men different from *all* women.

PHYSICAL SEX DIFFERENCES

The traits that make *most* males different from *most* females have to do with size, strength, and sturdiness. More males than females are born (105 for every 100) but about 33 percent more boys than girls die in infancy, and more girls survive childhood illnesses, perhaps because of the female's advanced maturation rate. (A newborn girl is physiologically comparable to a six-week-old boy.) Males are much more often afflicted with defects such as hemophilia and color blindness, genetic traits linked to the "X" chromosome. (Girls have a second "X" chromosome that buffers or cancels the defect, but boys have only one, unprotected "X.")

Most girls are about eighteen months ahead of most boys in bone development, eruption of permanent teeth, onset of puberty, and overall physical maturity. They reach full growth by age twenty-one; males start later and keep at it longer—until about age twenty-four.

From birth, most males exhibit a higher metabolic and respiratory rate, greater caloric intake, and larger lung capacity. Most girls sit up, crawl, and walk earlier and show more anatomical flexibility, while boys develop larger bones, superior motor skills, and greater muscle mass and physical strength as they grow up.

In height and weight, girls and boys are generally indistinguishable until thirteen or fourteen. By twenty, most males are 5 to 6 inches taller than most females and about 20 percent heavier. Whether due to physiology or social pressure, American females seem to reach the terminal stage of physical performance by age thirteen; most boys go on to improve their physical abilities until about age twenty, after which time the above-average male can usually match the performance standards (strength, speed, athletic prowess) of the most outstanding female.

What do these physical sex differences mean?

If one were to judge by organism vulnerability, incidence of genetic defects, slower maturity, and susceptibility to disease, males would be the "weaker sex." But because the balance changes in favor of boys on all measures but illness and longevity, we acknowledge that the reverse is usually true.

That one sex tends to be bigger and stronger than the other, however, is largely irrelevant to everyday life in the twentieth century. No longer do we survive by bow and brawn; we depend on talent and technology. And if size were integral to heterosexual attraction, then all women would be attracted to the tallest, heftiest men and all men would pursue the shortest, frailest women.

In those few contexts where physical endowments are relevant, they alone are not enough. On the basketball court, for example, height matters but skill matters more. If you need help moving a piano, strength matters, but gender doesn't necessarily predict effectiveness. Billie Jean King might be a more suitable assistant piano mover than Woody Allen; and since these average differences do not develop until puberty, a nine-year-old girl might be better than a nine-year-old boy for the purposes of child labor.

The assumption that all males will be he-men puts a dreadful burden on the fellow who doesn't measure up, just as the belief that all girls are weaklings undermines female self-sufficiency and creates a self-fulfilling prophecy. The point is simply that average known sex differences describe the center of a *range,* not a limit. In many areas, it is a question of what you do with what you've got.

One woman recalls: "During the sixties when I was a competitive swimmer, female swimmers were told they would reach their 'peak' at the age of fifteen. This theory fitted very nicely with the fact that my state had a *law* against high school women's participating in interscholastic sports. I only realized how ridiculous this precept was when I clocked my best-ever time at the ripe old age of twenty-one."[5]

After five months of training, a team of women (half of them typists) scaled nine-foot walls, leaped across water jumps on a

3½-mile run, and outshot a platoon of men on the rifle range by 50 points.[6]

A 114-pound speech teacher took up weightlifting and within one year was able to hoist 360 pounds in the "dead lift" to the knees. In 1977, she broke the state men's record for her weight by squat-lifting 225 pounds.[7]

In swimming events, today's women outperform Johnny Weissmuller's record in the 1924 Olympics.[8]

Female runners have also been gradually closing the gap between women's and men's records. In 1934, the fastest man ran the 800 meters in 1 minute 49.8 seconds and the fastest woman clocked 2 minutes 16.8 seconds. By 1976, the men's record was 1:43.5 and the women's time was 1:54.9.[9]

Among long distance runners, the average female's additional body fat and lesser muscle bulk make her the ideal endurance competitor. One woman finished a 50-mile run at a pace that translated to 6½ minutes per mile or almost 10 miles per hour. Another runner commented after the Boston Marathon, "I can't run much faster, but I can run much, much farther." And a woman who ran 100 miles in 18 hours came in 2 hours ahead of the only male finisher.[10]

It is probably important to add that the female reproductive system is no impediment to athletic performance. Olympic records have been set by women and girls at every stage of the menstrual cycle.[11]

BEHAVIORAL SEX DIFFERENCES

Physical sex differences are an open-and-shut case compared to behavior. This is where social science and biology meet stereotype and myth. Often one can hear the same questions debated in a graduate school seminar or a neighborhood bar. Are males "naturally" more aggressive? Is there a "maternal instinct"? Why do boys seem to excel in math and girls in writing? Do females and males *think* differently?

The answer is there are no answers. Despite all the age-old dichotomies mentioned earlier, behavior does not divide itself neatly in two. Researchers have observed both sexes at great length (and cost) to see who is more sensitive to jets of air and to the feeling of a baby blanket; who is more interested in human faces and who in geometric shapes; who is more willing to lie, to administer electric shocks to others, or to help someone in trouble; who is more afraid of spiders and snakes, more willing to reveal intimate feelings or anxieties, more responsive to infants, more able to get someone else to eat an unpleasant food, more relentless about finding a toy behind a barrier, more "suggestible," more timid, and so on. They have found some trends and patterns but *not one behavioral trait has been proved the absolute and exclusive consequence of sex.*

In 1968, Josef Garai and Amram Scheinfeld reviewed the research of the past hundred years and declared the following sex differences among those that seemed certain: females are more sensitive to sound, touch, and pain, males are more visual; males excel in spatial perception and arithmetical reasoning, females in verbal fluency and rote memory; girls speak earlier and use their language skills for success in personal relationships, boys use their language skills for theory development and problem-solving; boys have superior mechanical ability, girls have superior manual dexterity; girls remember names and faces, boys remember general information and things. And so it goes for 130 pages.[12]

Garai and Scheinfeld's compendium, and others like it that received less attention, were alternately verified or disproved study by study, case by case until 1974 when Eleanor Maccoby and Carol Jacklin, two prominent psychologists from Stanford University, published a book that seemed to settle all the arguments.[13] After painstakingly reviewing over two thousand contemporary articles and books on sex differences in motivation, social behavior, and intellectual ability, Maccoby and Jacklin dismissed most of Garai and Scheinfeld's (and everyone else's) list of differences as ambiguous, inconclusive, or flat-out "myths."

From hundreds of behavioral sex differences, Maccoby and Jacklin shrank the list to four "fairly well established" findings:

1. Males are more aggressive than females.
2. Girls have greater verbal ability than boys.
3. Boys excel in visual-spatial ability.
4. Boys excel in mathematical ability.

Within a year or two, this definitive research-on-the-research was under attack for "sliding definitions" and "slippages in the evaluational sequence"—psycho-jargon that criticized method more than substance.[14] But in 1977, a University of Michigan psychologist[15] objected to the Maccoby and Jacklin findings because "new data that have come out since the book was published, seem to indicate that . . . there is empirical support for the existence of many other sex differences." So here we go again.

Unwittingly, the feuding experts and conflicting experiments testify to the truth: we will never have a Sears, Roebuck Catalog of sex differences because human beings are too diverse for labels and measurements. But that doesn't mean the research is a waste. It can provide clues to sexist problems so that we can help repair the damage to the girls and boys whose lives we touch.

As you assess competing claims, keep the following caveats in mind; they help keep everyone's "definitive discoveries" in perspective.

• *Naming a difference doesn't tell what causes it.* The nature (heredity) *vs.* nurture (culture) argument is a diversion from larger questions of fairness and justice. However, if you find yourself caught up in it, the following criteria will help identify whether a sex difference is biologically determined:

1. It occurs cross-culturally (humans in New Guinea and New Jersey exhibit it).
2. It shows species continuity (humans and subhuman primates exhibit it).
3. It can be manipulated biochemically (a shot of hormones will alter it).
4. It appears early in life (before the culture can get to it).

Even with these criteria one cannot know how much the environment adds to or takes from each person's biological "givens."

• *The language of sex differences is imprecise.* When a study reports "Males are more restless than females," it means "More males than females are restless"; it does not mean *"All* females are less restless than *all* males."

• *The overlap counts too.* For any characteristic measured, large numbers of girls or boys may not fit the majority tendency. For example, psychologist Erik Erikson gave 150 girls and 150 boys, ages ten to twelve, hundreds of toys and props with which to build scenes exciting enough to be photographed and asked them to describe their set-ups.[16] Two-thirds of the boys made aggressive outdoor scenes with cannons, tall towers, protrusions, cars, animals, accidents, traffic, police arrests, and dangerous possibilities, while two-thirds of the girls made placid interior scenes with people or animals in a static position. From this Erikson concluded that anatomy is fate— that the boys were being their thrusting protruding selves and the girls were expressing their "inner space." He gave no weight to the decade or more of exposure to sex-role norms that these children brought with them into the toy room. Moreover, his experiment has never been successfullly replicated. But be that as it may. What interests me here are the *other* thirds, the 50 children in each sexual grouping who did *not* create these sex-typed scenes. What happens to those 100 individualists when the psychologists develop their profiles of "normal" sex differences in child's play?

This figure[17] may help you visualize the significant overlap population:

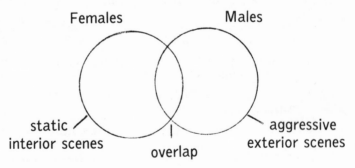

• *For every trait studied, the differences* within *each sex are greater than the average differences* between *the two sexes.* More inches on a ruler separate the shortest girl and the tallest girl, for instance, than separate the average female and the average male.

(What makes male/female comparisons so irresistible that science neglects *same-sex* differences, where the really surprising disparities occur most?)

• *Almost every "objective" study of behavior is culture-bound.* A person being studied in a lab or in the field—even an infant—is already the product of sex-differentiated parental handling and exposure to society's values and attitudes. One critic holds that behavioral analysis cannot even qualify as science. "Derived from persons already enculturated in the assigned sex-roles, such data tell no more about the 'real' nature of woman and man than did the ancient myths."[18]

• *Self-rating is a revealing but limited tool of inquiry.* When subjects are asked to report their own preferences or behavior, we get what they *think* but not necessarily what they *are,* and certainly not *why* they are. The error is to "ask the product to involve itself in the investigation."[19]

• *Results of sex-difference research should not be used to predict behavior.* Predictions based on the performance of the majority may constrict individuality and pressure the minority to conform to what the group is "supposed" to do.

• *Much of social science is contaminated by unconscious sexism.* One study conducted with newborn babies in a hospital nursery attempted to measure sex differences in activity levels before the environment has a chance to leave its mark. The babies' nameplates and all pink and blue clues were removed so that observers would not be affected by their biases while watching the infants kick, squirm, sleep, or cry. But sexism triumphed nonetheless: the hospital nurses had automatically styled the boys' hair in a side part and the girls' hair in a center swirl.[20]

Selective neglect is another by-product of sexism. For example, scientists have always considered the male rhesus monkey a classic male chauvinist and hopelessly indifferent to infants, but it was years before anyone thought to actually investigate his parenting potential. (*Male* parents?) When they did, the rhesus males proved to be adequate caretakers.[21]

At bottom, social science sees the female as a nonmale, and

treats male characteristics—"boys are analytical; girls are less analytical than boys"—as the human standard and the social norm.

When several groups of clinical psychologists were asked to choose attributes that described a healthy adult "male," a healthy adult "female," and a healthy "adult," *sex unspecified,* they chose identical traits for the "male" and "adult," but totally different traits for the "healthy female."[22] This double standard for mental health betrays the belief that only a male is a normal person.

• *People do and say what's expected of them.* One famous experiment found that when teachers were told to expect exceptional performance from some randomly selected students, "the I.Q.s of these students increased significantly."[23] But children don't only rise to high expectations, they shrink to fit low estimates of themselves. When parents, teachers, or psychologists expect that girls will be different from boys—more fearful or inept at math, for example—the expected traits materialize. Males also internalize expectations that they will be different from girls—less emotional or more stoic and tough—so boys hide their feelings, play sports while injured (rather than "give up"), bully someone so as to establish dominance. Observing such behavior doesn't teach us about girls and boys; it teaches us the power of gender roles and cultural expectations to mold behavior.

• *Other variables than sex may be the more compelling organizers of behavior.* Age, ethnic or religious background, economic status, general body type, and geographical origins probably affect personality more dramatically than femaleness or maleness. A skinny six-year-old Baptist boy from a poor family in rural Alabama will undoubtedly have more traits in common with a girl of the same general description than with a well-fed, urbane sixty-year-old Episcopalian man from Scarsdale. It is absurd to claim affinity between boy and man strictly on the grounds of their sex.

Overlooking the *age variable* can be seriously misleading: In a grade school population, more boys than girls suffer depression, but from junior high school on, far more girls than boys are chronically depressed.[24]

Subcultures often outrank sex: Among Orthodox Jews, for

example, the pale, serious, studious boy wears the mantle of manhood, but in El Barrio you'd be laughed off the street if you supposed that scholarship makes the man.

The *situation* is the most often underestimated of all the variables: where something is happening, who are the subjects and who are the observers, what are the consequences—all these factors affect behavior. In a rape situation, a pacifist woman might kill, and in an army situation, a combative man might laugh off his sergeant's insult. It all depends . . .

• *Capacity does not define purpose.* Because females have the capacity to bear children does not mean their purpose in life is to conceive and raise children. Because males can fight doesn't prove they should be boxers, bouncers, or wife-beaters. The belief that sociology follows physiology might just as easily lead to the conclusion that men should work in an upright position and women should do best seated. After all, several times a day, the male stands at the toilet and the female sits; why shouldn't they just keep on doing what comes naturally?

• *Something may "function" well and at the same time not be moral, fair, or good.* Wherever sex roles are defended as a "sensible" or "efficient" division of labor, it's only a matter of time before you hear the functionalist say, "Man hunts, woman nurtures"; therefore "Man brings home the bacon, woman cooks and serves it." In Kate Millett's words, "Having found the status quo operable, they could proceed to find it 'natural,' hence biologically necessary . . ."[25] However, we must learn to ask, Whom is it operating *for?* And whom is it hurting?

• *The study of sex differences tends to overshadow human universals.* As long as the differences make news in professional journals and the nondifferences do not, the literature of polarization will continue to grow and seemingly objective research projects will continue to support "the assumption that sex differences are more important than similarities."[26]

• *The study of sex differences is pernicious if it promotes the notion of "deviance."* If restlessness is declared a "normative masculine trait," then restless girls may be classified as "boyish," not simply as restless girls, and peaceful boys may be classified as "girlish," not just as peaceful boys. When sex differences are twisted to serve the rigid yardstick of "masculinity" or "femininity," those peaceful boys and restless girls end up on a file card stamped "deviate."

Thus far I've attempted to survey the limited knowledge we have on sex differences and to equip you with tools of skepticism with which to analyze the broad range of problems connected with such research. Now I want to use those tools to examine one trait, male aggression—certainly one of the most commonly observed sex differences. Let this question-and-answer format serve as a dialogue of clarification:

Q: *How do we know boys are more active and aggressive than girls?*
A: Parents' comments about their sons confirm the mountain of research that has found boys more aggressive in play, mock fighting, fantasies, and a wide variety of other settings from the age of two years on.[27]

Parents describe boys with such words as "dynamic," "a bombshell," "bold," "belligerent," "so much energy he can't use it all up," while little girls are described as "well-poised," "enjoys being a cute little girl," and "wants to do what might please people."[28]

Teachers frequently report that boys fight with fists and weapons; girls with words. Even the preschool boy is a different challenge to his teacher. "He grabs toys, attacks others, ignores teacher requests . . . laughs, squeals and jumps around excessively, is more tense at rest time, stays awake in naps, breaks toys, rushes into danger. . . ."[29]

Q: *Isn't that what we mean by "Boys will be boys"?*
A: Yes, of course, and that slogan epitomizes the allowances our culture makes for male children. If we believe fighting and hyperactivity are normal male traits, we may tolerate more "acting out" from boys. We may also revise reality to match our expectations: In a kindergarten classroom, teachers rated more boys than girls as "active and impulsive," even though the activity gauges attached to each child's arms and legs registered no sex differences in actual gross motor movement.[30]

Q: *Can it be that teachers and parents encourage aggressive behavior in boys because it is seen as a masculine norm?*

A: As a general rule, adults do not encourage or approve of aggression in either sex. But because it is thought to "come naturally" to boys,[31] and therefore to need more civilizing controls, boys are punished for aggressive acts more often and more harshly than girls. As we'll see in subsequent chapters, this is in keeping with other differences in parental treatment, such as boys' being handled more roughly and played with more vigorously. The sum of these differences may telegraph to boys that they really are expected to be rough and vigorous themselves.

Rather than directly encouraging sex-typed activities in boys, parents seem to actively *discourage* "inappropriate" behavior ("sissy stuff").[32] This might incline a boy toward aggressiveness just to prove he's not a "sissy."

Q: *Would there be fewer aggressive males if there were fewer differences in the treatment of the sexes?*
A: Who knows? Since there are no totally nonsexist societies, the best we can get is a cross-cultural perspective. Several exhaustive reviews of studies covering nearly a thousand existing cultures or subcultures[33] yield the same bottom line: Males are more aggressive than females.

One of the reviews that concentrated on children found that "young boys the world over tend to be somewhat more aggressive than the same aged girls" regardless of the society's general level of aggression. "In no case were girls within any cultural system more aggressive than boys."[34] (The anthropologist-author does concede that females' aggressive styles may differ from males' and investigators may have been alert only to the male brand of violence.)

Although nearly every society trains boys more than girls in self-reliance and achievement,[35] less than 25 percent of the societies actively encouraged boys to be more aggressive.

Q: *Does that mean aggression isn't learned, it comes naturally?*
A: Maccoby and Jacklin (still the last word on sex differences in aggression) insist that it *is* learned—but boys are more biologically prepared to learn it.

Q: *Why only boys?*
A: Among the indisputable biological sex differences discussed earlier you will recall the surge of androgen secreted from boys' testes at birth and again at puberty. Girls do not experience these secretions. Now, since androgen has been associated with aggressive behavior in certain nonhuman mammals,[36] and since only boys get this

extra shot of androgen, it was assumed that androgen caused aggressive behavior in boys.

But there was no proof until the 1950s, when progestin, a synthetic androgen given to pregnant women to prevent miscarriage, inadvertently provided the human guinea pigs. Girls born to these women had received artificially the same hormonal surge that boys experience naturally during gestation. John Money and Anke Ehrhardt studied these girls along with matched groups of unaffected girls, and their results tell us more about gender identity than centuries of "science" have.[37]

The androgenized girls developed normal bodies and experienced normal female puberty (no surge of androgen occurred at puberty, of course, because their original dose was artificial). Despite all expectations, Money and Ehrhardt found they could make only one tame statement about these girls' difference from other girls—and that statement was not based on sound, objective observations, but only on interviews and leading questions. The difference? "Genetic females masculinized *in utero* and reared as girls have a high chance of being tomboys in their behavior."[38]

"Tomboyism" is a phenomenon of sexism. A "tomboy" only exists in the eye of the beholder who chooses to believe that to be an active girl is to be "like a boy." But for the sake of argument here is John Money's description of these girls' "tomboy" behavior: They liked

> strenuous physical activity, cavorting about on their bicycles, climbing trees, hiking and exploring. . . . The test girls aren't rebels. They don't mind dressing up for church or for a visit to grandma, or a party, but they prefer everyday clothing that doesn't restrict them or hamper energetic play. . . . Some of them, however, like to wear perfume. . . . the test girls take it for granted that they will eventually marry and have children, but . . . their ambitions center on their future careers, both before and after marriage.[39]

Are these the children of a biochemical tragedy—or models of physical and mental health? Let's test the double standard mentioned in the caveat section. Read John Money's excerpt once again, this time substituting the word "boys" for "girls." You will find that the one interest that seemed to make the girls normal—the perfume—becomes on second reading, the one interest that makes the boys abnormal!

Q: *Did the parents treat these daughters differently since they knew the girls had been "masculinized in utero"?*
A: Family interaction was not observed extensively. However, it is certainly plausible that parents gave freer reign in play and behavior to children they knew to have male hormones coursing through their bodies. But because plenty of girls become "tomboys" *without* exposure to excess androgens, we may still conclude that parental attitudes have more effect on the freedom behavior of girls ("tomboyism") than do hormones.

Q: *But at least Money and Ehrhardt proved once and for all that hormones cause aggression, right?*
A: "In point of fact," write the authors, "this did not prove to be true. The fetally androgenized girls . . . were not rated by themselves or their mothers as aggressive children who like to pick fights."[40]

Here is the crux of this extraordinary human experiment: "Rather surprisingly," says Money, "they have kept their dominance toned down below the boys' level, although they are well able to assert themselves. . . . First, they aren't much interested in outrivaling other girls, and second, they sense—or learned early— that boys won't easily tolerate a girl who is too pushy."[41]

Even male hormones could not overcome the "feminizing" pressure of culture and environment that takes the fight out of females.

Q: *I'm confused again. Do the sex hormones have any effect on behavior or not?*
A: No one has proved that even they do, or even that they establish *predispositions* toward certain kinds of behavior. In any case, culture can, and does, seem to triumph. Most powerful of all are how we raise our children, how they feel about being female or male, and how the culture evaluates and defines the *function* and characteristics of gender.

Which brings me to the last enemy of nonsexist childrearing: *Evolution,* or more precisely those who look to evolution for a biological base for sex differences. The word "evolution" means change by sequential stages, or effecting a "new arrangement by passing from one formation to another,"[42] but many of those who study evolution seem unable to tolerate the idea of our society's "passing from one formation to another." Where females and males are concerned, they are Social Darwinists deciding what should be according to what is and has been, and espousing what *works* regardless of who is damaged by it.

These "theoreticians of the status quo" use the same methods with which nineteenth-century English scientists were able to "prove" that the English were descended from the angels and the Irish from the apes.[43] If we continue our inquiry into male aggression, you'll see what I mean.

When Charles Darwin first published his *Origin of Species* and *Descent of Man,* people refused to believe humans had evolved from animals. Now, under the influence of such books as Robert Ardrey's *The Territorial Imperative,* Konrad Lorenz' *On Aggression,* Desmond Morris' *The Naked Ape,* and Lionel Tiger's *Men in Groups,* people refuse to believe that humans are any *better* than animals.[44] We are merely pawns of our instincts: the female of her "maternal instinct," and the male of his "killer instinct." Man's innate aggression makes war and murder inevitable, some say. Fighting for food and mates among animals is merely a primitive incarnation of modern man's perpetual fight for status and power. It's all the same, they argue. You can't change human (animal) nature.

Two Tennessee psychologists think that because male aggression and female nurturance are so indelibly imprinted on our evolutionary memory, most girls cradle their schoolbooks against their chests like babies, and most boys carry their books at their sides like spears.[45]

Konrad Lorenz sees no real difference between a cockfight, a dogfight, "boys thrashing each other, young men throwing beer mugs at each other's heads, and so on to barroom brawls about politics, and finally to wars and atom bombs."[46]

For Lionel Tiger, "Man is essentially an ape—just another primate—with woman presumably standing even lower, a kind of sub-ape."[47] Tiger maintains that humans inherit " 'genetic packages' which arranged matters so that males hunted cooperatively in groups while females engaged in maternal and some gathering activity."[48] Curiously, he reasons that "aggression is an intensely co-operative process—it is both the product and the cause of strong effective ties between men." And this suits him fine. In fact,

Tiger warns, "To reduce opportunities for such aggression is to tamper with an ancient and central pattern of human behavior."[49]

Sociobiologists are convinced there are genetic imprints for just about everything, including intelligence, social class, sex roles, and aggression: ". . . the trick in becoming an evolutionary winner is to hit just the right level of aggression."[50] Edward O. Wilson, inventor of sociobiology, summons the behavioral habits of jellyfish, honeybees, termites, elephants, and chimpanzees to establish that all life—including ours—is nothing but a struggle to reproduce.[51] War, machismo, and aggression evolved so that males could muscle out competitors and advertise to females, "I have good genes; let me mate."[52]

If this reads like an out-take from a Tarzan script, other zoological analogies more closely resemble Disney cartoons; for example, Ardrey's description of antelope males as "champion gladiators" and antelope females "gamboling along like high school girls on their way to an ice cream soda."[53] Authors who use cross-species analogies to create sexist scenarios "are revealing far more about their own sexual preoccupations and limitations than they are telling us about animal behavior."[54]

Is it fair to ridicule these books?

Eminently fair. For their distortions and inaccuracies and for creating propaganda on behalf of authoritarianism, ridicule is mild retaliation indeed. But ridicule is not enough. If we believe that *a child is more than a domestic animal,* we must ensure that these theories don't contaminate our childrearing attitudes and that we understand why they are not only ridiculous but wrong.

First, analogies between humans and insects, birds, or rats are genealogically incorrect since humans evolved from a different phylogenetic tree.

Second, even analogies with groups from which humans descended (shrews, moles, marmosets, baboons, apes, and so on) do not settle any arguments. Since "behavior does not fossilize," we cannot know whether aggression exhibited by today's moles or apes would show genetic continuity back through the evolutionary line. Humans may have evolved from a line of creatures who were *behaviorally* different from today's moles or apes, which may be one reason why that line of creatures became us instead of moles

or apes. In short, "Contemporary monkeys and apes are not the equivalents of human ancestors."[55]

Third, comparison with other animals ignores the fact that animals have undergone only one evolutionary process (organic evolution), while humans have experienced a million years of *social* evolution, plus language, brain development, tool-making, labor activities, and culture.[56]

Fourth, if aggression among animals is to be given any weight at all, it must be acknowledged that "the females in natural groupings of primates are usually the aggressors and initiators of sexual responses."[57] Since humans are animals, and animals are primarily motivated by sexual reproduction (as sociobiology claims), then it must be the female's particular aggression that is most crucial for species survival. The obvious question is, If aggression is an animal instinct and humans are animals, why not call *human* females "the aggressors and initiators of sexual responses"? It might spruce up women's image.

Fifth, just as animal analogies are inadequate, so is extrapolating from primitive cultures to male aggression in the schoolyard or on Wall Street. Among primitive peoples, males hunt and females gather because a female can pick berries or dig roots while pregnant or carrying a nursing child, but she cannot chase or transport game. In a society whose main function it is to survive, whose women have no control over their rate of childbearing and no alternative to breastfeeding, whose meat supply is unreliable and whose vegetable foods provide subsistance, a division of labor based on biology may make sense—and the consequent rise of male dominance based on control of the protein supply may be understandable.[58]

Our daughters, however, will not be perpetually pregnant from puberty to menopause and our sons, like everyone else, will be able to get their protein supply from the supermarket—and those two simple facts invalidate the hunter/childbearer paradigm as a model for our time.

Finally, the theory of innate, ineluctable male aggression must be rejected because it lets us off the hook. "He's not responsible, his instincts made him do it" is one version of this moral surrender. "Boys will be boys" is a more endearing way of saying the same thing, but it gets harder and harder to draw the line between "boyish" mischief and the savagery of juvenile crime. We cannot give our sons an evolutionary "excuse" to commit mayhem. The next logical step is congratulating ourselves for *resisting* the "killer instinct"—as Lionel Tiger and Robin Fox do when they arrogantly state, "Since we are primates and do have hand grenades it is amazing that we molest one another so little and kill so rarely."[59]

It hardly seems "so little" and "so rarely" when one man has been killed by a fellow man every 68 seconds over the last century and a half or so, a stunning statistic of war and murder that inspired Dr. Peter Corning, a geneticist, to suggest, "In an age when the masculine virtues are becoming less adaptive for our survival, government by women might actually prove to be a superior adaptation in evolutionary terms."[60]

Dr. Corning's heart is in the right place, but there's a simpler answer: *Stop making aggression a "masculine virtue."* It is tempting to conclude from the data that males with their raging hormones of aggression should be kept from the nuclear button and other affairs of state, but again there's a simpler answer: *Stop making manhood dependent on domination.*

Male aggression is bad for society and bad for males. It may have been an adaptive advantage to cave dwellers but it doesn't help our sons to win friends and influence people now that punching one's way to the top is generally frowned upon and persuasion and performance are the preferred means to success.

However, like parents of sons, our entire culture sends conflicting messages. "Boys will be boys" applies to children but blatant aggression is unacceptable for grown men. What do men do with aggression after it has become an inculcated "masculine virtue"? They reroute it. It emerges as a socially approved relentless quest for dominance and supremacy (*i.e.,* money and power) and eventually it kills them. The diseases of stress and "masculine" imperfection begin in early adolescence when 65 percent of boys (and only 21 percent of girls) worry about "achievement"[61] —and end on the actuarial tables where man's life expectancy is nearly eight years less than woman's.[62]

If violence is a "masculine" role requirement, it is very hard on men and boys. Although no strangers to victimizing the female, more often males aggress against each other or themselves: Little boys usually dominate and attack other little boys, not little girls; fathers use more physical force than mothers and use it on their sons more than their daughters; boys get into more trouble in school; and more boys than girls kill themselves.[63]

Perhaps now we can agree that the cult of sex differences hurts boys. Had we chosen to scrutinize any of the supposedly innate "feminine" qualities (such as compassion or passivity), we would have ended with an even worse litany of suffering on behalf of girls.

How much better for everyone if the cult of sex differences gave way to the views held by my three children when they were much younger and more protected from the sexist world. Abigail and Robin were eight and David was five the day I overheard this conversation and scribbled it on a pad.

ABIGAIL: I can't think of what makes men and women different besides their bodies.

ROBIN: Let's see, both can feel sad, mad, happy, surprised, and both can look forward to things.

DAVID: Both have glasses.

ROBIN: Both can type.

ABIGAIL: Both are patient.

DAVID: They both make Cream of Wheat.

ROBIN: Both of them can build houses.

DAVID: They can swim and dive and drive trucks and cars.

ABIGAIL: They can build bookshelves. And tell stories.

DAVID: I forgot seaplanes.

ABIGAIL: I know . . . only women can wear rouge or earrings.

ROBIN: Yeah, except for man clowns and pirates.

ABIGAIL: What about uncles? I don't think women can be uncles.

ROBIN: That's right. Only men can be uncles. I'm almost sure about that.

And I'm almost sure that it takes this kind of anyone-can-do-anything spirit to find out who can do what and whether they want to. Without freedom of exploration, how can a child discover the boundaries of the self?

The way out of our gender ghettoes begins with the recognition that the alternatives presented to parents have been false from the start.

We do not have to choose between raising children to be "sex-typed" and raising children to be "the same." We can simply help each child to become the fullest person possible.

We needn't prove girls and boys radically different from each other in order for our daughters and sons to feel good about being themselves.

We don't have to label them to love them.

And we needn't prove them the same before we can offer them the same chances and choices.

3

The Politics of Sex Roles:
Who Needs Them and Why

Here come the "buts" . . .

"But how will my son know he's a boy unless he learns all the ways he's different from a girl?" And vice versa.

"But my daughter might turn out masculine if we don't teach her to be feminine." And vice versa.

In a society that favors either/or simplifications, such concerns make sense. But stop and think for a moment and they become suspect: Why do sex differences alone inspire such paranoia? Parents show absolutely no concern about teaching children about everything *else* they're different from. No one asks, "How will my son know he's different from a dog, or my daughter know she's a person, not a houseplant?" No one worries that without intervention children might think they are chairs.

Such rudimentary lessons in identity are considered unnecessary because humanness is perceived to be a "felt reality." Obvious. Basic. Certain. After humanness, being female or male is the most salient fact in every person's who-am-I or what-am-I profile.

If adults were not so hypertense about "femininity" and "masculinity," the same knowingness, the same "felt reality" that is taken for granted about one's human identity would develop in connection with one's gender identity. Since the anatomical, biological, and physical sex differences are among the most visually obvious human characteristics, gender is one of the earliest concepts children understand. By the time they can talk, they know girls from boys as surely as they know humans from dogs, chairs, and houseplants.

CORE GENDER IDENTITY

A child learns that she is a girl or he is a boy sometime between eighteen months and three years of age, a period considered critical for the establishment of gender identification.[1] During these months, children learn their gender label by hearing the word girl or boy applied to themselves over and over again. ("What a good boy you are!" "That's my brave little girl." And so on.) At the same time they learn to generalize sex labels by organizing information they see and hear about other people. ("He's a nice man." "She's a friendly woman." "Look, that boy is running after that girl!") We may not know exactly how children organize all this information, but we do know how the sequence progresses.

By interviewing thousands of children—asking such questions as "Is this a girl doll or a boy doll?" "Are you a boy or a girl?" "Is this a picture of a woman or a man?"—developmentalists have been able to trace the stages of gender comprehension.[2]

At twenty-four months, many children were not quite sure of their own gender but could identify the women and men even if the pictured females had short hair or wore trousers. By age three, almost all children were aware of their own sex as well as other people's.[3]

In the three-year-old's mind, however, gender identity is still subject to a childhood phenomenon known as "magical thinking," the belief that under certain conditions, things can turn into other things on whim; for example, a cat could become a dog if its whiskers were cut off.

Ask a three- or four-year-old girl, "Could you turn into a boy if you wore a boy-style haircut or boys' clothing?" and she will nod confidently. By age five she may equivocate; sometimes gender is stable, other times not. But ask her at age six and she'll think you've lost your mind.[4]

Once the concept of "gender constancy" is absorbed, the healthy child knows that each person's sex is unchanging; the girl knows that she was a girl when she was a baby, will remain a girl no matter what she wears or does or plays with, will become a woman, not a man, when she grows up and a mother, not a father, if she has a child. This knowledge becomes a "felt reality" to children at about the same time that their minds make the link between genital differences and the girl-boy labels that go with them.[5]

Once *core gender identity* has been established, it is "probably the most entrenched, unchangeable psychic structure in the human psyche."[6] *So invincible are feelings of boyness or girlness after the critical period that if a child with male genitals somehow believes himself to be a girl* (parental and medical ignorance or ambiguous infant genitals have created such errors in sex assignment), *it is easier to surgically change his body to match his belief than to try to psychologically change his gender identity to match his body.*[7] (And the same is true for incorrectly assigned girls.)

With normal children under normal circumstances, once core gender identity is established, there is no reason why children should not spend the rest of their lives exploring the infinite variations of their who-am-I profiles. In a nonsexist society, that open vista would stretch out before us all. But in our present culture, the facts of biological and physical sex differences and the "felt reality" of gender identity are overlaid with layers and layers of irrelevant sex-linked rules.

It is not enough today to *be* a girl or *be* a boy; one must *play the part* of a girl or a boy. Society reintroduces "magical thinking" in a new guise: Watch out, child; the haircut may not change her into a boy but it can make her *masculine.* The whiskers don't make the tomcat male, but without them he might turn *feminine.* Watch Out.

How sex differences can be touted as "natural" (see Chapter 2), and at the same time must be hammered into us, is one of sexism's craziest contradictions. Nevertheless, the hammering is accomplished by a catechism of sex role rules and regulations expressed in absolutes and extremes and embodied in the sex role stereotype.

THE STEREOTYPE AS
CULTURAL SLEDGEHAMMER

Literally, a stereotype is a printing block from which pages of type can be duplicated. The essential "permanence and unchangeableness"[8] of these blocks are the features that have come to symbolize rigidity and regularity.

Stereotypes oversimplify human complexity. They bang people into shape with a cultural sledgehammer that flattens the wonder of individuals into monotonous group characteristics.

Stereotypes assert themselves through caricature, name-calling, and idolatry: "Poles are dumb," "Children are destructive," "Blacks are lazy." All stereotypes are "a substitute for intimacy"[9] —and sex stereotypes, in particular, are a *barrier* to intimacy. One doesn't describe a friend or lover in lumpish generalizations.

Here's a quintessential example of the bizarre results of polarizing males and females to such an extreme that they become strangers acting out a farce:

> He is playing masculine. She is playing feminine.
> He is playing masculine *because* she is playing feminine. She is playing feminine *because* he is playing masculine.
> He is playing the kind of man that she thinks the kind of woman she is playing ought to admire.
> She is playing the kind of woman that he thinks the kind of man he is playing ought to desire.[10]

What could drive sensible adults to such contortions?

A childhood in which sex role stereotypes were made the standard of human development and the means with which our culture taught them the roles to be and not to be. Let's look at these sex role lessons through children's eyes at each stage of development.

THE PRESCHOOL CHILD

Because children have to decode two sex roles—the one to play and the one to avoid—each sex must be familiar with the approved "norms" for the other sex.

This is an acquired talent. Before age two, there is little evidence of sex-typed awareness or preferences, but by two-and-a-half or three, both girls and boys know which toys "belong" to each sex and which tools, appliances, clothing, and activities go with mommies or daddies.[11]

Between infancy and early adolescence, research shows that more boys than girls feel heavily pressured by sex role standards. For example, to protect their "masculine" image, tiny little boys will assiduously deny themselves a highly attractive "feminine" toy and choose to play with an unappealing sex-neutral toy instead, whereas girls feel free to pick the "opposite" sex toy if it is more attractive, and they don't give the boring neutral toy a second glance.[12]

In nursery school, boys who cross the sex line to play with dolls, dress-up clothes, kitchen toys, or art materials are criticized by their classmates six times as often as other children, while girls who try out such "masculine" activities as blocks, hammers, transportation toys, or sandbox play may be ignored by their peers but are not criticized.[13]

Kids don't just know sex linkages, they have a pretty clear picture of the power differences involved. A child between about three and five knows enough to say, "Mommy never really has things belong to her." Or "He's the daddy so it's his but he shares nice with the mommy."[14]

Preschoolers' ideas about adult occupations are already ossified stereotypes. I often tell the story of a friend who took a childrearing leave of absence from her job as a newspaper reporter. One day, when her three-year-old, Sarah, expressed interest in a TV story about a crime reporter, my friend decided to explain her own career: "Before you were born, I used to have a job like that," the mother said, building to a simple but exciting description of journalism. "I went to fires or to the police station and the stories I wrote were printed in the newspaper with my name on them."

After listening attentively, Sarah asked, "Mommy, when you had this job before I was born, did you used to be a man?"

Obviously, the child had not yet developed the concept of gender constancy; but what necessitated the magical thinking that turned her mother into a man was Sarah's inability to associate the exciting job of a newspaper reporter with the female sex.

Seventy Wisconsin children, ages three to five, had much the same problem.[15] When asked "What do you want to be when you grow up?" the boys mentioned fourteen occupations: fireman, policeman, father/husband, older person, digger, dentist, astronaut, cowboy, truck-driver, engineer, baseball player, doctor, Superman, and the Six-Million-Dollar Man. Girls named eleven categories: mother/sister, nurse, ballerina, older person, dentist, teacher, babysitter, baton-twirler, iceskater, princess, and cowgirl.

Next, the children were polled on their more realistic expectations: "What do you think you *really* will be?" they were asked. The girls altered their choices toward even more traditional roles —changing from ballerina, nurse, and dentist, to mother—while the boys changed to *more* active, adventurous futures—for instance, from husband to fireman.

Taking into account the narrow range of occupations familiar to nursery-school children, it still seems pitiful to have had job options closed to you before you are three or four years old.

Pittsburgh children of the same ages were asked "What do you want to be when you grow up?" followed by "If you were a boy (girl), what would you be when you grow up?" For the first question, most chose stereotyped careers: policeman, sports star, cowboy, and one "aspiring spy" for the boys; nursing and the like for the girls. To the second—what they would be if they were the "opposite" sex—the children answered with stereotyped other-sex occupations as well. But their *reactions* to that second question were striking: The boys were shocked at the very *idea* of being a girl. Most had never thought of it before, some refused to think about it, and one "put his hands to his head and sighed. 'Oh, if I were a girl I'd have to grow up to be nothing.' "

The girls, on the other hand, obviously had thought about the question a great deal. Most had an answer ready. "Several girls mentioned that this other-sex occupational ambition was their *true* ambition, but one that could not be realized because of their sex." More poignantly, the gender barrier had become so formidable that it even blocked out fantasies and dreams. "Thus, one blond moppet confided that what she really wanted to do when she grew up was fly like a bird. 'But I'll never do it,' she sighed, 'because I'm not a boy.' "

The metaphor is haunting. "I could not help wondering," said the researcher, "how many little children believe that only males are capable of something as grand as flight."[16]

STEREOTYPES ACCORDING TO
FIVE- TO ELEVEN-YEAR-OLDS

When kindergarten children were asked to imagine a typical day in their futures, the girls talked about getting up to clean house and feed the baby; the boys talked about performing an operation and being on a space ship.[17]

To find out whether children increase their knowledge of sex stereotypes between kindergarten and fourth grade, researchers showed children pictures of a man and a woman and asked which one would match a range of behaviors or characteristics. For example, "One of these people is a bully. They are always pushing people around and getting into fights. Which person gets into fights?" Or, "One of these people is emotional. They cry when something good happens as well as when everything goes wrong. Which is the emotional person?"

Additional questions elicited information about which person daydreams, owns a store, talks a lot, says bad words, is confident, and so on. Comparing the age groups, examiners found an increase in the number of items stereotyped between kindergarten and second grade, but no change between second and fourth grade —which suggests that with the basic stereotypes under their belts, children need little additional elaboration.

One more intriguing result: *Both girls and boys learn the male stereotype earlier than the female one. The male ideal obviously demands greater attention.* [18]

By age five or six, almost all children claim (in their own vocabularies, of course) that every male is more powerful, invulnerable, punitive, aggressive, fearless, and competent than every female.[19]

Eight- to eleven-year-old boys say that adult men need to make decisions, protect women and children in emergencies, do hard labor and dirty work, fix things, support their families, get along with their wives, and teach their children right from wrong. Men are the boss, control the money, get the most comfortable chair and the daily papers, get mad a lot but laugh and make jokes more than women do and are more fun to be with.

The boys say that female adults are indecisive, afraid of many things, get tired a lot, need help often, stay home most of the time, are squeamish, don't like adventure, are helpless in emergencies, do things the wrong way, and are not very intelligent. Women always "have to keep things neat and tidy, take the pep out of things, easily become jealous and envy their husbands, feel sad more often than men, and are pests to have along on an adventure."[20]

Eight- to eleven-year-old girls have similar stereotypes in their repertoire: child care, the interior of the house, clothes and food are "feminine"; manipulation of the physical environment, machines, transportation, the structure of the house, most recreation, and most occupations are "masculine."[21]

Primary school children also classify being good at games as "masculine," being quiet as "feminine."[22] Trucks, cars, and boisterous self-assertion are "masculine"; jump ropes, dolls, cuddling, and dependency are "feminine."[23] Arithmetic and athletic, spatial, and mechanical skills are "masculine"; reading and artistic and social skills are "feminine."[24] School objects, such as a blackboard and a book, are "feminine";[25] chess is "masculine."[26] Interview any child between the ages of five and eleven and I defy you to find ten objects or behaviors that they consider sex-neutral.

STEREOTYPES ACCORDING TO
TWELVE- TO SEVENTEEN-YEAR-OLDS

Many of the tensions of adolescence are attributable to one unfortunate misconception, which begins here and persists into maturity: *the confusion of sex role standards with sexual competence.*

Lack of experience and a frame of reference for their developing sexuality leads teenagers to equate extremes of "femininity" and "masculinity" with the ultimate in sexiness. They are anxious about everything: their physical appearance, hormonal changes, popularity, desirability as a romantic and sexual partner, academic standing, and destiny in life. Understandably, many adolescents therefore seek an identity within the clearcut outlines of stereotype. At this age, digressions from the "norm" are imagined to bring social ostracism and worse.

Sex-typed interests peak for girls at thirteen and for boys at sixteen, years that roughly correspond to the peak transformations of puberty.[27] The sex-typing itself trots out a parade of high-camp caricatures. Take, for example, the montages created from magazine pictures by some eighth-graders. The boys were asked to express "Boys' Ideas of Their Maleness"; the girls, "Girls' Ideas of Their Femaleness"; and then each group did "opposite" sex evaluations.

One group of boys plastered a large number 2 on their montage about femaleness and a number 1 on their maleness poster. Seeing this, the girls' group immediately pasted a big zero on their "Girls' Ideas of Maleness" montage. In later discussions, the girls poured out their resentment of men and boys: "They think they're superior because they bring home all the money; boys are inferior and always in trouble; they are lazy; they act like animals."[28]

Verbally, the boys characterized girls and women as being bossy, nosy, self-centered, talkative, and interested in their looks, breasts, menstruation, birth control, getting married, and having babies.

The "Girls' Ideas of Their Femaleness" montages concentrated on beauty, marriage, love, sex, make-up, cooking, money, dieting, cleanliness, perfume, jewelry, clothes, and skin. Yet the girls objected to the boys' idea of their femaleness because "all it is is sex, sex, sex, sex, making love, bust developers, work, cooking, children and cleaning. They think we're their slaves."[29]

On their own maleness montages, the thirteen- and fourteen-year-old boys pictured sports, hunting, cars, cycles, muscle development, military service, careers, and work. In some posters, family scenes appeared minimally; in others not at all.

These posters, and their creators, depict two different worlds and the brand of male-female alienation that is all too familiar among adults.

As the plot thickens on the adolescent social scene, an about-face is happening in the intellectual sphere: Children stop stereotyping school achievement as "feminine" and start stereotyping the whole academic package as "masculine."[30] To test this finding, I asked some thirteen-year-old girls which gender label they would put on mathematics:

"Math is a girl's thing because all the girls are better at it."

"No, it's a boy's thing when you think of how boys need it when they grow up."

"Women need it too—for adding up prices and budgets."

"Yeah, maybe if you think of arithmetic, it's female. But when you think of a mathematician, it's male."

Sex role standards for achievement become more definite and extreme with age. By the time they are seventeen, both sexes almost unanimously stereotype athletics and arithmetic as male, and reading and social skills as female.[31]

High school seniors are also relentlessly judgmental about what is inappropriate for adults. In one national survey, 30 percent of them said a woman's place is in the home and 4 percent think women are totally incapable of working outside the home.[32]

STEREOTYPES
ACCORDING TO EIGHTEEN-PLUS

Sex role attitudes vary considerably by socioeconomic group, but opinions of a college population tend to be closest to adults of the educated middle class. Therefore the following findings might be assumed to predict not just college kids' future behavior as parents, but social policies in the near future when many of these students become leaders in their fields.

• Despite their professed belief in legal equality for the sexes, both females and males said the characteristics of "masculinity" are more socially desirable than those of "femininity."[33]

• Of the traits that 90 percent of the students agreed belonged to one sex and not the other, ten of the male traits were positive and five negative, while ten of the female traits were negative and five positive.[34]

• One study found that college students stereotype women as "secretary, sexpot, spender, sow, civic actor and sickie."[35]

• Sex-typing of occupations seems to have subsided somewhat by college age. For eighteen-year-olds, only hazardous jobs and jobs requiring physical strength still carry gender labels. Two-thirds of the males and four-fifths of the females agreed that housework and child care should be equally shared except that the man should do repairs, and the woman should do laundry, sewing, and infant care.[36]

• Finally, when asked to rate behaviors of typical two-year-olds, young men and women called several activities sex-specific: for boys—rough-house play, aggressive behavior, and play with transportation toys; and for girls—doll play, dressing up, and looking in the mirror.[37]

So we've come full circle, from the two-year-old's stereotyped view of adults to the young adult's sex-stereotyped view of two-year-olds. This foolproof closed circuit of sexism doesn't happen by accident. Having briefly reviewed the content of sex role stereotypes, we now turn to their *intent.* What do they all add up to? What do they mean and what do they want from us?

THE HIDDEN AGENDA OF SEX ROLES

Because stereotypes are by definition extravagant overstatements blunt enough to be understood by children, they are also blunt enough to advertise their intent. What sex role stereotypes tell children and the rest of us is this:

Boys Are Better.

Girls Are Meant to Be Mothers.

These two messages—male supremacy and compulsory motherhood—are the raw essentials of a patriarchal system. In order for the system to perpetuate itself, children must be trained to play their proper roles and to believe the system natural and just.

Male supremacy—the paradigm for white supremacy or any oppressive form of hierarchy—begins at home. Big Daddy is in charge in the family, and some men are expected to be in charge of other men (and all women) in the corporations, universities, governments, and playing fields of the nation. Boys, therefore, must be trained to become men who can exercise their rightful power and believe themselves worthy of it. Girls must be trained to admire and depend upon the men who exercise power, and to believe themselves unworthy of controlling their own or others' destinies.

Because male power is to be spread across all of public life, boys must be motivated to produce in all arenas—business, policy, art, academia, everywhere. Not only are females to stay out of the action in those arenas, but they are themselves to be incentives that motivate males to strive for power, the sexual and ornamental rewards that the male controls and sometimes marries. As a wife, "his woman" further rewards him with offspring (she "gave" him a son) to carry on his name, the continuity of the patriarchal line, and to provide the larger patriarchal system with workers, soldiers, and more mothers. (History shows that in wartime and during periods of decreasing population and underemployment, motherhood has been vigorously promoted and abortion and contraception are more likely to be made illegal.)[38]

For this gender arrangement to come into being, girls must learn to see themselves as sexual entities after puberty and be motivated to be mothers after marriage. Only when she is under male control (married) can a woman be exalted in motherhood (unwed mothers are not) and her child be officially recognized ("illegitimate" babies are not). A girl must be so well trained that she relinquishes the desire to *produce*—business, policy, art, and so on—in favor of *reproducing.* When she succumbs to the definition of her optimum self as Mother legitimatized by marriage, she locks male supremacy into place.

As Simone de Beauvoir has said, woman's "creation results only in repeating the same Life in more individuals," whereas man "remodels the face of the earth, he creates new instruments, he invents, he shapes the future."[39] Man transcends. Woman repeats. Or, as I have chosen to formulate it for purposes of this discussion: *Boys Are Better. Girls Are Meant to Be Mothers.* That's how children see it.

Thus, vastly oversimplified, we have the intent of sex stereotypes and the hidden agenda of sex roles. The name of the game is power and one's relationship to it: Someone wins because someone else loses. All the players learn the rules in childhood. The objective of the game for boys is to grow up to be President. The objective of the game for girls is to grow up to have a baby. For him, the one and only pinnacle position; for her, a destiny available to every female of every species on the face of the earth.

There is nothing wrong with the stereotype of the attractive young woman who becomes a mother—other than the fact that she is the *only* woman a girl is supposed to become.

There is nothing wrong with the fearless leader stereotype either, except that since it cannot be fulfilled by 99,999 out of 100,000 males, it dooms most boys and men to a deep sense of "masculine" failure, which must then be relieved by reaffirmation of the one manageable component of the male stereotype: superiority over women.

THE SEX ROLE SEESAW

Whoever he is and however he performs, at least he can feel strong if she is weak. Her "femininity" and his "masculinity" have been made such a seesaw of opposites that if she refuses to be powerless she "emasculates" him. His sex role and his phallic potency rise and fall in unison. If she agrees to be powerless, his "masculinity" rises and from his full height on the seesaw, he looks down and proclaims her "a real woman."

This dynamic springs from the original fallacy outlined in Chapter 2:

> The two sexes are different;
> the two sexes are opposites;
> one sex is better than the other.

Making sure that boys know they are better and that girls accept lesser status and eventual reproductive duty is the basic agenda of patriarchy and the conscious or unconscious foundation of sex role learning. This intent can be tested against the content of the sex stereotypes we found children assimilating from nursery school to college, and the following rules they internalize about the way the two sexes are meant to function in society:

Rule #1: Boys Are Better—therefore males are meant to be powerful; or males have power, therefore boys are better.

Psychologist Lawrence Kohlberg calls power and prestige a "major attribute of children's sex role stereotypes."[40] Gloria Tischler Hirsch, another psychologist, says power is the most crucial and influential variable affecting the child's feelings of self-worth and self-esteem, without which no individual can "feel in charge of his or her own life."[41]

Power, according to writer Susan Sontag, is not a substance to be seized; "power exists only as a series of relationships."[42]

What sense do children make of the power relationships in their lives?

They may see Mother with the immediate power to reward and punish them but it doesn't take them long to learn that Father has the ultimate authority over Mother. The very young, with their concrete thinking styles, extrapolate very simply from the average man's superior size to male superiority in all things. First, they think "that fathers are bigger and stronger than mothers, next that they are smarter than mothers and next that they have more social power or are the boss in the family."[43] (Remember, "He's the daddy, so it's his.")

Small children may think of the mother as the economic provider because she actually buys the food. But between ages five and seven, almost all of them understand that men really control the money and usually earn most if not all of it. They have figured out that money is received in exchange for work and, as we've noted, they label most work "for men only."[44]

By about age seven, children know that men play the most decisive roles outside the family, too. The police officer, mayor, priest, firefighter, bank guard, and school principal are usually men, and men are power figures all the way up to the President and the Pope. This is indeed grandiose corroboration of Boys Are Better. And the "power aura"[45] that accrues to fathers, simply because they are men like these other authority figures, increases even more when mothers are discernibly dependent on fathers.

Studies have shown that women become further removed from economic and psychological autonomy and more and more dependent on their husbands as the number of children in the family increases. Then, as the wife's neediness grows, her status in the family decreases. Inevitably, it seems, the person who most needs a relationship has the least power in that relationship.[46]

Also, the tendency for women to marry men who have more education and economic wherewithal than they do and the fact that job bias almost guarantees that those mothers who do work will be consigned to lower-level jobs with less pay, further increase the power disparity and decrease the woman's status in children's eyes. Married or single, Mother is seen as powerless.

In husband-wife families, the main criterion of power is who has the greatest influence in decision-making, which is connected to who controls the resources, which is why, even in "woman's place"—the home—man rules.[47]

Thus, Mother is diminished by economic dependency, psychological neediness, inferior credentials, and lower job status, factors that children evaluate as negatively as everyone else. That her work or childrearing activities free Father to get through graduate school, to work long hours, to be a weekend athlete, or to entertain and impress clients doesn't register on children as an equal contribution to the family. It registers as proof that Mom is there to sacrifice herself and to serve others.

In the same way, seeing Mother as the purchaser of food and clothing cuts no ice with youngsters past the age of innocence. It is the person who *possesses,* not the one who consumes, whom they most admire. When tested, children will choose to imitate an adult who, they are told, "owns" a lot of candy, rather than someone they actually *see* eating the goodies.[48] In most families, Dad owns the candy and the children know it. Even those with working mothers in father-absent households believe that a Daddy *should* own the candy; the stereotype has enough force to contradict reality.[49]

Rule #2: Boys Are Better—therefore a girl who tries to excel is trying to be a boy, i.e., *she's "unfeminine."*

This item on patriarchy's hidden agenda is captured in the much-quoted aphorism "Men are unsexed by failure, women by success." If she's competent, she couldn't be a real woman; if she were a real woman, she wouldn't be competent. Rather than be impaled on the horns of this dilemma, a girl is supposed to step out of the competition to be sure she doesn't beat a man and thereby lose her sexuality.

Recently, 35 percent of Americans agreed with the statement "As women become more independent, assertive and successful, men may find them less attractive sexually and men may even become impotent."[50] Thus, not only is the female's own sexual identity in direct conflict with her potential for excellence, it is also responsible for the well-being of the male's ego and *his* sexual competence.

Sounding almost like a businessman faced with aspiring women executives, an eleven-year-old boy complains:

> They're getting too smart now. Before, only the boys gave wise-cracks; now, girls do too. Now, some are too advanced. . . . They talk, well it's like a college man to a junior high— they make us look like fools in front of everybody.[51]

Another young man objects to a girl who broke the "femininity" barrier:

> Everybody was scared of her, even me. She played football and did everything that boys did. . . . One day she gave practically all the boys in the class their social science lessons. . . . There is one [tomboy] in my class again this year. There always is.[52]

In a society that educates its male children "on the simple device of teaching them not to be women,"[53] the female's function is to remain at the opposite pole of behavior; to represent everything the male *isn't;* to complement him, not compete with him. By the time they enter college, girls have incorporated this rule to the point of imagining the kind of woman that men want as even more submissive, passive, and unachieving than the actual "ideal woman" described by the men.[54]

In our society, the only female who is allowed to exercise power and competence without "losing her femininity," is the widow. Inheriting status, the family business, or a husband's seat in Congress is "feminine"; *earning* them is not.

Rule #3: Boys Are Better—thus boys are preferable to girls.

Children seem to absorb this patriarchal precept by osmosis. When she was nine, my daughter Robin asked, "How come girls aren't people's favorite people?" In one way or another, women have been muttering that question throughout history.

Did you ever wish you were the other sex? Polls show that five times more women wish they were men than vice versa.[55] This overwhelming preference for maleness begins with parents:

> SPRINGFIELD, ILL. Aug 3 (UPI)—Gov. James R.
> Thompson of Illinois and his wife, Jayne, became
> the parents of a 7-pound 4-ounce girl today. It
> was their first child.
>   "I just held the baby, the baby is beautiful,"
> said Gov. Thompson, 42. "The next one is going to
> be a little Jim, but I couldn't be happier."
>   —*The New York Times,* August 4, 1978

In other words, she'll do until the real thing comes along.

Preference for a boy, especially a first-born boy, is so widespread in all cultures that statistics almost humiliate beyond belief. (See Chapter 5.) And preference quite naturally translates into privilege: When asked, "If your son and daughter were both good students but you could only send one to college, who would get to go?" 4 percent of those surveyed said the daughter, but *40* percent specified the son.[56]

In a patriarchy, the boy inherits the family name, property, business, talent, money, land, or trade. The boy becomes "a chip off the old block." A girl is just so much sawdust. A waste of seed. She marries and the family name disappears; and her father has to pay for the ritual besides.

Joe and John and Bob and Ted were groomed for greatness but the Kennedy daughters, offspring of the same clan, were groomed to marry well. When they became Pat Lawford and Eunice Shriver, they became wives and mothers first, Kennedys second.

Daughters are supposed to inherit money, but not authority. Because Aristotle Onassis had expected his only son, Alexander, to take over his shipping empire, there was no thought of educating his only daughter, Christina, for a lifetime in the business. When Alexander was killed in a plane crash and Onassis died a few years later, Christina was totally unpre-

pared to be an active "heir" instead of a glamorous "heiress."
To become, quite suddenly, a shipping magnate, when she had
been educated to be a "lady," was an impossible task. Judging
from the news reports, she married "impulsively," the third
time, in 1978, when she announced that she would live with
her newest husband in a two-room apartment in Moscow
where she would wash the dishes for him like any "normal
woman."[57] By Christmas 1979, the marriage had broken up.
Yes, a waste of seed.

*Rule #4: Boys Are Better—therefore it is natural for females
to envy, imitate, and favor males, and for both sexes to diminish, dismiss, and devalue females.*

Beneath every sex role stereotype is a rating, positive or
negative, like a door prize under one's plate, and the rating system
is known to all. From age three up, both girls and boys express
a strong preference for boys' toys, activities, pursuits, and for
being male.[58]

Little girls "know" that boys are better. "They admire boys'
activities. Boys despise theirs. The tomboy tags along after her
brothers; the sissy lives his rejection in private secrecy. A communion of little girls is a communion of failure."[59]

Up to 70 percent of girls would rather work with building
tools than with cooking utensils. And only 5 to 20 percent of
girls prefer becoming a mother to becoming a father, while a
full 95 percent of boys prefer becoming a father.[60] Wherever
the adult division of labor creates sex-typed tasks, both girls
and boys give the male tasks higher ratings.[61] Boys' opinions of
girls get progressively worse throughout childhood, while girls'
opinions of boys get progressively better. At eight, for example, less than half the girls in one study said boys make "the
best leaders"; by fourteen, more than *80* percent of the girls
called boys "the best leaders."[62]

Learning to prefer males is one thing; learning to despise
females is another. "I don't like females," says a sixth-grade boy.
"I say that men could live better by themselves." The origins of
misogyny (woman-hating) may be traced to sex role training:
"Through their conditioning away from 'femininity,' " says one

psychiatrist, "boys learn not only avoidance of the 'feminine' behaviors but hostility and contempt for the female."[63]

Rule #5: Boys Are Better—therefore the male role, the more important role, requires more rigorous training.

"Masculinity" is important and precious, but also fragile and vulnerable to distortion. That's why boys must begin learning their sex role earlier and be punished more severely for deviations from it. Studies have found that while general awareness of sex-appropriateness increases with age, boys are always clearer about their sex roles than girls, and working-class children are clearer than middle-class children[64] (perhaps because the working-class male compensates with "masculine" bravado for his low job status).

"Femininity" is not so highly valued that it must be carefully and constantly defined, so girls are given more opportunity to explore boys' clothes, toys, and activities. However, boys' activities are monitored closely and censored.

In New Milford, Connecticut, a few years ago, factions of the community almost came to blows over the sex-integration of home economics and industrial arts classes in grades six to eight.

"I'll take my son out of school before I'll let him take this course," said one father about home ec. "My son doesn't want the course and I don't want him to be a sissy."

Said a local minister about boys' learning to cook, "You take some boys that have homosexual tendencies; this could be the thing that tips the scales."[65]

The football coach of a Texas junior high school saw as a personal insult to his "masculinity" the fact that his players wore long hair: "It is time that American coaches stopped allowing themselves to be personally represented by male athletic teams and individuals that look like females."[66]

Defining maleness by its negatives boils down to not looking like, acting like, or playing with girls. But affirmative proof of manhood is also required. As Margaret Mead's pithy phrase puts it, maleness must be "kept and re-earned every day."[67]

The boy learns that the sooner he purifies himself of "sissy" behavior, and the better he decodes the signals of "masculinity," the more he can enjoy its advantages. His slogan might be *Learn Now, Reap Later.* I'm not suggesting his childhood isn't fun; but because it is also more complicated by sex role rules than is a girl's, it is a much more anxious time. Being a "sissy" isn't considered a cute transitional phase, as is "tomboyishness"; it is a scandalous failure to join the privileged caste.

In their desperate flight from "sissyness," many young boys are *"compulsively* masculine"[68] to answer what seems to be society's nervousness about their gender. This is understandable. First, the boy is confused by the fact that girls can do what he does but if he does what girls do, the gods roar. Second, the ideal male behavior is most often passed along to him not with "do's" but with "don'ts." ("Don't giggle, you sound like a girl." "Dammit, don't touch that ball again until you stop throwing like a girl.") And then, after society insists that for him, everything "like a girl" is wrong and sissy and what he must not be, they leave him under the domination of "the epitome of all sissy things—women. In other words, he is compelled to knuckle under to that which he has been taught to despise."[69]

In order for this crucial contradiction to do no damage to patriarchal order, men make certain that women believe in male supremacy so intensely that they are able to tutor others in its permutations. Which is why—as I hope has become crystal clear —both girls *and* boys must learn that Boys Are Better.

What of girls? I've said that the other side of the patriarchal coin bears the legend Girls Are Meant to Be Mothers. Let us briefly consider how this imperative serves male supremacy.

Rule #6: Girls Are Meant to Be Mothers—therefore until puberty girls are functionally meaningless.

Because the female role is less important and less desirable, it needn't be paid as much attention in childhood. Studies show that from infancy to adolescence, girls do not receive comparable reinforcement, rewards, or punishments concerning "femininity," as boys do re "masculinity."[70]

In childhood, however small and weak a boy may be, he can fulfill the imperatives of the male role as long as he strives to be

better than other boys (and all girls) in sports or daring or whatever. But girls can only pretend at their ultimate female role,
because their bodies betray the truth. For him, there is the concept
of proving his manhood; for her there is no act or effort because
the proof is biological: womanhood *happens* to her whether or not
she lifts a finger.

Since the female role depends on sexual maturation—a girl
needs breasts and hips to be a sex object and menstruation to
become a mother—she cannot hope to fulfill true "femininity" in
childhood. And since no one seems to care about girls before
puberty anyhow, she may choose to play with preferred boys'
things and activities, if she wants to. Her "tomboy" behavior is
usually excused as a transitional phase, acceptable while her body
is lithe and boyish, but disciplined out of her when puberty puts
her womanly body in business.

If the boy's childhood slogan is *Learn Now, Reap Later,* the
girl's is *Play Now, Surrender Later.*

The rise in rates of depression among adolescent girls may
well be a result of this startling loss of the liberty of childhood.

*Rule #7: Girls Are Meant to Be Mothers—therefore women
need men to fulfill themselves.*

A message on feminist T-shirts reads "A woman without a
man is like a fish without a bicycle"—humor that derives more
from wishful thinking than emotional truth. Most single women
today still feel like "spinsters," not "bachelor girls," and married
women feel "unfulfilled" if they are not mothers. A boy becomes
a man by proving himself; a girl becomes a woman when a man
proves her worthy of him.

If the montages of those eighth-grade girls are reliable clues,
it seems that the tasks of attracting boys, planning marriage and
children, and being beautiful are still the main occupations of
female adolescence—not to mention the main profit base for the
fashion, cosmetics, magazine, and television industries.

In order to be a worthy reward for the best boy, a girl must
have "sex appeal." Other girls are her competition and her own
inadequacies are her curse. ("My fat legs, my pimples, my flat
chest! How will he ever *like* me?!!") Until her wedding day, she

never knows if she's a reward worth claiming, and after motherhood transforms her from a girl with "sex appeal" to a drudge
with diapers in hand, she's never sure if she's worth keeping.

A female who gains personal affirmation through male approval has chosen a slippery route to selfhood—yet it is the most
traveled route of all. If her self-esteem comes from him and not
from within herself, then it can be withdrawn at will, leaving her
with nothing but her motherhood. Mothers without husbands or
self-esteem are a drug on the market. Since we as a culture tend
to see women in terms of their relationship to men, wrote philoso-
pher Georg Simmel, "one ends up concluding that they are *nothing* in themselves."

That sentence echoes the statement of the little boy in Pittsburgh: "Oh, if I were a girl I'd have to grow up to be nothing."
And it tells us that the original disservice to women happens way
back when little girls say they want to grow up to be mommies
and we fail to ask, "Why, and what *else?*"

*Rule #8: Girls Are Meant to Be Mothers—therefore mother-
hood must be exalted.*

The patriarchy's big guns are brought out for this propaganda effort: television, women's magazines, Mother's Day mythology, and religion all glorify motherhood.

Despite the inescapable statistic that nine out of ten girls will
work outside the home, motherhood is still presented as though
it were a lifetime full-time job, when at most it's a part-time job
with built-in obsolescence. The average woman is thirty when her
youngest child enters school, which leaves her with about 45 more
years to fill from 9 A.M. to 3 P.M. and eventually all day, every day.
To prevent her from perceiving the void, she has to swallow a lot
of lies . . . and ignore the contradictions.

Motherhood is so glorified it would seem that only the elite
few are capable of it, yet it is available to every woman and there
are no educational requirements. Mother is put on a pedestal, yet
no one wants to get stuck talking with her at a party. Her job is
supposedly the most valuable in the world, yet it counts not at all
when she goes looking for a "real job." They tell her, "The hand
that rocks the cradle rules the world." If that were true, why

couldn't generations of black "mammies" rule an end to white racism? Why were those hands tied? Because the hand that rocks the cradle is under the thumb of the men who have the real power. They are the ones who make sure that it is Mother and not Father who sits beside the cradle rocking her life away.

The patriarchy needs a class of people at home where they will consume goods and services produced by another class of people who leave the house each day. The patriarchy needs an exalted mythology of motherhood to justify assigning one parent major responsibility for the offspring of two parents.

Rule #9: Girls Are Meant to Be Mothers—therefore whatever else they do is unsuitable or superfluous.

"Sex roles assign domestic service and attendance upon infants to the female," writes Kate Millett, "the rest of human achievement, interest and ambition to the male. This tends to arrest her at the level of biological experience."[71]

See how the patriarchal catechism works wonders. The motherhood imperative keeps women out of the upper reaches of the marketplace. ("Why bother to train someone for whom a career is secondary?") It invents maternal guilt. It marks certain fields of endeavor as incompatible with motherhood (though not with fatherhood), such as the executive's "long hours," or the "unsafe conditions" on a job that happens to pay twice as much as traditional women's occupations.

The expectation that girls are meant to be mothers establishes occupational stereotypes so rigid that children find it twice as unthinkable for women to work at "men's jobs" as for men to work at "women's jobs." They assume that any man has the expertise for any job automatically, just because he is a man,[72] but their reluctance to see women in competent roles is so strong that when a male and female performed equally well on a "masculine" task (using a wrench), most children attributed the male's performance to skill and the female's to luck.[73] They come to believe that a profession depletes women's capacity to mother.

"No, don't be a lawyer," cried a child whose mother had enrolled in law school. "You won't be my mommy anymore."

The view that other-than-mother is wrong has squelched the dreams of who knows how many girls. Usually, we hear only from those who fought back.

"I think what galvanized me into becoming a doctor," says one now-successful woman, "was the biology teacher who said to me, dead seriously, 'But, women just don't DO that!' "[74]

Women *do* motherhood. To want to be someone other-than-mother isn't quite "feminine." Or nice. That's why a prosperous woman who loves her job felt she had to tell her daughter that she works because of financial necessity; otherwise "what excuse would I have for working?"[75] A father need never defend his working no matter how independently wealthy he is. For men, it is taken for granted that work brings dignity.

If a woman *must* work outside the home, the *types* of work considered proper—teaching, social work, and nursing—utilize "motherly" skills of nurturing, empathy, and sensitivity.

Sex-typed jobs are sorted out by children before they are five. A group of preschoolers were shown a picture of a female telephone line worker on a pole with a bird *upside down* on the telephone wire nearby. When asked to specify what part of the picture was "not O.K." almost twice as many children mentioned only the woman line worker as "not O.K." as mentioned only the upside-down bird.[76] That is the lesson in a nutshell: *Girls Are Meant to Be Mothers, so a woman in a nonmothering role is not O.K. It's worse than an upside down world.*

When the women's movement first criticized compulsory motherhood, a hue and cry went up as though the suggested alternative were *no* motherhood. Such artificial extremes obscure the reasonable middle ground where a woman can choose among many options during each phase of her life, thereby giving the children around her (her own and other people's) a glimpse of their own infinite possibilities.

Study after study shows that daughters of employed mothers perceive women less negatively, see women as more competent and themselves as more worthwhile, see male and female roles as less polarized, and see themselves as more able to combine love and work happily.[77]

If a doll was not thrust into a little girl's arms as soon as she can sit up, and if television serials didn't hawk "mother of seven" as the archetype of American heroines, and if childless women were spared our collective pity and all women were recognized for their intellectual or creative offspring, then we might find out the truth about female human beings.

Fewer of us might become mothers but those who do might be less ambivalent about it. The patriarchy would lose its brainwashed breeders of soldiers and workers, and its polished ornamental prizes—but humanity would gain a new phenomenon: little girls who choose their roles without coercion or guilt.

The motherhood compulsion and male supremacy are opposite swings of the same pendulum ticking back and forth in our children's brains. Few of us bother to analyze how it hammers away at them, clocking in day after day of service to the patriarchal system. But once you see through those nine rules of sex role conformity, the ticking becomes a roar, and you will want to put an end to it for good.

4
Everything to Gain, Nothing to Lose:
Why Nonsexist Childrearing Is
Good for Your Child

People who are skeptical about nonsexist methods should ask themselves not only what they're afraid of, but what they're hanging on to. The old ways hardly seem worth defending. In fact, there is much evidence that traditional childrearing is *bad* for your child. To drive home that point, I want to focus on five areas where sex-typing does the most damage.

ACHIEVEMENT

The Nonsexist Objective: Achievement is a sex-neutral human need. All children should feel free to excel in any field and to enjoy fully the fruits of their performance.

The Status Quo: One after another, studies have shown that present sex-role standards hamper the intellectual efforts of both sexes—although at different ages and with different effects.[1] "Masculinity" prevents many boys from doing well in elementary school,[2] while "femininity" interferes with girls' achievements in high school, college, and thereafter.[3]

We've seen that young children seem to characterize school as a "feminized" environment. Most elementary teachers are women and classroom life stresses stereotypically "feminine" values such as neatness, obedience, and conformity. It makes sense: girls who are raised to value those qualities become women who are consigned to low-paid, child-oriented work roles such as teaching: Therefore females bring those sex-typed qualities with them into the classroom. This inevitable cycle is intersected by the equally inevitable "masculinist" resistance to the taint of "feminine" teachers, objects, and ambience. To be a "real" boy, he may find it necessary to renounce teachers, books, homework, or good grades rather than feel himself a "sissy."[4]

This picture changes drastically in adolescence when the academic sphere is gradually transformed into a training ground for the "man's world." If they want to assume the privileged male role the patriarchy has cut out for them, boys must begin to let their abilities show and grow. Most of the more intelligent ones respond to the school's pressures, become focused on college preparation, and think seriously about their future careers.[5] Achievement is no longer a "girlish" value but a male merit badge to be won by those who will be in charge in a world far larger than the classroom.

The intellectual casualties of school sex-typing are usually lower-class boys who get little motivational impetus from their homes to tide them over during the years when they lose interest in the "feminized" school. As the school stereotype makes its about-face sometime during junior high school, these underachievers experience a sudden loss of "masculine" status; academic endeavors that are beyond their grasp have suddenly become not "sissy" but "manly." To overcompensate, these boys spend more time on sports; drive cars earlier; prefer boxing, playing pool, judo, karate, and football; get into trouble more often; and score higher than their peers on measures of heterosexual interest and activity.[6]

"These kids must have a girl friend," says one school counselor, "because it gives them greater self-image and assures their masculinity. Sex gratification is a motivating force great enough to take the place of achievement."[7] School has lost these boys forever.

Meanwhile, what's happening to the girls? They have superior attendance records,[8] get consistently better grades than boys throughout primary school,[9] and teachers consider them neater, better-behaved and harder-working.[10]

One writer says this brief "reign" of female superiority may explain why so many grown men "believe that it is neither necessary nor important that women be given equality: 'the girls got *theirs* in school, didn't they?' "[11] Only if the comparison graph ends at the sixth grade.

In the seventh or eighth grade (age twelve or thirteen), most of the bright girls begin to back away from academic achievement, preferring instead to be popular in the nonintellectual "feminine" mode.[12] In high school, the "demotivation" process solidifies with each passing year,[13] and the more a girl cares about her "proper" role, the less likely she is to maintain high educational aspirations.[14] Between 75 and 90 percent of the brightest students who do not go on to college are girls.[15]

Girls tend to feel less *entitled* to be smart. Raised to "face the facts," a boy can say, factually, "I'm an 'A' student and I'm going to be a physicist when I grow up." But girls are often "criticized for stating high, albeit realistic, expectations. They are taught that 'boasting' is unfeminine."[16]

Without self-esteem, confidence flags; with it, a child gets an energy charge. The brighter a boy is, the better he says he expects to master a new task; but the brighter a girl is, the worse she predicts she'll do.[17] Grade-school girls presented with a tough puzzle asked for more help from adults than did boys.[18] By the time girls are in high school and college, they have lost so much faith in their problem-solving ability that they attribute their academic performance to "hard work"[19] or "sheer luck,"[20] while boys credit *their* achievements to their basic abilities and skill, and blame only their failures on bad luck.[21]

All the "feminine" virtues—modesty, need for approval, conformity, and obedience—turn out to be antithetical to our daughters' intellectual performance.[22] Nevertheless, you'll still hear plenty of different-but-equal double talk about "feminine-style" achievement motivation, such as this from Lawrence Kohlberg:

> In the case of girls, feminine roles award an ample if somewhat lesser scope for power and competence . . . channeled into values that are not competence or achievement values in the usual sense. However the [girl's] pursuit of attractiveness, goodness and social approval is ultimately based on the same needs for control of the environment, for self-esteem and for successful achievement as are the more obvious masculine values.[23]

All that jargon can't mask a double standard of power and competence that doesn't help get a girl into college. "Attractiveness" is no *achievement;* it's a triumph of artifice superimposed on lucky genes. It also has a nasty tendency to fade with the years, while the more obvious "masculine values" are enhanced by maturity. And although "goodness" is indisputably good for both sexes, it rarely appears on job descriptions or Pulitzer Prize qualifications.

Finally, positing "social approval" as the motivating force for "feminine-style" achievement means that when the sought-after approval is denied, girls who have been conditioned "feminine" tend to give up.[24] Does it make sense that a child should need permission to strive for excellence?

Kohlberg sees the male's achievement as "the usual" but reduces the female's efforts to the antics of a child performing for a pat on the head. In fact, he finds the comparison of woman and child rather comforting: "While the stereotype of adult femininity is inferior in power and competence to the male, it is still superior to that of a child of either sex."[25]

For both sexes' sake, the status quo must go. Sex-typing inhibits boys from early school achievement and restrains girls from trying to excel as they get older. Certainly, that's not good for your children.

FEAR OF SUCCESS—FEAR OF FAILURE

The Nonsexist Objective: Success is sexless. Parents should help both girls and boys strive freely, take pride in their accomplishments, and be realistic about their failures.

The Status Quo: We've already noted the female's double bind: if she becomes a competent *person,* she's not a "real" woman; if she becomes a "normal" (that is, underachieving) woman, she's not the fullest person she can be, which is to say failure is "feminine."

One young poet quit writing for a year when her male seventh grade teacher told her, "You write like a man."[26] That scared her. As Margaret Mead put it, "Any success in a woman calls men's manliness into account."[27] Boys wouldn't like her. To outperform or even to equal males is to defy the culture's edict that Boys Are Better.

It's as though there were a limited amount of achievement to go around and the successful female automatically deprives males of their rightful share. A forthright exponent of this viewpoint was a former Harvard Law School dean who every year accused the few young women in the entering class of usurping the seats of young men.[28]

Mead warned women decades ago that nobody likes an uppity underdog:

> ... there are no rules in American life for the good behavior of underdogs ... for the woman who makes a success in a man's field, good behavior is almost impossible because the whole society has defined it so. A woman who succeeds better than a man ... has done something hostile and destructive.[29]

No wonder psychologist (now Radcliffe College president) Matina Horner found so many bright women anxious about "intellectual competition and leadership potential,"[30] and thus "contaminated by ... the motive to avoid success."[31] Horner asked college students to imagine what happens when "After first-term finals, John (Anne) finds himself (herself) at the top of his (her) medical school class."

Almost all the male students wrote cheerful stories about "John's" success, while a good majority of the female students wrote grim stories about "Anne," whose medical school distinction, they imagined, would make her abnormal, unhappy, lonely, ugly, hated, envied, acne-faced, sad, and unpopular, or would cause her to drop out of school, get beaten up by her classmates, decide to be a nurse, or have a nervous breakdown. One female found it so difficult to deal with a woman at the top of her class that she decided "Anne" was "a code name for a nonexistent person."[32]

Imagining a younger "John" or "Anne" at the top of a high school class, 6 out of 10 children from ten to seventeen, boys and girls alike, expressed fear of success imagery,[33] which may reflect a typical childish reluctance to stand out above the crowd. However, by eleventh grade the fear of success imagery was declining in boys but was on the increase in girls, especially girls who were headed for college.[34] By the end of high school, the brightest boys not only lost their success anxieties, they wanted to be remembered as "the best student"; the brightest girls did not.[35]

In college, 9 out of 10 female students show success anxiety, with the most marked depressions experienced just when a girl is about to complete a course or degree program.[36] Such crises don't stem from some fatal flaw in the female psyche, but from anticipating the *consequences* of the success she is on the brink of achieving.

Is it worth it? she asks herself. Women still have to work twice as hard to go half as far in a sexist society in which men react negatively to the achieving woman. Many boys and men characterize a female as "unattractive, immoral and dissatisfied"[37] merely for overstepping the sex role norms. They assume she used her body to get to the top, or else that she denied her sexuality to pursue "masculine" goals. Some college men even accused "Anne" of becoming "muscular and unfeminine" and developing "a five o'clock shadow" after she turned up number one in her medical class.[38]

The Mind-Binding of the American Girl

These male attitudes are felt as an implicit threat: "Certainly you can be equal in this society, honey, but we will punish you for it; we will desex you, we will not love you."

Raised to want male approval above all, girls take the implicit threat to heart, thus negating the supposedly democratic access routes to success. Girls will "play dumb" rather than be ridiculed or rejected. If the task or situation has a "masculine" label (such as medical school), girls will purposely underachieve whether their audience is female or male.[39] But if the task is labeled "feminine" (such as nursing or secretarial school), or if the achiever is not isolated (being one of three top women in medical school,[40] for example), then a girl's fear of success decreases.

Girls, it seems, are supreme realists. They fear not success per se, but sex role deviance and the *consequences* of it. Often they choose mediocrity rather than have to apologize for excellence, as did the little girl who won the spelling bee in Whittier's poem:

> "I'm sorry that I spelt the word:
> I hate to go above you,
> Because,"—the brown eyes lower fell,—
> "Because, you see, I love you!"[41]

Why and how do girls learn to fail for love, or more broadly, for "femininity"? When I started dating, the facts of (social) life were made clear to me, courtesy of my mother, girlfriends, teen magazines, and advice books:

"Get high grades but don't flaunt them. Why run for class president when vice president is good enough? The most popular girls are flirty, pretty, and act helpless in front of boys. Ignorance and gullibility are "cute" and make a boy feel important.

"Don't be a bossy know-it-all. Don't be a brain. Don't be too athletic. Don't beat a boy at his own game; flatter him, admire him, and let him boast. Don't match him medal for medal. Follow him up the wrong path even if you know the way. Take an interest in whatever interests him. Don't bore him with your enthusiasms. Stop *trying* so hard!"

By the time I was fifteen all that information was rolled up into one cardinal rule of middle-class womanhood: be smart enough to attract good "husband material" but not too smart to scare him away.

It was—and still is—hard work for many females to keep themselves second-best. I remember a high school friend who turned down a full scholarship to an Ivy League college because she didn't want to outshine her boyfriend, who was attending a city school. One study found that women tend to get pregnant when their professional accomplishments begin to nudge past their husbands'.[42] And I can think of several women who paid for their fear of success with lost opportunities and hard cash.

Shirley Polykoff, for example. An advertising genius (creator of Clairol's "Does She . . . Or Doesn't She" campaign, among others), Polykoff consistently refused her employer's promotions and raises: "I was trying to keep my career within manageable bounds, at least as far as my salary was concerned, so as not to threaten my husband's psyche," she explains.[43]

When her husband died, Polykoff felt free to succeed; she "let" her employer immediately quadruple her salary and make her Senior Vice President. How ironic. For the sake of her husband's ego, there was less money for both to enjoy while he was alive than was there for her to spend alone after he died. And how perverse that 1 of every 2 husbands polled nationwide agreed it would be "slightly difficult" to "impossible" to have a wife earning more than he,[44] even if her income goes into the same pot and is sorely needed by the family unit.

Sexism takes money out of our pockets two ways: first, by perpetuating an economic system that discriminates against females in the workplace; and second, by prescribing that boys are better and thereby causing girls to fear success, and hold *themselves* back.

I thought about this when one of our daughters was suffering the slow tortures of puberty while her more "developed" friends, a clique of simpering, giggling nymphets, "were having all the fun."

"But you're terrific at sports and you sing beautifully and write poetry," I ventured, amazed that giggling and simpering could be equated with my daughter's talents.

"Writing poetry isn't worth diddly if you don't have breasts!" she burst out. *"Boys like breasts!"*

My husband confirmed the truth of her statement but promised that breasts would fall into perspective, so to speak, as she and her friends grew older. At the same time, I was remembering how much easier it was *with* breasts than without them. I also knew that whatever her age, it would always be tempting to succeed "as a woman," sexually and superficially, without bothering to earn notice through her labors or her art. I vowed to help her guard her talent.

It is not enough to inspire my daughter and your daughter individually. Studies show that in society at large, females are more "positively evaluated" if they fail.[45] Therefore, we must care about altering society's judgment of the successful female and teaching all our sons to appreciate and love those accomplished daughters. Otherwise, the competent young women we send into the world will be met by young men who are afraid of them, men who are more interested in their breasts, or who see muscles and "five o'clock shadow" where there is only a woman's fervor to excel.

Fear of Failure

In those few communities where "eggheads" are branded "sissies," bright boys also fear success. But for the most part, the spectre that haunts males from boyhood to death is fear of failure.

Failure is so "emasculating" that even admitting *anxiety* about failing is "unmanly."[46] And success is so important that the bribe, as Margaret Mead wrote, is nothing less than the parents' love:

> ... rewards are so great for displaying to admiring and helpful parents those qualities of initiative, independence, and assertiveness ... only a sissy takes defeat as anything but a stimulus to try harder. . . .
>
> The chief trap for the boy in this pattern of maturation lies in the conditional nature of the whole process. . . . Mother loves you *if* you succeed; Father is grinning and proud, *if* you succeed.[47]

Rather than value his achievements as a measure of his competence, the boy begins to view them as amulets against failure; each success is a temporary reprieve from the downfall that must lie somewhere in his future. His fear of failure is "a realistic admission that an upward thrust cannot continue indefinitely,"[48] and that there is not enough room at the top to accommodate all the boys trying to get there.

Then, too, there are the moral questions: Who defines success for each of us, and what price should one pay to get it?

Whereas females can evade such questions by retreating into underachievement and "affiliative" satisfactions,[49] males who reject Upward Mobility imperil their "manhood." The patriarchy does not forgive those who rebuff the emoluments reserved for the chosen.

Can anyone believe this situation is good for a boy's development? Without suggesting that the suffering of the oppressor ever equals that of the oppressed, one can recognize that it is its own kind of pain: having to constantly re-earn his maleness; not allowed to question the morality of supremacy as a motivating goal; terrified of symptoms of weakness—of getting hurt, needing help, being sick, giving up, losing face, feeling frightened or indecisive or alone. As Jimmy Carter's book title asked, so every little boy is challenged: *Why Not the Best?* "If you're a woman doing more than your mother did, you feel successful. If you're a man and you're not President, you feel like a failure."[50]

Boys seem to adopt two strategies: either they set ridiculously high goals "so that success is not really expected and failure is not a disgrace"—like hoping to become President or a major league pitcher—or they set ridiculously low goals "so that failure is highly unlikely." Since females generally lack the first option (high goals, realistic or not, are reserved for males), they are left with the second option, ridiculously low goals that damage them as surely as males are damaged by their demons.[51]

The third area where the status quo is bad for children is the area of health and body image where, sad to say, sex roles literally make people sick.

PHYSICAL HEALTH AND WELL-BEING

The Nonsexist Objective: Children should be able to accept and enjoy the bodies they were born with and should not compromise their health to satisfy the dictates of an ideal "image."

The Status Quo: How sex role imperatives distort the female body is all too obvious: shoes deform feet; hair coloring causes cancer; make-up clogs pores and irritates allergies; clothing styles impede mobility; some birth control methods, plastic surgery, and fad diets wreak bodily havoc; and such "innocuous" self-improvement weapons as "speed," silicone, DES, estrogen, and liquid protein sometimes kill.

The pernicious physical payoffs of "masculinity" are just as familiar: high blood pressure, ulcers, hypertension, heart disease, anxiety, stroke, suicide, and early death.[52] A review of all medical evidence available through 1977 "confirms that male sex role socialization contributes to the higher mortality rate of men."[53]

Beyond these sadly familiar perils are two less frequently studied sex role imperatives affecting the body and health: *Men Must Be Taller than Women,* and *Women Must Be Thin.*

Height Makes Might

The movies show us that He must be taller than She. So do the picture book illustrations of taller Kings and shorter Queens, taller fathers and shorter mothers, taller brothers, boyfriends, grooms, and heroes, and shorter sisters, girl friends, brides, and damsels-in-distress. Despite the fact that about one-third of all women are taller than the average man and one-third of all men are shorter than the average woman,[54] somehow we are all expected to pair up like Big Daddy and the Little Woman. What does this sex role imperative do to those who cannot comply?

"I always yearned to be small and delicate like a girl is supposed to be," laughs one friend bitterly. "But I've been five-foot-ten since the sixth grade, so it's hard for me to find a guy I can look up to." While expressing the romantic ideal, what she seems to want is a man who will look down on her.

A much-maligned five-foot-six-inch man sarcastically calls for an "Equal Heights Amendment" to be added to the U.S. Constitution. Not quite so glib are his recollections of his youth:

> I was the kid who took vitamin B-12 to speed up my growth so I wouldn't develop an inferiority complex. I was the small fellow who agonized before dances, calculating not whom I wanted to invite, but what girl was short enough not to tower over me in heels. If they wore flats, I felt patronized.[55]

Another short man remembers stuffing socks into his shoes to elevate himself at school dances. A tallish woman used to shrink by contorting one hip. My friend Marsha perfected a slump that knocked two inches off her five-foot-seven frame when her boyfriend was five-foot-five.

The "opposite" sex standard requires a partner who sets one off by contrast. If you are a girl aching to look "feminine," the taller the guy, the smaller you look.

Some point to Woody Allen and Diane Keaton to refute this, or to Nancy and Henry Kissinger, but jet set standards haven't filtered down to kids. When asked "If you could change one thing about yourself, what would it be?" little boys most frequently wished they were taller.[56] Boys care because of all the cultural propaganda, but also because many have parents who care, parents who take slow-growing boys and fast-growing girls to the endocrinologist's office to be treated for their gender-inappropriate heights.[57]

I am not confusing "gender-inappropriate" height with pathological growth problems, such as that of Sandy Allen, a victim of pituitary malfunction. Medical treatments finally stabilized her growth at seven feet, seven inches, but she still has to contend with size 22 shoes, a 440-pound frame, and the inability to fit into a seat in a movie, restaurant, automobile, or airplane. With such formidable physical problems and their emotional toll, it is astonishing to discover that Sandy Allen has inflicted another impediment upon her life: she plans never to fall in love with a man shorter than herself. "I'm an old-fashioned girl," she explained to the *New York Times.*[58]

I know an old-fashioned man who was afraid his son, age seven, would be "too short," meaning not six feet tall like his father. He measured the boy every month or so, made him stand back-to-back with his playmates for a comparison check, and finally took him to a doctor.

The boy was perfectly normal. At ten, he caught up with the average for his age and his father finally let up on him.

It's natural for a parent to worry about a child who appears to be growing like a dwarf or a giant, but few cases merit a visit to the doctor. It's also natural to comment when an unusually tall or short person passes on the street, but not to make height into a component of someone's gender.

Your child will grow to her or his genetically determined full size regardless of what you think. But what you think *can* make the difference between raising children who feel physically disqualified for their gender and raising children who stand tall at any height.

The Weight of the Matter

Apart from the pleasures of good eating are the issues of food, "femininity," and fat—a complex set of connections that begins with the breast as a milk source, the mother as cook and nourisher, and the girl learning to see herself as a "real dish"[59]—contoured just so, not too fat and not too skinny, but definitely *thin.*

Getting fat can be understood as a deliberate challenge, either conscious or unconscious, to sex role stereotyping and to the culturally-defined experience of womanhood."[60] Girls have fattened themselves into a false pregnancy,[61] perhaps the most pathological fulfillment of the sex role dictum that Girls Are Meant to be Mothers. There are girls who put layers of flesh between themselves and the world[62] to make themselves asexual,[63] to make it "safe to be friendly,"[64] or to become an observer rather than a target. It may be that getting fat is one way that a female "asserts her need for space—by literally taking up more of it," trying to carry more weight than most females are allowed.[65] There is also the girl who puts food into her mouth rather than let anger out.

Obesity, the most obvious physical rebellion against the "feminine" ideal, is matched at the other extreme by compulsive underweight, an increasingly common form of sex role pathology.

Sixteen-year-old Susannah was five-feet-four, weighed only 73 pounds, and looked like the living skeletons who stare out of pictures of Dachau. She thought she was "fat" and "gross."

Shaughn, a fifteen-year-old, had to take size 10 children's clothing to summer camp because she weighed 66 pounds. The year before, when she was five feet tall, 103 pounds, and developing ample breasts and hips, she remembers, "The boys said I was 'built' and my parents worried that, physically, I was too mature for my age . . . my boyfriends and father joked about my 'padded' hips."[66] In response to those comments, she stopped eating. She dieted, gave away the school lunches her mother packed for her, messed up the kitchen so it would appear she had eaten breakfast, was oblivious to her real appearance and health even though she couldn't find clothes to fit; her skin dried out, her hair thinned, her stamina disappeared, and she stopped menstruating. For a year she refused her parents' bribes—a dollar for every pound gained, a trip to Europe—until finally, for reasons no one understands, she admitted to her doctor father that she needed help, or else she would "starve myself to death."[67]

Susannah and Shaughn are victims of a disease known as

anorexia nervosa, which has been found in 1 out of every 200 high school and college girls.[68] (It rarely affects boys, and then only those boys who are raised like girls.) The condition seems most common among affluent or middle-class girls who are exceptionally attractive, intelligent, and "good."[69] In short, model daughters and perfect little ladies.

Some psychoanalysts attribute anorexia in adolescents to rejection of "feminine" maturation, fear of oral impregnation (food-equals-sex and fat-equals-pregnancy), and resistance to the traditional passive-receptive female role (signified by rejection of the mother, who is equated with food-giving).[70]

Others take the totally opposite view that anorexics adopt the "feminine" stereotype all too well, that "their obsessive pursuit of thinness constitutes not only an acceptance of this ideal but an exaggerated striving to achieve it."[71]

Under either interpretation, one finds in the backgrounds of these emaciated girls a history of sex roles run amok. Dr. Hilda Bruch, author of *Eating Disorders,* summarizes the typical anorexic's mother as a woman who gave up her career plans and became a "proper" subservient wife and an overprotective mother. The anorexic's father, a somewhat distant "hero figure," praises the girl for her looks and reinforces her "feminine" behavior. Neither parent encourages her to be self-reliant, self-expressive, independent, or assertive.[72] She is able to sustain a distorted body image (seeing fat where there is only skin and bone) because she has developed no identity other than her reflection in the approving eyes of others—remember Kohlberg's idea that "social approval" is female achievement.

Since this quintessentially "feminine" girl was trained to please, she loses weight with a vengeance at the mere suggestion that she has *dis*pleased her observers. Thus anorexia may be triggered by slight overweight, which causes a friend or family member to tease her (such as Shaughn's case), or by a boy's rejection of her, whether real or imagined.[73]

After a childhood of "goodness," this wind-up doll expects perfect male adoration in return for her perfect female development. When she experiences rejection, she blames her body. She starts dieting ("a woman is never too thin or too rich," they say) and eventually starves herself trying to match the elusive ideal that will make her acceptable.

Dr. Marlene Boskind-Lodahl studied 138 young "bulimarexics," girls who combine starving (anorexia) with periods of gorging (bulimia), then make themselves vomit, then take huge amounts of laxatives, then fast and gorge all over again.[74] Two of Boskind-Lodahl's case histories illustrate the deleterious sex-typed upbringing that can result in this behavior.

> Anne, a good, generally submissive child . . . had been socialized by her parents to believe that society would reward her good looks: "Someday the boys are going to go crazy over you." "What a face! With your good looks you'll never have to worry about getting a job." Clinging and dependent, she could not see herself as a separate person. . . . Anne's distorted body image was linked to a complete lack of confidence in her own ability to control her behavior.[75]

Peggy tells this story:

> I was always a tomboy. In fact at the age of ten to twelve I was stronger and faster than any of the boys. After I won a race against a boy, I was given the cold shoulder by the rest of the boys in my class. The girls teased me and my parents put pressure on me to "start acting like a girl should."[76]

"Acting like a girl should" almost killed Peggy and thousands more like her. Until recently the death rate for anorexia nervosa and bulimia approached 20 percent of those afflicted with the condition.[77] Today's most effective treatments include a family therapy approach that emphasizes the very same values embodied in nonsexist childrearing: a less controlling, less family-obsessed mother, a more family-involved father, equal status between brothers and sisters and reinforcement and praise awarded to a girl for what she *does,* not for her docility or her looks.

At all ages females "experience" the body as the *self* far more than do males,[78] a finding consistent with girlish preoccupation with body weight and image. Although American males suffer from the "masculine" height imperative and are generally considered less appealing when fat than when trim, they do not punish their bodily infractions with quite the same savagery as females do, and they rarely use food and flesh as tools of rebellion against their sex role destiny. Remove that "sickening" destiny from your daughter's crystal ball and she might be healthier, feel better about herself, and live longer.

CREATIVITY AND INDEPENDENCE

The Nonsexist Objective: Girls and boys should be encouraged to express themselves with originality and enthusiasm, however iconoclastic their interests—and to make independent judgments based on facts, feelings, logic, pleasure, and consideration for others, without regard for sex role "propriety."

The Status Quo: Sex-typed people tend to be "dependent in their interpersonal relations, suggestible, conforming and likely to rely on others for guidance and support," writes Eleanor Maccoby.[79] Because they see the world in stereotypes, they also are prone to other kinds of prejudices and tend to have authoritarian personalities.[80]

Conformists don't think for themselves. Even when presented with physical evidence, such as two straight lines of different lengths, they will go against their senses in order to agree with what others say is the longest of the two lines.[81] That sort of "socially defined" (as opposed to "self-defined") behavior makes sex-typed girls and women less able to cope with stress, less likely to take "vigorous, appropriate action to solve a problem,"[82] or even to resist smoking when a male lights a cigarette in their presence.

Sex-typing retards creative and independent thinking in boys, too. Among grade-school boys, lower originality correlates with high scores in traditional "masculinity."[83] And in a study of adult male architects, it was found that "the more creative a person is, the more he reveals an openness to his own feelings and emotions . . . and wide-ranging interests including many which in the American culture are thought of as feminine."[84]

Someone once said that to be creative, a woman must have been a "tomboy" at some point in her childhood. What this means, of course, is that a girl (like a boy) must be given *indepen-*

dence training, the freedom to explore her environment and to have her high spirits admired—as a boy is grudgingly admired when he uses the electric tools without permission, and secretly builds a go-cart.

Those characteristics absolutely necessary to creativity—assertiveness, initiative, independence, and analytic thinking—are the very characteristics that are bred *out* of the female in the traditional family or school.[85]

And it doesn't take long. At age three, children who were creative problem-solvers were the "active, confident, expressive, less compliant" children. Two years later the boys were unchanged but the girls had become inhibited, less vital, and "frequently scapegoated and victimized by their peers."[86]

The pressure to conform to sex roles can have the power of the Spanish Inquisition in a nursery school classroom. Yet the nonconformist, high-intellect boys tend to rebel against sex role expectations from early childhood, resigning themselves to taunts of "sissy" or "weirdo," while creative girls do not rebel and express their full nonconformity until adolescence.[87] From our earlier discussion, you'll understand that this happens because the heavier coercion of the male sex role regimen forces an earlier showdown for the "different" little boy.

Girls need the strength to be "different" in high school. Unlike comparable boys, creative girls, whether artists or mathematicians, exhibit a "pervasive and continuing interest in their chosen fields,"[88] a single-minded dedication that totally eclipses other adolescent social activities. Gifted girls, first of all, need to be twice as committed and intense about their interests in order to be taken seriously. Secondly, since the conventional female role is antithetical to intellectual achievement, and since a girl's energies are so relentlessly channeled by peers and pop culture into being popular and pleasing others, the creative girl seems to build a wall of concentration around herself in order to resist the sex role imperatives and pursue her goals in peace.

There is an uncanny resemblance between the typical family background of creative, independent children, and the egalitarian nonsexist household. The bright children's families were "expressive, undominating, and gave the child much freedom . . ."[89] They

had fathers who were "especially warm and accepting and listened...
rather than imposing their own opinions"[90] and mothers who were
"distinctly autonomous," with interests and careers of their own.[91]

Put it all together and creativity—just as achievement—
clearly prospers best under nonsexist childrearing.

The fifth category in which children gain from role-free living
is the vast area of individual psychology where the cultural sledgehammer has done some of its worst damage.

MENTAL HEALTH AND
EMOTIONAL WELL-BEING

The Nonsexist Objective: Children and adults alike should throw
off "the curse of the ideal"[92] and emotional self-censorship—and
should reach beyond the clichés of gender to discover who we are,
what we really feel, and how happy we can be.

The Status Quo: Most experts have assumed that "masculine"
boys and "feminine" girls are the most "normal" children and
grow up to be the most effective, well-adjusted adults.

But recently a small minority of investigators have worried
in print about possible detrimental effects of sex role standards,[93]
which some have called maladjustments[94] and which I understand
to mean lack of "positive self-concepts, personal security and
feelings of adequacy."[95]

No wonder we're "maladjusted." Faced with an ideal for
each sex that no one can live up to, an ideal that makes virtually
everyone feel inadequate. However, instead of blaming the sex role
system for our distress, we blame ourselves. And we want our
children to do better.

"How people continue to believe so fervently in values and
norms according to which they can only be failures, is an awe-
inspiring phenomenon," says sex role expert Joseph Pleck, who,
like many men, was raised with all the Byzantine agonies of "masculine" inadequacy:

> I was so rarely allowed to experience myself as all right—in
> sports because I was a complete failure and in intellectual
> work, because though I performed well, I would never be
> perfect.[96]

Julius Lester, raised in the black community, suffered so desperately as a boy that he actually found reasons to envy girls:

> I thought of the girls sitting in the shade of porches, playing with their dolls, toy refrigerators and stoves. There was the life, I thought! No constant pressure to prove oneself. No necessity always to be competing. While I humiliated myself on football and baseball fields, the girls stood on the sidelines laughing at me, because they didn't have to do anything except be girls.[97]

Whoever said *that* was easy? Just as a boy felt compelled to play sports, we girls felt we *had* to be beautiful.

Talk about self-hatred and violence: I grew up hating my nose, so I learned to gracefully (I thought) cover it with my fist whenever I was in profile. My hair was too straight and fine, especially compared to Shirley Temple's, so I had a torturous permanent wave on a circa 1949 curling machine that resembled the head set of an electric chair, and that burned my hair to a frizz. As I grew older I decided my ankles were too skinny and my chest too flat, so I wore two pair of thick wool socks every day, and an Exquisite Form bra that kept its exquisite form on or off my body. When I was fourteen and weighed barely 90 pounds, tiny waists were all that counted in the "femininity" sweepstakes, so I wore a boned corset that cinched my middle to a circumference of 20 inches. "If you wanna be beautiful, you have to suffer," we girls told each other.

Around that time, my father had a favorite joke about a couple on their wedding night: When the bride took off her false eyelashes, her wig, her padded bra, and shaped corset, and put them all in the bureau drawer, her new husband looked at her disdainfully and said, "Thanks, I think I'll spend the night in the drawer."

My worst fear was that I wasn't pretty enough for any boy. My second worst fear was that if I ever did win a husband, as soon as he saw my natural self, he too would leap into a drawer. I just didn't think I could measure up.

When children are raised to measure up rather than to become their best selves, childhood is a Procrustean Bed on which they must stretch or shrink themselves before they can have a night's rest. The effort produces *role strain*[98] ("No matter how I try, I'm not as athletic as a boy should be"), *role conflict*[99] ("Can I grow up to be a good doctor and a good mother?"), and eventually *role dysfunction*[100] ("I'll show them I'm a man; gimme a gun!" or "I can't be Superwoman, gimme a Valium").

Misery, Male and Female

Let's face it: our sex roles make us suffer. Boys have to learn theirs early, so they suffer more in childhood. One child in 3 has difficulty with school, self-esteem, friendships, or family life; most of them are boys.[101] In childhood boys also outnumber girls 2 to 1 as institutionalized mental patients.[102] At five or six years old, when "masculine" strain is severe, boys' dreams become more frightening, stressful, and nightmarish, while girls' dreams get more docile and passive in early adolescence, when "femininity" becomes important.[103]

The dysfunctional extremes of each sex role also show up in the symptoms, or at least the diagnoses, of mental distress.[104]

Boys end up in child guidance clinics for "aggressive, destructive and competitive behavior" while girls are referred for "excessive fears and worries, shyness, timidity, lack of self-confidence, and feelings of inferiority."[105]

Most of the children who run away from home each year are girls; boys are more apt to be allowed to "act out" their frustrations.[106] Those who continue to feel insufficiently "masculine" may become hostile or violent.[107] From age fourteen on, more males commit criminal offenses while more females seek counsel for mental problems.[108] Boys fight, steal, and destroy property to prove their "manhood"; girls use sexual behavior for similar ends: "adulthood, independence from parents, and femininity."[109]

Too often, boys who feel insufficiently male by society's standards refuse to identify as male at all (see Chapter 16, "Homosexuality, Hysteria, and Children"). Others try to escape life altogether.

> When Jimmy was 10, he made his second try to get into
> ... Little League, and was turned down. His father, who had
> been a college football star, was so disappointed that he
> refused to talk to Jimmy all evening. Later that night, Jimmy
> swallowed some pills from his parents' medicine cabinet.[110]

Suicide is the tenth major cause of death in this country. More females attempt it, but boys and men are three times more successful at it.[111] "Either men are more skilled in killing themselves," says one doctor, "or they have more to kill themselves about."[112] Perhaps, they succeed at killing themselves because they can't face living having failed at dying, a failure women can accept along with all their others. ("I just can't do *anything* right!")

It's too facile to say they're killing themselves because of the male role; obviously there are many contributing factors. But one can't ignore the data: high sex role conformity in men correlates with the highest rates of anxiety, neurosis,[113] drug abuse, and alcoholism.[114] And the only period during which "masculinity" correlates with boys' happiness is the teens when "their masculinity itself confers status on them in adolescent male culture."[115]

A decade or more of "Boys don't do that!" or "You look like a sissy!" and suddenly the teenager experiences the joys of male privilege. Bigger than girls finally, and taken somewhat seriously as a "future man," he enjoys many of the pleasures of male supremacy and few of its burdens. He's a hero to younger boys but not yet a competitor to men; he's suitor and sex object of preening girls but not yet the overburdened provider and protector for grown women.

Ironically, many of these "automatic" adolescent heroes never learn to develop the interpersonal skills that adults expect from one another.[116] Boys who enjoy a golden adolescence are all the more rudely shattered by maladjustment or driven by adult sex role pressures to drink, fight, rebel, or work themselves to death.

Growing Up Girlish

"Where one sex suffers, the other sex suffers also."[117] If male suffering can be headlined "The Compulsion to Be Number One," then female sex role suffering can be abstracted to "The Commandment to Be Number Two."

Puberty is the great leveler. Budding breasts and menstruation remind a girl and everyone around her that Girls Are Meant to Be Mothers. Your daughters' individuality and my daughters' individuality disappear, subsumed under that one sexual persona, Mother.

The training for motherhood is not overt. (If we told girls about labor pains and cracked nipples they might be somewhat less enamoured of their dollies.) No, the training is just holding back, learning to fear success, putting yourself last, learning to live through others, learning helplessness.[118] "High sex-typed interests are actually associated with poor adjustment throughout the life cycle for females."[119]

The more your daughter conforms to the "feminine" stereotype, pressed upon her in her teens, the more she is likely to feel inferiority and low self-esteem,[120] envy and anger (and internalized rage because she cannot ventilate either and still be a "lady"),[121] anxiety, neuroticism, and guilt;[122] the more she's likely also to suffer withdrawal, alcoholism and drug abuse,[123] and most of all depression, the epidemic that never leaves the country of the "feminine" damned.[124]

Historically, being female has often been synonymous with being sick. Once there was supposed to be a link between women and sorcery, then women and hysteria, then women and fainting spells;[125] now it's women and depression. In almost any era, every girl raised to fit the "feminine" role has had good reason to become a basket case.

In the language of social science—

The pressures of sex role conformity have been determined to have a direct relationship upon the maladjustment of young adult females. . . . Therefore, it would appear that a reduction of stereotyping should be a goal towards developing psychologically healthier persons.[126]

Konrad Lorenz cautions all theorists to begin with the "knowledge of what is good and what is bad for the organism."[127] In this chapter, we have reviewed just a small part of the evidence that nonsexist objectives are good and gender role stereotypes are bad for the male and female organism in five crucial areas of learning and development:

1. Achievement
2. Attitudes Toward Success and Failure
3. Physical Health and Well-Being
4. Creativity and Independence
5. Mental and Emotional Well-Being

This evidence should impress upon parents the urgency of our task. To help you remember the main objectives of nonsexist childrearing, I am repeating them all together below: copy the list, if you like, tack it to your wall, and reread it when the going gets rough.

FIVE MAIN OBJECTIVES
OF NONSEXIST CHILDREARING
(or, why it's worth the struggle)

1. Achievement is a sex-neutral human need. All children should feel free to excel in any field and to fully enjoy the fruits of their performance.

2. Success is sexless. Parents should help both girls and boys to strive freely, take pride in their accomplishments, and be realistic about their failures.

3. Children should be able to accept and enjoy the bodies they were born with and should not compromise their health to satisfy the dictates of an ideal "image."

4. Girls and boys should be encouraged to express themselves with originality and enthusiasm, however iconoclastic their interests—and to make independent judgments based on facts, feelings, logic, pleasure, and consideration for others, without regard for sex role "propriety."

5. Children and adults alike should throw off "the curse of the ideal" and the burden of emotional self-censorship—and should reach beyond the clichés of gender to discover who we are, what we really feel, and how happy we can be.

II
Self and Parent

5

Bias Before Birth

"So you're going to have a baby! What do you want?"
"Well, naturally, we'd like a boy first. But we'll love whatever we get."

"Pregnant *again?!!*"
"I know. I know. We were going to stop after the fourth boy. But we decided to try just once more."

Eavesdrop on conversations with expectant parents and more often than not, you'll find that sex bias begins *before* birth. They may say they're expecting "a baby" but usually they are imagining a boy baby or a girl baby for particular reasons, and their sex preferences are so widely shared in this culture that few listeners challenge them.

"Naturally," a boy first. "Of course," at least one of each sex. It goes without saying.

But when such things go without saying, parents may never understand why sex preference proves sex prejudice. People only prefer a girl or a boy if they believe that the two sexes are two different *givens,* different inside and out, different in worth and potential; and if that is their belief, the children they will bear are "preconceived" long before they are actually conceived. Their parents have built a prison of gender, brick by brick, in advance of ever meeting the little inmate.

SON PREFERENCE

The most common sex preference is for a first-born boy. Of course. If people believe that Boys Are Better, then it's better to give birth to boys.

Nature, too, seems to favor boys at first, dealing out an average of 105 boys for every 100 girls, but then equalizing the ratio with a higher rate of infant mortality for males.[1] To stack the deck with more boys, almost every culture has elaborate rituals, such as the one in my family, carried to the American suburbs from a Jewish shietl in Hungary. It required the pregnant woman to eat the two heel ends of every loaf of bread encountered during the entire nine months. My older sister "proved" the superstition true. She indulged to excess in bread tips and had three boys in a row before overcoming the yeasty overdose and producing a daughter.

College-educated, cynical, and well-aware of the absurdity of phallic transubstantiation, I nevertheless gorged myself on bread tips during my 1964–65 pregnancy (pre-feminist consciousness) and succeeded in delivering up twin girls.

If you are unacquainted with the wonders of bread tips, perhaps you inherited one of the other male-making recipes that have survived the age of enlightenment.[2] For example, according to folklore,

• The couple should have intercourse in dry weather, on a night with a full moon, after a good nut harvest, and/or when there is a north wind.

• The man should wear boots to bed, get drunk, tie a string around his right testicle, cut off his left testicle, take an ax to bed, hang his pants on the right bedpost, and/or bite his wife's right ear.

• The woman should lie on her right side during intercourse, eat red meat or sour foods, let a small boy step on her hands or sit in her lap on her wedding day, sleep with a small boy on her wedding eve, wear male clothing to bed on her wedding night, and/or pinch her husband's right testicle before intercourse.

In those rare cases when a girl child is wanted, a few "Old Husband's Tales" recommend that:

• The couple must copulate facing south, during a south wind and in rainy weather.

• The man should hang his pants on the left bedpost and focus all aforementioned rites on the left testicle.

• The woman should concentrate on happy thoughts and eat sweets.

PREDICTING SEX

Many sophisticated folks who call such pre-conception rites "primitive" nonetheless swear by their own formulas for sex detection *after* pregnancy. Far and away the most accepted it's-a-boy clues are the belly that "sticks out in front" rather than one that looks "heavy all over," and the active, kicking fetus. Thus, even into the womb children are described by sex stereotypes: the thrusting, assertive boy and lumpish, passive girl.

Furthermore, nearly every sex prediction method establishes positive clues for boys and negative clues for girls. As in the pre-conception rituals, the birth of a boy is associated with the right side of the body, traditionally the side of justice, rightness, and goodness; the girl is left-oriented. The woman's body is thought to respond more hospitably to a male fetus; the female fetus is more "sickening." The boy is also signified by something extra (an odd number), something more, longer, faster, better, as indicated by the following ethnic and folkloric predictions:[3]

The child will be a *BOY* if:	The child will be a *GIRL* if:
The pregnant woman carries high.	The pregnant woman carries low.
Her complexion is rosy.	She is pale.
Her disposition is cheerful (Arab), happy (Indian), untroubled (Jewish).	She is bad-tempered and cries a lot.

Her looks improve; she glows.	Her right eye is bloodshot; her face is bloated; she has complications of pregnancy— swollen legs, skin discoloration.
A coin slipped down her back falls heads up.	The coin falls tails up.
The fetus has a fast heartbeat.	The fetal heartbeat is slow.
The fetus moves by the 40th day.	The fetus doesn't move until the 90th day.
The number of seeds in a handful of grain is uneven.	An even number of seeds turn up in your handful of grain.
When a wishbone is pulled between the woman and the man, he gets the longer part.	The woman gets the longer part of the wishbone.

Son preference has been so universal for so long that jokes about it are commonplace: "I'll send it back if it's a girl," a man tells his wife as she is wheeled into the delivery room.[4] A nurse shows a man his newborn baby and the man says, "That's O.K. A girl was my second choice." An insurance company brochure quips, "Certainly, next to the phrase, 'It's a boy!' the most beautiful phrase in the English language is 'It's deductible!' "[5] The plight of Tevye in *Fiddler on the Roof* arouses sympathetic laughter. The only comfort for a man with nothing but daughters is the reminder "Look at all the sons-in-law you will have!"

Everyone laughs. Everyone understands the "problem": daughters must be "married off"; fathers have to pay for the wedding, the hope chest, the dowry; and most daughters are assumed to be incapable of supporting their parents in old age. But even where these economic considerations are secondary, son preference still persists. It persists without too much acknowledgement of its darker side: daughter-hatred, the by-product of misogyny and, throughout human history, the justification for gynocide.

FEMALENESS: PUNISHABLE BY DEATH

Some facts are too painful, too "extreme" to have anything to do with *us.* Yet these facts can be allowed to speak for themselves—from ancient times to just yesterday:

A Roman father could . . . expose his infant daughters on the hillside to die of starvation, he could condemn his wife to death.

—the Roman republic, circa 500 B.C.[6]

The Greeks practiced infanticide at times, leaving babies on temple steps or in wild places. Baby girls were killed more often than boys, as would be expected in a warrior society that valued men more highly than women.

—classical Greece, circa 400 B.C.[7]

Henry VIII annulled his marriage to aging Catherine of Aragon because of his craving for a legitimate male heir to the throne. Anne [Boleyn] became pregnant . . . only to disappoint the anxious King by presenting him with a daughter, Elizabeth. Anne did become pregnant with a male child, but it was born dead. Henry then demonstrated his dissatisfaction with his wife by having her beheaded.

—England, 1536[8]

> If the tenth too, is a girlchild
> I will cut both of your feet off,
> To the knees I'll cut your feet off,
> Both your arms up to the shoulders,
> Both your eyes too, I will put out,
> Blind and crippled you will be then,
> Pretty little wife, young woman.
> —Bulgarian folk rhyme[9]

For the father can decide whether a girl will be kept or killed so the wife can get pregnant again to bear, hopefully, a boy.

—Thule, Greenland, 1918[10]

"Girls . . . died from the same causes as boys but their parents gave boys higher quality medical care and possibly more supplementary food."

—India, 1950s and 1960s[11]

The seventh or eighth child in a poor family was the one doomed to die. The means of killing were starvation and neglect. As far as could be ascertained, the doomed child was always female.

—South America, 1973[12]

Her father broke into the hospital room and shot her mother
for giving birth to a fifth daughter.

—Israel, 1975[13]

An all-male jury found the father of three girls guilty of
tossing his youngest child out of a sixth floor window because
he wanted a son.

—New York City, 1978[14]

In times past, to rid the world of a daughter, one could,
quasi-legally or not, expose her to the elements, starve her, turn
her over to the *balia* (the wet nurse who specialized in infanticide),
suffocate her "accidentally" by overlaying,[15] or just neglect her to
death. This is sexism's "final solution": the killing of girl babies
and of the mothers who bear them. We don't like to think about
it. It's barbaric, inconceivable, a grotesque and abhorrent crime.
Yes. But its psychic and political sources are still with us, tamed
and lightened and laughed about.

Decapitation is passé, but kings still trade in queens who
"give them" no heirs and husbands still complain that "the wife
keeps turning out daughters," and the daughters themselves still
know they are less valued, less celebrated, less wanted.

HOW DO WE KNOW
GIRLS ARE SECOND CHOICE?

Polls and surveys tell the story. Reviewing more than 40
years of research on sex preferences, Dr. Nancy Williamson of
The Population Council notes that American attitudes have not
changed very much since 1933 when the first such study found boy
babies preferred over girls by a ratio of 165 to 100.[16] Despite the
feminism of the 1970s, son preference is as strong as ever:[17]

• For an only child—Over 90 percent of the men and two-
thirds of the women preferred to have a boy.[18]

• For a firstborn—about 80 percent wanted a son; only 4
percent of the men and 10 percent of the women preferred to have
a daughter first.[19]

• For a three-child family—most preferred two boys and a
girl, rather than two girls and a boy.[20]

It isn't just that boys are preferred in the abstract or in "what-if" musings during pregnancy. Many parents who vow to "love whatever we get," never resign themselves to the second choice.

"We have three adorable daughters but have wanted a boy from the start," writes one Kansas City woman, asking a doctor for help conceiving a male child.[21] More than 1 out of 3 parents of firstborn daughters would have preferred a boy, while "almost none of those having a boy first would have preferred a girl."[22]

The birth of a girl baby when a boy was preferred can be the cause of more conceptions than a couple originally intended: those who have two girls are more likely to have a third child than those whose first two are boys;[23] couples with a firstborn girl conceive their second child an average of three months sooner than couples whose first was a boy;[24] and mothers of daughters are happier about their new pregnancy (relishing the possibility that it may be a boy this time) than pregnant mothers who already have the treasured son.[25]

Although modern women are rarely murdered for bearing girl babies, it is not unusual for women to apologize for giving birth to a daughter, as though it were their personal failure.

An obstetrician remembers attending at a horrendous emergency birth in a cold-water flat in Chicago. The baby's placenta was attached to the mother's cervix, labor contractions were tearing the cervix causing alarming blood loss and cutting off the baby's oxygen, the exit from the uterus was blocked, and the baby was lying in an impossible transverse position. After many hours, a special operating team miraculously delivered a healthy baby girl and saved the life of the mother. "As she regained full consciousness," the obstetrician recalls, "she glanced at her newborn infant cradled in her arms and turning to her husband, moaned apologetically, 'Oh, John, I'm so sorry it wasn't a boy.' "[26]

When Liv Ullman was born, her mother remembers "a nurse bending down and whispering apologetically: 'I'm afraid it's a girl. Would you prefer to inform your husband yourself?' "[27]

This is serious business: a father's disappointment, a mother's shame. What does woman apologize for if not for reproducing *herself*, for delivering the lesser of two lives, a creature of inferior morphology and minimal potential.

*Delivery Room dialogue at the moment of birth
(verbatim transcript)*

DOCTOR: Come on, junior. Only a lady could cause so much trou-
ble. Come on, little one.
(Baby is delivered)
MOTHER: A girl.
DOCTOR: Well, it's got the right plumbing.
FATHER: (laughs)
MOTHER: Oh, I'm sorry, darling.
DOCTOR: What are you sorry about?
MOTHER: He wanted a boy.
DOCTOR: Well, you'll have to try again next week, won't you![28]

If at first you don't succeed . . . We've progressed beyond
murdering wives who bear daughters, but not beyond women's
seeking forgiveness or women's bodies' being used to keep trying
for the production of the desired son.

Some fathers want a boy so badly that they alter reality to fit
the wish:

In Mrs. D.'s delivery the baby is held up for the father to see,
who says "It's a boy" though in fact it's a girl. The midwife
and the mother correct him, and he admits "I got my things
sorted out wrong." They all then exchange bantering remarks
about the fact that she won't be able to play rugby.[29]

The above quote is from *The Psychology of Childbirth,* a
volume in the prestigious Harvard University series on The Developing Child. The book offers no comment on the psychological
ramifications of the father's "mistake" about his baby's gender
identity. There is no comment on parental sex preferences in
general. The flat assertion that this unknown new person "won't
be able to" play a certain sport—as if she were born with a
physical handicap—goes unchallenged, and the possible effects of
such typecasting on the rearing of that child are not explored.
There is only the author's brief speculation:

I think that behind this banter there is a very serious grap-
pling with the baby's being a girl, an adjustment that starts

at this moment and probably takes a considerable time to complete.[30]

The problem with which readers are expected to sympathize is the poor father's adjustment to "the baby's being a girl."

Occasionally the possibility of "the baby's being a girl" is *so* problematic that it isn't even entertained. In one case, a woman reports that her parents so resolutely expected a boy that "the cigars they bought to announce my birth, each with a band reading 'it's a boy,' had to be tied with pink ribbons."[31] And in another situation, the sex preference (this time for a girl) was so role-stereotyped that *neither* gender could satisfy the mother's expectations:

> Joan had always dreamed of having two little girls—girls she could sew for, buy dolls for, and share good times with. . . . She was so sure that she was going to have a girl that she went right ahead and painted the nursery pink.
> The baby (of course) was a boy. Her husband was delighted and Joan eventually squelched her disappointment. But when Lisa was born two years later, Joan was so thrilled that she taped a pink bow in her hair. And she immediately chose a super-feminine wardrobe for her little girl . . . (who turned out to be) not the girl-type girl Joan had envisioned. She preferred playing with dirt rather than dolls, and she was more vigorous and rambunctious than her older brother.[32]

Joan resented both of her children—"one for being a boy and the other for not being the kind of little girl she'd wanted."[33]

For some parents, there is never an adjustment to their child's sex no matter what sort of person the child may be. More often than not, the dissatisfaction is focused on the female. In China, daughter-hatred is embodied in such old sayings as "Even a deformed son is better than the brightest, most skilled girl."[34]

My friend Antoinette, who attended Catholic school in California in the 1940s, remembers learning that

> missionaries in China collected money to rescue the girl babies that the Chinese parents threw away. There was a large chart on the [school] bulletin board every year. At the top was a picture of a nun picking up a baby out of a heap of garbage.

... We were told that when we sent five dollars we fed a baby for a whole year. We could even name them. Somewhere in the Orient there are at least ten Chinese women named Antoinette.[35]

Somewhere within Antoinette is the silent knowledge that she, too, was unwanted. She grew up hearing her Italian-American family and friends "bless people in response to a sneeze with *Salut' e figli maschi,* which means 'Good health and male children!' "[36]

SELECTING SEX SCIENTIFICALLY

Now people intent upon influencing the sex of their next conception can move beyond blessings and rituals into the realm of science:

Emulate Girl-Prone or Boy-Prone Families

After accumulating a list of all the single factors found among boy-prone couples, one body of research tells us more boys are born during and after wartime, if the mother is fifteen years old, if the woman has orgasm before the man, if the couple practices Orthodox Judaism,[37] and to "families of higher socio-economic status, Caucasians, couples with higher frequency of intercourse, those conceiving in certain months, and mothers who have had toxemia of pregnancy."[38]

The drawbacks of this sex control method should be especially obvious to those who cannot alter their age, race, or socio-economic status prior to copulation.

Selective Abortion

Sex identification of the fetus is one of the ancillary data that result from amniocentesis, a process in which amniotic fluid is drawn off from the uterus to test for genetic abnormalities.[39] Some scientists are working on simpler sex-detection tests that utilize blood[40] or saliva samples.[41]

In any case, when the fetus is the "wrong" sex, the "corrective" is abortion, and therein lies the problem. If abortion is discredited by its abuse for capricious gender selection, it may be politically compromised as a birth control method of last resort and as a basic right that guarantees women reproductive freedom.

What's more, gender selection should not become a euphemism for a pre-birth purge of firstborn females. In China, which permits sex detection and abortion after seven weeks of pregnancy, out of the first 30 selective abortions performed, 29 of the rejected fetuses were female.[42]

Sperm Favoritism Through Timed Intercourse

Since the father's sperm determines the baby's sex, and since X-bearing and Y-bearing sperm have different properties and do better in different vaginal and cervical environments at different times of the month, two theories recommend that intercourse be timed for a specific day during the menstrual cycle depending on which sex is wanted. However, not only do both theories rely on a woman's ability to predict the exact day of her ovulation, but sex control fanatics are stymied by the fact that the two theories directly contradict each other.

To conceive a boy, Dr. Landrum Shettles advises coitus at the time of ovulation; for a girl, he says intercourse should precede ovulation by several days.[43]

Dr. Rodrigo Guerrero, on the other hand, says it is boy babies that result from making love four or more days before ovulation. The recipe for girl babies calls for copulation the day before.[44]

Both theories claim high success rates but Dr. Nancy Williamson, the maven in this area, says neither approach is very satisfactory.[45]

Sperm Selection and Artificial Insemination

Because of the different size, weight, motility, longevity, and speed of the two types of sperm, various filtering procedures can be used to separate X-bearing (girl-making) from Y-bearing (boy-making) sperm in the father's semen.[46] The chosen sperm are then introduced into the mother by artificial insemination.

Although this process may improve the odds for the preferred sex by 90 percent,[151] the depersonalized act of artificial insemination may limit the method's popularity.

FUTURE SHOCK IS
SOONER THAN YOU THINK

Will the capacity to order babies by sex affect your family planning? What impact will it have on society? Here is what the experts say:

• Almost everyone using sex selection will choose to have a first-born boy, creating more uniform family sex stereotypes—father older than mother, brother older than sister—thus institutionalizing male supremacy in yet another form.[47]

• First-born children of either sex tend to be "more ambitious, creative, achievement-oriented, self-controlled, serious and adult-oriented . . . more likely to attend college and to achieve eminence";[48] more musically talented;[49] more likely to have high I.Q.s,[50] to be gifted children, distinguished scientists, and to be listed in *Who's Who.*[51]

At present, at least some first-born girls have a crack at these special advantages. But, with sex control, boys will monopolize the eldest-child bonuses in addition to other male privileges.

• If, as expected, the one-child family becomes more common, chances are that child will be a boy, adding to the predicted imbalance in the normal sex ratio.[52] Some sociologists predict a female shortage so alarming that it leads to epidemic prostitution, homosexuality, excessive bachelorhood, and "frontier town macho lawlessness,"[53] war, aggression, crime, murder, suicide, and diseases to which males are particularly vulnerable, "more sexual pressure on women, more alcoholism, more autism and retardation. . . . More of everything, in short, that men do, make, suffer, inflict and consume."[54]

• Political analysts and population experts point out that governments can use sex control to breed boys when soldiers are needed and girls when it is important to increase the pool of workers or to repopulate a country decimated by war. Conversely, fertility can be reduced without cost or bothersome birth control; just eliminate future women.[55]

• A British microbiologist drily assumes that during the period when males heavily outnumber females, "a form of purdah would become necessary. Women's right to work, even to travel alone freely, would probably be forgotten transiently."[56]

• Even without state control, experts say families would have fewer children if they could have exactly the sex mix they want.[57] (A great many women alive today owe their births to their parents' decision to "try again," for the son they'd missed.[58])

• The child who is unwanted because of its sex would be a thing of the past. Although very little is known about the fate of such children, experts say that they may be "resented and rejected," feel worthlessness, irrational guilt, and deflated self-esteem, and suffer abuse, malnutrition, and economic and emotional neglect. With scientific sex preselection, every girl born in the new age would know she was wanted, not just tolerated, which is far from true right now.[59]

Sounds great: Solve overpopulation and prevent the birth of unwanted children by giving people an Rx for sex. Until we ask, Why? Why does anyone care about anything but having a healthy baby? Why are sons wanted as firsts and onlys, and why are girls wanted less often by fewer people and only *after* boys?

12 COMMON REASONS FOR SON PREFERENCE

1. *To carry on the husband's family name.* This, the most frequently cited reason,[60] is formal homage to the patriarchy. In John Galsworthy's novel *A Man of Property,* one character is so desperate for a son that

> after a complicated labour during which he has had to decide whose life should come first, his wife's or the child's—and he has chosen the child's . . . when after all this, the doctor tells him that his child is a girl, he feels cheated, swindled. . . . He goes to see his father who is dying and there tells him a lie

rather than disappoint the dying man by letting him know that the child is the wrong sex.[61]

Wrong for what? Wrong for dynasty, legacy, continuum, property, power transmitted one generation to the next through the link of maleness and a name. The fathers are "cheated" of their immortality by a baby girl whose crime was simply being born. Her name will be lost as her mother's name and all the mothers' names are lost, like footprints in wet sand. No one worries about those names. The sighs are for the fathers.

2. *To bring status and prestige to the family.* It's a self-fulfilling prophecy: people want a son who will become a man who is worth more because of his maleness, which maleness gives him the right to his achievement. The daughter is restricted in her activity while en route from her father to her husband and her obligatory motherhood. Daughters give grandchildren; sons give honor.

3. *To take over the family business.* This reason generalizes from gender to business acumen: If it's a boy, somehow people assume that he will care about the family real estate holdings, that he will be good at banking or running a hardware store, that he will want to "take over." And before the girl is born everyone "knows" that she won't *want* the burden, she'll *want* to raise a family. The family business and the power and control that go with it are snatched from her while she is still in the cradle; then, when she grows up and her *husband* steps into her father's business, the family clucks, "You know, she didn't want it, she wanted to raise a family."

4. *To play the protector role for younger siblings.*[62] Parents who view female and male roles as distinct want their desired second-born female to have a "big brother" who will watch out for her as Father does for Mother. "Masculine" responsibilities are among the parents' birth "gifts" to their tiny baby boy.

5. *To prove the husband's virility.* Among Puerto Rican men, for example, those "who produce females are teased and called chancleteros (makers of chancletas—cheap slippers, a revealing slang term for little girls)."[63] A black father confessed that having a boy "kind of makes a man's chest stick out,"[64] and a white father of six sons admitted he always tried to "find some way to call attention to our family and enjoy the admiring responses . . . it was the *macho* thing."[65]

Some men contemplating the birth of a daughter feel upset at the idea of their male bodies' spawning a female baby, as though there were something vaguely homosexual about creating the "opposite" sex with one's sperm. Nancy Williamson adds,

> In the U.S. the "masculine" is partially defined as a rejection of the "feminine." This way of defining masculinity puts men in a household of women in an awkward position since they do not want to reject their family.[66]

> Yet they must reject what their daughters represent. The confusion between sex roles and sexuality seems to require the father to prefer sons as a demonstration of his preference for all things "masculine" and of his ability to exude enough maleness to create another entire male person. The creation of a female, on the other hand, might suggest that the "feminine" in himself has literally come to life.

6. *Women want sons to please their husbands.* Because all the polls show men, much more than women, want sons,[67] it may be that women *say* they want boys just to please their husbands. Perhaps the mother fears the father's rejection of the female child, or fears his disappointment in her for producing the "second choice."

7. *To provide a companion for the husband.* Because fathers want "to have someone like them whom they can teach and who will be a male like themselves,"[68] "someone he can play football with,"[69] if not rugby or poker or stickball or any number of fun-filled activities that cannot be visualized with a girl in the picture.

8. *Because boys are easier to raise.*[70] The "easier" rationale does double duty: boys are supposed to be easier because they don't need so much supervision, are less fragile, and are not sexually vulnerable. But when the same parents are ready for a girl, they say girls are easier because they are so sweet, agreeable, and so on. (See Number 4 under "Why Some People Want Girls Some of the Time," below.)

9. *To support the parents in their old age.* This may be a motivating factor in Third World cultures or among recent immigrant groups, but in the U.S. today there is no evidence that boys are seen by their parents as "economic assets."[71] This reason seems to be sheer rationalization for existing son preference.

10. *For Freudian reasons.* To solve her "penis envy" and resolve her "castration complex," a woman is said to prefer a boy baby who offers her psychosexual deliverance. Writes Freud:

> A mother can transfer to her son the ambition which she has been obliged to suppress in herself, and she can expect from him the satisfaction of all that has been left over in her of her masculinity complex.[72]

Freud is half right. But Adrienne Rich says it better:

> When I first became pregnant, I set my heart on a son. . . . I wanted to give birth, at twenty-five, to my unborn self, the self that our father-centered family had suppressed in me, someone independent, actively willing, original. . . . If I wanted to give birth to myself as a male, it was because males seemed to inherit those qualities by right of gender.[73]

Among other things, this reason for son preference also puts an unfair burden on sons who are expected to live the lives their mothers covet. As women's autonomy increases, the need for vicarious living vanishes: women active in the Women's Movement "were more likely to specify no preference in the sex of their first child."[74]

11. *Because of "the surprise factor."*[75]

> No one can guess very accurately how a male baby will spend the majority of his time when he is an adult; his future depends largely on his native talents, opportunities, intelligence, and social class. On the other hand, one can predict with considerable accuracy that the female child will be a wife and mother and that these duties will consume the majority of her time. Heretofore the girl child has not had the same possibilities of being a source of pride.[76]

Nancy Williamson finds the speculation provocative but dismisses "the surprise factor" as a singular reason for son preference:

> Many sons have brought their parents unpleasant surprises: they have become criminals; they have died in battle; they have deserted the family for greener pastures; or they have married the wrong woman. Yet son preference persists.[77]

12. *I don't know; I just prefer boys.* This inchoate attraction to males can be explained by a host of psychoanalytic theories. In my view, however, Dorothy Dinnerstein, a Rutgers University psychologist, holds the master key—to misogyny, male supremacy, divided gender relationships, and incidentally to son preference. In her book, *The Mermaid and the Minotaur,*[78] Dinnerstein says that the female monopoly of early child care puts each of us, male and female alike, exclusively in the domain of the mother's body and will for the first two years of life. During a prolonged infancy in which our physical neediness, helplessness, hunger, and rage depend for relief upon this all-powerful first parent, no mother can satisfy and fulfill, cleanse and feed, bring comfort and pleasure flawlessly and totally because Mother is only human and is ultimately separate from her child.

The slow dawning of the fact of maternal separation—the awful truth that mother and her omnipotence are not connected to the self—is the first betrayal, the first *You* to impinge upon the original *I,* the first suffering and the first chilling intimation that in giving us life the mother has also started us on the lifelong journey toward death. The brute power of this adult who initiates us into the human condition and whose "frailties are worse because they are encountered earlier"[79] is, in Dinnerstein's words, the "original center of human grief."[80] Female authority overwhelms us in early childhood and will continue to be "a force that must be overthrown"[81] as long as mothers are given primary or sole responsibility for babies.

One way that we overthrow that force is to underwrite male supremacy as "a reaction to, a revolution against, earlier experience of female dominion."[82] Another way is to deprive mother-like creatures, that is females, of their very being—not flagrantly, through female infanticide or mother murder, but silently and bloodlessly, by wishing them never to be born. Son preference is perhaps the psyche's revenge against the mother who was always too powerful and who could never be good enough.

DOESN'T ANYONE WANT GIRLS?

An analysis of 18th- and 19th-century literature found scores of characters wanting sons, but in only 3 instances in the 300 novels reviewed was there ever the vaguest mention of preference for a girl.[83]

In the only *five* cultures worldwide that are daughter-preferring, females are not dominant. Their status as "valued goods"[84] may stem from matrilineal transfer of property; the custom of the brideprice; or women's usefulness as a medium of exchange, as superior workers, and as producers of more daughters.[85]

In 20th-century America, there is one category of parents that consistently and overwhelmingly prefers girls: those who want to *adopt* a child.[86] Only when the adoption is between relatives are boys once again the preferred sex.[87] This should not surprise anyone. Patriarchal imperatives apply only when paternity can be assured by blood. An adopted boy would always, in that sense, be another man's son. And with an adopted boy the "surprise factor" seems more likely to turn sour "given the uncertainty of his genetic heritage."[88] An example of this dramatic flip-flop in sex preference is the fact that Jews (along with Catholics) show the strongest son preference for births, but for adopted children, 72 percent of Jewish families wanted a girl.[89]

WHY SOME PEOPLE WANT GIRLS SOME OF THE TIME

Nonadoptive parents, of course, want a girl baby too—but only in her place (after a boy) and for very different reasons:[90]

1. *For companionship to the mother around the house.* The son is expected to be active outdoors, the daughter to be home-oriented.

2. *To help with the housework and child care.* Daughter provides domestic labor while Mommy provides role-training.

3. *Because they are sweeter, more affectionate and cuddly.* Parents who believe girls are temperamentally different tend to treat them accordingly, and girls thus *become* what they are thought to *be.*

4. *Because they are easier to raise, more obedient, neater.* Another self-fulfilling prophecy. And a convenient rationalization to balance the claim that boys are easier because they're tougher.

5. *Because girls are cuter, more fun to dress and fuss over.* This reason for daughter-preference would hold true equally for

Barbie doll and Baby Tenderlove who, better still, never eat, make messes, or grow up. But for women who view "feminine" ornamentation as one of life's main events, having a little girl to mold and beautify is as close to playing God as a woman can get.

6. *Because the woman fears or resents males.* If the "opposite" sex is alien enough, one can imagine a woman's recoiling from the act of mothering one of *them.* There may be psychological resistance to the male as stranger, conqueror, and threat, no matter what his size (not to be confused with feminists' political ambivalence about raising another male who might oppress women—or preference for daughters on the grounds of "sisterhood" and solidarity).[91]

7. *Because girls stay close to the family.* Boys have this nasty habit of breaking free and leading independent lives. Even after they become parents themselves, girls are thought to never quite leave home emotionally—and are expected to keep in touch on a more regular (and willing) basis than sons.

8. *Because Father wants "a little princess" in his castle.* A daughter may not constitute a proper heir, but she doesn't constitute competition either; she doesn't unseat the male from his throne by outgrowing him, outperforming him, and outearning him. She just adores him.

A GIRL FOR YOU AND A BOY FOR ME

Even in the most patriarchal, son-preferring subcultures in the United States, almost every couple wants at least one child of each sex. However, as Nancy Williamson cautions, "this does not mean they are necessarily being egalitarian since boys and girls are usually desired for quite different reasons."[92] We have seen that these different reasons are direct outgrowths of sex role stereotypes, that girls are often valued for their qualities as children and boys for the adults they might become,[93] that each sex is expected to provide different rewards to the parents, to involve the parents in different activities, and to be pint-sized replicas of Father and Mother in their gender hierarchy.

The truth is that the twelve reasons for wanting boys and the eight reasons for wanting girls are twenty different ways of saying two things:

Real Reason #1: Boys are preferred because parents want to cash in on patriarchal privilege. In other words, as long as male supremacy is the rule of the culture and maleness comes with automatic entitlements, then boys are the sex to have first, the sex to have more of, and the sex to have if you're having only one.

Real Reason #2: Children are wanted by specified gender because parents have two sex role scripts in their minds and they need the "right" sex child to play each part.

It's as simple as that. Rather than send down to central casting for a fully grown "feminine" or "masculine" stereotype through which parents can live their sex role illusions, they grow their own.

Prospective parents can avoid pre-birth bias and veteran parents can bring clarity to hindsight by asking themselves some probing questions and thinking through what effect their answers might have upon their childrearing styles or their subsequent gender favoritism.

A CHECKLIST FOR BIAS BEFORE BIRTH

1. Do/did you care about the sex of your first child? Your next child? Why?

2. Have you ever wished any of your present children were other than the sex they are? When and why?

3. What do you want from a boy (girl) that you can't do, have, or experience with a girl (boy)?

4. Before its birth, do/did you fantasize about your child? If so, describe your image. (Pregnant women, it's been found, dream twice as often about male babies as about daughters.)

5. Describe a day in the life of your soon-to-be born child at age five; at age twenty-five. Does gender affect your imaginings?

6. Have you practiced or would you practice sex-selection methods, if perfected?

7. During pregnancy, did/do you and your mate refer to the fetus as "he"? Sometimes? Usually? Always?

8. If you decided to have two children and gave birth to two girls in a row, but could be guaranteed a son the next time, would you have a third child?

9. When you were born, were your parents pleased about your gender?

10. Did you ever wish you were the other sex?

There is no "failing" this test; the idea is to explore just how much unconscious sexist baggage women and men carry with them into a relationship with a brand new, unseen, unmet child. Those who believe in parenting-without-predestination will use the test to rid themselves of those twenty excuses to raise cardboard characters or patriarchal piglets.

Honesty demands that I pose one more question: *Since there is* some *difference between girls and boys* (see Chapter 2), *isn't it only natural to want to experience both?*

I think so. But only for the same reason people climb mountains: because they are there. Because there *are* girl babies and boy babies, not because girl babies and boy babies will necessarily give you different experiences in some preordained pattern.

I think, moreover, that the only valid reason to affirmatively prefer having "one of each" is the same reason why a bias-free parent might want "either": if you can say "I want a boy so that if, in becoming himself, he is different from other boys, I can be the parent to help him do so," *or* "I want a girl so that if, in becoming herself, she is different from other girls, I can be the parent to help her do so."

The nonsexist parent might have a sex preference based on the desire to provide reparations—to help a girl feel good about being strong in a society bent on taming her, or to support a boy who might want to be something other than what the world expects him to be. But since both sexes need reparations for, and armor against, sex role coercion, we come back to the fact that a child of either sex will have enough needs—and enough promise —to suit any parent's giving impulse or revolutionary fervor.

6

Decisions: About Pregnancy, Delivery, Furnishing the Nursery, and What to Name the Baby

If your mind is free of sex preference, you'll have more energy to consider the really important decisions, such as should we have a baby at all, and if so, how can we ensure a positive pregnancy and birth experience?

DECISION: TO HAVE
OR NOT TO HAVE A BABY

Most people reading this book already have, or have decided to have, one or more children.

But if you're a couple that is still undecided, or a single person considering having or adopting a baby on your own, you might examine your motives for parenting and your philosophy about rearing children. You can do this with the help of a few specialists,[1] or by asking yourself the following questions:

• *Why do I/we want a child?* Those men most in favor of feminist principles also seem to be most eager to have children and to "personally rear" them, while traditional men wanted "to conceive children who will be cared for by their wives," and "viewed childrearing as less creative . . . than did the proliberation men."[2]

It's the difference between wanting children and wanting "to parent." Some like the first idea but not the second.

Men threatened by egalitarian roles, who want to increase male dominance, may desire larger families so that their wives will stay home and be submissive. . . . These attitudes may be expressed in the statement, "Keep 'em barefoot and pregnant." . . . Husbands may see the presence of children as a hostile way to chain their wives down and make their lives less pleasant.[3]

A woman on the other hand may see the pregnancy as a way of being noticed, as reassurance of her "true womanhood," a way to feel important, avoid boredom, postpone proving herself, or gain her husband's solicitude.

> I love being pregnant. I've never gotten so much attention in my life, from Alan and everybody else. . . . I don't think Alan would have considered [cleaning the bathtub] if I weren't pregnant.[4]

Both partners might want to conceive a child to extend their egos, cut the cord with their own parents, keep up with the child-bearing activity in their social set, prove the husband's capacity to impregnate, save a failing marriage, or simply because both people are ready to be parents.[5]

• *What will happen to our relationship with each other?* Can our sex life survive pregnancy?[6] What are we/I willing to give up: time? self-indulgence? career advancement? money? peace and quiet? sleep? freedom?[7] In a recent experiment, a psychology professor gave each of her college students a doll and put them on a forty-eight-hour regimen that duplicated the schedule of parents of newborns. Even without the "real" dirty diapers, fussing, and crying, 40 percent of the class lost much of its original interest in parenthood because of the constant drain on their time and personal lives.[8] You might consider "borrowing" a niece, or a neighbor's or friend's baby for a week or more to try on the actual daily life of a parent (while incidentally bringing precious relief to the baby's exhausted parents).

• *Is this the right time for me/us?* Economically? Professionally? In terms of personal maturity? Is it safe to conceive a baby at this age? One's psychological or financial readiness will never be as measurable as the condition of one's sperms or eggs. For your sake and the baby's, clarify the physical risks and precautions: read,[9] talk to doctors, and interview parents who postponed conception until their thirties or forties. Be sure that you're prepared in mind as well as body.

Whatever your age, no conception should be contemplated

unless and until the woman involved is in good health and *wants to become pregnant.* [10] Women who make that affirmative choice have far less depression, anxiety, and complications of pregnancy, labor, and delivery.[11] Furthermore, wanted babies enjoy better health and fewer learning problems and are less accident prone than their unplanned counterparts.[12]

• *Can we agree on role-sharing and childrearing methods (or am I ready to do it all alone)?* You'll be able to answer that question fully after you have finished this book. For the moment, see how you feel about discipline, childhood sexuality, morality, education, or any potentially controversial area relating to kids. Discuss possible division of household and child-care tasks. Think about the way you were raised and what you plan to do differently with your children.

• *How many children are the right number for us?* One intriguing study found that if the marriage was egalitarian or if the wives believed it was primarily the husband's job to take care of the children, men reduced the number of children they wanted.[13] Other research shows that women who reject the "feminine" stereotype have fewer children than women who incorporate "undesirable feminine characteristics" such as "incompetence and immaturity."[14] Thinking about the ideal size family should bring you right back to who you are, why you want children, and what you expect of parenthood.

Assuming the answer is "Yes, let's have a baby," must you put yourselves passively in the hands of medical experts—become infantilized by doctors before you can become a parent to your own infant? Can a woman retain control of her own body and can a man stay involved enough during pregnancy so that his transition to parenthood is nearly as organic as hers?

DECISION: HOW TO RETAIN CONTROL OF PREGNANCY AND BIRTH

In the last decade or two, mothers- and fathers-to-be have been demanding more sensitive obstetrical care. Women's health advocates have written their own textbooks,[15] and demanded that the mostly male medical establishment demystify the birth process and return it to the family and to female dominion.[16]

Both parents now expect to understand gestation and to participate in decisions involving amniocentesis, natural childbirth (which can be ecstatic for some, but must never be a test of "real" womanhood or an occasion for "failure"[17]), and alternative delivery methods from Leboyer to midwives, to home birth, to Caesarian section.[18]

The decision to make father a partner during pregnancy and a coach-assistant during labor and delivery[19] is a crucial step in the direction of nonsexist parenthood—as long as the father doesn't take over the show, as doctors have done in the past. When a doctor says "I delivered the baby," or a husband says "*We* pushed" the mother's singular labor is diminished.

As you consider breast or formula feeding—and there are good arguments for and against both[20]—never let the decision get out of the mother's hands. The use of a woman's body is that woman's business and no one else's.

This sort of advance planning is something you'll never regret. Especially if you are the mother-to-be. For, as Adrienne Rich has written,

> What we bring to childbirth is nothing less than our entire socialization as women. . . . To change the experience of childbirth means to change women's relationship to fear and powerlessness, to our bodies, to our children.[21]

One example of a decision that can reverberate unexpectedly is whether or not to have "rooming in"—that is, to keep the baby with you immediately after birth rather than in the hospital nursery.

Psychoanalyst R. D. Laing calls early mother-child separation "a precondition of insanity. The mother-child interaction is most significant. The disruption of bonding can be one of the causes of schizophrenia in later life."[22]

Two Cleveland pediatricians, Marshall H. Klaus and John H. Kennell,[23] claim that putting the baby against the mother's chest, and encouraging touching, gazing, and other mother-infant attachments during the first 45 to 90 minutes after birth, triggers many biological interactions (such as the baby's cry's stimulating production of the mother's milk), and determines how close the mother-child dyad will be for years to come. The lack of immediate skin-to-skin, face-to-face contact, doctors say, may account for a woman's loss of affectionate feelings and maternal interest, a child's lower I.Q. and less cheerful disposition, dissolution of the family, anxiety, child abuse, and higher divorce rates among the parents—all of this depending on which doctor you read.[24]

It certainly sounds alarming . . . and plausible. So why not demand that your doctor and hospital permit your baby to stay in or near its mother's bed?

Because you need to know more: If the emotional bonding works so magically, isn't it important for it to happen between the infant and *both* its parents?

BONDING: THREE WAYS OR NONE

Childbirth has very definite effects on the father, from sympathetic labor pains or parallel post-partum exhaustion[25] to more common feelings of exclusion, displacement, and alienation from both wife and child.

> It is impossible to allow a husband to play no part whatsoever in the pregnancy and childbirth of his baby and then demand that he share equally in the childrearing. The pattern has already been established . . . at an extremely sensitive time in the man's life. Also, for the woman, this separation from her husband leads to her substituting the child in his place.[26]

Some bonding proponents acknowledge that the father's interaction with his infant for even one hour during the first three or four days of life can increase his absorption and interest in the child from that time on.[27] Yet how many delivery-room bonding programs actively bring father into the magic circle? Not many. Most experiences are like Carol and Frank's. Frank assisted Carol as much as possible throughout pregnancy, labor, and delivery. When their baby was born, Frank laughed, cried, and hugged Carol vigorously but the little boy was given exclusively to Carol.

Then, she began cooing and talking to him. Her attention was all his. She checked his fingers and toes to make sure everything was intact, then gazed at his face some more. Frank might have been jealous, but the beauty of this union between his wife and his son produced feelings of awe and protectiveness.[28]

Several things strike me wrong. A union between "his wife and his son" excludes *himself;* "awe and protectiveness" are remote patriarchal concepts; and feeling "jealous" is no basis for father-son closeness and love. Unless bonding embraces all three members of the new family, give it serious second thoughts.

More questions arise. Is the bonding as good in all respects for the mother as it is for the baby? One follow-up study found a year after bonding that mothers "hover about their children more . . . [and] are less eager to leave their children with anyone."[29] What conflicts will this instill in the mother who must return to work or who is committed to her career?

Does the bonding theory imply that a premature baby or a baby to be given up for adoption or a baby born of an anesthetized delivery will be forever disadvantaged because its mother could not establish instant attachment—and is it useful to program mothers with this added source of guilt?

I know some mothers who remember needing sleep far more than those extra few hours with the baby. An arduous labor and the need to take on all the responsibilities of a new baby and perhaps a toddler or two may be so fatiguing as to make energy conservation more urgent. Other women (whether poor, jobless, or otherwise troubled) may need more than mere proximity to create an emotional bond with a baby they possibly did not plan and cannot afford. Special counseling would seem more practical than mystical attachment procedures. As for the babies born to such troubled women, researchers found some of them less responsive to cuddling and comforting from the very first, another suggestion of more complex factors to be considered than the idealized generalizations about bonding.[30] One woman's idyllic bonding is another's bondage.

If mother-infant bonding is presented as the baby's be-all and end-all without regard for the mother's circumstances, women may find themselves shouldering yet another "right thing to do" —which means yet another potential for feeling inadequate.

A final question to ask is whether the bonding theory may be a neo-scientific resurrection of the discredited "maternal instinct." (See Chapter 8.) One writer asserts that "the first hours may have a lot to do with shaping the mother's attitude toward the child, the strength of her commitment to him (sic) and her capacity for mothering."[31]

Aha! It sounds as if, without a push in the baby's direction, the fabled "maternal instinct" may be lacking. If it *isn't* "natural" and "instinctual," who wants us to have it? Shouldn't we consider whether a *stronger* mother-infant bond is in the long-term interest of our society or if, as Dorothy Dinnerstein has argued, it is at the root of human malaise?[32] Do we need another blame-the-mother theory to add to the Oedipus Complex, the Jewish Mother, Momism, and Portnoy's Complaint? Where are the innovators when it comes to the father-infant bond, which is in far more desperate need of repair because it hangs by a thread: paternity and little more. Shouldn't we be stimulating *men's* commitment to babies?

It's tricky—and I am suspicious. Although rooming-in has been an option in some hospitals for decades, why is it *now*—when women are trying to redefine themselves as more worldly and less child-bound—that the experts are giving us the hard sell, the supposedly new concept of mother-or-madness?

DECISION: WHOM TO HEED

As soon as a woman's pregnancy becomes public, it's open season on advice to prospective parents. Unfortunately, few hot tips are ignited by nonsexist fervor. That terrific obstetrician may have the annoying habit of calling pregnant women "Honey," a term actor Alan Alda says should be reserved for a bear talking to its lunch. The "one good hospital" may have superlative technical equipment but treat Father as an intruder. And the pal who knows just what to do with a colicky baby may end up blaming all baby's problems on working mothers.

Actually, friends are more likely to be tuned in to your values than are the "experts" whose biases may be woven like subtle threads into their otherwise comforting blanket advice. As a general rule, watch out for experts who:

• assume all women have a natural talent with babies and all men are inept (or adorably intimidated).

• use "she" when referring to "the parent" and "he" when referring to "the baby" or "the doctor."

• suggest that the nuclear family with a stay-home mother and employed father is the optimum and most common arrangement.

• assume the two parents should play "complementary" roles, a euphemism for the sexist division of labor in childrearing and housekeeping.

After surveying fifty-three parenting manuals, John De-Frain[33] found that only two of them[34] "openly question" conventional sex-linked role playing. These are typical statements from the worst of the books:

Haim Ginott: "In former times, mother represented love and sympathy, while father personified discipline and morality. . . . In the modern family, the roles of mother and father are no longer distinct. Many women work outside the home in the 'man's world' and many men find themselves involved in mothering activities such as feeding, diapering and bathing the baby. Though some men welcome these new opportunities for closer contact with their infants, there is the danger that the baby may end up with two mothers."[35]

Arthur Janov: "I cannot express strongly enough my contempt for this sort of motherhood. If a woman is not planning to do mothering in the true sense, she shouldn't become one!"[36]

Fitzhugh Dodson: "Father has a crucial role to play in giving preschool boys the physical interaction and rough-housing they need. And fathers display the tenderness and softness a little girl needs to encourage her coquettishness and femininity."[37]

To avoid such advice, consult "The Politics of Parenting Books: Rocking the Cradle Without Rocking the Boat"[38] before you decide what books to depend on in the coming years.

My personal favorites are:

• *Baby and Child Care* by Dr. Benjamin Spock[39]—but only the revised edition, published in April 1976. After twenty-seven years and sales in the tens of millions,[40] Spock rewrote portions of his "baby bible," leaving intact his common-sensical advice on health care but making important nonsexist improvements, such as the following:

1968: A man can be a warm father and a real man at the same time. . . . Of course I don't mean that the father has to give just as many bottles or change just as many diapers as the mother. But it's fine for him to do these things occasionally. He might make the formula on Sunday.[41]	*1976:* I think that a father with a full-time job—even where a mother is staying home—will do best by his children, his wife and himself if he takes on half or more of the management of the children (and also participates in the housework) when he gets home from work and on weekends.[42]

And notice the difference in the two editions' advice about the father-daughter relationship:

1968: She gains confidence in herself as a girl and a woman from feeling his approval. I'm thinking of little things he can do like complimenting her on her dress, or hair-do, or the cookies she's made.[43]	*1976:* She gains confidence in herself as a girl and a woman from feeling his approval. In order not to feel inferior to boys, she should believe that her father would welcome her in backyard sports, on fishing and camping trips, in attendance at ball games. . . . She gains confidence in herself from feeling his interest in her activities, achievements, opinions and aspirations.[44]

• *Ourselves and Our Children* by The Boston Women's Health Book Collective.[45] There is nothing here on runny noses, tics, stuttering, mumps, or the heartbreak of adolescent acne, only the voices of real parents and children, a high feminist consciousness, and an excellent bibliography.

Two books directly address the daily challenges of nonsexist childrearing:

• *Right from the Start* by Selma Greenberg.[46] A readable narrative full of insight, anecdotes, and sound advice from an early childhood specialist with a loving respect for children.

• *Non-Sexist Childraising* by Carrie Carmichael.[47] Interviews with families who are struggling with the problems of sexism offer a glimpse of parents and children in the act of change-making.

DECISION: WHAT TO DO, BUY, GET, OR SAY IN ADVANCE

Most couples begin purchasing baby things during the last two or three months of pregnancy—partly because the baby doesn't seem real until then and partly because major purchases can take about ten weeks for delivery.

You can get layette lists anywhere. My only concern is to make you aware of the areas where sex-typing can become an unnecessary impediment to your efficiency. Instead of looking at practicality and durability, many people focus on *incidentals:* color and decoration.

What if the best buy in a crib bumper happens to be available only in blue or all the little buntings and hand-knits your niece has outgrown are pink? Suppose your heirloom bassinette is pink-painted wicker laced with pink satin ribbons? Do you tell your parents to keep it in the attic? Do you repaint it? After accepting a nephew's expensive one-piece snowsuit, the one designed like a Los Angeles Rams uniform, do you dress your baby in it if she turns out to be a *she?*

Your answers will depend on whether you choose to revise reality, or to neutralize it.

The Revisionist Position

First, you resolve to be color blind. Then you buy or accept any item you like, regardless of its color, drawings, or ornamentation.

You don't care if the lamp in your baby daughter's room is mounted on a statue of a Space Man, so long as the lamp is cheerful and provides light. And you don't get upset when passersby comment about how your little boy in his pink snowsuit is such a "sweet little girl."

People who make gender-color assumptions often do it within earshot of a baby old enough to hear—and that's where the revisionist position gets you into trouble. When each human infant becomes *conscious,* something that doesn't happen to other experimental organisms, she or he learns her or his gender identity from the comments and labeling statements made by others. Since very young children are not able to understand that those "sweet little girl" labels may be incorrect assumptions based on color coding, it might be easier on them if you choose the second policy on the pink/blue issue.

The Neutrality Position

Very simply, ban pink and blue from babyland. Insist on such gender-neutral infancy pastels as pale yellow, lime green, or white, or search for furnishings and baby clothes in red, royal blue, kelly green, and bright yellow—the colors that babies find most appealing and adults find least sex-linked.

As for decoration and ornamentation, the idea is to provide all sorts of visual stimuli so that, as children develop consciousness, many you-can-do-anything images are within view: airplanes *and* dollies on the playpen mat, for instance, not boys playing with airplanes or girls playing with dollies.

Finally, there is the example of lace-trimmed socks. Now, no baby *needs* lace-trimmed socks. It is even questionable whether a baby needs socks, period. Yet teeny-tiny socks come plain or with bands of lace around the ankles. If you are a revisionist, you might buy your son lace-trimmed socks hoping that everyone around you and eventually the boy himself will think of lace as lace, and not as "girlish." If you are opting for neutrality, both your daughter and son will wear plain socks until lace becomes as genderless in our society as blue denim.

Preparing Other People

In addition to priming yourself and your house for nonsexist childrearing, it would be wise to explain the basics to those who will be closest to your baby—neighbors, nurse, grandparents, other relatives, babysitters, or friends of the family.

For openers, tell them—especially the person planning your baby shower—your feelings about color-coding so that friends' gifts will take your preferences into account. If someone offers to cook for the new father while the new mother is in the hospital, thank them but explain that he knows how to cook for himself and will be doing so for the family, so he may as well keep in practice. Nip incorrect assumptions in the bud, even if you end up refusing the delicately caned rocking chair your own mother used when you were a baby.

"I'm afraid I'd break it, Mom," you might say. "Janet and I plan to alternate feeding the baby, so we'll need a rocker that can support my weight as well as hers."

When people express interest in your "newfangled" ideas, explain them. If you're lucky, those closest to you will not just humor you; they will reinforce you. It's a great bonus for children when their parents' values are reflected in the world beyond the home.

DECISION: WHAT SHALL WE NAME THE BABY?

Names are a Big Subject. Possibly, you have to name the baby after a saint or a deceased relative, or after the wife's family name. There might be a problem with various first names in conjunction with your last name (Charles Charles?) or with the set of initials a child's name creates. One friend was so humiliated by his monogram, B.M., that he adopted a fictional middle name when he was eight, and he's been B.S.M. ever since.

I'm not thinking about any of that. Nor am I thinking about etymology, about fads in naming children after movie stars or biblical figures, or trends that made Linda and John *in* during the 1940s and put Jennifer and Michael on top during the 1970s.[48]

What I care about here is making you aware that your baby's name, in a sense, will forever stereotype him or her, because unconsciously, subliminally, Americans are nearly unanimous about what sort of person "goes" with what sort of name.[49] Children seem to agree on the names that describe "someone who runs" as opposed to the names appropriate for "someone who sits,"[50] and most of us seem to believe that[51]

Harvey is weak. John is trustworthy and kind.

Patricia is plain. Maureen is sultry and surly.

Bertha and Leo are fat. Barbara and Kenneth are thin.

Michael, James, Adam, David, and Daniel are "masculine" but Isadore and Shelly are not. Wendy, Sue, Linda, Sophie, and Elizabeth are "feminine" but Florence and Gerry are not.

Ann is nonaggressive. Pamela is ambitious and domineering.

So when you choose to name your daughter Ann, it could be because your mother's name was Ann, or because you like simple, old-fashioned names, *or* because you have the subliminal hope that your daughter will be "nonaggressive."

By the same token, let's say you have an unconscious association between the name Steve or Stephanie and the quality of being "athletic." If you choose one of those names, are you telegraphing your expectations for the child? Will you be seriously disappointed if she or he is unathletic? Think about it.

The power to name is a godlike power. It is the power to put a label on a *self,* a *me,* and *I.* Among some American Indian tribes, a child was not named until he or she was about six years old "and had shown some special trait or skill."[52] Then the name matched or described that specialness.

In the 1960s I met a "hippie" couple who named their son "Son"—temporarily. The parents said that when he was ready to take a permanent name for himself, it would be his right to do the naming.

However, since you will undoubtedly exercise the parental prerogative to name your children before you know them, you should consider what name stereotypes, which seem buried in all of our psyches, might mean to your daughter or son.

If your chosen male names are conventional, such as Robert or Joseph, while the girls' names that appeal to you tend toward a fancier Marisa or Lizette, it's because common names are seen by most people as "better, stronger and more active than unusual ones."[53]

You should also know that neuroses, psychoses, flunking grades, and other handicaps seem to accrue more often to boys with unusual names, but not to odd-named girls.[54] Females seem to like their unusual names and males prefer the common names they're generally given,[55] a measure perhaps of conformity rather than real preference. Conformism may also explain why fourth- and fifth-graders with the most popular names, such as Karen, Lisa, Jonathan, and Patrick,[56] were also the most popular children, and kids with unpopular names were less liked by their peers.[57]

The unique name turns out to be a plus for a boy who grows up to be an army officer, college president, aristocrat, or otherwise privileged white male—but not for a girl who happens to be an underprivileged black.[58]

When parents give a child a name, they give more than a legal identity on a birth certificate; they create an image, a prediction, an advertisement, an ideal.

Thus, your momentous decision—*What shall we name the baby?*—boils down to two choices: capitalize on the positive associations attached to certain names and give your child that subliminal edge in the world; or follow your personal taste and help your child give his or her name its life and its meaning.

I think a case can be made for either choice. The pragmatic parent will probably take the first route and pick a name that "works" for the child; idealistic parents might disregard group psychology and shared stereotypes, and pick a name that has content for them or "feels" right for their child.

My aim is to have you make your decision with heightened awareness, so you catch yourself before branding a child with a name "to live up to" rather than a name *to be.*

7

In the Beginning:
Nonsexist Infancy

"It's a baby!"

Obviously, that is *not* the sentence you hear in the delivery room.

Sex is the first noun attached to a human life at the moment of birth. Sex is the first self: "It's a girl!" or "It's a boy!" In that primal instant, gender is being and being is gender. Then, as the minutes and hours pass, your baby is given elaboration: it is "a healthy baby," "a 7-pound 4-ounce baby," a "restless," "docile," or "alert" baby.

Days go by. Adjectives are added. As you feed, hold, touch, kiss, cuddle, coo to, gaze at, change, dress, bathe, burp, stroke, comfort, and love your baby, this unknown creature gradually becomes defined, like a sculpture emerging from a lump of clay.

You get to know your baby's look, feel, and smell; the way your baby cries, sleeps, nurses, reacts to light or music; the grip of your baby's tiny hand on your finger; the gummy little smile that rewards you for materializing beside the crib.

Weeks turn into months. Your baby develops more personality, more individuality: you know the funny way she turns over, the expression on his face when he eats his peach purée, her favorite song, his beloved toy, her creep-and-crawl locomotion, his gurgling monologues. This is no longer a baby born to thus-and-so parents on such-and-such date; this is a beginning *person,* with a discernible temperament and special qualities all its own.

Or so you think. But how much of your baby's uniqueness is really developing freely? And how much is a result of that first fact duly noted by all—"It's a boy" or "It's a girl"—and all the unconscious acts of "genderizing" that flow from there?

Watching an adult with an infant, you may not notice what systematic research observation has proved to be true.

From the first millisecond after its sex is known, people act and react, think, speak, and move differently with a baby girl than with a baby boy. Many parents say "it would be 'unfair' to treat boys and girls differently,"[1] and insist "I treat all my children the same."[2] But that's not what really happens.

IN THE DELIVERY ROOM

"Isn't she beautiful? Look at all that hair!"[3] is a common reaction to a daughter, for good looks and long hair are instant emblems of "femininity." The fact that boys are born just as good-looking and just as long-haired is immaterial.

"A boy! Wow! He's peeing all over the interns!" That's the way I reacted to David in the delivery room, and I have since learned that although many babies are born urinating, far greater notice is taken when a penis is responsible.[4]

Another delivery room. Another set of parents:

Mother: Oh, she's gorgeous.
Father: Looks like you.
Mother: Well, Dr. Murphy, I was right. I had a sneaky feeling it was a girl, just because I wanted a boy.
Doctor: Often tactically best to have a girl first—she can help with the washing up.[5]

Mother notes the most salient "feminine" fact: "She's gorgeous." Were it a boy, she might have said "He's a buster." Father establishes the girl as her mother's genetic responsibility. ("Looks like you.") Mother establishes that she didn't really want the lesser sex; that the girl is fate's spite. Doctor offers reassurance, the compensatory promise of a household helper.

In a modern urban hospital, "She can help with the washing up" proclaims a girl's future, just as in a village in Italy, when a boy is born, a pitcher of water is poured into the road to symbolize that the newborn baby's destiny is to travel the roads of the world. When a girl is born, water is thrown on to the hearth to show that she will lead her life within the walls of the home.[6]

Disappointment and the assumed domestic future—all sewed up within minutes of the birth of the little girl.

ARTIFACTS, ACCOUTREMENTS, AND CUSTOM

Why is gender so important in babies? For the same reason people are afraid of adult "unisex" fashion, of a journey without signposts, of a wine without a label, of having to make judgments without first reading the reviews. Once a person is presented to the world as female or male, everything else follows.

When a mystery guest came out on the "Dick Cavett Show" dressed in amorphous black cloth coverings, the usually glib Cavett was nonplussed: "I don't know what to say," he sputtered. "I can't even tell if you are a man or a woman."[7]

In the fable *Baby X,*[8] a government "x-periment" requires a chosen set of parents to refuse to divulge the sex of their baby to the outside world. The child, too, keeps its gender identity to itself. Because no one knows if X is a girl or a boy, X is allowed the entire range of girl-type and boy-type activities. Baby X grows to be a happy, well-rounded, loving child, but friends, neighbors, relatives, and school authorities are outraged and confounded because they do not know "what" X is.

"You don't know how to treat it if you don't know what it is."[9]

Parents use the sight of their babies' genitals as a cue to trigger their own attitudes. Otherwise, they could not tell their baby's sex from its appearance or behavior.[10] Since babies are not generally left naked, everyone else needs some signal to telegraph its gender so *they* can know "how to treat it," too.

In the hospital, the swaddling blanket, the wrist identification bands worn by mother and baby, or the name card on the nursery bassinet gives a pink or blue sex identification signal.

Floral arrangements in maternity wards announce what "kind" of baby each woman had. When I gave birth to our twin girls, people sent bouquets resplendent with pink satin ribbons, pink roses in a lacy basket, tiny sugar cubes nestled in nosegays, daisies in an old ice cream goblet. For my son, the flora ran to blue-tinted carnations, ribbons of bold plaid or stripes, big pom-pom blossoms strung with tiny bats and balls, and a no-nonsense potted plant or two.

Sex is proclaimed on the bands of the cigars Dad hands out, on the gift-wrappings, in the baby book, and by the color of the booties, bonnets, and blankets presented by visitors.

Congratulations cards parents receive from friends are among the most extreme sex discriminators:

WHAT IS A BOY

A boy is a composite—he has the appetite of a horse, the digestion of a sword-swallower, the energy of a pocket-size atomic bomb, . . . the lungs of a dictator, the imagination of a Paul Bunyan. . . . He likes ice cream, knives, saws, Christmas, comic books, . . . large animals, trains, . . . and fire engines. . . . Nobody else gets so much fun out of trees, dogs and breezes. . . . A boy is a magical creature . . . he is your captor, your jailer, your boss and your master —a freckled face, pint-sized, cat-chasing, bundle of noise.[11]

WHAT IS A GIRL

A girl is innocence playing in the mud, Beauty standing on its head, and Motherhood dragging a doll by the foot. . . . A little girl likes new shoes, party dresses, small animals, . . . dolls, make-believe, dancing lessons, ice cream, kitchens, coloring books, make-up . . . tea parties. . . . She is the prettiest when she has provoked you . . . and the most flirtatious. . . . Who else can cause you more grief, joy, . . . and genuine delight than this combination of Eve, Salome and Florence Nightingale?[12]

"Excitement," "fun," "noise," and action fill the congratulations cards for boys; "enchanting," "giggle," angel," "charmer," "sugar-sweet," and "precious treasure"[13] describe the delights of girls.

At the top of the line are these three-dollar hardcover greetings:

What Is a Little Boy?

crawler over, in and out . . .
grabber . . . chewer. . . . That's a
little boy. . . .
Speaker . . . climber of cribs . . .
and before you know it, trees. . .
Skinner of elbows, knuckles and
knees . . . Giver of orders, sage
advice . . . Winner of races and
games . . . That's a little boy.
Explorer . . . Inventor . . .
Leader of wagon trains, treks
into space and races to supper
. . . Rider of things like sleds
and swings, ferris wheels,
scooters and skates . . . Jumper
. . . Taker of dares . . . Helper of
fledglings . . . Maker of kites . . .
Asker of why, what and when
. . . Thrower of "long bombs,"
fast balls and curves . . . Joiner
of teams and clubs that meet in
treehouses . . . Teaser of sister
and sitters . . .[14]

That's What a Little Girl Means

. . . embroidered blankets as soft
as down, elfin gowns as pink as
cotton candy . . . bonnets
trimmed in regal lace . . . a
ribboned rattle, . . . bibs with
sunny scenes . . . That's what a
little girl means. . . . Her
highness in her high chair
finger-painting dainty pabulum
pictures . . . A pixie-perfect
smile and a beguiling style of
toddling . . . That's what a little
girl means. Brand new shoes . . .
A giggle that's so charming and
a wiggle that's disarmingly
delightful . . . little tip-toe peeks
at things she can't quite reach
. . . A bedtime beauty . . . A
little light left on at night in case
a "dream beast" wakes her . . .
A day when you become aware
you just can't toss her in the air
quite like you used to . . . A
sudden grace that makes you see
the lady she will be . . .[15]

Besides the differences in active verbs and passive nouns the cards foretell that he will become Paul Bunyan, bring "a lifetime of joy," be a winner, an inventor, a leader; she will become a "lady."

A printing company dares to imagine your child's future. A friend feels free to tuck such predictions into an envelope. And parents display these cards proudly. Why? Because the values embodied in their corny rhymes are *shared* values. In this culture, it's perfectly all right to tell parents that their children will be like everyone else as long as the generalizations are based on sex, not race or ethnic stereotypes. The "dictator" and "lady" don't raise an eyebrow. But let Hallmark publish a couplet about the black child who will become a good dancer or the Jewish child who will grow up to be a clever money-lender and watch the fur fly.

If you receive sexist greeting cards from close friends, you may not want to embarrass them with your objections, but at least send the cards back to the printing company with your criticisms. If enough new parents protest, the publishers may have to create more nonsexist messages, such as "One little baby . . . so much happiness! Congratulations!"[16] That says it all.

ANNOUNCING THE BIRTH

When parents want to put out the word that a chid has been born, they send birth announcements to friends, relatives, and often to their local newspaper listing the baby's name, details about its size and birth time—and sometimes a lot more:[17]

Their first smash hit

"It's A Girl!"

starring
Jennifer Susan
Hailed as a Howling Success
World Premiere: September 2, 1976 at 1:43 P.M.

Producer . . . . Richard Richardson
Associate . . . . Donna Richardson
Technical Advisor . . . . . Dr. Johnson

I'm curious. Did Donna, whose body sheltered and nourished Jennifer, accept the credit "Associate" without a fight? Did Richard think it his right to be called Producer, even in fun? Did either parent think about it at all? If so, they might have understood that a family in which the parents are arranged in hierarchical order, with Father getting top billing for everything including childbirth, is a family already committed to raising their girl to be number two.

From the birth announcement columns of a San Francisco newspaper:[18]

BORN TO:

Thompson, David A., . . . June 20, a son
Wong, Kenson, . . . August 15, a daughter

> Young, Walter . . . August 12, a daughter
> Zelaya, Robert . . . June 12, a son

Line after line, column after column, of babies "born to" men. Mothers are invisible. Womb envy? Perhaps. Or perhaps just institutionalized patriarchy—a recitation of newly acquired male property, borne by women *for* men.

Other newspapers report births more "creatively":

Births

EASTMAN—Dawn and Tricia are happy to announce the arrival of their new sister Valerie Jeanne on Wednesday, July 9, 1975, at 4:01 A.M. weighing 7 lbs., ½ oz. at the Kingston General Hospital. Another girl to wait on daddy and a Susie Homemaker for mommy.[19]

One's imagination fills in the missing dialogue. Maybe the doctor said, "She can help with the washing up." Or maybe the parents exclaimed, *"Another* girl! Dammit."

Whatever was said, Valerie Jeanne's life is now set in cold type: daddy's servant, Susie Homemaker—not Paula Bunyan.

When you publicize your blessed event, the idea is not to ignore sex, but to avoid sex stereotypes; to announce a birth, not a destiny.

Home from the hospital. The visitors have gone, the celebrations are over, and the baby's life is in your keeping. But how do you raise a free child if sex stereotypes are so deeply entrenched that few of us can even recognize them without help? Where do you start?

I think you start by becoming aware of how others treat girls and boys. Just as we speak better once we notice other people's speech affectations, when you're alert to other parents' sex prejudices, it's almost impossible to fall into those habits yourself. At first, you'll be hyper-conscious, but soon enough nonsexist attitudes will be second nature, and you'll know what to watch for.

DIFFERENCES IN
INTERPRETING INFANT BEHAVIOR

People react differently to the exact same baby behavior (a movement or sound, say) depending on the baby's sex. That's how life becomes an entirely different experience for girls and boys; that's why they "live in two different worlds" and "don't speak the same language": a different world has been created for them by their parents and a different language has been spoken to and about them from birth.

At One Day Old. Within 24 hours after the birth of their first child, thirty sets of parents were asked to "describe your baby as you would to a close friend or relative." They, fathers especially, rated sons as "firmer, larger-featured, better-coordinated, more alert, stronger and hardier. They described daughters as softer, finer-featured, more awkward, more inattentive, weaker and more delicate."[20]

Were the parents being particularly alert to the looks and behavior of their own babies? Quite the contrary. Just because they knew the sex of their baby, they saw in him or her sex-appropriate characteristics that were not there at all: *hospital records show that the fifteen boys and fifteen girls were virtually indistinguishable from one another in terms of weight, height, muscle tone, reflexes, and general level of activity.*

Fathers, who had not yet even touched their babies, hauled out every sex stereotype to describe them intimately. Mothers, who measured their acquaintance with their babies in hours and minutes, also typed them with authority. Thus, conclude the researchers, "sex-typing and sex-role socialization appear to have already begun their course at the time of the infant's birth, when information about the infant is minimal."[21]

In that sense, we are as prone to "primitive" fortune-telling as the Mundugumor people in New Guinea. They believe that only those born with their umbilical cords twisted around their necks can become great artists, and lo and behold all the talented, recognized Mundugumor artists turn out to have been born that way.[22]

Our society believes that children born male are strong, alert, and hardy, and wonder of wonders our strong, alert, hardy citizens turn out to have been born male.

At Three Months. A small rubber football, a Raggedy Ann doll, and a flexible ring were placed on the floor for the adults to "use" while interacting with a three-month-old baby dressed in yellow.[23]

Researchers found that when the adults were told they were playing with a girl baby, they used the doll. When they weren't told if the baby was a girl or boy, the men took the "safest" course and played with the neutral toy (the ring) while the women chose either the football or the doll.

Several other findings are noteworthy:

1. People were anxious when they did not know the sex of the baby. ("You don't know how to treat it if you don't know what it is.")

2. With the cue "it's a girl," people pressed a doll upon a three-month-old. (Girls Are Meant to Be Mothers.)

3. People played differently with the same baby depending on its announced sex. (Males and females "live in different worlds.")

4. When asked to guess the baby's sex using only physical and behavioral clues, the great majority of adults were *wrong.* (There are no innate sex differences in infancy; differences are in the eye of the beholder.)

At Six Months. The "Adam/Beth" experiment tested the same principle with a child who was old enough to provide feedback.[24] This time, a six-month-old was dressed in blue pants when introduced as "Adam" to half of a group of young mothers, and in a pink dress when presented as "Beth" to the other half. The toy choices here were a fish, a doll, and a train.

Results: When the women thought they were playing with "Adam" they handed him the train more often; when they thought they were playing with "Beth," they gave her the doll. The mothers also tended to smile more when playing with "Beth."

"The infant emitted essentially the same behavior for all mothers, yet their treatment of him systematically differed depending on whether he was perceived as male or female."[25]

At the end of the experiment, when asked if they could tell the baby's sex had there been no clothing cues, one mother said she absolutely knew "Beth" was a girl because she was "sweet" and girls are sweeter; another knew because of the soft way "Beth" cried—"a feminine trait" in that mother's opinion, although it has been proved that adults cannot distinguish male and female babies from their cries.[26]

All the mothers who thought they had been playing with a girl were "very surprised" to find "Beth" was actually a boy.

Before the experiment, these mothers had said that they do not treat their own children differently by sex. After the experiment, the women did not recognize that they had actually treated "Adam" and "Beth" differently. If people are totally "unaware of their stereotyping" under supersensitized laboratory conditions, imagine how biased they can be in casual everyday life.

At Nine Months. After watching a videotape in which a nine-month-old baby responds to a teddy bear, a jack-in-the-box, a doll, and a buzzer, many people saw different attributes in the baby depending on whether they were told they were watching a girl or a boy: ". . . where the infant cries, 'the boy' was seen as angry and the girl as afraid. Further, both men and women considered 'the boy' to be more 'active' and 'potent' than 'the girl'!"[27]

Same film, same baby, same behavior, but what a difference a label makes.

DIFFERENCES IN
MOTHERS' TREATMENT OF INFANTS

Girl and boy infants do the same amount of vocalizing (babbling), fretting and crying, smiling, and moving about. Accordingly, you cannot tell the sex of a baby from watching the baby. However, "the skilled observer can tell from a mother's behavior with her child whether it is a girl or a boy."[28] In fact, several key differences in mothers' behavior "seemed to be determined by the sex of their infants,"[29] and nothing more.

Mothers of Girls:

- pick up the crying baby more often and faster.
- are more responsive to the infant's smiling and crying.
- vocalize and look at the infant more.
- smile more at the baby and try to elicit more smiles from the baby.

Mothers of Boys:

- let the baby cry longer.
- are more responsive to the infant's movement and playfulness.
- hold, touch, and rock the baby more (up to age six months), then gradually decrease such "proximal" behavior until, by the first birthday, boys are touched, held, and kissed much less than girls.

What accounts for these differences and where do they lead? We can follow some educated guesses. Michael Lewis, a long-time infant watcher, says mothers may touch boys more at first because boys are more valuable in this culture, but by age six months, "mothers start to wean their sons from physical contact with them," because "mothers believe that boys rather than girls should be independent and encouraged to explore and master their world."[30]

Female infants are allowed to touch and stay close to their mothers throughout early childhood because females are being "socialized" for dependency. (*Socialization* is the way children are trained to think about themselves and act with others in their environment.) When these more clinging infant girls become women, no wonder they are less confident about their autonomy.

Another result is that American males do not learn to be comfortable with touching behavior except in such defined situations as sex or contact sports, while American females are raised to *need* the touching behavior most men cannot give them.

The cry and the smile are forms of social communication at which females are thought to excel. If mothers respond to these behaviors more readily and enthusiastically in girls, crying and smiling are reinforced "in keeping with cultural expectations."[31]

Similarly, the additional time spent babbling to girl babies, and encouraging their vocalizing in response, tips the developmental scales in favor of girls' becoming more verbal and word-oriented than boys.[32] If mothers treated boy babies to more "conversation" in infancy, perhaps Johnny would be able to read better later in life.

DIFFERENCES IN
FATHER-INVOLVEMENT

Fathers, too, touch male infants more than females; they are more attentive to first-born boys,[33] and more active playing with year-old sons than with year-old daughters.[34] New fathers "tend to get more angry and irritated with female infants" for no apparent reason; they roughhouse with boys but treat girl babies "like porcelain."[35]

Such preferential treatment may be explained in various ways. For example, like attracts like, therefore, the father is drawn to the miniaturized version of himself. (That theory would not explain mothers' preferential treatment of sons.) Others say that the father values his special relationship as a "role model" for the son's manly behavior; but what is so man-to-man about relating to a newborn?

I'd say the preference emanates from the father's unconscious evaluations of the two sexes. Boys Are Better: better babies to touch, play with, and whittle into chips off the old block. And if daughters happen to miss out on the full energy of a man's fathering attentions, oh well, Girls Are Meant to Be Mothers anyway, and that's not something a Dad can teach a girl. The perfect alibi for the crime of sex preference.

DIFFERENCES IN
MATERNAL ATTENTION TO
SECOND-BORNS

It's logical that mothers spend less time caring for, fussing over, and adoring their second babies than they did their first-borns.[36] What isn't immediately logical is this: When the second baby is a girl, the mother's attentions are reduced *more* than if the second is a boy. "Virtually no decrease occurs in maternal attention for males who had first-born sisters."[37]

A girl is most welcome and fussed over if she arrives *after* one or more boys. How does this differential attention from the mother (and presumably, the father, to whatever extent he cares for the baby directly) affect the rest of the child's development? No one knows for sure, but we can imagine.

DIFFERENCES IN FEEDING PATTERNS

Studies have found mothers more likely to breastfeed boys than girls, to nurse boys up to 20 minutes longer per feeding, and to wean boys from the breast later than girls.[38] Among bottle-fed babies, boys get an average of 15 minutes per feeding, girls 8 minutes; bottle-fed boys weren't weaned to the cup until fifteen months, girls were off the nipple by the time they were one year old.[39] In a baby's short life time differences count a lot.

Maybe this feeding favoritism happens because heterosexual women feel more comfortable with the semi-erotic nursing experience when the suckler is a male. Maybe it's because women are trained in general to service males but not other females. Maybe mothers believe boys get hungrier (despite no evidence to that effect) or need extra nourishment so they can grow big and strong. Or maybe by nursing, holding, and feeding boys longer than girls, mothers are proving with their bodies the son preference they hold in their hearts.

Some of the effects of this feeding pattern are quantifiable: the longer-nursing baby gets more nourishment, more sucking pleasure, more maternal attention, and has fewer eating problems later on. Some of the effects are less obvious. The boy who is preferentially breastfed

> . . . obtains tangible proof of the availability to him of his mother's body and thus of the importance of his own body . . . of the importance of his well-being to his mother and of the place he occupies in his mother's life and therefore in the world. . . . It is precisely this complete acceptance of the baby's body by his mother that engenders that self-love which is so rare in girls and often so excessive in boys.[40]

DIFFERENCES IN TOILET TRAINING

Despite the fact that most doctors now believe babies are physiologically ill-equipped to control elimination before age two,[41] many parents choose to start toilet training much earlier. One study found that on the average, training is begun with girls at five months but with boys not until eight months.[42]

> Mothers are also more tolerant of little boys when they soil their pants. . . . If a boy is dirty and untidy, this seems to be in the natural order of things. If a girl is, she is looked upon as an annoyance and is attributed with the malicious intention of not wanting to keep herself clean.[43]

DIFFERENCES IN
PATTERNS OF MISTREATMENT

Studies published by the U.S. Public Health Service found that in all socioeconomic groups, girl children are consistently punished at earlier ages than boys. By nine months old, 31 percent of girls but only 5 percent of boys were being punished. Among eighteen-month-olds, 70 percent of the girls were receiving punishment for misdeeds, but only 50 percent of the boys. A portrait emerges of the typical abused infant: a second child, born very soon after the first child—and female.[44]

DIFFERENCES IN
VOICE AND LANGUAGE

It's not news that parents talk baby-talk to babies. But did you ever notice that fathers talk to babies differently than mothers do, and both parents talk differently to girl babies than to boys?

Fathers address their sons in "a sort of Hail-Baby-Well-Met style: while turning them upside down, or engaged in similar play, the fathers said things like, 'Come here, you little nut!' or 'Hey, fruitcake!' Baby girls were dealt with more gently, both physically and verbally."[45] Fathers also tend to talk in a high-pitched voice to little girls and a deep bass voice to little boys.[46]

From this combination of hardy handling and mock rough

talk, perhaps boys are toughened up for the real world, while girls, being "dealt with more gently," are readied for vulnerability.

On the other hand, perhaps the Hail-Baby-Well-Met approach, the withholding of physical and verbal gentleness to boys, is what rears unexpressive adult men who equate a soft word with "femininity" and weakness. Can parents learn to speak in a full range of voices to each child, regardless of gender? Yes, if we learn to *hear* sexism before it rises in our throats.

EQUALIZING INFANCY

Psychologist Jerome Kagan says that "males and females are more similar during the first week of life than they will ever be again."[47] However, Kagan writes,

> . . . sex differences arise in part because each parent holds a representation of what the ideal boy or girl should be like. . . . Since the ideals are different for the sexes, familial treatment will not be the same."[48]

Find an "ideal" that works for both sexes and you will find yourself treating your infant daughters and sons with equal vigilance and equal license, with equal hopes and equal frolic. Examine your "ideal boy" or "ideal girl" image. Think about how one differs from the other. Cancel out the physical incarnations of that difference. Think about what ideals are left. Think about which of those ideals require training for "femininity" or "masculinity"— and whether you really want to impose such training on your baby. Don't try to compose a formal list of Do's and Don'ts to check your biases. Just let the material in this chapter sink in, and very gradually and naturally you will act on your new consciousness by streamlining the way you behave with your baby.

You won't be raising your girl and boy babies to become "feminine" or "masculine" ideals. You won't be raising them "the same" either. You'll be raising *this particular baby* responsively, individually, and the best way you know how. And infancy will be a much richer, happier experience for your baby, and you.

8

Parity Parenthood:
Who Does What How Often
And Why It Matters

As an important, if not *the* most important role model in your child's life, you should be asking yourself the question I have often asked lecture audiences: *"Would you do anything different if you knew that your children were watching?"*

Well, they are. Watching, listening, learning, and imitating. Deciding what they can become by observing what you are and what you do.

Awareness begins earlier than you think. Days after birth, infants who *seem* to be oblivious to everything, except the delivery of milk and comfort at regular intervals, are actually absorbing the nuances of adult behavior during every interaction, and drawing conclusions about their parents' roles based on who does what, how often—and who doesn't.[1]

At three weeks old, babies already react differently to each parent's voice:

> . . . when the father is placed behind the child so he cannot be seen, and then speaks, the baby's face lights up with joy. . . . It appears the baby is ready to play, to be tousled. When the mother does the same, however, the baby's face is much more composed. It seems that the child is waiting to be fed, clothed or changed.[2]

By eight months, babies show more pleasure in their interactions with their fathers[3] but turn to mothers when in distress.[4] Before they can walk or talk, they know Mom as the caregiver-comforter and Dad as the exciting playmate.

Sex roles come in self-fulfilling cycles. Acting out parental roles *they* learned as children, mothers and fathers consistently picked up and held their babies for very different reasons. . . . Mothers were most likely to hold their babies for caretaking purposes whereas fathers were far more likely to hold babies to play with them or because the babies simply wanted to be held.[5]

Mothers free fathers to have fun with their children. Indeed, fathers spend four to five times more time playing with their infants than taking care of them.[6] But the imbalance exacts a toll. Father-child closeness is not nourished by a steady diet of "fun" any more than a love affair can deepen from nothing but laughs. Eventually, children consider their mothers "more loving and affectionate" than their fathers, and also, significantly, "less ignoring and neglecting."[7]

The play styles of the two parents also differ according to how *they* learned to play. With newborns, mothers speak softly, repeat words, and imitate babies' babble, while fathers are less verbal, touch their babies more, tap them rhythmically, and pay attention to them in fits and starts.[8] When playing with older children, mothers prefer "conventional games like pat-a-cake"; fathers are more active overall, initiating "physically stimulating and unpredictable or idiosyncratic types of play."[9]

Thus do traditional parents unconsciously pass on sex roles —gender "personality" and gender-linked activities—to the next generation. But in the nonsexist family, the cycle stops. With consciousness can come parity parenthood: shared nurturing, caregiving, and playful loving, which teaches infants and children that everybody does everything.

PARITY PARENTHOOD

The dictionary contains two entries for the word "parity":[10]

1. equality, as in amount, status, or character
(derived from the Latin *par,* or equal)

2. condition or fact of having borne offspring
(from *parere,* Latin, "to bring forth")

Since parity means both life-giving *and* equality, and since *par* and *parere* both suggest "parent," I propose that "parent" also is meant to encompass both definitions.

Very simply, it takes two parents to "bring forth" a child. That parity sets the stage for the other: for "equality, as in amount," of caregiving; "status" of both mother and father; and "character" of rewards and responsibilities.

I am not suggesting that Latin derivations prove my case. Nor do I blithely prescribe equal parenthood because it is what feminists want.[11] I am for it because without it, you cannot raise free children.

To begin with, think of the alternatives this way:

Traditional parenthood: one parent is half of human potential, the male half or the female half; two parents are whole.

Sex-linked divisions of labor in traditional families are based on the assumption that each parent will specialize in half of life's activities (one parent is half), and combined, a mother and a father will provide a complete picture (two parents are whole).

Parity parenthood: one parent is whole; two parents are double.

Nonsexist childrearing, on the other hand, assumes that each person should be a competent, self-actualized, and nurturant human entity (one parent is whole), and combined, mother and father can enrich children with twice as much (two parents are double).

If each parent is a competent, loving childrearer, it follows that two such parents are a double bonus for children. It's also a bonus for the adults in the unit. Rather than cover half the waterfront all the time, each parent can cover all the waterfront half the time, a revision that offers diversification, more leisure per person, and resentment-free marriage.

The eight million children living with their single mothers and the nearly one million living with single fathers[12] would also benefit from parity parenthood. Instead of considering those children automatically handicapped in a single-parent situation, we might find one full, totally functioning parent more desirable as a childrearer than the half-person who plays a traditional sex-linked role in the so-called intact family.

Separately, each nonsexist parent is a "renaissance" person (one parent is whole)—someone with both expressive and instrumental competencies, someone who can meet children's emotional needs while individually embodying many possibilities for being and becoming.[13] Coupled or single, such a person represents not a model for role conformity but an admirable, effective model for optimum *human* development.

In the two-parent household, what is usually needed to achieve parity is an overhaul of the power balance in the marriage, the distribution of housework and child care duties, the job-family priorities of both partners, and, eventually, the social system and labor market in which the family functions. To even begin dealing with these changes, we have to get to the tap root of patriarchy —the myth of "natural motherhood."

THE "MATERNAL INSTINCT"

It goes like this: Because the human female menstruates, gestates, and lactates, Girls Are Meant to Be Mothers while males, lacking the biological predispositions, are unsuited to child care. Thus, it is claimed, egalitarian parenting "fights against nature."

The "maternal instinct" theory, scientifically discredited for more than half a century,[14] has been ostentatiously revived by sociobiologists of the 1970s, despite overwhelming historic evidence of its opposite. Women's *flight* from motherhood through infanticide, abortion, and birth control; the current trend toward fewer children; and the grim statistics on child abuse would seem to disprove the theory on its face. If not, there are these contradictions:

If mothering is an inborn urge, like sex or eating, why does acting on it often lead to depression[15] rather than satisfaction and ecstasy. And why doesn't it behave repetitively, like copulating or eating, making us crave baby after baby after baby?

If it's an instinct, why does society have to sell it so hard? Why all the sentimental pieties, pro-family bromides, and religious pressures to bear children?[16]

If it's an instinct, why do women need mothering courses[17] and how-to books to teach them how to do it?

If it's natural, why do so many women need therapy and drugs to make it tolerable?[18]

WHAT'S REALLY HAPPENING?

The fact is, the "maternal instinct" is a manmade myth that assigns the entire child care responsibility to the female and desexes her if she won't accept it.[19] George Bernard Shaw saw through the ruse nearly a century ago:

Now of all the idealistic abominations that make society pestiferous, I doubt if there be any so mean as that of forcing self-sacrifice on a woman under the pretence that she likes it; and, if she ventures to contradict the pretence, declaring her no true woman.[20]

The myth of the "maternal instinct" implies that it is easy to be a good mother; it comes naturally; therefore, any woman can do it and if you can't, you're a failure. That is the wellspring of mother-guilt for all women, but especially for traditional or working-class women for whom motherhood "comes to be the most eventful experience in their lives."[21]

If mothering is an *instinct,* society can undervalue the real *skills* involved in childrearing, giving mothers points for quantity ("Nine kids! Wow!"), but not quality.

If it's an instinct, we can take mothers for granted ("They do it for love and love to do it"); we can pay low wages to those whose jobs parallel mothering functions (teachers, nurses, or household workers); and we can resist training women for top management or space engineering ("They'll just get pregnant and leave").

If females have a special biological predisposition, then introducing fathers into the nursery is redundant (They're not fathers, they're "mother substitutes"), contrary to nature, and insulting to women's expertise.

Occasionally, a piece of research unmasks the propaganda; for example, one study found both men *and* women equally unprepared for the practical realities of parenting.[22] But if research isn't handy, language usage gives away the truth.

SEMANTICS SPEAKS

Have you ever noticed that "to father a child" refers to the momentary act of depositing one's sperm, while "to mother a child" means years of loving care? (What's more, that entire motherhood is delegitimatized if that one moment of fatherhood is not acknowledged.[23])

Have you ever noticed that a child who grows up without a mother is said to be suffering maternal "deprivation" (dictionary definition: "loss, dispossession, bereavement")?[24] Life without father, however, is merely father "absence" ("a state of being away").[25] And the difference between deprivation and absence, as value-ridden concepts, allows men routinely to walk out on their families and be bad guys at worst, while women who do so are unnatural monsters.[26]

What about the fact that when the man is the breadwinner, a family is called "traditional," but when the woman is head of household, they call the family "matriarchal"[27]—as in the Moynihan Report on what's "wrong" with black families in America.[28]

Each of these discrepancies reflects what belief in the "maternal instinct" does to women. It predestines them, despite unique abilities, to end up in the same role. (The quality of the role is not the point here; the sausage-grinder sameness of millions of women's destinies *is*.[29]) Momma-mania roots role-playing in the species psyche and ennobles the role with the cloak of species survival. "To mother" is to save the race by raising its children; "to father" is to give sperm, money, and one's name.

Not to mother is to deprive children of a basic right like food, clothing, and shelter. Not to father is just not showing up.

Patriarchy means "power of men." Matriarchy has come to mean "power of *mothers.*"[30] Yes, semantics speaks the truth. For patriarchy is the name of a social system where men rule over women and matriarchy is the name of a house without a father, in which a woman—even one who is playing her proper role—has taken more power than men will allow.

BELIEVING MAKES IT SO

Men don't *make* women stay home with the babies. Most women say they *want* to; in fact they "do it for love." In the words of children:

A mom is someone who cares about you. So she cooks for you.

A mom is supposed to love you and wash boys' smelly socks.[31]

Sometimes satisfying her "maternal instinct"—staying home with the babies and working for love—can shrink a woman's world, and make her into a small-minded, incompetent person who is unfit to be in charge of children.

My mom is a Jack of all trades and a master of none.[32]

A mother should be fun! I hate boring mothers. Who wants a boring mother?[33]

Yet the "maternal instinct" continues to herd women into full and exclusive responsibility for children. You can hear it in all the familiar axioms: "No one can love a child like its mother." "A woman shouldn't have children if she doesn't want to raise them." "Surely a mother can give up her own plans and devote herself to her children during their formative years."

Father is the volunteer parent, the back-up man. Lacking "the instinct," everything he does is a miracle, or a favor. For instance, diaper-changing seems to be a key area for male martyrdom. From a child care advice booklet comes this:

Some fathers, and they are entirely within their rights, will have nothing to do with it . . . or perhaps only in an emergency. Others are willing to try.[34]

And this dialogue excerpt is taken from a book on conflict resolution:

INTERVIEWER: Who is going to be changing the diapers?
IRENE: Uh, he says me. He can't stand messy diapers.
INTERVIEWER: Do you have a desire to change diapers, Irene?
IKE: She likes all those things that go along with motherhood.
IRENE: I never thought about it. I just knew it was something you had to do whether you like it or not.[35]

When fathers care for their own children, mothers are supposed to be impressed and grateful. "You wouldn't believe how

well he managed when I was sick!" Or "He watched the baby for
me *all day* Sunday." *For* me. Man doing woman's work. How
lucky she is.

How convenient, too, for men, that the exhausting, repetitive,
often unpleasant and isolated work of rearing and socializing
babies automatically—instinctively—falls to women who are subordinate to and financially dependent on their husbands. That
way, father keeps the power while mother does the dirty work and
runs interference.

> A mother is the parent that cooks your food, washes your
> clothes and tells your father when to spank you.

> Moms are people who end up doing chores your father told
> you to do.[36]

That way, men keep control of the next generation without
having to get involved until children are older, more civilized, and
more rewarding. When there are dirty diapers and spit-ups and
squirming creatures in playpens, children belong to their mothers.
But when things get interesting, in steps father, father the glamorous, father the fun-lover, father the powerful parent.

> My father is a proud and kingly man. The ruler of the house
> and television set.

> A father is a person who most little boys fight over who has
> the strongest or the smartest.

> A father is the man who sits at the head of the table.[37]

Powerful-father is the other side of the coin from Natural-
mother. Father is respected but remote, admirable but not available. The patriarchal division of labor that assigns mother to early
child care leaves father forever distanced from his children. First,
the "maternal instinct" kept him on the outside of the mother-
child circle by making pregnancy, birth, and lactation the criteria
for admission.[38] Then the Powerful-father ideal makes a man who
does feel love for a baby repress that feeling as unnatural and
unmanly.[39] Eventually, the repression becomes a way of life.

No matter how much fun and respect and power Dad represents to his children, the trade-off is that he becomes an emotional
outsider.

My father is not ideal because I can't tell him anything. . . .
He doesn't understand me. I wish he understood me better.[40]

WHERE IT ALL BEGINS

Most psychologists believe that "the infant is preprogrammed to seek proximity to a protective person."[41] This person
is the mother, who is likewise "preprogrammed" to be maternal.
The attachment to Mother, the most "significant other," creates
a lifelong anchor of personal security from which children can
explore the world. Without this anchor, children rarely achieve
competence and autonomy.[42]

Other psychologists question whether babies even remember
human beings, experiences, separations, or reunions encountered
during the first year or two of life.[43]

Whichever camp is right, both sides have been father-blind
on the issue. Investigators used mothers and babies to test "separation protest" (crying) and "proximity seeking"—so, not surprisingly, their results proved that babies need mothers and mothers
respond to babies.[44]

Only recently, when researchers began to interview the *other*
parent and observe him with his child from behind a one-way
mirror, was it discovered that fathers, too, given the opportunity,
touch their babies, kiss, adore, and embrace their babies as enthusiastically as mothers. And babies (now that someone has given
them the chance to show it), "contrary to our earlier assumptions,
are indeed attached to both their mothers and their fathers."[45]

To put a fine point on it, study after study conducted
throughout the 1970s has confirmed men's capacity for father-
infant connections[46] so intense that leading researchers have declared fathers "just as nurturant as mothers."[47] Meaning they *can*
be if we let their childloving abilities develop.

FATHER FEELINGS

Maybe, after all, there is a *"fathering* instinct."[48]

Certainly, in ritual, legend, and myth, men have gone to great
lengths to appropriate women's life-giving powers. Zeus gave birth
to Athena from his head and Dionysus from his thigh. The Bible

tells us males are the first mothers: God, the father, created Adam, and Adam delivered Eve from his ribs. "The man is not of the woman, but the woman of the man" (I Corinthians 11:8) is paternal revisionism at its scriptural best.

Among various fish, birds, and animals, the male exhibits "mothering instincts" such as nest-building, incubating eggs, and feeding, protecting, and tending his offspring.[49]

Furthermore, "there are demonstrated biological disposi- tions to the father-child attachment in humans"[50]—and psycho- logical dispositions that are only beginning to be explored.[51]

In some cultures, the fathering urge is so compelling that the husbands of pregnant women undergo *couvade,* a sympathetic birth experience complete with labor pains and postpartum recov- ery symptoms.[52] In Western society, before sex role pressures get to children, little girls and boys both enjoy doll play and both show the same basic "attraction to infants."[53] Under conditions that are not ego-threatening, adult men too, are as attracted to babies as adult women.[54]

Starting with Karen Horney, several psychologists have said that in some profound way the human male suffers from womb-envy,[55] and that laws establishing paternity are men's compensatory bid to connect themselves to childbirth.[56] One writer points out that the experts who have "spoken most categorically about women's maternal drive are men whose own lives have been dominated by children."[57] These are Bruno Bet- telheim, author of *Symbolic Wounds,*[58] which deals with womb- envy rituals; Erik Erikson, who defines women by their "inner space," which only pregnancy can fill;[59] and Benjamin Spock, "who, like the Madonna, is forever associated in our minds with achild."[60]

By stating this rather convincing case for the "fathering in- stinct," perhaps we can argue away the whole premise of innate behavior, get rid of the "motherhood mandate,"[61] and start from scratch. Here are the ABC's:

A. To learn about motherhood, don't ask a sociobiologist, ask a mother. (Or read one of the honest books written by mothers about their feelings and experiences.[62])

B. Not all women are meant to be mothers, and no individual woman is meant to be only a mother and nothing else.

C. Two parents want a child. Two parents make a child. Two parents raise a child. Neither parent was born knowing how to do it. Both parents can learn.

PARENTAL SPECIALIZATION

Even after the "maternal instinct" is put to rest, women are called the better childrearing parent on the basis of the efficiency of the division of labor: "Somebody has to bring in the money and somebody has to take care of the children; somebody has to fix things and somebody has to cook the food." If parents have different skills and responsibilities, but together they make a good team, this argument asks, what is wrong with their having separate but complementary roles?

Nothing is wrong with division of labor so long as the role split is based on individual specialties, not on sex. But the usual spheres of influence for each parent suspiciously parallel sex-role stereotypes. And the sexist division of labor is defended with muddled notions that it aids children's gender identification.

The idea is: Children are supposed to learn their sex from their parents' sex roles.

The fear is: Without sex roles there is no sex.

The truth is: Separate-but-complementary roles do not help gender identity any more than separate-but-equal education helped racial identity.

Dividing work, love, power—the whole human agenda—between two parents (and by extrapolation, between two sexes) gives children the half-parent I warned you about at the beginning of this chapter. Now let's reunite the human parts in a parity relationship that calls for the basic reapportionment most families need: *More Dad in the home, more Mom in the world.*

OH, DAD, MORE DAD

In terms of time alone, the typical American father has a long way to go to achieve parity parenthood. One famous study found that the average father interacts with his baby for less than 38 *seconds* a day.[63] In 38 seconds, you cannot even change a diaper or sing three verses of "The Farmer in the Dell." The *most* any father in this sample devoted to his infant in one day was 10 minutes, 26 seconds—barely time enough for a bottle and a burp.

Other fathers have logged up to 15 minutes a day feeding their babies, compared to 1½ hours daily for mothers; almost half these fathers said they had *never* changed the baby's diapers, and 3 out of 4 had no regular caretaking responsibilities whatsoever.[64] With one-year-olds, fathers spend between 15 and 20 minutes per day,[65] and although no one is quite sure how to measure father involvement with older children, we have only to look at children's survey responses to learn that it is not enough.

Father alienation is so severe that half of the preschool children questioned in one study preferred the television to their fathers;[66] 1 child in 10 (aged seven to eleven) said the person they are most afraid of is their father; half wish their fathers would spend more time with them; and among children of divorce, only a third said they see their fathers regularly.[67]

I am most moved by the thirteen-year-old boy who earnestly told the *New York Times* that he would not do to his children what his father has done to him: "If I decide to have children, I couldn't let myself have a real career. Being a father takes so much time. . . ."[68]

Despite all this father-hunger, the American man is paid to spend time *away* from his children, not to be a good father. The successful adult male is a cool leader and a big money-maker, not a warm, gentle, egalitarian, and an adored dad.[69] As one pragmatic employer put it,

> Hell, when I'm interviewing a young lawyer, the *last thing* I'm interested in is his emotional openness or how much housework he does. I want a tough, ambitious son-of-a-bitch who'll stay at his desk until midnight.[70]

The family man is actually penalized in the business community: if he cares too much about his children, his career "commitment" is suspect. He is likely to be overlooked for promotions and he may even lose his job.

A man who explains to his superior that he cannot work late one night because he has to prepare dinner may only be looked at askance and even commended for his consideration for his family. But should he repeat this behavior, he will probably be told that he needs to reassess his priorities if he intends to remain a valued member of the organization.[71]

Further along the same line, fathers who voluntarily devote *all* their time to children, even temporarily, are seen as social deviates. When writer-critic John Leonard quit his job, he discovered "Our neighbors, strangers, disapproved. The idea of a grown man staying home during the day to care for a baby was subversive."[72]

Another full-time father internalized public opprobrium and began to doubt his own worth because his *work* was childrearing:

> I get an empty feeling when people ask me what I'm doing. Most of my energy in the last six months has focused on Dylan, on taking care of him and getting used to his being here. But I still have enough man-work expectations in me that I feel uncomfortable just saying that.[73]

Before men can comfortably devote more time to their children, the values of the workplace must change. But that is the task of the whole society, not of the individual father. What *he* must do is recognize housework and child care as intrinsically important work and free himself from the "masculine" compulsion to be the achiever-provider no matter what the cost. One father, a formerly compulsive academic, recalls:

> I had to give up this image of being a scholar sitting in the library 'til all hours of the night. Then I started to enjoy being at home. After all, [my son] would grow up and I might have missed all that. The library would always be there.[74]

KIDS NEED FATHERS, AND FATHERS NEED FATHERHOOD

It surprises some people to learn that a man who . . . can meet the purely practical needs of children—bathing, feeding, getting them to school on time—begins to feel more effective. . . . Once the feelings of competence begin to be introduced into the area of dealing with children's emotions, reinforced by the child's well-being, the whole area of emotions becomes less threatening. . . . For men socialized to believe that feelings must be kept hidden and are a barrier to effective functioning, experiencing competency in this area can be a source of positive self-regard.[75]

In other words, it feels good to father well. It also feels good not to mess up at something that matters so profoundly. As Gerald Jonas, father of two daughters, admits,

> I put as much effort into raising children as I do into earning a living, partly because I get so much satisfaction from it, and partly because I believe that the sins of the fathers are visited on the fathers.[76]

The sins, of course, are sins of omission. Fathers who neglect infancy, who tolerate toddlerhood, and only tune in on their children at mid-childhood, when they are "interesting" and "companionable," usually find it is too late then to do anything about the child's development and too late to understand the person inside the child.

Many women were roused to hopeful enthusiasm when, in a 1978 cover story, *Newsweek* proclaimed that "men are changing," turning down job advancement offers, setting aside time for their children, sharing housework and wage-earning with their wives, "opening up and feeling better about it."[77] If it is not a nationwide groundswell, it is certainly more than a ripple. Polls show that city and farm fathers alike want to be "closer to their children than their fathers had been to them." They want to be "more sensitive to the feelings of the child . . . and involved in decision-making" related to children's activities and welfare.[78]

Although it is never too late to begin, the easiest way to achieve this father-child intimacy is to get in there from the very start. Men who participate in the childbirth process and in "bonding" infant care during the earliest months adjust better to family life, feel less parental anxiety, and enjoy "a special warmth and ease" with their children.[79] Involved fathers eventually reduce the time they spend in the workplace,[80] "develop a stronger self-image, view their careers as less important, say they are more able to express emotion [and] claim they understand children better."[81]

From the experience of divorced fathers, psychologists have learned what feminists have been saying for years: shared parenthood is better than full-time or almost-no-time parenthood. The divorced father with full custody tends to sound like the harassed full-time mother in a traditional "intact" family: "O.K. I'm it. There is no one else I can rely on. I wash the clothes, I feed the kids, I put them to bed. I yell at them, I love them. I am it."[82]

The divorced father with every-other-weekend or similar occasional arrangements to see his children is comparable to the busy, traditional father who uses his rare time with his children to entertain them like visiting clients: "I went to every park, museum, playground, movie, zoo and what-have-you imaginable. I was constantly on the make for things to do."[83]

But the divorced father who shares child custody with the child's mother, and the married father who shares child *care* with the child's mother, both are able to relate to the child authentically and intimately. Instead of playing Judicial Authority, Daddy Moneybags, or Playmate-Coach, the sharing father is a flesh-and-blood person—sometimes fun and sometimes cross, sometimes knowing and sometimes defeated by the details of lamb chops, mittens, birthday presents, and crumbs. Children can turn to such a father not just for playtime and problem-solving, but for sharing secrets and needing hugs. No more or less loving or depriving than their mother, no less familiar with their wastes and mess, no more responsible for their genius, their sweetness, or their beauty, he becomes the man in their life who *deserves* to matter most.

THE BEST MOTHERS
ARE LESS MOTHERS

Simply stated, get Father into the house a lot more, and let Mother out of it. Just as the exclusive provider-achiever role is too burdensome for one man, the full-time mother role is too much responsibility and too little stimulation for one woman. To wit:

• When asked how a person's life is changed by having

children, four times as many mothers polled gave totally negative answers as totally positive ones.[84]

• The peak rates of mental illness for women occur in the first months following delivery.[85]

• Women report the most psychiatric symptoms when they are immersed in their most role-related activities: getting married, having babies, and caring for preschool children alone at home.[86]

In the past, postpartum depression—irritability, anxiety, unrelieved sadness, tears, hostility to the baby,[87] insatiable demands for the husband's attention or antagonism toward him and sexual retreat[88]—have either been attributed to fear of the feminine role;[89] dismissed as another of those mysterious "women troubles," like cramps and cravings; or trivialized, as in an ad for hair coloring: *"We had the post-partum blues. So we became blondes!"*[90]

Against a backdrop of such reductionism, psychologist Edward Pohlman understood, and sensitively explained, the enormous implications of epidemic maternal despair:

> The decade that follows a woman's first pregnancy is often a dreary, lonely, frustrating one. This is true even though the mother may later look back with pleasant fondness on these years. The heavy psychological costs women experience during this period cannot but affect their husbands, their marriage relationships and the parents' relations with their children. . . . Since so many American women have highly similar reactions to their first 10 or 12 years of parenthood, a broad cultural problem seems involved.[91]

Since that was written in 1969, hundreds of scholars and researchers have identified that "broad cultural problem": *the female sex role.* Whether a woman is reacting to her first baby or her fourth, she is *not* depressed by the baby, but by the concomitants of what I will call Total Motherhood—the loss of freedom, lack of emotional support and economic autonomy, feelings of helplessness; the unassisted, incessant labor of child care, the fatigue, the sense of decreased "sex appeal" and self-esteem; the absence of a life of her own outside the home.[92]

Here is the sound of that depression in *anticipation:*

My pregnancy turned me into an agoraphobic housewife who would not even drive two miles into town because "something" might happen. My husband had married an extremely independent, outgoing, career-minded woman but he was now living with an insecure, terrified housewife who sat at home and worried all day. If he was fifteen minutes late coming home from work, I had planned the funeral and was sobbing from grief.[93]

And here is the sound of depression after the baby arrives:

Faced with the crushing truth: that I am totally responsible for the life of a helpless human being, I sit down at the kitchen table and cry.[94]

Depressed by dependence, loneliness, and shrinking boundaries to her life, a woman may be reminded that she is "free to choose" to work outside the home as well. But assuming her husband "lets" her get a job (which many, especially working-class men, will not),[95] she is expected to do so without inconveniencing anyone. She must *add* outside activities to her "primary" roles: maintaining her "femininity," mothering, and having dinner on the table by six o'clock. She must be able to do it *all*, and if the marriage fails or the children have problems, it is her fault and it is proof that a woman cannot do it *all* without her family's "suffering."

Marya Mannes described the superwoman syndrome this way:

Nobody objects to a woman's being a good writer or sculptor or geneticist, if she still manages to be a good wife, a good mother, good-looking, good-tempered, well-dressed, well-groomed and unaggressive.[96]

Because this is an impossible order, most women succumb to Total Motherhood, at least during their children's youngest years. Total Mothers are women who ritualize domestic chores, who dramatically recount every spill, mishap, repair visit, and household crisis, to convince themselves that something *happened* to them each day. They are women who—for the first time in human history[97]—have distended child care into a twenty-four-hour-a-day job. They are women who learn to live through others.

One young mother remembers that after she watched everyone fuss over her new baby, *her* mother said to her, "I guess now it's your turn to live vicariously." The younger woman recalls,

> Her remark went through me like a knife. . . . I felt enormous waves of anger and fear rising inside of me. Anger that my own role model, who spent what could have been her most creative years in frustration, living vicariously through her daughters, had no qualms about passing on this legacy to me. And fear that I might find myself accepting it.[98]

Millions of women accept it. But millions more have discovered that living vicariously is like eating prechewed food, and for all the joys and challenges of childrearing, Total Motherhood is in many ways a cop-out.

> It is really much faster and easier to make a baby than paint a painting, or write a book or get to the point of accomplishment in a job. It is also much easier in a way to shift focus from self-development to child development—particularly since, for women, self-development is considered selfish.[99]

Many women are discovering now what Antoinette Brown Blackwell recognized over a hundred years ago:

> A mother's child is but an incident in her life. Love it as she will, it will grow up; and in a few years it is gone. But a lifework remains for a lifetime![100]

Understandably, those who give up their own needs, hopes, and dreams make their children their lifework. But the result is more often mockery than honor (*e.g.,* "the Jewish mother," "the stage mother," "smother love," and so on). Even when mothers make *extraordinary* children their lifework, the rewards are tainted. Jimmy Connors' mother is ridiculed for her single-minded devotion to his tennis career. And when a gifted young clothing designer was heralded by the fashion world, *Life* magazine sneeringly commented on "his omnipresent mother"[101]—even though the boy genius was only ten years old and could hardly be expected to deal with Seventh Avenue business interests on his own.

When a father takes a similar hand in a child's career, his actions are perceived differently. If he is passing on a skill of his own (like dancer Jacques d'Amboise to son, Chris, or skier Mickey Cochran to his children), he is celebrated as a coach and mentor. If he is a "nobody"—like Mr. Mantle, the farmer, who trained his son Mickey for a pro baseball career—he is lavished with praise for "giving his life" to the betterment of his child. Mothers in the same position are condemned for "living off" their children's glories.

No wonder so many mothers see themselves as martyrs. No wonder they expect their sacrifices to be repaid by children (who can never do enough) or husbands (who can never atone for stealing their wives' freedom).

> Ann Owens is, like her husband, 47-years-old, and like many of her contemporaries, beginning to wonder what she had ever done with her life besides raise two children and fix hundreds of thousands of meals.[102]

The mother role comes with a guaranteed midlife crisis. It has built-in obsolescence. For many women, the departure of grown children is experienced as abandonment, and the husband, if he is still living, cannot fill the gap because his salience has so long been eclipsed by the children. For such a woman, the "empty nest" is synonymous with an empty life.[103]

For other women, studies show, "when day to day care ends and the children leave, relief comes."[104]

Total Motherhood cannot be good for women if, when its prime years are over, the mother either falls into despair or breathes a sigh of relief. And Total Motherhood cannot be good for children if it puts in charge of them someone whose distinguishing characteristics are passivity, other-directedness, and self-sacrifice.[105]

Unfortunately, due to cultural propaganda, the women who want children most, and who become mothers most often and most exclusively, are "self-protective, fearful of danger, risk-avoiding, resistant to change and low in flexibility,"[106] whereas the best mothers are women who are independent, self-sufficient, creative, flexible, nonauthoritarian, and incidentally, pro–women's liberation.[107] "The persons we would want to employ for childcare (if we had standards for evaluating its quality) would be persons —educated, intelligent, etc.—who are probably already employed."[108]

Someone once said that the best mother is not a person to lean on but a person to make leaning unnecessary. The woman who is nothing-but-a-mother needs to be leaned on in order to feel needed. But the woman who is someone in her own right knows that to be leaned on is to be rooted in one spot, and she will have none of it.

Because she loves her children for themselves and not for her own self-affirmation, she welcomes their independence. And because she values herself and her own aspirations, she can let them go, knowing there will be a full person left over when they leave.

WHAT'S IN IT FOR YOUR MARRIAGE?

At some point within the first few days after a baby's birth, almost every parent I know has been stunned by this insight:

> The thought came to me one morning that she was my blood relative and he wasn't, and that while there were things that [my husband] could do to make me stop loving him, and stop being his wife, there was no way Audrey would ever not be my daughter.[109]

The impact of a baby on a marriage is both thrilling and traumatic. That one tiny creature can cause so much chaos and ambivalence in two adults is perhaps the greatest shock of first-time parenthood. "No one, ever again, will wreak such havoc on our lives. It's easier for three people to become four than it is for two people to become three."[110]

Parenthood has been blamed for marital crises attributable to lost companionship, no sleep, being tied down; to arguments and anxieties about the care and discipline of the child; to lowered self-esteem of both parents; to conflict about their work roles, privacy, communication patterns, and new demands on their time.[111]

Rather than cementing the marriage bond, the birth of a baby often lowers a couple's satisfaction with marriage,[112] reduces the frequency of their sexual relations,[113] cuts in half the time they spend in conversation (alarming, if it's true that marital satisfaction is "directly related to the amount of time a couple spends talking together each day"[114]), and changes the subject of their conversations from themselves, their feelings, and their sexuality, to discussions about their child.[115]

In truth, it seems that husbands and wives become parents primarily and marriage partners second. Marital morale slumps during the children's school years and doesn't pick up for years.[116] Psychologist Angus Campbell offers this reassurance: "Wait 17 years or so until you are alone again with your spouse. Your satisfaction with life and your all-around good mood will return to where it was before you had kids."[117]

Some reassurance! Why does parenthood take seventeen years out of a love relationship, and what can we do to prevent it? An answer is suggested by this sociologist's explanation:

> Many young people are egalitarian peers in school, courtship and early marriage. With the birth of a child, deeper layers of their personalities come into play . . . the acting out of old parental modes that have been observed and internalized in childhood, triggering a regression to traditional sex roles that gradually spreads from the parental role to the marriage and self-definition of both sexes.[118]

"Regression to traditional sex roles" is just what parity parenthood can avoid. Establish that Mother is not the primary childrearer and Father is not the sole breadwinner. Otherwise, you will find, as hundreds of thousands have, that with each child born, Mother loses more personal power and authority,[119] and Father loses emotional connections, becomes estranged, and . . . is put in his place, which is after the children. No wonder the assertion of his patriarchal controls becomes louder and louder— how else can the father keep his place in the family?[120]

When sex roles harden and the division of labor separates the two parents, there *is* "a place" to be kept in the family. In *his* place, the husband suffers financial anxiety, and jealousy at the felt loss of his wife's love.[121] He resents the restrictions a baby imposes on their social life and even wishes, occasionally, "to return to pre-baby days."[122]

"When we were married," goes a typical complaint, "I thought my wife was going to take care of me. As it turns out, she takes care of the baby and I take care of them."[123]

In *her* place, the wife experiences work-family conflicts, loss of identity, and altered priorities. When asked what was most important to them, traditional mothers ranked children first, being a husband's companion *fourth,* and being a sexual partner *seventh.* [124] Rating their husband's key roles, women put "bread-winner" first, "father" second, and "husband" third.[125] Is it any surprise, then, that marriages turn sour?

What I'm leading up to is this: Sex roles in childrearing are deceptive. They seem to make the marriage partnership more efficient, but they can actually destroy married love and diminish married sex. Parity can change the picture completely.

Postpartum depression and father resentment have been found less likely if the father is prepared for parenthood tasks and his highly participatory role is spelled out in advance,[126] and if the mother is "deeply involved" in roles other than motherhood.[127] Financial strain can be avoided if two adults remain contributory wage-earners, *and* the by-products of work—new friends, achievement, stimulation—enhance the couple's interest in one another.[128]

There are no secret emotional debts accruing for payoff later. Because neither parent's life is weighted disproportionately toward family or work, wife and husband are about equally appreciated or taken for granted, equally energized or exhausted.

> When my daughter, Emily, and I are together in the house for an entire day, somewhere between five and six o'clock, when she is tired and hungry and cranky, and I am tired and hungry and cranky, I want to run away from home. I am resentful that my husband gets such a thrill when he comes in and sees her little face light up.
>
> When Emily and I are apart during the day, somewhere between five and six o'clock, I want to get home. When I come in, I can understand precisely how my husband feels, and I am no longer resentful. It is an incredible thrill to see my daughter's little face light up.[129]

Empathy. Sharing. Closeness. Husband doesn't outgrow wife, nor wife resent husband. Working side-by-side, they finish faster and have more time together for talk, family life, romance. Jointly deciding how to bring up their children gives two parents a sense of mutuality instead of hostility and fault-finding, and lets children thrive in an atmosphere in which there are fewer marital conflicts and misunderstandings.

Research proves my point: Marriages "characterized by shared power, flexible division of tasks, and a high level of companionship" contain *healthier* men and women than do traditional marriages;[130] and couples "who were not tied to traditional concepts of husband and wife roles" experienced *more* "wedded bliss," *more* love and interest in one another, and *more* mutual commitment as years went by.[131] In sum, "there is considerable evidence that egalitarian patterns of marriage result in high marital satisfaction for both spouses."[132]

So. We have established that for our sake and our children's, fathers need more time in the family and mothers need more outside-the-family activities. Now, how do we get from here to there? How do parents, single or cohabitating, change their old habits, reapportion housework, revise family-job priorities, and alter the marital power balance so that when our children are watching, we'll be proud of what they see?

Since no one set of how-to's could apply to all situations (black parents, for instance, shoulder the added burden of racism,[133] and working class parents have fewer economic options), what I shall present in the next chapters is a basic menu for change, cafeteria-style: choose the advice that suits your family and pass the rest right by.

9

Advice for Adults:
More Dad, Less Mom—
And a Balance of Power and Love

So often, people ask, "What should I do?" "How can we change?"
"Start us off." These suggestions—for mothers, fathers, and marriages—are only the beginning . . .

ADVICE FOR MOTHERS

Demystify Child Care

Feeding, cleaning, and dressing a child are not acts of love.
They're functions you perform lovingly. *Not* performing them
constantly or exclusively does not constitute bad motherhood. No
one should feel guilty about wanting to share the work of child
care, because that's what it is: *work*—repetitive, tedious, often
lonely and exhausting work, like scrubbing and folding and picking up and sponging and washing and so on. To romanticize it,
as our culture has done, is to mislead women (and men) and make
real-life parenthood ultimately disillusioning.

> I would tell him how I would finish a day and feel as if
> I hadn't done a thing, not a *thing*. David would say, "But of
> course you have! Look at this marvelous child you're bringing
> up."
> I don't think David understood what I meant until I was
> bedridden for a week. The first day he had Seth for 24 hours.
> You know the man in the Alka-Seltzer ad? . . . Well, David
> looked like that.
> The point is that Seth's doing it, not me. He's growing;
> I'm not really growing him. And day after day, I have no
> sense of growth myself.[1]

When you demystify child care, you can distinguish between two aspects of parenthood: one is challenging and creative (the growth part), and the other contends with menial chores and maintenance (the no-growth part). Mothers have to keep telling the truth about the no-growth parts—to ourselves, each other, our husbands (and eventually to our sons and daughters)—not just to our psychiatrists or pediatricians.

One New York pediatrician with a huge practice[3] told me he had never known a mother who had not confessed one or more of the following secret disasters during the first six months of her child's life:

- Overdressed the baby on a hot day; underdressed the baby during a blizzard ("*I* gave her this cold!")

- Stuck the baby with a diaper pin ("His tetanus infection will be *my* fault!")

- Lost grip on the baby in the bath ("Good God, I almost *drowned* her!")

- Turned away long enough for the baby to roll off the changing table ("Is it brain damage? Have I killed him?")

Only pediatricians know for sure how truly trial-and-error is the experience of caring for a first baby, no matter who does it. If men were not so obsessed with success, they could view their blunders with babies as a learning process, not as evidence of lifelong inadequacy. And if women told the truth about child care, instead of pretending to be "instinctually" proficient, men would find children quite as manageable and unmanageable as women do.

Give Up Your Domestic Throne

This second bit of advice for mothers is tougher than it sounds. Let go. Stop getting an easy high from being maven of the manse and honcho of the household. What's tough is relinquishing your expert status and sharing domestic power before you are sure of gaining any external power to replace it. But you have to start somewhere, and unless men are let in on the mysteries of home management, women will remain trapped in their groove.

Don't view a man's way of doing housework as a personal attack. His method is not a criticism of your methods; it is *his* method. And don't view his participation as a favor or a gift; it's a *normal* obligation: "We both eat, so we both shop, cook and do dishes. We both contribute to the mess, so we both clean it up. We both wear clothes, so we both do laundry."[3]

Let go for your children's sake, too. When a man shares housework (not just "helps around the house"), it's easier to rear your son to *be* that kind of man, and your daughter to expect that kind of behavior.

Think of it this way: give up one-woman rule and your children will have a head start on a good marriage of their own.

> He was an only child but his mother worked outside the home and he carried his share of the load as his father did also. He was brought up to be a caring individual toward other people, whether male or female. I have to give his parents credit for him being the supportive husband he is today.[4]

Do for You and Don't Feel Guilty

The last chapter described how more Dad at home and more Mom in the world is advantageous to everyone involved. Let that be your keynote, your permission to think about *you,* for a change.

This is not the place to discuss goals clarification or strategies for your career development. But it *is* the place to assure you that your children's connection to your own career decisions is not what you've been led to believe:

> On weekends, from 7 P.M. Friday to 1 P.M. Sunday, my husband completely took over the house and four children. I was glad for it, but I had a really rough time when the kids started calling Daddy when they were cold, sick, thirsty or frightened in the night. Had I lost them? Had I abdicated motherhood to selfishly pursue Fulfillment?[5]

No, it turns out her children stopped calling Mommy for the most pragmatic of reasons: they couldn't wake Mommy up. Mommy had become so tired from her weekend nursing shifts that once she finally got to sleep, she slept like the proverbial log. So the kids switched to Daddy for their nighttime needs. And Daddy was delighted to *be* needed. And the children couldn't care less which parent responded so long as someone loving and patient came to them in the dark.

Doing things *for* you does not mean doing things *against* your children. Making time for your activities out of the family makes room for the children's *other* parent *in* it. Remember that you do not constantly have to play the *role* of your child's mother —you *are* your child's mother.

Be Honest About Your Own Needs

If working outside the home is what you need to make you happy, or what the family needs to "make ends meet," deal with it. Do not be deterred by a shrieking child barring the front door or wrapped around your legs. Children, like the rest of us, become addicted to the full-time service and attention of another person. This doesn't mean it's beneficial for them to have it, and it doesn't mean they won't get used to it if they don't.

Dr. Ruth Hartley found that when asked about their parents' jobs, children expressed "almost as much bad feeling about fathers leaving for work as about mothers."[6] It's just that with fathers, they learn fast that the departure is nonnegotiable.

Of course, one does not suddenly up and leave the house without notice. A sensitive mother explains her plans far enough in advance for the children to get used to the idea. For very young children, a storybook about working mothers might be a helpful discussion aid. With older children, a straightforward presentation of "mother-is-a-person-who-needs-etc." should be followed by lots of talk about changed family roles and a dry run or two so that everyone knows his or her obligations.

Many women seem more comfortable telling children they are working for financial need, whether or not it's true. (You'll remember the affluent mother who said, "Otherwise, what excuse would I have for working?") Ironically, anything but the truth about your motives could backfire in your children's minds. For example, in answer to the question "Why do you think mothers work?" one little girl said, "Some work for the money, some . . . because they like to, and some . . . to get away from the children."

Dr. Hartley warns, if more mothers could admit to the second reason, "perhaps there would be less need for children to believe the third."[7]

Nobody Suffers If You Are Not Suffering

Millions of mothers worry that going to work will affect their children's academic and social development, but decades of research show "no evidence of any negative effects traceable to maternal employment. Children of working mothers are no more likely than children of nonworking mothers to become delinquent, to show neurotic symptoms, to feel deprived of maternal affection, to perform poorly in school, to lead narrower social lives," and so on.[8]

The impact on children—good, bad, or nonexistent—is not connected to a mother's work status, reports psychologist Judith Bardwick: "The attitude of the mother—whether she is pleased with what she is doing, or resentful, gratified or guilty—seems more important than whether she is employed or at home."[9]

A mother's self-esteem, energy level, and feelings of personal worth—whether they derive from an executive job, blue-collar work, *or* homemaking[10]—determine not only the quality of her maternal behavior, but the messages she transmits to her children about female competence and dignity.

If you are happy with your work and your children are well cared for, the fact that you have a job might even have a positive impact on your children's values and personalities.[11]

Daughters of employed mothers have been found to have greater educational and career aspirations and higher academic achievement;[12] more assertiveness, independence, and autonomy;[13] less anxiety or rigidity about sex roles;[14] more self-esteem and self-reliance;[15] and higher mathematical and spatial abilities.[16]

Finally, children of both sexes whose mothers are both affectionate and intellectually active tend to develop more flexible, well-adjusted personalities—personalities that are balanced between "forceful and cognitive as well as emotional, affective and sensitive" characteristics.[17]

Do Not Expect Child Care Help to Come Easy

After reviewing all available data, Dr. Lois W. Hoffman, co-editor of *The Employed Mother in America,* [18] wrote:

> The working mother who obtains personal satisfactions from employment, does not have excessive guilt, and has adequate household arrangements, is likely to perform as well as the non-working mother or better. [19]

Of course, the magic words are "adequate household arrangements." Indeed, it seems to take a magician to make child care arrangements at all. Until more men "unlearn" male privilege and take on a larger domestic role (more about that later), women will continue to feel overburdened, guilty, and driven to Supermom extremes. Until a national child care program becomes a political priority, household arrangements for children will remain "a source of constant stress" for white and minority women alike. [20] In the meantime, patchwork arrangements with neighbors, relatives, and babysitters are the best we can do.

If you are fortunate enough, however, to find space for your child in a wonderful local child care center, be prepared to feel two contradictory fears: "Will my children begin to think of the day care staff as their family?"—and "Can communal care (especially for babies and toddlers) equal the loving one-to-one attention of a child's mother?"

Then focus on the facts: Children from three months to three years of age entrusted to day-care centers for eight hours a day still show a *strong* preference for their mothers over their teachers. Also, these children are neither more aggressive nor more cooperative than a comparable group that's home-reared. [21] They're just regular kids.

Although 51 percent of American parents are still skeptical about child care centers, Harvard psychologist Jerome Kagan is convinced that "when you have conscientious and well-trained caretakers, then it is difficult to find any psychological differences in the children so reared." [22]

Am I suggesting that all children should be raised in communal centers or that women have to work at paid jobs to be happy? Not at all. I am trying to get rid of all the "have to's," "musts," and "shoulds." I am saying that women who work because they *have to,* but would rather stay home, are fulfilling an economic "must." Women who stay home because they think they *should,* but who would rather go out and work, are fulfilling a sex role "must." But women—and men—who work when and because they *want* to, or who stay home when and because they *want* to, are fulfilled human beings. They are the people to whom children should be exposed most.

ADVICE FOR FATHERS

It has occurred to me that in this age of catastrophe, when it takes a Three Mile Island to arouse anti-nuclear activism or a DC-10 tragedy to assure safe aircraft, it may require a death sentence to put a person's values straight.

If you were told you had six months to live, would you want to spend it primarily on the job or with your family? For most men, family life counts more than moneymaking,[23] but wins less of their time and dedication.

Robert Townsend, a brilliant business success and author of *Up the Organization,* once told me his greatest regret was that he missed his children's childhoods. He had operated as though his family could wait, as though there would be time to catch up later, as though the prime years belonged not to those he loved, but to those he "administered," "managed," and made money from. Then, suddenly, it was too late: the children were off with their own friends, busy with their own lives; gone.

How can you reverse gears? How can you change your attitudes and actions before it's too late? Accepting your wife as an equal, primary, or sole wage-earner might be the first prerequisite. At the very least, once you can get past the feeling that economic dependency is a strictly "feminine" condition (and a dirty word), you can make economic and occupational decisions on the merits. As a married couple, rather than a single parent, you have optimum flexibility: if you want to, you and your wife can underwrite each other's dreams.

The second prerequisite for change is to analyze the state of your finances. Naturally, if both you and your wife are working full-time and still can't stay out of debt, then there's little room to maneuver. But if you are working harder than you have to, making more than you *really* need just because of the onward-and-upward habit, or pursuing a Big Shot Job just for the victory of winning it—or if your wife is *not* working because you need the "masculine" status of being sole support, or if she is holding back on her earning potential to protect your ego—then the two of you are cutting off your options and spiting your children.

If you can financially afford to make radical changes in your work schedule, think of the process as reapportionment, not sacrifice. Here are some possibilities:

• *Drawing the line:* Make 6 P.M. the absolute cut-off between your paid job and your father-job; give up all overtime work; stop bringing a briefcase home; never take business calls in the house; do not go to the office on weekends; refuse all voluntary assignments, optional conferences, union meetings, and so on.

• *Exploring flexible schedules:* Could you live nearly as well on two part-time salaries as on one full salary? What about a combination of part-time and freelance work? Or a paired job where you and a co-worker split the time and pay of one job between you?

• *Reassessing what everything means to you:* Maybe you are on someone else's treadmill; maybe you really want to be a poet, or a potter. Think about going back to school, changing fields, taking a year or two off to be a "househusband,"[24] to immerse yourself in family life, to relieve your wife after all her years at home, to get to know your children.

Whatever economic or scheduling adjustment you can afford should have one objective at heart: to balance love and work more sensibly so that your children can have a real father, and you can have the pleasure and humanity most men find out too late that they missed.

Adjustments of attitude and time make a man *available* for fatherhood. What makes him a father (and not a mother's helper) is involvement in the dailiness of children's lives at every level. Specifics here are endless, but I'll venture some generalities:

• *You will have to learn the physical how-to's*—the feeding, holding, diapering, bathing, dressing, toilet-training—the way most mothers learn them: by doing them, reading about how to do them, and talking to experienced parents who do them well.

• *You will make many mistakes.* And you will feel boorish and inept. But you will not weasel out of parity parenthood by the escape route experts like Dr. Henry Biller hold out to fathers:

> . . . you may not be as patient, enthusiastic or adept at it as your wife . . . you may feel uncomfortable about it . . . you may be put out by the demands of the baby for nighttime feedings and diaper changes.
> . . . if your wife doesn't feel a burden in caring for the child, and you really are uncomfortable, don't feel guilty about skipping it."[25]

Imagine if both parents took such a "when I feel like it" approach to an infant. Imagine a mother's "skipping it" when she feels "put out" by baby's demands (and show me a woman who doesn't feel put out by a full diaper at 4 A.M.). Optional fathering is an attitude as intolerable as optional mothering; it is a "luxury" neither you nor your children can afford. And ineptitude is no excuse. Feminist psychiatrist Robert Gould sees right through it:

> The stereotype of the he-man awkwardly holding the infant and feeling foolish is just that—a stereotype. How do those "big clumsy hands" fumbling hopelessly with diaper pins and feeding spoons magically become infinitely patient, steady, surefingered and dextrous "surgeon's hands" in the operating room or "craftsman's hands" in the workshop?[26]

• *You will either learn the tricks of the trade or make up your own.* Not only can fathers feed babies successfully, they can pick up babies' distress signals as well as mothers,[27] and they can invent child care techniques as well as any woman—if they *must.*

I've seen a father change his baby in a train station using his attaché case as a changing table. I watched a man put a fresh paper diaper around his baby's neck for a make-shift bib, and another give his child shaving soap and an old bladeless razor to "shave" with when entreaties to "wash your face" fell on deaf (not to mention dirty) ears. I've heard men brag about their innovations just as mothers have for centuries: One father wears garden gloves so his newborn won't slip out of his hands in soapy bathwater;

another uses the empty tub as a feeding "environment" because his daughter tends to fling her meal in every direction (then he removes the child and washes the strained spinach down the drain).

When our children had trouble falling asleep and Bert ran out of lullabyes, he used to sing them his college alma mater and assorted football cheers. (And because they literally knew the cheers in their sleep, they became the most well-versed, high-spirited fans on the Rutgers side of the stadium.)

• *You cannot let your money speak for you.* "I realized we had no relationship at all," says a grown-up daughter. "He brought home the money and that was it . . . he gave me a bike before I wanted it and gave me a car when I really didn't want it. I feel sorry for him."[28]

If you suspect you might be bartering money for love, try this: leave all the exciting purchases and gifts for the children up to your wife for the next three months. Let it be known that the wagon, the pony rides, or the trip to Disney World came from Mommy's wallet, and see if you can show your affection for your children without spending a penny on them. Once you have confidence in your nonmaterial expressions of love, you can share the big, fun purchases with your wife as a symbol of your shared finances and your equal power to issue tangible rewards.

• *You may need help with your emotional life.*

In our house, where, like everybody else, I have accidentally become an adult, they are trying to teach me that money and authority are not substitutes for details of feeling.[29]

Those "details of feeling" may be learned from your family, from books that analyze male socialization,[30] or from a men's discussion group or a sensitive therapist. One psychologist says that in his twenty years of practice, men came to him for many kinds of help, "but no one ever asked me to help him become a better father."[31] Yet that kind of help is what many men need most.

Although fathers' interest in children's *activities* may increase as kids mature, one study found that fathers move away from children *emotionally*, while mothers move closer, as if to compensate for the loss.[32] However, children are not fooled when mothers try to be fathers' emotional surrogates: "Mother would say 'kiss your father goodnight . . . you know your father loves you,' but my father never said that to me."[33]

Even those men who apprentice themselves to their wives until they learn the "details of feeling" eventually must go it alone. And that does not necessarily come naturally, even if you start from the very beginning. Fatherhood is no more reflexive than motherhood. Closeness develops only with intensive exposure, care-giving, and interaction. Said one schoolteacher,

> At first I really didn't have that proud father feeling. But as I hold the baby, I'm getting prouder and prouder, stroking his face a lot, feeling his skin, smelling him—it's a kind of enjoyment that I can have now while we're alone.[34]

Although this father talks in terms of paternal "pride" (love words don't come easily to some men), what he is describing is a growing emotional connection to his son. To develop that further, he would need to unlock the demonstrativeness and sensuality that were probably suppressed when he was a boy being socialized for "manhood."

Transform that useless "manhood" into fatherhood. Try to say your feelings aloud, no matter how fleeting or "corny." Hearing yourself admit "I love the smell of his hair" or "I feel so wonderful when she runs into my arms" prepares you for the habit of intimate communication with your children as they grow older —and eventually gives them a signal that it's okay to express their most "corny" feelings to you.

Practice listening without asking questions, and without giving advice (unless it is sought), and without jumping to conclusions before the child has been fully heard. Many fathers try to be instant problem-solvers, when all a child wants is a confidante or a word of fatherly support.

The man who knows the difference between quiet time and other times, between ten minutes rocking a child in his lap and ten minutes playing catch with her, between *being* there for a teenager with love problems, or tossing him the keys to the car—the man who knows those differences, and can act upon them appropriately, knows emotionally how to father a child.

• *You will be surprised.* Men only believe babies are fragile until they learn, from necessary invention, that you can carry one under one arm, while stirring the stew with the other and talking on the phone with the receiver cradled in your neck—and the baby *likes* it. You may think babies are weak, until you struggle with one who is powerfully opposed to taking its medicine. You may think you'll gag if you have to change a diaper, until you *have to* change diapers five times a day because no one else will and you have already discovered you can't "cheat" because the baby's rash will advertise your neglect.

You will also be surprised at how delighted a baby can be by its own toes, how exhilarated you are by that first "Da-da," how the same five-year-old can be indefatigable when working on her Tinker Toy rocket but too tired to brush her teeth, and how downright smart your twelve-year-old can be about *your* problems.

Being surprised is one of the unsung "perks" of parenthood, although some of the surprises are less gratifying than others: "Nobody had ever told me how *humorless* it is, staying home with an infant. Whether or not the baby sleeps, there are no jokes."[35]

Worse than no jokes is no relief. Nobody ever tells you about the relentlessness of child care, the voracious, spasmodic bites it tears out of each day, the incessant interruptions, the impossibility of concentration, the futility of work. Mothers find this out. Women's lives reflect this. Men inexperienced at childrearing are unprepared for it. In this excerpt from a poem written during his early child care years, Kenneth Pitchford describes the phenomenon with succinct force:

POEM DESPERATE IN NAPTIME

5:10 P.M.
October 16, 1970
Blake is 15 months, 6 days old.

Story complete in one typing,
    not for the reader's convenience,
    but for the writer's.
    Time for long forms gone.
    A new life takes a total of one
    complete adult's constant attention.

Even divided exactly in half
  (not even counting the free half
  that must still be saved for
  laundry, groceries,
  some sleep for the adult(s) involved)
  there's too little left for long forms
  and revolution, too.
And then they say that women have had centuries
  to show genius in nearly
  every field—ha.[36]

• *You will not have the right to feel like a hero.* Just because "most men" eschew meaningful fatherhood does not entitle you to embrace it expecting prizes, praise, or pity. You will have to be a participatory father for yourself and for your children's sake. You will have to understand that it is not something you do only when your wife can't, or to prove that you can do whatever you set your mind to. It is something you do because your child is *there.* It is something you do to make children's lives better now and to make them better people later. In his revised edition, Dr. Spock wrote:

> When a father does his share as a matter of course when at home, it does much more than simply lighten his wife's work load. . . . It shows that he believes this work is crucial for the welfare of the family, that it calls for judgment and skill and that it's his responsibility as much as it is hers. . . . This is what sons and daughters need to see in action if they are to grow up without sexist attitudes.[37]

Spock and other experts who talk mostly to mothers address children's needs in a straightforward way. However, when psychologists talk to fathers in print, they play to male self-importance, almost *flattering* men into fatherhood by extolling the "special role" a man supposedly plays in child development.[38] They claim a father's presence in a child's life can do everything including inspire conscience development, motivate achievement, prevent a son from becoming a homosexual and promote a daughter's "femininity," validate boyish mischief and masturbation, and counteract an overprotective mother. Finally, a man can make his wife feel secure so she is a more effective mother; he plays

". . . an important role in the childrearing process through his relationship with the mother, even if he does not spend large amounts of time with the infant."[39]

Isn't it amazing how fathers can accomplish so much by doing so little? But if men have such magical effects on children, why does recent father-absence research indicate that fatherlessness seems "to have no detrimental effect on the children's development"?[40]

I am not contradicting myself. I am not saying on the one hand that children need fathers, and on the other hand that children do just as well *without* fathers. I am saying that having a Man-of-the-House is not enough; having a man *in* the house and *in* the children's daily lives is what counts. And what *kind* of man is what counts most. If it is not a man who is available *and* accessible, it might as well be no man at all.

Traditional father-present families are really mother-nourished families in which children rarely enjoy a palpable, caring relationship with their male parent. Such a family is only minimally different from a fatherless household, and sometimes—if the single mother is financially secure and spiritually energized—the father-absent household can be a better environment for the child than a hostile "intact" family.

The father *per se*—that is, the parent *as male*—is not necessary (as we have learned from children raised in lesbian families). He is not necessary for delinquency prevention, for "masculinizing" sons or "feminizing" daughters, or for any idealized "Life with Father" function. Therefore, if you become a caring father, you have no right to feel like a hero. Like any mother, you are only as important in your children's lives as you—by your love and your heedfulness—choose to make yourself.

ADVICE FOR THE MARRIAGE

Single parents need to make nonsexist childrearing one of the top priorities of mutual concern to the ex-spouses (as the child's education is, for instance). Their attention to parity will be a matter of detail, logistics, and listmaking, not a day-by-day dynamic. In an intact marriage however parity parenthood is an organic expression of a marriage based on equalities of power, effort, and competence. Don't forget, the children are watching. And your marriage is the prototype for all the two-sex relations they will engage in for the rest of their lives. (Single parents, presumably with a greater variety of friends and "dates," will offer children a more diffuse set of models for heterosexual relations.)

In the most enduring nineteenth-century definition of an ideal marriage, John Stuart Mill posited two people,

> between whom there exists that best of equality, similarity of powers and capacities with reciprocal superiority in them so that each can enjoy the luxury of looking up to the other, and can have alternately the pleasure of leading and of being led in the path of development.[41]

The "companionship marriage" formulated by Ernest W. Burgess[42] comes closest to the ideal in twentieth-century language. Its emblematic words are self-expression, not subordination; democratic, not autocratic; companionship, not duty. Happiness is considered the *right* of both marriage partners and the key measure of the success of the union. To assure your own "companionship marriage," and to establish a healthy dialogue between you and your spouse, try the following suggestions:

• *Be at least as considerate as two roommates.*

> If a white male and a black male were living together, surely the typical white student would not blithely assume that his black roommate was to handle all the domestic chores. . . . But change this hypothetical black roommate to a female marriage partner and somehow the student's conscience goes to sleep.[43]

In an egalitarian marriage, conscience never sleeps: labor is divided just as if two single women or two bachelors were sharing a home; chores are assigned by preference, by drawing lots, or whatever, and no assumptions are made about who will do what.

• *Establish your definition of "equality."* Do you agree with this statement: "Many women are as strong, intelligent, clever and ambitious as their husbands"?[44]

You do? Then you may *not* believe in sexual equality. That statement supposes that all men possess those positive traits and "many women" measure up to the male standard. To see how patronizing it is, let's turn it around: "Many men are as strong, intelligent, clever and ambitious as their wives."

True egalitarianism does not seek to reverse stereotypes. Nor does it panic when a woman happens to be in the superlative position. You believe in true equality if you find it "normal" when a wife earns more than her husband, or a father gains child custody.

• *Consider yourself dispensable.* What I mean is—consider what would happen if you died tomorrow. Who would have to fill in what gaps? What financial, occupational, child care, and housekeeping adjustments would be necessary if the husband died, and what would be necessary if the wife died? Would there be any difference in insurance collected, chances of going on relief, ability to sustain the family on one income, need for domestic help?[45]

An egalitarian or "equitable marriage"[46] is one in which the loss of either parent would be experienced as equally depriving and the family's welfare would be equally likely no matter which was the surviving parent.

• *Eliminate extremism.* The mistake mothers (and fathers) make is role extremism, which ends up short-changing children. For instance, Total Mothers may spend a lot of time in the same room as their children, but they *interact* very little. Less than five percent of a baby's waking day is spent in affectionate contact or stimulating play with Total Mom. (She's too busy with caretaking and housecleaning.)[47]

Just as infants prefer, not the parent who dresses and cleans them, but the one who is *care*-free enough to play with them, older children—as their lives become more complex and their needs more varied—seek the versatile and self-assured parent, not just the parent who is always there. In truth, the parent who is always there ends up needing her children more than they need her:

All my mother ever seemed to do was make good food and nag me when I ate too much of it. . . . My disappointment with my mother was typical of the low estimation in which all my friends held their own mothers. . . . Familiarity breeds contempt. . . . It seems only natural that we grew to resent our mothers' unrelenting presence.[48]

Thus do children rationalize mother-presence into suffocation, and father-hunger into idolatry. For his part, father usually has the resources to make his limited time into a big event; he may be an emotional stranger but at least he is child-fresh after a day in the adult world.

> Since father does not provide the more routine comforts, he is almost forced to invent and improvise signs of affection by bringing things home, taking the children to circuses and parades, telling them stories, playing games, making jokes, and so on, although he runs the risk of becoming little more than a stunt man in the process. . . .
>
> If father attends almost *anything* with his children, the occasion usually becomes a much more important one than it would be otherwise. Children are quite accustomed to mother's companionship on mundane visits to the dentist, to buy shoes and the like; therefore her presence cannot add the luster of a paternal companion.[49]

To equalize the luster, distribute the mundane more equitably between both parents, and the fun part too. With less parental extremism, you can give children *two* exciting, patient, recharged parents, instead of one rarely seen stunt man and one omnipresent old shoe.

• *Know thy partner as thyself.* Trouble between peoples, races, sexes, or any disparate individuals often originates in the belief that the other person is an "Other." Simone de Beauvoir coined the word to describe how we see someone who is not-like-Self, someone alien, different, a secondary kind of being who can be assumed to have second-rank feelings.[50] With an "Other," it is easier to justify victimization or to make demands one wouldn't expect of oneself—as in "She'll address the invitations; women like detail work," or "He'll check the noise in the cellar; men are fearless."

To learn if you harbor any "Otherness" notions about your spouse, write down five things you believe your partner would *never* want to do (plausible things, not walking on hot coals), and five things you think she or he would love to do if money or time permitted. Show him or her the lists and see how right you were.

• *Do not romanticize the good old days.* Was your parents' marriage happy? How about your in-laws' marriage? The marriages of your mother's and father's sisters and brothers? Can you think of any traditional, "male-headed," nuclear families that match your ideal of a mutually satisfying union? I can't think of one. But even if each of us could identify two or three among all the married people we know, is that enough to support living by leftover myths of patriarchal wedded bliss?

• *Be "no-fault" partners.*

"Why the hell can't you teach your son to behave!"
"What do you mean *my* son? He's your son too."
"He's my son when he's good. He's yours when he isn't."

Because women rear all of us, mothers have been blamed for everything from homosexuality to crime, war, and disease. "Billy can't come out to play," reads the Public Service ad. "His mother forgot to get him his measles shot."

Even though women have not had the option *not* to rear us, and even though mothers have been carriers, not creators of cultural values, it is easier to blame women than to spread the responsibility for childrearing to men.

Most people seem to hold mothers responsible for a child's emotional problems, overdependence, obesity, and failure in English—all disorders of the stereotypically "feminine" sphere—and for "neutral" disturbances such as asthma, mental retardation, bedwetting, and stuttering. Fathers are held accountable, in the public mind, only for such "masculine" disorders as excessive aggressiveness, rebellion against authority, school failure in math and science, and athletic incompetence.[51]

If both parents share responsibility for all aspects of childrearing, mothers will cease to be the scapegoats when things go wrong, which would considerably reduce women's guilt feelings and many causes of marital conflict. More importantly, when the energies and resources of two adults are directed toward healthy child development, there are twice as many chances for problems to be avoided, recognized, and/or treated.

• *Rout out the double standard.* Identify similar actions that arouse different reactions depending on the sex of the parent; for example—

- Mother's meals are taken for granted; father's cooking is lavishly praised.
- Mother is expected to attend school conferences; Father is nearly knighted if he does.
- Everyone's upset if Mother comes home late from work; everyone's solicitous if Father has to put in long hours to support the family.

An egalitarian marriage must espouse a single standard of acceptable behavior for the adults before it can teach equality to children.

• *Make sure you're a partner, not a boarder.* If you really *live* in that family of yours (rather than being a kind of honored guest), you should know where things are and what's going on. Which means neither spouse should have to ask the other:

- Where is the grapefruit knife?
- What grades are our children in?
- When is Grandma's birthday?
- Which child hates broccoli?
- Where is the screwdriver?
- Who are our children's best friends?
- Did we pay the mortgage (rent, car payment) this month?
- How much is a dozen eggs?
- What size shoe does our youngest wear?
- How many quarts of milk do we have in the refrigerator?

• *Analyze the marital power balance.* For people who are serious about nonsexist family life, this final exercise is perhaps the most important.

I may be wrong, but I think most men enjoy jokes about spendthrift wives, not because such stories put down women but because they build up men. They establish where the power lies. They tell us that he earns enough for her to spend money foolishly; that he can decide to "let" her spend, or he can turn off the tap. They remind us that a woman's buying power is not necessarily decision-making power.

I may be wrong again, but it seems to me that it is *women* who laugh loudest at the joke that goes something like this:

My wife is in charge of the house, the children, the food, the bankbook; I'm in charge of the *important* things—solar energy, Puerto Rican statehood, and the national debt.

Women laugh loudest because we need to believe men are little boys playing War and Monopoly in the big world, while *we* are the real adults holding life and limb together. In many ways, this view approximates the truth. But in many ways, too, it is a hype, a panacea for the powerlessness women feel at the bottom of it all. Powerlessness not just about solar energy, but about their own everyday lives. When asked "Who is the real boss in your family?" three-quarters of the wives sampled said "the husband."[52]

Now, in *your* marriage, which of you (if anyone) has the last word on:
- moving to a new city?
- what car to buy?
- the children's sleepover plans?
- each spouse's spending money?
- the choice of a family doctor or dentist?
- getting the roof fixed?
- whether the wife should get a job?
- which job the husband should take?
- where to go on vacation?
- which dry cereals to buy?
- whether to invest in land or municipal bonds?
- tonight's menu?

These questions[53] are more penetrating than "Where's the screwdriver?" These questions define "Where's the power?" and in what spheres it operates. Your answers will uncover the intriguing tip of an iceberg. But you can dive deeper.

As we saw in Chapter 3, power in marriage is based on material attributes; the spouse with the greater occupational prestige, status, and income is usually the more "powerful."[54] Power is expressed in marriage in two ways: *freedom to exercise options,* and *participation in decision-making.*

In most cases, the more children a woman has, the less likely she is (in this society) to have occupational prestige, status, and income, hence the more limited is her freedom to exercise options.[55] Minus two points for the woman. On top of that, if decision-making is split on sex role principles, into public and private spheres for husband and wife, the power balance tips completely.

Men often gladly give up power at home. As long as they maintain the role of breadwinner and have interesting, well-paid and possibly even prestigious work, they are safely superior to women and in control. As is the right of persons with power, they can choose to "delegate" power . . . to endow women with some degree of power, usually regarding things that they have little interest or concern with, such as issues surrounding the house and children. This is because it is a sign of masculinity *not* to be involved in domestic issues.[56]

Thus, the division of decision-making into His and Hers domains—even if it turns out to be a 50-50 split—is not the same as participation in all decisions, or pooled judgment and mutual consultation on matters large and small.

Among black, white, and Chicano couples alike, who makes which decisions is usually a symptom of who holds the economic power,[57] which often connects with physical power—its threat and its use. (Husbands who batter their wives, and wives who are victims, tend to share a belief in sex roles and male supremacy.[58] The man-in-charge model of marriage is "directly influential in men's taking the license to use force . . . to maintain control, discipline or superiority."[59])

Decision-making patterns and economic and physical uses of power all add up to determine what a marriage *feels* like to each of its members and what it looks like to each of its offspring. That is why nonsexist childrearing usually requires a redistribution of domestic power. The marital balance has a ripple effect on the children; it communicates both the particular worth of their mother and father and the generalized worth of women and men —including the women and men the children will become.

In crisis situations, children fare best if power and leadership have been exercised by father *and* mother so that "both partners are able to take charge of a situation when the need arises."[60]

In everyday life, children should see neither parent with fixed authority over the other, and neither receiving more deference than the other[61]—if parents are to serve as models for fair and just human relations.

The separation of love and power is one of the hallmarks of role orientation in families.[62] In nonsexist homes, where love and power are blended, children can turn in either direction, to father or mother, for the guidance, leadership, and security they need.

III

Family and Feelings

10
Role-Free Family Life: Working Together

These are the givens:

First, that your family operates as a socializing environment —a unit of affection, education and support.

Second, that it is beyond the scope of this book to inquire into the origin of the family,[1] its political, economic, and social functions within the patriarchy,[2] or the relative merits of the nuclear family as opposed to kin networks, communal structures, and other conceptual frameworks.[3]

Third, that The Family—as in "What effect will unemployment have on the family?"—does not exist. What we really have are *families*: different kinds of households in which the *people who live together make moral and emotional claims on one another.*[4]

Though two or more single adults or a childless married couple make a family, for the purposes of this book, the word family implies a unit of at least one child and one adult whose moral and emotional claims on one another create a tapestry that each member acknowledges as "my family."[5]

"My family" can refer to:

- two employed parents and their children (18.5 percent of all American households);
- a father who is sole breadwinner and a mother who is full-time homemaker (15.6 percent of all households);
- a single mother and her children (6.2 percent);
- a single father and his children (0.6 percent).[6]

The high rate of divorce and remarriage has produced 25 million stepparents in America; 1 child in 8 is a stepchild.[7] Therefore, let's try another way of looking at families: Of every 100 children under age eighteen[8]

- 67 live with two parents, both married once, who are the child's original biological or adoptive parents;

- Of the remaining 33,
  16 live with mother only,
  1 lives with father only,
  13 live with two parents, but not both original parents,
  3 live with other custodians.

Whatever its components, your family life—not The Family —exerts the most important influence on the development of your children.[9]

The fourth given in this chapter is my assumption that you and your children feel *good* about the family constellation in which you live. If not, extraneous pressures (for example, the "wicked stepparent" syndrome) could confound the nonsexist childrearing effort which should be practicable in any family set-up. All else being equal, children seem to be as happy at home and as competent at school whether they live with their original parents or their stepparents.[10] And family specialists have affirmed time and time again that the single parent family "is a valid family form, not a pathological condition."[11] So whatever their marital status, all parents with nonsexist commitment theoretically start from the same place.

As I write, however, I'm aware that single parent households are more apt to be strained by poverty (40 percent of all single mothers do not receive any financial assistance from their children's fathers)[12] and by severe occupational disadvantages (half of all female heads of households receive wages below the national poverty level).[13] Custody and visitation arrangements, logistical problems, and emotional tensions between divorced or stepparents also may make nonsexist family policy more difficult to sustain.

Because 8 out of 10 children do live with *two* parents, most of the ensuing discussion will be pegged to that family constellation; however, I encourage single and blended families to adopt as many suggestions as possible to their own special situations.

MAKING CHANGE

"If you want to understand something, just try to change it."[14] Truer words were never written.

Whenever one talks about changing the dynamics of family life, there's always a hard-liner in the room muttering "role reversal," worrying that change is a "threat to the family."

A *New York Times* editorial answers, "The women's rights movement did not cause the undeniable erosion of family life. Rather, it is more nearly the result of that erosion."[15]

Which is not to say that "role reversal" is women's idea of the cure for the ills of the family. (It's more often a scare word reflecting men's fear that they'll have to do what women have been doing all along.) While a few families do thrive on a househusband–working-wife set-up, most prefer not to perpetuate the same game with different players. They deal new cards to everyone, and the winning hand varies from house to house.

Let's begin with housework, because that is usually the toughest struggle of all. The conventional family has operated for so long on the free labor of women and belief in the maternal instinct that it's hard to think of house*work* without thinking of house*wife,* and without attaching child care to the role.[16]

While the housewife-mother is esteemed in the abstract, the work she does is demeaned. Housework is fragmented, its result short-lived (how long does a bed stay made, a baby stay clean, a meal stay on the table?), and its standards of excellence defined by advertising slogans, not by the nature of the work itself. As a result, people who don't *do* housework don't *understand* housework and have trouble seeing it as *work,* and people who *do* do housework have trouble complaining about something that seems so trivial. ("What's the big deal about washing a few dishes? Or mopping a goddam dustball?")

People who don't do housework avoid it on the grounds that[17]

• they don't do it well, so it will take twice as long and look half as good.

• they don't know how, so you'll have to spend time teaching them; isn't it easier to do it yourself?

- they have more important things to do (*i.e., real* work).

- O.K., they'll do it but they'll do it badly and they'll grumble all the way and make you regret you asked.

- O.K., they'll do it if you really think it's worth creating such an unpleasant issue over something so trivial.

This inconsequential, unpaid job, which takes an average of 99.6 hours a week,[18] was worth $13,364 in 1973 U.S. dollars.[19]

Unlike other job categories, housework hasn't benefited from technology. "Labor-saving" devices notwithstanding, the time spent on housework today is the same as 60 years ago.[20] Modern society has simply upped the ante on cleanliness and domestic creativity.

Nevertheless, housework remains invisible labor—unless it is neglected long enough to inconvenience someone, or must suddenly be undertaken in its entirety by someone previously oblivious to how things get "done," someone like the physician whose wife went abroad leaving him at the home front, with his consciousness rising like a rocket:

> First, work that I had taken for granted and had never done (meal preparation, kitchen clean-up, laundry), I quickly recognized would not be done unless I did it. Second, being a good parent required more than a cheery smile and willingness to help with the homework—it meant car pools, making sure snacks were taken and gloves were worn and that someone was available when our youngest son came home from school. Third, my day was not done until each of our three children was in bed and no one was left to mess up my spotless kitchen. (I really became compulsive about cleaning up after meals). . . .
>
> There were no grateful patients thanking me for keeping a clean kitchen. No applause from a large lecture hall after making certain the children left happily for school. No praise from a professional colleague for having kept up with the laundry.[21]

In another family, when the wife had to spend several weeks away, her husband moved his office into the house and took up the slack as follows: He hired a full-time babysitter for the children and planned a dinner party by having his secretary write out the invitations and hiring a caterer to cook and deliver the dinner, and a waitress to serve it. Said the wife incredulously:

> Can you believe he called me in California the next day to say working at home and giving dinner parties was easy? And then he said of course when I got home he couldn't afford the four people it took to replace me.[22]

Barring the employment of four in help, a nonsexist approach to the labor of keeping house is the only fair substitute for the oppressed housewife.

CHART THE STATUS QUO

Before you reapportion tasks (or argue about them) make a list of who does what now, or be more precise and keep a minute-by-minute record of everyone's activities for an ordinary week (not during vacations or illness). Log the time you spend on paid work, driving, cooking, shopping, paying bills, reading, and so on. Record the *content* of the time spent with the children, whether you are playing with or caring for the baby, having a talk with an older child or watching TV together.

Time without substance is almost meaningless: two hours in a movie with a child are not comparable to two hours spent teaching her to tie a shoelace, mediating a brother-sister quarrel, or getting bubble gum out of his hair.

Your completed time chart will probably mirror the results of recent studies:[23]

• While men say they approve of their wives' working and claim they share housekeeping and child care, most are not willing to make personal adjustments to help out.[24]

• Working wives spend 40 hours on their paid jobs and up to 40 hours more per week on home chores.

• Married working mothers do four times the amount of housework as married working men.

• Husbands of job holders do *not* do more housework than husbands of full-time homemakers; however there is some indication that as men increase their family involvement, they also increase their performance of family work.[25]

• The more children a couple has, the more leisure the father has and the less the mother has.

• Husbands tend to do marketing, yard and car maintenance—activities that can be deferred until a convenient time. Wives devoted more than half their time to food preparation and clean-up, laundry, and child care—activities that can not be postponed.[26]

• In one study, women were found to be doing 80 to 95 percent of all household tasks, *including* the supposedly "masculine" work of shoveling snow, paying bills, and emptying garbage.[27]

• In other samples, men were more likely to shovel snow, mow grass, and perform minor repairs, chores that are "infrequent, seasonal and, for apartment dwellers, mostly non-existent."[28]

• "Even the 'now' generation, whether cohabiting or married, are still dividing the work along traditional lines with the women bearing the brunt of the labor."[29]

The work your children do around the house may surprise you as well: if these findings are any indication:

• In conventional families, adolescent children have only slightly more responsibility for household chores when the mother is employed than when she is at home all day.[30]

• In urban communes where sexual equality is essential to the group ideology, housework is rotated among the adults but children have been found to get off scot-free.[31]

• Where children of both sexes are expected to do the same *amount* of work, their task *assignments* are sex-differentiated: girls set the table, do the dishes, dust, and make beds, while boys are asked to empty ashtrays and wastebaskets, take out the garbage, shovel walks, and wash the car.[32]

How the labor of the family enterprise is split has been shown to have long-term effects on children's competence formation, their ability to surmount stereotypes, and their lifelong interests and occupational choices.[33] If parents' home chores are sex-typed and if they assign their children to comparable tasks, they are in effect apprenticed to sex roles.

Thus housework is *not* trivial. It tells children how valuable males and females are, what their time is worth, and what they can expect to be and do in this world.

WORK-SHARING AS YOU LIKE IT

Although 6 out of 10 Americans believe husbands should share the housework, nearly 9 out of 10 oppose formalizing an arrangement in writing.[34] A contract may strike you as a cold way of working out a relationship, but "often it is the only way of coping with 2000 years of tradition."[35]

Written Contracts

One couple with an agreement on paper say they relish "all thirty-five deadly serious pages" of it:

> Some of our work is divided semi-permanently (laundry, kitchen clean-up); some work rotates (bill-paying, vacuuming); we do cooking, housecleaning and care of our nine-year-old as a team; and personal responsibilities are divided on a list we revise twice a year.
>
> For instance, Wayne is now in charge of birthdays. If he doesn't get our son a present and plan his party, those things won't materialize.
>
> Remembering everything isn't my job. My husband or son isn't my job. Only certain things are my jobs and all of us know what they are.
>
> This contract has saved my dignity and my sanity.[36]

Both Mike and Corinne McGrady have been homemakers, Corinne for fifteen years and Mike for one highly publicized year, when he stayed home and Corinne went out to support the family. It took Mike's experience with housework to bring about a signed contract that included "freedom for everyone in the family to grow, to realize their potential, to enjoy life to the full"; a totally shared exchequer; one night out per week for each adult; one week at the beginning of each of the four seasons set aside for doing jobs everyone hates (dubbed "Hell Week"), and five areas of firm responsibility for the three children to perform in turn.[37]

You don't have to be married to love justice. When Clark and Sharon welcomed Clark's fourteen-year-old son to spend the summer, all three sat down and rewrote the work contract Clark and Sharon had been "cohabiting" by for months. Says Clark,

> Not only did Frank not resent his part of the contract, he actually bragged about being "completely in charge" of certain things around the house. Our housework contract is the first serious document Frank has ever been asked to put his signature on.

Verbal Agreements

Most people prefer a spoken commitment flexible enough to change with new circumstances, such as more job demands, more children, or a change in finances.

• We had to re-discuss our arrangement when we discovered that Al made 60 percent of our total income and I made 40 percent. To split our bills 50-50 would have been unfair.

• We never considered that I would quit my job and stay home with the baby any more than Ken would quit his. We both chose to have a child so we're both accommodating our lives to the change.

• I went back to work as a flight attendant when Nicole was three months old. We found a wonderful woman whose children are grown to take care of Nicole daytimes when I'm out of town, which is about three days and nights each week. Vince is home every night, which lets him and Nicole develop a really close relationship. He bathes her, reads to her, changes her sheets, sings to her—and she knows her father better than most children from coast to coast.

Six children in a combined "stepfamily" rearranged their habits when the woman of the house went on strike against housework, an event responsible for several epiphanies:

Now that the boys are doing laundry it is amazing how long they can wear clothes before they hit the hamper.

My husband used to complain that we didn't have tacos often enough. Now that *he* is the one who stands and cooks three dozen tacos he understands why.

Getting married and having children was my seventeen-year-old daughter's only desire in life until she experienced dirty bathrooms, smelly garbage, heavy grocery bags, being tied down to her turn babysitting for the eight-year-old, and then doing everything all over again. She may well decide to get married and have children, but with her eyes wide open.

The other day, my sixteen-year-old stepson said he hoped to raise his family just like we were doing.

The greatest opposition has come from the oldest boy. He has lived the longest in our sexist society and it's harder for him to give up the role he thought was his privilege for life. He is still positive that he wants a traditional "feminine" wife and as I've told him, who wouldn't want a wife who's as good as a servant and as adoring as a child. But I can see that he has new respect for the work done in this world by traditional women.

These personal accounts raise a half dozen issues basic to every housework-sharing agreement, verbal or written, whether reached before marriage or the morning after your twentieth anniversary:

1. Neither partner's work is more important than the other's.

2. The work that brings in the most money is not necessarily more *valuable* than the work that brings in less or none.

3. Because a person earns more, his or her *time* is not worth more. (As things now stand, most men earn more because their sex is more valued.)

4. The woman who earns less cannot be penalized twice: once on the job (because of sex discrimination in wages), and again at home (where she is expected to do more housework, pay for child care out of her salary only, and so on).

5. All tasks are gender-neutral. No task is "inappropriate" or "humiliating"—there are only those one is or is not equipped to handle. (The most sex-typed tasks in the public mind are repair of faucets, lights, and appliances [male] and laundry and sewing [female]. The least sex-linked chore is food shopping.[38])

6. Involving children (whatever their legal relationship to the adults in the house) in family roles, to the degree that their maturity allows, is not an imposition but a gift of self-reliance.

Agree on these points, then structure a sharing plan from the following alternatives.

Fifty-Fifty

Split each job in half (I chop, you sauté; I mop, you wax). Or split the total list of chores down the middle (I plan meals, shop, cook, and clean the kitchen; you make the beds and clean everything else in the house). Or split the time in half (I do everything Monday through Wednesday and every other Sunday; you do everything Thursday through Saturday and the other Sundays). Variations are endless.

> After work and school on Fridays, we all meet at home to clean the house together. The ten-year-old and I usually start in the front with the kitchen, and the thirteen-year-old and my wife start in the back with the bathroom, and we meet somewhere in the middle.

> We both do the chores together weekday nights after work; we split the child care on weekends. Saturday is my husband's day to himself and Sunday is "Mother's Day," a whole day with no responsibilities. Whatever I do is my choice—no explanations, no excuses, no guilt!

Your Turn, My Turn

First agree on a fair division of tasks, then alternate who does which bundle of chores for how long.

> We switch jobs each week on Sunday. This week, for instance, I do laundry, clean half the rooms, and supervise the children in the evenings. Meanwhile, my wife is responsible for meals, including school lunches and afternoon snacks, and for clean-

ing the other half of the house. Our girls, ages eight and six, take weekly turns on pet care, kitchen-helper duties, emptying wastebaskets, dusting, and sweeping; each is responsible for her own bed-making and for putting clothes and toys away. Our house runs pretty smoothly.

Instead of rotating by the week or month, one couple has alternated from one childbirth to the other. In their case, what seems to be "role reversal" is actually a democratic division of responsibility no matter who stays home.

I stayed home for a year and a half with our first baby so he's staying home with our second. Regardless of who is at home, the plan remains the same. The home spouse cooks, cleans, and does the wash. The work-going spouse feeds the baby his evening meal and prepares everyone's dinners on weekends, and handles baths and bedtimes to assure some private time between the children and the employed parent.

The "Your Turn, My Turn" plan is ideal for the four-way cooperative devised by two couples who live in the same city loft building. Each couple has two young children and all four adults have flexible schedules: the men are artists and the women are a college teacher and a writer. Each of the adults is "on duty" for three consecutive hours every day (which amounts to the total twelve hours of waking time of the children). An intercom system keeps both of our apartments in touch. Once a week, one of the four adults does the marketing for both families. Babysitting, meals, laundry, and housecleaning are pooled on the same four-way rotation, which gives each adult nine hours of free time every day. It's heaven!

Laissez-faire

"Pick up after yourself, pitch in without measuring, and somehow it all comes out even" is a policy founded on more than the honor system: it requires unselfish people who notice what needs doing and harbor no secret desire to get away with the cushy life.

My husband and I have a sort of ad hoc system for dealing with care of the children, house and dog. Each morning we compare schedules and work things out, a task roughly equivalent to coordinating the raid on Entebbe.

We share all the work so we can have time to share all the fun. It all works out because my wife and I are both easygoing. We have only one set rule in this house: whoever leaves the bed last, makes it.

Children raised in this atmosphere can either absorb their parents' generous behavior by osmosis or be oblivious to the casual way things get done. In the latter case, a more conscientious sharing policy should be discussed, as a recently divorced mother realized:

Benjamin had taken our services for granted because my ex-husband and I never made a big thing about it. (The marriage foundered over sex, not housework.) So when Benjamin and I set up house alone, I had to make it clear to him that whatever he didn't do, I would have to do and I wouldn't be a very pleasant mommy if I had to do everything myself.

The 5-2 Plan

When one spouse stays home, child care can be divided by this formula: the at-home person covers five weekdays plus two weekend nights, and the other parent is on duty five week nights plus two weekend days. I should tell you that although some swear by this plan because each parent has such well-defined and uninterrupted time off, at least one couple I know found it did not give them enough time *together*. Which makes me think it might work well for divorced parents with shared custody and two nearby households, who aren't interested in togetherness.

Whoever Wants To, Does

Dividing housework by "talent" tends to perpetuate sex roles because most of us are "talented" at what we've been socialized to do. But dividing things by *preference* circumvents this. It makes it all right for a woman who cooks well to do all the cooking if she wants to, but it also allows her to refuse to cook, despite her "talent," if she prefers mowing the lawn. Just to give you an idea of the possibilities for division of labor by preference:

> Bob loves to cook and it's a matter of family survival that I be kept out of the kitchen. I actually enjoy cleaning as much as he likes cooking. We each iron our own clothes because I like to iron in bulk and he in time of need. I do the snow shoveling because our philosophies about snow are so different. He belongs to the "if it's below my knees, I'll just stamp it down" school, and I'm out with a broom at the sign of the first flake. Bob is in charge of the children's health since I forget dental appointments and do not panic at a hundred-and-two-degree fever the way he does. But I handle all travel arrangements since Bob is constitutionally incapable of arriving an at airport before his plane takes off.

This may be a good opportunity for the two-parent family to practice *skills-exchange,* a two-way training program that capitalizes on the one-sided upbringing most of us cart with us into marriage. If she was raised to scour a sink until it glistens and he was raised to understand the interior of a toilet tank like the palm of his hand, they should teach each other their expertise and save years of bickering. (Couples who share housework frequently find fault with one another over jobs poorly done because of inexperience, not ill-will.)

The mutual skills-exchange training period shouldn't last long, but when it's over, both spouses will have doubled the number of jobs they can do well. By witnessing their able-bodied, sure-fingered parents at work, your children will become Renaissance men and women themselves. But beware: during his parents' training period one eleven-year-old worried that they were going to separate, otherwise he couldn't imagine why his mother was teaching his father how to do the marketing.

Obviously, the single parent can't apportion housework according to the preference plan. She or he has to cook *and* mow the lawn, like it or not, at least until the children are old enough to become part of the preference system—and when they are, you can:

• List every job in the house.

• Organize the jobs by a point system or separate them into categories, such as boring jobs, messy jobs, hard jobs.

• Let the children choose first from each category.

• Then choose the chores you want.

• For the jobs left over after all preference picks, flip a coin and alternate who does them, or draw a wheel and spin.

• Permit trade-offs of two easy jobs for one unwanted job.

Whether yours is a single- or two-parent family, you'll notice a remarkable change in children when they have a stake in household cleanliness.

Our ten-year-old son chose to clean the upstairs bathroom and went about it diligently. At bedtime, when the usual teeth-cleaning routine was about to begin, the ten-year-old realized what was soon to happen and yelled at his older brother, "You're not brushing your teeth in *my* clean sink!" Click!

WATCH WHERE THE BUCK STOPS

Some people are *able* to do everything interchangeably; they are *willing* to do anything that needs doing; it's just that they never seem to *remember* to do it or notice that it needs doing.

Let me be specific. I knew a man who never claimed to be too important for housework. Not once in sixteen years did he say that a job was inappropriate for a man. He never used fatigue or business demands to shirk even the most unpleasant task. But he also never, not once, remembered without being told, that the babysitter has to be reserved a week in advance; never noticed when the children's nails needed cutting; never remembered to stop for toothpaste or eggs even if he used the last one himself.

You know the buck stops with you when the toothpaste and eggs are on your mind and not your mate's, even though you didn't use the last one. The buck stops with you when your children's nails would curl under in their shoes if *you* did not cut them. Equality stops whenever the ultimate responsibility resides solely within one or the other person's consciousness.

Showdowns do not work. They elevate small inconsiderations into apocalyptic marital crises. Outwaiting one's mate sometimes penalizes the children (ingrown toenails, for instance). Playing dumb requires superhuman will-power and a capacity for self-mockery. When asked "Where are the ice cubes?" for instance, one must practice saying "I don't know" with a straight face. Caving in and saying "in the freezer," or getting the ice tray, or filling the tray that one remembers is empty keeps relations civil and puts ice in the drinks, but leaves one with disproportionate responsibility and a gnawing tapeworm of rage.

I think, although I have never been successful at it myself, that the only solution is to count *remembering* as labor, and to trade it for other work in and around the house. Such as:

- I make the lists; you do the shopping.

- I keep track of immunizations; you sit in the pediatrician's office with the children.

- I remember the children's nails; you clip them.

When the doing begins to seem more arduous than the remembering, your spouse's memory might improve.

SHOULDER-TO-SHOULDER CHILD CARE

Children are more important than toothpaste, eggs, or ice cubes. Although more men say they are willing to share child care than housekeeping chores,[39] they don't seem to be doing much of either.

Who Is Responsible?[40]

Activity	Mother (%)	Father (%)	Both (%)
Prepare the meals	77	1	22
Stay home when children* are sick	72	1	26
Shop for children's clothes	66	1	32
Clean the house	65	1	33
Take children for checkups	63	1	35

Go to Open School Week	22	1	76
Help the children with homework	20	5	72
Speak to teachers if children are in trouble	20	8	71
Decide on children's allowances	9	20	67
Discipline the children	7	9	83
Teach the children sports and bike-riding	4	36	57

*All children between ages six and thirteen.

Two Los Angeles psychologists questioned parents on how they apportioned 89 typical childrearing items from "toilet training" to "teaching self-defense." They found only 34 items were shared; 47 were Mother's sole responsibility and 8—none of which involved children's emotional or physical care—were Father's.[41]

What little fathers *do* is more likely to involve public or intellectual matters, issues of power and policy (allowances and disciplinary actions, for instance) or teaching children sports and skills. Most often father acts as mother's helper not as "the buck stops here" parent.

The fact is plain that mother-only responsibilities exceed father-only responsibilities by great numbers, but more important is the *significance* of the task differences. Look at it this way: You remember your school principal better than the school custodian. The executive who decides your salary carries more weight in your life than the cafeteria worker who decides whether you'll have pears or plums for dessert. Your development was more deeply affected by the person who taught you to swim than by the one who bought your underwear.

Rather than use these truths to justify elitism, use them to demand egalitarianism. In my office, we call it "spreading the shitwork."

As you evolve a new way of working together as a family, keep two caveats in mind.

1. *Don't abandon unselfish spontaneity.* Don't let any work agreement stop you from packing a lunch with a love note in it or offering a cold glass of wine to a spouse returning from work, even if it's not your turn to be in charge of food and drink. No division of labor should prevent you from helping voluntarily, asking for help when you're overwhelmed, and spending as much time with your children as you want to.

2. *Don't expect any work-sharing plan to be an adequate solution.* It makes life more tolerable and pleasant, but work-sharing doesn't change the essential dilemmas of running a family within an unresponsive, inhospitable society. To find real solutions, we must first confront vast economic inequities and the paucity of social support systems.

"I can't think of one single institution which helps make our way easier," said one sharing father.[42]

We raise our children virtually without help and in isolation from one another because the myth of individual self-sufficiency dies hard.[43] Yet we know that most families in which father is the breadwinner and mother is untrained, except as a housewife, are families that are only one man away from welfare. We know that although most families cannot make do without two paychecks, "the second earner in a family is the most heavily taxed of all Americans."[44] We know that although few working mothers and fathers have the option of staying home full-time with their children, there are only one million licensed day-care slots for the twenty-eight million children who need them. We know that the government spends *sixty times* more equipping each soldier than it spends educating each child;[45] that rather than examine how national policies might strongly support families, the government supports welfare laws that prohibit payment to intact families; and that rather than provide services to keep a family together, the government pays more money to put children in foster homes and pays the most to institutionalize children. We spend billions incarcerating youth and shuttling children from one place to another when we could spend millions to help families better care for their own.

Think how much easier it would be if we could count on a few systemic changes to right the balance between family and work:

• *Parental leaves* so that fathers as well as mothers would have the right to stay home with their babies without prejudice to their income and career prospects.[46] (One recent study found employers much less likely to approve a leave of absence for a male worker than for a female, and some employers even viewed the man's request as a sign of his unsuitability for the job.[47])

• *Twenty-four-hour child care and enrichment centers* staffed by qualified professionals, and workplace creches for infants and nursing mothers.

• *Parent education courses for both sexes,* preferably introduced in the elementary grades, continued through high school, made as compulsory for graduation as basic reading competence, and kept available at the community level for all adults.

• *A variety of work options:* part-time jobs with pro rated benefits,[48] job-sharing arrangements so that two people can split one job, flexible schedules, whether the four-day week or flexitime, so that parents can arrange their professional and home lives more equitably.

• *Alternating periods of study, employment, and homemaking* as an accepted accommodation to different life-cycle needs.[49]

• *Federal stipends for new parents,* such as Sweden has had for more than a decade,[50] to give child care a monetary value (and some new prestige), to relieve the economic crunch on young families (who are socializing the next generation in the same sense that subsidized farmers are cultivating the next generation of food crops), and to encourage fathers' greater participation in young children's lives.

• *Community cooperatives* to provide surrogate extended families, integration of single parent and two-parent families, and operation of communal kitchens and maintenance services to free parents so that they can be with their children without always having to *service* them.

Sound impossible? No more so than getting a man on the moon. With the same kind of commitment, we could make families more functional and take a great step for humankind.

11
Living Together

Besides everyday chores, what is family life made of?

Kisses and crying, mealtimes, bedtimes and bathtimes, helping and teaching, laughter, money matters, privileges, rewards and punishment, territoriality, feelings, fighting, making up, and living by the rules, whatever they may be.

I am not going to tell you how to run your family in each of these arenas. But I think you may want to reconsider your ways after we look at a number of situations in which, for no good reason, parents' actions are determined by their children's sex.

COLOR

I happen to loathe pastel colors. Most especially, I hate pink. Four hot pink towels with hippopotamuses on them are the only pink items under our roof and their pinkness was overlooked in favor of their hippos. Otherwise, whenever I'm even slightly attracted to something pink—say a frothy pink peignoir or a pink organdy bed canopy—I have a habit of remembering the dyed-to-match brainwashing that several California girls and women wrote about for Sheila de Bretteville's poster, "Pink":

We did not choose pink. Pink is the color they gave to us. . . . Pink is the color of curlers, dollhouses, deodorants, girdles, baby talk, pablum, Sadie Hawkins, playpens, Valentines, . . . pacifiers, pills, girlie shows. Pink is a jail.

When I was a little girl I was dressed up in pink dresses and my room was pink and so I learned that dirt really shows up on pink!

Pink is the color my mother wished for me, Thinking it sweet, thinking it pure, Thinking it all things not violent or cruel. She did not notice, hidden in the heart of the sweetheart roses, the seed of blood deepening into crimson.

As a little girl, I was pale—not pink-cheeked, pale—and I frowned and was called pickle-face. I never looked right in pink.

. . . pink contains no pigment, only psychosocial ramifications."[1]

Pink is the one color so unquestionably synonymous with the female gender that few notice when pink-sexism intersects with pink-racism, as in the lyrics to this song from *Carousel:*

> *My little girl, pink and white as peaches*
> *and cream is she,*
> *My little girl is half again as bright*
> *as girls are meant to be.*[2]

Girls are not meant to be bright—or vigorous or black, brown, or yellow. Girls are meant to be pink. The "feminine" ideal in the language of the palette. Petal pink and delicate. Cotton-candy pink and sweet. Baby pink and tender, vulnerable, fragile, dainty, and helpless.

The male version of that sappy message is, of course, pink stinks. Avoid it at all costs. My son, David, who will face down his teasing peers on most feminist issues, would not allow the hot pink towels in his camp trunk, hippos or not. But somehow my husband escaped untouched by this color aversion. I know that because at various times over the years, Bert has owned a pink toothbrush, a fact that astonished a six-year-old houseguest who once saw Bert poke his head out of the bathroom door, toothbrush in mouth.

"Your Daddy has a *pink* toothbrush!" the boy whispered to our daughter Robin, in the tone of voice one uses for a tornado warning. Oblivious to the sex-typing implied, Robin made her own sense of the child's overreaction.

"Oh, *you* must hate pink like my Mommy does," she said.

Actually, what I hate is what happens to pink when it's called into service to decorate a little girl's room or clothing. It colors ruffles that cannot be sat on, and lace that costs a fortune to clean. It also seems to coordinate with spindly-legged furniture and fabric that tears easily, thereby restricting girls' mobility and activity as effectively as shackles and chains. Pink is warm. But pink is suggestive of delicacy, of small, controlled motions in a small, confined space.

Blue is cold. Blue is the color guard for no-nonsense "masculinity." A "practical" blue decor can make a four-year-old's bedroom as inviting as a U.S. Navy recruitment office. Or blue can be the wild blue yonder: the sky behind the airplane print curtains or the ocean on which clipper ships sail across the wallpaper. Blue suggests that the big world out there is relevant to the little boy growing up in that room. Blue hides a multitude of stains.

A while ago, when David had a sleep-over party, there were too many guests for his small room. He negotiated a switch with his sisters, who, at that time, shared a larger space. David spread his friends' sleeping bags on the floor of their room, and never had to feel he had invaded sugarplum castle. The ability to move a bunch of nine-year-old boys into a room belonging to two twelve-year-old girls, without the scene taking on a "what's-wrong-with-this-picture" quality, marks a home free of gender color-coding. Abigail and Robin's room, like David's room, was bright and functional, forest green, orange, and yellow.

If you failed to resist the pink-blue connections at birth (see Chapter 6), chances are orchid, fuschia, purple, magenta, and mauve have by now joined pink as forbidden colors for boys. By the same token, baby blues have probably darkened to navy or aged into tan, brown, and gray to the point where the males in your house only feel comfortable when a room resembles the Yale Club.

Boys are not likely to want to sew in a sewing room decorated in the recommended "feminine" hues, nor will girls feel welcome in a "den" that *House Beautiful* might call a "saddle tan haven for the man of the ranch." When colors are linked to gender, the rooms of a house become ghettos—as divided and alienated from each other as the urban ghettoes that separate blacks and whites.

This is not only divisive, it is downright uneconomical. With wallpaper, bedspreads, curtains, carpeting, and furnishings, just as with clothes, hand-me-downs do double duty if they can be passed from girl to boy or vice versa *without* a dye job or a paint job.

SPACE

Architecture is the sum of "physical detail, social reality and style."[3] But what else is it? Think about the politics of space utilization: the way architecture affects human relationships;[4] its power to mold "the structure and functioning of the nuclear family";[5] the fact that women and children have little say in the design of the space they are intended to occupy the most—and what it might look like if they did.[6]

Think about how a family's appropriation of interior spaces (rooms for common use, individual use, children's or adults' use) might affect siblings' interactions, create power struggles, arouse feelings of anger or intimacy, and provide "security, stimulation and identity."[7]

"What I always wanted from my childhood was my brother's space," one woman remembers. "He always seemed to get the priority spaces, his own room, his own choices."[8]

Think of how architecture organizes behavior and sex roles on a broad cultural blueprint. For example, nearly every household has its own kitchen instead of several families being served by a communal kitchen as in the Israeli kibbutz.[9]

Ideally, although not actually, the communal kitchen situated in a central location rotates chores among all its members, of both sexes. The American household kitchen *privatizes* those chores, and the American family lacks the ideology of shared tasks. Thus, in a sense space forces function.[10] The mere existence of a particular space (the kitchen) imposes a role (cook) upon someone (in our society, it's usually the female). In a communal society, with kitchenless homes, the issue is moot.[11]

Think about your house: How is interior space appropriated, utilized, and regulated? What makes a family member feel comfortable in one area of space and not another? Is privacy an equal right? Who takes up the most space? If, as one sociologist puts it, "Household space is a scarce resource for which there are competing uses,"[12] how does someone "win" the competition?

When we were renovating our apartment to get more rooms into the existing square footage, we had many family discussions about where new walls should go and which child would get what room. Because of structural considerations, the rooms would have to be of unequal size and would have slightly different features. We also knew the bathroom would be at one end of the hall and the phone at the other. The rest —design, space allocation, room assignment—was up for grabs.

Not once during our discussions did David, Robin, or Abigail make a claim based on gender. But when I mentioned the project to adult friends, many of their suggestions were keyed to the children's sex:

• "David ought to get the biggest room; boys need lots of space for their activities."

• "Just make sure the girls are near the phone. You know how teenage girls love to talk."

• "Keep the boy near the bathroom. He'll have less excuse for missing the hamper."

Perhaps they were speaking from experience. Or maybe they drew their advice from the bag of unconscious stereotypes we all carry around with us. In any case, the willingness to generalize without knowing my children, their likes, or their habits, reflects the fact that family space usage and household territorial rights are decided according to gratuitous male/female assumptions, not simply on the more defensible basis of adult/child.

> Architecture is also a physical language and can be used in the same way as the spoken language to condition us to sexism. . . . Expressions such as the "master" bedroom, the "family" room and the "powder" room reinforce role stereotyping and teach us about ourselves.[13]

Family members come to recognize what sociologists call "territorially defined and encapsulated zones of autonomy"[14]— meaning private spaces or areas that seem to belong more to one family member than another—and the "rules of trespass"[15] that apply to them:

Never bother Dad when he's in his study, if you know what's good for you.

Mommy lets us ride our trikes in her kitchen.

Please return the hammer to Daddy's workshop.

In affluent families, "His" and "Her" spaces are defined by walls: the garage, library, or study, let's say, is Father's; the laundry room or sewing room is Mother's.

More modest households or crowded apartments accomplish space demarcation with the assignment of furniture. The hi-fi area may be tacitly known as Father's. The biggest chair is his, whether he is six-two or an inch shorter than Mother. The desk in the living room is Dad's. (Mom's "desk" is the catty-corner angle at the end of the kitchen counter.) Even for professional couples, such as wife and husband academics who need home offices, her work space is smaller than hhs. In virtually every circumstance, the man in the middle-class home tends to take up more room than the woman. He spreads out. He even occupies more space in a double bed than his size would justify (and he usually decides who sleeps on which side). He feels a greater entitlement to household spaces.[16]

Whether Father's private space is a room or an area, it is usually as out-of-the-way as possible: a workplace over the garage or in the basement, a "den" or a corner where he can get away from the hubbub, read, tinker, build, make repairs. When Father is in his space, he is not to be capriciously disturbed. No running through, no nagging, no interruptions allowed. Often, because of the location of his private space, the father cannot even hear the children.

Mother's space is another story. Either "her kitchen" is right out in the open, or it is centrally located, a placement that is said to contribute to warm family life and the integration of the mother into the activities of the family.

This type of kitchen plan seems to be associated with a special view of the housewife's role which gives less importance to the craft aspects of cooking and homemaking and more prominence to the expressive aspects of the role.[17]

In other words, Mother should be emotionally accessible and physically available at all times. Her work is interruptable. Everyone can drop in for a snack or drink, ask her questions, use the kitchen table for homework or other projects, see and be seen, hear and be heard. She can "pick up sounds indicating potential trouble —e.g., the click of scissors from the living room when only the baby is there, or the incipient fight in the bedroom."[18]

Maybe she likes her accessibility, maybe not. The point here is the double discrepancy: Father gets the right to retreat but loses contact with the truth of family life while Mother is too "in touch" and almost totally deprived of privacy. Her kitchen is communal space; her bedroom is shared with her husband;[19] the children's rooms are theirs; the living room, dining room, and bathroom belong to everyone.

Children's perspective on these spatial relations generalizes to sex roles: Mother's time is our time; her space is our space; her work is visible, predictable, nonmysterious, and family-oriented. Helping Mother in her space is prosaic. "Oh, do I have to set the table *again?*"

Father, however, has space of his own, the right to privacy or the right to limit access to space of which he is recognized as "the principal occupant."[20] Children's perception: We must respect Father's space. We must not wander through it or touch things in it. Usually, we have to get invited into it. Sometimes going into Daddy's garage or tool room to help is an apprenticeship experience. However,

> the extent to which family members are likely to be in or to come into, each other's presence *without having meetings programmed or arranged* is . . . an important determinant of . . . the "texture" of family relationships.[21] [emphasis added]

In terms of crossing the gender skills barrier, a boy can pick up the basics of, say, salad-making by hanging around the kitchen during his afternoon snack. But to enter the traditional "masculine" spaces of the home, a girl would have to be affirmatively chosen to watch her father fix the toaster. Or she would have to be sufficiently motivated to ask if she can help, if she has not been invited.

As I see it, children should expect their parents both to be sometimes casually "around" and sometimes private and concentrated. To the extent that spatial usage contributes to that balance, it is important to the nonsexist home and important to the child's conclusions about male and female dignity.

How can you make space gender-neutral if one parent is exclusively associated with that space? You cannot do it by proclamation. It must be an organic by-product of parity parenthood—a natural result of the shared chores, responsibilities, and competencies discussed in the previous chapter.

Father doing his normal part in the kitchen and laundry room, and Mother comfortably ensconced in the study working on a speech or holed away in the workroom rewiring a lamp, are the only kinds of legitimate scenarios through which space is de-sexed.

THINGS

Material things are not supposed to matter, but they do. Possessions and objects are compared, bartered, coveted, exchanged. Some "things" can be so inextricably identified with someone that the sight of the object makes one see or smell that person. Things can be utilitarian, aesthetic, taken for granted or cherished. Things can also be sex-role artifacts—"the living archaeology through which we can extract the actual values held by society."[22]

First there are the physical realities. Most things, even objects meant for women's use, are designed by men who think of "man" as the norm and consequently "things" can be physically inconvenient or even hazardous for women.

Most chairs and couches are made for the average man, who is five inches taller than the average woman—a strain on female backs and legs. Desks, tables, and kitchen counters are usually too high for women (the work surface should be about 2 inches below the elbows), and automobiles, says an expert on occupational biomechanics, are thoroughly inhospitable:

A man designs a steering wheel, for example, based on how comfortable it feels in his hands. He doesn't consider that the proportions of a woman's hands are different. Even the seats and controls put a woman at a physical disadvantage.[23]

(It often appears as if men make things and buildings that are uncomfortable to women, and then women decorate interiors and objects in such a way that they become uncomfortable to men; *i.e.,* the chair is too big for her but the chintz fabric is too cute for him. Is this the retaliation of the unconscious?)

Tools, such as the soldering iron, the crimper, and the wire stripper, fit the average male hand (19.7 cm long), not the female's (17.3 cm). A woman who uses one of these tools may need two hands to span its grip.[24] She is not likely to use it effectively under those conditions—and children watching are not likely to gain an impression of her competence.

Just as with color and space, there are many other psychological effects on children when *things* are sex-typed. We noted that female-stereotyped school objects (books, chalkboard, and so on) make boys resistant to the school environment. The same phenomenon applies in both directions at home. Try these tests:

• With older children, ask them to list five nonpersonal gifts they would buy each parent if they had a thousand dollars to spend. Then ask if they think mother and father could be happy with one another's gifts. Why did the oriental rug go on mother's list and the video-tape recorder on father's list? Will only one parent use and enjoy those items?

• For younger children, put the following objects on the floor in a random arrangement:

electric blender/mixer	*electric saw/drill/sander*
egg beater	*pliers*
mop/broom	*snow shovel/rake*
body thermometer	*keys to the car*
shopper's catalog	*newspaper*

As you point to each object ask the children to tell you whether it is "anybody's," "Mommy's thing," or "Daddy's thing."

If they consistently identify things in sex-typed categories (as I grouped them above), several concerns seem warranted: How will they develop broad skills if they associate with gender those objects that are associated with certain jobs? Is it possible for them to feel "normal" about developing proficiency with an object if it is identified with the "opposite" sex?

Some parents dismiss these concerns. So what if objects and gender are linked, they say; as long as children see each parent being good at *something,* it shouldn't matter if the tool is an egg beater or pliers. But it *does* matter because sex-typed objects are value-laden in other respects as well.

"Mommy's things" are usually the accoutrements of domesticity, labor that receives little recognition or status. Pots, cutlery, spools of thread, and the like tend to appeal most to babies and young children; they can be used for noisemaking, water-play, and imitating the cleaning jobs around the house that small children can approximate respectably well.

On the other hand, "Daddy's things" have high status, or glamorous counterparts in the outside world. His objects are often large, productive, electrical, electronic, exciting, fun, related to "real" jobs (carpenter, plumber), and require some dexterity. Babies and young children cannot use Daddy's things. These objects become more attractive as children get older because mastery of them denotes maturity and accomplishment.

The car is the most obvious example of a value-laden object. In addition to the influential advertising campaigns that make people equate the automobile with success, sexual potency, and status, behavioral scientists have found that the car extends "one's limited physical abilities, giving enormous power and speed. Being in direct control of a powerful or agile vehicle greatly enhances feelings of dominance."[25]

If this thing, this hunk of metal, glass, vinyl, and steel, contains such formidable symbolic power, who can afford to be casual about its being a male-sex-typed object?

Parents need not become "thing-obsessed," but we can be less unthinking about who slides behind the wheel of the car—not just to ferry kids around the neighborhood on weekdays, but to drive on long trips or family outings when *both* mother and father are in the car.

Being less unthinking might also mean alternating which parent—

- takes a child's temperature.
- expresses a desire for a food processor.
- checks the bank statement on the calculator.
- refills the flour canister.
- keeps track of things the children need.

And being less unthinking might mean looking analytically at the "things" in our children's lives, the presents we buy them, the hobbies and collections we encourage. Why, for instance, should it be "original" when a twelve-year-old boy collects lizards but "weird" when a girl does it? Must musical instruments be sex-typed to the detriment of children's opportunities?

> His father . . . laughed at him and called him a girl . . . when Allen once said that he wanted to learn to play the violin. "I thought I had me a son. Violins are for girls."[26]

Many parents say they are guided by their children's interests. But a study of children's rooms found that long before they are old enough to have developed interests—that is, from ages one to five—children are surrounded by things that their parents think they should have. Boys in this study had more vehicle toys, girls had more dolls; boys' decorations, pictures, and mobiles were of animal motifs, girls' were floral. The researchers comment:

> The rooms of children constitute a not inconsiderable part of their environment. Here they go to bed and wake up; here they spend some part of every day. Their rooms determine the things they see and find for amusement and instruction.[27]

Little things mean a lot. Whether in a low-income family where purchases are saved for methodically, or in a more affluent family where things may be bought more uneventfully, my point remains the same: the more clearly an object is sex-typed in the larger society, the more critical it is for your children that it be seen as "anybody's thing" in your house.

MONEY

Most parents and experts hold very firm opinions on money.[28] They know when and how children should "learn the value of a dollar." Some contend that an allowance should be given with no strings—like food, clothing, and shelter; that children's pocket money need not be earned by chores or good behavior. Others consider a weekly allowance a child's salary for fulfilling family obligations, an introduction to the work ethic, and a privilege that can be withdrawn as punishment. I hold no brief for either policy so long as parents are not sex-selective in its enforcement, or in any other money matters. Complains an eleven-year-old girl:

> My brother is eight and he gets fifty cents a week for doing nothing. I get two fifty a week for helping with the housework. My thirteen-year-old sister gets five dollars for starting dinner every night before our parents get home from work, and my brother, who's fifteen, gets ten dollars just because he has a girlfriend to take out, and *supposedly* he takes the trash to the recycling center.

A Gallup Youth Survey found that nearly 4 adolescents in 10 receive a regular allowance from their parents, of whom 85 percent have to do chores to earn it. The survey further reported that boys earn their allowances by doing yard work for the most part, and girls by working around the house.[29]

I have heard of many other sex-discriminatory financial practices: from the family that bought their daughter an expensive nose job but thought so little about male appearance that they neglected their son's seriously protruding teeth, to the father who insisted that his son get an afterschool job while doling out "pin money" to his daughter whenever he paid his wife her household allowance, to the family whose sons had bank accounts of their own at eighteen but whose daughters remained on the take until they married.

Perhaps the most typical situation is the one described by a forty-eight-year-old plumber who has changed his views: "If I could only have afforded to pay for one college education ten years ago, it would have been for the boy. Today, I would have to say that I would pay for the best student, which happens to be my eldest, a girl."[30]

Adults hold the economic power; children are the dependents. That's hard enough for children to accept, but it's harder still if gender creates a complicating subtext. A few guidelines cover a lot of contingencies:

• *Kids' sex-role rationales for money demands should carry no weight.* Your son might argue that it costs him more for entertainment because sometimes he has to pay for his date. Your daughter might claim she needs a higher clothing allowance to keep up with high school fashions. Both arguments may be accurate, but they are irrelevant to the family. If your son finds the dating system unfair, he should campaign for the kids in his circle to go dutch; your daughter could innovate her own styles, boycott high-priced stores, resign herself to being less "in." Accommodating children's allowances to sex role imperatives implies acceptance of them. One should not have to suffer one's sex role and pay extra for it to boot.

• *Spend for the individual, not the stereotype.* For instance, buying a $30 softball mitt because "a boy needs a decent mitt" and a $9.95 mitt because "she's only a girl and she probably won't play much" are two unjustifiable reactions, especially if you don't yet know which child likes softball.

• *Don't be doctrinaire about equal pay.* It is all right to buy singing lessons for the gifted soprano but not the child who is tone deaf, or to buy a juice extractor for your suddenly fanatic vegetarian child without getting something of comparable expense for your meat-eaters. As long as gender is not the reason for special treats or denials, children escape having to pay a price for a biological fact they cannot help and should never have to regret.

• *Expose children of both sexes to the financial facts of life.* Let them be aware of your paying bills each month, of the meaning of installment buying, and of economic realities outside of your family. When our children were small, Bert and I used to play a game with them at the dinner table. "What's more expensive," we'd ask, "a motorcycle or a week's worth of groceries?" "Who do you think earns more, a teacher or a baseball player?" Little by little, they developed a concept of price and an awareness of social-economic inequalities that would not normally be explained to them.

• *Savings should be sexless.* Putting AT&T stock in a safe for a boy's future and linens in a hope chest for a girl's marriage is just plain crazy. Saving for a boy's college education and not a girl's is just plain cruel. (And yet 1 parent in 3 still believes the son, not the best student, should get the college money.[31])

• *Be sure your girls as well as your boys understand budgeting, checking accounts, and other mechanics of financial management* by the time they graduate from high school. If boys are expected to work after school or during summer vacations, you had better have a good reason why if your girls have no such obligation.

• *Allowances should be known to come from parents' pooled resources;* mothers and fathers might alternate payroll duty to clarify that both control the purse.

MEALTIME, BATHTIME, AND BEDTIME

Banish all generalizations from your mind. "Boys need more food and less sleep," "It's more important for girls to be neat and clean,"[32] and similar statements about personal habits will always hit the mark about *some* girls and boys some of the time, but when the statements aren't true they tend to be coercive. Armies operate by common-denominator expectations, but a family can afford to respond to the individual.

A few test questions in each category will alert you to potential problems:

Mealtimes

Writes Craig Claiborne, food critic of the *New York Times:*

> It is a long-known fact that there are, in this country and elsewhere, sexist implications in certain foods. Perhaps the most obvious examples are the tendency to relate steak, the rarer the better, with masculinity and salads with femininity.[33]

If you believe meat-and-potatoes make a "man's meal" and cucumber sandwiches a "ladylike lunch," ask yourself which meal you would serve to a *person* who was really hungry? Wouldn't you try to make a cucumber sandwich attractive to a *person* who hates vegetables? Would you force meat and potatoes on someone trying to lose weight? For health's sake, shouldn't you keep sex out of menu-planning?

Then, there's mealtime role-playing: At breakfast (assuming all family members are over age six), who scoops out the soft-boiled eggs? Who butters everyone's toast?

Who sits at the head of the table? How did you decide which was the "head" and which the "foot"? Does it have anything to do with the sex of the parent and the location of the kitchen?

Who brings things to the table? Who gets up to clear the plates? Who has to remind the children to clear the plates?

Is the conversation of each family member given equal attention at the dinner table, or does Father's report of *his* day take precedence? Is conversation divided mother-daughter, father-son, or adults-talking-over-the-heads-of-the-children, and if so, are there other times of the day when family community is established? (Children of divorced parents particularly need those other times since they seem to be more likely to eat "pick-up meals at irregular times," and less likely to eat with their parents.[34])

Is drinking a means of confirming masculinity? Does Father boast about his capacity to "hold my liquor," or the fun of getting drunk with "the boys"? Is wine "effeminate," and beer, "macho"? Are all your teen-age children subjected to the same rules about drinking regardless of sex? (A survey of ten thousand seventh- to twelfth-graders found that 23 percent of the boys and 15 percent of the girls are "problem drinkers!"[35])

Bathtimes

> Perhaps I have been brainwashed by Madison Avenue, but I happen to believe that a man should bathe daily, and a woman can't bathe enough!
>
> —Abigail Van Buren[36]

Are your daughters and sons bathed, or expected to bathe themselves, equally often? Do you believe it more important for females to be clean, especially after puberty, than for males? Were you indoctrinated with a fear (loathing?) of natural female odors?

Do you equate cleanliness with "femininity," and dirt with healthy "manly" toil? When your sweaty, grimy son comes home from practice late and goes to bed sweaty and grimy, do you chuckle "Isn't that just like a boy?" or do you send him to the tub? When your sweaty, grimy daughter comes in from working in the garden, do you say, "Ugh, you look like a slob! Go straight to the tub!" or do you admire how she staked her tomato plants?

Has your son had a bubble bath lately? Do you think (as do many questioned in a recent study[37]) that baths are childish and "feminine," and showers are "masculine"? If your daughter is in a hurry, which makes sense: a bath or shower? And if your son is in the mood for a soothing, luxuriant tub bath, where's the harm?

What equipment or products do you think a boy or girl needs for personal hygiene? How did your son learn that soap, washcloth, and shampoo are enough, if your older daughter uses bath beads, sponge, back brush, callous stone, soap, washcloth, shampoo, conditioner, bath powder, and cologne?

Bedtimes

> One study found that "children not going to bed on time" was one of the ten childrearing issues that most "irritate parents, create tensions and generate arguments."[38]

Are your bedtime rules logical and consistent? Logical means age-related (bedtime at escalating hours as children get older), not sex-related (*i.e.,* girls need their "beauty sleep"); and consistent means your son cannot get an extension to finish his model plane if your daughter was not allowed to stay up reading.

Is the bedtime ritual nondiscriminatory? (I pity the boy whose father tosses him a businesslike "Goodnight, son" after having kissed his sister in the next room.) Tucking in, goodnight kisses, bedtime stories, lullabyes, bedtime chats, final bathroom visits and drinks of water are comforting transitions from an active day to a restful night, regardless of sex.

Do you feel uneasy when your son exhibits nighttime dependency symptoms: the need to suck his thumb, stroke his "security" blanket, sleep with a teddy, or keep a light burning in his room at night? Did or would any of these habits bother you in your daughter? At what age should they be discouraged for a girl? A boy?

At bedtime one evening, a twenty-month-old boy who was

"extremely lively and all over the place . . . reduced his mother to tears of exhaustion and despair. As she sat crying on the bed, he ran to fetch his security blanket, which he habitually sucked in moments of tiredness or upset, and gave it to her, trying to push it into her mouth."[39]

Would you want to wean your son of his blanket at the expense of his wonderful empathy and kindness?

Do you respond comfortingly whether the child having a nightmare is female or male? Have you ever said anything like "A big girl doesn't let a little dream scare her"?

Are pre-bedtime activities sex-differentiated? (Fathers sometimes overstimulate boys with rough-and-tumble play—a bid for "masculine" cameraderie[40]—while the most a girl gets is some tickling, a fatherly activity "almost completely reserved for daughters; only one boy out of 250 . . . mentioned having been tickled by his father."[41])

Do you have a bedwetter in your family? Have you thought about the intriguing connections between bedwetting and sex roles? Dr. Spock says: "Four out of 5 cases occur in boys and 10% of boys are still wetting the bed at 12 years of age. Most of these stop wetting in adolescence." The rarer female bedwetter is likely to be the "spunky sort who is highly competitive with her brother or . . . resentful about being a girl because of the discrimination so often involved."[42]

We know that many more young boys than girls are pressured to measure up to their sex role stereotype. Often, the pressure lets up when the boy's status is socially and physically augmented after puberty. Therefore, boy's bedwetting in childhood and cessation of bedwetting in adolescence parallels sex role tensions and their release after puberty. Although bedwetting may be caused by a small bladder capacity or psychologically triggered by an event such as homesickness or a new baby, it is most commonly brought on by criticism and pressure to perform.

Thus, wet sheets can be a symptom of sex role strain. Boys wet their beds in resistance to the demands of "masculinity"; it is their retreat to a stage when less was expected of them. Girls wet to resist "feminization"; the girl is telling her parents, "O.K., you won't let me be strong and free as a boy, so I'll be weak and helpless as a baby."

Nonsexist childrearing is a kind of general antidote against bedwetting. But if your child already has the problem, try to use the quiet bedtime moments to find ways of reassuring your son or daughter that he or she is entirely adequate as a human being, that you admire his or her activities, and that you consider him or her "normal" and lovable as is.

12
Family Feelings

Disapproval of me was his main thing. I never seemed to be able to do things right for him. Once . . . I remember I had to clean out the garage. I really worked hard at it, hoping for once to do a really good job for Dad. But his only words were, "How come you didn't wash the windows?"[1]

How do parents hurt children's feelings? Let me count the ways: by lovelessness, ridicule, belittlement, coldness, sarcasm, harsh words, neglect, and outright abuse.

Sexism hurts feelings. Feelings are "feminine." So when the father rules the roost and the "masculine" style sets the emotional mood of the home, expression of feelings is discouraged or punished and gaining control of one's feelings is an overt goal, especially for sons. Boys' tears are despised.

Sometimes me and my father box. He gets me down and he starts punching me, and then when I start crying he says, "Stop those crocodile tears," and keeps on punching.[2]

So many youngsters cannot communicate their feelings to their parents (most often fathers) that *Children's Express,* a collective of child writers, devoted a section of their book to the subject. When asked "What do you do when you're upset and can't tell your parents what's bothering you?" children from eleven to thirteen said they "take it out on the [teddy] bear" . . . "tell my friends" . . . "I eat; I drown my sorrows in pizza" . . . "punch something like the wall." The need for a parent confidante is so great that the listening parents are sometimes imagined: "I sit in my room and I pretend that I'm talking to them . . . sometimes it makes me feel better."[3]

Children reveal themselves most to parents who create a

nurturing, accepting atmosphere; in conventional homes this means mothers,[4] but in nonsexist families with warm, understanding fathers children disclose their feelings to both.

Fearfulness is one example of the many normal human emotions children would share if it were not squelched and distorted by sexism. A ten-year-old reports,

> In my family we don't talk about our emotions much because I think they have the feeling that if you tell, you'll be vulnerable. Like, if I said to them, "Oh, there is one thing that I hate: I hate snakes," or whatever, then they might tease me about that. So I don't really talk a lot, except to myself.[5]

Interestingly, among children from two to six, the same percentages of girls and boys show fear of a snake, of a large dog, of going into a dark passageway, staying near a menacing stranger, or investigating a loud noise. The only difference is that girls are more willing to admit their anxiety,[6] probably because of the "learned helplessness" socialization of the female (see Chapter 4), and parents' greater tolerance for fearfulness in girls.

Both sexes lose something from sex-typing: the girl is "free" to be afraid but loses the impetus for adventure; the boy grows brave (maybe) but loses the emotional truth of a situation and the flexibility that would allow him to retreat from danger. This difference makes it hard for them both to share experiences, comfort and be comforted, or act rationally under stress.

Just as fear supposedly desexes a male, anger desexes a female. To retain her "femininity" a girl learns to bottle up her rage, to smile or turn her rage inward rather than let it show. Emotional dishonesty[7] in the form of pouting, baby-talk, sulking, manipulation, flattery, false mirth, and other "feminine" ways and wiles may "work" to get a girl what she wants, but may also "seriously damage a woman's self-esteem and diminish the respect she gets from others."[8] Then her low self-esteem starts the rage-repression-dishonesty cycle all over again.

Not only are females supposed to repress their own anger, they're expected to absorb the anger of others. Be the calm island in man's storm. Males tend to explode suddenly and with little provocation as a result of having "compulsively kept feelings in check as men have been trained to do."[9] That explosive anger can only be directed, safely, downward toward the powerless. The powerless in turn, can survive best by comforting, pleasing, and appeasing the powerful. Hence females have become "the complaint clerks of society,"[10] smiling, serving, and hiding their pain behind a smile.

It's sensible to be angry at belittlement and afraid of menacing strangers, poisonous snakes, dogs that bite, unfamiliar passageways, and explosives. Confusing fearlessness with "masculinity" can literally get a boy killed, and will surely kill the sensitive, help-seeking impulses within him. Likewise, permitting fearfulness and sweetness to become a badge of "femininity" consigns a girl to the life of a china knickknack, and condemns her to unnecessary distress in benign situations. So, be sensible about feelings. Teach your sons and daughters to respond to the unknown, the infuriating, and the threatening with an emotion that fits the situation and best serves the child.

COMMUNICATION COMPETENCE

Whether fear or ecstasy, feelings need an outlet. Children should be able to bring their feelings to a parent in the expectation that they will be dealt with, not ridiculed or repressed. Parents do not have to accept all feelings as valid or admirable but we should keep the lines of communication open, give kids our honest reactions, and let them see *our* feelings now and then.

A friend told me how visibly choked up her husband was when their son announced that he wanted to go away to boarding school.

"Your mother is not sure she's ready to let you go," the father said to the boy, although the parents had never discussed the issue before.

My friend looked hard at her husband. "If that's what you're feeling, *tell* him," she said. "Don't make me your emotional surrogate."

Embarrassed by this exposure of his feelings and his need to filter them through a woman, the father broke into tears. For the first time in his twelve-year-old life, the boy had an inkling of how much he meant to his father.

Why do parents keep such secrets? Dr. Alice Ginott answers:

> It is our incompetence in communicating, *not* our lack of love, that drives children crazy. Most of us love our children. What we lack is a language that conveys love, that mirrors our delight—and that makes a child feel loved, respected and appreciated.[11]

Parents really need the same thing from children: love, respect, and appreciation. When we get it, childrearing is the most rewarding project in the world: "Just think Mom," said a small boy to the mother who raised him singlehandedly. "Nine years together and we still love each other!"[12]

When we don't get it, it may be because we closed off the access routes between ourselves and our children. Because mothers are usually the primary care-givers, their greater exposure to their children gives them early understanding of, and practice responding to, the babbling gestures and beginning speech of little ones.[13] But fathers are often inept at such communication. They tend to speak to two-year-olds in questions ("What is this? "Is this a camel?") which, psychologists say, lets them control the conversation and consequently feel more comfortable with the child. Fathers speak to five-year-olds mostly in imperatives. ("Get that book." "Come here.") They seem uncertain about how to talk to their children, how to teach them without being overbearing, how to *be* with them verbally. They often talk down to children or over their heads. In sum, fathers' language and communication style "is less attuned to the child's needs than is the speech of mothers."[14]

When fathers spend more time caring for children, they become familiar with children's levels of comprehension, their enthusiasms, feelings, and speech habits, establishing a verbal intimacy that cannot result from the noncommunicative "pals" relationship typical of so many fathers and children. (While getting to know their children better, fathers also contribute to their greater language development—an intellectual bonus for the child.[15])

Is it ever too late to build communication? Too late for whom? Answers Dr. Ginott:

Certainly not with adolescents. Teenagers seem so disorganized because they are in the process of reorganizing themselves. We, as parents can influence the direction. How we talk to them can make the difference [and] demonstrate to our teenager that feelings are to be taken seriously since emotions alert one to what often the mind can only later learn.[16]

Boys who feel most "understood" by their fathers attribute this to shared interests, the reasonableness of their father's punishments, and their father's *interest in them*. Boys who feel "misunderstood" describe themselves as "unfairly disciplined and coerced into father-son activities that they didn't relish ... [they felt] lonely, frustrated and unimportant whenever they approached their dads. Explained one, 'It's the problem of talking to someone whose mind is somewhere else.' "[17]

DEMONSTRATING AFFECTION

What is true about expression of feelings is true in spades about affection. Once again it is fathers more than mothers who need the most help changing. Actor Paul Dooley told the *New York Times* that he was able to play the character of the father in the film *Breaking Away* because of its similarity to his own father:

He is not able to show affection for his wife or his son directly, and his style is to sort of grumble in a kind of comic way, to sort of complain, to put his son down. It's a very subtle thing because it doesn't seem to be mean-spirited ... you knew that he cared for you, but he didn't show it directly. It's not an uncommon disease in our country.[18]

This common "disease," complicated by fear of homosexuality, prevents men from showing love, especially to another male. Understandably, then, daughters very often report their fathers far more demonstrative than do sons in the same family.[19] Toward boys, men restrain their affectionate feelings in dread of the supposedly "feminine" and "feminizing" trait of loving kindness, but with girls they can let go to some extent at least.

Are the girls in your family enjoying a warmer brand of fathering? What a cheat for boys. And what a dividend when Father *is* affectionate. However banal it is to restate, "Love is the most important ingredient in happiness." We can learn this from poets or psychologists: "A shortage of love in childhood causes people to choose other sources of happiness, such as money, that don't work as well."[20]

Boys with affectionate fathers showed "strong achievement strivings"[21] and were less apt to drop out of high school in later adolescence.[22] In sum,

> the young men who turned out the most well-adjusted had very loving fathers who were around a good deal of the time, while the sons of unloving fathers who were also around a lot tested out as undependable and immature.[23]

Affectionate behavior can be learned. Go for walks with your child. Stroll hand-in-hand or toss an arm over the child's shoulder. Take a child to lunch, just the two of you. Or share a milk shake and conversation the way you'd have drinks with a friend. Talk about your experiences in simple details that your child can understand. Keep up with your children's lives.

Kiss children hello, good-bye, goodnight, or for no special reason, until *they* show *you* they're too old for it. Tell them you love them; use the words "I love you"; don't be afraid. Tell them how wonderful they are. Pick them up until their weight strains your hernia. Hug them, stroke their cheeks, tousle their hair. Be vulnerable. Show fallibility. Accept their criticism. Enjoy their adoration. They will only be children once in their lives, and yours.

PARENTS AS PEOPLE

Family life sustains itself and grows strong when there is parent-child empathy in both directions, when children understand parents' feelings almost as well as parents understand children's, and when children's perceptions of their parents bear more than a chance resemblance to their parents' reality.

What do our children think about us? Eight-year-old Susan who lives with her mother said she felt "funny" about having only one parent because there were no other children like her in her second-grade class. How did Susan's mother let her child think their situation was so "different," when in fact, 21 out of the 33 children in Susan's class lived in single-parent families?[24]

Nine-year-old Steven asked his parents for books to prove in print that other families in the world are like his: that is, families in which both Mother and Father are lawyers.

Eight-year-old Mitzi lies about the fact that her mother goes out to work and her father stays home.

Most of us are much better at telling children what we think of them than at discovering what they think of us. In nonsexist families, where children experience much that is contrary to the cultural "norm," keeping tabs of their impressions of us is particularly essential.

I kind of liked myself when I heard my son David, age nine at the time, talking with a friend during their gin rummy game: "Most mothers tell you to keep your feet off the couch," he said, "but my mother always has her *own* feet up on our couch."

I also liked the story of the little girl who "trotted from door to door saying: 'Come see my momma, she is under the car!' And of course, the neighbors trooped out, fearing the worst."[25] However, what the mother was doing was draining the oil, and her daughter was calling attention to her as a *doer,* not a victim.

Most children more often boast about their fathers than their mothers. For instance, boys tend to claim that their fathers have more education[26] and are much taller[27] than is actually the case. Rather than signifying children's love for their fathers, these grandiose overestimates may just be superman braggadocio in the patriarchy's "My dad can beat your dad" sweepstakes.

In terms of emotional evaluations of their fathers, children rate them as "more fear arousing, more punitive, more restrictive, colder and less understanding than mothers."[28]

Mothers who work outside the home have a particular need for their children's understanding—of what they do, why they do it, and why their work is not a betrayal of motherhood. Since our culture promotes the homemaker ideal, children of stay-home mothers rarely feel ambivalence; they can observe Mom around the house and can respect her labor if she enjoys it and does it well. Such children frequently consider employed mothers peculiar and pass that opinion on to other children. However, since half of all mothers work outside the home, there is no reason—except failure of parent-child empathy—for children of wage-earning women to feel the least bit odd about their situation. Here is one child who went completely the other way in his perceptions:

"I was at Lorraine's today, and her mother was home sick," he reported.

"Oh? What was wrong with her?" I asked.

"I don't know. She didn't look sick. But she was home *all* day."

For a big boost to parent-child empathy, take your children to your workplace. Introduce them to your co-workers and explain your job in child-scaled terminology or let them watch you at work.

Eugenia Zuckerman, flutist, and Pinchas Zuckerman, violinist, do this with their two young daughters who, they say,

> constantly surprise us with their ability to understand and accept the very structured life of performing musicians. They see us practice every day, want to come to all our concerts, and while the pain of leaving them when one or both of us are out of town is very real, we hope that by letting them share our career—not only our accomplishments but our joy in music—they will have the security children need.[29]

Visualizing you at work helps children accept your absences. It anchors you in the vast space "out there." It explains your occasional fatigue, work pressure, or excitement for what you do —and introduces healthy fantasies of what they might do "someday."

To learn how your children perceive you, ask them to role-play *being* you. (Psychological games can be as much fun for a family as intellectual or athletic games—and far more revealing.) Give them several situations to act out, for example:

• one of the children has a fever of 104 degrees.

- the car gets a flat on a deserted highway.
- the living room is a mess and guests are coming.
- two hundred Christmas cards have to be addressed.
- a child hit a ball and broke the neighbor's window.
- the Sunday papers arrive.

Notice who is portrayed as competent in a crisis, who gets the news section of the paper, who takes responsibility for the illness, the visitors, the greeting card obligation.

If you could overhear your children describing you to a friend, would you recognize yourself? Would you *like* yourself? Can you accurately guess whether your child would fill in the word "mother," "father," or "parents" in the following statements:

- Before I can go on the hike, I'll have to ask my _____.
- My _____ will be furious that I lost my school bag.
- Of course I know what my _____ does/do all day.
- Don't worry, my _____ will fix it.
- My friends all tease me; maybe my _____ know(s) what I should do about it.

The word "parents" in most of those fill-ins would augur well for nonsexist family life, and for the security of your child.

CONFLICT

There are infinite reasons why parents and children disagree and siblings squabble, but those that are caused by sexism are among the most avoidable of all family conflicts. With all the things there are to fight about, why not avoid the avoidable?

Generally speaking, boys resent girls' being "put on a pedestal and treated with kid gloves just because they are girls,"[30] and girls are angry or envious when boys are favored, allowed more freedom, or given more responsibility just because they're boys.

Sexist conflict does not necessarily require two sexes. In fact, an expert observer of two-child families found sibling rivalry "at its most intense when children are of the same sex—and of traditional sex roles."[31]

"Why can't you ever look as neat as your sister?" or "When your brother was your age, we could leave *him* in charge of the store" are the kind of comparisons that start fights and create envy, hurt feelings, and loss of confidence—all in the name of a sex stereotype.[32]

When a child has had her or his parents' exclusive attention, the arrival of another child is a predictable cause of anger and jealousy. ("Wasn't I good enough?" "Why did they need another one?" "It's not fair that I suddenly have to share everything.") But children's natural reactions are worsened if the cult of sex difference is added to sibling rivalry. I'm thinking of a little boy who was angry because his mother kept carrying around his newborn baby sister. When told she was too young to walk, he replied, "Isn't that just like a girl? She doesn't even try."

Margaret Mead made this trenchant analysis of the conventional sister-brother relationship in sexist America:

> The sister becomes a double rival as she grows faster than he, does her lessons more dutifully, gets into fewer scrapes, learns the woman-taught lessons more easily. . . . The boy is taught both that he ought to be able to beat her record, as he is a boy, and that it is fair to compare their achievements on the same scale at the same age, because they both ride bicycles or sleep alone on the third floor. . . . They are treated as alike whenever it suits the rest of the world, and as unlike whenever that proves a better goad . . . when she outstrips him, he is told it is even worse than if he had been outstripped by a boy, and yet she may be almost twice his size and he has also been told not to hit her because she is a girl. Side by side they sit in the nursery to be compared on neatness and punctuality as well as reading and writing and arithmetic. She sits and challenges him, and beats him at least half the time . . . until high school provides the blessed relief of science and shop, where girls aren't encouraged to succeed any longer. And as he sits and is beaten . . . he learns that girls can do most of the things that boys can do for which rewards are meted out and that it is intolerable that they should, because it has been made humiliating.[33]

To reduce the resentment/hostility level in your house, follow these three suggestions:

1. Don't make comparisons between children.
2. Keep gender out of the granting or denying of privileges.
3. Don't assign blame on the grounds of sex.

How do these precepts apply to everyday conflicts?
SITUATION: At a school raffle, your family wins two tickets to a Yankee-Dodger World Series game. Who goes?

    a. father and mother
    b. father and son
    c. father and daughter
    d. mother and son
    e. mother and daughter

In many households, answer b would be automatic and might arouse hostility. When the tickets were won by our family (with one extra daughter in the mix), all five of us wanted to go. We argued on the merits: the parents were oldest and had never yet seen a World Series game. Each child claimed a recent deprivation ("I was sick when all of you went swimming"), or a turn-taking rationale (Daddy already took Abby to the opera).

While answer b might start the conflict for most families, answer d ended it for us, and everyone agreed it was as fair a resolution as any. I got one of the tickets because I was the person who bought the raffle in the first place, and David got the other because, in truth, he was the family's only Yankee fan.

SITUATION: Your family is at a carnival. It's your daughter's turn to throw the darts at the balloons in one of the twenty-five-cent carnival games. From all the other games, your family has nine coupons toward a ten-coupon transistor radio that everyone wants to win. This is the last quarter in your carnival budget. She throws the darts: misses once, misses twice, misses altogether.

Your son is hysterical. "That was our last chance to win the transistor, you nerd!" he shouts at his sister. "I should have taken your turn! Girls can't throw anything to save their lives." Your daughter shouts back and punches her brother in the arm. In seconds, a battle royale is underway. What went wrong?

Blaming a disappointment on a flaw supposedly attributable to gender makes a person mad. Gender can't be helped and shouldn't have to be defended. In a nonsexist family, the situation might have been different in any of these ways:

a. When everyone realized it was the last chance at the tenth coupon, the family might have given the turn to its best dart-thrower (whether Mom, Dad, or one of the kids) so that the whole group could have the optimum chance to win the transistor.

b. If no player was clearly superior, the children could have taken one dart each and flipped for the third.

c. Sister and brother might be equally good at darts in the first place if they had been given equal opportunity to develop their throwing ability in various sports.

d. The brother might have blamed his sister's performance on bad luck, bad lighting, or dull dart tips, because gender generalizations would simply never occur to him.

CONFLICT STYLES

Some people think family fighting is an art, a rapport builder, "a crucial ingredient of intimacy between parent and child."[34]

As one who grew up during wartime—the one between my parents as well as the one in Europe—I have little affection for confrontational conflict. I like arguments, discussions, debates, and "talking things out." I think grievances should be aired and rage should be released and people should be able to shout or sulk and still know they love each other. But I hate fights, by which I mean I hate self-indulgent screaming, throwing things, slamming doors, name-calling, and other grandstand gestures associated with "letting it all hang out."

That approach to family conflict, called "therapeutic aggression,"[35] considers extremes of verbal and physical fighting a catharsis and a learning experience, whereas I have always found it a mind-numbing experience, sometimes terrifying in its accelerating violence. Reviews of the research on anger[36] seem to prove me right and the catharsis theory wrong: instead of serving to let off steam and ventilate anger, that sort of all-out aggression does little more than raise the level of violence in any fight.

As a feminist, I can't help noting too that the higher the level of permissible aggression and violence, the greater the male advantage. Women and men are on equal footing when family arguments are conducted with words, but introduce slaps, pushes, and punches, and the male, who is generally larger and more likely to have been socialized to fight, has the distinct edge over the female.

Not only is this unfortunate for the woman of the family but for the children as well. Upping the ante on permissible violence between parents raises the threshold of tolerance that children will feel in the presence of violence for the rest of their lives. It also means conflicts between parents will be resolved by male force, not gender-neutral justice. The outcome of a fight may have no connection whatsoever with right or wrong. Children who witness such fights learn nothing about disputation, effective advocacy, constructive resolution of differences, or right and wrong. The issues are lost in the result: might wins and might is usually male.

Before adolescence, it is age, not sex, that determines who is the physically bigger, more powerful sibling in a family. However, the reason one often sees a bigger, older girl being bullied by her younger brother is the sex role duplication of the parents' conflict styles, and parental expectation and acceptance of greater physical aggression from boys than from girls. Studies find that both girls and boys quarrel equally often with their brothers and sisters,[37] but like a self-fulfilling prophecy, boys (whether older or younger) are more likely to strike their siblings than are girls,[38] and parents are more likely to hit a son who is found beating up his brother or sister than to hit a daughter.[39]

The lesson: Physicality is a male thing and boys must be able to dish it out as well as take it.

For a sure-fire "consciousness razor" you and your family should list all the fights you have had over the past month (or six months, if you can remember them). Put the subject of the fight in the first column on paper. In the second column, record who was the angriest; in the third column list how the anger was expressed, and in the fourth list whether or not the angriest person got his or her way.[40]

"Then figure out if one style of anger (crying, shouting, fist-pounding, name-calling, pouting, etc.) is more 'efficient' in your family than any other. Do the males or the females in the family practice the 'efficient' style of anger most frequently?"[41]

While you're at it, look carefully at the subjects of most of the fights. Do they form a pattern? You may find as one twelve-year-old did, that whatever the subject, your family is actually fighting over one thing: "power and who has the right to what."[42]

The power-love balance in the family and the parents' policies regarding violence are learned by the children through observation and emulation. And the rate of family violence is *lowest* in homes where wives and husbands share decision-making.[43]

FAMILY CONSTELLATIONS

Family fights and family feelings very much depend on whether the household contains an only child, sons and daughters, or an all-boy or all-girl family.

The singleton tends to be more confident, verbal, and resourceful, and her or his family is closer and more democratic than average.[44] Instead of apportioning certain privileges to a son and others to a daughter, parents tend to let the only child try everything and share both adults' interests.

If they have more than one child, parents' attitudes toward sex roles seem to be significantly affected by children's birth order and sex composition.[45]

First-born sons are usually subjected to the most intense parent pressure. They tend to grow up to be stubborn, heroic individuals with extremely high expectations.[46] (One investigator discovered that all the wars in which the United States has been involved, except for the Spanish American War, were instigated or escalated by presidents who were oldest sons.[47])

First-born girls in an all-girl family (like the female only-child) seem to get whatever advantages might otherwise have gone to a son: education; parental encouragement; athletic, cultural, and intellectual exposure.[48]

The effect of a brother on a girl's development seems arguable: one study found that having brothers makes a girl more active (presumably due to her proximity to male-type playthings and sports),[49] while another found that "having no brothers probably provides an opportunity structure for girls. Their absence removes an important obstacle . . . a male who is supposed to act for her."[50]

You might imagine that families whose children are all one sex would track toward sex-typing. For instance, in a traditional family where there are only sons, all the toys would very likely be "boys' toys." If one of the boys were to bring home a doll from nursery school, it would be more jarring than if he had a sister whose playthings had occasionally attracted his attention around the house.

Indeed, research shows that sex role rigidity *is* worse in single-sex families—but only if that single sex is male. It's as though parents of boys work overtime to keep "feminine" influences out of their all-male enclave.

So if a child had to be born into a traditional family and wanted the family constellation with the greatest tolerance for individuality, a girl would do best choosing an all-girl family, but a boy should arrange to get born into a brother-sister situation.

Better still, let's create nonsexist families where the gender mix will never work against children's development—or hurt children's feelings.

13

Managing Freedom: Rewards and Restraints

"Here is how you fertilize houseplants."
"Let me show you the easy way to splice film."
"Just remember: *i* before *e* except after *c.*"

When you help or teach children—when you show them how or tell them why—you are doing more than imparting information or skills. *Helping efforts also transmit competence impressions about the gender of the helping parent.* For instance, a child surmises, "My father taught me to thread a needle; that means men can sew." Another example: buying your daughter a train set is fine as far as it goes. But, as Dr. Lisa Serbin points out, what matters most is which parent sets it up and shows her how it works. When mother is the helper-teacher, the girl learns females can have mechanical skill, not just the right to own toy trains.[1] *When parents can help with different things, children learn that someone who is competent in one skill area is competent, period.* A study of kindergarten girls found that "daughters of working mothers were more likely than daughters of nonworking mothers to name their mother as the person whom they would ask to repair a broken bicycle."[2] *When both parents are "pan-competent," children gain an optimum choice of learning "sources."* There is growing research evidence that in some cases, girls learn best from and for male teachers and boys from and for females.[3] In other situations, the reverse is true.[4] Having both fathers and mothers in diverse teaching roles creates the broadest possibility for girls' and boys' receptivity to learning.

With two helping parents, both adults' strengths can be passed on to all their children instead of granting only same-sex apprenticeships. The familiar moan "If only you had been a boy" expresses fathers' perceived loss of an heir to their skills. Few men have breached tradition to share learning with their daughters—as did the fathers of astronomers Maria Mitchell and Caroline Hershel, for example,[5] or a modern father who has taught his teenage daughters to fly a plane as well as he does (while the mother has passed on to their daughters her polished skiing style).

In an article entitled "Sexism and the Family Tree,"[6] Karen Bruno deplores the loss of her Mexican great-grandmother's legendary cooking secrets, including, among other things, a recipe for "the best tacos in the mid-west." Three generations removed from this woman, her great-granddaughter laments:

> I have thought about the recipe for tacos and have determined that it was lost simply because my grandfather was a male. Had he been female, he would have learned his mother's recipe and kept it alive within the family for more generations.
>
> . . .
>
> I have observed my family to determine what aspects of our family are dying out with this generation. The Brunos are skilled mechanics and all of my male cousins who descended from my uncles . . . possess this talent. They can fix anything with amazing ease and rarely need to pay for repairs.
>
> My male cousins who descended from my aunts do not possess this trait, however. My aunts were not welcomed around my grandfather's tool bench and did not learn the wonderful secrets of repair. Thus, they could not pass these things on to their sons.
>
> I have been denied the secrets of fixing things, as my grandfather was denied the secrets of his mother's recipes, simply because I am the wrong sex. The best taco recipe in the mid-west is gone from our family forever because society has set up strong rules for passing knowledge from one generation to the next.

In that very deep and lasting sense, it is sexism, not feminism, that destroys families. "It forbids the sharing of priceless information. . . . It distorts and destroys identity forever."[7]

What is taught, who does the teaching, and finally *how* parents teach are the key elements of learning at home. Because of the "how," some learning is not worth having. I'm thinking of the boy who remembers "my father never letting me make mistakes when he was showing me how to do something . . . grabbing the tool from me [saying], 'Jesus Christ, you'll never finish that way!' and me learning to hate."

I've seen parents' helping and teaching efforts drive children to tears, especially when sexist goading is the motivating pressure. Samples:

"You're the only boy on the block still using training wheels."

"It's hopeless. I don't know why the schools even *try* to teach girls calculus."

"Dammit! If it's not too cold for that *girl* to go swimming, it's not too cold for my son."

Whether it is helping with homework or teaching a teenager to drive, if you find yourself short-tempered, if you lose patience or belittle your child for not "getting it," you might as well quit the whole thing. Let the teacher give extra tutoring or send the teenager to driving school. Inferiority and hatred are *not* what children should learn from their parents' "help."

INDEPENDENCE AND FREEDOM

Freedom is the existence of alternatives among which one may choose.[8]

When you let children go to school alone for the first time, or play far from home, or stay out past their bedtime, you are giving them precious gifts—autonomy, trust, respect, freedom.

You know the feeling yourself: experience success on your own, and your self-esteem soars. Act independently, make your own judgments, and you get hooked on self-determination. In childrearing, freedom need not mean license, nor independence total permissiveness. But letting out the leash is the only way puppies learn to run, and letting children explore, experiment, and choose among alternatives is the only way they learn to be competent human beings.

One mother remembers with regret:

When my daughter asked my permission to be a traffic scout when she was in sixth grade, I said no. I was upset about her projecting herself into a male role (it was 1973), and I was concerned for her safety. Yet I had given my son permission, and I was proud of him directing traffic.

Had I attached more importance to my daughter's safety than my son's? Had I cared more for his independence training than hers? Why?

Because parents actually believe they are preparing their children for "two different worlds." The fact is that independence training is part of the family heritage for boys, while protectiveness and fearfulness-training are for girls:

• Although nine-month-old girls and boys are equally fragile, parents consistently express more fear of possible illness and physical harm to their daughters than their sons.[9]

• Mothers of two-year-old girls warn them of a nearby open cellar door; mothers of boys tend to ignore the danger in the same situation. (About the effect of this difference on girls, Jerome Kagan says, "These [kinds of] warnings occur several times a day, seven days a week, month after month, and must have a strong influence on the child's fearfulness and inhibition."[10])

• At toddler ages, "boys are left alone more often . . . even when parents have no conscious desire to give boys more freedom than girls."[11]

• Children experience the environment differently according to their sex. Parents let boys play further from home without asking permission.[12] Girls "are more closely controlled than boys."[13] Girls receive more "chaperonage"; they are escorted to and from school, they must report their whereabouts, they are more often in adult company, being supervised, "leading a more protected and sheltered existence . . . under consistently greater pressure towards conformity with adult standards and values."[14]

• "During adolescence parental anxieties concerning dating behavior of girls lead to increasing restrictions, conflicts, and use of physical force in asserting parental control."[15]

So much for a girl's independence training. It is foiled and displaced by fear—in infancy and childhood by the belief that girls are dainty and fragile, and in adolescence by the paranoid protection of virginity. (More about sexist sexuality and its consequences in the next chapter.)

Intellectual repercussions are just as serious. Free exploration of a far-ranging environment seems to foster something called "field independence," a cognitive skill essential to all problem-solving tasks, especially the ability to visualize and analyze spatial relationships. In the words of a cognitive specialist:

> We have seen that girls tend to be restrained by parents, teachers and peers in their environmental exploration and manipulation because such activities are considered masculine. Thus, not only is a possible area of competence and adventure denied them [but] both lack of experience and lack of confidence would in turn tend to diminish girls' spatial abilities and perhaps generalize to other types of problem-solving. Certainly, the stereotypes and their related restrictions do not support the development of skill in using the environment for attaining goals.[16]

In plain words, let your daughters go. Question your impulse to warn them, restrict them, or protect them. All children are smaller and more vulnerable than adults. Any child can get lost, run over, mugged, drowned, assaulted, or sexually attacked. (Homosexual abuse of boys is just as dreadful as heterosexual abuse of girls.) If you love your daughters and sons equally, give them equal safety rules and an equal chance to feel free.

It may be necessary for a father to keep asking himself, with his daughter, whether he would impose the same restrictions on a son. A mother might have to check her own fears, swallow that "No, dear" before it leaves her lips, battle her own "learned helplessness" and "femininity" hang-ups.

For instance, going fishing . . .

Don't find it "natural" when your daughter is squeamish about baiting her own hook. Don't do it for her (assuming *you* aren't squeamish) or let her brother do it for her; *show her how.* If she wants the fun and rewards of fishing, she must take on the effort and boredom of fishing. That is, the whole of the experience.

Don't protect her excessively from the cold, or overload her with gadgets and lures, or spare her the physical work of hauling in her catch and removing the fish from the hook. Whatever the day brings, don't patronize her. If she didn't get a bite, say "better luck next time" and praise her persistence.

If she hauls one in, regardless of its size, it will be a Big Catch because it was all hers. Fry it, stuff it, mount it on the wall. Talk it up among the cognoscenti. Take a picture of her holding it by the tail. Make it known that you're proud to have an able daughter who wouldn't give up until she caught herself a winner.

REWARDS AND PUNISHMENT

One of the most important determinants of personality and behavioral outcomes is the pattern of parental rewards and punishments.[17]

Just as the hip bone is connected to the thigh bone, so the disciplinary policy in a family—"the pattern of parental rewards and punishments"—is connected to the conception of "the ideal child" that parents harbor deep in their souls.

It's quite straightforward: "Discipline is essentially programmed guidance."[18] With your image of "the ideal girl" or "the ideal boy" as your unconscious model, you reward the behavior you want to encourage and you punish the behavior you want to abolish. Because this "programmed guidance" is often used to trim and polish children's sex role behaviors,[19] it's understandable that girls and boys raised in the same house by the same parents can turn out so different from one another.

Although parents may articulate a consciously held egalitarian ideal—for example, that both boys and girls should not do dangerous things and that both should be clean and considerate[20]—underneath it all, parents believe certain behaviors are "natural" for each sex,[21] which influences their demands for "good" behavior from each of their children.

In general, parents are more actively involved and firmer in socializing children of the same sex—mother to daughter, father to son; they are more lenient with their cross-sex children—mother to son, father to daughter.[22] For instance, boys are more often spanked by their fathers, girls by their mothers,[23] and children report that the cross-sex parent is the one who "kisses most."[24]

Fathers more than mothers are concerned with sex-appropriate behavior (especially in sons) and are more apt to punish inappropriate behavior, whether or not it makes sense.[25] (Punishing a boy for hitting a girl but not for hitting another boy is an expression of role over rationality.)

Both parents, but especially fathers, are more task oriented with sons and socially oriented with daughters.[26] (His rewards are won for excellence, hers for getting along with others.)

Boys are punished for such "feminine" behaviors as dressing up for "let's pretend," and acting helpless, significantly more than girls are for such "masculine" behaviors as running and climbing.[27] Also, parents tend to reinforce daughters' help-seeking by offering assistance when asked, whereas requests from sons are apt to be ignored or criticized.[28] Furthermore, girls are rewarded with their parents' attention when they stay close, but boys who linger around adults are quickly sent off to play.[29]

Girls get more physical affection and are allowed to express a broader range of emotions than are boys.[30] Boys experience more prohibitions for a wider range of behavior.[31] Although parents permit more of boys' aggressive acts to go unpunished, within any given time period, boys receive more reprimands than girls.[32]

HOW AND HOW MUCH
ARE CHILDREN DISCIPLINED?

An act of . . . correction occurs between mothers and their two-year-old children on the average of once every three minutes.[33]

Despite distinct differences in disciplinary styles depending on their income level, marital happiness, race, ethnic group, and occupation,[34] most parents still believe girls and boys cannot be raised by the same rules.[35]

After reviewing the differences in parents' disciplinary treatment, two prominent researchers comment: "Adults respond as if they find boys more interesting and more attention-provoking than girls."[36] In all socioeconomic groups, boys receive more of every kind of behavior control—more physical punishment, more "negative reinforcement," more criticism, more disapproval, but also more praise, encouragement, compliments, and attention.[37]

When a society operates according to the cult of sex differences, gender itself (especially for boys under male supremacy) becomes both a disciplinary tool and a disciplinary rationale. As Margaret Mead put it:

> A society without a rigid sex-dichotomy merely says to the child . . . "Don't behave like that! People don't do that." "If you behave like that, people won't like you."
>   . . . Consider in contrast the way in which children in our culture are pressed into conformity: "Don't act like a girl." "Little girls don't do that." The threat of failing to behave like a member of one's own sex is used to enforce a thousand details . . . cleanliness, ways of sitting or relaxing . . . sportsmanship . . . personal vanity, interest in clothes or interest in current events.
>   . . . "Girls don't do that." "Don't you want to be a real man like Daddy" . . . Every time the point of sex conformity is made, every time the child's sex is invoked as the reason why it should prefer trousers to petticoats, baseball bats to dolls, fisticuffs to tears, there is planted in the child's mind a fear that indeed, in spite of anatomical evidence to the contrary, it may not really belong to its own sex at all.[38]

Some parents are positive reinforcers; they might be full of praise when a son lifts weights and just ignore him when he tries on his mother's bracelets. Negative reinforcers might spank him for wearing bracelets but say little or nothing about the weightlifting because they take sex-appropriate behavior for granted.

In either case, parents seem to use three basic disciplinary techniques to regulate children's behavior:[39]

1. Power assertion—spankings, beatings, deprivation, denial of privileges.

2. Love withdrawal—acting upset or hurt, yelling, implying "If you're bad, I won't love you."

3. Teaching—praise, criticism, reasoning, discussion, explanation of consequences.

Traditionalists tend to discipline girls with the teaching approach and boys with the two punishment techniques. (Single parents[40] and parents of large families seem most sex-stereotyped in their discipline style,[41] perhaps because they have less time to tailor it to the individual child.)

Praise and criticism register with great effect on young children; older children get the message simply from their parents' neutral reactions (the absence of praise or criticism), or from tone of voice or facial expressions.[42] Nevertheless, most parents do not limit themselves to a frown or a shout; 81 percent use corporal punishment on their children.[43] Leaving aside the immense subject of child abuse, which also reveals consistent sex-linked patterns,[44] more than 6 out of 10 "average" parents spank or beat their children an average of once a week, and boys are typically subjected to up to three times as much spanking as girls.[45]

There are several reasons for this: the traditional "prohibition against inflicting physical pain on girls"[46] (which still applies to children if not to adult women[47]); the cultural axiom that girls are (and should be) weak, since a woman's life does not require physical toughness or courage;[48] and the belief that spanking is unnecessary because girls are docile and pliable enough to obey spoken commands.[49] And girls *will* obey because they have been raised to need approval more than they need adventure, autonomy, or any of the desires that get boys in trouble.

Women seem to remember their childhoods more clearly and intensely than males.[50] They remember parental punishment as harsher whether they were spanked or not.[51] When you rear children for sensitivity, dependence on others' approval, and weakness, a little anger goes a long way.[52]

Thus, sex-typed discipline in childhood yields sex-appropriate behavior.

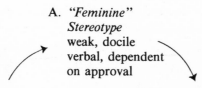

A. *"Feminine"*
Stereotype
weak, docile
verbal, dependent
on approval

C. *Developmental*
Result
conditioned to
perform for approval
to be timid and docile
especially in the presence
of aggression

B. *Parental*
Treatment
verbal constraints;
teaching but also
making approval
contingent on
obedience

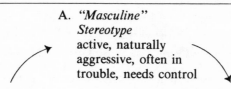

A. *"Masculine"*
Stereotype
active, naturally
aggressive, often in
trouble, needs control

C. *Developmental*
Result
conditioned to accept
aggression as means
of expression, prone
to violence

B. *Parental*
Treatment
fight fire with fire;
physical constraints,
tough them up;
teach them to take it

MORAL DEVELOPMENT

Parents want their children to "be good." They spank children to "teach them a lesson," "knock some sense into them," "teach them right from wrong." Yet the art of making moral judgments is not learned via physical threats and penalties—that we know for sure. No matter how painful the punishment, spanking and beatings do not "alter the behavior of children,"[53] do not make children able to resist temptation,[54] and do not produce children with internalized moral standards.[55]

Moral children are those who will behave decently *without* a parent, a cop, or a soldier threatening harm if they don't. Moral children carry their knowledge of right and wrong inside themselves (otherwise known as having a conscience). They are children who understand and care about the consequences of their actions. For the most part, it is children who are punished least and reasoned with most who are the more moral human beings[56] —and more often than not, that means girls. Conversely, boys, the more-punished sex, turn out to be the more violent, corruptable adults.[57]

How logical for sex differentiated discipline to bear this result. Boys, who are rewarded most for achievement and punished most for failure, grow up to sacrifice morality for the "success" they've been bullied to seek. Of course, they will be less moral if their actions are motivated by fear of detection and punishment. And of course, girls will be more moral if they have been taught, not terrified, into good behavior.

When parents discipline with the teaching approach (rather than power assertion or withdrawal of love), they usually give children one of two kinds of reasons to regulate their behavior:

1. *The person-oriented reason*—"Don't climb that tree; I'm worried that the branches are too weak to support you."

2. *The position-oriented reason*—"Don't climb that tree; nice girls don't do that sort of thing."

Research indicates that parents are "more person-oriented in regulating their same-sex children and more position-oriented with their opposite-sex children."[58]

The position-oriented appeal, which relies on "rules" keyed to one's position or status in society (*i.e.,* one's sex), teaches children rote, stereotyped do's and don'ts that are arbitrary, limiting, and irrational. Typically, parents use "position," or sex role pressure, to mold their sons.

In contrast, the person-oriented appeal, used more often with daughters, tunes children in to the needs, intent, feelings, or well-being of themselves or other people. It imparts useful information and helps children sort through standards that can be applied to future situations.

In sum, the teaching style of discipline is most effective and the person-oriented explanation is most beneficial and educational. The teaching-reasoning approach is the one we use to persuade our friends of our point of view. Why not use it with our children? Girls *and* boys.

IS THERE A FOOLPROOF ROUTE
TO GOOD CHARACTER?

Apply every principle even-steven to girls and boys across the board and up and down the line—is that the answer? Not necessarily. There is no virtue in consistency, even democratic consistency, if it blinds you to your child's individuality.

Remember: Nonsexist childrearing values the person behind the gender, but it does not *ignore* gender. In this context we must deal honestly with some curious research findings: The fact that the *same* parental treatment seems to have *different* effects on boys and girls in some areas. Not only that, but the same treatment can have different effects on girls and boys depending on whether it comes from the mother or father.

As an example, what parenting attitude would you imagine might most effectively motivate children to perform well in school and feel good about themselves as a result?

Dr. Roger Loeb found that girls do best when their fathers make rewards contingent on performance. However, highly directive or demanding fathers are *not* conducive to boys' best efforts. Boys' self-esteem has been found to flourish when their *mothers* are demanding. Adds Loeb,

> It is interesting to note that the form of directive behavior found with low self-esteem is what we expect from traditional sex-role stereotypes; *i.e.* fathers use physical modes, mothers use verbal ones.[59]

The point is complex but crucial. Before you can judge the effect of your actions in a given situation, you should consider which of the four possible parent-child pairs is involved —mother-daughter, mother-son, father-daughter, or father-son —and then add the mediating factor of the sex stereotype that usually operates in that situation. *If both the personnel and the behavioral goal are in line with the sex stereotype, the outcome is likely to be negative for the child. If both the cast of characters and the behavioral goal are counter-stereotype, the result will probably be positive.*

To continue with the example of Loeb's study, low self-esteem (the negative outcome) results from either of two stereotypical scenarios: a tough, directive father pushing a boy to excel, or a talky, manipulative mother imposing her will on a girl. On the other hand, the *counter-stereotype* scenario with a different mix of players has a highly positive effect: gentle verbal fathers give their children a real boost when they do not make big demands on their sons, and when they *do* reward their daughters for performance, because the culture does just the opposite.

What is true for self-esteem is also true for children's achievement orientation. Heavy doses of motherly affection seem to foster superior intelligence in boys,[60] but not in girls.[61]

Again, the same parental behavior has a different effect on each sex because it resonates against the cultural stereotype. The boy, who, according to the American ideal, is supposed to be toughened up with coldness and emotional withdrawal, actually puts out more when he is demonstratively well-loved.[62] The girl, who is usually appreciated for sweet passivity, not for what she *does,* actually performs best when she is subject to criticism, cognitive encouragement, and objective standards of excellence, instead of being smothered by love and misguided by unconditional acceptance.[63] (Too much affection and praise seems to "oversocialize" a child; that is, it creates a need to please, which induces conformity and makes a girl take the safe road, rather than take the risk to explore and innovate.[64])

Like warmth and discipline, parents' permissiveness also has different effects depending on a child's sex. It seems to have a salutory effect on girls because it reverses the culture's restrictiveness and gives girls a bracing dose of autonomy, whereas extra permissiveness has a negligible effect on boys, who already enjoy greater freedom in the world at large.[65]

Permissiveness is one of the childrearing styles that foster what psychologists call "masculinity"—which only means assertiveness, adventurousness, high aspirations, and a sense of personal effectiveness. Take away the loaded word "masculinity" and ask yourself whether you want those four character traits for your children of both sexes. I know I do.

GETTING-ALONG GUIDELINES

Parents can only do so much, in the face of so many other cultural forces, to assure that gender is not an impediment or a burden to their children. But whatever we accomplish to build character in the family setting—whether the lesson is how to share, how to argue, how to express feelings, or how to live by a moral value system—will be enhanced by these nonsexist guidelines for family life:

• Remember the four coexistent variables that determine whether any situation is growth-producing or not:

1. the behavior in question
2. the sex of the child involved in that behavior
3. the sex role stereotype associated with that behavior
4. the sex of the parent reacting to the child

Think about behavior such as fighting or crying, think about a girl or boy, think about the stereotype that pops into mind when I say fighting or crying, and then think about the effect of the mother or father reacting to a son or daughter who is fighting or crying. Obviously, different mixtures yield different results. You should consider all four components when you encounter a difficult childrearing decision. The variables may make this a confusing exercise at times—but nobody ever said a parent's job was easy.

• Try to enforce rules and grant privileges on a gender-neutral basis, but do not let this blind you to problems that are gender-*related.* Suppose your daughter has been asked to play left field tonight for a neighborhood baseball team, but tonight is her night to do the laundry. If your son faced this conflict, you might expect him to refuse the invitation and fulfill his family obligation, because you know that he plays baseball all the time and is sought after by every team in town. But your daughter has a different history: she has been practicing with fierce determination and praying one of the teams would accept her as they have accepted very few girls. If she refused tonight's offer, it might be her last chance to play. As an aware and sensitive parent, you bend the rules for this gender-specific situation, and you suggest that your daughter trade laundry nights with your son.

• Do not fall into the good cop/bad cop routine. Few things are more destructive of family relations than the relegation of one parent to the role of disciplinarian and the other to mediator, informer, or co-conspirator. The harping, overcritical mother and the stern patriarch with hairbrush raised and purse strings pinched are one-sided characters who maintain order at the cost of their children's love. Divorced parents should beware of acting the indulgent, permissive pal to make an ex-spouse seem cruel by comparison,[66] or of abdicating disciplinary responsibility to the other parent,[67] or of allowing children to play off one parent against another or stepparent against "real" parent.[68] Two-parent units should avoid the "Wait until your father gets home" trap, or the mother-scolds-daughter, father-scolds-son habit. Let your children know that the family's acceptable standard of behavior will be upheld for girls and boys by mother, father, and stepparents alike—and make sure all the adults know what that standard is.

• When parents disagree about some aspect of childrearing that one parent considers sexist or sex role coercive, treat the dispute as you would any intra-marital disagreement: compromise, negotiate, think of the best interests of the child. Try to spare children from adult hangups if you can. I know one man who thought his five-year-old son had too many girl playmates, particularly that he spent too much time with two little girls who lived nearby. The father got upset enough to threaten prohibiting the boy from playing with the girls. Fortunately, the mother persuaded him that would be a very foolish and confusing response to the situation. It might make the boy suspicious or afraid of girls in general, and it would certainly create hostility in the neighborhood. "If you insist on judging Larry's friends by a sex count, that's your problem," the wife said. "He plays with the children who live close by and they happen to be girls. If you want him to play with boys, you should enroll him in the after-Kindergarten group, which is sex-integrated, or you'll have to transport Larry to visit boys from school who live out of our area." The father took on that responsibility, and rather than banish Larry's female friends from his life, several male friends were added.

• The metaphor that people relate to best can tell a great deal about the kind of parents they are: Do you see yourself as a game warden and your child as a creature to be tamed? That is often the metaphor expressed by parents of boys. Or do you see yourself as a sculptor and your child as the clay to be molded—the typical metaphor for girls? Instead of these two images, try to think of your children as plants to be nurtured and of yourself as the farmer cultivating their growth, providing the best possible growing conditions but not trying to make a vine into a tree—or a child into something she or he is not.

• The final guideline is deceptively simple: put yourself in your child's place. Imagine how you would feel. Do not allow the fact that your child may be the other sex to interfere with your imaginings. Remember all the times *your* parents reacted irrationally, put barriers in your path, or made you obey just because you were a girl, or a boy. Make sure that you are not raising your child to be "the ideal boy" or "the ideal girl" that your parents wanted.

IV
Sex and Sex Roles

14

Nonsexist Sexuality

Children, even infants, are sexual in their fashion.[1] Not only do they respond pleasurably to warm baths and baby oil, but—

> One of the earliest things a boy baby does after the first cry is to have an erection; the girl baby's vagina lubricates within 24 hours of birth. . . . Masturbation and almost unmistakable signs of orgasm have been identified by observers for boy and girl babies under one year. Many men and some women testify that their first remembered masturbation to orgasm was at four or five years of age.[2]

And recent research shows that the clitoris is physiologically analogous to the penis and the female sex drive and orgasm are as strong as the male's, if not more so.[3] Despite these and other similarities, "the lessons taught each sex regarding sexuality and love are opposite and contradictory."[4]

To countermand sexist sex education, your child needs:

1. permission to feel sexual pleasure;
2. a positive attitude toward the body—her or his own and others';
3. the right to sexual knowledge without sex role distortion;
4. protection from sexual abuse.

PERMISSION TO
FEEL SEXUAL PLEASURE

About 40 percent of Americans still believe masturbation is immoral and harmful,[5] even though it is openly discussed in the media, endorsed by diverse experts,[6] and known to be an "all but

247

universal habit."[7] Nevertheless, most of us were raised to feel guilty about it. Our parents' anger and disgust, or their less-than-casual attempts to "distract" us from our bodies, told us that "when you feel good, you are bad." Like it or not, many of us have inherited that negativism. Regardless of all the research and sex surveys attesting to the normal and beneficial nature of masturbation,[8] people still find it difficult to act on this enlightenment when it comes to their children—especially their daughters.

Today's parents punish girl babies more than boy babies when erotic activity is discovered,[9] and, as is clear from an important Cleveland study of sexual attitudes in the family, parents think masturbation is more "all right" for sons (ages three to eleven) than for daughters.[10]

Apparently, attitudes haven't changed much in twenty years. A typical 1950s mother scolded her daughter,

> Your eyes are to see with, your mouth is to eat with and that part of your body is to go to the toilet with.[11]

And in the 1970s, a Cleveland woman told her five-year-old

> that she would get the germs on her fingers and I would appreciate it if she would wash her hands after she was playing with herself because she could get sick from it.[12]

Parents' discomfort arises not only from their own upbringing or their reaction to unbridled sexual expression in such small "innocent" humans, but from the notion that it is their responsibility to "civilize" the child's body and teach control of its "animal" leanings. Thus, taming masturbation is lumped together with toilet-training, teaching acceptable eating habits, and other social controls.[13]

Whatever its origins, parents in general cannot conceal their discomfort from their children or overcome it by sheer force of will. It needs to be reasoned away.

Since science has no definite answers about the effects on children of their parents' responses to masturbation,[14] we must be guided by experience and common sense.

Girls who do not masturbate at all are unlikely to discover that they have a clitoris, "the small organ of erectile tissue that plays an important role in every female orgasm."[15] In most families, the clitoris is never seen and rarely even named. Not *one* parent in the Cleveland survey reported mentioning the clitoris to either daughter or son.

Boys experience their genitals differently, partly because the penis is held and observed during urination, and easily stimulated, and partly because of the "masculine" stereotype.

Only after their sons are old enough to be expected to make heterosexual connections do parents begin to object to male masturbation, because they associate it with homosexuality.[16] Until then, boys are believed to have pent-up "animal" sexual energy for which childhood masturbation is an acceptable outlet—so acceptable in fact, that many boys are comfortable masturbating in front of their friends.[17]

For the boy, then, self-stimulation is seen as a phase, a socially validated, parentally condoned rehearsal for eventual heterosexual activism. And by the time he teams up with a girl, masturbation has taught a boy that male sexuality needs no object, is its own subject, and delivers its own orgasmic pay-off. As a result, sexologists maintain, boys have

> a capacity for detached sexual activity, activity where the only sustaining motive is sexual; this may actually be the hallmark of male sexuality in our society.[18]

If "detached sexuality" is the negative side of masturbation, the positive side is "sexual self-sufficiency"—and for the libido, that's like money in the bank.[19]

Girls have no such luck. First, because the clitoris is unknown or unacknowledged by parents and peers, a girl who has found the "magic button" keeps it a secret, often thinking herself a freak of nature. She does not boast or masturbate communally because, crazy as it sounds, the female orgasm seems shamefully "unfeminine." Anything *that* autonomous must be "masculine."

Secondly, since the clitoris has no function in reproduction, and the female is so totally associated with reproduction (Girls Are Meant To Be Mothers), the very idea of a girl's being sexual when she is not yet fertile is hard to accept. (That's why premenstrual girls and post-menopausal women are considered neuter to nearly the same degree.)

Third, parents intent on training a girl for the female role imagine their young daughter poised between two historical archetypes: the lustful siren—modern version, the multi-orgasmic "libber"—whose aggressive sexuality makes men impotent; and the innocent maiden—virtuous and properly indifferent to sex. Boys as well as girls are made aware of the distinction:

> We were brought up to believe that nice girls—the goddess next door—didn't like sex, or at the very best would permit us to "use" their bodies after we got married.[20]

In some American communities in the eighties, perhaps the alternatives are slightly less polarized. Most girls, even "good girls," are expected to *have* sex (when they're older)—but they still aren't being raised to enjoy it, and certainly not all by themselves.[21]

Since traditional parents still believe chastity is a girl's only bargaining chip (college students listed it *last* among eighteen criteria wanted in a mate[22]), they discourage masturbation, to reduce her libido, to assure her chastity, to make her eligible for a good marriage, which, in turn, is necessary for "legitimate" female sexuality.

A "good girl" is supposed to be good at servicing others, not the self. A good girl is flirtatious, not carnal; sexy, not sexual; affectionate, not orgasmic. Twisting Daddy around her little finger is "feminine," but putting that little finger to erotic uses is not.

Once a daughter completes puberty, however, parental policies change. Now, promiscuity is the calamity for girls and homosexuality the stigma for boys. Therefore, parents would rather their sons fornicate than masturbate, but prefer masturbation to premarital intercourse for their daughters.[23] After all, the sexually "self-sufficient" virgin can still be a madonna.

Sabotage of girls' sexuality has been an unfortunate success. While nearly 100 percent of American boys (virgin or not) have experienced orgasm by age eighteen, only 40 percent of our girls have had the pleasure. To live two decades of one's life without ever utilizing the body's hormonal fuel and orgasmic fervor is like having healthy eyes and never opening them.

The consequences are not minor. Early sexual deprivation may cause physical damage in the sensory system and parts of the central nervous system.[24] If she has little or no masturbatory outlet, and if her sexual activity is confined to petting, the young girl is prone to vasocongestion, which has been found to cause cystic changes in the breasts, ovaries, and uterus.[25] Sexual deprivation after puberty has been correlated with adult inability to reach orgasm.[26]

> Socialized from infancy to inhibit and repress their sexuality, women can't just switch to uninhibited enjoyment as the changing culture or their husbands dictate.[27]

Dr. Wardell Pomeroy, co-author of the Kinsey reports, prescribes masturbation as a matter of health routine: *wonderful*

> Girls who have orgasm when they are young—as early as three or four—but anywhere along in preadolescence, have the easiest time having orgasm in marriage, or as an adult. It's a real learning experience.[28]

To give your children permission to feel pleasure, be matter-of-fact about masturbation; stay silent if your personal style makes that the most comfortable positive response, or be affirmative and comment, "I'll bet that feels good." Either reaction says, "It's all right. We approve."

Later you can attach the word to the act. Explain what's happening in the child's body. Talk, point, draw pictures, identify your son's erection by name, differentiate your daughter's clitoris, urethra, and vagina. (Some women illustrate anatomical discussions with their own bodies.[29] It's my feeling that, although a mother should never hide her body, mature female genitalia are too different from those of a young girl to serve as a relevant educational model.) Under age five, girls seem comfortable opening their own labia (vaginal lips) to inspect the vulva and have their questions answered. Older girls can be encouraged to examine their own genitals with the aid of a hand mirror in the privacy of their rooms, and to ask questions later. For children of all ages, make available books that show or discuss the clitoris as well as other genital parts.[30]

Many parents believe it wrong to volunteer sex information.

I find it absurd *not* to. How can we expect kids to raise these sensitive topics themselves in our repressed culture? They may not know what they should know, or they may already be too ashamed to admit what they *do* know.

They need us to initiate discussion and give guidelines; tell them where and when children can feel free to masturbate and when it will lead to embarrassment; establish that pleasure-seeking is a private but normal activity—so normal that it even has a code of appropriate locales; teach the wisdom of discretion, since "some people" are upset by masturbation and might even punish the child for it; talk about how orgasms are good for the human body and how everyone is entitled to have them.

For girls, especially, your talk can be their ticket to sexual sanity. Sex counselors were amazed when a group of thirteen-year-old girls submitted a long list of questions about sex of which the first two were "Do any girls masturbate?" and "Does masturbating harm intercourse?"[31]

Perversely, masturbation—one of the biggest subjects on kids' minds along with V.D., wet dreams, and menstruation—is among the last subjects parents discuss with their children.[32] Don't be one of those who would rather explain pregnancy and birth to a six-year-old than talk about the penis, clitoris, and orgasms that refer directly to the sexuality of the child.[33]

A POSITIVE ATTITUDE TOWARD THE BODY— HIS OR HER OWN AND OTHERS'

The second contribution you can make to children's libidos is to teach them to accept and like the human body as conscientiously as you teach them to conceal it. "Children want to know what the other sex looks like. Children want to know what bigger people look like . . . and they want to know for sure."[34]

By eighteen months of age, babies show great interest in anatomy. They inspect one another during diaper changes or in the nursery school bathroom.[35] They check out the bottoms of their dolls, pets, and stuffed animals. Before long, they are asking impertinent questions in loud voices on crowded buses. With their friends they play "doctor" or "marriage." They experiment: girls try to urinate standing up, boys squat. They pretend: boys puff out their tummies and say "I'm having a baby"; girls put a stick between their legs and sing, "I have a pee-nus."

Such "preoccupation" with male and female anatomy is natural and good. If a child was as actively inquisitive about architecture or horticulture, you would think you had a genius in the family. Why not be as positive about sexual curiosity?

Use children's "mistakes" and malaprops as conversation openers. Create opportunities for comparative anatomy lessons. Let girls and boys peek at one another, have sleep-over dates, bathe together when they are small. Arrange visits so they can watch a baby being changed or watch their friends toileting or getting undressed. "Your aim is not to keep children apart because they might become curious. Your aim is to bring them together because you know they are."[36]

Children are students, not voyeurs. Don't panic if you happen upon "show-and-tell" between a brother and sister. (Why should pornographers be able to co-opt the genitals? Looking and learning from one another need be no more obscene than listening to each other's heartbeats through a stethoscope.)

Visual familiarity in the very young years, when children are matter-of-fact about their bodies and unconcerned about privacy, might make the vulva less frightening or "funny looking" than it has been for past generations, and might establish that "what girls have" is just as substantial as "what boys have."

Keep an ear tuned for phallocentric bias. If a girl says, "He has a penis and I don't," you might answer, "Right. But you have a vulva, clitoris, and vagina, and he doesn't."

Define the female by what's there, not by what isn't. We don't say the face has eyes, a nose, and a "non-nose"; we name the mouth and all its wondrous properties. "Mostly inside," like the mouth and female genitalia, and "mostly outside," like the nose and male genitalia, should be facts, not judgments.

Girls actually learn the correct anatomical labels for the male sex organs sooner than they learn their own. Only 8 women in 100 remembered knowing the right names for female genitalia when they were children; the rest learned euphemisms or nonsense names (like "your nasty" or "down there"), or inaccurate designations, such as calling the entire genital area "the vagina."[37] (If she learns that the tiny urinary opening is "the vagina," a girl may well be appalled when someone tells her babies come out of the vagina.)

Parents' failure to acknowledge female genitals, says Dr. Harriet Lerner, is a key cause of female sexual difficulties:

> Because neither girl nor boy [is] informed that the clitoris is an important part of "what girls have," this organ may unconsciously (and even consciously) be experienced as a small and inadequate penis rather than a valid, feminine part of the growing girl's sexuality . . . an unconscious message that her parents do not want her to achieve sexual pleasure and genital fulfilment. It is as if mother and father are saying "The vulva (including the clitoris) is not important, must not be spoken of nor thought about; it does not exist."[38]

Dr. Lerner concludes that what makes girls devalue their sex and diminish their sexuality is not the "mysterious and concealed nature of the female anatomy" but the mysterious and concealed nature of our communication about it.

Family Nudity

Healthy acceptance of the body would be more likely for children if nudity were less a problem for their parents. In the Cleveland study, the majority of parents said "nudity is bad." They tell their children, "You should be careful of who sees your body," a warning fathers most often gave to daughters.[39]

Parents more readily leave boy babies naked (often admiring their "equipment") but cover up girls in the presence of strangers, as if "to instill in them from the start a so-called innate sense of modesty."[40]

That "innate" modesty is made, not born. From the time the chest of a two-year-old is covered with a bikini bra, through years of instruction to keep her legs crossed, girls learn to show enough skin and contours to keep boys interested, but not so much that they think her the "wrong" kind of girl. She learns the paradox

of female existence: her body incarnates both innocence and evil
—and a millimeter of exposed flesh can make the difference.

Good girl/bad girl. Good girls show themselves only to their
husbands, and good women teach the rules to their daughters, and
thus does "modesty" keep female sexuality in check from one
generation to the next.

The boy, on the other hand, is allowed to display his favored
male body in infancy, but not as he grows older. Admiring one's
own image is "feminine," nonproductive, unmanly. After all, Nar-
cissus was a weakling. Only in homosexual subcultures is male
nakedness overtly appreciated, and then usually in its more glorified forms. For most males, it's as if the adult penis is too prized
and too vulnerable to be exhibited—as if men fear comparison,
exposure, and judgment, even from their kids.

A friend of our daughters confessed her father has *never* been
unclothed in the presence of his children, and says she is "terrified" of the time when she will "have to" see a naked man. A
six-year-old boy who asked to look at his father to satisfy a question about the penis met the man's uneasy refusal. Looking might
"cause trouble," said the father. The boy might "get the wrong
idea."[41]

Actually, boys get the wrong idea from concealment:

> I never saw his cock, limp or hard. I wish I had. For lack of
> a real look-see, I substituted a vision in which it became a
> monstrous engine, a veritable battering ram.[42]

The fig leaf is passed from father to son. The once-proud
naked boy joins the secret fraternity of men whose oath demands
that the presence of the penis be heralded but the proportions of
the penis be shrouded in awe and mystery.

Children of both sexes are confused by parents' ambivalence.
Fathers who read *Playboy* and mothers who wear low-cut dresses
are often shy violets about their own natural, naked bodies. Well
over half of the surveyed parents said they have trouble undressing
or using the bathroom in front of a child.[43] Many admit they avoid
nudity specifically to evade their children's questions about sex.[44]

A century of Victorian, religious, and psychological prohibitions have left a mark on parents and experts alike.[45] Many fear

that parent nudity may "overstimulate" children,[46] a child's "castration anxieties" may be aroused,[47] or the Oedipal attraction to the parent might "inhibit" children's heterosexual development.[48]

> Little boys may feel small and weak in comparison with their big fathers. . . . To be repeatedly reminded by the sight of the father's naked body that they are smaller may emphasize over and over again inner feelings of inferiority and resentment despite reassurances that they will grow up to be as big as daddy.[49]

How familiar. Rather have them imagine the "battering ram" than expose the real organ. In the guise of protecting children, are we merely protecting ourselves from being seen in human scale? Are we also unwittingly perpetuating the myth of the modest maiden and the phallic god?

Despite the highly charged connotations of the sexual portions of our bodies, seeing one's father's penis and testicles need not necessarily make a little boy feel hopelessly inferior, any more than seeing Daddy's larger hands or feet makes his son feel doomed to lifelong littleness. Children understand that they grow larger with age. Boys assume their sex organs will grow along with the rest of them, unless *we* isolate the penis and make it mythic.

Dr. Alayne Yates comments, "As a culture we remain preoccupied with penis size and penis envy. When will we begin systematically to develop penis pride in our boys and feelings of clitoral worth in our girls?"[50]

If taboos against parent-child nakedness are supposed to guard against incest, sexual deviation and turmoil, why do Western societies have so much incest and sexual deviation, and so many crowded mental institutions?

Among 250 cultures studied, ours is one of the three most restrictive.[51] Millions of us have honored the taboo against family nudity and yet we are not a generation of psychosexually healthy people. It's time for another way.

Many experts[52] dispute the standard warnings about family nudity: Dr. Gloria Friedman[53] says, "If a kid is overstimulated it's because the parents are sending out sexual vibes, not because they're naked on the way to the shower. Children raised in more permissive cultures, or even in American nudist colonies where the body is natural and accepted, seem to suffer no unusual sexual problems. It isn't nudity but our *attitude* toward the body, or parents' sexual hanky-panky with their children, that creates the problems."

Dr. Robert Gould[54] blames the popular culture for making nudity prurient. "Pornography, X-rated movies and popular indoctrination that isolates breasts or buttocks makes it difficult to normalize nudity in natural family settings," he says. "But a parent who gets coy or tries to hide the body when children happen upon him or her dressing or coming from the bathroom indicates that there is something dirty or wrong about it."

Dr. Warren J. Gadpaille, himself a conservative psychoanalyst, says this about parental nudity:

> Data from other cultures [do] not support the fear of emotional damage, nor does information gathered informally from sexually well-adjusted western adults, who frequently recall the bodily freedom of their parents during their early years as a major source of their comfortable acceptance or their own physical sexuality. . . .
>
> Both common sense and authoritative reasoning lead to the conclusion that casual and natural parental nudity is not only harmless but beneficial.[55]

Common sense tells us that concealment negates body positivism and mystery makes for estrangement. If our bodies are to be lovable to one another, females and males must become physically familiar and unfrightening. This can happen most easily if parents are comfortable in their nakedness. If a mother's body is shamefully concealed during a child's observant years, he or she is left with only those exaggerated memories of her body as it appeared in an infant world, when mother was the nurturing-denying, omnipotent "center of everything the infant wants and feels drawn to, fears losing and feels threatened by."[56]

Instead, the casual occasional sight of her body year after year may help children make a more gradual transition from mother-as-manna, to mother-as-woman, to woman-as-human. By the same token, the sight of the father's body demythologizes the penis. Together and in contrast, the truth of both parents' bodies spares children upsetting fantasies and fears.

I'm suspicious of a culture that hides from children the *factual* evidence that girls and boys are different but spends so much energy embellishing the sex *role* differences.

Why not let our bodies speak for themselves instead of making pink and blue or dolls and trucks define our genders? Casual but observable family nudity gives children a physical reality-check for their own gender-identity clarification process.

Your nudity is an invitation to young children to ask questions and draw conclusions about differences and samenesses.[57] Your nudity is the older child's guarantee that puberty comes to all who wait, and that sexual maturity runs in your family.

Family nudity gives children a nonsexual, nonthreatening context within which to get used to what the other sex looks like in finished form, and what they might look like fully grown.

Nudity is not just for learning, it's for good feelings too. From the time our children crawled until about age six, they enjoyed a daily fifteen minutes before their baths when they could run around the house, play, or lounge while completely undressed. "Naked time," as we called it, was a time for joyful sensual abandon, and we were kind of sorry when it gave way to their sense of privacy (and to the demands of homework).

When that moment of modesty arrives, you'll know it by a clear signal: the sound of doors closing.[58] During the middle school years, most children begin to need privacy just as they need space in which to define the boundaries of the self.[59] They will refuse to let parents bathe them, or to be seen naked by brothers and sisters. Maybe they'll ask everyone in the family to be more circumspect about nudity. Honor their wishes. Privacy is not the same as secrecy. Privacy means you can close the door of your own bedroom; secrecy means refusing to acknowledge that parents make love or kids masturbate behind that closed door. Secrecy is founded on sexual shame, but privacy recognizes individual needs and respects them. Make sure everyone in your family knows the difference.

If you can accept healthy sexual curiosity and family nakedness, your child should be well on the way to a positive body image. But the issue of "good looks" introduces a sexist stumbling block.

Beauty and Body Pride

In our culture, "what is beautiful is good."[60] That is, attractive individuals are believed to have more good qualities than unattractive individuals. As a result of their looks, they experience better treatment from parents, teachers, and friends, which in turn helps them feel better about themselves.

Since people *expect* girls to be more attractive than boys,[61] a girl has to be even more attractive, on a scale of one to ten, in order to enjoy the same treatment that accrues to a boy who is less attractive on that same scale of appearance. In other words, to be called "cute," and treated with special adoration, a baby boy might be average looking, but a baby girl must be exceptionally attractive. Therefore, right from birth, says one researcher, "male and female infants may receive differential treatment as a function of the interaction between their sex and their perceived attractiveness."[62]

Subliminally, girls learn how important it is to be pretty but boys learn that sheer good looks are not enough, nor quite appropriate. ("Such gorgeous eyes belong on a girl.")

A boy's appearance is not for others. A girl is told "Look pretty for daddy," and by inference, "Look pretty for men." Sons are never haunted by a parent's admiration for the handsomeness of the boy around the corner, but daughters hear raves about this beauty or that, about how homely so-and-so's daughter is, or how stunning a niece looked in her party dress.

Day after day, year after year, female appearance is what wins notice and approval. It doesn't take long for a little girl to ask herself not how do I feel, but how do I look. To wonder not who do I like, but who will like me? To become so completely an object of erotic focus that her "female sexuality gets twisted into narcissism"; so relentlessly is she trained to think of her physical surface as both target and source of all sexual interest that in the sex act the adult female almost makes love to herself vicariously, through the excitement she arouses in a male.[63]

The girl's preoccupation with her face, figure, and clothing comes with other previously mentioned risks and burdens: the retreat from intellectual success, dread of aging, and obsession with body weight. Body pride and self-esteem are nearly unattainable for someone whose inner voice is always gnawing: "Will they like me? Am I too fat? Is this skirt too short? Should I curl my hair? Should I shave my legs? Am I as pretty as other girls?"[64]

Mirror, mirror on the wall . . .

Comparisons and envy poison female friendship as surely as the apple poisoned Snow White.[65] While boys compete for honor and acheivement, girls compete for boys' admiration.

Mirror, mirror on the wall . . .

Before puberty, girls seem self-accepting—"as if they had not yet turned an observing eye to their own body."[66] But between eleven and eighteen, most white, middle-class girls learn to dislike their weight, complexion, nose, ears, body hair, and breasts.[67]

When asked what they *did* like about their bodies, many girls answered that their hair was their best feature, with their eyes in second place, and hardly anything in third place. In contrast, a fourteen-year-old boy liked these things about his body: "It's alive, it's smart, it moves; I can talk, I can see, I have all the senses."[68]

Such reactions reflect the different conditioning of female and male physicality—"girls in the direction of being observed, boys in the direction of action, of the body as machine, in keeping with our cultural stereotypes."[69]

It is almost a blatant quid pro quo: "feminine" upbringing yields cosmetic beauty and sex-object polish without core body image, while "masculine" upbringing with its emphasis on athletics and activity "seemingly goes hand in hand with healthy ego development" and a realistic body image. The girls who were active in sports or who danced regularly generally felt better about their bodies than did the nonathletic girls.[70]

Long-term studies have found that people who are most satisfied with their bodies tend to have the most confidence, self-esteem, and satisfying sex lives.[71] People who feel good about themselves "are not available for exploitation."[72] Every girl might be unavailable for exploitation if the "feminine" stereotype didn't stand in the way of her self-esteem.

The "masculine" stereotype also impinges on some boys' self-images, though to a far lesser extent. Boys may want to be tall, to have a he-man physique, be muscular, and have a large penis.[73] If this he-man ideal goads your teenager, he should know that in the estimation of most females, the least important physical attributes for a male are height, muscles, and penis size.[74]

As a parent you alone cannot defeat the He-man Ideal or Beauty Contest mentality, but you can accept your child's appearance for what it is. Compliment girls and boys profusely, but keep your adjectives genderless and free of stereotype. "You look great!" or "Your hair is so marvelously healthy-looking!" or "That shirt is terrific with your coloring!" endorses the total person far better than "You look so manly in that suit," or, "That coat makes you look so dainty and feminine."

Notice a daughter for her radiant health and physical *effectiveness,* not for her physical *effect* on others. Tell her she's beautiful when no one else will—when she is concentrating intensely, or working up a sweat. Tell your son he looks wonderful when he's gently rocking the baby to sleep or when he's feeling tired and small. And in the presence of both sexes, express your admiration for women and men in public life who fall short of the body beautiful but whose dynamism or humanity eclipses the wan and sexist American ideal.

THE RIGHT TO SEXUAL KNOWLEDGE
WITHOUT SEX ROLE DISTORTION

The usual answer to "How do you make a baby?" goes something like this: "When a man and woman love each other, they get married and the Daddy puts his penis inside the Mommy's vagina and plants a seed and it grows inside the Mommy's tummy and nine months later, a baby comes out."

Sounds right, but this tale is rife with misinformation.

Regardless of how young the child, no basic sex education conversation should give the impression that the anatomical sex difference is solely for making babies. This is not just a half-truth, it's a lie. People have sex without love, marriage, or procreational intent as kids soon enough learn from news about rapes in the neighborhood, or from witnessing a friend's mother share a bedroom with a man who is not her husband.

People make few babies in a lifetime, but they make a lot of love. Let your children think of their parents as lovers. Let them know that male-female sex is primarily for fun. You can add your own morality to that, but don't misrepresent the physical truth.

And ask yourself whether, in hiding your sexual intercourse from your children (which I happen to believe wise), you may also be hiding inadvertently, gestures of affection, a stroke of a wife's or lover's cheek, or a hug that communicates the warmth of adult physical love without its clinical detail. When was the last time your children saw their parents kiss?

A few more suggestions: Don't call the uterus a "tummy," or give Daddy all the moves and let his "seed" upstage her egg. Instead of father "puts," it could be that mother "takes" the penis into her vagina. A verb can change the whole dynamic of the act.

What happens when your children ask for sexual rather than reproductive information? Do your moral standards have double standards?

Most parents say they want their children to know about erotic activity by the time they're teenagers. Yet only 12 parents in 100 have ever talked about sexual intercourse to their children, and fewer than 4 in 100 have ever discussed contraception.[75]

What have they discussed? They've "cautioned their sons about not acting like a sissy and their daughters about not acting like a tomboy, or warned their child about sex play and child molestors. On most other aspects of sexual learning . . . parents are remarkably silent."[76] Not because they're prudish, I think, but because they're confused, uncertain, and limited by their own upbringing. They want to have heart-to-heart talks but they're not sure what they believe, and what they fear.[77] They want their children to know more but not to *do* more.[78]

They believe their daughters should have sexual and emotional fulfillment, but are afraid they'll become promiscuous and unmarriageable. They want their sons to be gentle, open and emotionally expressive but are afraid the boys will become sissies or homosexuals.[79]

You can't have it both ways. You must give up sex role stereotypes if you want to help your children prepare for happy, healthy, and responsible sex lives. You can't hope your daughters will find emotional fulfillment if other parents are not raising sons who can give it. You can't tell your daughter to be good and your son to be careful.

A mismatch is fated for women and men in the future if girls continue to be programmed for romance without sex and boys for sex without emotion. (Or as one boy put it, "To me, fucking *is* feeling.") And a boy will not learn to be open and affectionate if his father isn't (70 percent of men rarely or never hug anyone[80]), or if his parents stand ready to call him a "sissy,"[81] or if affection wins absolutely no points from his friends.

Friends become the sex experts when parents offer little more than silence. Like the blind leading the blind, kids teach each other that[82]

- masturbation gives you pimples or brain damage.

- virgins can't use tampons.

- girls can't urinate when wearing a diaphragm.

- boys get "blue balls" if they get excited but don't reach orgasm.

- no one gets pregnant the first time.

- you can't get pregnant standing up.

- you can get pregnant from a toilet seat.

- you can only get pregnant if you do it during your period.

- a girl loses her virginity when she masturbates to orgasm.

- if there is penetration but no ejaculation, you're still a virgin.

Friends misrepresent sex. Parents repress sex. The culture exploits sex. How can children make sense of their bodies, especially when such sensitive issues as puberty, menstruation, and contraception are involved?

Puberty

Boys who mature early tend to become self-confident adults. Girls who develop early become self-conscious, but late-maturing girls grow up to be more active, buoyant, cheerful, sociable, and prone to leadership.[83]

The discrepancy makes sense. Physical manhood gives a boy more power, size, and sexual agency. But the arrival of physical womanhood seems bereft of bonuses. Menstruation is seen as a burden. Breasts are always too big or too small, the butt of jokes or the object of obsession. As soon as a daughter is capable of maternity, many parents limit her activities and oversee her friends and her whereabouts as never before.[84] No wonder girls are less than ecstatic about early sexual development.

By mirror-sexist reasoning, the *late*-maturing boy child suffers the agonies of hell. In a world that expects male superiority in all things, it is bad enough that girls are *normally* two years ahead in physical development during adolescence. If, on top of that, a boy's growth is slower than average, his "emasculation" is compounded.

How can parents cushion the blows of puberty's capricious timetable without patronizing sex stereotypes?

1. Compliment your children's appearance no matter how awkward or clumsy they appear. Reassure them that almost *everything* is temporary or transitional. Tell stories of your own adolescent experience.

2. Avoid comparisons with other children. Renounce sarcasm or teasing about puberty-related phenomena. Shaving twenty-two whiskers, losing his voice mid-sentence, or waking up to wet bedsheets are serious matters to an adolescent boy. Advise and explain without laughter.

3. Characterize puberty as "maturity," "a consolidation of your mental, emotional, and physical powers." Do not present it to your daughter as "Now your body can make a baby." Puberty should enhance your children's feelings about themselves in the present. Why make it into a utilitarian event with relevance only to a girl's future?

4. Find a sensitive (preferably female) gynecologist to answer your daughter's puberty-related questions in the privacy of the doctor's office. I gathered a group of four girls—Abigail and Robin and their best friends—for a two-hour session with Dr. Marcia Storch, and the girls reported how relieved they were to learn how *normal* they were, no matter what "horrible" truth they confessed about their bodies or their sexual fantasies and fears.

5. Don't penalize your daughter for becoming a woman. That means do not withdraw your affection and trust. A father should neither avert his eyes nor fixate on a girl's physical development; only admiration and casual acknowledgement are appropriate. A mother should not sigh that a woman's body is a "sacred vessel," *or* "a vale of tears." Don't make puberty the occasion to object to a daughter's clothes or to restrict her social life. Don't assume every boy is after her body or she may wonder if that is all she has going for her.

Menstruation

Although girls may begin menstruating as early as age nine, by twelve (the average age of menarche[85]), about half still have learned nothing about this major physiological event.[86] Even among mothers who remembered how *they* had been frightened by menstruation, few had explained it to their twelve-year-old daughters.[87] One young woman remembers:

> My mother said to me, "Well, dear, you're going to be going through a change." That was the end of the subject. I had no idea what kind of change . . . whether I was going to turn into a frog or what.

When menstruation is discussed, it is often in derogatory terms (getting sick, unwell, the curse, on the rag)[88]. It is packaged with myths (menstruating women attract reptiles, kill wildlife, give babies cramps, bring bad luck in coal mines),[89] prohibitions against baths, shampoos, swimming, sports, and sexual intercourse,[90] and other frightening or debilitating misinformation (blood loss is weakening; "every" woman gets premenstrual tension, and so on).[91]

The impressions given to both boys and girls about menstruation are predictably in keeping with "feminine" sex role socialization:[92] girls are physically vulnerable, emotionally moody, and mentally irrational; pain is the lot of a woman; hormones will triumph.

"What you expect is often what you get," notes one scientist.[93] Women who are told they are premenstrual have been found to suffer from more severe distress than those who are made to believe they are between periods. What's more, female socialization propaganda has a measurable somatic effect: girls who test highest on conventional "femininity" scales also report the most menstrual discomfort![94] Therefore,

1. Don't give your daughter any ideas. Although many adolescents experience menstrual cramps, many do not. Don't condition your daughter for fragility or suffering. Cope with *her* symptoms, not your expectations.

2. Make it clear that physical and sexual activity, baths, and sports are not only possible but beneficial. Let her know that "an American Olympic swimmer recently broke a world record and won three gold medals during the height of her period,"[95] and that life can go on as usual for her, too.

3. Explain *everything* when your daughter is eight years old, and review the whole subject at least once a year thereafter if she doesn't ask about it again. When her breasts and pubic hair seem to be developing is the time to prepare her for the logistics of getting her period in public, and for the use of sanitary protection. She should know that virgins *can* wear tampons; and for the sake of her mobility and comfort, persuade her to give them a try. Help her experiment with the various tampon styles and offer to assist in learning how to insert them. (It can literally change a girl's life to wear her protection on the inside, where it is forgettable.)

4. Fathers can describe menstruation as well as mothers, although mothers add that "I know how it feels" element. But fathers must show an accepting attitude toward menstruation—

not gag at the sight of a bloody panty, and not insist that the Tampax or Kotex be kept out of his view.

5. Menstruation should be explained to boys, too. The more time they have to get used to the facts of female physiology, the more likely they will develop the same casual, accepting attitude exhibited (one hopes) by their father.

I am always glad when one of my children notices me taking a tampon with me in my briefcase, or hears Bert remind me to pack the Tampax in my tennis bag. The unspoken message to the children is, Mommy has her period but it's no big deal—it's nothing to be afraid of, it's nothing to hide.

Of course, menstruation *is* a big deal. It marks sexual maturity and reproductive fertility, awesome realities in a girl's life. Many women experience premenstrual syndrome (tension, headaches, pain, irritability), and cramps (dysmenorrhea), usually on the first day of their periods.[96] One gynecologist estimates that just under 50 percent of his patients report symptoms of real discomfort[97] which matches the national data.[98] No one should suggest that these are imaginary or psychosomatic reactions. They are hormonally determined and the more painful ones may require special adaptation or medication. But the start of three or four decades of ovulation needn't be the end of freedom. If your daughter feels menstruation is a sickness or a mystery, dirty or weakening, it can adversely affect her body image, her sexuality, dietary habits, even her adult attitudes toward medication, contraception, and family planning.[99]

> The notion of menstruation as a mystery is a profoundly androcentric [male-centered] notion—one might just as well speak about the mystery of the dry male body if one took the female body as the norm rather than the deviation.[100]

One psychologist insists "it is an extraordinary jump for women to accept the idea that bleeding means health."[101] I have not found that to be true. "Health" is an ever-changing concept. It's also remarkably responsive to cultural values. (A century ago, the "healthy" people were fat, not slim.) Bleeding *can* mean health if female body equals human norm. Bleeding can mean health if our daughters understand the physiology of menstruation, if they control it rather than let it incapacitate them, and if we help them celebrate it both as proof of nonpregnancy now and potential for childbearing later.

Can anything be healthier than that?

Sexual Activity and Contraception

"That male adolescents may 'sow their wild oats' premaritally while females save themselves for marriage is one of the most durable aspects of sexual polarization."[102] That double standard is also laced with hypocrisy: whether or not mothers themselves had sex before marriage, they still disapprove of it for girls up to three times more often than for boys.[103] One mother was barely joking when she quipped that her son could have sex at eighteen, but her daughter should "wait until she's forty-three!"[104]

Another mother defended having never told her twelve-year-old daughter about intercourse and birth control because "she's not into that yet."[105] Of course, when she is "into" sex, it may be too late for a parent to help her out of it without scars:

> *Fact:* In a representative group of 100 teenagers, 3 girls and 10 boys will have intercourse for the first time before age twelve. Nearly 40 percent of all thirteen- to fifteen-year-olds are no longer virgins.[106]

> *Fact:* The younger a girl is at first intercourse, the more likely she is to become pregnant.[107]

> *Fact:* At least 1 teenager in 10 (about a million girls) will become pregnant this year (30,000 of them will be under fifteen years old) and half of those pregnancies will occur during the girls' first six months of sexual activity,[108] activity that parents often believe does not exist.

> *Fact:* Eight out of 10 unwanted pregnancies happen to girls who use no contraception.[109]

> *Fact:* Up to 95 percent of all parents have *never* discussed contraception with their children prior to puberty.[110]

Let me be blunt. Parents who fail to provide contraceptive information to both girls and boys are guilty of child abuse. Having a child while still a child abuses a girl's body and ruins her life. "Teenage pregnancy is not only a health risk for the mother and child, it is a major cause of high school drop-outs, unemployment and poverty."[111]

Why are Americans willing to tolerate an epidemic of teen pregnancies rather than provide their children with simple contraceptive information? Why are parents unable to face the truth of a daughter's sexual activism even at the risk of destroying her future?

Because virginity, chastity as an institution, helps men assure their paternity, which is basic to the patriarchal transfer of power. But making contraception openly available to girls removes the threat of pregnancy that policed female chastity and instead accepts nonreproductive sex as a female prerogative. And that clear a crack in the links between virginity and "femininity," and between female sexuality and maternity, effectively destroys the sex role imperative: Girls Are Meant to Be Mothers.

Rather than break the back of the patriarchy, we allow one million girl children to become mothers each and every year.[112]

Suppose you agree with Dr. Calderone that "Babies should not be used as a 'punishment' for sexually active girls."[113] But you also disapprove of sex before marriage, or sex without love, or sex before a certain age, or whatever. What then? Then, I think, there are several points for you to ponder:

• If most young people subscribe to a single standard and disregard female virginity, why do you care about it? Might you be using your daughter's chastity as a mark of your own virtue?

• Have you taught your children technical virginity, but neglected sexual ethics? A respected sex educator writes: "Instead of worrying about the distinctions between necking, petting, heavy petting . . . and real intercourse, young people would be better advised to examine their motives. After all, a boy can do wrong even by simply kissing a girl, if he knows that she is not ready for it and that it upsets her. In other words, it is not the type of sexual activity that counts, but the intentions behind it."[114]

• Are you unconsciously programming your daughter for the kind of "feminine" passivity that leads to just the "promiscuous" behavior you fear most? Raise a girl on romantic notions of being "swept off her feet," and she may be prey to any sweet-talking seducer. If premeditated sex (using contraception) strikes her as incompatible with the female role, but being "taken" excuses her sexual activity, she's the perfect potential "victim" of early pregnancy. It is the "good girl" who doesn't ask her parents for birth control advice, and who believes only boys should be "ready for sex."

• Do you know that sexual sophistication reduces rather than increases teen sex activity? "Young people who talk with their parents about sex and contraception tend to delay sexual intercourse and to use contraception. When they do enter into relationships, they tend to be more mature and less exploitive."[115]

• Have you objectified your daughter's body? Warnings such as "No boy will buy the cow if he can get the milk free" imply that a girl is a piece of property with finite and depleting value. Parents cannot constantly monitor boys' access to a daughter's body. We can only make her strong enough to define her own boundaries and self-respecting enough to think herself more valuable than a cow.

Eventually you will find the truth unavoidable—as well as nonsexist: The sex drive is comparable for both sexes and their levels of heterosexual activity (kissing, necking, petting) show "remarkable similarity."[116] Although girls, as well as boys, are "doing it," they needn't do themselves damage to pay for their sexuality. They can know about sex—and be prepared for sex— and still decide not to *have* sex.

Certainly, they can refuse to be premature mothers. Girls raised to play a meaningful role in life do not "turn to a baby as a source of identity . . . instant adulthood, an instant role and instant femininity."[117] Girls raised to take responsibility for themselves are not likely to be victimized; they want more from a boy —and from a relationship—than the assurance that they satisfy.

The best sex education you can offer your children, therefore, is an anti–sex-role education. For a girl, dignity, self-respect, and unabashed authority over her own well-informed, authentic sexual self; for your daughter, good-bye to Sleeping Beauty, or "I only did it because I was drunk," or "What kind of girl will he think I am?"

For a boy, good-bye to Mr. Macho, Don Juan, "Get any lately?" For your son, who is growing up alongside girls who will expect equality in the bedroom as well as in the boardroom, the new sexual ideology affirms that

• "scoring" is stealing unless a girl is as willing, as risk-free, and as sexually satisfied as he is.

• "knocking up" a girl is a sign of stupidity, not virility.

• "It isn't any fun that way" is no excuse for not wearing a condom.

• if the responsibility for birth control is not shared, the responsibility for the pregnancy will be.

• "losing respect" for a girl after sex signifies contempt for female sexuality, not high-toned morality.[118]

• it is not a girl's "job" to restrain a boy's sex drive, or her "fault" if he can't restrain himself.

• his sexuality is neither so wild it cannot be controlled, nor so vulnerable it can be ruined by rejection.

• he doesn't always have to "know what to do" or "take charge" or "perform"; he is "masculine" when he follows, as well as when he leads.

If you can communicate these ideas to your son throughout his childhood, he should be able to tell you what a fourteen-year-old boy told Mary Calderone after three days of discussion: "You sure taught me that there is more to sex than just doing it!"[119]

Finally, for parents who are still troubled by the issue of morality *vs.* the risk of pregnancy, Dr. Sol Gordon seems to offer the best summation: wanting children not to have sex while at the same time giving them birth control information "is not a double message to our young people; it means simply that we respect them enough to give them our best advice, and love them enough to help them if they choose not to listen."[120]

PROTECTION FROM SEXUAL ABUSE

After giving your child permission to feel sexual pleasure, a positive body image, and sexual knowledge without sex role distortion, the last guarantee is the hardest to make good on. Children inevitably leave the house and go out into the world. We do the best we can issuing cautions, warning children about suspicious situations, dangerous neighborhoods, not taking candy from strangers.[121] Unfortunately, however, child abuse often begins at home where those whom children love most take advantage of their weakness and dependency.

Incest, the greatest of all family secrets, has been brought out of the closet. Books, surveys, and confessional seminars[122] have begun to delineate a veritable epidemic of child molestation in the home setting. The subject is far too complex and serious to explore here; however, an understanding of sexual abuse as a by-product of misogyny and male supremacy may be illuminating for the nonsexist parent.[123]

People (usually men) sexually abuse children (usually girls) when sex becomes confused with power. As more grown women refuse to be passive and innocent, some men move down the age range to little girls who are still *powerless,* who can still be controlled and *used,* who cannot assert their will.

Frequently, when little girls complain about molestation by their brothers, uncles, neighbors, but most often by their own fathers, their reports are dismissed. This is the legacy of Freud's denial of his women patients' accounts, one after another, of having been seduced or abused by their fathers. He attributed their reports to wishful fantasy, the Electra complex of adoring daughters. To accept that all those fathers molested their little girls would have been too unspeakable, too damning of *Man*—and by inference of Freud's own father.[124]

On the heels of Freud, generations of parents and doctors have discounted children's accusations, and blamed little girls for "wanting it." Like blaming the rape victim, like firing the woman member of the couple who has sex on the job, like punishing the teenage girl with pregnancy for the intercourse a boy engineered, it is always the female who pays twice—once with the original abuse, and again for "allowing" the loss of her own innocence.

I do not know how to prevent sexual molestation of children in the home or on the streets. But I believe deeply and surely that such abuse is intrinsic to gender inequality. It's a short step from the infantalized, "baby doll" woman, to the female child. There isn't a clear line between patriarchal rule and following father into his bed when so ordered.

No one should be surprised when the women-and-children dyad merges and blurs in sex as it does in the family, the economy, and the minds of some men. Sexual abuse of children will not disappear until power-inequity pornography disappears, until idealization of the big man–little girl disappears, until rape is not a hair's breadth removed from the ideal of sexual seduction, and until men cease to believe themselves emasculated by taking no for an answer from a woman, or a child.[125]

A parent's only hope is that the autonomous, self-respecting child will not tolerate victimization and will not accept degradation as her (or his) sexual obligation. We cannot truly guarantee our children protection from sexual abuse, but perhaps we can raise sons who disavow violence as a badge of manhood, and daughters whose bodies belong to themselves and not to any man.

We've given our children life; now we must give them non-sexist sexuality to enjoy it.

15

Homosexuality, Hysteria, and Children: How Not to Be a Homophobic Parent

Let's be honest. I may have persuaded you that sex stereotypes are bad, role-free family life is good, and nonsexist sexuality makes sense. But for many parents, apprehension about nonsexist child-rearing boils down to one question: *Will it make my child a homosexual?*

In the words of Dr. Robert Gould, director of adolescent psychiatry at New York's Bellevue Medical Center, "Allowing boys to do so-called feminine things, or girls to be what is considered masculine, has absolutely nothing to do with homosexual development."[1] So, the answer is emphatically *no,* but it is within the question that we find three of the most erroneous assumptions of our culture, assumptions that can poison every parent-child relationship:

1. that sex roles determine sexuality;

2. that specific ingredients *make* a child homosexual; and

3. that homosexuality is one of the worst things that can happen to anyone

After dispensing with these assumptions I will give you ten guidelines to eliminate such worries altogether.

ASSUMPTION 1:
SEX ROLES DETERMINE SEXUALITY

It was inevitable that the cult of sex differences would lead us to the familiar romantic bromide—*opposites attract.* Most people truly believe that the more "masculine" you are, the more you'll love and be loved by females, and the more "feminine" you are, the more you'll love and be loved by males.

If you believe this quid pro quo, you will systematically raise your daughters and sons differently so that they become magnets for their "opposites," and you will fear that your children's resistance to stereotyped sex roles might distort their behavior in bed as adults.

Clever, this patriarchy. In return for conformity, it promises a "normal" sex life for our children. But it can't deliver on that promise, because all available evidence proves that *sex role does not determine sexual orientation.*

During the last decade thousands of homosexual men and women have "come out" from behind their "straight" disguises, and we discovered that except for choice of sex partner, they look and act so much the same as everyone else "that they may not be identified as homosexuals even by experts."[2] Most female and male homosexuals have tried heterosexual intercourse; many have been married and have children;[3] and sometimes they are remarkable only for being so *unlike* the "gay" stereotype.

Take a quintessential "man's man," David Kopay—six-foot-one, 205 pounds, ten-year veteran of pro football. "I was the typical jock," writes Kopay in his "coming out" autobiography. "I was tough. I was successful. And all the time I knew I preferred sex with men."[4]

Interviews with more than sixty players, coaches, sports officials, and psychologists convinced a Washington *Star* reporter that Kopay is far from unique: "The percentage of male homosexuals in sports is probably close to the same . . . as in society at large. Only about 10 percent of the entire male homosexual population fits the stereotype of limp-wristed, effeminate 'queens.' "[5]

Just as the male athlete is assumed heterosexual because his looks and interests conform to stereotype, the female athlete is often thought to be a lesbian because she does *not* conform: She doesn't cheer on the boys, she's in the action herself. The Washington *Star* found, "Almost every female sports star in U.S. history, with the exception of an occasional outstanding beauty, has been rumored to be homosexual at some point in her career."[6] To neutralize their perceived loss of "femininity," Chris Evert's romances, Evonne Goolagong's baby, and Laura Baugh's good looks have been highly promoted.

And yet, great beauties, "feminine-looking" women, married

women, and mothers of many children have, for centuries, had lesbian love affairs with one another, disproving the opposites-attract theory with a vengeance.[7] "The preponderance of homosexual females are not 'bulldykes,' " says Dr. Alan Bell of the Kinsey Institute for Sex Research. "They are passive and traditional females."[8]

What does this add up to for parents?

A deduction that begins with the proof and works backwards: If adult sexual orientation is unrelated to stereotyped sex role behavior, then stereotyped sex roles cannot guarantee your child will become a heterosexual adult.

ASSUMPTION 2:
SPECIFIC INGREDIENTS MAKE
A CHILD HOMOSEXUAL

Although no one knows what causes homosexuality,[9] there is no shortage of theories on the subject:

Genetic Theory

E. O. Wilson, the sociobiology guru (see Chapter 2), breathed new life into this moribund area when he "invented" a breed of homosexual ancestors who bore no children but functioned as hunting or child care helpers. Wilson's thesis has been nicely squelched by Harvard biologist Stephen Jay Gould: "Since exclusive homosexuals do not bear children," Gould asks, "how could a homosexual gene ever be selected in a Darwinian world?"[10]

Meanwhile, other behavioral scientists pursue the idea that "genetic loading" can create a predisposition toward homosexuality,[11] a theory that will remain far-fetched until researchers can find many sets of identical twins both members of which became homosexual although reared separately.[12]

Hormone Theory

No definitive connection between testosterone level and homosexual orientation has been established because biochemical studies of the last decade have directly contradicted one another's results.[13] Even when hormonal differences are found, no one knows whether the hormones cause the homosexuality or the homosexual activities cause the hormone production.[14]

The biochemical "explorers," like the geneticists, perpetuate the idea that homosexuals are a different species with a hormonal disturbance that chemistry might "cure." So far, attempts to alter sexual orientation with doses of hormones have only succeeded in increasing the *amount* of sex drive, not changing its direction.[15]

Conditioned Response Theory

This theory holds that sexual orientation depends not on biology or "instincts" but on learning "in the context of one's experience" from the same reward and punishment process as any other acquired behavior;[16] learning from trigger mechanisms,[17] such as pictures, music, or certain memories, that set off homosexual or heterosexual responses the way the bell set Pavlov's dog salivating.

If playing doctor in a girl-boy situation is your daughter's first pleasurable sexual experience, it may chalk up a point for heterosexuality. Two girlfriends playing "you tickle me, I'll tickle you" may outrank playing doctor in intensity, leaning the girl toward homosexuality. But then, frequent and pleasurable girl-boy kissing and petting may outshine everything that happened before, adding up to learned heterosexuality. By adolescence, "most sexual preferences, whatever their nature, tend to be fairly stable."[18]

The conditioning theory, logical as far as it goes, leads us down several blind alleys. Why might one child experience a certain kind of stroking as pleasurable when a same-sex friend does it but *more* pleasurable when a friend of the other sex does it, while another child feels the reverse? Why do some children "learn" to overcome the effects of a frightening early sexual experience, while others may be hurt by it forever, and still others "learn" to merge pain with pleasure?

Doesn't cultural pressure itself "teach" children to avoid a particular sexual response, no matter what the body has learned to like? Otherwise, how do millions of adolescents move from masturbation to homosexual experimentation—often the *only* interpersonal sexual pleasure they have known—to heterosexuality, which is unknown to them outside of fantasy and books?

Perhaps the conditioned response theory can explain the man who has felt homosexual since childhood, but how does it account for the woman who, after twenty years as an orgasmic, exclusive heterosexual, had a lesbian encounter and found she didn't have to "learn" to like it?

One research psychiatrist reminds us that we don't yet understand the basic mechanism of sexual arousal in the human central nervous system, and until we do, questions about homosexual or heterosexual arousal are entirely premature.[19]

Psychoanalytic Theory

This is the most steadfast and intimidating of all the causation theories, the one that "blames" homosexuality on the family. To challenge it, we must begin at the beginning.

In 1905, Sigmund Freud declared that human beings are innately *bisexual* at birth and their early psychosexual experiences tip the scales one way or the other.[20]

In 1978, at a two-day conference on homosexuality sponsored by the University of Pennsylvania, Dr. Paul Fink, a psychiatrist and sexuality expert, launched the discussion by announcing: "Each of us has had one intense homosexual love affair (with the same-sex partner) and one intense heterosexual love affair (with the parent of the other sex). When we unlearn our erotic feelings for one of our two parents, we determine our sexual *object choice* —the kind of person who turns us on."[21]

To insure a heterosexual outcome, the child is supposed to identify with the same-sex parent, to "kill them off" so to speak, as an object of sexual interest. For example, a girl's psychodynamic is "I become like Mother therefore I no longer desire Mother; I desire Father, but I can't have him so I desire those who are like him."

If instead the girl identifies with the other-sex parent ("I become like Father"), he is killed off as object choice ("therefore

I do not desire Father"), and the girl will be a lesbian ("I desire Mother or those who are like her"). For the boy, obviously, the same psychodynamic is true in reverse.

Freudians say this homosexual refraction happens because of an "arrest" in the following schedule of sexual development:

Oral stage (birth to about 18 months). A baby starts with no distinction between its mother and itself. Because she relieves its hunger and discomfort and gives it pleasure, the mother becomes "the first and strongest love-object and the prototype of all later love relations for both sexes."[22]

Anal stage (1½ to 3 years old). Children find satisfaction in urination and defecation, learn to control elimination by toilet training, exhibit stubbornness and negativism—all signs of developing autonomy and separation from the symbiotic mother.[23]

Phallic phase (3½ to 5). The pleasure zone moves from the oral and anal areas to the genitals where the child's exploration of the penis or the clitoris brings sexual pleasure. This arouses sexual curiosity and leads to the discovery of male and female genital differences. A boy compares his proud organ to the bereft female apparatus, and fearfully concludes that he *too* could lose his penis. A girl sees her genitalia as a non-penis and feels envy, not pride. For both children, the emotional reaction is called the "castration complex."[24]

At this point, the theory goes, the child realizes the mother is a sexual entity, not just a source of power or gratification, and understands that she or he is part of a primal triangle—mother, father, self—and that the parents have a relationship that excludes the child.

Enter the famous Oedipus complex.[25] Little boy wants to get rid of Father and have Mother to himself, but Father has the power to castrate the boy for his incestuous desire, *i.e.,* make him penis-less like Mother. To avoid this horrendous fate, the boy properly destined for heterosexuality will give up the mother, identify with the father (rather than compete with him), and eventually turn his erotic interests toward other females.

Little girl blames Mother for passing on to her this inferior penis-less condition of hers, and so ceases to love Mother. She is supposed to be en route to heterosexuality when she transfers her erotic interests to Father and eventually to those like him, who possess the envied penis.

But two more giant steps are necessary within the Freudian master plan before the girl's Oedipal (or Electra) complex is resolved, and frigidity and lesbianism avoided. She must move her pleasure zone from the "infantile" phallic clitoris to the "mature" receptor vagina; and she must replace the wish for a penis with the wish for a child—ideally "a little boy who brings the longed-for penis with him."[26]

Freud is sanguine about the totally unequal demands he has posited for each sex. He writes: "The girl has then, in the course of time, to change both her erotogenic zone and her love object while the boy keeps both of them unchanged."[27]

According to this theory, female homosexuality derives mainly from too much *hostility* toward the mother for passing on her inferior genital equipment.[28] The lesbian girl identifies with Father and compensates for her hatred of the inferior mother by loving women, while rejecting "femininity" (meaning passivity, masochism, lifelong penis envy, and inferiority) for herself.[29]

Male homosexuality derives mainly from too much *attachment* to the mother; *i.e.,* a Momma's Boy can't be a woman's man.

To get right down to cases, if children do not successfully shift weights from bisexuality to the heterosexual side of the balance, psychoanalytic theory usually finds Mother's thumb is on the scales.

Poor Mom. "Her dual crime," writes Dr. Dorothy Tennov in a trenchant critique of psychoanalysis, is "her combined 'domination' and 'overprotection,' terms which in the psychoanalytic lexicon can cover the entire range of possible maternal behaviors."[30]

There are so many ways for Mother to fail, but Father, according to some psychiatrists, merely by being present in the household, "practically insures a heterosexual outcome."[31]

Unless he commits one of the few paternal sins: is too abusive or too passive, or overvalues "masculinity" and deprecates women to such an extreme that his daughter refuses to become, and his son refuses to love, a devalued woman.

Those are some of the family interactions that psychoanalysts claim establish sexual orientation long before children reach puberty, fall in love, or choose a sex partner. Psychoanalytic theory now takes us beyond the Oedipal period to the remaining stages of development:

Latency (roughly 5 to 9). Biological drive is diminished, or "sublimated," so that the child's sexual energies may be converted to intellectual curiousity and creative energies.[32]

Pre-adolescence (10 to 12). Children become preoccupied with the functions and intactness of the sex organs. Phallic fantasies and active "tomboyism" are said to represent a last fling for girls before they resign themselves to "femininity." For boys, bragging, showing off, and antagonizing girls indicate that boys are battling a recurrence of castration anxiety; they don't want to be reminded of what girls represent (the penis-less mother and the Oedipal triangle). Supposedly, at this time same-sex friendships and father-son palships flourish as a hedge against castration. ("See, Dad I like boys and I hate girls; therefore I'm not in love with Mother, so don't cut off my penis.")[33]

Adolescence (the period from puberty until "independence and social productivity".[34]) At this point, according to psychoanalytic theory, the child's object choice becomes evident in the cast of characters who play out her or his masturbation fantasies or boyfriend/girlfriend scenarios.

"For those who at puberty feel shocked or guilty when they learn what turns them on and how they respond, it's too late to do too much about it," writes John Money. "The pubertal hormones regulate the strength of the libido but not the stimulus to which libido responds."[35]

Even if what turns them on is the other sex, some homosexual experimentation is common at this stage.[36] Boys have "circle jerks," girls have crushes on one another, and most psychiatrists agree these are normal developmental events that cannot in themselves make someone homoerotic.

Psychoanalysts predict that youngsters returning from the homosexual detour, will choose, as their first serious heterosexual love object, someone who is wildly "anti-Oedipal." If a girl's father is an introverted Caucasian plumber, her boyfriend might be an extroverted Black poet—a love object who infuriates the parents but allows the child to enter full-fledged heterosexuality cleansed of the taint of Oedipal incest. ("I love a male, but he *certainly* isn't my father.") However, within ten years supposedly they will end up with a textbook copy of the Oedipal parent. That is the denouement for *The Making of a Heterosexual According to Psychoanalytic Theory.*

The Making of a Homosexual presupposes that the child enters adolescence with an unresolved Oedipal struggle, which impels her or him to continue seeking a surrogate for a lovable same-sex parent.

There you have it, the psychoanalytic decoding of homosexual causality, a drama as densely plotted and neatly solved as an ancient myth. Like any good fairy tale or legend, it makes perfect sense as long as you swallow the fantastic premise on which it is based. If you believe a goose can lay golden eggs, the rest follows plausibly. And if you believe in the Oedipus complex and penis envy, you create an "explanation" for every sex role rebellion, a modern fairy tale that can advance the politics of the sexual status quo and provide a custom-made infrastructure for patriarchy's agenda.

Boys Are Better comes off the analyst's couch as "everyone wants a penis." *Girls Were Meant to Be Mothers* becomes a prescription for female mental health. ("Pregnancy: Guaranteed to Cure Penis Envy in Nine Months!") Psychoanalytic theory faithfully serves the values and goals of institutionalized law and religion. It is easier to pronounce homosexuality "criminal" or "sinful" if it is also considered "abnormal."[37] Orthodoxy in religion requires "married sex"; law requires "legal sex"; both recognize sex for procreation, not for pure pleasure. Conveniently, this tenet is buttressed by the mind-doctors' declaration that homosexual, *i.e.,* nonprocreative, activity is "infantile" ("It is babyish not to make babies") and that childbirth is woman's psychic salvation.

Law, religion, and psychoanalytic theory have the same rules; only their styles of enforcement differ. Law and religion say, "Obey." Psychoanalysis says, "Adjust."

Although many contemporary psychologists now believe otherwise, and despite Freud's views' being unsupported by "an iota of objective evidence,"[38] it is his ideas that millions of lay people have accepted—the view that human beings grow "healthy" by the Oedipal resolution: fearing and thus respecting one parent (Dad) and disdaining the other (Mom). Since our parents stand as our first models of male and female, this primal fear and disdain tend to form a paradigm for lifelong sexual enmity, suspicion, betrayal, and rejection.

Father is supposed to represent reality and Mother is associated with infant dependency. In order to gain their independence, both girls and boys must form an alliance with Father against Mother. Politically, this translates to male supremacy ("alliance with Father") and cultural misogyny ("against Mother"). Psychologically, the message is buy it, or you might turn out "queer."

The threat of homosexuality is the fire hose forcing us into sex roles, and psychoanalysts are the riot cops holding the nozzle. (See my phallic symbols?)

The hitch is, as indicated earlier, sex role and sexual orientation have been shown to be totally unrelated—and responsible psychiatrists know it. (Various kinds of aversion therapy and behavior modification have reoriented no more than one-third of those treated, and most of those have reverted to homosexuality in time.[39]) Modern practitioners may disavow Freud but since they have not loudly and publicly revised psychoanalytic theories on homosexuality, they are in effect supporting the old lies and allowing the threat of homosexuality to continue to underwrite sex stereotypes.

What's more, their silence leaves unchallenged these fatal contradictions within the theory itself:

• A human *instinct* should be the same for everyone, everywhere; yet in societies where sex stereotypes do not exist, the supposedly instinctual Oedipal psychodrama doesn't exist either.[40]

• If the castration complex, the fear of losing the penis, is the founding element of "masculinity," how is it that boys who were born without penises believed themselves boys anyway?[41]

• How do we account for millions of children who become

heterosexual though raised by their mothers? Without a father around, how do these mothers arouse fear and respect in the boy and the requisite penis envy in the girl?

• Why do batteries of psychological tests *fail to show any significant difference* between lesbians and heterosexuals on the psychological criteria that are supposed to "cause" female homosexuality?[42]

• How can one say male homosexuals identify with Mother and take on "feminine" ways, when mothers of homosexuals are supposedly "masculine," dominant, and aggressive?[43]

• If a woman's compensation for her missing penis is a baby boy, then of course she'll overprotect her son as a hedge against a *second* castration—losing him. It's a cruel tautology to posit motherhood in these terms and, at the same time, to hold mother responsible for overprotection of the one treasure she's supposedly spent her whole life seeking.

• Could it be that girls and women envy the *privileges* that accrue to people whose distinguishing feature happens to be the penis, without envying the penis?

• Freud declared the "vaginal orgasm" the diploma of heterosexual maturity, yet William Masters and Virginia Johnson have proved the clitoris to be the physiological source of all female orgasms.[44] Why require a girl to unlearn clitoral pleasure when in every other instance Freud believed that "urges dissipate when they become satisfied"?[45] Is it because the clitoral orgasm is active, not receptive; because it doesn't require a penis and it doesn't result in procreation? Was the promotion of the "vaginal orgasm" patriarchy's way of keeping females passive, male-connected, and frequently pregnant?

We could devote pages and pages to poking holes in psychoanalytic theory, but these final points should do the trick: studies show that the classic "homosexual-inducing" family produces plenty of "straight" children; other kinds of families raise both heterosexual and homosexual siblings under the same roof; and totally "straight" traditional family constellations rear homosexual offspring.

"What are we to make of this paradox," asks Robert Gould, "if not a skeptical view of all the explanations?"[46]

And so, all speculations—genetic, hormonal, psycho-analytic, and conditioned reflex—have been found wanting, and we are left with a final indisputable fact: *no one knows what causes homosexuality.* But I want you to have no doubts about another crucial point: Of all the possible influences on the development of a child's sexual orientation, nonsexist childrearing is *not* one of them.[47] Therefore, if you allow fear of homosexuality to impede your efforts to raise fully actualized children, you've been duped.

We began this chapter with the three assumptions underlying the question "Will nonsexist childrearing make my child a homosexual?" We know now that sex roles do not determine sexuality, and that no specific formula determines a child's sexual preference. Both of these points lead directly to the third assumption, the one that most damages parent-child relations.

ASSUMPTION 3:
HOMOSEXUALITY IS ONE OF THE WORST THINGS THAT CAN HAPPEN TO ANYONE

Because penis and vagina *fit,* and the combination reproduces the species, heterosexuality must be normal, natural, and good for us, and homosexuality must be wrong and unnatural, as well as queer, perverted, sick, and bad for us. This sort of biological determinism explains why 62 percent of the American public wants homosexuality "cured," nearly half feel "homosexuality is a social corruption which can cause the downfall of a civilization,"[48] and most parents believe homosexuality is one of the worst things that can happen to anyone. Yet, the facts—when this volatile subject can be viewed factually—prove that homosexuality is neither uncommon, abnormal, nor harmful to its practitioners or anyone else.

When the "naturalness" of heterosexuality is claimed via examples in the animal kingdom, one can point to recorded observations of homosexuality among seagulls, cows, mares, sows, primates, and "most if not all mammals."[49] But more important, among humans, "there is probably no culture from which homosexuality has not been reported,"[50] and no matter what moral or legal prohibitions have been devised through the ages, none have ever eliminated homosexuality.[51] In fact, homosexuality is a greater problem in countries that forbid it than in those that don't.[52] With all the fluctuations of public morality, about 10 percent of the entire population consider themselves exclusively homosexual at any given place and time.[53]

Physically, almost all homosexuals have normal chromosomes, sex hormones, genitals, secondary sex characteristics, bodily proportions, and age of puberty.[54] Psychologically, they are quite unremarkable too.

Even Sigmund Freud (who wasn't always wrongheaded) wrote in a 1935 letter to the mother of a homosexual, "Homosexuality is assuredly no advantage but it is nothing to be ashamed of, no vice, no degradation, it cannot be classified as an illness."[55]

Nearly forty years later, the American Psychiatric Association caught up with Freud and declared that homosexuality "by itself does not necessarily constitute a psychiatric disorder."[56]

Aside from choosing to love members of their own sex, lesbians and homosexual males are, on the average, no different from heterosexuals in gender identity or self-esteem,[57] in "drinking, drug use, thoughts of or attempts at suicide, number and sex of friends, relationships with parents, satisfaction with world and many lifestyle issues."[58] One study actually found lower rates of depression among lesbians;[59] another study measured higher competence and intellectual efficiency;[60] still another found more lesbians (87 percent) than heterosexual women (18 percent) experienced orgasm "almost always";[61] and two important recent reports revealed that homosexuals seem to have more and closer friendships than do heterosexuals, more communication and consideration in lovemaking, are less preoccupied with orgasm and are far *less* likely than heterosexuals to commit child abuse or other sexual crimes. In short, many homosexuals "could well serve as models of social comportment and psychological maturity."[62]

Hence, we have this "condition" that has been around for

about five thousand years. It is not an illness, a threat, nor an affliction. It is not the worst thing that can happen to anyone— rather, it usually makes its participants happy and doesn't hurt other people, the economy, or the environment. And yet, parents feel obliged to protect their children from it.

Why?

In a word, *homophobia*—fear and intolerance of homosexuality. Despite the facts just enumerated, millions still believe homosexuality *is* the worst thing. Nearly half of all college students questioned labeled it more deviant than murder and drug addiction.[63] Others reveal their homophobia by sitting an average of 10 inches further away from an interviewer of the same sex wearing a "gay and proud" button than from an interviewer wearing no button.[64] Most said they wouldn't be able to form a close friendship with a gay person.[65]

A Gallup/Field poll found that 43 percent of adult respondents considered homosexuals tolerable "only if they don't publicly show their way of life"[66] (another way of saying "Disappear. You scare me").

A homophobic society excludes homosexuals from politics, friendships, and jobs; ridicules them, denigrates them, segregates them until they become "untouchables," pushes them into hiding, calls them freaks, and then hates them for being different—all because homosexuals remind "straight" people of what could "happen" to them.[67]

HOMOPHOBIA AND MEN

Throughout their lives, many men feel compelled to guard their precious, hard-earned "masculinity" against perceived challenges.

A few years ago, a sixteen-year-old boy was stabbed to death (knife = penis?) by a man who had "to assert his manhood after homosexual advances were made to him" by someone else entirely.[68]

When a ten-year-old couldn't do all the push-ups and chin-ups required by his gym coach, "the coach made fun of me. He said 'I hope none of you guys are like this one here. He's weak.

He's a sissy.' This went on for most of a year. I used to go home crying every day."[69]

In a society that works as hard as ours does to convince everyone that Boys Are Better, homosexual taunts, whether "sissy" or "faggot" say *non* boy; in pure form, "the most horrendous insult" one boy can scream at another is "you girl!"[70] That curse is the coming home to roost of the cult of sex differences. Indeed, sexism and homophobia go hand in hand.[71] The homophobe *needs* sharp sex role boundaries to help him avoid transgressing to the "other side."[72] His terror is that he is not different enough from the "opposite" sex, and that his "masculine" facade may not always protect him from the "femininity" within himself that he learned as a boy to hate and repress. Homophobia is, at bottom, contempt for everything female.

It may also be fear and contempt for his own sexual history. At least 1 of every 2 men (according to Kinsey's statistics on adolescent homosexuality) knows that he is capable of the very acts he despises.[73] And since homosexuality obviously lies on a continuum with male friendship, the homophobe knows that his golf pals, poker buddies, or fraternity brothers could be mistaken for gay lovers.

Also by virtue of his homophobia, a man cannot love a woman with abandon, for he might reveal his vulnerability; he cannot adore and nurture his children because being around babies is "sissy" and child care is "women's work." According to his perverse logic, making women pregnant is "masculine" but making children happy is a betrayal of manhood.

Never was the madness of homophobia more evident than when one man complained that his child wouldn't shake hands and was getting too old for father-son kissing. How old was "too old"? Three.

If it makes a father recoil from his own son's innocent love, then homophobia, not homosexuality, is the disease of our times.

"Surveys have shown," writes Robert Brannon, "that a majority of all men have been worried about being latent homosexuals at some point in their lives."[74] The flight from this homosexual taint is most desperate in those whose sense of maleness is most insecure.[75] For such men, just *being* a man is not enough. And for the sons of these men, the pressure to make the team may be the unfinished business of their fathers' "manhood."

Homophobia, the malevolent enforcer of sex role behavior, is the enemy of children because it doesn't care about children; it cares about conformity, differences, and divisions. In this society, Gregory Lehne says, "Homosexuality is not the real threat, the real threat is change in the male sex role."[76]

HOMOPHOBIA AND WOMEN

If women seem to be less threatened by homosexuality than men and less obsessed with latent homosexual impulses,[77] it's because the process of "becoming" a woman is less arduous to the female and less important to society than the process of "proving" one's manhood.[78] "Masculinity" once won is not to be lost. But a girl needn't guard against losing that which is of little value.

There are other reasons too. First, "a sexual act lacks emotional significance unless a penis is involved."[79] Second, to want to be "masculine" is more normal in a society that prefers boys. That's why a "tomboy" is kind of cute. That's why parents are less upset when a girl paints a mustache on her face or wear cowboy boots[80] than when a boy wears lipstick or high heels. Girls are forgiven for imitating the favored gender while boys are excoriated for resembling the "second sex" when their physiology entitles them to be First.

Finally, while American society considers homosexuality the major pitfall for males, heterosexuality (loss of virginity or sexual promiscuity) is the pitfall for females. (Example: if a thirty-year-old unmarried, nonstudent male has a roommate, the rumor is he's gay; if a thirty-year-old unmarried, nonstudent female *doesn't* have a roommate, the rumor is she's a whore.)

The most important thing for a man to be is "masculine," but the most important thing for a woman to be is chaste. He must be "masculine" because *Boys Are Better.* She must be chaste because *Girls Are Meant to Be Mothers,* and no man wants plundered property to mother his children. However, if the epithet "Whore" doesn't shape up a rebellious woman there is still the female equivalent to the challenge "What are you, a fag?" The words "dyke" and "lesbian," "are charged words calculated to send shivers of horror up the spines of women who want a more independent life style."[81]

Like male homosexuals, the lesbian doesn't need the other sex for physical gratification. But the lesbian's crime goes beyond sex: She doesn't need men at all. Accordingly, despite the relative unimportance of female sexuality, lesbianism is seen as a hostile act because it is an alternative to heterosexual marriage, family, and patriarchal survival.

However, since prepubescent bodies are as yet incapable of performing the reproductive role, young girls may be given a kind of breathing space in which to discharge their "tomboy" sparks. Homophobic parents rarely crack down on unconventional daughters until late adolescence or even several years past the usual marriageable age.

They might tolerate a spunky little girl because activity and adventure belong to childhood. They might tolerate an unmarried young woman because they know sex role etiquette requires that a "lady" wait to be asked, or if the "swinging singles" scene has postponed the average age of marriage in their social set. But in time, she'll be coerced into the woman's role by the insinuation that she's living "like a man."

"When *any* woman behaves as a human being," writes de Beauvoir, "she is declared to be identifying herself with the male.[82]

The woman who is called a "dyke" not because she's wearing man-style clothes but because she lives her own life, owns her own time, and earns her own keep, understands that this culture's definition of lesbian is "autonomous woman." Our fear of lesbianism for our daughters may simply be fear of female freedom and selfhood.

HOMOPHOBIA AND CHILDREN

Before children have the vaguest idea about who or what is a homosexual, they know that homosexuality is something frightening, horrid, and nasty. They become homophobic long before they understand what it is they fear.

They learn that "murderer" and "crook" are tepid blasphemies compared to "cocksucker" and "lezzie." They learn that "What are you, a sissy?" is the fastest way to coerce a boy into "masculine"—or self-destructive—exploits. Occasionally a boy hears the taunt as prophecy. If applied to him often enough, and if his self-esteem is low, he may conclude that the word accurately describes him. In psychological terms, he may "internalize" the taunt and incorporate it into "a self-concept in which inadequate masculinity is recognized by the self and advertised to others."[83] He becomes what he has been told he already is.

Let's be specific. A little boy puts on nail polish in nursery school because he fancies the little brush or the smell of the polish or the look of color at his fingertips. When he gets home, his father calls him "sissy" and his friends laugh at him. With the help of the sex-stereotype checklist that children memorize from infancy on, he determines that he just doesn't measure up. Not enough snails and puppy dogs tails. Today it's his experiment with nail polish, yesterday it was his tears, the day before, his fears that brought the cries of "sissy." The standards are too high; the path of least resistance for such a child is surrender: "I will be the nonboy you say I am."

He takes all the information he has learned about nonboys (*i.e.,* the "opposite" sex) and assumes their characteristics as his own. The result may be caricature, or "effeminacy," or simply a withdrawn little boy with a secret fantasy life. Or it may be the beginning of a commitment to the homosexuality that he learned about from those who fear it most. One wonders how many children could have been spared unhappiness if girls and boys were free to pursue their interests without sexual stigma. Let's be sensible: What is so terrible about a boy with polish on his nails?

While homophobia cannot prevent homosexuality, its power to destroy female assertiveness and male sensitivity is boundless. For children who, for whatever reason, would have been homosexual no matter what, homophobia only adds external cruelty to their internal feelings of alienation. And for those who become the taunters, the ones who mock and harrass "queers," homophobia is a clue to a disturbed sense of self.

"The worst 'fag haters' I knew in high school, college, and

in professional football were also the ones who seemed most confused about their own sexuality," writes David Kopay.[84]

A psychiatrist has found that "kids who tell the most jokes about homosexuality and who scapegoat others are the ones who are having the most trouble with homosexuality themselves."[85]

Boys who are "fag haters" are often bullies, brawlers, and young delinquents who affect the behavior of the stereotyped "he-man" because they "suffer from an almost desperate fear that they might be considered as a 'she-man.' "[86]

It's all so painful. And so unnecessary. Eliminate sex role stereotypes and you eliminate homophobia. Eliminate homophobia and you eliminate the power of words to wound and the power of a stigma to mold a person into something he or she was never meant to be. So here's my best advice on the subject:

Don't worry how to raise a heterosexual child; worry about how not to be a homophobic parent.

Since people consistently "report feeling better about themselves as their homophobic attitudes decrease,"[87] why not get rid of them completely? You'll be more relaxed with your children—and maybe "free-up" your own sexuality a notch or two.

TEN COMMANDMENTS
FOR NONHOMOPHOBIC PARENTHOOD

1. *Don't try to "prevent" homosexuality.* It won't work and it may backfire. Studies show that homosexuality cannot be reliably predicted from either childhood[88] or adolescent behavior.[89] Therefore, any misgivings you may have because of your child's taste in toys, play, friends, or hobbies, reveal more about *your* biases than about your child's sexual development.

Homophobia has spawned a number of homosexuality "preventors" nonetheless. On the endocrinology front, one who believes he can diagnose "it" during pregnancy wants to give hormones to the "suspect male fetuses."[90]

An educational advisor wants speech therapists to "properly correct an effeminate boy whose voice pitch is too high," (the patient parent might await puberty to lower the pitch) and wants gym teachers to prevent homosexuality by providing "activities for girls which are less competitive in nature, such as gymnastics or rhythmics."[91]

In a more ambitious prevention effort, Dr. Richard Green intervened in the lives of fifty boys aged 4½ to 10 who seemed "to be headed toward a homosexual adulthood."[92] By rewarding "masculine" behavior such as a strutting walk, and imposing penalties on such "feminine" behavior as "refusal to join in outdoor games," the regimen was supposed to "straighten" out these little boys.[93]

Four years after the start of his program, Dr. Green admitted that its capacity to prevent homosexuality is unclear, and that behavioral intervention may reinforce "the very societal bias which the therapist would like to change."[94]

Take the word of another psychiatrist who has had years of experience with homosexuals: resist the urge to intervene.

> There may be 670 variables in terms of how one gets to be heterosexual, or homosexual. No one can police every one of those variables and still be a good parent.[95]

A good parent with anxieties about his or her child's sexual happiness, or a homosexual youngster who feels the strain of being "different" in this culture, should feel comfortable about seeking counseling—as long as the goal is helping children to feel positive about themselves.

2. *Don't worry about homosexual "conversion."* If people could be seduced into a sexual orientation, more homosexuals would have been seduced into heterosexuality by the hoards of experts who've tried to do it.

Seduction doesn't cause homosexuality even in those rare instances when a child is the target.[96] Only 4 percent of homosexuals in one study were seduced into their first homosexual act, none by force, and in any case, all the youngsters said they "were aware of their sexual orientation . . . about four to five years before."[97]

Campaigns against homosexual teachers, for instance, are based on fear of conversion and on the mistaken idea that while heterosexual impulses are civilized, homosexual impulses are uncontrollable. In fact, heterosexual rape "is much more common than homosexual rape,"[98] and seduction of girl students by straight male teachers is more frequent than the seduction of boy students by homosexual teachers.[99]

Several studies of children raised by homosexual parents provide additional evidence that young people are not influenced by the sexuality of others;[100] if they don't imitate their parents, presumably they don't imitate their teachers either.

These letters to the *New York Times* responding to Anita Bryant's war on homosexual teachers are my idea of great rebuttals to the "seduction" and "conversion" argument:

> *I do not understand fear of children growing up to be homosexuals because they may emulate the life style of their teachers. If that were the case, I should have grown up to be a nun.*
>
> —JAMES C. CLAIR
> *November 10, 1977*

> *Two of my high school teachers in Florida were male homosexuals. One taught Latin and the other English, and both had a great effect on my life. Because of their intellectual interest in me they encouraged me to develop my writing talents. Today I make a very comfortable living by the use of the English language.*
>
> *During my years in that high school, not one faint hint or suggestion of improper conduct was made to me by either of those teachers. I was, however, seduced by a 30-year-old lady who taught, appropriately, biology.*
>
> —JOHN W. CONNOR
> *November 6, 1977*

Accept the fact that being "converted" to homosexuality is a false fear and concentrate on preventing sexual suffering—as the next eight commandments suggest.

3. *Don't make children feel they are the "wrong" sex.* Said a gifted violinist:

> Both my parents wanted me to be a boy because they thought my talent was wasted on a girl. I live with a woman whose parents also wished she was a boy. Last year, when she had to have a double mastectomy because of breast cancer, she wanted to tell her parents, "Here, this is what you wanted."

As we saw in Chapter 5, if the "wrong" sex child is born to parents with a sex preference, she or he can become an "unwanted child" and later feel like an unacceptable person.[101] In some cases, the result is "latent or overt homosexuality and some degree of psychological confusion and disturbance if parents try to make a boy out of a girl or vice versa."[102] Without sex stereotypes, there would be no "wrong" sex concept and perhaps fewer unwanted children.

4. *Don't use sex stereotypes as a vaccine against homosexuality.* Trying to mold children to match stereotypes sometimes inspires just what parents meant to avoid. The all-male military school where fathers send boys to make them into men and the convent that was supposed to turn little girls into "ladies"[103] are often the scene of active homosexual experimentation.

A boy may become so convinced of male supremacy that for sex, as for everything else, he comes to believe Boys Are Better. Or else he may resist force-fed "masculinity" by mimicking the worst elements of swish "femininity." The more rigid the prescribed role, the more irresistible rebellion may be.

"My father was an aggressive business man," a young man told me. "My older brother was a star athlete. Both of them tried to make me into *them*. In order to be myself, I guess I had to become what I am: a social worker and a homosexual."

"My mother called me 'truck driver,' " remembers a friend. "My sister was the pretty, feminine one. In high school, I purposely got pregnant to show them I was a woman too."

It is a rare child who shares her or his feelings about sex role coercion as forthrightly as Stephen Rourke did at fifteen:

> *I haven't ever wanted to be*
> *What people have always been telling me*
> *Is a man.*
> *The type of man they want me to be*
> *Has little of the qualities that I would see*
> *In a man.*
> *Yet I must conform, and be their way*
> *If I want to be considered "straight" not "gay."*
> *But still I disagree with what they say*
> *Is a man.* [104]

5. *Don't assume anyone can "just change" their sexual orientation.* It's not easy to be a young homosexual, and those who are do not seem to have any choice. In a survey of 140 lesbians, most said they "had determined their sexual orientation by their early teens, apparently in the face of great pressure not to be homosexual."[105] Although many male homosexuals say they "were born that way,"[106] Kinsey found the mean age of first homosexual contact was just over nine years old. Truman Capote said he was eight when he started "going to bed" with other boys, and there was no question of an alternative.[107]

Says one gay man, "As I got older and understood what I was, no one tried to resist it harder than I."[108] And another: "My parents always wanted an all-American boy and Christ how I wanted to be that. I always felt different . . ."[109]

At thirteen, David Kopay felt his first attraction to another boy at military school. He spent the next twenty years tortured by his homosexuality, hiding it, trying to respond to women, visiting prostitutes, marrying a beautiful woman—but nothing could change him.

Dr. Judd Marmor suggests that we think of homosexuality as "a normal difference," like left-handedness, to understand how difficult it is to change. Attempts to make "righties" out of lefties can result in severe emotional problems, stuttering, or learning disabilities. Conversions are rarely successful. The same is true for homosexuality.[110]

6. *Don't make it hard for children to love the other sex.* Television personality Phil Donahue wonders how he ever overcame sixteen years of Catholic education to become an adult male heterosexual: "We boys were taught that dates were always occasions of sin."[111]

David Kopay had to go to confession because he engaged in "heavy petting with girls at fifth grade parties," and he never did overcome the Church's anti-sex teachings. "I learned a lot about fear and guilt through the church," he writes, "and very little about compassion and love."

Kopay learned no love of females from football either. The uniform exaggerates maleness, the sport excludes girls, coaches prohibit socializing before a game, and girls are mentioned only as insults. "If you don't run fast enough or block or tackle hard enough, you're a pussy, a cunt, a sissy." The surprise is not that Kopay is a homosexual, but that any male in that environment is ever heterosexual after "so much time idealizing and worshipping the male body while denigrating and ridiculing the female."[112]

Children can also develop an aversion to the other sex if they feel heterosexual stimulation "at the same time they're taught that heterosexual activity is evil."[113] Witnessing one's parents' unhappiness or listening to the moral pronouncements of their elders can also turn children off heterosexuality.[114] Girls are warned that all boys want from them is sex. Boys learn to separate love and lust, and good and bad girls. They are given little choice but to find sexual pleasure with other males or with females "degraded enough to be insulted safely."[115]

Boys get these contradictory messages:

Before, they'd beat the hell out of your for touching a little girl but now all of a sudden . . . you're supposed to be interested in girls' bodies.[116]

Sex was dirty. Little girls could be gotten into trouble . . . it scared me off girls. I actually thought it was much less sinful to have sex with a boy.[117]

Girls got negative messages, too.

[my father] said to me that there's only one thing that every man wants. And I thought, very logically, "Well, if that's true of every man, it must be true of you, too." What a horrifying thought.[118]

My parents made a rule: no boys in the house. They were sure I'd be doing bad things with boys.[119]

Because sex segregation is common in this culture (*e.g.,* all-boys' schools or all-girl teams), and because parents sanction same-sex best friends more readily than girl-boy relationships, the homosexual child is able to be more sexually precocious than other children of the same age. Boys can go off to the treehouse or hang around in the locker room together; young lesbians can call each other, hold hands, kiss and hug, and plan sleep-over dates, whereas a heterosexual girl would die before initiating such contacts with a boy.

All these factors discourage cross-sex experimentation but facilitate homosexuals' expression of their sexual orientation and pursuit of their object choice.

Even more than religion, sex-negative parents, or sex-segregated friendships, the entire system of male supremacy makes it hard to love the other sex. If Boys Are Better, why should a male choose to love an inferior female? If a penis is so great, two penises should be even greater. In large and small ways, boys are actually conditioned against heterosexuality because society is so relentlessly *for* "masculinity."

As for girls, why would they want to love a male, a member of the sex that exploits them, degrades them, or reminds them of their lesser status? They wouldn't, contends Janis Kelly, a proponent of "Sister Love":

> ... because equality is necessary to the full growth of the ability to love, and because of the essential equalness of women, the most perfect development of the ability to love, where women are concerned, can occur only in a homosexual context.[120]

It's a wonder the two sexes ever get together. The idea of "opposite" sexes polarizes us. Segregation and the sexual double standard estrange us. Casting girls as saints and boys as satyrs hardly inspires a suitable partnership. The wise parent will call a permanent truce in "the battle of the sexes." It's a war no one ever wins.

7. *Don't underestimate the father's role.* Although single mothers are perfectly capable of raising well-adjusted children of both sexes, when the father *is* part of the family, he must be held accountable for children's development, too.

"We are unused to attributing responsibility to men for how children grow up," writes Dr. Phyllis Chesler. "We find it is easier to deny, explain away or at least 'understand' paternal child abuse, or emotional and physical abandonment."[121]

But fathers who allow their homophobia to prevent them from tender, caring relationships with their sons need help, from a therapist who believes in loving fathers, from a men's consciousness-raising group, or a peer counseling service. A truth-telling session in such a men's group helped a California businessman break out of his tough Big Daddy veneer and start reconsidering what made him a "masculinity" junkie. While sobbing, the man told the group he had flashed back over a set of mental pictures:

> his father giving him a nightly ritual back rub in bed that ended at about age ten with no explanation; a . . . sex play scene with a playmate at about age six; comforting a close Navy buddy in his arms . . . after he had been wounded . . . and sitting in the living room at home looking at his eleven-year-old son and not knowing how to touch him. His face fell into a mask of mourning as he said, "Now my dad's dead, my buddy's dead, I never even got to know that kid back home and my son and I are afraid to touch each other.
> . . .
> "Things may turn out different for my son."[122]

If you're a well-meaning father who wants things to be different for your children, now is the time to begin to be different *with* your children. Don't be the "man" you think you "should" be; be the father you wish you had had.

8. *Don't react intemperately to children's questions, interests, or confessions.* One psychiatrist who should know better became hysterical when his eight-year-old son brought home a homosexual magazine.

> I threw it in the garbage in a rage. I know I wouldn't have destroyed heterosexual pornography, even though I deplore the kind of sex it depicts. I would have used my son's interest in it as an opportunity for sex education. The sad thing is, the next time he's curious or disturbed about homosexuality he may be too scared to come to me.

Parents' overreactions to questions about homosexuality, or to children of the same sex exploring their anatomies or declaring love for one another, may imbue a heterosexual child with the suspicion that she or he is a homosexual[123]—or may signal the child that all kinds of sexual love are shameful and nasty.[124]

Since nothing good can come of parental puritanism, get rid of it. Don't let it allow you to panic and pass on to your children the worst of your own hang-ups.

Finally, should one of your children someday "come out" as a homosexual, try to remember that homosexual children aren't *only* homosexuals, they are all the rest of the things that you have helped them become. Their homosexuality may well be the one thing about them for which you are *least* responsible. Don't waste energy blaming yourself, pleading or threatening, worrying about what "people" will think, or shouting things that you can never take back. There are several books and organizations[125] that can help you understand your child's sexual choice, and make it easier for you to talk, share, and make peace with this thing that you should by now realize is far from "the worst thing that can happen to anyone."

9. *Don't confuse transsexualism with homosexuality.* With all the headlines about Renee Richards, some have lumped together these two very different "conditions." Most experts[126] agree that the homosexual accepts her or his body (and just happens to prefer that same gender as a sex partner), while the transsexual feels trapped in the "wrong" body because she or he cannot behave the way people with that body are "supposed" to behave.

Rather than transgress gender lines, transsexuals mutilate their bodies to match their sex role preference. Many psychologists consider transsexuals people who cannot handle the guilt of their homosexual object choice in a heterosexual culture.[127] They are the ultimate homophobes: they'd rather switch bodies than be "queer."

Actually, transsexuals have relatively low libidos.[128] They want different genitals not for sex but for sex role congruence:

> A lady walked a certain way, talked a certain way . . . She disliked sports, rough and tumble. . . . I'd been a rebel since childhood, keen on doing the things boys do, and no one was going to change me. Become a lady? I would not![129]

So that tough, spunky little girl grew up and became a man. For the right to move freely and be outspoken, she cut off her breasts, had her uterus and ovaries removed and nearly died in an operation to graft an artificial phallus on her body.[130]

We can sympathize with the misery that inspires such extreme measures. But it is more to the point that medical science cooperates and profits from that misery rather than challenge its cause.[131] Homophobia and patriarchal conformity demand that, "If the shoe doesn't fit, change the foot."[132]

Thus, transsexuals (and there are now tens of thousands of them) represent not proof that some men want to be women but rather "the ultimate homage to sex role power."[133]

10. *Don't let other people's homophobia hurt your children.* You can't always control what people in the outside environment do to your children; however, there are some personality types to watch out for—for example, athletic coaches with a he-man mentality. Their philosophy "is deceptively simple: A winner is a 'man' "—and, conversely, a man must be a winner.[134]

When such people are in positions of power over your children, you may not know the harm they do until it is almost too late. One eleven-year-old boy begged his parents to take him out of summer camp. His letters complained of fierce intergroup competition, tough and nagging counselors, and a "wilderness" hike that the boy swore almost killed him. The parents resisted his letters, hoping he would adjust, but finally, on parents' visiting day, they agreed to withdraw him from the camp.

When they went together to inform the camp staff, the head counselor growled, "If you leave this camp, boy, you'll always be a quitter! You'll never be a man!"

The father responded angrily, "If this camp is your idea of a turning point for manhood, I feel sorry for you."

In the car on the way home, the boy said admiringly, "Gee, Dad, thanks! Thanks for being on *my* side."

Too many parents are on the side of sex roles, not on the side of their own children. Too many care more about what friends or strangers *think* than about what children *feel.*

If you value your children above social conformity, if you use nonhomophobic judgment and insight, your ultimate test of every childhood choice or activity should be, not "Will it make my child a homosexual?" but "Will it make my child a happier, better person?"

16

My Sex Role/My Self: How "Children" Learn to Be "Girls" and "Boys"

O.K. Sex isn't sex role and sex roles don't determine sexual orientation. Then what are sex roles for? And how do children learn them? Are we our children's sex role mentors whether we like it or not? Will they do as we say or as "most people" do? In short, how do children decide what it means to be a boy or a girl?

Sex role socialization is the academic name of the process by which children identify as girls or boys and acquire what society considers appropriate behavior for their gender. Academics have various theories about how this process works, but most share the assumption that children *should* be socialized to play a role in life.

Because I challenge the role, I challenge the routes that supposedly lead there. After considering how various experts define "becoming" a girl or a boy as a healthy personality goal, I hope to persuade you that "being" a girl or a boy is enough, and that the proper goal of childhood socialization is *becoming human,* as fully, gloriously, individually human as every child can be.

Instead, the cult of sex differences, the idea of "opposite" sexes, a wide range of sex stereotypes, the "maternal instinct," the tradition of dividing love, work, power, the whole human agenda between two parents—all those bulwarks of patriarchy figure to some degree in each of the major theories of sex role socialization.

I have simplified the main features of these theories[1] and arranged them in chart form to give you a graphic sense of the gender polarization prescribed. Read through each theory horizontally. Then if you cover the Female Role column and read down the Male Role column, and cover the Male column and read the Female column vertically, you'll see that traditional sex dichotomies are not "complementary" halves; they're half-lives, period.

COMPETING THEORIES OF SEX ROLE SOCIALIZATION

I. Traditional/Religious

Children learn what females and males are supposed to be from the Bible, the Church, and the family. Parents teach through rules, discipline and example. Identification with the same-sex parent is accomplished through sex-segregated activities (mother-daughter hair styles, father-son teams), sex role apprenticeships (do it just like Daddy), and direct instruction via punishment and praise ("You look prettier in a dress").[2]

Child's View	Female Role	Male Role
I do what I am told. I am told I am female.	child care	breadwinner
I am told to act like my mother who is female like me.	housekeeping	producer
I become like my mother.	submissive	dominant
	subordinate	authoritarian
	duty to obey	duty to earn
	dependent	autonomous
	deferential	commands respect
	love-giver	disciplinarian
	sympathetic	demanding
	religious sphere	secular sphere
	behind the scenes influence	responsible for standards

II. Psychoanalytic/Identification

Children learn psychological maleness or femaleness by total identification with the same-sex parent. Mothers and fathers must exhibit gender-appropriate behavior in order for children to resolve the psychosexual struggle and identify with the right parent during the Oedipal period. Sex role socialization is a libinal process motivated by wishes and fears: for the boy, fear of castration; for the girl, fear of loss of love. Parents are the "tamers of the child's animal nature and agents of civilization."[3]

Child's View	Female Role	Male Role
I discover my male genitals.	passive	active
I discover the other kind of genitals.	nurturant	worldly
I love my mother.	masochistic	aggressive
I fear my father.	affectionate	punitive
Rather than fight my father to possess my mother (and risk castration),	caretaker of early childhood ages	emancipates child from mother-dependency
I become like my father.	gives unconditional love	gives love conditionally
	needs approval	performer
	pleases others	individualist

III. Sociological/Identification

Sex role socialization is a learning process linked "directly with the role structure of the social system." In the nuclear family, the division of labor between mother and father along the expressive/instrumental axis provides children with information about sex differences that facilitates their identification with the same-sex parent. The child identifies not with the parent as a total person but with reciprocal roles being performed. [5]

Child's View	Female Role	Male Role
I discover there are males and females.	expressive	instrumental
Females do "A" when males do "B."	solicitous	judgmental
Males act "C" if females act "D."	warmth and stability	discipline and control
I am a female, therefore I do "A" and act "D."	socio-emotional	occupational
	mediator and conciliator	executive and managerial
	responsible for relationships	link between family and the world
	manages home	externally oriented
	gains status from family	gains status from job and achievements
	communion[6]	agency
	togetherness	separateness
	interdependence	independence

IV. Cognitive-Developmental

Children are born with curiosity and an intrinsic motive for learning and competence. Using their innate cognitive skills, they categorize their own gender identity because of physical clues. Then, with increasing mastery at each stage of childhood (Piaget's stages, not Freud's), each child consciously seeks and processes information about both sexes based on physical and social reality, and thus participates in her or his socialization. Sex roles are not instinctual or cultural. The right one is chosen by the child because of the belief that like-self things are best, and because it is seen as "morally right" to conform to a role pattern. [7]

Child's View	Female Role	Male Role
I am labeled male.	smaller	bigger
I learn what males should be by what they are.	weaker	stronger
I learn that males like certain things and females like other things.	rounder	angular
I choose male things that are liked by people who are like me.	long hair	short hair
I am a male who does male things, which are the best things.	vulnerable	powerful
	child care	worker
	nicer	dangerous
	sexual charm	economic status
	attractive	adventurous
	conservative	fearless
	inside the home	outside the home
	safe	smart
	ornamental	pragmatic
	body is the negative of the male	body is the positive human form

V. Social Learning

Appropriate sex role is conditioned by modeling (observing behavior and attitudes exhibited by same-sex models), and through reinforcement (reward and punishment). Models may be parents, peers, siblings, or culture heroes. Models most influence children's behavior if the model shows "expertness, attractiveness, legitimacy, coerciveness and rewarding power."[8] Children envy and imitate those who control resources, not those who consume resources. Sex socialization does not come from inside the child's biology or brain. It comes from outside: from others observed or acting upon the child in different situations. The learning process is not necessarily conscious.[9]

Child's View

I get rewarded for doing female things.
I get punished for doing male things.
Therefore I am female.
I will continue doing female things to get more rewards.
I will imitate other females (especially the Mother-female) to be sure I get it right and win more rewards.

Female Role

raise children
keep house
passive
comforting
nurturant and serves children's needs
cautious
critical
attention-seeking

Male Role

go to work
make money
active
angry
nurturant but not involved in child care
impulsive
demanding
task-oriented

Attempting to critique these theories (which are at odds amongst themselves)[10] is like picking one's way through a minefield, but it's another way for you to defeat sex role dichotomies and internalize a commitment to equality before we discuss the influences of the outside world upon your children.

The core fallacy in theories I, II and III is the contention that "proper" sex role socialization requires every child to have two parents who maintain a sex-linked division of labor and personality. Studies of father-absent homes have proved that "requirement" unfounded.[11] In fact:

• boys know they are male (gender identity) whether or not they have fathers with whom to identify, and girls know they are female without the "masculine" contrast.

• whatever maladjustments father-absent children exhibit are not due to the loss of a male role model, but to "the train of circumstances triggered by father absence,"[12] meaning the social and economic strains of life with an overburdened, underpaid single mother.

• boys without fathers learn not only their gender identity but also the conventional "masculine" role ideal, which suggests that the outside culture can substitute for—or overshadow—the family situation. (It's the same with daughters of physician mothers who, at young ages, may insist that women can't be doctors.[13])

These citations are not mentioned to demean fathers but to put all parents into a more realistic perspective. Since the family cannot be an island in the surrounding culture, parents cannot be the sole influences on their children. And when parents are models, they must be looked at as individuals, not as a matched set or a gingerly balanced seesaw on which their child's sexual identity teeters.

All five of these theories may be dismissed, in my opinion, on the basis of their totally erroneous starting point: they all confuse gender (I am a girl) with sex role (I act "feminine")—and they assume that learning one's proper sex role is a healthy developmental goal. Beyond that, one by one, I find the theories inadequate to the issues as follows:

I. TRADITIONAL/RELIGIOUS:
THE OBSOLETE THEORY

Although still espoused by Total Women,[14] fundamentalists, Mormons, and various orthodox sects, this philosophy has been widely challenged from within modern churches, and seems to be going the way of animal sacrifice.

Among some working-class communities and ethnic groups, "man's work" and "woman's place" remain lip service ideals. Changes in the traditional family frequently lag behind social change,[15] but fewer children, longer lives, the need for two incomes, rising maternal employment,[16] the high divorce rate, and new media images of American family life have made the traditionalists' division of labor ethic an oppressive anachronism, if not a joke.

In such homes, children get discordant messages. They see women as manipulators who must act weak but be strong enough to hold a job and then come home and do all the child care and housework in order to "retain their femininity" and protect Dad's ego. They see fathers trained to link their maleness to their job, who play the strongman-provider but who are vulnerable to unemployment or a wife's earning power. These rigid sex roles teach posturing and pretense, not identity.

II. PSYCHOANALYTIC/IDENTIFICATION:
THE THEORY WITH NO PROOF

Theories of parental identification are in professional disrepute today for several reasons (some of which were touched on in our discussion of homosexuality). They fail to show cross-cultural or cross-class consistency;[17] they fail to account for "parents' shifting behaviors as models" or for different outcomes when two children model the same behavior;[18] they lack research validation;[19] and they have been clinically contradicted in these areas, among others:

• The idea that identification takes place via the Oedipal struggle sets it at age three to five, yet many recent studies find that gender identity is almost immovably in place by the child's second birthday.[20]

• The idea that fear of the castrating father motivates a boy's identification is disproven by findings that children identify with parents who combine power with warmth and affection, not those who are threatening or punitive.[21]

• The idea that a woman's identity is only complete when she has a husband and children[22] goes up in the smoke of modern feminist rage—and is contradicted by findings that marriage and children create feelings of *loss* of self.[23]

III. SOCIOLOGICAL / IDENTIFICATION: THE MYOPIC THEORY

As articulated by Talcott Parsons[24] and others, this is basically psychoanalytic theory translated into sociological terms. In one of the most interesting critiques of it, Philip Slater objects that Parsons' instrumental/expressive dichotomy (see chart) could actually *impede* the desired identification of the child with the same-sex parent (by which Slater meant the boy child).[25] Parsons' strict division of roles—for instance, that mothers are always permissive and fathers always denying— makes parental conflict inevitable, "whenever there is the slightest contradiction between the two directions of specialization."[26] Either the parents would have to avoid interacting with the child at the same time, Slater warned, or the mother might try to make up for her lack of status in society by subverting the father—gaining control of the children and teaching them "that the father is the source of all discomfort and she the source of all good."[27]

If the father is always the heavy, boys might end up identifying with the nicer mother, Slater worried. He calls for "de-differentiation of parental roles" primarily to prevent the scapegoating of the father and to enhance son-father identification.

For a deeper analysis of sex stratification systems that "assign women to domestic, or private, and men to public or politicized domains,"[28] one must look to feminist thinkers. Interpreting patriarchal culture "as a problem, rather than a given,"[29] feminists understand the expressive/instrumental or domestic/public dichotomies as polarizations that rationalize female oppression in the name of complementary roles.

Beginning with the greatest dichotomy of all, *female is to male as nature is to culture,*[30] a grand design takes shape. Since culture must subordinate nature for the sake of civilization, male must subordinate female for the sake of efficiency and the socialization of children. And if we accept male-culture and female-nature, then we can accept

> male = technology, instruments, invention
> female = birth, child care, food, waste, death

> . . . and male = achievement, advancement
> female = maintenance, cycles

> . . . and male = creator of relatively lasting objects and ideas
> female = creator of relatively perishable human lives

> . . . and male = social and political institutions
> female = biological and sexual functions

Which brings us back to Parsons' long list of sex role divisions (see chart) that scale down the grand design to fit within individual men's and women's lives.

The ultimate objective, according to some, is male control of women's sexuality: privatize a woman's life and tie her to marriage and the domestic role if you want to be sure of her dependence, fidelity, and the paternity of her children.[31]

Other analysts see sex-linked role-playing as a balm for male suffering in a wounding economic system. When women do housework and child care for love, "they allow men to represent the autonomy of the wage-dependent nuclear family unit, while women symbolically absorb the pressures that contradict that autonomy."[32] In other words, the man-works-for-money/woman-works-for-love dichotomy lets men project their sense of powerlessness onto women while men retain the illusion of having power within capitalism.

All of this ends in the same place: dichotomies divide up life to the disadvantage of female human beings. But it's not just a matter of "sex role life is unfair"; the point is that sex role life is unworkable. A survey of American families found that few parents live according to Parson's expressive/instrumental dichotomy.[33] It certainly doesn't work for the single parent who "must both 'bring home the bacon' and apply the psychological Band-aids."[34] But it also doesn't work for two-parent households the minute a mother takes on a career and ceases to orient herself strictly to home and kin.

IV. COGNITIVE-DEVELOPMENTAL:
INTRIGUING BUT TOO LITERAL

This theory differs from the others in that it sees the child as "an active and independent intellect,"[35] not a passive creature of instinct or victim of cultural forces. While this seems to impart dignity and grandeur to the child, it is actually a pessimistic view of human potential.

First, it postulates stages of cognitive development that are as preordained and irreversible as those that underpin biological determinism. Second, it sees the child as an *interpreter,* and the environment as merely the setting, not the cause, of those interpretations, a view that derogates the need for social change. (Why change a child's environment if sex stereotypes are formulated from the brain *out,* not from the world *in?*)

Third, a cognitive rationale for the superiority of the male (big = male = better) leaves little room for alteration of sex role hierarchies. One can take issue with all three items:

• The accuracy of Piaget's stages is challenged by recent findings. One small example: Piaget claims the ability to imitate doesn't develop until eight to twelve months old. Seattle researchers showed infants capable of imitating an adult pursing his lips, sticking out his tongue, and clenching his fists—when the infants were twelve to twenty-one *days* old.[36]

• The idea of child as interpreter and environment as setting-not-cause does not answer the problem of "cognitive dissonance."[37] For instance, we're told that the "masculine aggression" stereotype derives from body image (men are bigger, thus more powerful) *plus* from "differences in extra-family roles"[38] (*i.e.,* men are soldiers, firefighters, police). But what happens when children see women soldiers, firefighters, and police? Cognitive dissonance sets in when social realities contradict physical realities—and since women are becoming soldiers, firefighters, and police, it would seem that this theory falls under the weight of change.

• The idea that physical differences between the sexes will always be interpreted by the child as symbols of other differences does not necessarily mean those differences are assigned different *values.* Indeed, children see the differences. But our culture tells them what those differences mean and how to evaluate each of them.

V. SOCIAL LEARNING THEORY: CLEAR BUT NOT COMPLETE

This is the most commonsensical and optimistic of the standard theories of sex role socialization, although, like the cognitive-developmental approach, it lacks "unequivocal research support."[39] Yet, it makes a strong case for conditioning through reward and punishment, for reinforcement and shaping, imitation and modeling, environment over biology. It explains what I have described in previous chapters, how children learn from their parents' treatment and from the consequences of their actions.

It explains how a three-year-old girl who sees her mother sweeping, then drags the broom across the floor to the accompaniment of her parents' applause, will repeat that action and feel encouraged to try similar activities to gain similar praise. Conversely, if parents don't pick up on her curiosity about the toolbox, or if they scold her for trying to hammer like Daddy, she will eventually conclude that such activities are not meant for her.

But the social learning theory doesn't explain everything quite as neatly as that. A few discontinuities:

• If children supposedly get their primary sex role cues from the same-sex parent model, why has research found children to be no more similar to their same-sex parent, on most measures, than to any other same-sex stranger?[40]

• Why do girls frequently select fathers or other males with whom to identify without losing their sense of their own femaleness?[41]

• What makes some remote pop culture heroes more influential role models for some children than their own beloved on-the-scene parents?

• If the environment is so determinative, why do so many children raised in nontraditional households express highly sex-stereotyped ideals at certain times of childhood? (In our family, I have been downstairs meeting with women to plan a demonstration while my daughters have been upstairs "dressing up" and acting the parts of damsels-in-distress.)

• If the most attractive models are people with prestige, warmth, aggressiveness, competence, power, dominance, and experience—and if 6 out of 7 of those characteristics are not considered "feminine"—how would *any* girl want to identify with the "feminine" women in her life?

Everything points to one conclusion: social learning theory is structurally accurate but politically skewed by the male bias and analytical myopia of its theorists. They chart the child development routes expertly, but they cannot see the grand map of sexism. They know, from countless studies, that girls prefer the male sex role, yet they fail to see the sex role system as the problem and persist in questioning the girls' "maladjustment." Their studies tell them that girls can prefer "masculine" objects and activities without wanting to *be* boys, yet they persist in welding sex role conformity to gender identity; they insist that "femininity" and "masculinity" are each separate, mutually exclusive psychological entities and see them as the ultimate goals of child development. The few who recognize that sex roles *are* the problem cannot seem to imagine a world without sex-linked specialization—or when they do, it is a world without sex.

But there are exceptions.[42] Dr. Joseph Pleck, a leading expert on sex roles, is one of those who recognize that roles dichotomies are dysfunctional and that the happiest people are those who *outgrow* role rigidity. To help us think through a new set of goals for child development, Pleck creates a synthesis[43] of cognitive-developmental and social learning theory to explain how children in a sexist society can and do pull off the miracle of growing up free.

Pleck's "alternative paradigm" is hopeful, useful to parents, and positively accommodating toward "the change in sex roles now underway for both women and men in contemporary culture."[44]

PHASED FREEDOM

Pleck identifies three phases of sex role development:[45]

1. *Amorphous.* "The child has amorphous and unorganized sex role concepts including confusion over the child's own gender."

2. *Conformist.* "Children learn the 'rules' of sex role differentiation and are motivated to make others and themselves conform to them."

3. *Transcendent.* "Individuals transcend these sex role norms and boundaries and develop psychological androgyny in accordance with their inner needs and temperaments."

By conceptualizing these phases, Pleck has simply made sense of the research and analyzed the known results without filtering them through the sexist status quo. And *voila,* instead of characterizing sex role behavior as the *final* stage of child development, Pleck finds conformist "femininity" and "masculinity" to be an *intermediate* stage to be supplanted by a more responsive, individualized, and flexible humanism.

To support this concept, he draws the analogy between sex role phasic maturation and the phases of children's moral development, a process that has been studied in reliable detail.

Here we know that, as children mature, their moral thinking progresses from phase 1, where they try to gratify impulses but avoid punishment ("I won't do that because I'll get spanked if I do"); to phase 2, in which they try to maintain the approval of others, especially those in authority ("I won't do that because I want to be liked or accepted by people who consider that wrong");

to phase 3, where children make moral judgments based on internalized, refined moral principles ("I won't do that because I consider it wrong").

Just as we would not want our children to stall in phase 2 of their moral development, we should not want them to get stuck in phase 2, the conformist stage of sex role development.

Let's dramatize Pleck's stages by imagining several typical situations:

1. *Amorphous phase.* The preschool boy loves and nurtures his doll. ("I love my doll because it's mine, it's fun to play with, and it makes me feel good to cuddle it.")

2. *Conformist phase.* The six-year-old boy abandons his doll disdainfully and wants it thrown in the garbage. ("I hate my doll because I'm a boy and boys aren't supposed to like dolls.")

3. *Transcendent phase.* The mature teenager works in a child care center or the young father loves and nurtures his own baby. ("I care for babies because they need care; I love my baby because I am its parent and it needs love.")

The three-phase formulation helps us understand why children, even those raised in nonsexist families, go through periods of almost fascistic sex role rigidity. "No girls in the block corner!" and "Boys can't be nurses" are familiar pronouncements in the early childhood classroom. Boys with pacifist fathers brandish carrot-guns and strut like soldiers, and girls with full-time working mothers can be heard declaring "Daddies work. Mommies stay home."

This happens because after they have solidified their gender identities—sometime between eighteen months and three years old—children seek literal clues, labels, and embellishments to help clarify their new discovery ("I am a girl" or "I am a boy") and establish that there are others in the world just like them.

Pleck compares the move from phase 1 to phase 2 to the symbol-learning process by which children acquire language. There is the cognitive component of language-learning—children possess intellectual structures that can receive and process words as symbols or gender, and sex roles as "images and linkages."[46] And there are the social learning components of language-learning

—hearing and seeing words in different sentences, combinations, and contexts, or experiencing and observing females and males in various settings.

Where do parents fit in?

"Parents provide a basic part of the sex role corpus the child observes—as they do with language—but their role is not paramount," says Pleck. It is "supplemented by many other inputs. This is why children whose parents show deviant language or nontraditional sex roles still seem, in large part, to learn both 'standard English' and 'standard sex roles.' "[47]

As sex roles blur and lessen in the family and society, children will get their early clues and labels from the *real* differences between the sexes: voice, appearance, size, and feel—without value judgments and status hierarchies attached to those differences.

By describing sex role learning as an organic, evolving process of individual self-definition, one understands why young children show role rigidity and why, as noted before, sex-typed interests peak in adolescence (about age thirteen for girls and sixteen for boys).

In adolescence, the discovery of active, genital sexuality has the same seismic effect as did the discovery of gender identity. Once again, girls and boys seek rules to guide them. In this time of new interpersonal stimulation, old rules become obsolete and the peer group reigns supreme.

Adolescents display socially approved uniforms to advertise to one another that puberty has made them women and men. Long-haired, spunky girls, who wore sneakers and flannel shirts in seventh grade, turn up coy and flirtatious with stylized hairdos, strappy sandals, and tight blouses in eighth grade. The tenth- or eleventh-grade boy chooses a "masculine" style—"cool," "jock," or whatever sends out sexual signals to his counterpart girls. Thus, phase 2, a time of sex role literalism, serves the purpose of clarification and establishes group security and belonging. Once that is in place, young people can begin to explore the luxury of self-definition and transcendence of sex role rules.

If they're lucky—or if *you* are their parents and role models —teenage girls will not succumb to permanent passivity and fear of success at the end of this phase of heterosexual discovery. Teenage boys will, likewise, not turn arrogant with male size or privilege. And neither girls nor boys will let the tight little world of teenage posturing narrow their life options. Joseph Pleck writes:

> Change in sex-typed traits occurs, in fact, through the life cycle as individuals encounter the many life experiences that have sex role meaning—parenthood, same and cross-sex intimacy, experience in work, adult psychosexual changes, and aging. These later life experiences can be experiences which enrich and loosen one's conception of oneself as a man or woman, or they can be occasions of still more distress, discomfort, and feelings of inadequacy.[48]

Those occasions of distress and inadequacy can be avoided if we take sex out of nonsexual activities—meaning take sex out of the apportionment of housework and child care responsibilities, take sex out of decision-making, money-making, and bed-making functions, and out of emotional or temperamental expression.

As we leave behind the sections of the book dealing with parents' singular impact, and turn outward to the influences of the larger world, we should answer the question posed at the beginning of this chapter: How do children learn what it means to be a girl or a boy—and what do parents have to do with it? With Pleck's phasic sequence in mind, we can draw several conclusions:

• Gender is a fact; sex roles are invented and must be learned (just as the voice is a fact and language is invented and must be learned).

• Sex role learning is not a developmental goal but a developmental *transition* to a higher goal.

• Sex roles are "a symbolic system which has a concrete reality outside the individual in the same sense that language does."[49] Therefore, sex roles can be changed.

• Parents are major but not exclusive models of how females and males function in the home and society.

• The more extreme the sex-role conformity during phase 2, the longer the journey to phase 3 transcendence. Therefore, as sex roles blur and disappear in the environment, children will have less difficulty reaching a self-defined state of being that works best for them.

• At various points during phase 2, children may choose to imitate cultural stereotypes (which they absorb very early in life[50]), rather than the behavior and values you have taught them. However, having nonsexist parents as models for adult behavior and for marital and childrearing attitudes provides a marvelous foundation of human possibilities that children can call upon later "as a resource for change and growth."[51]

• Other cultural forces (TV, schools, and toys, for example) may influence sex role learning at least as much as parents. Therefore parents should concern themselves with broad social change as well as with at-home influences. (See Sections V through VII.)

Remember, one can decide to be a housecleaner after one has learned to be a housebuilder, but a housecleaner cannot become a housebuilder quite as easily. Your job as a nonsexist parent is to teach children to build and let them decide how they want to clean, decorate, or rearrange; teach them to fly and let them define where they will go; teach them transcendence is possible and let them find their own way to achieve it.

In Pleck's words, sex role conformity is "a phase that children go through which should not set the pattern for later living. Its role in the life cycle is limited. The great risk in development is not that the person may fail to reach this stage, but that [she or he] may never leave it."[52]

V

Friendship and Fun

17
Liking and Loving,
Friendship and Courtship,
Female and Male

Life is not a one-character play. It's a crowded stage and we want our children to hold their own in dialogue or din. We hope their report cards will say, "Works and plays well with others." We wish them pals and chums, confidantes to trust, companions in delight and, someday, a beloved.

All would agree that "Friendship is not a superficial luxury . . . but a necessity in childhood socialization."[1] As to what *kind* of friendship and what experiences a peer group should provide to children, agreement is more difficult.

The traditional idea is boys should be boyish together, girls should be girlish together, and all in good time, the sexes will join two-by-two, fall in love, and marry. But has it ever been so simple? Think about your own childhood friendships, the times you felt left out, your adolescent heartaches, and your present grown-up problems with love and friendship.

Is eveRRRyboddy happy? And if not, why not?

For many of the shortcomings of interpersonal relations, I blame the all-boy and all-girl play groups characteristic of childhood under sexism. This early sex segregation stunts friendship *within* each same-sex cluster because peers reinforce gender stereotypes rather than relating as individuals. It also distorts the relationship *between* the sexes by casting it as strictly sexual while teaching children to rely on members of their own sex for everything else but sex.

Childhood separation of the sexes is what makes traditional American culture "homosocial."[2] It sets the pattern for sex-split fraternity/sorority, his poker game/her coffee klatsch, his fishing trip/her shopping spree, his friendships/her friendships—the inescapable facts of homosocial preference within a culture preoccupied with its myth of heterosexual "normalcy."

Right now, "the one way in which neither sex is taught to view the other is as potential friends and peers."[3] For friendship to occur, parents must renounce the cult of sex differences that slowly but inexorably divides girls and boys and makes them strangers in the service of sex role dichotomies.

THE RISE OF SEX SEPARATISM

It does not happen by itself. Raised differently, treated differently, the two sexes develop different emotional styles and play interests. Although they may be mutually compatible in the preschool years, by four or five they have differentiated themselves across the widening abyss until each becomes "the opposite" of the other.

They have different playthings. If he likes her toys, he's a "sissy," which makes it risky to be her friend.

They have different rules. If she runs where he is allowed to run, it's too far, which makes it frustrating to be his friend.

Being with him gives her extra freedom and status; she already knows the world thinks Boys Are Better. But being with her, however he might like her, is a "downer." The inferiority of her gender-caste rubs off. Father complains if he has too many girlfriends. Mother pushes him outdoors to make his way with his male peers. Not only don't girls count as friends, they *detract.*

"Bobby's playing with the *girls!*" the boys jeer. "He likes them so much he must be one himself!"

That ultimate insult, or the threat of it, "cures" the boy of sex-blind friendships forever. Society has made him an offer he cannot refuse: *being one of the boys*—and girl-hating is part of the deal.

Although girls of nursery age also discard their male friends, boys' abandonment of the "opposite" sex is far more avid and purposeful because of the greater pressure on them for early sex role conformity.

For the male mold to set properly, boys must not be polluted by female company and influence. (Mothers and women teachers are uncorrupting because they are caretakers rather than heroes or peers.) Isolated in all-boy groups, young males can take dares, compete for The Best and The Bravest, and together march onward and upward to "masculinity," using their distance from girls as one measure of their proximity to manhood.

Egalitarian separatism would be one thing. But boys' exclusivity functions not just to reward them with peer group acceptance but to codify their differences from girls and proclaim their superiority.[4]

In their own words, "Boys are best! Girls are gross!"

From the girls' group, we hear, "Same to you, so there! Boys stink! Who needs boys!" But girls' taunts, clearly more reactive than active, have a hollow ring. Girls feel boys' growing disdain, and with increasing exposure to the culture, they too develop an improved opinion of boys and a lower opinion of their own sex.[5]

For that reason among others, until puberty, "a tomboy is as well-liked as a 'young lady'—and sometimes better."[6] Girls harbor no secret belief that they are best, or even good enough. Most tellingly, the anti-boy taunts are quickly repealed when a girl is accepted into the boys' game. And she who returns to the female fold after such a foray is treated far less harshly than would be a boy who returned to his peers from the society of girls.[7]

Thus, while there appears to be volitional sex segregation in both gender groups, on closer scrutiny, we see that girls' separatism is defensive, boys' is offensive. Furthermore, girls erode the psychic part of sex segregation sooner, orienting themselves *toward* boys long before they are *with* boys,[8] which won't be until about the tenth grade—when boys are ready to have them.[9]

For a decade or more, from before kindergarten to well into high school, girls and boys establish "separate social systems," have "only limited contact with each other," and act as though "members of the opposite sex are 'horrible' and to be avoided at all costs."[10]

Some parents welcome the separatism; they fear that girl-boy friendships "might result in pre-pubescent sexual experimentation."[11] Others think "mutual scorn" is cute, harmless, or "only natural." Nonsexist parents, on the other hand, recognize childhood sex segregation as a stepping stone to male supremacy. We see the single-sex peer group as a cloistered training ground for traditional sex roles. We worry about what our children are getting, and what they are missing, as a result of their lopsided exposure to only one-half of humanity.

GIRLFRIENDSHIP AND
BOYFRIENDSHIP AND
HOW THEY DIFFER

During those separatist years, when children spend an average of three hours a day with their peers,[12]

> Boys flock; girls seldom get together in groups above four whereas for boys a group of four is almost useless. . . . In boys' groups the emphasis is on masculine unity; in girls' cliques the purpose is to shut out other girls.[13]

That's an efficient summary, but let's be more specific. "Masculine unity" is not a superior character trait linked to the male chromosome; it is a result of male socialization. As we've noted before and will discuss in the next chapter, boys are encouraged to be outdoors where there is space for the sports and games important to "masculinity." Team sports require large numbers of players, not one or two dear friends. To amass large groups, boys must be rather open-minded and tolerant. Personality aside, a boy can play his way into a crowd if the others need what he has to offer—the running, batting, or ball-throwing skill that is, to a great extent, within his control to achieve. It is all very logical and above-board, so much so that boys are often interchangeable; someone who can do the same thing fills in for someone absent.

Large groups seem to require dominance hierarchies. In boys' groups, who leads and who follows are public, organized, and "not intensely personal issues."[14] I've seen boys unknown to one another organize a pick-up game, determine during warmups who is best at what position, and sort themselves out in just so many words.

Whether in first grade or ninth, boys seem to agree that a leader is "a real boy," someone who "takes chances," is "good at games,"[15] and has "the guts to scrap when he has to."[16] Leaders or "most popular" boys gain the power to set standards for others;

but that power is used to stratify, rarely to exclude, because for boys' activities, more is always better. Extras can wait on the bench, but not-enough can kill the whole game.

Boys who do not make any team have an alternative to isolation: the gang. The gang is family and fraternity to many boys from lower socioeconomic backgrounds, who have been raised with rigid sex role rules and scant experience with male loving kindness.

Writes John Leonard:

> My own father disappeared when I was eight not bothering to leave behind much information on how to be a friend or a father. It was necessary for me to improvise. . . . The purpose of a peer group is to substitute for imperfect fathers.[17]

The gang provides reassurance of "masculinity" and ritualized ways of rejecting "the feminine principle." It does this heavy-handedly, to say the least, with such caricature symbols of machismo as leather jackets and motorcycles, and showy acts of violence and rowdyism.[18] Gang boys are not afraid of teachers or cops. They stand together against the adult world and they do not rat on someone in trouble.[19]

For the gang, a criminal adventure substitutes for The Big Game, and "masculine unity" facilitates not team sports but team resistance to authority and "assertion of hypervirility."[20]

Boys, whatever their class, cannot just *have* friends and *be* friends. A boy must *do* something against a backdrop of his peers. As long as dominance defines "masculinity" in America, he needs a competitive arena—a league, gang war, drag race—in which to prove himself a man among men.

At any age and in any set, male camaraderie has its dark underbelly: casual violence toward life and property—communal torture of animals,[21] cruelty to younger children and to girls who tag along. I remember once playing hide-and-seek with the boys in my neighborhood. Secluded behind a wooden fence, I waited what seemed like hours for someone to find me. Finally, I understood that I'd been tricked; they had left me in my hiding place and run away to play without me.

Boys can be bruising to a peer who is the slightest bit different. Nearly 40 percent of the nicknames boys assign to boys are based on physical defects (less than 7 percent of girls' nicknaming exploits handicaps).[22] Teasing is often so brutal that a boy will refuse to go to school or out to play rather than endure attacks on his size, his glasses, the fact that he succumbed to a mock marriage at age seven,[23] that he is known to like knitting or takes music lessons,[24] that he kissed a girl, messed up in a ball game, or was favored by a teacher.

Even among *friends,* "sarcasm, 'put-downs,' as well as physical threats and violence are all commonplace."[25] One boy felt impotent when his "friends" put his bike up in a tree. Another had to beg a "buddy" to let go when his "good-natured" arm-twisting became unbearably painful. "I knew I couldn't get angry or protest too much," he remembers. "I didn't want to spoil the fun."[26]

"Goody-goody," "spoil-sport," "sissy"—*fear* of such labels has propelled boys into insane initiation rites to prove themselves, ironically, fear*less*. They step off cliffs, die of exposure, allow themselves to be force-fed raw alcohol or buried alive rather than be "unmasculine" or let their "friends" down.[27]

In pursuit of sex role adequacy, boys' peer groups routinely spawn young alcoholics:

"I feel that because I don't drink as much as the other guys, there might be some doubt if I am a 'real' man," says one of the affluent and educated.[28]

"There's something between men and liquor," says the drinker in the ghetto gang. "Liquor makes hair grow on your chest."[29]

Humiliation, brutality, self-destruction, "interpersonal atrocities"[30]—these too are components of "masculine" togetherness, and reasons for parental concern about the all-boy half-life. Since most boys are not kept as close to their families as girls[31] and few have positive male role models available for close study, the male peer group has inordinate impact. When there is more Dad in the family, a more humane definition of "masculinity" in the culture, and more male teachers in early childhood classrooms, perhaps the all-boy group will not be solely entrusted with the delicate task of turning boys into men.

What of the friendships that turn girls into women? Thanks

to the Women's Movement we have discovered there is more to female bonding than the commonality of our second-class status. We have learned about great female alliances in literature and history,[32] and we have recycled female competition for men into support systems for one another.[33] Sad to say, however, we have not alleviated the destructive aspects of girlfriendship for little girls growing up today.

GIRLPOWER: MEASURING POPULARITY AND EXCLUSION

Abigail and Robin, at thirteen, co-authored an article for a children's magazine that summed up female "Friend Problems":

It usually begins in fourth grade: secrets, exclusion, worries. Worries about who likes you, who hates you, who's talking behind your back, and what they're saying.

Girls start becoming conformists, doing what everyone else does just to be accepted. If you let yourself get too involved in the unpleasant, unnecessary arguments that take place so frequently, you suffer a lot of hurt. . . .

We've been experiencing these conflicts for four years and only now is the situation beginning to clear up.

We started being our own persons, saying what we wanted to say, wearing what we wanted to wear, living for ourselves and not for others. We began ignoring the secrets and whispers. We started speaking out.

It wasn't easy. It's nice to be liked and popular, but not if you have to give up your true self. . . .[34]

How does it end up as a choice between being liked and being "your true self"?

Today, as in my time and my daughters' time, little girls have "intensive," not "extensive" peer relations.[35] Because adults like to keep an eye on girls, girls tend to play indoors. Because large groups of children playing active sports would be disruptive indoors, girls' games are small, domesticated, and confined: "house," "store," board games. And because just about any child can play these games as well as any other child, there is no skills-based justification for leadership and no objective measure of achievement.[36] As a result, girls "know their worth only from others' responses,"[37] and what others respond to is a pretty face or nice clothes, those being the few quantifiable specifics that distinguish one girl from another.

"Dulcie has got lovely hair," says a nine-year-old girl. "That's partly why I like her."

"My best friend is Vera," reports a twelve-year-old. "She always dresses nicely and walks with her shoulders back. Sometimes she wears brown slip-on shoes, a green cardigan and a dress."

(Those quotes come from two of the 340 essays on "My Friends and Why I Like Them."[38] Not one of the essays written by a boy includes a description of a friend's clothing or looks.)

In the all-girl group, an attractive girl becomes popular and then reigns by force of personality, arousing the loyalty of a few peer constituents. Clusters develop around such popular girls as early as second grade (age seven),[39] but cliques really hit their stride between fourth and ninth grades.

The power of girls' groups is the power to exclude. Letting some girls in and keeping others out creates the superiority of the Ins by virtue of the jealousy of the Outs.[40] The "activities" of the Ins are staying In; displacing best friends; jockeying for the favor of the favored; flattery; manipulation; slavish conformity to clique dress, language, and interests; competitive acquisition of material things; whispering (to arouse insecurity); deception (to incite antagonisms); and gossip (to put someone down and build oneself up).

Since overt aggression and dominance behavior are "not sanctioned" for females,[41] a girl either learns devious "feminine" tactics or suffers impotent despair, not understanding why others are popular and she is not. She may be willing to give up her "true self" in order to be popular, but that does not mean she knows what to do next, because *doing* has little relation to popularity among girls. Just as being pretty is a passive accomplishment, *being liked* is capricious and beyond her control. What is worse, *not* being liked isn't an indictment of a particular correctable failing (a weak arm, for instance), but rather a rejection of her total self.[42]

In adolescence, a new criterion is added: to be popular with most girls' groups, a girl has to be successful with boys. This boy-based popularity also seems to *happen* to a girl whether or not she does anything to cause or deserve it. Since something so externally activated can cease as mysteriously as it started,

> nearly all the girls suffer from . . . never knowing where they stand with the boys: why they are liked or not liked, how long it will last. . . .[43]

All in all, girls' peer group dynamics train women well for their role in a patriarchal system. The clique's pattern of "alternating intimacy and repudiation . . . establishes a core sense of distrust which has a powerful impact on women's relationships with each other."[44] This distrust prevents females from forming alliances threatening to males. Likewise, the aggression that might be turned against men because of women's shared oppression is deflected into intra-group hostility.

Girls' experience with whole-self rejection instills caution, inhibits assertiveness, and makes them play it safe. Their experience with popularity has taught them women are valuable only when they are liked, so they work hard to please, though they believe themselves basically helpless to affect the reactions of others. Having witnessed the success of those who look pretty, act "nice," and are clever at manipulation and flattery, girls develop no expertise at persuasion, argumentation, task persistence, or power management—the crucial qualities for leadership.

It is therefore absurd to say boys are "natural leaders" when their peer groups have tutored them for dominance—or to say girls "choose" popularity over power as if they had not been drilled to make that choice.

FRIENDS AND FEELINGS

The all-boy group is a hotbed of achievement motivation but an emotional desert, especially compared to girls' groups. While boys are shooting baskets or BB guns, girls are talking, sharing secrets, confessing fears, and comparing fantasies. Their clique melodramas make them "considerably more self-conscious than boys [and] more vulnerable to criticism,"[45] but also teach them to be good listeners, to comfort and reassure, to put feelings into words, and to enjoy making another person happy.

Girls braid themselves into one another's lives. One girl's family problems are agonized over like a continuing soap opera. Each friend gathers items to add to the others' "collections." (Piles of yogurt tops, match books, and coins have been accumulated in our house for various pals.) They comb the shops for individualized little surprises—an obscure brand of candy, the perfect message T-shirt. They know one another's favorite colors, foods, and rock stars, wear each other's clothes, read each other's most private diaries,[46] write poems to each other's kindness. In their twosomes and tiny groupings, they are continually practicing "self-disclosure"—the bedrock of human intimacy[47]—and refining the art of knowing someone else inside out.

Their highly developed sensitivity to feelings and uncanny insights into human behavior would be considered evidence of genius if they were male-linked traits. Known as women's strengths, they are relegated to the realm of the mystical, and called "female intuition."

Because girls' emotional and affiliative skills count so little in our culture, their "intimacy-competence" does not contribute to girls' self-esteem the way achievement-competence does for boys. As one psychologist describes it, the emotional lot for the female is *doing good and feeling bad.*[48]

Boys have feelings too, of course. They experience sadness, love, anger, and fear exactly as girls do.[49] But their sex role demands action and not emotional expression, especially within the male peer group.

Once, after my son admired some baby rabbits, commenting that they were "sweet," "adorable," and "gentle," he volunteered that he would never have been able to say those words in front of 9 out of 10 of his friends without taking a razzing.

Boys' feelings are to be conquered, not aired. Getting hurt, touched, or moved means a boy is too soft. Emotions in general are so relentlessly degraded that eventually they are completely denied.[50] Whereas girls openly care about being liked and are liked because of it, among boys, someone who "works hard at winning acceptance . . . is *disliked.* "[51] Neediness is weakness. And weakness is "feminine."

Two types of inexpressive males result: the Cowboy (or John Wayne type), who has feelings but won't express them for fear they would compromise his "masculine" image; and the Playboy (James Bond type), who is nonfeeling and "dead" inside.[52] Later in life, both types will disappoint women, but for the time being, in the boys' peer group, being emotionally closed is the only way to succeed at interpersonal relations.

Again, the male sex role calls the shots: a. If a boy has to be *competitive* with other boys, how can he afford too much empathy? b. If he must beware of *homosexual innuendo,* dare he show another boy any affection? c. If *personal vulnerability* would destroy his "masculine" image, how can he disclose his real fears and feelings? And d. if there are no expressive and affectionate *male role models* around him or in his group, can he afford to be alone against the grain?[53]

Because the peer group serves to police the sex role, best friendships among boys are worlds apart from what we catalogued among girls.

"I like him because he is a good sport and kind to animals," says a ten-year-old of his best friend. "At games he never cheats and he sits out if he is out."[54]

"He's President of the Student Council . . . drives a car . . . got a real nice personality . . . active in sports . . . goes out with girls a lot" is how a sixteen-year-old describes what he sees in his best friend. "We play basketball together and play games and cards at home. We have a lot of fun together."[55]

That is "closeness." Spending time, admiring a pal's accomplishments, doing the same things, talking about "safe topics."[56]

"I wonder if sports, politics, work and the weather—not to mention war and sex—were invented to give men something to talk about besides our feelings," writes John Leonard, who goes on to confess, "I tend not to admit that I love someone if he is male, until after he can't hear me. This is a cold witness."[57]

Men become each other's cold witnesses—speaking their love only in foxholes or at deathbeds—because in early life the warmth has been bred out of them. They don't know each other's middle names, not to mention favorite colors, impending divorces, or secret terrors. To be sure, best-boyfriends *do* more together and perhaps have more "fun," but unlike best-girlfriends, each has no idea *who* the other is. They can let out anger in front of one another but not a whimper or a tear; they can take a punch at each other but they cannot lean on a pal for strength. Joy too is imprisoned behind the athlete's modest shrug, the smack on a teammate's backside, or the street kid's, "Hey, man!" and soul handshake.

In sum, among boys, "time is rich and full, but basic problems are not handled. This is the girlfriend's job."[58]

At the same time as boys are perfecting a "sluggishness of emotion,"[59] their potential girlfriends are practicing the emotional scales to a fare-thee-well: kissing, crying, "talking it out," hugging, hurting, making up, sorting feelings like fruits and vegetables, and saying "I love you" to each other when they just mean, "See you later."

GETTING TOGETHER

After some ten or more years of such different conditioning, these two groups of hostile gender "types," these emotional strangers, are expected to make heterosexual couplings. They are supposed to be tender and considerate, open and trusting, mutually supportive. They are supposed to fall in love, exchange intimate thoughts, and fulfill one another's most vital needs.

How can they?

The affection that girls have learned to need, boys have not learned to give. The anger boys are allowed to express, girls are raised to fear. The openness and vulnerability girls consider honest, boys consider contemptible.

In fact, the entire female sex is considered either contemptible or not worthy of notice until boys are 14½ or 15. But girls have been noticing and fantasizing about boys since 11 or 12—not because romance is a female genetic trait, but because boys are expected to become the "project" of the adolescent peer group, just as men are supposed to be the focus of adult women's lives.

When Robin and Abigail had barely turned 12, they received a chain letter that closed with these words:

Think of the boy you love. In 4 days, something will happen. In 77 days he will tell you he loves you.

Neither my daughters nor their friends had anyone who could remotely be called a boyfriend, but all of them could indeed think of the boy they "loved." And savor the possibility that "something will happen."

In a study of youngsters in ninth grade (age fourteen), 100 percent of girls and 90 percent of boys said they intend to marry.[60] But only adolescent girls said they think about and talk about the other sex,[61] and consciously refine their ideas about a suitable mate.[62]

... twice as many girls as boys worry about dates; twice as many boys as girls worry about study and career. Thus boys ruminate about their place in society and girls ruminate about boys.[63]

What observers glibly call "boy crazy" behavior in teenage girls is fueled by male supremacy and the girl group's collective inferiority complex. It's not that female friendship is less important than male friendship but that girls are less important than boys.

I'd rather be seen with a boy I even dislike than with a girl I like. You know, nobody is terribly impressed if you just run around with a bunch of girls. ... Girlfriends are just for when you don't have a date.[64]

By herself, she's nobody. In the company of others as secondary as herself, she is still not much. She becomes someone—that is, gains value and self-esteem—when a member of the superior caste (even one she dislikes) approves of her.

Through the years, she has learned to be quite picky about her girlfriends, but a boy need only be a boy to be basically desirable. A boy is not a person, he's a status symbol. Only 36 males in 100 said they would marry someone they did not love if the person had other good qualities, but 76 females in 100 would do so[65]—because the woman marries male status as well as a particular man.

Conventional parents worry about their daughters' popularity with boys, and their sons' popularity—also with boys.[66] In both cases, the target is *male* approval. The higher caste status of the male gives an individual boy the power to render social judgments on *both* sexes.

Think about it: Boys are socialized to be independent of everyone, but they must have other boys' validation of their "masculinity." Girls are socialized to need approval from everyone, but only *boys* can validate their "femininity." Parents, accommodating to current reality, want their daughters to be accepted by men in marriage, and their sons to be accepted by men in the "man's world." Proof that sex-segregated peer groups in childhood are of vital service to the patriarchy lies in the fact that boys' groups function to train and validate that hallowed "masculinity," while girls' groups function to orient girls toward boys—awaiting their judgment.

In the teens, girls' and boys' societies begin to interweave. The peer group becomes a place to rehearse for the adult world without having to pay for one's mistakes, a home base away from adults, a kid-created subculture wherein children can find an "identity" and try on roles like wings. Too often, for girls this period marks the end, not the beginning of flight.

With all its conformity pressures, the all-girl group had made room for bona fide individuality; witness the popularity of "tomboys." But the girl-boy coupling of early adolescence demands a fresh burst of sex stereotypes, as if to compensate for the loss of sex separatism by giving them *new roles to divide them lest they suddenly appear to be equals.*

Boys notice girls because of their awakened sexual interest in the female body. However, they do not change their *minds* about girls, they only change their *feelings.* The difference is crucial. The male libido causes boys to *overlook* what was formerly despised in girls, but not to *disavow* their belief in female inferiority.

A black-white parallel sharpens the point. Given America's history of racial separatism and mutual suspicion, we understand that a black and a white may not become friends as easily as two blacks or two whites. The best intentions will not undo what racist indoctrination has painstakingly wrought until an entire generation of blacks and whites starts out from the beginning experiencing one another's humanity up close, day after day, year after year.

Similarly, what sexist indoctrination has wrought through ten years of sexual separation and mutual suspicion, the adolescent libido cannot undo. Boys may call this sexual pull "love" because it so overwhelms their prior feelings of distaste. But do not imagine that hormonal surges make them drop the view that girls are their social inferiors[67] any more than whites who have loved and slept with blacks have necessarily dropped their racism.

Girls may call the attraction "love" because if it isn't love they would have to repress or deny their "unladylike" sexual feelings. They may call it love because otherwise it might reveal itself as status hunger.

Whatever girls and boys call it, what they feel during the awakening of heterosexual interest is not friendship. They have no experience with friendship, no history of friendship, and once there is sex, no impetus for friendship. And that is how the patriarchy needs it to be.

As everyone knows, sex can flourish between unequals. Love can also thrive between unequals—witness the love between parent and child or student and tutor. Because of the vast discrepancy in female and male status and power, romantic love is also love between unequals. It only looks equal because when a culturally superior male loves a female, he elevates her above the rest of her sex "in order to justify his descent into a lower caste . . . [and] this idealization process acts to artificially equalize the two parties."[68]

But friendship—and only friendship—requires equality as a precondition of its existence. True friendship, as opposed to love and sex, is founded on total mutuality. Unlike love, friendship cannot be unilateral or unrequited.[69] Unlike sex, it cannot be imposed by force. Two people *elect* to be friends because both get satisfaction from their closeness. To a friend one would not say I love you because you have status or a good body, or because you give me what I cannot give myself. To a friend one says, *I love you because you're you.* That "youness" is what is felt and known between equals.

That "youness," achieved in homosocial peer groups, is what is missing between male and female children, to the tragic detriment of male and female adults.

Without a history of friendship, boy meets girl across a gulf of discrepancies too wide for romantic love to bridge. After a decade of bifurcation and gender enmity, estrangement at the deepest level of the soul is virtually inescapable. The sex role-playing characteristic of adolescent dating[70] compounds this alienation with an act: He's supposed to play the pursuer, planner, bill-payer, and seducer. She's supposed to play the accepter, admirer, incompetent, and virgin. Despite all the "counterculture" hoopla, young people "continue to expect a sexual dating script in which the male attempts to gain access to the female's body and the female either passively accepts . . . or actively blocks his efforts."[71] And after years of talk about the male ego and female equality, even enlightened young men tend to find an assertive, independent girl likeable "as a person," but not lovable as a girl-friend.[72]

Separatism has made it difficult for friends to be lovers and for lovers to be equals. Sexism has put friendship and fun in the homosocial column, and love and sex in the heterosexual column, and the dichotomy has perverted dating, courtship, and marriage so that nothing that goes on between us is quite what it seems.

Studies show that among adolescents, the main motive for girls' accumulating boyfriends and boys, sex partners, is *to impress their same-sex peers!*[73] The pursuit of the other sex is thus an intermediary courtship through which to woo the real friend, the equal—the one they've been playing to for the last ten years.

Girls and boys flirt, make out, fall in love, and have sex together to be sure. But boys turn to *their* friends for fun and girls turn to *their* friends for intimacy because that is the togetherness pattern they understand.

Girls and boys double date so that when conversation fails, the two boys can talk about sports and the two girls can escape together to the powder room to mine the emotional terrain.

Lovers have little in common when the heavy breathing is over. Newlyweds sit in restaurants without speaking. Behind the scenes in the "love match" marriage, the requirements of affiliation and intimacy that she learned among girls, and the requirements of "getting ahead" and "staying cool"[74] that he learned among boys, are in mortal conflict.[75] She needs him to be a "close confidante" to "protect her from depression."[76] But he finds her talk about feelings "petty."[77]

He lives for his weekly night out with the boys, she talks about their sex problems with her girlfriends, and the two of them never quite agree about what makes for a fun vacation.[78]

In a sane, nonsexist world, a world without false dichotomies, we could find friendship, fun, love, and sex in the same person. But for now it's hard to outgrow the feeling that when we're with the "opposite" sex, we are once again, as in our childhoods, in enemy territory.

WHAT IS THE ALTERNATIVE?

I am not saying that girls and boys must play together and only together, or that boy-boy and girl-girl friendships are intrinsically inadequate. Children deserve experience with all three human permutations. Moreover, what goes on within each of the gender-combinations, if not poisoned by sex-typing, can offer rich varieties of liking and loving.

What I envision is free-flowing, gender-blind alliances that satisfy children's needs rather than train them for sex role conformity. I see much reduced cross-sex hostility because boy-girl friendship throughout childhood will have kept the two sexes real and human in one another's eyes. They will have a history of intimacy, experience with integrated fun and feeling, and none of the lunacy of separating to become sex stereotypes only to come together as strangers.

We would not train a girl and boy to play championship mixed doubles together by having them spend ten years playing on separate courts.

Within the larger patriarchal society, there is only so much individuals can do to alter gender arrangements (and only a minimum role for parents in their children's social lives). But some do's and don'ts are practical:

1. *Let children see cross-sex friendships among adults:* a single woman or man whom both mother and father like as a friend. Do not equate male-female relations only with sex and marriage.

2. *Don't identify children always by gender.* Say, "Let's invite a friend over on Saturday," not "Let's invite a little girl."

3. *Don't divide activities by gender.* Rather than have chil-

dren see the women get together for talk or shopping and the men for sports or TV, have friends over for bridge, backgammon, dancing, or whatever all can enjoy.

4. *Don't tolerate cross-sex cruelty, teasing, or exclusion.* A five-year-old planning his birthday party told his mother, "Only boys can come, I don't like girls." "But I'm a girl, don't you like me?" asked the mother. "Yes . . . but you're a mommy . . . not a girl." The mother recognized the early stirrings of misogyny and took her son's logic to task. Boys who divide the loved-Mommy from the hated-girl grow up to see women as either madonna or whore—neither of which is a friend nor an equal.

5. *Don't make your daughter praise-dependent.* Encourage her to stand by her beliefs and preferences rather than adjust them to please others. Tell her, "You can't go through life failing just so your achievements won't make your friends feel bad. The sad fact of life is that some people are never going to love you, no matter what you do."[79]

6. *Put popularity in perspective.* Point out that grades, health, talent, self-respect, and personal dignity matter more and last longer than "being liked" or "fitting in." Explain that lack of social success in grade school does not mean the same will be true in high school, college, or adult life. Suggest that your child might be too *mature* for her or his peers, might be better appreciated later by brighter, more discriminating friends. (Can *you* remember the names of your three best friends in fifth grade? Do you still see any of your friends from junior high? Should anyone sacrifice one iota of personal authenticity for such temporary acquaintanceships?)

7. *Underwrite breakaway cliques.* If your child has been rejected by the "popular" crowd, point out what she or he has in common with other loners. Maybe all the out-groups would add up to an In-group: girls who like to hike, not hang-out; boys who like to paint or act, not play sports; girls and boys together. Pay for a pizza party to get the new group going or let your house be used as a meeting place. Reinforce tentative new alliances by getting together with the new friend's parents, or helping new twosomes get involved in a backyard game.

8. *Be a back-up buddy.* When your child complains "Nobody likes me," or "Everyone else was invited but me," don't insist on a stiff upper lip or moralize about the school of hard knocks. Step into the breach. Depending on the child's age, offer a suspension of bedtime rules in favor of an extra story, make a favorite dessert together, go out for a walk or a special weeknight movie —try anything that helps assuage the rejection. Be glad if your company or comfort is an acceptable alternative to suffering in silence. Not every parent is allowed to take second place to a friend.

9. *Talk about love.* Make "love" a subject long before it becomes a hormonal reaction. The light-headed ecstasy of romance will not be compromised by conversations with the child (from eight years old on) about the meaning of love in a girl's or boy's life. Parents prepare children for every other crucial human experience, why not love? Talk about who says "I love you" and who doesn't. Ask should one "sacrifice" for love; is love "blind," is love losing the self or finding another? Collect quotations about love. Two of my favorites: "Sexual love is lust plus trust."[80] And "Love is that condition in which the happiness of another person is essential to your own."[81]

10. *Help children recognize sex role exploitation in cross-sex relationships.* Typically, a boy confides to a platonic girlfriend problems that he cannot admit to other males, or he uses her to plot "feminine" strategy or spy on a girl he likes romantically. The trouble is, the two of them have nothing in common besides his problems; he needs her only for her "expressive functions";[82] he doesn't provide the same services in return and rarely owns up to their friendship in front of his male peers. Your daughter may want to accept the terms of such a relationship, but first you should help her see it for what it is.

11. *Explain nonsexist principles, don't just impose them.* Many people will attack your nonsexist beliefs as emanations from female self-interest. Your children should understand that emotional freedom and love between equals are matters of human urgency, not partisanship. For instance, your son should be emotionally liberated for his own sake, not for the girls he may someday meet. (What's more, male affection isn't necessarily good for women, as misogynist but demonstrative male Latins, Arabs, and homosexuals will testify.)

12. *Prepare your children for the perils of nonconformity.* This point is too important for a "To Do" list. It requires a deep breath.

Adrienne Rich has written, "If we wish for our sons—as for our daughters—that they may grow up unmutilated by gender roles, sensitized to misogyny in all its forms, we also have to face the fact that in the present stage of history, our sons may feel profoundly alone in the masculine world, with few, if any, close relationships."[83]

My answer is, our sons have few if any close relationships *now*. The male friends who accept our sons, without the shared ritual of girl-hating to keep them together, will be friends worth having. Perhaps our sons will be leaders of entirely new kinds of peer groups, open, nourishing, and bristling with healthy rebellion against stereotypes and lies. Or perhaps they will indeed, suffer, as Dr. Joseph Church says.

> The liberated child will often be at odds with his peers and their families. He may even suffer ostracism, which is nothing less than capital punishment for children. We have no right to use our offspring as instruments of the social change we wish to effect.[84]

Church is right about the penalty of ostracism, but wrong in assuming our children are merely pawns of our ideologies. Social change is *for* children. Suffering for social change seems cruel until one remembers that the alternative is suffering with things as they are.

Ostracism hurts, but it must not be given the power to deal a death blow to "the liberated child." Teasing, bullying, and ridicule leave scars. But they can be overcome. Children can talk back, fight, make converts, organize alliances, or stand alone if they *are* alone on justice's side. Ostracism from a destructive group is better than surrender to its values.

[handwritten in left margin: good Ex. of enduring]

[handwritten at bottom: need to △ at all costs.]

18

Having Fun:
Sports and Child's Play

Life must be lived as play.
—PLATO'S LAWS

Play is older than culture.
—JOHAN HUIZINGA[1]

In the playgrounds and gymnasiums of this country, the words "sissy" and "tomboy" police the culture's sex roles. Although there is no connection between human sexuality and passing a football,[2] the accusation "You throw like a *girl*" can banish a boy from his team and from his gender. The nickname "butch" can move a girl to defend her "femininity" with ribbons in her hair or lace on her tennis clothes, or to apologize for her competence ("Y'see, my brothers needed someone to pitch to them"), or even to quit a sport rather than risk defamation.

Why tar children with accusations referring to their sexuality when the activities involved have nothing to do with the sex act? Because play situations are patriarchal power relationships in microcosm, and patterns established in sports and games carry into adult life.

While "having fun," children are supposed to learn the sex role basics: boys must be competitors and girls cheerleaders, boys must be fleet of foot, girls full of grace, et cetera, et cetera, and *not* vice versa. Certain activities must be understood to be "congruent" with one's gender while others "detract."[3]

Horses are a good example. Many more girls than boys are attracted to horseback riding. More than 85 percent of horse magazine readers are girls. Margaret Mead has speculated that riding can give a girl a sense of mastery that is very appealing at times to one who has grown up in a society in which dominance is frowned upon in a woman.[4]

Despite their passion and proficiency, girls either give up horses in adolescence or direct their skills toward mannered horse shows and jumping exhibitions. They don't grow up to be the Marlboro Man, riding rugged and alone. And they don't grow up to ride often enough with the U.S. Equestrian team in the Olympics, where male riders outnumber females two to one.[5] Dominance in the saddle is permitted a girl but not a woman.

Other sports are "unfeminine" from childhood on, yet some girls have managed to resist the stereotype and withstand the stigma. They play championship marbles although marbles has always been a "boys' game";[6] and championship chess, which is typecast as a "man's game."[7] They include the girl who started shooting pool when she was nine and became women's U.S. Open Pocket Billiards champion at thirteen.[8] And the five girls who completed all 25 miles of a swim down Oregon's rough Columbia River as a fund-raising event for their swim club, "while the seven boys who participated stopped short."[9]

I especially admire the girl who weighed 100 pounds at age eight, dieted, ran, trained, lost 35 pounds and by age eleven was the only female Golden Gloves boxer in her state—and a straight "A" student besides.[10] And I marvel at the nine-year-old who put on headgear, passed as a boy, and defeated her male wrestling opponent in a rout;[11] and the twelve-year-old who ran the 1500 meters 27 seconds short of the world's record;[12] and finally the girl who spent two years restoring a World War II airplane with her own hands, and logged 135 hours of solo flying time in it before she was seventeen.[13]

We all admire girls like these from afar. We exclaim, "Gee, she did *that!* And she's a girl!" But in their home towns and often, in their own homes, when a girl gravitates to "unfeminine" play or sports, the exclamation she hears is "Gee, she *can't* do *that!* She's a girl."

FIGHTING FOR FUN

That's why, for one girl after another, having fun hasn't been easy, from the much ballyhooed struggle to get girls into Little Leagues,[14] to the countless unknown little girls like these:

• One ten-year-old had to sit on the bench and watch her team, playing without a goalie, lose the North American Silver Stick Hockey Championship, while she—the team's only goaltender—was ruled ineligible to play on account of sex.[15]

• Another waited eleven months for the West Side Tennis Club to process her application and hire her as the first ball girl in the history of the U.S. Open.

• Three girls were admitted into the Soap Box Derby only after the mother of one of them, who happened to be president of the local N.O.W., threatened suit.[16]

• Some girls—including golf star Nancy Lopez—had to institute legal action to force their schools to let girls play on the same team as boys.[17]

Jody Lavin's experience seems to epitomize the psychology behind the struggle. When she was chosen to receive her high school's "Outstanding Senior Athlete" trophy, administrators "felt that giving the award to a young woman would upset male students (and alumni)."[18] So, although no boy matched Jody's high academic average and extraordinary record in three varsity sports, the administration announced they would give two awards that year—one to the best male and one to Jody, the best female.

Thankfully, enough women and men of the community protested so that, after much acrimony, the administration gave Jody Lavin the singular trophy she deserved.

THE POLITICS OF PLAY

Male problems with girl athletes stem largely from the must-win mentality of "masculinity." Boys Are Better, so how can a girl be best? In almost those words, coaches and psychologists worry about the boy-ego and sacrifice the girl-ego to it. They warn of a "heavy psychological cost" if boys compete with girls.[19] Not just because girls are invading the last male preserve of team sports and sharing in its "unforgettable . . . click of communality,"[20] but because girls were the cushion that stopped a boy from hitting bottom: no matter how bad one was at games and sports, girls could always be counted on to be worse.

The loss of that soft female cushion is the "heavy psychological cost" they are warning us about.

Few have been troubled by the cost to girls of female weakness-by-predestination. Nor, for that matter, the effect of wiring a direct line between a boy's sports aptitude and his "balls."

To be a "real" boy in America your son doesn't have to do fractions, know the scientific name for common salt or tie a square knot in 10 seconds. Yet *every* boy in America is expected to play team sports—baseball, basketball, and football, at minimum.[21]

For a boy, "athletic skill is remarkably disproportionate to its role in adult life."[22] Judging by the emphasis on scores, averages, and trophies, you'd think that schools were grooming every boy for the pros. Social success is measurably advanced by sports aptitude and retarded by athletic incompetence.[23] And a vast majority of boys would rather be known as an "athletic star" than as a "brilliant student."[24]

VIRILITY TO THE VICTORIOUS

"You have to win or they hate you" says one man of his youthful sports experience. "The athletic role is a prototpye of the male role. It separates the men from the boys."[25]

It seems to me that having fun is no fun if you *have* to have it to preserve your sexual identity. The only difference between the anxiety of an athlete and the misery of a klutz is that one boy is *afraid* he won't do well, and the other is *sure* of it.[26]

One man remembers anguish in every physical endeavor from first-grade dodgeball to daily lunch periods when, whatever the sport, he was always picked last. His most dreadful memory centers on a father-son softball game:

I was the only person on both teams, the fathers and the sons, not to get a hit: I struck out every time. I don't think I have ever felt so ashamed of myself as I felt then, or felt that anyone else was so ashamed of me as my father was then. In the picnic which followed, my father and I avoided each other completely. Driving home with him was excruciating. I didn't attempt anything even remotely athletic on my own initiative for about five years after that experience.[27]

At sports, the only thing worse than being clumsy or inept is being beaten by a girl. And at play, the only thing worse than choosing to play a game "inappropriate" to one's sex is running away from a fight.

Physical strength and physical courage become identified with moral strength and moral courage, and the willingness to fight other boys for one's rights is an emblem of manliness. The physically weak boy may be bullied or left out of group play while the stronger boy will be selected for leadership positions and in most games becomes the chooser of sides or the captain of the team.[28]

Many parents as well as peers condemn the noncombatant:

When I was a little boy and had come home crying after a beating from some local bully, my mother would push me out and lock the door, demanding that I go back to give as good as I had gotten. She said boys who didn't fight back were sissies.[29]

AMERICAN MACHISMO

If you ain't tough, you're a sissy. If you won't fight, you must be a "faggot." Violence and "masculinity" are one.

Like bullfights in Spain, big-time sports in the United States are our "hostility rituals,"[30] romanticized, idealized combat scenes choreographed by rules and referees, but potent enough to explode into savagery at any moment on the field, court, ice, track, or in the stands.

American machismo is pre-game demonstrations with a strong military flavor: the Air Force band on the field and phantom jets in the sky dropping American flag "bombs" on the Super Bowl crowd.[31] It's temper tantrums (Coach Woody Hayes slugged a lot of players before he was fired[32]) that pass for team spirit, sadism masquerading as character formation, and "training drills" that humiliate[33] and sometimes kill boys[34] en route to "building men."

The all-American star-spangled hero-idol is no longer Mickey Mantle signing baseballs or Joe Louis going to bed early —idols who were idealized but admirable. Today's heroes gouge and elbow under the boards, and admire a coach who crows, "I'd like to be known as the Idi Amin of football."[35] Today's boys are raised on the gospel according to Vince Lombardi:

"Winning isn't everything. It's the only thing."

SEXISM IN THE FIRST QUARTER

As unfailingly as girls and boys peel off to their separate locker rooms, that is how divided and separate their play experiences have been from birth.

Remember what we've seen of parents' differentiated handling of girl and boy infants, rough-housing with him, tickling and peek-a-boo games with her, the different stimuli placed in girls' or boys' rooms, and the different expectations for independence.

Remember which sex is encouraged to play outdoors, allowed to explore further from home, rewarded for problem-solving; and which sex is restrained, protected, chaperoned, raised to please, hooked on adult help, and encouraged to be overcautious.

Think too, about the sports that children see on television, and the gender of most of the players; the type and amount of leisure activities traditional mothers and fathers engage in; and which parent is likely to throw a ball to which sex child.

After so much sex-differentiated conditioning and exposure, it's no miracle of biology that girls and boys play differently and "avoid opposite-sex activities by the time they enter nursery school."[36] The miracle is that it take as long as three years for it to happen. And the shame is that we have accepted these sex differences as "normal" despite their differential rewards and serious lifelong repercussions:

• Boys' block-building play teaches them to be rational, constructive, and inventive; girls' dolls, dancing, and dress-up play teaches them to be dependent, domestic, and decorative.[37]

• With their outdoor play, boys learn to master their environment and exercise their bodies. Boys' group games encourage cooperation. Girls' sedentary one-on-one activities do neither.[38]

• Girls graduate from free play during early childhood to "helping adults," which is considered "fun." Boys graduate from free play to organized sports. Girls learn to give pleasure; boys learn to perform.[39]

• Boys' games are intricate and involving; they last longer and may be played for years with increasing mastery. Girls' games (dolls, jump rope) become boring with age.[40]

• "With no fouls, no rule disputes or choosing sides and few areas of ambiguity (like a slide into third base) girls gain little experience in the judicial process."[41]

• In girls' play, there is no mentoring or apprentice system as there is in boys' sports. Littler girls are only used as "live dolls" and the oldest have to play on the level of the youngest, while the reverse is true of boys.[42]

• Overall, boys learn strategy, group dynamics, problem-solving, mediation, and reaching beyond their grasp; girls do not. Overall, girls' games teach nurturance and empathy. Boys' games do not.[43]

HEALTH MYTHS AND
WISHFUL WARNINGS

I grew up believing that a girl could get cancer from an elbow jab to the breast, so I lost my enthusiasm for basketball. They said I might ruin my reproductive life by riding horseback during a menstrual period, so I never felt entirely comfortable in the saddle at any time of the month.

Fears about the effect of strenuous exertion or contact sports on a girl's health probably quashed more female athletes than any other single influence. Not surprisingly, since sex roles decree that

Girls Are Meant To Be Mothers, the fears focused on damage to girls' reproductive capacity. This was so even though doctors have known for generations that the uterus is perhaps the most shock-resistant organ in the human body, that the breasts need no more protection than the male genitals, and that "young women who have engaged in athletic training are less likely to have complications during pregnancy than nonathletic women."[44] Doctors and coaches also should have known that

• *girl athletes do not develop Amazon builds and big muscles;* "heredity alone dictates the size of the body frame,"[45] and only the hormone testosterone contributes to muscle development. In fact, athletic girls "more nearly approximate the ideal weight (for their height), not only during the period of training but also in the years that follow."[46]

• *girls are not more injury-prone than boys.* Both sexes participating in four high school athletic programs experienced one injury for every 650 hours of play.[47]

• *girls are not more physically vulnerable than boys.* Girls' reaction times are no slower, their bones are no weaker. "The physical performance of girls up to thirteen is equal to that of boys. At five years of age, the development of girls is about a year ahead of that of boys. The superiority in height and weight (up to thirteen) of girls over boys gives them a slight advantage in running and body contact activities. In muscle strength, agility and endurance, however, there is no significant difference."[48] In other words, physical vulnerability is in the eye of the male and the mind of the female.

• *girls are not more likely to be injured when competing with boys.* The issue is size not sex. An eight-year-old girl is safer playing with an eight-year-old boy than with a twelve-year-old girl.[49]

• *girls are not more likely to be injured in contact sports than in any other physical activity.* Football and basketball may be rough in the pros but in school it is softball and gymnastics that lead the injury list. Yes, gymnastics—the "feminine" sport![50]

Just as most of these medical facts are becoming generally accepted, a new health "hazard" is being touted: *amenorrhea,* the cessation of menstruation or the delay of an adolescent's first menstruation, a condition common to strenuously athletic women and girls, especially runners. The possible "threat" to a girl's childbearing capacity has inspired rumblings to the effect that a female's sports activity should be curtailed "for her own good."

One women's track coach calls amenorrhea "just the ammunition male chauvinists are looking for."[51]

Indeed, the sudden outcry is suspicious. Ballet dancers, gymnasts, and swimmers have always experienced some amenorrhea; why are the experts "concerned" only now that girls have begun to forge ahead in track and other "boys'" sports? Male runners have been found to have decreased testosterone levels after a marathon;[52] where is the solicitous concern for their low sperm count?

The fact is that the overwhelming majority of female athletes do not experience amenorrhea or any menstrual irregularity, and those who do seem to bounce back to regularity when training stops, and go on to bear as many children as they want.[53]

Amenorrhea seems to occur when the amount of fat in the female body drops below 15 percent of total body weight.[54] Girls who regain that portion of fat find menstruation restored with no ill effects. So don't let your concern for your daughter's future maternity scare her away from the joy of sport right now.

WHY PARENTS SHOULD CARE ABOUT CHILD'S PLAY

The amenorrhea "panic" is one reason why you need to keep on top of the facts about play and sports. The uninformed parent too easily becomes the misinformed parent. We cannot just leave girls and boys alone "to make their own fun" because left alone with their peers they may be bullied into stereotyped activities and out of the sports they love.[55]

From every point of view, play is just too important to be ignored. "To the young child, play is life itself."[56] Play is the developmental *work* of childhood[57] and "a precursor of adult competence."[58] Play builds the body, the senses, the personality, and the powers of the mind. To different children at different stages, play can be emotional therapy and a means of coping with disturbing events, a rehearsal for adult roles and relationships, a dry run for "the game of life," a laboratory in which to experiment with language, communication, shared expectations, creativity, leadership, fantasy, and invention.[59]

I am not exaggerating. Play is all that and more. And, as touched on before, the *kind* of play matters. Block-building, climbing, riding, and playing with transportation toys lead to better visual spatial development than dolls, playing house, art-work, or board games,[60] which may account for boys' superior spatial-relations skills after age eight.[61]

Another example is marbles. If Jean Piaget, the dean of child psychologists, could not find "a single collective game played by girls in which there were as many rules and, above all, as fine and consistent an organization and codification of these rules, as in the game of marbles,"[62] then girls should learn to play marbles.

Another play category vital to child development is fantasy or dramatic play. Children who have imaginary playmates, make up wild stories, and act out elaborate pretend dramas (starting well before age five), are more creative, original, and flexible intel-lectually, and less aggressive than low fantasizers.[63] Parents might encourage a boy's fantasy life as much as they encourage sports if they knew that too much physical activity tends to reduce the frequency of that healthy fantasy play.[64]

Paying attention to your child's dramatic play will tell you a great deal about her or his sex role ideology. One mother watched her five-year-old son join in make-believe with a group of older boys. Since he was the smallest, and there were no girls, the big boys assigned her son the role of "the little girl." He cried and carried on terribly: there was nothing worse than being the girl. So the other boys let him be "the dog"—and he was happy.

Important as toy play, games, and fantasy are for early child-hood, sports is as crucial for middle childhood and beyond. Sports is play that lasts a lifetime, play that grownups never have to give up, play that is transformed from physical *education* to *recreation* the minute there is mastery. If it is not too competitive or compulsive, sports can be a pleasureful shortcut to health, fitness, self-respect, social camaraderie, fun, and occasional ecstasy, for as long as the body holds up. Sport also socializes and civilizes children:

> The lessons learned on the playing field are among the most basic: the setting of goals and joining with others to achieve them; an understanding of and respect for rules; the persistence to hone ability into skill, prowess into perfection. In games, children learn that success is possible and that failure can be overcome. . . . young athletes develop work patterns and attitudes that carry over into college, the marketplace, and all of life.[65]

Children who have the opportunity to play the sports they like become more enthusiastic sports fans,[66] just as those who learn to play a musical instrument become more cultured listeners. And being a player, not just a fan, gives a child a rich ceremonial life, a sense of belonging to the language, lore, costume, and custom of her or his chosen sport.

While traditional girls' games (such as gymnastics, jump rope, ice-skating, and swimming) contain some of the above attributes, they are usually practiced in isolation, under minimal competitive stress. Such individualistic activities leave a girl with the mistaken impression that if you're good, you'll be rewarded. Out in the real world, girls are shocked to discover that what matters is what team sports taught boys: group strategy and interaction, performing for the common goal, and experience with leadership.[67]

In our generation, some girls learned these lessons despite sex role contraints. The most successful, achieving women in a wide range of fields were "tomboys" in their youths.[68] And among today's high school girls, the athletes have higher grade averages and educational aspirations than other girls in their classes.[69]

Because sports offer so many "basic benefits"[70] to the growing child, it is essential that your daughter as well as your son has full access to all forms of play.

WHAT YOU CAN DO—IN CHILD'S PLAY

• *Make sure both sexes have three types of play experience from infancy on: solitary play, peer play, and parent stimulation.* Playing alone develops problem-solving. Peer interaction, even among ten- to fourteen-month-olds who play *parallel* rather than together, promotes positive social behavior.[71] Parent stimulation, which might include reading to children or teaching them games, develops verbal acuity and global thinking.[72]

Since girls usually get more of this parental supervision and boys tend to be left to play by themselves, it makes sense that more girls than boys are good with words, and more boys than girls are good with figures.[73]

• *Encourage the explorer in your child.* Simone de Beauvoir writes of female weakness:

> . . . if she could assert herself through her body and face the world in some other fashion, this deficiency would be easily compensated for. Let her swim, climb mountain peaks, pilot an airplane, battle the elements, take risks, go out for adventure, and she will not feel before the world that timidity.[74]

While de Beauvoir's agenda may be ambitious, you can counter the common tendency to overprotect a daughter by encouraging outdoor play, a climb to the top of the monkey bars, trying out for the team, joining the big kids on a campout. Mastery is the "liberating" experience every child deserves.

• *Promote the widest variety of play experiences.* To assure children's access to all kinds of games, toys, and activities, you may have to *affirmatively negate* the labels that society has attached to them and actively challenge the stereotypes that close off whole categories of fun.

Studies show that children do best at games that are forthrightly labeled appropriate for their sex.[75] They need to know that sex role conformity is *not* required[76] and to be told that it's definitely okay to play with a socially sex-typed item:

> This tool kit looks like fun! It has almost as many tools as my friend Kathy, the carpenter, has in her toolbox.

> Of course, boys can knit and sew. Look at this picture of

football player Rosey Grier doing his needlework,[77] and this man who makes lots of money designing clothes, and these boys in China who weave beautiful rugs. If they can do such great things with their hands, so can you.

Don't be silly. If chess was meant to be a man's game, why is the Queen the most valuable piece on the board?

Boxers use jumping rope to develop endurance. Double-dutch jumpers do it for precision, cadence, and timing. A rope is just a rope until you feel like using it for whatever exercise you like.

I know enlightened parents who give nontraditional toys to their children and then telegraph their discomfort nonverbally. If you are like most parents, when you give a doll to a girl you show her how to cradle it in her arms. If you coldly thrust a doll at a boy, you may as well give him a truck. Instead you might say, "Isn't this a wonderful doll! Here's how I held you when you were a baby. Would you like to see how I bathed you so you'll be able to do it when you grow up to be a daddy like me?"

• *Watch your children at play and see how many sexist stereotypes are already writ large on their small canvas. Then decide how much parental intervention is needed.*

Preschool girls spend 75 percent of their time playing "house"; boys spend 30 percent.[78] When either girls or boys take the part of "the mommy," they play her as a domestic laborer: someone who is good with babies but helpless with appliances and emergencies; someone who dresses up a lot, cleans, cooks, talks on the phone, and waits for her husband to come home to pick up dropped objects and fix the iron.

When playing "the daddy," boys portray him as a leader and expert in all situations, while girls play him as competent in the role of husband-worker, but not very good as a father.[79]

There are other revelatory sex differences in child's play.

Up to age four, about one-third of both sexes are willing to be "the baby" in dramatic play; after four, girls still like being "the baby," but boys become increasingly interested in adult roles.[80] Boys are disadvantaged in fantasy play only for as long as they can imagine no other role for themselves but "the daddy," a part most boys have trouble fleshing out since they see their fathers fulfilling it so minimally.

When preschool children make up stories, boys fill their tales with machines, rockets, cars, outdoor elements (storms, sun); and girls' stories revolve around flowers, people, and home events[81]— imagery that precisely matches the stimuli to which each sex has been exposed.

In children's fantasy worlds, barnyard animals and jungle creatures conform to gender stereotype: fluffy little rabbits are "she's," but very big cows might be "he's" regardless of their udders, and very attractive roosters are frequently "she's."

I have witnessed two little girls pretending to be huge dinosaurs call each other by male names. The possibility of being a powerful, fearsome mammoth of the female persuasion seems beyond the reach of the imagination.

Before age six, most children fantasize being wild animals such as lions, tigers, and bears to help them cope with the discovery that the world can be hostile and dangerous. At eight years old, boys are still pretending to be ferocious, but girls have been tamed: a girl who was a lion at four is "a sweet, little kitten lapping up cream" at eight.[82]

While observing your children at play, you may remember Erikson's experiment referred to back in Chapter 2, in which two-thirds of the boys made towers and outdoor action scenes while two-thirds of the girls depicted interiors, enclosures and people in static positions. Should such forms appear in your kids' block play, resolve to set role-free examples and kindle brighter fantasies by joining in (without taking over) children's play. Girls' "inner space" constructions enlarge noticeably when they believe outer space belongs to them and not just to the male of the species.

• *Get involved. Be creative. Indulge the child inside you.* Think up wild "what ifs" for Let's Pretend. What if you could change five things about your life? What if all the women in the world disappeared tomorrow morning? What if you were the other sex?

Be elaborately fond of a "gender-incongruent" toy. A same-sex role model with lots of confidence and gusto can pave the way for children to play unconventionally.[83] (I remember a boy proudly showing me, "This is my father's favorite doll, and this is mine.")

Take a nontraditional role. When I was "the doctor," David, five, chose to be "the hospital man." I wasn't maneuvering for him to be "the nurse," just to accept me as "the doctor." Does your son want to play school? Father might be the kindergarten teacher, and mother the principal.

Props invite drama. Sailor hats put little girls at sea and pilots' wings put them in flight. Our children often played office with old briefcases, file folders, a dead phone, a stapler, and paper-clips. Robin once delivered a political campaign speech because a big dress-up hat reminded her of Bella Abzug; then she responded to questions from the "press," alias Abigail and David. Props and dress-up clothes can help anybody "be" anything, so fill a box with hats, costume jewelry, baskets, menus, old tools, whatever, and let children try roles they only dreamed possible.

• *Be a "positive interventionist."* When children are playing, you would unhesitatingly interrupt if you heard a racial slur (such as "catch a nigger by the toe"). You'd intervene if they were doing something physically dangerous or if it became necessary to break up a fight. You should also

• intervene when one three-year-old tells another that she can't sit in the pretend truck because "ladies can't drive trucks." Set them straight and then withdraw.

• intervene when someone chants "No Boys Allowed." Tell them that any group that cannot include everyone cannot continue meeting in your house or yard because you know how much it hurts to be left out.

• intervene when you start to hear a lot of "I'm afraid," or "I'll get dirty" or "I don't know how." The four most important words a parent can say to a child are, YOU CAN DO IT . . . and how rarely those words are said to girls.

• intervene when one child is repeatedly bullied. Try to mediate. Help the child formulate dazzling verbal parries. If the attacks persist, encourage rational self-defense: fighting back not to prove toughness or bravery, but to establish that she or he refuses to play the victim. Physical aggression must not be permitted to intimidate children or establish ruling hierarchies based on sex or size.

• intervene when you hear a jump rope chant, cheer, or clapping rhyme that offends. Some think this too doctrinaire, but if the subject was an ethnic group or old person rather than the two sexes, more of us might find these ditties objectionable:

Boys have the muscles,
Teachers have the brains,
Girls have the sexy legs,
But we win the games.
    —NEW YORK CITY CHEER

Boys are rotten,
Just like cotton.
Girls are dandy,
Just like candy.
    —SOUTHERN BLACK CHANT[84]

Fishy, fishy in a brook,
Daddy caught it on a hook
Mommy fried it in a pan,
Baby eats it like a man.
    —ORIGIN UNKNOWN

• *Do not overreact to "excessive" cross-sex play behavior.* We've noted that parents tend to be far more punitive when boys play "inappropriately" than when girls do.[85] If a boy shows what you consider "too much" interest in dolls, dressing up, or playing with girls, or any of the so-called "childhood indicators of homosexuality,"[86] reread the chapter on homosexuality and question your own homophobia before you make snap judgments about children's sexual orientation from the evidence of play.

Compulsive play preferences of any kind should be read as a signal of your child's unfulfilled needs: a girl who insists on *always* and *only* being the father in fantasy play may use the pretend male role as a vehicle through which she can freely express her dominance and assertiveness. She needs your permission to be a dominating, assertive *girl.*

A boy's enthusiasm for dress-up play is not a sure sign of transvestism; it may be his way of saying "It's too hard being a boy all the time; sometimes I want to be someone else." Take the pressure off and give him permission to be laid-back, expressive, demonstrative or whatever he feels like being—while still being a *boy.* Don't make children conjure up a complete sex change in order to play or act as they wish.

Before calling the child psychiatrist, think about Dr. Sirgay Sanger's advice to a father who was upset that his three-year-old son liked to wear earrings:

interesting

Let him. Eventually the world will inform him in no uncertain terms that boys don't wear earrings. Either he will notice it by himself, or outsiders will instruct him. Let the world teach him, not his father. By angrily forbidding them or ripping the earrings off his son's ears, a man is saying much more than "boys don't wear earrings." He is saying, "I'm scared you're not a boy." No child should see that much "masculinity" panic in his father—and besides, if the boy is actually headed for homosexual or transsexual adulthood, nothing the father says or does about something like earrings will stop him.[87]

Actually, no play is "deviant" unless we make it so. If we can free ourselves of sex role straitjackets and let our children try out all imaginable roles, costumes, activities, and behaviors during childhood, we might rear far fewer fetishists than did our parents' generation.

• *Playmate-mentor is an important function for mothers.* You'll recall that children often prefer Father to Mother because of Father's playfulness (which is made possible by Mother's relieving him of the caretaking chores).[88] How can children learn to see Woman as carefree, strong, physical, and fun-loving?

Don't just ferry your children to swim class or ballet; take classes together, exercise together in the house, play hide-and-seek, toss horseshoes, run races, climb trees, make mud pies outside—let kids think of Mother as alive and kicking, not just as the sensible parent who teaches them to cook or dress neatly.

Let Father get the dinner while Mother and the boys play. Those idyllic images of the woman approvingly watching her "men" cavorting beyond the kitchen window as she scrubs the grass stains out of yesterday's playclothes or warms the soup for their lunch are propaganda for woman-as-spectator. Your daughter is more likely to want to be a woman if it doesn't mean giving up the action for a view from the kitchen window.

WHAT YOU CAN DO—IN SPORTS

Many of the nonsexist principles that enhance playtime also work wonders in sports.

• *Cross the gender barrier wherever possible.* Father can take his daughter away on a ski trip or shoot baskets with her in the school yard just as comfortably as he might take tap dancing, pottery, or art classes with his son on a Saturday. He might offer to hit high flies or grounders to a girl and her friends, help them start a soccer league, volunteer to coach them in whatever sport might be lacking a woman coach.

Women sports experts are still pretty rare. If you have one in your house, use her. Mother might start a field hockey team, take a carload of kids to a lacrosse game and be the only one who can explain the plays, advise her children on the best bowling shoes, teach them a Ping-Pong slice, or volunteer to coach or manage teams of either sex.

Margaret Ellis, who was never allowed to play baseball when she was a girl, remembers when she first started coaching her son's Little League team:

> Many of the boys would not look me in the eye. One boy told his mother he would not play for a woman coach. Still, we finished with the best won-lost record in the minors.[89]

And by the end of the season the boys were *bragging* about their coach. In much the same proud way, my friend Wendy Weil talks about her mother the fisherwoman, who for twenty-five years has made an annual excursion to a certain upstate trout stream:

> My brother and I leave schools and jobs to join her. We come to be with her, to share her excitement, and to try to catch her style as well as a few fish.[90]

Another "sportsy" mother (as my son puts it) is the woman who played third base on a small-town softball team. One of her seven children describes his childhood:

> It was always baseball. . . . Mother could really hit. When I was real little I batted right-handed but when I saw the way Mother hit left-handed, I turned around. . . . Sometimes on a family picnic, Mother would play third with my sisters at first, second and short and another sister playing roving shortstop.[91]

After emerging from this family of "female jocks," the boy made high school all-America in baseball, was a running back in football, played basketball, and was a track star. Many colleges offered him scholarships but he chose pro baseball. At this writing, Terry Whitfield, son of a third basewoman, is batting .289 for the San Francisco Giants.

• *Don't settle for "locker room" love.* Father-son, man-to-man relationships forged by shared sports interests have been glorified in popular mythology from Ernest Hemingway to *Boys' Life,* from *Bad News Bears* to a baleful statistic: "More than 50 percent of the time that fathers spend with their sons is spent either talking about or participating in sports."[92]

If sports provides such a vast opportunity for father-child closeness, then daughters should get in on it. But if sports is a *substitute* for real intimacy, then boys should not have to make do with locker room camaraderie in place of fatherly love. Only you can judge which function sports serves in your family and whether it should be extended to girls or minimized with boys.

• *Teach girls to win and boys to lose.* Well, not literally. However, since girls get the message not to compete too hard and boys have been pressured to win at all costs, parents need to release children *out loud* from society's obligations to conform to stereotype and thus take the onus off sports as a sex role proving ground. That means lots of loving ego-building when a boy does not excel and lots of family enthusiasm when a girl *does.*

• *Expose girls and boys to role models of both sexes (and all races) engaged in every possible sports activity your child might enjoy.*

Like most women over thirty, I grew up with male heroes because that was the gender heroes came in. Heroes were giants grown from ordinary American children; they were courageous, physically transcendent, adored—but if you wanted to grow up to be one, you had to start out a *boy.*

Such female heroes as Amelia Earhart, Althea Gibson, and Babe Didrikson were rare, remote oddities. Ordinary little girls couldn't grow up to be *them;* you had to start out as supergirl.

Besides, the whole notion of a female *hero* was off-track. Women were *heroines.* They "endured" until rescued.

In 1977, however, the top six sports heroes of ten-year-old girls *and* boys were rated in this order: Dorothy Hamill, Nadia Comaneci, Bruce Jenner, O.J. Simpson, Chris Evert, Lou Brock.[93]

Now you can expose your sons and daughters to heroes in two genders, those six and many more who open vistas of human potential, who inspire girls to strive and boys to admire girls who strive—and whose exploits peel the sex labels off every kind of fun.

I mean women in golf, tennis, and basketball, of course, but I also mean women racers; whether auto racers, swimmers, runners, or horse-racing jockeys, the idea is to free girls to experience *speed*—the exhilaration of it and the triumph of beating a clock or a field of competitors. And I mean rugby, where 125 active women's teams are putting an end to the male monopoly of this all-out sport; and football, where thirteen teams mix it up in the National Women's Football League.[94]

For boys, the expanded horizon includes field hockey, a formerly-female sport, and figure skating, where men "have blended athletics and grace to a degree that gets spectators jumping out of their seats,"[95] and gets little boys out on the ice for the *beauty* of it.

Exposure to role models means taking children to live games, tuning in televised matches or tournaments featuring these athletes, tacking up magazine stories about nontraditional heroes, and subscribing to special-interest sports magazines.

The objective: to create heroes *of* both sexes *for* both sexes.

• *Encourage girls to take credit for their accomplishments.* Most girls are uncomfortable about their athletic triumphs. They attribute success to luck; they don't brag the way boys do:

> If you listen to a couple of ten-year-old boys talking about their performance . . . you'd think you just tuned in on a conversation between Ty Cobb and Joe DiMaggio. They tell of smashing hits and diving, one-handed catches . . . and pretty soon they convince themselves that they are in fact as good as they say.[96]

As we saw in the discussion of peer dynamics, girls worry about making friends jealous by their achievements. We've also seen how girls can "fear success." Yet "taking credit" helps children delineate their self-image and inspires them to live up to their own notices.

For example, this fourteen-year-old's letter from camp radiates enough heat to warm up several future performances:

> Mom and Dad,
>
> I played the game of my LIFE! All the
> guys were older than me. I was playing second
> base, batting first. Nothing went by me in
> the field. I caught flies, dove for grounders
> and caught bullet throws to the bag. Once there
> was a ground ball to me that I fumbled and
> dropped but I ran after it, picked it up and
> fired it to third to get the lead runner out.
> I was up at bat four times. Once I hit
> a smash out to center which they caught, twice
> I walloped solid singles and once I got an
> R.B.I. which tied up the score. . . . I was playing
> my *best!* I wasn't nervous at all and I stopped
> feeling like I needed to prove myself.

The author of that letter was Abigail Pogrebin, the only girl on either team. She could take credit for her game because she's always been encouraged to face the reality of her own competence. Give your daughter permission to brag occasionally, thereby giving herself enough confidence to hold her own even if she's a minority of one.

• *Don't let cheerleading pass for a real sport.* I know the arguments: it's a pep squad, it's like dance, it's acrobatics, it's entertainment.[97] That may be true for cheering squads made up of both girls and boys with gymnastic talents and big voices, wearing reasonable outfits and spread out so the whole crowd can hear the cheers.

But when it's pretty girls only and no talent necessary and a low-cut go-go "uniform" and all the girls clustered near the team bench where no one can follow their cheers, which come at the wrong times anyway because no one ever bothered to teach them the game—then cheerleading is a school-sponsored sex object parade and your daughter should not be seduced into it.

If you need more convincing compare the *purpose* of the exposed flesh of a cheerleader with that of a girl running track: "Which body is passively bared for ogling and which for power and skill? Which flatters [the male] ego and which commands respect?"[98]

A surprising number of present-day feminists were cheerleaders in their school years, myself included,[99] so this critique can't be written off as sour grapes. For us, cheerleading (then "clean cut," non–go-go at least) was the only way a girl could get out there on the field. For our daughters, there is a more genuine route to glory.

• *Try anything.* With that rule of thumb, I have managed to compensate for my creampuff childhood. Research indicates that women raised as I was usually gave up trying long ago, and now merely put themselves down, especially to their sons.[100] Certainly, I've watched my contemporaries giggle, screech, self-deprecate, and opt out when faced with an athletic endeavor, whether a sailing lesson or a parents' potato race. I just tell myself that my children are watching, and it helps me plunge in. (That's the feminist version of "sacrificing for the kids.")

Bert, who spent every day of his childhood playing outdoors (while I was guarding my reproductive organs), does not realize the enormity of the fact that if I were not setting an example for the children I might never have taken up tennis, baseball, touch football, sailing, skiing, or windsurfing. Once I couldn't run for a bus without needing mouth-to-mouth resuscitation; now I run a mile. I might never have known I could.

I tried all these sports because I take being a role model seriously. And I ended up loving all but two: ice skating is boring and scuba diving scares me to death.

The "try anything" attitude marks a mother as a woman of action. Don't worry about how good you are; it takes children years to notice. At eleven, David confessed that until he was ten he thought his father and I were equally terrific softball players.

It was inevitable he'd find out otherwise. But during his age of innocence I had ten great years.

I don't mean to suggest that fathers are automatically more agile and athletic than mothers. Often it is even harder for a father to "try anything" because sports is so emotionally charged for men and when a father is learning something new alongside his children, he has to risk being more inept than most men care to feel.

• *Don't overorganize, oversupervise, or overpressurize kids' sports.* Sociologists find that kids want to play, parents (usually fathers) want to win; kids would rather bat and field on a losing team than sit on the bench on a winning one.[101]

Adults are impressed by coaches, uniforms, formal teams and schedules, referees, and crowds in the stands, but children "do not learn skills well under pressure."[102] They learn from sandlot games, pick-up teams, peer foul-calling, and lots of chances to shoot baskets or hit baseballs without whistles blowing and parents blaring orders from the bleachers.[103]

Nonsexist parents (especially men who have unsettled scores from boyhood) must strike a balance between overinvested adult hysteria and not showing up for games. There is a huge point spread between those extremes for parents, and between the extremes of *spectator* and *varsity* for children.[104] Having fun can and should be an end in itself.

If fun and games don't come naturally to you; if you need help understanding the function of fun, how to motivate girls to play sports, or learning the rules of any game, read a few books pre-season.[105]

SEPARATE ISN'T EQUAL, IT'S SUSPECT

One more thing remains to be said about having fun: fun, like friendship, should be "haveable" by girls and boys *together.*

The recent ruling by a federal judge in Ohio that high school girls may not be barred from playing on boys' athletic teams. . . . [is] a truly radical decision because real equality in sports will break down forever the traditional male and female roles.[106]

There's the crux of it: playing separately consolidates sex roles; playing together breaks them down forever. Playing together from toddlerhood, as friends, playmates, and eventually teammates would create a shared history. It would give girls and boys an interest in one another beyond the relatively narrow objective of sexual arousal.[107]

Playing together would require boys to stop belittling and sabotaging girl athletes.[108] If their sports destinies are intertwined, boys will want girls to be well trained for the good of the team.

Playing together would mean death to the notion of "proving manhood" through sports, because what then are the girls doing out there?[109]

One school stopped giving team letters when the women's varsity was formed. They claimed that the letters had lost their meaning. "Generally, when women get involved in formerly all-male activities, the 'rating' of that activity goes down."[110] Playing together in every activity would nullify that pernicious phenomenon.

Playing together from the beginning would eliminate that period of sex role "consolidation" when boys learn to become pathologically competitive and girls learn to fear success and prefer to "lose handsomely."[111] The two sexes might "modify the extremes of each others' behavior,"[112] or the extremes themselves —male aggression and female helplessness—might lose their gender linkages.

Playing together as children would make living together as adults more *sensible*. Women and men would very likely enjoy the same sports, understand the same games, prefer the same kinds of recreational activities and vacation sports.[113] Husbands wouldn't have to "escape" wives in order to pursue their interests, and wives wouldn't have to feign enthusiasm for alien sports in order to promote family "togetherness."

Finally, the routine exposure of boys to girls' competence[114] would revolutionize the deepest relationships between women and men. It would accustom both sexes to the experience of females who are not only lovers and friends but leaders, heroes, high-scorers, and champions.

19

Toys Are Us

Once upon a time, there were two enlightened parents who decided to liberate their children from sex roles.

"No more domestic toys for our daughter," said mother.

"No tough-guy toys for our son," agreed father.

So under the tree on Christmas morning was a shiny new truck for their little girl and a sweet baby doll for their little boy. The parents beamed as their children took the toys into the playroom.

"This will be the beginning of a new life," said father.

"Down with sexism in the nursery," agreed mother.

Later, the parents tiptoed in to observe their emancipated children at play. They saw the little girl cradling the truck in her arms and singing, "Aah, Aah, baby," while the little boy was pushing his doll across the floor, bellowing, "Vrroom, vrroom, vrooommm."

That's the gist of a television comedy sketch that was never produced because the writers were afraid it would be misinterpreted. "People might take it as a boost for biology-is-destiny," explained Renee Taylor. "They don't realize it takes more than one toy to undo a whole childhood."[1]

True enough. Unless the adults around them are practicing flexible roles, children will ignore toys they fear are gender incongruous. In other words, there's not much sense in giving a doll to a little boy whose father wouldn't be caught dead rocking a baby. But if more men knew how important toys can be for child development, more fathers might reform their role rigidity for the good of their children if nothing else.

365

A variety of toys gives children "a sense of being in control"[2] of a small part of life, lets them experiment with many roles, express love, and vent frustration and anger. Different kinds of toys also help children learn to reason, count, create, manipulate, spell, read, analyze, categorize, construct, and dismantle. A toy can teach them to compete or cooperate. A toy can change their behavior and influence their futures.

A friend who is an oceanographer discovered her affinity for sea life when she got a snorkel mask at age ten. When I was nine, I started writing a monthly "magazine" because my parents gave me a Hectograph, a primitive copying machine with which I could "publish" my work.

Finally, toys can leave an emotional imprint for life. How many of us still remember the tragedy of a broken or lost toy, and how many more have kept a favorite toy or stuffed animal from then 'til now. In *Citizen Kane,* the hauntingly mysterious "Rosebud" turned out to be a child's sled.

Despite this impressive potential to enlarge a child's world, toys have usually been used to constrict it for sex roles' sake. Maybe that's why many of us can remember the toys we *didn't* get better than those we did.

> *Video:* Close up of a woman sitting on the rug beside a Christmas tree, wrapping a package of Lionel trains.
>
> *Audio:* "You know the very worst Christmas I ever had when I was little was the year my brother got a Lionel train set and I got another doll. I wanted a Lionel, but I was a girl. . . . Well, that's not going to happen to my little girl. This Christmas I'm giving her a Lionel of her own, with all the trimmings. . . . Because who ever said Lionel trains were only for boys?"[3]

This "breakthrough" commercial was too ingenuous to be commendable. Whoever said electric trains were only for boys? Everyone said it, starting with the company spokesman, who quipped "We're doing this for all the frustrated Daddies who couldn't enjoy model trains because they had daughters."[4] The packages said it by using only pictures of boys and men, and the stores said it by setting up the train sets in the "Boys' " section of the toy department, and the ads said it by touting trains for "Dads and Lads."

In keeping with its high price and because of its intricacy, a model railroad has enormous play potential. It can teach children about transportation, city planning, engineering, electricity, ecology, geography, history, and sociology. Yet generations of girls have been cheated of this multi-layered experience in families that could otherwise afford it.

Manufacturers, advertisers, and retailers are all culpable. But it is primarily a parent's decision that puts a toy such as an electric train in a child's life. It is your hand turning the pages of the store catalog until you see a sex-"appropriate" selection, and your voice asking a salesperson for a toy suitable for "a six-year-old girl," instead of something for a six-year-old who loves animals, or a six-year-old musical genius.

I was one of those parents, too, until I started reviewing and testing thousands of toys and games for the annual "Gifts for Free Children" feature in *Ms.* magazine. From this saturation exposure, I developed a simple checklist of toy standards, which many parents and educators have found useful:[5]

A good toy must be 1. safe; 2. made to last; 3. respectful of a child's intellect, self-esteem, and creativity; 4. nonracist and nonsexist in the way it is packaged, conceived, and planned for play; 5. moral in terms of the values it represents.

Let's be specific about the latter two criteria:

A TOY MUST BE NONRACIST* AND NONSEXIST IN THE WAY IT IS PACKAGED, CONCEIVED, AND PLANNED FOR PLAY

A toy has no gender and no idea of whether a girl or boy is playing with it.

It's often necessary to make that preposterous statement to

---

*Here my emphasis is limited to sexism, however it should be understood that the patterns discussed are usually applicable to issues of racism as well.

remind people that *we* are the crazies who ascribe to inanimate objects a sex-linked identity and we are the sensible people who can decide to do otherwise.

Sexist Packaging

Illustrations don't just show the toy, they show (or tell) who is supposed to use it. As we've noted, children feel *entitled* to play with something if they see others like themselves playing with it. Overall, boys appear on game packages twelve times more often than girls, and on science toys, boys are pictured sixteen times more frequently.[6] A mere body count, damning as it is, misses the subtleties:

• A walkie-talkie package shows both girl and boy using the toy but the girl is chattering on her end (just like a woman) and the boy is listening on his end with a bored, superior expression.

• "A busy working dashboard just like Dad's" is the subtitle on a package showing a boy operating the toy as a girl looks on.

• Both items do the same thing (pick up small objects into a catch-all bag) for the same age group (two to seven), but the pink, orange, and yellow push-toy is called a vacuum and labeled "Just like Mommy's," and the red, blue, and green push-toy is called a lawn mower, "Just like Daddy's."

• Four pictures on a Young Erector set show boys making intricate structures. In the fifth, a girl is building a doll house.

Sexist packaging can be a serious stumbling block to the purchase of sports equipment. Inevitably, they picture a boy getting the big catch with a fishing set, the hole-in-one with a golf club, the bull's eye with a dart game, the strike with a bowling set —and if a girl is shown at all, she is usually clapping or jumping for joy on his behalf.

Occupational Tracking

Inside those packages are materials that, in the adult world, would be cause for a job discrimination suit:

• Many doctor's kits still show boys only, and nurse's kits show girls; doctors get medical paraphernalia, nurse's kits are as likely to contain food service trays as nursing items.

• A matching game contains pictures of twenty-one males to match with jobs from mason to milkman to sailor to scientist. The three females match up with teacher, violinist, and dancer.

• Flash cards show fathers who ride off to work, mothers who cook.

• A preschool puzzle gives a boy diverse role choices; for a girl the options are mother, ballerina, or nurse. Another puzzle shows a male in the driver's seat of every car, truck, bus, or van.

• A multi-piece playset comes with a Mommy figure wearing a permanent painted-on apron.

• A set of masquerade masks could transform a boy into a cowboy, doctor, football player, fireman, clown, monster, pirate, or spaceman. The girl masks include nurse, bride, majorette, movie star, and princess.

• One Sears Roebuck catalog devoted forty pages to housekeeping toys, and dolls to make every girl "feel like a real Mommy."

Behavior Tracking

If I tell you there are games called *What Shall I Wear?* and *Mystery Date Game,* you'd have no trouble knowing for which sex they're intended. In both games, a girl's objective is to outfit herself properly before her friends complete their wardrobes. The "fun" is provided by female rivalry, getting dressed, and snaring dates.

The competition cards in the *Miss America Pageant Game* judge a girl's "personality, talent, swimsuit and evening gown." There's no category for brains, money management, or independence. Nor is there a male counterpart game judging boys on "personality, talent, swimtrunks and tuxedo."

Emblematic of the trivia-is-your-life message is a girls' game in which a sample card reads: "You handled your first date with a new boy very well. You made an excellent impression and got another invitation." A similar product, *The Bride Game,* is "For the girl who wants to be a bride one day (and who doesn't)." Although all those brides presumably marry men, American boys are not up in the tree house preparing themselves with *The Groom Game.*

The Effect of Separate Toys for Girls and Boys

Girls' toys teach girls "to sit and play quietly and just accept things the way they are," says psychologist Florence Denmark. Boys' toys teach boys "to have an effect on the environment . . . taking things apart, putting them together and moving things around. They can see themselves as creators of society."[7]

Boys' toys are more varied, expensive, complex, active, and social, while girls' toys are generally simple, passive, and solitary. Report two Yale University researchers, after thirty hours of observation and interviewing customers in a toy department:[8]

- not one scientific toy was bought for a girl.

- people spent more time choosing toys for boys.

- for boys, buyers were more apt to choose activity items; for girls they were more willing to buy such nonactivity gifts as jewelry, clothes, furniture, and books.

- sex-neutral toys were the most creative and educational.

Competency training is another by-product of boys' toys. It's the difference between *Just Like Dad's* tool box with shop plans "designed to demonstrate the relationship of plans, tools and labor," and *The Popularity Game,* which demonstrates how to "make a good impression" on a date.

It's the difference between being the one who *does* and the one who *uses:*

> *Construction set brochure:* "If his sister Carol is nice to him, he will let her drive the car across the bridge which he himself has built."

It's the difference between being the target of great expectations, and not:

Construction set brochure: "I am Nathalie, the secretary. Here are John, the architect who designed this house, Alexander the engineer and Philip the plumber."

(We don't need Fannie the feminist to tell us who has more status.)

Boys' toys aren't all construction sets or constructive values. Take the example of male superhero dolls, known as "action figures" because what boy would play with a "doll"? These characters usually come with a hyper-masculine persona (Big Jim, G.I. Joe, Super Slade) and various weapons, uniforms, and props intended for fantasy play that involves rescue, ambush, beatings, victory, and death.

A few exceptions—the official Boy Scout dolls who fight the elements, not the "enemy," and such sports figures as O. J. Simpson—can be positive role models and surrogates for the child's best self. Similarly, unless children see them as reminders of their own inadequacy, comic book heroes such as Superman and Wonderwoman are conducive to futuristic make-believe that stretches the imagination. But there's nothing redeeming in such action figures as Action Jackson, Torpedo Fist, Warpath, The Whip, and Dr. Steel, who make "tough, mean, and menacing" the thing to be. For children who are just learning what it means to be human, such superhuman representations of manhood are nothing but trouble.

Double-Standard Heroism

New lines of female superheroes give the appearance of equality among the demi-gods, but look closely. See Batman, Robin, and Aquaman with bendable, jointed limbs suitable for action poses, while Cat Woman, Supergirl, and Batgirl have straight rigid limbs suitable for a mincing walk or fashion pose.

In the *Bionic Woman Game,* labeled "for girls," Lindsey completes her assignment with "special assistance" from Steve. In *The Six Million Dollar Man Bionic Crisis Game,* Steve's crisis is a matter for "the world's best scientists." As for attachments, he gets the "Bionic Transport and Repair Station"; she gets the "Bionic Beauty Salon."

Double-Standard Play Figures

The active/passive dichotomy in human sex roles translates to action/fashion in the play figure population. Girls get fashion figures with accompanying pamphlets suggesting play ideas. Barbie doll comes with suggested strategies for eclipsing the other girls, winning Ken doll's attention, and getting married. For this sequence she absolutely *must* have a dozen fashionable ensembles, several hair pieces, cosmetics, fragrances, a Barbie Beach Bus, Backyard Pool, Cabin Cruiser, and of course, a wedding dress.

When his daughter was seven, Art Buchwald confessed in print, "I bought a $3 Barbie Doll and ended up spending $400 to protect my original investment."[9]

Unlike the boys' kits, which emphasize what the doll can do, Barbie, Dawn, and B.J. lead occupational and recreational lives entirely dependent on their wardrobes. However, in the mid-seventies, a few companies brought out brisk, modern girl figures that were meant to perform great feats (while also dressed to the teeth): Debbie Lawler, the motorcycle stuntwoman; Dusty, the all-around sport; Derry Daring, who took up mountain climbing and journalism; and Wanda, formerly solely a nurse, stewardess, and ballerina, who turned to skydiving, racing, tennis, and big-time show business.

The message of the active female couldn't be missed. But what did millions of parents buy for their girls?

"Growing Up Skipper," the first doll that undergoes perpetual puberty. Twist her arm and she grows breasts and an indented waistline; untwist and the curves disappear. The mind reeled at the possibilities for "creative" play—eight-year-old girls twisting one another's arms trying to grow their own breasts, or small boys staging neighborhood sex shows headlined "Watch Skipper Grow Up. 5 Cents a Peek."

"We'll be happy when the development of a girl's mind receives as much attention as the development of her bosom," said N.O.W.'s letter to Mattel toys.

Somehow I can't see Mattel marketing a Growing Up Buster doll: "Twist his leg, his penis grows and his testicles descend." Not bloody likely. The male body is its own subject, not an object to be exploited or "toyed" with.

The Doll Dilemma

At worst, the action or fashion dolls communicate negative values and sex-stereotyped behavior. But without the accoutrements of the killer or the clothes-horse, these figures could serve as fantasy alter egos for the child's future self. A child, who has never been a teenager, uses the doll figure for "guesswork" pretend situations in which she or he can imagine being a more powerful and independent person.

To help children deal with the unresolved scenarios of the present and recent past, however, children need a doll that can represent themselves as they are now or were as babies.[10] Benjamin Spock explains:

> Dolls can be used to dramatize all the human relationships a child is sensitive to and has a compulsion to work through. A boy or girl playing with a doll has it break things or wet its pants or be rude in order to express his [or her] own rebelliousness and hostility. But then he [or she] scolds or spanks the doll as a way of placating his [or her] conscience for the naughty impulses and as a way of practicing his [or her] future role as a parent.[11]

In a straightforward retraction of his earlier position on boys and dolls, Spock says,

> I used to think it was important to emphasize maleness in boys by giving them boys' toys and clothes. But I no longer believe that is the way to do it. I refused to get a doll for our boys when my wife suggested it, but now I believe I was wrong.[12]

The millions who swear by Spock's advice in all other areas are still too insecure, he says, to accept dolls for boys.[13] One of my friend's experiences illustrates that insecurity:

> My son was wheeling his doll carriage and I was walking alongside. First, a fireman standing on the street said, "Tell

your mommy boys should have guns, not dolls!" Then a storekeeper told my son, "Your mother should give you a little sister if she wants a girl that badly."

Those guys were really disturbed. But they chose to speak man-to-man to a three-year-old rather than directly to me.

A doll in a carriage is not an "effeminate" object. To be strictly logical, most heterosexual men become fathers and most homosexual men do not. Proud adult fathers wheel babies around all the time without compromising their virility. In fact, quite the reverse. Once, when Bert was pushing the twins in their double carriage, some guy in a leather jacket quipped, "Hey, man, you must be twice the man to make 'em two at a time."

The contradictions are maddening: Dolls are thought to be bad for the boy in the child, but they are absolutely essential for the child in the boy. They are also useful for the father the boy may become. Yet dolls are denied to the sons in a traditional family, and recently have been denied to the daughters of feminists.

(Betty Friedan's parents were so troubled by her refusal to play with dolls that "they hauled her off to a child psychiatrist." Almost as retribution for their own brainwashing, many women shy away from dolls for girls.[14])

Parents should beware of solving their own sex role hang-ups through their children's toys. Consider dolls to be staple items in a balanced toy diet. Not fifteen to eighteen dolls per girl under age six, which is the national average,[15] but three or four dolls for each girl *or* boy. And I don't mean a Polly Pretend dress-up, makeup, hairstyle doll who appears to be around three but wears lipstick, high heels, and a "fun fur." I mean a simple cloth, rag, or soft vinyl doll, preferably one with anatomical accuracy, who stands ready to be the child your child needs.

Blinder-Vision: Where Are the Girls?

Would you rather be ignored or ill-treated? This Hobson's Choice approximates the general state of affairs in the history division of the toy trade.

I don't dispute men's commanding influence on past events,

but I believe the manufacturer of an educational plaything has an obligation to ferret out women's history, to tell children of both sexes what the other half of the population was up to, and to give us inspiring female ancestors. Instead, we have

• *Dioramas* that let a child create handsome scaled-down scenes of the Wright Brothers and Lindbergh's flights, but no comparable set for Amelia Earhart.

• *Famous Black People,* a biography game that offers thirty notable black men and six black women. If I can think of more than six, why couldn't the manufacturer?

• *Your America,* a bicentennial quiz game that mentioned only six females—and one of them was "Her," Lyndon Johnson's dog. So much for two hundred years of womankind in "Man's America."

How to Play Sexism

Before our daughters learned to read, I used to read game directions aloud to them, altering the inevitable male pronoun to "he or she," or, more often, "you"—as in "You should roll the dice and move clockwise on the board."

One day, after Robin could read by herself, she brought me the instructions for a game she was starting to play.

"This game isn't for girls, Mommy," she told me. "Look how it says a player should move *his* piece when *he* draws a card."

I had to explain that in gameland, as in English usage, *"He* means *you."* (See Chapter 24.)

Two men who strongly objected to the 109 "he's" in the directions for Monopoly spent years badgering Parker Brothers and seeking popular support for a change. Finally, the company's Vice President For Finance answered:

Since Monopoly is Parker Brothers' most valuable trademark, I'm sure you can imagine that we are very careful to protect our interests and we would not want to take any actions which would not be in the best long-term interest of Parker Brothers.[16]

A TOY MUST BE MORAL IN TERMS
OF THE VALUES IT REPRESENTS

This final guideline of mine brings up a point of definition. Since sexism is a kind of cosmic immorality, very often it takes something as ordinary as a toy to make feminism's large moral issues emotionally understandable.

Several years ago, a toy manufacturer introduced a series of torture kits for boys called Monster Scenes. In one, a semi-nude female figure could be assembled and then strapped to a platform with a razor-sharp pendulum guillotine at her throat. For bigger and better thrills, a boy could imprison his "girl victim" in a "hanging cage" or "pain parlor" equipped with blood-flecked spikes or "hot" coals to force her to stand on.

Chanting "Sadistic Toys Make Violent Boys," members of various parent and women's groups picketed the company's New York headquarters and announced a boycott of all its products. We charged that such toys "condition boys to accept as normal a sadomasochistic relationship between men and women and to believe that manhood is achieved through power over others."[17]

The grotesqueness of his pain parlor and hanging cage was lost on the company spokesman who said of the protest organizer that he'd like to put her "in a cage."[18]

Before the torture kits were discontinued, *eight hundred thousand* of them had been sold. A French TV commentator gave a trenchant epigram: "The French may have invented the guillotine but it took the Americans to make a toy out of it."[19]

You needn't save your outrage for such extremes of savagery. Children's values are corrupted enough by toys like Rock 'Em Sock 'Em Robots ("You can knock his block off"), or Knuckle Busters ("One punch in the nose and zap!"), which project a swaggering, bullying, "masculine" ideal.

Or by an "entertainment" like Chutzpah, the game that asks the question "Can a toy be sexist, anti-semitic, and unfunny all at once?" (The answer, Yes, if it contains game cards like, "Get your nose fixed," "College for Marvin, the genius," and "A catered wedding for daughter Shirley.")

Or by war games—whether of the cowboys-and-Indians ilk, which blind children to the genocide committed by white settlers against America's native population, or the racist-type that pit good-guy G.I. Joe against "Japs" or "Gooks." Or games of world domination—"Fire away . . . sink ships, capture islands, and become King of the Sea," or better yet, "Occupy every territory on the board, eliminating all other players, thus conquering the world!" What more effective way to teach boys such patriarchal imperatives as conquer, dominate, and rule, than through the step-by-step ritual of game-playing. Only weaponry can beat it.

A Gun Is No Fun

Forget about the phallic symbol business for a moment and think of the gun as a tool of power—the great persuader that eliminates negotiation and silences dissent. Because man perceives himself to be the legitimate power wielder, the tools of power belong to him whether he keeps them well oiled in a gun rack over his mantle, or "keeps" them only symbolically in the form of toy guns given to male children.

Unfortunately, some sons take the heritage seriously. There are over two hundred thousand gun crimes in the U.S. every year and more than thirty thousand deaths.[20] "Guns don't kill people; people kill people," says the weapons lobby. But of course, without guns, countless hotheaded altercations would end in a fistfight instead of a murder, and children would not shoot themselves or their friends with real guns mistaken for toys, and ghetto kids playing cops and robbers would not be shot by real-life cops who say they can't always tell the difference between a toy and a gun.

For all this, I won't deny that most little boys love guns. Which takes us back to the gun as a phallic symbol. I've watched our two daughters grow into adolescents without a single request for a toy gun. They've played chase games in which there are pretend fighting, horrific injuries, and melodramatic dying scenes of victims rolling down hills or falling in a heap. But there has been no shooting. When I asked them why, they said it never occurred to them to add guns to the dramas.

On the other hand, our son—raised on the same values and

toy gun prohibition—has occasionally come under the spell of a fancy toy tank or shiny revolver, and has attempted a feeble plea for "just one." His play sometimes has included pretend finger guns, war whoops, and "Bang, bang, you're dead." When I've walked in on such a fracas, he has always looked sheepish. Although I've never stopped the action, David can read my mind.

Once, when he was about six or seven, he fashioned a gun-shaped object out of a piece of wood and announced that "it's a miracle gun that shoots life back into people who get dead." David reveres life. He covers his ears when someone tells a story about suffering. But he retains a definite fascination with guns. If it wasn't obvious from his dramatic play as a small child, it would be crystal clear from the meticulously detailed drawings of artillery, bombers, and gunboats he has produced throughout his later childhood years.

Is this because he's a boy, or is it because he's seen guns everywhere defined as the accoutrements of male power and glory? We'll never know the answer until our culture tells its children that weapons are not symbols of strength but signs of weakness.

In the meantime, you must decide whether to ban toy guns, as our family and many others have done, or to accept one of the rationalizations for gun play, most commonly the argument that children who work out their hostilities in make-believe situations are less likely to do it for real.

Dr. John Speigel, former director of The Center for the Study of Violence and past president of the American Psychiatric Association, refutes that claim:

> Today's kids have plenty of opportunity to release their aggressions in ordinary play in a healthier manner. The problem with the violent toy is that when a child shouts "Bang-bang! You're dead!" he has no realistic control over his aggression. But if your youngster's aggression comes out in sport and play and he realizes that he may hurt somebody, he learns what the consequences of his aggression are.[21]

When the consequences of aggression in Vietnam appeared on the nightly TV news, sales of war toys dropped dramatically, but since the U.S. pull-out, toy guns have made a comeback.[22] Military toys always sell better in peacetime when there are fewer reminders of the gore guns leave behind.[23]

Gun "play" does not reduce aggression, says Dr. Jerome Frank of Johns Hopkins Medical School. "The mere sight of a gun will *increase* violent behavior." In an experimental situation, "children who played with toy guns were more likely to destroy the work of a friendly playmate than children who had not."[24]

No one expects to protect children from all the violence in life. But to protect them from the glorification of violence and to deny parental *approval* of weapons as tools of power is a parent's right and obligation.

Certainly, if every toy has the potential to teach a child something, then a toy gun will teach some boys to need a real gun and to enjoy pulling the trigger. Yet the most moral and responsible parents ask their children to accept a contradictory message: *We think crime and killing are dreadful, but here's a cute little toy rifle for Christmas.* Says Dr. Frank,

> By giving our children toys of peace instead of war, we show them that we disapprove of violence. This discourages them from resorting to it and may lead them as adults to search for new nonviolent ways of resolving conflicts that do not endanger human survival in the nuclear age.[25]

Dr. Lee Salk forbade his children to have guns on more personal grounds—"because guns stand for killing, and killing upsets me terribly." One day, Salk's son pushed his father toward the curbside. "Don't look to the right, Daddy," said the boy, "or you'll be terribly upset." Salk did as he was told, but he'd already caught a glimpse of the store window full of war toys.

Another rationale proposes that toy guns compensate for the anxiety boys feel about their genitals. To that, nursery and kindergarten teachers report "they can often spot students who are the most fearful by the number of toy guns they carry and the persistence with which they carry them."[26]

Dr. Emanuel Tanay, an expert on homicidal behavior, admits guns are "a universal male fascination and affliction." But that doesn't mean he *prescribes* it.

I don't forbid my five-year-old son to engage in gun play when he uses a stick or a carrot, but I do refuse to allow toy guns in the house. Parents have to walk this middle ground. Our attempts to eradicate all forms of gun play would fixate the gun obsession as surely as if we bought our son a dozen B.B. guns.[27]

Whether culture or castration anxiety inspires boys' interest in guns, you needn't give in to it by providing the weapons and thereby endorsing the violence they symbolize. Let your son *invent* the gun play he needs; don't give him the Saturday Night Special and the shooting script to go with it.

TOY INVENTORIES TELL ALL

The name of the game is fun, don't forget—and the world is full of playthings that both complement a parent's consciousness and warm a child's heart. Does your child have enough of those kinds of toys? To find out fast, use our test for nonsexist children's rooms: Could you move a six-year-old girl's toychest into a six-year-old boy's room in confidence that he would enjoy its contents? If not, how many and which toys would you remove to make the collection more "suitable" for a boy; what toys would you add, and why?

Chances are the switch can't be made so easily, and yet the disparate impact of one-sided sexist toy collections, such as were found in a study of children's rooms,[28] suggests that the switch is absolutely essential for girls.

Boys' toys (that is, toys traditionally given to boys), more than girls' toys, allow children to be more creative[29] and foster more competence and originality. The most successful professional women are those who played with boys' toys when they were children.[30]

If our society cared about men's being more loving, we might have some data on the effects of depriving boys of the nurturant play associated with traditional girls' toys. But we know enough about the effects of an unbalanced toy diet on girls to draw some reverse conclusions and to start taking toys seriously for both sexes.

Start with a toy inventory; it's an enlightening experience just to sort and count. You may find your daughters' toy collection is suffering from terminal "femininity," while your son doesn't have one soft, cuddly object to call his own.

Even without such extremist toy environments, most children would benefit from more balanced play options. For young children, simply introduce new toys one by one until some diversity is achieved. Once gaps are filled, stereotyped toys blend into the collection and become part of the range of choices. With older children, discuss your own past biases, point out what's one-sided, and talk about unexplored areas of fun. If that seems too self-conscious, let your kids guide you to their repressed wishes: Notice which of her brother's toys your daughter is always "borrowing," or what toys attract your son at a female friend's house or in a toy store. Ask the child's nursery school teacher if any classroom toys are particular favorites.

For a treat one day, let your child pick out five toys, each of which costs under five dollars or whatever, as long as you get to choose the one that is actually bought. Then pick the one that seems the least predictable for that child, the toy most unlike others in her or his collection. (When President Carter's daughter Amy was nine, the "toy" she wanted most for Christmas was a chain saw. And when the president of the F. A. O. Schwarz toy emporium told his three-year-old grandson to pick *any* toy from the store's huge selection, the boy chose a tea set.[31])

I once watched a little boy select a flower press as a gift for his friend in such a way that it was clear he coveted the item himself. "Are you kidding?" said the boy's father. "We can't get Peter such a sissy present." Judging from the crushed look on the boy's face, I'd say his interest in preserving flowers died on the spot.

Other children's birthdays are a great excuse to discover what your child likes. You can also use toy ads as a clue. A spirited "Doesn't that look like fun?" might awaken a request for a racing set from your daughter. If mother or father has a nontraditional skill that the children admire, look for toys that might inspire imitative play.

Wishes are the most direct route to children's hearts' desires.

When we had to buy Abigail ballet slippers and tights for her first dance class, David, who was four at the time, whined, "Can't I get something new, too?"—a request I'd normally consider annoying. But since I was curious to see if David might want something associated with ballet, I asked him what he'd like. He brightly answered, "A sewing kit."

Older children might keep their hearts' desires more deeply buried. To get at them, ask, "If you could have any toy in the world and never have to show it to anyone, what would it be?" Or, "Can you think of ten great toys you wish someone would invent?" Or the old standby, "If you were a boy (girl), what toys would you like to play with?"

To be sure, some children have too many toys as is, and a corrective toy-buying campaign could spoil the child as well as strain the finances. In time, though, the inventory should be revised, either through bought toys or made toys, or—

COLLECTIVE COLLECTIONS

At little or no expense, you can create a toy lending library if you can find a central place to store the toys, someone to gather donations of used toys in good condition, and a few volunteers to help kids check out toys the way they borrow books. Or else, try a toy exchange—an organized hand-me-down procedure that lets children own a variety of toys by trading with others as they outgrow or tire of their own playthings.

Both toy-sharing plans let kids from low-income families play with toys their parents might not otherwise be able to afford. Everyone's toys would be recycled rather than discarded, and sex role stereotypes could be eliminated from the playroom through judicious borrowing and bartering.

WHAT'S GOOD? WHAT'S FUN?

The best toys are "yes" toys—playthings that are unstructured, open-ended, and positive. A "yes" toy is always nonsexist because it decrees no roles and is as pliable as the child's imagination. The best "yes" playthings are basic materials—dirt, water,

paint, paper, cardboard, dolls, blocks, fabric, boxes, cooking utensils, clay, building materials (whether raw wood, nails, and tools
or commercial sets, such as Lincoln Logs).

A "no" toy is one that has a right way and a wrong way of
playing with it. It breaks or spoils easily, needs adult supervision,
or comes pre-cut, pre-designed, and almost pre-played-with. Often
it suggests particular roles for girls or boys *(The Popularity Game),*
or it requires one person's discomfort for another's pleasure.

In reasonable proportion, "no" toys teach kids to live in the
real world where people play by the rules, endure failure and
frustration, and compete with others. The idea is to strike a balance among all kinds of toys: those that say an open-ended "yes"
and those with a qualified "no," those that challenge and those
that offer quick mastery, large muscle toys and think-toys, toys
that teach and toys that evoke feelings.

If I had to name the one play item in our house that lasted
the longest and gave the most, it would have to be wooden blocks.
For more than ten years our set of unpainted wooden blocks in
the shapes of arches, squares, rectangles, columns, half circles, and
triangles gave all three children thousands of hours of fun. We've
watched the blocks be transformed into bridges, castles, space
stations, zoos, highways, farms, street scenes, and split-level
homes, accessorized with little rubber animals, wooden people
figures, cars, trains, street signs, fresh flowers and weeds (for
landscaping), aluminum foil mirrors and lakes, homemade curtains, wallpaper, and murals. Other structures have been used to
hide in, jump off, climb up, perform from, and balance on. Blocks
are an expensive investment (in our case a gift from Grandma for
Robin and Abigail's third birthday), but I can think of nothing
more durable, versatile, economical (on a cost-per-use basis),
pleasure-giving, and educational. Which brings me to the myth of
the "educational toy."

TOYS THAT TEACH

During a workshop on nonsexist toys, a mother once admitted that she buys her son "educational" toys, which, more often
than not, he tires of quickly, while her husband buys only toys that
he *likes* himself and the son seems to adore them. Other parents

offered explanations of this phenomenon: one ventured that children may be more influenced by their father's enthusiasms because it's such an "event" when a male parent takes an interest in child's play. Another said that men are just grownup little boys who understand fun better than women because they maintain a relationship with play by playing at sports, playing with tools, and playing with money in business. A third thought that men, acting out of confidence in their judgment, make toy choices based on the inherent qualities of a toy, while women lack that basic confidence and thus rely on the authority of an educational expert to guide their choices. I find some truth in all three theories.

In any case, the most "educational" toy of all is a percolator coffee pot. A child can take apart the lid, basket, and stem and reassemble it; use the pot as a hollow drum, as a vessel for filling and pouring and measuring liquids, or as a make-believe "real" coffee pot; strain things through the coffee basket; blow through the hollow stem or use it as a water pipe; look at the world through the percolator glass bubble on top; load the pot with smaller objects and shake it like a noisemaker, or actually use the pot to learn how to make coffee beans and water into fresh-brewed coffee.

This wondrous "toy" comes into the house with no fancy psychological phrases, expert endorsements, or packages that decree who should play with it—and it probably gives twice as much play value as most "educational" toys at double the price.

BEYOND THE TOY STORE

Just as labels don't guarantee learning, finding an object on a toy counter doesn't mean it's a better plaything that you can get elsewhere. Go to an *art store* and buy better paints, brushes, and paper. Add a *dime store* picture frame and display a child's masterpieces in style. At a *garden shop,* get seeds, soil, flowerpot, spade, watering can, and sprinkler bottle, for the price of one plastic "plant kit."

The *stationery store* is a gold mine: pipe cleaners for wire sculptures; a pencil compass makes op-art; a hole puncher is great for Swiss cheese; graph paper for work charts; ledger books for scorekeeping or playing store; labelmakers help kids spell; wall calendars teach numbers and months, and help kids keep track of events; a steno book can contain a diary or a full-length novel. And needless to say, a stapler, tape dispenser, scissors, note pads, and file folders make a school child's desk as important as an executive's.

Don't leave the *notions counter* without colored yarn, beads, sequins, buttons, appliques, hooks and snaps, trim, and braiding. Put them in separate plastic bags, pop them in a box, and give the child a first-rate collage kit.

The hardware store is a prime source for no-nonsense tools, nails, and screws—but have you thought about more exotic items such as hinges, sandpaper, and wood stain for the creation your child brought home from shop; self-stick shelf paper for home-made book jackets or wall paper for the dolls' house; a selection of weird light bulbs for the child's room fixture (our hardware store has colored bulbs, black light, flickering candle bulbs, silver-tipped bulbs, globe and chimney shapes)? The best chess set in the world is the one your child makes from such hardware goodies as nuts, bolts, eyelets, and hooks.

At the *supermarket* the shopping list and the toy list can be combined. Mild detergent is bargain-priced bubble bath; food coloring (diluted in water in a plastic squeeze bottle) is good for "painting" the tub at bath time; cake and frosting mix plus a few bottles of sprinkles guarantee the joy of cooking, or at least cupcake-decorating. When everyone has finished eating, why not use the empty food cans for playing "supermarket," the empty milk cartons for bowling pins, the little grocery bags for handmade hand puppets, the big grocery sacks for over-the-head disguises, and the delivery cartons for trains, cars, beds, or houses.

Finally, the *rummage sale!* Where else can a feather boa be had for a buck, a top hat for fifty cents, and a Legion of Honor medal (or lookalike) for a dime? When gender identity ceases to be confused with sex-role identity, a child is free to try on various roles, lifestyles, and personality types with just a change of clothes.

Thanks to the treasures from bazaars and tag sales, you need never buy another sexist tot-sized uniform. Instead of that princess outfit, your daughter might relish a leather helmet, circa 1914, a white silk muffler, and goggles—just the thing for playing Amelia Earhart in the cockpit of a grocery carton.

BECOME A PACKAGE ALTERER

Our children have always done very well at rummage sales. With a dollar in hand, each one will come home with a find. But in conventional toy stores, I've always preferred to shop without them. First, I think kids are overwhelmed by the array of merchandise. But more importantly, they're influenced by the store's "Boys" and "Girls" departments or toy groupings and by the sexist package illustrations.

When you do the toy shopping alone, you can select items your children will enjoy and then do some creative repackaging before giving the toy to the child.

If sports equipment comes sheathed in "masculine" imagery, rewrap it and put it in a plain brown wrapper or an empty shoe box. A tool set labeled "Handy Andy" or "Mr. Fix It" can be repackaged in a neat metal tool chest from the hardware store. Voila! A grown-up container that is sex-neutral and practical enough for years of use as larger tools are added.

If you wait for a small broom, mop, and dustpan to be packaged under a picture of girls *and* boys cleaning, you'll have quite a heap of dust in the children's rooms. Buy the "Golden Girl" cleaning set, throw away the box with the picture of a housewife wearing a crown, spare your four-year-old the visual brainwashing, and present the broom and mop in the raw, secured with bright ribbons. Or get a long box from the florist; a container big enough for a dozen long-stemmed roses will hold a toddler-sized clean-up set nicely.

Package dishes, crafts, rockets, trucks (whatever comes with a sex-role commercial on its box) in shiny party bags, burlap, cheesecloth, aluminum foil, empty boxes covered with self-stick paper—anything cheerful and anonymous enough to make the toy inviting to a child of either sex.

DOLLS AND GUYS

Male resistance to dolls is understandable. "Doll-like" describes a vacuous girl about whom not much else can be said. A generally agreeable female is "a real doll." Toy dolls have namby-pamby names: Sweet Blossom and Wispy Walker. They're usually female, dressed in pink, and packed in boxes labeled "For girls 2 to 6," or "For the little mother."

Add these cultural cues to the boy's sex role socialization and the aversion he shows toward dolls becomes an instinct for survival. Parents too have strong anti-doll biases for boys. But both of you can get over your resistance, so that the boy from two to six can have the chance to play "little father."

First, buy the most lovable *boy* doll you can find—preferably one that resembles your son's hair and eye coloring, and certainly, a black doll for a black child. Call the baby Tommy, Buddy, or whatever. Then rename the object itself. Suppose you borrow your terminology from the play *Guys and Dolls,* and called the boy doll a "guy"? Might he (and you) feel more comfortable announcing, "I'm going to take my guy for a walk?"

Frivolous as it may seem, a generic name change could neutralize the fluff-and-femininity aura of a doll. The power of naming or renaming things, always a prerogative of the ruling class, has often been used to change minds (the term "unemployment insurance" removed the stigma of "going on relief"), and to reshape negative auras (such as changing The Secretary of War to The Secretary of Defense).

Calling male hero dolls "action figures" relieved masculinist anxieties about doll play but left little boys with Big Jim and G.I. Joe, not with objects of love and tenderness. With man-to-man reassurance, *Mattel* announced in its press release that "Big Jim is acceptable to many fathers as a doll for their sons because Big Jim is involved in masculine pursuits. And Big Jim is a doll that is not an assault on a father's masculinity." (What can one say about a grown man whose sexual identity is vulnerable to "assault" by a child's doll?)

SEX AND THE SINGLE DOLL

Anyone who knows children at all knows that two minutes after receiving a new doll they will examine all its features, undress it and inspect the area between its legs. In most cases, they will find no genital detail because toy manufacturers claim that modesty, good taste, and puritanical parents dictate a policy of sexless dolls.

Yet toymakers have managed to persuade supposedly puritanical parents to buy "Growing Up Skipper" and girl baby dolls that suck, urinate, and defecate.

My hunch is that the absence of anatomical accuracy is attributable to the fact that most toymakers are men, and men, as we've noted, show reluctance to expose the penis. Since most baby dolls are meant to represent girl babies, male designers can demarcate the vague definition of external vaginal lips with psychic equanimity, or can consider it quite sufficient to denote femaleness by flatness; i.e., the absence of a penis. However, I've also seen boy dolls that are flat "down there."

It may take time for you to track down anatomically correct baby dolls that have nothing to hide, but it's worth the effort. When we provide a doll with equipment for suckling, urinating, and defecating, but lacking genital definition, we imply that there is something shameful about children's sex organs.

Instead of giving them hairstyle and make-up dolls or bride dolls that reinforce a girl's traditional sex role identity and make a boy feel silly even holding one, why not give all children dolls that reinforce gender identity by affirming the *factual* genital differences between the sexes?

WHAT TO DO WHEN YOU'VE HAD IT IN TOYLAND

We can report unsafe toys to the U.S. Product Safety Commission,[32] but no federal agency or law court recognizes the danger of sexism. It's between us and the toymakers. Unless we complain to them about packaging, advertising, and display, and about toys themselves, the industry can continue to claim "We only give people what they want."

Send your complaint or request to the manufacturer, the retailer, the Toy Manufacturers of America trade association,[33] the media that run the toy ads, and whatever publicity outlet might run a story about your complaint.

If the problem is bad enough, boycott, demonstrate, picket, visit toy buyers responsible for stocking offensive items, call a press conference, make toy reform a priority of your club or parent group. Join *Public Action Coalition on Toys* to get their "Guidelines on Choosing Toys,"[34] and to remain an informed toy activist.

Educate others by organizing panel discussions on toys; the panel should comprise parents, teachers, psychologists, toy manufacturers, and consumer advocates. Share information about good toys and warnings about bad ones. Get your newspaper to print your checklist. Hold speak-outs where parents can air their concerns and children can explain their likes and dislikes. Get your money back when a toy is a sexist, racist, or low-quality lemon.

Not enough people make life uncomfortable for toy manufacturers, but when we *do* they are exceedingly sensitive to criticism because of their direct relationship to children.

At one of the TMA's Toy Fair press conferences, the industry's paid psychological expert answered a reporter's question about guns by declaring that toy guns helped children prepare for hostile forces in "everyday life." I asked the psychologist if he would similarly condone a children's game about rape since it's a part of "everyday life," too.

Murmurs and whispers spread through the room as the psychologist answered, Yes, "if rape comes in as an everyday affair." I sat down, knowing that his absurd reply would make tomorrow's paper. Which it did. When dealing with the toy industry, I don't care if we humiliate them, sue them, bully or beg them—as long as we keep trying to change them.

Someone once said that a thousand years from now, the archeologists who find the toy chest will find the culture. Assume it's *your* child's toy chest that they dig up; what will it tell them about humanity in our time?

VI
Media and Culture

20

Television Is Sexistvision
Or—Beware of Furniture that Talks

Before we begin, please try to absorb these staggering numbers. Without them you'll surely accuse me of exaggerating TV's effect on children.

- More American homes have television than have heat or indoor plumbing.
- The average TV set is turned on for 6½ hours per day.[1]
- Most children begin watching television at 2.8 *months* of age.[2]
- Three- to five-year-olds watch TV 54 hours a week.[3]
- By the time a child enters kindergarten, she or he has spent more time in the TV room than a four-year college student spends in the classroom.[4]
- By the time a child graduates from high school, he or she will have spent less than 12,000 hours in front of a teacher and more than 22,000 hours in front of a television set.[5]
- By age seventeen, each child has seen 350,000 commercials.[6]

What can one say about a nonhuman presence that, in some children's lives, outpulls parents, teachers, and peers put together. TV is not just an object giving forth words and pictures; it's a force with the status and persona of a friend.

When children aged four to six were asked "Which do you like better, TV or Daddy? TV or Mommy?" 20 percent preferred television to their mothers and 44 percent liked it better than their fathers. Another survey found junior high school students believe television more than parents, teachers, friends, books, radio, or newspapers.[7]

What are they believing *in?*

The answer seems to be sex role propaganda, materialism, and violence.

SEX ROLE PROPAGANDA

Since there's no sex difference in television viewing habits by gender,[8] both girls and boys are absorbing TV's version of both sex roles to an equal degree. For example, a girl learns that women seek men's approval by cooking "man-pleasing" meals, and at the same time, boys learn that men can expect to be fed and served.

Because young children have scant life experience against which to compare television's "reality," they more or less swallow it whole—especially since it comes with the implied sanction of parents and society-at-large. After all, grownups bought the set and grownups are clearly in charge of what's televised, so at both ends of the tube, adult authority seems to underwrite TV's output. And here is what's put out:

Cartoons

In this most frankly child-oriented of all entertainments, males outnumber females up to four to one. Cartoon daddies are ambitious, aggressive, adventurous, and employed, while cartoon mommies are passive, timid, emotional, and almost exclusively domestic. Rated on a forty-point personality chart, both sexes make a strong showing in all the stereotype categories, from boy-is-brave to female-is-fragile.[9]

Public Television

The Task Force on Women in Public Broadcasting, which studied one week of children's programs televised on PBS, found that overall, male characters exceeded females by two to one on every show but *Electric Company.* [10]

Sesame Street, so widely hailed by educators, came in with a three-to-one ratio, and the males were far more likely than the females to be interestingly and gainfully employed. The authors of the report are concerned

> because of the relationship of occupational role models with sex-role identification. *Sesame Street* in particular was designed so that children could "model" or learn behavior from what they see on television. . . . Therefore, the numbers of occupational roles presented to children, as well as the kind of roles, are important as sources of learning.[11]

I sampled a *Sesame Street* program and turned up these boners (along with some admittedly fine features):

• Susan says, "Maybe I can get my husband to take me to the movies tonight," suggesting that she is financially or physically incapable of going herself. (Reverse it and give Gordon the line to see how it signals dependency.)

• Two boys and one girl seem to be assembling a wooden box cart, but actually the boys are doing all the work while the girl is scampering around them trying to get in on it. Finally she gives up, clasps her hands behind her back and stands in the classic female posture—watching from the sidelines.

• A black boy narrates the events of his day. (Dad goes off to work; Mom shops and watches Son in the playground; Dad comes home, gets a big welcome, sits down to the dinner Mom cooked. Then Mom washes the dishes while Dad and Son draw pictures until bedtime. Dad reads Son a story.) It's admirable to show a black man as a worker, family man, and involved father, but the black woman is, to say the least, one-dimensional. Certainly, the cure for race stereotypes is not sex stereotypes.

Soap Operas

With fifteen million kids tuned in,[12] preschool, during lunchtime, vacations, and sick days, the soap opera qualifies as children's programming. And although there has been some improvement it is still pretty traumatic programming.

A N.O.W. survey[13] found that 15 percent of the female characters on the "suds" were portrayed as mentally and physically ill. These women share the screen with miraculously successful men, 60 percent of whom hold professional jobs, and with other women who either stay home worrying about divorce, disease, incest, and infidelity, or hold jobs in nursing or office work.

At best "women past thirty are depicted as sexual beings, desired and desiring."[14] At worst, pregnancy seems to be the soap opera's ubiquitous plot device. (There are plenty of doctors and nurses in these stories but apparently they're ignorant of contraception.) Women who pursue careers or express personal autonomy are punished with sterility, miscarriage, tragic abortions, or an impotent mate.

> Normal women stay home and have babies . . . the birth rate on daytime TV seems to rival that of Latin America! . . . Strong impressions are conveyed here: pregnancy will save your marriage; motherhood will fulfill you; bearing a man's child will make you supremely important to that man.[15]

In other words, Girls Are Meant to Be Mothers.

For all this obsession with childbearing, children themselves are virtually absent from the soaps except as behind-the-scenes pawns in their parents' melodramas.

These sob stories may offer misery-loves-company solace to isolated housewives. But the kid who's sick in bed with the TV on is getting an even sicker message about what men and women say and do to each other in the grown-up world.

Prime-Time Programs

In case you haven't noticed, not all kids are asleep during adult viewing hours. Fact is, even between 10:30 and 11 P.M., five million children under twelve are still glued to the set.[16] What they and millions more have seen of an evening is a parade of brainless wives, dumb-but-pretty secretaries, sex kittens, Big Momma blacks, rape victims, floor waxers, and other cardboard characters who either shill for the status quo or perpetrate lies about women. After a year monitoring sixteen adventure and situation comedy shows, a Princeton group found, for example, that women characters were twice as likely as men to be incompetent. On a broader scale, the U.S. Civil Rights Commission accused the networks of systematic sex and race stereotyping. One sample: the Commission's 1979 report found white males account for nearly 63 percent of all TV roles but only 40 per cent of the U.S. population.[17]

The networks aren't exactly in a ratings war over who has more nonsexist male characters either. One study found only three instances of nurturant men in fifty-eight half-hour programs.[18]

Commercials

Where life is measured in thirty-second "spots," there is one reigning star: Dirt. Pitted against Dirt is the Hysterical Housewife caught in the act of battling those grimy collars, gritty floors, greasy dishes, and clogged drains that have brought shame upon her house and reputation.

The plot thickens. Neighbors compete for a wash that is "cleaner than clean." Mothers and daughters gossip about "telltale gray." Friends destroy the perfect bridge party by noticing water spots on the stemware.

But a germ-free bathroom can restore a wife's peace of mind. Outwitting the "Ring Around the Collar" Patrol can save her marriage, and soft, sweet-smelling baseball uniforms can endear her to her children. ("Your Mom sure does love you because she uses Final Touch.")

Who helps H.H. clean up her act so well? Janitor in a Drum, the White Knight, Mr. Clean, and a chorus of knowing male voices who instruct from afar. (Josephine the Plumber, who has never so much as changed a washer, is expected to get right at the sink stains herself.)

A housewife who successfully tames Dirt still runs the risk of disaster at mealtimes. Her mother-in-law might find her spaghetti sauce thin, her kids might not like her green beans, and worst of all, her husband might commit coffee infidelity: accept a second cup from another woman's pot!

It's easy and fun to mock commercial messages, but how many realize that the real mockery is of us, the millions who are molded and moved by their sex role propaganda:

• Women's products are *essential* to her "femininity." Men's products only *add* to his appeal.

• A man's voice can sell a woman bras or feminine deodorant because male approval is supposed to motivate and reassure women. A woman's voice never sells a man's product unless she's purring the sexual tease.

• Women's self-improvement is hinged to others. ("No headache is going to make me snap at my child.") Men do things for themselves. (*The Wall Street Journal* is for the "man on the move.")

• Men care about how something is made, how it works, and whether it will last; women care only about how it looks.

• "Here's to good times . . ." Beer "quenches a man's thirst" because "one crack at life is all a man gets." Beer is a masculine beverage drunk by men in locker rooms and taverns despite the marketing fact that most beer is bought by women for home consumption.

• Tea is a "feminine" drink—though British men seem unaware of it. In America, if you want to get a man to drink tea, you need a sports hero to tell him it's okay. Then, for good measure, you need sexual innuendo: "Don Meredith is a Lipton Tea lover."

• Men take no-nonsense showers; women take narcissistic baths. That's because men have to get on with all the important things but women can soak in the tub.

• Women will buy products even if you show them as scatterbrained fools who squeeze the Charmin and panic over "housitosis." Men must be sold on the facts.

• If dirt and food are "feminine," travel and locomotion are in the men's column. Airlines are "the wings of man," but they offer "take me along" rates for the wife. Men are on camera when the commercial touts engine construction or on-time schedules; women sell the lure of sexy faraway places.

• Automobiles named for animals (Cougar, Pinto) and weapons (Dart, Javelin) are transparent virility symbols. Although women bought 42 percent of the first million Mustangs sold, it wasn't until 1977 that Ford briefly ran its "women's commercial": *Mustang gives me the feeling I can be everything a woman can be.*

New York N.O.W. studied 1,241 commercials and found only 0.3 percent of the women in them leading independent lives.[19] That's only 3 full human beings in a 1,000. What are our children learning about womankind from the other 997 clean freaks and food fetishists? And are we letting them believe that love and intimacy can be summed up by "Good coffee is grounds for marriage"?

News

In a one-month survey of three local California stations, the American Association of University Women watched 5,353 straight news stories and counted only 523 that included women at all—most of whom were victims of kidnaps, rapes, murders, and disaster.[20]

My own seven-month study of network news[21] turned up serious inadequacies in their supposed "public service":

• General interest stories (energy or employment, for instance) are reported as if they affect only men. Rarely are women experts asked to comment, or women-in-the-street asked their reactions to events other than fashion or gossip.

• Networks devote more time to either sports or weather than to activities of 53 percent of the population.

• They sensationalize women's stories. (Coverage of a women's equality march focuses on the one man carrying a "male chauvinist pig" banner, or the one woman wearing a helmet and combat boots.) Thus girls are unlikely to see women activists as role models, and boys' schoolyard ridicule of "tomboys" and "women's libbers" is reinforced.

• Networks undervalue events that would be given historic weight if men, not women, were the subjects. For example, they ignored the formation of the Coalition of Labor Union Women. Had men representing fifty-eight separate trades gotten together across union and industry loyalties, it would have been the top story of the day.

• They label women by maternal status. Golda Meir was always "grandmotherly," but Menachim Begin, of similar age and type, was never "grandfatherly."

• Feature stories favor women who are attached to prominent men (Margaret Trudeau, former Canadian "first lady," rather than Margaret Atwood, the Canadian novelist).

• They emphasize conflict and ignore harmony. Two women arguing instantly attracts the camera. Two hundred women forging a coalition can't get ten seconds.

• They "lighten" the news at women's expense. (The low point of this genre was Tex Antoine's comment on a rape report: "If rape is inevitable, relax and enjoy it," a comment Antoine regretted only when he learned the victim was a child.)

News is supposed to be the only acre of the "wasteland" that prides itself on fairness and objectivity, yet both its *subject* and its *target viewer* are almost always male. Two examples:

• After announcing that Princeton University's valedictorian *and* salutatorian were both women, NBC's commentator smirked: "If it's any comfort to male chauvinists, the valedictorian at least is the *daughter* of a Princeton man!"

• At CBS, one newscaster hoped out loud that the "women around your house" aren't kicking up trouble like those on the news.

I somehow doubt that the networks would let its people reassure whites that the black-looking valedictorian is at least the child of a white man, or hope that the "blacks around your neighborhood" don't kick up trouble.

If children cannot get gender-blind objectivity and fairness on the news, then it's questionable whether TV has it to give.

Sports

Men's sports dominate the imagination of America partly because men's sports dominate the small screen. There's no telling what passionate devotees of women's sports we might be if women's games were telecast as extensively as men's; or what sports jobs women might hold if not for sexist ridicule, such as this from KING-TV, Seattle:[22]

> The New York State Supreme Court goofed today. They ruled that a 41-year-old housewife from Queens can be an umpire in professional baseball. . . . Assuming Mrs. Gera is a lady, her position isn't behind the plate in baseball, but behind the plate in the kitchen provided by her frustrated husband.

Bernice Gera, a graduate of an accredited U.S. school for umpires, eventually quit baseball rather than stand the harassment she got on and off the field.

Girl athletes may quit before they begin unless networks and local sports departments do better than they did early in the seventies when NBC devoted 365 hours to men's sports and 1 hour to women, and CBS managed 10 women's sports hours to 260 for the men.[23]

Game Shows

A network vice president explains how the game show is tuned to the housewife's cleaning routine:

> That's why we have buzzers and chimes and bells that tell her each step of the progress of the game . . . so she can rush back into the room for the jackpot question. By the time late morning or afternoon rolls around, the chores are finished . . . and she can sit down, relax and watch her serials![24]

What does this pragmatic programming mean for the young child who is at home with the homemaker?

Since the quiz questions are usually too sophisticated to be even subliminally educational for preschoolers, what children absorb is the sex role "theater" of the game shows: the bells and buzzers, the frantic contenders, manufactured tension, and outlandish prizes; the fact that most of the contestants are women and all of the hosts are men.

"The MC has to be in charge," says a CBS V.P. "When a female does this, somehow it doesn't work."[25]

After a while it might "work"—if the image of a female in charge was ever allowed to register on the retina long enough. But game shows prefer to use women at their least "in charge" and most childish—squealing, jumping up and down, begging, performing for a prize—while the MC teases and comforts like a dog trainer.

As contestant after contestant introduces herself as "just a housewife" or "mother of five" (who else can be at a TV studio at 10 in the morning?), children conclude that homemakers can't buy their own prizes; things must be given to them or won by chance with the benign assistance of Big Daddy.

How Children Are Affected

It's not the church which interests me, but the congregation.
. . . A television set without viewers doesn't interest me.
—JERZY KOSZINSKI[26]

What about the littlest congregation? How do we know if television's sex-role propaganda is sinking in or leaving scars?

First, listen to your kids recite advertising jingles verbatim (how much poetry do they know by heart?) and think about the sheer mass of rote learning involved. From Davy Crockett hats in my youth to the family tree fads inspired by *Roots,* from Farrah Fawcett's hairstyle to The Fonz's "Aaaayyy," television's awesome power to teach and children's susceptibility to imitation cannot be missed.

Advertisers have always understood the power of "role models" to affect behavior,[27] even if parents haven't. Bacon and eggs were banned from breakfast scenes in one show because its sponsor, a cereal manufacturer, knew kids would follow the hero's example and eat bacon and eggs. Years ago, the cigarette sponsor of a crime show instructed scriptwriters not to show "any disreputable person" smoking. Cigarettes were for the good guys.[28]

If children copied only the *style* of their heroes, I'd be unconcerned, but they model the *behavior,* and as we've seen, heroes free of sex stereotyped behavior are few and far between. Thus, kids transform idealized sexist behavior into future aspirations.

Heavy viewers, aged three to twelve, held more stereotypical views of occupational sex roles than did light viewers of TV.[29] In another study, when eight-to-eleven-year-olds were asked "Are there any people on TV that you want to be like when you grow up?" boys named more TV characters as models than did girls—which makes sense, given television's more frequent and more positive male characters. Boys often explained their choices on the basis of strength or toughness; girls chose a role model because she was "pretty" or "dressed nice"—probably the most favorable attributes that one could ascribe to TV's women.[30]

Nevertheless, the main finding of this study is remarkably encouraging: after exposure to five somewhat counter-stereotypical women (the school principal on *Lucas Tanner,* the police officers on *Get Christie Love* and *Police Woman,* the park ranger on *Sierra,* and the TV producer on *Mary Tyler Moore*), children of both sexes were much more likely to say it was appropriate for girls to try for such jobs.

In a comparable experiment, children shown some specially prepared commercials that portrayed women in traditionally male jobs later endorsed those occupations as suitable for women; kids who saw standard commercials did not.[31]

Before it went into reruns, *All in the Family,* the most provocative adult program on TV, was also the program with the largest young audience: every show was seen by nine million kids under twelve. A researcher interviewed 320 representative children about their favorite characters on the show. The top draws were Archie, because he "yells at Edith when she acts so stupid," Edith, because "she was nice no matter how mad Archie got," and Gloria, because she was "pretty" and "nice."

The study concluded that what had the greatest impact on most children was not the moral/ethical lessons that were the focus of the show, but the physical appearance of the characters, the role stereotypes, and the comedy behavior associated with them.[32]

MATERIALISM:
SEXISM'S FINANCIAL PAYOFF

A drawing in a children's book shows a little girl basking in the light of a boy's homemade lamp. The picture is captioned: "Boys invent things. Girls use what boys invent."[33]

In rather more elaborate form, this is the principle that supports the economy of a patriarchal society. "Boys invent things, girls use them" extrapolates to a larger economic principle: "Men make things; women buy them." Men are the producers, women the consumers. The only production culturally approved for women is reproduction; women and their "product," children, together make a market of users for the things that men produce.

The number of commercials directed at women far exceeds those directed at men. Advertisers estimate that women do up to 85 percent of the purchasing in America. And they *know* that the modern housewife buys more than the woman who works outside the home.[34] That's why the sex role formula means to keep each woman isolated in her nuclear household, feeling inadequate to her cleaning tasks, wondering if she's as good a wife and mother as the next woman, and worrying about her fading looks. The only way to "do" something about her problems is to *buy* the promised solutions: Youth in a cream, fulfilment in a can, love in a brand name. Ad men characterize spending as "decision-making" in the supermarket and "accomplishment" at the cash register.

Despite convenience foods and labor-saving devices, as we've noted, the homemaker spends more hours at housework and shopping today than sixty years ago. "The housewife is urged to find new crevices to clean and higher standards of innovation and creativity against which to measure her domestic abilities."[35]

Women in the labor force spend less than half as much time at housework as housewives and don't, as a general rule, live less hygienic or civilized lives. However, these women who clean less compulsively use fewer products and spend less money.

So advertisers glamorize homemaking, to make it a noble and "natural" calling, to create a full-time job out of keeping the self and others clean and fed. How? Romanticize routine, the thrilling waxed floor and so on, and if you're lucky, a woman won't realize she's working up to 99 hours a week without pay, and probably without much appreciation either.

The mercantile payoff of TV's sex role images is the manufacture of a class of female people who labor "for love," stay out of the job marketplace, and buy the products that make the male-run economy run so well without them.

What has all this to do with children?

Like many women, children are not producers. Linked to women by the caretaking relationship and by their shared "weakness" (embodied in the rescue call "women and children first"), kids are seen by advertisers as conduits to mothers.

In Vance Packard's words, children are "consumer-trainees." If they can be taught to *want* things, to *need* things, to spend and to make their mothers spend, they are useful to men's economy. The cynicism is not my own. Listen to an adman's view:

> When you sell a woman on a product and she goes into the store and finds your brand isn't in stock, she'll probably forget about it. But when you sell a kid on your product, if he can't get it, he will throw himself on the floor, stamp his feet and cry. You can't get a reaction like that from an adult.[36]

Mothers succumb to kids' entreaties because, as we have seen, a mother's role is to make her children happy. To reach her through her persuasive child consumer, sponsors buy time on cartoon shows and children's programs that give advertisers a clear path to the child's psyche.

> Before the advent of television, it was almost impossible for an advertiser or a salesman to reach a young child without first encountering a protective adult. Door-to-door selling was dealt with by a parent, the salesman was barred from the classroom and magazine and newspaper ads were beyond the comprehension of most children under the age of nine or ten. With television, however, all this has changed.[37]

The "talking furniture" that babysits for children, that supposedly makes Mom's day easier and kids' lives livelier, is actually a shill for man's economic gain. The show excuses the sell. *We'll be right back after this word . . .* —and the word is exploitation.

The exploitation of children's appetites brought the networks nearly a quarter of their total profits for the year.[38]

Mothers knock themselves out planning nutritional meals, schools teach balanced diets, health experts warn of empty calories and mood-altering additives, but television beats them all with a few well-chosen words about Choco Puffs.

Exploitation of dissatisfaction is another "consuming" device: making children dissatisfied with their toys and other possessions means parents will feel guilty about not providing what the child wants and what kids on television have. The pressure is felt most by the "masculine" provider. Fathers have to work harder and spend beyond their means to alleviate the dissatisfaction.[39] Then the materialism that makes them work longer hours also requires them to buy more things to make up for their increased absences and to prove their love, materially. Dissatisfaction is bad for family life, but oh so good for business.

Exploitation of feelings of inferiority has the same result: "Step right up, ladies, your natural skin, hair, and everything you do are inadequate, but luckily, perfection is yours for a price while supplies last."

That message is brought to you by the same people who promise children "strength, energy, athletic prowess, almost anything short of sexual satisfaction for the use of certain products."[40]

All children feel small, insufficient, and overwhelmed by events beyond their control. By suggesting that a toy or snack can bestow power or make children happy, commercials teach the First Commandment of a materialistic society: *You are what you own.* With television's help, the lesson will last a lifetime.

Advertisers' argument that commercials give children an education in consumerism collapses in the face of reason. If kids can't touch, taste, or try advertised products, and haven't lived long enough to compare products on claims alone, how are they learning good buying habits?

When they do buy something and it falls short of its video glories, as too often is the case, they've learned only that grownups are free to deceive children and that people are allowed to make things that don't work and aren't good for you. Children are not educated into the consumer economy, they're educated to be cynics and spenders in the profitable land of patriarchy.[41]

VIOLENCE: SEXISM'S "HIT MAN"

If commercials are the appetizer and dessert of each TV time slot, violence is its main course, the meat and potatoes that make the sponsor's message stick to your ribs. "To the advertiser, violence equals excitement equals ratings."[42]

How much violence? Three in ten programs are "saturated" with it or the threat of it; cartoons contain an average of one aggressive act per minute; and overall, an hour of children's "entertainment" contains six times more violence than an hour of adult fare.[43] It adds up to some "18,000 murders and countless detailed incidents of robbery, arson, bombing, forgery, smuggling, beating and torture" seen by each American child between birth and eighteen.[44]

The blood and bullets have attracted a lot of attention—from the White House Task Force on the Media,[45] to the Surgeon General's Scientific Advisory Committee on Television and Social Behavior,[46] to parent and child advocacy groups locally and nationally,[47] all of whom have lobbied, held hearings or issued reports that made headlines—even on television.

Meanwhile, the networks issued denials, recruited educational advisors, appointed special vice presidents for children's programming, and declared themselves serious about self-regulation. They were very showy throughout the seventies about their "commitment" to children's well-being.

Yet in March 1977, Dr. George Gerbner, who tallies the annual *Violence Profile,* told Congress that all three networks showed more incidents of extreme violence during the previous year than in any of the preceding ten years; in fact the percentage of programs showing violent acts "rose to the highest on record."[48] At the close of the seventies, sex was edging out violence in prime time.[49] But whether annual violence quotient rises or falls by a few points, the basic tolerance and justifications of violence persist—and most parents don't like it.[50]

Who's at fault? Advertisers say they're only paying for what people want to see. Producers say they need "action" or viewers get bored. The networks say, in effect, just because violence riddles the tube doesn't mean children are adversely affected or moved to commit violence. Some even claim TV action has a cathartic effect.[51] But child specialists find it disturbs and upsets kids:

> They cannot understand why Tom keeps hitting Jerry; they worry about how much it hurts. As a result they themselves feel confused and vulnerable.[52]

Children who watch many hours of TV suffer an increase in nightmares, fears, and appetite disturbances.[53] They develop greatly distorted ideas about death and suffering.[54] Their behavior is altered in small and large ways.[55] They become insensitive to the sight of someone being hurt. They use violent scenarios as a guide for their own actions when playing with others. They are capable of reproducing hostile acts exactly as they saw them on TV eight months earlier. When given the opportunity to either help or hurt a child in need, kids were more likely to *hurt* after seeing a fighting scene than after seeing an exciting sports event. And an appalling number of juvenile crimes—torture, kidnappings, rapes, and murders—have been traced to events portrayed on television dramas.[56]

Most sobering of all, I think, is this fact that affects all children, not just the criminal few: Kids who watch four or more hours of TV a day tend to overestimate the number of violent crimes that happen in real life and exaggerate the danger of their own victimization.[57] Children needn't mimic violence to be damaged by it; they are wounded spiritually by the *fear* of violence and the suspicion that they are unsafe in our world.

One sex is influenced more than the other:

> A boy's television habits at age eight are more likely to be a predictor of his aggressiveness at age eighteen or nineteen than his family's socioeconomic status, his relationship with his parents, his IQ or any other single factor in his environment.[58]

Correlations between aggressiveness and TV-watching do not hold for girls. Why? Because although television teaches both sexes how to be aggressive, boys learn that men are rewarded for it while girls learn that women are punished for it.[59]

When television's female characters are involved in violent situations, their usual role is victim. In the relatively few instances when women are aggressors, they are less successful than men and less likely to get away with it. As victims, they are more likely to be single than married. As villains, they are more often working women than housewives.[60]

Kids get the message, the moral, and the role models all rolled into one. The most powerful characters on television are males who are young, white, middle class, single, involved in violence and not only not punished for it, but usually rewarded with admiration and possessions—including beautiful women. Independent women end up victims of violence; married women and housewives who fulfill their proper role are spared some death and villainy. Violence by bad guys is punished because it's unjustified. Violence by good guys is justified ". . . for reasons of vengeance or self-defense or both."[61]

Violence does pay when you're a good guy defending your manhood—or when you're a vast patriarchal institution like television, defending your team's social order.

Violence is the "hit man" for sexism, the last-ditch defender of the status quo, the gold coin of man's realm. To devalue it is to divest men of their ultimate advantage over women: that is, when all other power politics fail, a man has his muscles.

The mere capability of inflicting physical pain upon the female lies like a sleeping tiger in the male body—even in those who never batter, rape, or kill. But on behalf of all *man*kind, television lets the tiger off the leash, reminding us that it's there and showing us what happens to female pussies and housecats who overstep their bounds.

MASTERING THE MEDIUM

Nonsexist parents should watch television with a third eye, responding to its sex role propaganda, materialism, and violence with one of three options: teach in, talk back, or turn off.

Teach-in

If television is, as many have called it, an addictive drug, then parents are the pushers. We let our children get hooked because *their* habit frees *us* to work, sleep, whatever. Surely, one critic writes, "there can be no more insidious drug than one that you must administer to others in order to achieve an effect for yourself."[62]

To cure the addict in your house, "cold turkey" is not recommended. A ban on certain programs may be obeyed ("I can't watch because I'm not allowed"), but not necessarily believed ("What could be so terrible about that program?"). Withdrawal symptoms of the "cold turkey" approach are anger and distrust of parents—not quite features of a warm family life.

No, you'll have to make up for all those hours TV gave *you* by giving some hours back to your children. Sit with them; watch television together, not for escapism and not in a shared stupor like most families[63] but as active, critical viewers. Help them bring their own life experience, however limited, to TV's version of life; show them it's all right to contradict, ridicule, mimic, decide to turn off the set. Use TV, don't let it use you.

When Robin and Abigail were ten, I took them to a women's march down Fifth Avenue that ended in a rousing rally in honor of International Women's Day. Back home, we turned on the evening news to watch the coverage of our event (and maybe catch a glimpse of ourselves). Despite its being a Saturday night with few hard news stories, our item was reported late in the newscast and very briefly; the speeches by notables at the rally weren't covered at all and the estimate of the crowd size was absurdly low. I decided to comment on the easy discrepancy:

"How many people do you guess were marching with us?" I asked the girls.

"Oh, thousands and thousands and thousands," was the answer.

"The TV reporter said it was only about five thousand," I

reminded them. "Why do you think they would underplay the size of the crowd?"

"Maybe they couldn't count us all."

"Or maybe they didn't want the people at home to think *that* many people care about women's rights."

"Yeah. They're probably afraid that the next time there's a demonstration even more people will show up."

This conversation led us down some interesting paths. We talked about a book Robin had read that described how early suffragist demonstrations were mocked and trivialized; we realized that it can be important to know how many marched in a demonstration because some people avoid acting on their beliefs if they think they will be a too-visible minority. We talked about the power of TV news to give an event historical significance—or to deny it significance by distortion or neglect.

The experience provided graphic proof that the TV isn't always the truth. Two ten-year-olds were there and they knew better.

Ask your children their opinions of TV programs; people rarely do. Leading questions, critical intervention, and open-ended conversation may be the most underutilized means of getting to know your children's values while raising their media consciousness. Some sexism-decoding exercises are fun too:

• Watch for euphemisms ("tired blood," "feminine freshness") that sell products by inventing problems—especially problems of sex role inadequacy.

• Keep two pads near the TV. On one everyone can list each stereotyped character seen in a program. On the other, list the nonsexist, nonstereotyped ones. Compare the length of the lists at the end of a week. Ask your children which characters they most admire.

• Analyze product names and find the "hidden persuaders." "Pride," "Bold," and "Imperial" glorify mundane products, for example. "Brut" makes perfume "masculine."

• Make up plot devices that could solve a program's conflict without violence.

• Imagine gender-reversed roles on your favorite shows. How would this week's *M*A*S*H* be different if Hawkeye were a woman surgeon and Hot Lips a male nurse?

• Write a truth-in-advertising commercial for a product that has disappointed you: "This overpriced Jane Doe doll is made of brittle plastic. She is guaranteed to lose a limb when you try to dress her in one of her skimpy outfits. Buy her anyway because you'll make your friends jealous."

• Count your way to consciousness: how many acts of kindness can you find in a half-hour cartoon; how many female voice-overs; how many women shown making money rather than spending it?

• At the end of each program ask children to forget about sex as a component and just indicate which role they would have liked playing. How often is it the female role?

After a few weeks of shared viewing, let children set their own schedules. Keep a record of how much they watch, and which programs. You may find the bloom off the electronic rose. But if they still seem prone to overdose you may want to limit viewing time, choice of programs, or both.

Pediatrician T. Berry Brazelton believes "one hour a day is the maximum amount of time a child up to the age of five can spend in front of a television set before he [or she] begins to show the signs of depletion and exhaustion."[64] Until our children were ten or eleven, we followed the one-hour limit fairly successfully, with several caveats: no violence, no TV in the afternoon, or while doing homework or eating meals—except for such super-specials as election coverage, ongoing events of an international crisis, or catching a classic movie on the set.

Of course we've made dozens of exceptions to the exceptions. You can review the upcoming week's offerings in *TV Guide* and agree in advance about the viewing schedule and the week's "extras." After a while you'll move to the honor system, I'm sure. Rules are most meaningful when the rulemakers are receptive to a good case for waiving them. Frequently, when we give in to a program we really don't like, the children go into a real tailspin if it turns out less than spectacular. The junk show reminds them of what they *haven't* been missing.

The goal of your teach-in is not a brainwashed TV-resistor but a skeptic with a firm finger on the "Off" switch.

Talk Back

After awareness comes activism. With their new critical powers and raised consciousness, your children—like you—will want to talk back to the television set.

Several years ago, Wheaties cereal commercials showed boys jumping, running, riding a motorcycle, climbing, and generally having a terrific time while a man's voice intoned, "He's ready for Wheaties; he knows he's a man."

The ad made our daughter Abigail furious. In July 1973, she wrote a letter and asked that I mail it to the right address (which is how I had the chance to photocopy it). A month or so later, an answer came from General Mills. (See pages 414 and 415.)

After receiving this rebuff, of course there was nothing left to do but make good on Abigail's threat. So, to our boycott list of California lettuce, grapes, and Gallo wine (who at the time would not recognize the United Farmworkers Union), we added Wheaties (who would not recognize female breakfast eaters).

We survived admirably without Wheaties for a couple of years and then one evening, Abigail shouted, "They did it! They changed their ad!", and there on the screen was a Wheaties commercial showing a woman and a man jogging. During the following months, we saw ads with girls as well as boys running, jumping, climbing, and playing.

When I questioned the ad manager for General Mills about the charge, he said he personally was offended by the "He's a man" campaign because "it was so macho. I'd rather a boy know he's a man because he can help a baby or an old person, not because he can ride a motorcycle. But the agency pressured us on it."[65]

A spokesman for the ad agency told me that the "He's a man" campaign, which ran from January 1972 to September 1975,

Dear Wheaties company, this is a 8 year old girl speaking when ever I see your wheaties commercial I sing the opposite of a boy knowing he's a man, I sing the girl knows she's a woman. ~~because~~ when I see that boy doing all those good things I get tempted myslef and I think that girls would love to have ~~the~~ the opportunity on being on one of your commercials about that great ~~cereal~~ cereal. NOW I'm not saying that you have to put a girl on that commercials I'm Just warning you that I'm not even touching one of ~~those~~ tasty bit of those wheaties till theres a girl on that TV commercials

Sincerely
abgail
Pogrebin

July 1973

DORIS W. POOTON
Coordinator of Consumer Response

August 22, 1973

Ms. Abigail Pogrebin
33 West 67 Street
New York, New York 10023

Dear Abigail:

Thank you for your recent letter concerning current Wheaties
television commercials.

In presenting the Wheaties story to the public, we have
endeavored to capitalize on the brand's long heritage as
a male oriented product. As you know, many products such
as Virginia Slims, Grape Nuts and Marlboro have spoken
primarily to one sex. This is not done to the exclusion
of the other gender. It merely speaks to those people that
constitute the majority of the brand's consumers. This
is true with Wheaties for although many women do eat and
enjoy the product, our research indicates that it is predominantly
eaten by men.

Our message for the product is that as a boy matures, his
taste matures and he is ready to eat an unsweetened, adult
tasting product. Wheaties is such a product.

As we do studies concerning our advertising and promotion,
we appreciate it when someone who feels strongly about a
matter takes the time as you have to give us his or her
comments. Again, thank you for writing.

Sincerely,

Doris Pooton

was phenomenally successful. It was dropped as a result of research on "the emerging woman concept and the fact that everyday folks of both sexes were becoming more concerned with sports and fitness."[66]

Whatever the advertising rationale, Abigail believed that her letter played a part in the company's change of heart.

Postage Power

Letter writing doesn't always bear such sweet fruit. But for the price of a postage stamp, it provides an outlet for mute rage and many advertisers admit that consumer letters do have an effect. In any event, unless you complain, you are giving tacit approval for television's bill of fare, or as one social scientist put it, "to do nothing is to do something."[67]

The first and only complaint letter Caroline Ranald, age seven, ever wrote (see facing page), got big results: Lionel Trains responded with a press conference and a new ad campaign featuring the female train fan.

Some children won't want to be bothered with letter writing; others will relish the chance to sound off, especially if they know that their parents both practice and encourage activist gestures, no matter how small.

Keep a box of stationery (with carbon paper for copies) and some postage stamps near the TV set so that any viewer can dash off a letter while the details of a program or commercial are still fresh. Mention the station's call letters, and the date and time of the televised nastiness; explain your reason for objecting to it and comment upon what you'd like to see in its stead. In letters to advertisers, include your intention to stop buying the product. As Abigail seemed to know instinctively, a complaint gains force when it is coupled with a boycott (or "girlcott" as Abby called it).

Obviously a great show should get a letter of praise. Whether complaint or commendation, you can send copies of your letter to the general manager or news director of the local station, the president of the network, the National Association of Broadcasters, the president of the company that advertised offensively or that sponsored the objectionable show, the president of the ad

Dear Sir: .23. Nov. 1972

I don't like your new
ads. Grils like trains too.
I am a girl. I like trains.

I have seven locomotives. Your catalog
only has boys. Don't you like girls?

                              yours truly
                    Caroline Ranald

7 years old.

I love the metroliner

agency that prepared the commercial, the Chairperson of the Federal Communications Commission, the Federal Trade Commission, or the Council of Better Business Bureaus.[68] You won't write to all those executives about every complaint, but the bigger the offense, the more people should know about it.

Talking back includes picking on their pocketbooks. (It cost Listerine ten million dollars to run corrective advertising to counter years of false claims that their product could cure colds.[69]) Individual sanctions multiplied by whole constituencies can mean economic disaster for a product or company. I've heard, for instance, that women's boycott of National Airlines during its "Fly Me" campaign brought about the ad's withdrawal.

Consumers can reach even further into the infrastructure and put pressure on churches, universities, union pension plans, foundations, and other large institutions that buy stock in the corporations sponsoring violent programs or offensive advertising. Companies such as Colgate, Sears, Kodak, Gillette and Schlitz have been known to respond.[70] To learn the identities of these institutional shareholders, write to the comptroller at the sponsor's executive offices and ask for the names of organizations holding sizable blocks of stock in the company.

Defensive strategies have their limitations. There may come a time when you'll want to challenge not just a particular ad or program, but the station's right to broadcast, period.

Since access to broadcasting channels is limited, only a certain number of stations in each geographical area are licensed by the government to use the public air waves *as trustees for the citizenry.* Each license is up for review every three years and the FCC has the power to deny renewal to stations who fail to broadcast "in the public interest, convenience and necessity."[71]

If your children are exposed to negative images of females and males, if excessive violence threatens their well-being, you may be justified in claiming that the station is in default and that renewal of its license is *not* in the "public interest, convenience and necessity."

Says a veteran of N.O.W. media actions, "Often just the *threat* of a boycott, picket line, or license challenge is enough to get serious negotiations going with a station. Local people want to avoid tying up their license or attracting bad publicity, so they meet with us and often make real changes in what our children see on the screen."[72]

For such a license challenge, you'll need many hands, eyes, and energies to monitor programs, collect data, file the "petition to deny" a license, and serve on the negotiating committee. It's more work than a cake sale but the results are more far-reaching than a complaint letter. All it takes, someone once said, is "the courage to plod."

The Backlash and How to Beat It

Granted, this might be a better world if they took all stabbings, shootings, maimings . . . off TV. But the problem with censorship is its tendency to "spill over." Soon frightened network execs may shy away from other controversial issues, such as homosexuality, rape, child abuse, pornography and abortion. And then all we'll be left with is Pat Boone and reruns of The Brady Bunch.
—*New York* magazine[73]

I'm not going to have any group tell me what I can do. I won't let any pressure group tell me how to be creative.
—CBS Executive[74]

[Beware of] . . . the current wave of feminist paranoid chic. . . . The equal-time equal-space technique of criticism employed by each successive power group . . . contains the germ of censorship . . . too much balancing could easily turn into a threat to the carefree, non-ideological fun.
—*New York Times*[75]

How do we answer these charges?

The claim that feminist objections will result in Pat Boone, *The Brady Bunch,* or a withdrawal of responsible coverage of controversial subjects presumes there are only two alternatives: Mostly-junk-with-rare-quality or Junk-only. I'm proposing a third: Mostly-quality-with-rare-junk.

To warn us that criticizing television is a threat to "carefree, non-ideological fun" suggests that what we have now is free-of-cares, non-ideological, and fun. As I hope this chapter has shown, present TV fare is none of the above.

Finally censorship accusations are based on the erroneous assumption that in its present state, TV is a neutral and nonpropagandistic marketplace of ideas, and that every challenge to it is censorship by "power groups." In fact, the only "power groups" involved at all are the broadcasters. They're the ones with the right of free expression and the access to the air waves. We are the *powerless* groups. We only have the right to challenge them.

When broadcasting interests represent the status quo as "normal" and call pressure groups "censors," they cloud the meaning of the First Amendment.[76] Freedom of the press is not supposed to belong only to those who own the press.

If you want to talk about censorship, let's talk about the way broadcasters censor the economic and social reality. When Nixon was equating peace groups with "traitors," one network told a scriptwriter that his Vietnam war drama would be unacceptable unless he agreed to "change the locale to Spain, make it a bullfight instead of a war, and make the soldier into a matador."[77]

During the years of civil rights activism, writers on *The FBI* series were told not to touch on the Birmingham church bombing, police brutality, FBI bugging, or corporate crimes; they might undermine the American way.

In other instances of network strong-arming, writers were warned to steer clear of such issues as racism, health-care scandals, and environmental pollution. One network rejected a script about the Pentagon's storage of nerve gas because "the subject would offend sponsors who had dealings with the Pentagon." Another script was turned back because it treated homosexuals too sympathetically.[78]

It seems that "censorship" in the service of the establishment somehow falls under the protection of free speech.

Then there is the charge that advocacy groups want "creative control." This one is laughable coming from an industry known for creativity-by-committee. If a show can absorb "input" from a team of writers and hordes of producers, sponsors, and network folk, it might sit still for—and benefit from—contributions from those who care more, and often know most, about a given subject.

Finally, to the statement that objections to sexism are voguish "paranoid chic," the answer is simple: The struggle against sexism is not just another single-issue protest cause, it is about the rights and dignity of half the human race and thus, the humanity of our species.

Keep talking back as long as you can stand the flak and frustration. Then move on to the third tactic and the only one that's foolproof.

Turn Off

Turn it off and it can't hurt your children. Don't have one in the house at all to be sure no one is tempted to "indulge." While it may seem heretical to propose this in the Telstar Age in a country where the water pressure drops at precise intervals because so many people go to the bathroom during commercials,[79] a TV-free home may be the only cure for media sexism.

Rather than battle with youngsters over which programs are permissible, a small number of parents have banned the set entirely the way some people ban nitrites from their diets. "We're too busy to waste time on TV," "We're a close family and television is a stranger in our house," and "We have so many better things to do" are some ways of presenting the no-TV policy as a gift of love, not an act of desperation.

In April 1977, seventy-five New York City children and their families took part in an experiment they called "No-TV Week," keeping diaries of their reactions and lists of things to do during the tube's blackout. One woman said her children got along better than at anytime she could remember. "I wish it could go on forever," she sighed.[80]

Living TV-Free

When children who grow up in a TV-free house play at the home of a plugged-in friend, they consider the set an elaborate toy, like a player piano. Some TV-free kids lead the kind of life many of us remember from before Milton Berle and Howdy Doody: they have pets, play stickball, do homework, listen to the radio or phonograph, practice an instrument, read books, pursue hobbies, do puzzles, draw pictures, seek out their friends, and weave daydreams.

Is it fair to remove children from the national media mainstream, deny them the shared experiences of prime time simultaneity? According to its defenders, television is the great equalizer, an instant password to the universal youth culture. Without TV, a child may be considered "out of it."

None of us wants to stigmatize our children for the sake of an ideology. However, consider the possibility that when we go with the TV crowd, we risk far more serious dangers.

The Mind Control Theory

Several critics have convincingly argued that television is democracy's dictator.[81] Among them is Cornell sociologist Rose Goldsen, who finds alarming parallels between the Pavlovian conditioning process described in *Brave New World* and modern TV's power to mold the masses, to homogenize us, and to indoctrinate our children into its own version of reality.

Dr. Goldsen asks:

> What will happen to the body movements and body rhythms of these children, their facial expressions and their emotive use of language, their dreams and their fancies and their fantasies? Will all converge toward some Universal Mean?[82]

Television's power to induce conformity and to colonize human diversity under one standard is already a proven fact. If a mass medium can sell us the patriarchal model with all its cruelties and impediments, it can sell us anything—a national toilet paper shortage, Tiny Tim, a *Führer*—anything.

The spectre of a brainwashed nation mesmerized by the cathode ray is reason enough to ban the set. But suppose the greatest hazard of television is not what we watch and what it tells us but what the *experience* of watching television does to the eyes, brain and body.

The Altered State of Consciousness Theory

In human beings, the right hemisphere of the brain affects spatial and visual abilities; the left, or dominant, hemisphere controls our verbal and logical activities. By age twelve, when "the brain attains its final state of maturity in terms of structure and biochemistry, it appears that certain functions such as brain specialization lock into place," writes Marie Winn,[83] who maintains that television alters a child's brain functions by overdeveloping the nonverbal, right hemisphere at the expense of the left hemisphere.

Nonverbal thought is "a mode of mental functioning that requires nothing but intake and acceptance . . . ," like recognizing faces, or watching television.

> If during the child's formative years [he or she] . . . engages in a repeated and time-consuming nonverbal, primarily visual activity . . . might this not have a discernible effect on his [or her] neurological development?
> . . . Might not the television child emerge from childhood with certain left-hemisphere skills—those verbal and logical ones—less developed than the visual and spatial capabilities governed by the right hemisphere?[84]

Marie Winn answers her own questions with staggering evidence: that TV causes sensory overkill; puts children in a trance-like state of consciousness; short-circuits their needs for fantasy, intellectual stimulation, and growth-producing human verbal exchange. (It feeds children words and images so that they need make no effort to form their own thoughts and feelings or put them into words.)

She identifies the post-television crankiness that many parents have observed as a "re-entry syndrome" from this altered state of consciousness.

Winn charges that "heavy viewers of *Sesame Street* demonstrated *fewer* gains in cognitive skills than light viewers!"[85]

Television dulls children's enthusiasm for real life. TV is closer than being there. Kids would rather watch a parade on TV than feel its sights and sounds on the street; they describe an immediate event with reference to television. ("A boy who lived through a devastating tornado says, 'Man, it was just like something on TV.' "[86]) Television fosters emotional detachment and a remoteness from humanity.

Television doesn't only reduce play time, adds Winn, it "has affected the very nature of children's play," making children more passive, unable to construct imaginary play situations with others, and impatient for instant gratification. (After all, TV wraps everything up in 26 minutes.) TV children have little experience with self-control or with the social aspects of play because they "have spent their childhood *watching* instead of playing."[87]

Winn winds up her indictment by reviewing the alarming results of one entire generation's having been raised on television: she mentions, among other things, declining college board scores, trends toward nonverbal obsessions (meditation, Eastern religions, parapsychology, drugs), use of TV deprivation as a form of punishment, an end to family rituals and shared experiences, children's increased dependency and resistance to risk (observed particularly at summer camps, where there has been a curious rise in homesickness attributed to the desire to "return to a more dependent situation in which the child need not function as a separate self"[88]), and parental expressions of impotence in the battle against television's take-over.

The late Dorothy Cohen, Professor of Education at Bank Street College, said teachers have noted disturbing intellectual changes in youngsters who were raised with television: in the primary grades there is strong resistance to reading and to "exerting any kind of effort," and in graduate schools many students "cannot cope with subtle ideas in print."[89] Television has not merely replaced books, it has subverted children's capacity to read, to conjure and to care. Other educators have found drowsiness, apathy, hyperactivity, dullness, and aggression in the children most hooked on TV.[90]

To avoid all of these hazards to the brain, emotions, intellect, and consciousness, Marie Winn says *turn off* the perpetrator. She reports on families who keep the TV in a closet, basement, or other inconvenient location so that they must go to considerable trouble to get it out and watch it. Others deliberately have an old black-and-white set with poor reception to help keep television unappealing. But the most satisfied (almost smug) and contented people were those who had no set at all. Winn says they experienced

> more interaction with adults . . . a more peaceful atmosphere in the home . . . a greater feeling of closeness as a family . . . more help by children in the household . . . more outdoor play . . . changes in bedtime and meals [more sensible hours, better mealtime conversation]. . . . Children play together more . . . more reading . . . better relationship between parents . . . more activities.[91]

These theories intrigue me; the reports of TV-free living sound like the nirvana of a bygone era. To think that we could obliterate television's pathogenic influences by simply giving our set to the Goodwill pickup truck is a tempting solution akin to the avoidance behavior of an ostrich.

It would ignore the children who inherit the set we give away and the children sitting in front of the other seventy-five million sets in the United States.[92] It would surrender the spirit and soul of these children to the electronic molester who could then prey upon them without restraint. It would relinquish the twentieth century's greatest technological tool to the forces of mediocrity and patriarchal oppression.

I'm not willing to turn off our set if it means turning it over to the hucksters, exploiters, and misogynists. I'm not willing to save my children from video sexism and let everyone else's children be damned. If television is, as it must be, here to stay, then all parents owe it to all children to stay tuned.

21

That's Entertainment?
Visual Arts, Film, Music, Print Media
and Theater Arts

Once tuned in to mass media stereotypes, you will help enrich your children's relationship with the rest of their culture by sharpening their attention to sounds and images and encouraging habits of observation and analysis.

Let's sprint through five more entertainment areas with those objectives in mind.

THE VISUAL ARTS

First, some questions. *Is art "feminine" or "masculine"?*

In the school years, most of us think of art as a girls' activity. Only when it's *Art*—serious, chic, and high-priced—is it "masculinized."[1] To counter this flip-flop stereotype, little boys need extra encouragement to survive childhood teasing and artistic girls need all the help they can get when they're older.

Another question: *If art imitates life and life is sexist, can art be nonsexist?*

The drawings of the very young suggest the answer is no.[2] By age five, more boys draw *things* (cars, planes, bombs), action figures (policemen, racing car drivers), and elaborate fantasies. More girls than boys draw *people,* the daily life of a family, affiliative scenes, and pictures with low-level fantasy. Ask children to draw girls and boys, and they will most likely show boys playing and girls watching or sitting. Ask them to draw adults and you'll probably get a man on his job and a woman at home. In most cases, the child will emphasize the face of the man and the body of the woman, "a tendency, conscious or not, to slight the intellectual qualities of women."[3]

Sex role conditioning comes out in children's art just as

surely as it went in—and sometimes it goes in pretty flagrantly. A book called *Drawing for Boys*[4] contains directions for drawing muscles, athletes in action, sports equipment, planes, cowboys, vehicles, and men landing on the moon. The companion volume, *Drawing for Girls,*[5] teaches techniques for drawing a kitten, teapot, lamp, house, baby carriage, flowers, birds, fish, ballet dancers, and a few action poses—of men.

These books were first published more than twenty years ago but I found them in a Manhattan art store in 1980, so be sure to thumb through art instruction books before you bring them home.

Question: *What about genius and gender; isn't Art a place where talent "rises above such ugly, commonplace phenomena as sex discrimination"?*[6]

Not quite. Until very recently, fine art (and photography) were graphic illustrations of the prejudices of patriarchy. For the most part, men created the product; decided what would reach the galleries, museums, and art publications; wrote the reviews that established "greatness."

Through the centuries, male image-makers also forged a set of sex role givens: Subjects were deemed worthy of art if they were "directly related to men's roles . . . [those] relating to the woman's role were automatically relegated to an inferior category."[7] The female was the artist's model, not the artist—meant to motivate art, not make it;[8] to serve the artist's needs, not to rival his reputation.

The undeniably gifted young girl might dabble at still lifes, be an amateur portraitist, a school art teacher, craft hobbyist, or maker of carpets, quilts, and other functional objects for the home. She certainly was not expected to paint visionary insights on a "feminine" canvas nor carve her own gods out of stone. The male artist has never been so "casual" about his vocation that women could slip in unnoticed:

> As a "useless" product, art is little respected in this society; [therefore] the men who have chosen such a "sissy" role have had to protect their virility images with a vengeance.[9]

There is yet another question, one that is supposed to silence all questioning: *If the sexes are equal, why have there been no great women artists?*

With children old enough to have absorbed the sex role stereotypes, that question is the place to begin. (It is as likely to be asked in terms of women composers or inventors, too.) Start by acknowledging that most famous painters have indeed been men. Then talk about the requirements of an artist's life: the long years of training and apprenticeship; the solitude, physical space, and undisturbed time necessary for one's work; the costly art supplies and instruments; the need for someone to provide food and clean one's clothes and keep visitors and children out of the studio for hours at a time.

Now ask your child to think about what it was like to be a girl in almost any period in history: born (disappointingly) female, she would have been trained for farm or home chores or, in the upper classes, for refined "ladyhood." Whatever talent she might have would be ignored. Art school or tutelage under an established artist would be unthinkable. Who would give her brushes or chisels, or time and place to work? What parent would invest money in or lose the labor of a child whose work would never be recognized, a person whose destiny would be bound to a man's, and yoked to enforced childbearing?

Great women artists? How? The artist's life would never even seem a dream worth dreaming for a girl. It is as foolish to ask "Why are there no Eskimo tennis teams?"[10] No brilliant stock market analysts among the poor? No black astronauts?

Tell your children how and why doors close when a dominant class, race, or gender guards the entry—*then* talk about women artists.

Fallacy and Forgetting

Does a tree fall soundlessly in the forest if no human ear is there to hear it? If we are not familiar with the names of great women artists, does it mean none existed?[11] Philosophers continue to debate the first question, but historians can now answer the second.

There *were,* in fact, a number of girls who defied all expectation, dreamed the dream and became women who made great art: *Artemisia Gentileschi, Sofonisba Anguissola,* and *Elisabetta Sirani* were each major celebrities of the sixteenth and seventeenth centuries.[12] *Luisa Ignacia Roldan* was a respected sculptor in seventeenth-century Spain;[13] the paintings of *Judith Leyster,* a seventeenth-century Dutch artist, hung in the Louvre, for years credited to Franz Hals. *Angelica Kauffman,* founding member of the Royal Academy of Art in 1768 (the next female artist was admitted in 1922), painted five hundred highly regarded pictures —and yet, have you heard of her?

Rosa Bonheur dissected carcasses to ensure accuracy in her animal paintings; *Lady Elizabeth Butler* posed hundreds of uniformed soldiers in battle tableaus for her military scenes; and there are ordinary and extraordinary stories attached to many other "great women artists" such as *Mary Cassatt, Berthe Morisot, Kaethe Kollwitz, Freda Kahlo, Georgia O'Keeffe, Audrey Flack, Alice Neel, Helen Frankenthaler,* and *Louise Nevelson,* to name a few.[14]

"Why were these women written out of art history?" your child might ask. Why, even today, do basic art history courses use a text that does not mention one woman in all its 570 pages?[15] It is impossible that not *one* woman was a great artist. Therefore it must be that not one man was an honest art historian. Help your children discover the lost geniuses through recently published books that record women artists' struggles and reproduce samples of their work.[16]

Read with and to your children; trace the common circumstances of women artists' lives: how many were daughters of artist-fathers who were willing to train them (an estimated 90 percent until the last century[17]); how many were restricted to small compositions and "ladylike" subjects;[18] how many were unmarried and childless, perhaps to be wife and mother to their art and free from the service of others; and how many were working in a total vacuum, unable to study the art of others because they were given no education, no art books, and no right to travel[19] to the major art centers?

Explain that until the late 1800s, women were thought too modest and chaste to study the naked body. Thus, they were not permitted to take a life drawing class, or to paint a male nude— the single most important image of history painting, which in turn was the ultimate fine art genre.[20]

The Naked Truth

Silly as it sounds, the best art awareness exercise is going "nude hunting." Take your child to the nearest large museum, park, church, (or wherever monuments, statues, and frescoes abound) note the number of male nudes and female nudes, the century in which they were painted or sculpted, the names of the artists, and the qualities personified by each nude (evil or innocence, power or vulnerability, shame or pride).

> Over the centuries of Western civilization, the male nude has carried a much wider range of meanings, political, religious and moral, than the female. The male nude is typically public: he strides through city squares, guards public buildings, is worshipped in Church. He personifies communal pride or aspiration. The female nude, on the other hand, comes into her own only when art is geared to the tastes and erotic fantasies of private consumers. . . .
> The relatively recent predominance of the female nude springs from a tendency to see nothing but sexual meanings in nakedness, to treat the nude purely as an object of desire.[21]

While you are looking for that difference, see if you notice another: the male nude is more likely to be consistently heroic and idealized; the female changes from ordinary, imperfect, distorted to ideal, "as if male fantasy constantly reshapes the woman's body to better fit his shifting desire, at the same time being careful to preserve the integrity of his own male self."[22]

In modern times, that "integrity" has been protected by a sharp decrease in the portrayal of the male nude as an image. When it has appeared, for instance in modern photography, this, from a male *New York Times* critic, is the typical response:

> There is something disconcerting about the sight of a man's naked body presented primarily as a sexual object [rather than symbolizing] some ideal of strength, skill or activity.[23]

Ask your children how they feel as they look at the nudes. Does the female seem to "belong" more to the viewer? The use of women's bodies to sell products and the proliferation of pornography has created that feeling. Even children pick it up; the *right* to look at woman in her vulnerability but the lingering discomfort when man is naked and defenseless.

Original insights? No, but for your young artist or art lover, the nude comparison-study puts sexism in raw perspective.

More Eye-Openers

From the time they can sit in a stroller, children should go with you to art shows, craft fairs, photo exhibits, and to the studios of working artists if possible. Most little ones respond to color, shape, texture, and interesting subjects. The mistake parents make (us among them) is prolonging the stay, but if you move along, stopping when the child is intrigued, offering biographical tidbits (especially about the women artists) or searching for specific stylistic elements, art can become an entertainment and an adventure.

Stand at the entrance to a room of, say, eighteenth-century paintings and see if you and the children can pick out any that were painted by a woman. Talk about what you used as clues: perhaps the size of the canvas, the delicate colors, the subject. Were you operating on historical knowledge or on stereotypes? Did you correctly identify the women's work?

At home, look through art books together. Cover up the names of the artists and guess gender from the artwork; test each other, speculate how a woman might have painted what Lautrec saw, or how Rembrandt's sister might have portrayed her life.

Bring one of the art world's contemporary controversies to your dinner table: Should art be genderless, ask the family, or should it express the iconography and experience of each sex?[24] Is there a "feminine" sensibility? A "masculine" style? Is it accurate to call someone a "woman painter"? Do we mean a painter of women subjects, or a painter who uses "adamantly female imagery,"[25] or a "less-than-man" painter (the way that "woman doctor" modifies doctor)?[26] Are the following motifs and genres worthy of the name Art: quilts, weaving, doll-making, paintings of a kitchen, brassiere, perfume bottle, beauty parlor, or baby food jar? (No? Then why are pictures of Dick Tracy, Campbell's soup cans, cars, motorcycles, superheroes, guns, and crushed scrap metal considered Art?)

Watch for TV specials, such as WNET's series, *Women in Art;* or for special exhibitions—for example, *Women See Men* (female photographers, male subjects), *Women Artists: 1550–1950* (Brooklyn Museum), the *Sister Chapel,* a traveling display of thirteen feminists' version of The Sistine Chapel, or *The Dinner Party,* Judy Chicago's monumental "table" with individualized "place settings" commemorating the lives of thirty-nine outstanding women in history (San Francisco Museum of Modern Art).

It is neither obsessive nor doctrinaire to emphasize or search out "the woman angle" in your children's art experience; it is simply making reparations for cultural amnesia and making certain both sexes can put themselves "in the picture."

FILM

Most movies are just TV without commercials. If you repudiate free sexism on the small screen, you certainly won't want to pay for it in movie theatres. So read motion picture reviews carefully, especially those published in media sensitive to children and to sexism.[27] Form a small group or a telephone network of parents willing to pool information about films they've seen. It shouldn't be hard to agree on plotlines or characterizations that would deserve an "S" (for sexist) rating. Talk to babysitters and friends' children. Adolescents are good advance critics; if one reports "A few years ago that movie would have made me afraid of girls," I wouldn't take an under-eight to see it.

In general, I don't believe in "sending" kids to the movies before age ten, even if it's a cartoon or children's feature. Go *with* them. Then you can share the pleasure of a good film, or neutralize the effects of a bad one by talking about it immediately afterward.

Audience popularity, "artistic merit," a famous director, or great acting do not make dehumanizing films tolerable—especially for children whose critical receptors are still too all-accepting and whose perceptions tend to go no deeper than the literal.

When children are old enough to see movies on their own, they should take a human value system with them. You wouldn't want them to watch a Ku Klux Klan lynching or Nazi propaganda film uncritically; similarly they should not take in cinematic sexism whole.

That doesn't mean you ban misogynist movies; the forbidden is only enhanced by inaccessibility. But you do send them off to see an otherwise worthy film alerted to sex stereotypes when you know something is riddled with them, and you make a story ridiculous or challenge its authenticity in advance so that children can distance themselves from it however hypnotic the imagery.

Don't be lulled by a "G" or "PG" rating. Some of the worst sex role lessons are in "safe" children's movies. Frankly, I'd rather take Abigail, Robin, and David to an "R" film with explicit but loving sex scenes than to some of the "G" shows we've seen:

> *Swiss Family Robinson.* Father and sons build, explore, and have all the fun on a deserted island while mother watches from under a parasol; sons rescue a young captive from the pirates, treat him as a companion and equal, discover "he's" a girl, then turn "chivalrous" and protective as she turns "girlish" and weak, and mother dresses her in clothes to sit under a parasol in. (At five, Robin said, "I'd like the girl's looks and the boys' adventures." That's the split that hurts.)

> *101 Dalmatians.* Two unappealing female archetypes in animated dog and human form: simpering, good wife and evil, independent vixen. Message: Single, fun-loving females are up to no good.

Those are old classics, you say; movies aren't like that anymore. But they *are.* One father wishes he'd been warned before taking his ten-year-old daughter to see this 1979 release:

> *Wilderness Family—Part II.* Mother and daughter cook and clean, while Dad and son go hunting. Mother gets hysterical while Dad calms her down. Dad teaches the eight-year-old (boy) who can hardly hold a rifle to shoot—but not the (teenage) daughter. When Dad has to leave the cabin to fetch a doctor (Mom—who else?—has gotten sick), he tells his son, "I'm leaving you in charge."[28]

In recent years my own pet peeve was *Star Wars,* the ultimate sci-fi flick that was likened to every morality play from *The Odyssey* to *The Wizard of Oz.*[29] All I saw was new weapons enforcing old power hierarchies, a simplistic polarization of good and evil "forces," and only two women: a princess and a housewife, the most reductive of all female sex role symbols.

Cartoons, adventures, science fiction films, and other supposedly safe categories for children—such as Westerns, crime and war movies—may be safe from explicit sex, but not from sex roles. Whether the actors are white or black, these movies give us almost parody paragons of "masculine" extremism:

> Pioneer, cowboy, outlaw, gangster, soldier, cop—all are glorified in film as the embodiment of strong sexuality. Women are noticeably absent from these men's lives. If they appear at all, they are ignored or raped or rescued or used and abused; men in combat, sport and power struggles cannot be encumbered with women.[30]

In movie musicals and romantic comedies (a dwindling category) there are plenty of females, but they're "types," not women:

- earthy sex-pot baby doll (Marilyn Monroe)
- ideal wife and mother (June Allyson)
- "tomboy" turned ideal wife and mother (Doris Day)
- "professional virgin" (Debbie Reynolds)[31]
- lovable dummy (Judy Holliday)
- asexual-tough-but-man-loving pal (Eve Arden)
- sexy-tough-but-tameable moll (Lauren Bacall)
- whore with a heart (Shirley MacLaine)
- the other woman (Joan Crawford)
- the bitch (Bette Davis)
- twinkly-eyed older woman (Thelma Ritter)
- "refined lady" (Norma Shearer)[32]
- headstrong beauty (Elizabeth Taylor)
- brainy sophisticate who can be humbled (Audrey Hepburn and Katharine Hepburn)

I've mentioned the paradigm actress of each "type," the woman who almost seems to have invented it, but you might ask your children to match current actresses to each category or to add new types to the list. Discuss why one type appeals to your daughter or son more than another. Katharine Hepburn's persona is by far our family's favorite. Even though she has to give up something to retain her "femininity" and keep her man, Hepburn's character—a lawyer *(Adam's Rib)*, missionary adventurer *(The African Queen)*, political journalist *(Woman of the Year)*, sports star *(Pat and Mike)*—always has enough substance to spare.

Someone is sure to notice that men don't fare much better than women in the lighthearted film entertainments. Male characters are "coarse conniving *brutes,*" "vulgar, wise-cracking *lowbrows,*" or "debonair, continental, suave, jaunty" *millionaires* sought after for their money.[33] One fading type personified by such actors as James Stewart and Gary Cooper, is *"the male naif,"* dense, tongue-tied, sexually innocent, "the child-man who was supposed to make women feel maternal."[34] And of course, there's *the bad guy,* recognizable by his moustache, dark shirts and light ties, or poor grammar.

Why don't these male and female "types" cancel each other out? Why not just laugh them both off? Because when they're on screen together, their interactions and "happy endings" tend to promote The Moral According to the Hollywood Musical:[35]

• He Teaches Her Everything She Knows. He Brings Out the Best in Her. He Gives Her Her Big Break. (courtesy of *My Fair Lady, Easter Parade,* or *On a Clear Day*)

• She Gives It All Up for Him. If You Love Him You'll Change Your Life for Him. *(Showboat, The Jolson Story, Grease)*

• Learn to Lose or You'll Lose Him. Don't Beat a Man at Anything. *(Annie Get Your Gun)*

• A Woman's Place Is in the Home. Two Careers Can't Coexist. *(A Star is Born, Funny Girl)*

• As Long As He Marries Her, All Is Forgiven. *(Guys and Dolls, Carousel, Fiddler on the Roof)*

• Women Cannot Survive Without Men—and Those Who Try, Suffer. *(Damn Yankees, Cabaret, Carmen Jones)*

Now let's look at the "good" films, the "serious" films—if you're letting your children look at them. In recent decades, major dramatic roles for females were "whores . . . jilted mistresses, emotional cripples, drunks . . . Lolitas, kooks, sex-starved spinsters, psychotics . . . zombies and ballbreakers." Says one critic, "that's what little girls of the sixties and seventies were made of."[36]

And what were little boys made of? Isolation and violence. Tough loners. Men with a mission but without women,[37] or with little use for women apart from sex and torture. In either case, men were big stars and women were bit parts. That's what your children saw in the seventies, unless they saw a lot worse.

The Gallup Poll found that 7 in 10 teenagers have attended an "R" and 1 in 6 has seen an "X"-rated film.[38] In movies with such titles as *Love Gestapo Style* or *Black and Chained* the "action" is bondage, brute force, mutilation, and enslavement, and the message is "that beating and raping women, urinating and defecating on women is erotic and pleasurable for men, and that women desire this kind of treatment or at least expect it."[39]

All too many parents shrug when their teen-age sons frequent "X" movies. Some argue that violence on the screen is a "safety valve," not a stimulus, a claim that would be lost on the nine-year-old girl who was raped with a broomstick the day after a TV movie containing that act was aired.[40] Ask yourself this:

> What would you think of a suggestion that parents who feel an urge to beat their children should have available to them movie houses in every town showing parents battering and torturing their children, and some of the children enjoying the experience? Do you honestly believe that such movies would prevent rather than promote child abuse?[41]

Far short of violent pornography are some other adult movies with fine writing and superb casts but some odd ideas about the sexes:

• *The female psycho-freak film*—modern variations on woman-as-witch—with—withering—powers. *(Carrie)*

• *"New heroine" films*[42]—much-touted strong women characters, female friendships, and "liberated lifestyles" that end up with no-win career-family choices (*Turning Point*), lesbian innuendo (*Julia*), and paying for unmarried sex with one's life, (*Mr. Goodbar*).

• *Men-are-suffering-too movies*—divorced and abandoned men reacting to the "new heroine's" treatment of them, and getting more sympathy than women ever dreamed of all those years when the tables were turned. (*Kramer vs. Kramer*)

• *The younger-the-better syndrome*[43]—Brooke Shields, Jodie Foster, Tatum O'Neal, and other heirs to Shirley Temple's legacy are far from the tomboy-in-crinolines. Baby talk and sweet selflessness have been replaced by cynical cussing and fierce loyalty while the madonna/whore dichotomy in the junior division is epitomized by high class "kiddie porn" on the one hand (*Pretty Baby*), and low-brow sentimentalized cherubs on the other (*Annie*).[44] Hollywood tells our daughters that the most lovable female is pre-mature, and the only satisfying male-female relationship is one that is vastly unequal. The message is that to win the heart of a grown man you have to remain a little girl: adoring, dependent, unthreatening.

My children see many of these movies just as yours do, but by now, they see through them. Don't worry about being a killjoy. Don't apologize for "overanalyzing" or for promoting movies you want them to see. The reprehensible thing is to let children relax and enjoy rotten films, because there aren't just two or twelve of them, there are hundreds, and if we don't get them one by one, then cumulatively, they'll get us.

MUSIC

I take piano lessons and the lines in the treble clef say "Every Good Boy Deserves Fudge. . . . That makes me sad so I want to change it to "Each Girl's Behavior Deserves Fudge." The boys can still choose the old way.

—Dana Turner, age 5½
Tampa, Florida[45]

Dana is right. Teachers could offer piano students a nonsexist mnemonic device to memorize the music staff. By the same token, in explaining the sonata form, music theory books needn't call the first theme "masculine" and the second theme "feminine," when what they mean is, the first theme is "dynamic, forceful, and rhythmic," and the second is "lyric, reflective, and expansive."[46]

Aside from these quibbles, music itself is no problem. The problem is in the additives—degrading lyrics in popular music, and the idea that certain instruments and musical genres are appropriate for one sex but not the other.

Instruments and Genres

Sex-typing never rests. Some divide the world between the "jocks" (macho) and the musically inclined (sissy). Among the musically inclined, they divide the world between "masculine" instruments —all the brass from trumpet to tuba, most of the winds, the percussion instruments, the double bass, and even the harmonica[47] —and the "feminine" instruments, harp and flute. Piano and violin, some say, depend for virility on the musician's "inflection" ("feminine") or "tigerish quality" ("masculine").[48]

Consistency doesn't enter into it. Bass and tuba are "men's instruments" because of their sound, size, and bulk, but the harp, certainly no lightweight to carry and no comfort to play, is "lady-like" on the grounds of tone and shape. Brass and winds are classified "unfeminine" because the *embouchure* (the lip formation required to play them) is considered unflattering to women. In that case, why the flute, which makes the mouth look like it's sucking a lemon, is considered "feminine" escapes me.

Although high school marching bands, chamber music ensembles, and other grass-roots groups increasingly practice instrumental "democracy," change is slower in the bastions of male musical domination—jazz, rock, and symphony orchestras— where the only instrument women have traditionally contributed to out-front performances is the female voice.

"A high voice has always been a potent symbol of eroticism in opera," writes one expert, "and that symbolism has carried over into popular music."[49] That's plausible; women are allowed to be successful when it serves male erotic needs. A woman in the first violin position isn't sexy, but a big band songbird, pop soloist, "girl group," or folk, soft-rock, country, or disco vocalist[50] in a tight gown has always added scenery to the sound.

Without detracting from female vocal skill, you should let your children know that a woman can be more than a singer. She can be a great teacher—as Nadia Boulanger was "musical god-mother" to Aaron Copland[51] and Mary Lou Williams was mentor to Charles Mingus and other jazz giants.[52] She can be a conductor, composer, and instrumentalist, as women have been from the Middle Ages to the present.[53] (There was even a female Mozart, Nannerl, his older sister who wound up a music teacher, as well as the child prodigy Elisabeth Jacquet de la Guerre, who played in French salons from the age of six, and became a favorite com-poser and harpsichordist in the court of Louis XIV.[54])

She can be a Tin Pan Alley tunesmith, like the women who wrote *Shine on Harvest Moon, Freight Train, God Bless the Child, Sunny Side of the Street,* and many more old favorites.[55] From Julia Ward Howe's *Battle Hymn of the Republic* to Carol Hall's *The Best Little Whorehouse in Texas,* women songwriters have surprising things to say.

She can also be a jazzwoman, hot or cool, like those who can be heard on recordings dating back to 1926,[56] or the many more who can be heard today at jam sessions and jazz festivals all over the country.[57]

My coda should be as clear as middle C. Expose your chil-dren of both sexes to music and musicians both conventional and off-beat. Look especially for a man like Jean Pierre Rampal (flutist extraordinaire) or a woman like Suzi Quatro (unexpected hard rock power on an oversized electric bass guitar). Give girls and boys every opportunity to respond to diverse music and perhaps to gravitate toward one particular instrument, without a word about the gender others attach to it.

Lyrics and Lies

There's more than a dash of sexism in nursery chants. "Peter, Peter Pumpkin Eater" is the original oppressive husband. Disney scores promise *Someday My Prince Will Come,* and Sesame Street tells kids the *People in Your Neighborhood* are all male people. And there's more than a smidgeon of sex roles in the traditional children's repertoire: the maids and mothers are found in the parlor or pantry, rocking babies or baking pies, and the men are workin' on the railroad, gone a'huntin', ridin' the range, settin' out to sea, or marchin' off to war.

By age four or five, kids start tuning in to the mass culture and memorizing the Top 40. I remember being slightly horrified to hear a six-year-old boy crow, "She's having my baby," from Paul Anka's macho ballad about impregnating a teen-age girl.

Studies of song lyrics of the seventies found that country and soul often contain "a rabid machismo." In country music, men are "frequently dependent on females yet fearful of this dependence . . . [while] women see themselves as victimized by men." In soul music, ghetto culture pits men and women against each other in the " 'finance-romance' equation." And in rock lyrics, males are "sexually aggressive, nonconforming, rigid and egotistical, and females are passive."[58]

No one has timed young children's radio exposure, but we do know that nearly twenty-two million youngsters over age twelve spend about three hours a day listening to radio.[59] Those tuned to conservative "easy listening" stations might hear some mellow musing about womanhood—"A woman's a two-face, a worrisome thing"—or advice on being a "lady" who always knows her place, or a wife who "doesn't wear curlers" when she sends her husband off to the office where a lot of pretty girls await him. The double-bind threat/warning for girls culminates in the ideal of "the every-day housewife . . . who gave up the good life for me"—or more bluntly: "Sadie, Sadie, married lady" . . . swears she'll do her "wifely job", "stay at home, become a slob."

On soul stations they might catch a lady singing the blues because she's been taken for granted, two-timed, or beaten up by "my ma-an," whether he's a liar, drunkard, or brute, her bottom line is, "But I love him."

Rock or disco stations favored by many children are purvey-ors of mindless twitterings glommed onto the all-important *beat*; lyrics demanding autonomy or fidelity, defining and bemoaning love, and glorifying the supportive, adoring girl who is "never far away, or too tired to say I want you."

Rock stations also serve up female masochism from the sadist's point of view, representing a woman as a "pet" to be kept under a man's thumb while he "can still look at someone else." A good girl is one who "can take what I dish out, and that's not easy." Lyric writers have countless ways to sing the praises of female subservience.

Even if you keep your radio glued to all-news stations or turned off completely, sexist songs will find a way to your children. At a school talent show, for instance, we saw and heard a girl dance roller disco to *Hot Child in the City* (a pimp's recruitment anthem?). The next day, the guitar teacher taught my son, a number about city girls learning to manipulate men "with just a smile," and something else about a boy preferring his power over his motorbike to his girlfriend's power over him.

And last week, at an off-Broadway revival of *The Sound of Music,* we sat through this:

> You wait, little girl, on an empty stage,
> for fate to turn the light on.
> Your life, little girl, is an empty page,
> that men will want to write on.

Whether she is demanding or submissive, the female described in most song lyrics is not a particularly lovable or admirable role model.

What to Do?

Isolate the negative lines. Speak them aloud to your children and talk about what is really being said. Have children write new lyrics to the melodies they love. If a message is beyond endurance, as was the Rolling Stones' 1978 hit, *Some Girls—*

> White girls are pretty funny,
> sometimes they drive me mad,
> Black girls just want to get fucked all night,
> I just don't have that much jam.

protest to the artists and record companies.

Stay alert for songs kids can grow on. Ask friends, check record stores, teachers, musical and feminist review media,[60] because you won't hear such things on the radio very often. Talk about the meaning of Willie Tyson's "I Wanna Be an Engineer," "Sister Suffragette" from the *Mary Poppins* album, "It's All Right to Cry," "Girl Land," and others from *Free to Be, You and Me;* and for teens, get into the music of Cris Williamson, Meg Christian, Kay Gardner,[61] and Holly Near.[62]

Be prepared for unexpected digressions, like this mother-daughter exchange when a three-year-old asked a question about the Davy Crockett song:

> She asked what "Kilt him a bar when he was only three" meant.
>
> I told her it meant that he had killed a bear when he was only three-years-old.
>
> She said, "His mother must have helped him."
>
> I was thrilled that my daughter would assume it was the mother who would help kill the bear. Later, it occurred to me that she was speaking from her own observation. Who was likely to be *with* a three-year-old when a bear came along? His mother, of course.[63]

Introduce children to grownup songs *you* like and sing them together. One of our family's happiest discoveries is the team of Gretchen Cryer and Nancy Ford,[64] whose lyrics are an education in sex role liberation whether they're singing about misguided "feminine" fantasy—

> Miss America, no wonder you feel bad,
> You bought the stuff they sold you
> and maybe you've been had.
> You ruled the land that never was,
> a princess in a play,
> But you've got time, it's not too late,
> you've still got today![65]

or whether they're writing a song for the overburdened man—

> I need a little time to get myself together,
> I've been working so hard for so long . . .
> Lately I've heard so much talk

about women wanting to be free,
and I just can't help but wonder, honey . . .
what about me?[66]

Not every decade will have a Cryer and Ford, a gentle James Taylor or a Helen Reddy proclaiming that woman is strong, resiliant, and invincible, but there *are* singers of conscience and marvelous lyrics to be heard if you listen.

PRINT MEDIA

Children's Books

By now, the complaints are familiar: the majority of main characters are boys—mischievous, brave, innovative do-ers—while the girls are lumpish, frightened, weak, shy, and giggling on the sidelines with their hands behind their backs. The men go to work, are fun, clever but nonnurturant. Aprons are welded to the women who are welded to their kitchens except when they are inept at problem solving or good at being kind to children and animals.

"If I were writing the books now," said Elizabeth Rider Montgomery, author of the *Dick and Jane* series, "I'd have Father washing the dishes or Mother mowing the lawn. Better yet, both Mother and Father doing things together."[67]

Some changes *have* happened to children's books in the last decade; "tomboys" are less likely to reform and mothers are more likely to earn money as most real women must do, and there are stories now of divorce, adoption, poverty, minority families, adolescent sexual experience, and other honest life situations.[68]

[margin note: Dies have occurred]

But you still have the problem of fairy tales.

In a book-length psychoanalysis of fairy tales, Bruno Bettelheim argues that children need such allegories to work out parental separation and Oedipal conflicts, sibling rivalry, sexual dread, and curiosity.[69] Hansel and Gretel is about oral greed, says he. Goldilocks is really snooping out the primal scene in Mommy and Daddy Bears' bedroom. Jack and the Beanstalk represents "phallic self-assertion."[70] The everpresent slimy frog symbolizes sex—disgusting to a child but later revealed to be a prince, "life's most charming companion."[71]

I find the theories more fun than the fairy tales, which I do not agree solve "existential predicaments"[72] or "convey the advantages of moral behavior."[73] Mainly, I believe that children take their Gretel and Goldilocks quite literally; they see one girl being comforted by her *brave brother* and another envious of the mother-father-*son* triad. They see hateful, sadistic witches and stepmothers.

One needn't unravel the unconscious to determine that 80 percent of the *negative* characters in the Brothers Grimm's tales are female.[74] Decoding themes and symbolism from a feminist perspective thus hangs the picture on a firm statistical peg; the lessons and warnings cannot be missed.[75] A girl must be beautiful to be a princess worth saving, delicate enough to be bruised by a pea (or any other environmental strain), mindless enough to fall under spells despite frequent alerts and admonitions, so dim she can mistake a wolf for her own grandma, and so malleable she'll marry the first guy who wakes her up.

But first she has to be put to sleep. At puberty but before her sexual power can be explored, it must be taken out of the action. To use Bettelheim's symbolism, the frog can only turn into a prince *after* they're married.

So, when *Rapunzel* turns 12, she is imprisoned in a tower, her hair (her childhood strength, her rope to freedom) cut off. *Snow White* eats the red apple (menstruation? sexual knowledge?) but before she can lose her innocence, she's out cold. *Sleeping Beauty* pricks her finger and before the (menstrual) blood is dry, she's asleep too. For a girl coming out of childhood, passive is good but catatonic is better. She mustn't get into any trouble en route from her father to her husband. She mustn't be lured, cursed, or tempted by autonomy—which is embodied in the wicked witch.

Witches are ugly, depraved, and carnivorous in order to warn girls against "unilateral actions by aggressive, self-motivated women."[76] To be nonmaternal, to have power of her own, makes a girl a witch.

What happens after happily ever after? Nothing. Marriage is not seen, only courtship; the *second* marriage exists so there can be a context for the stepmother (Bad Mommy) to be pitted against the king (Nice Daddy). An entire literature of make-believe helps little girls focus their goals on being "good" in childhood, passively beautiful in adolescence, securely married and Good Mommies in womanhood. So much for fleshing out the length of her days. *Not* witch-like is the only thing a girl must be in that invisible thing called woman's future.

For boys, the curse is to remain a frog or to be eaten by the giant. The cure is to join the patriarchy as a proper prince and giant-killer. Happily ever after consists of a kingdom to rule, young princes to initiate into manhood, and a princess to confine and marry off so that land and riches may pass from man to man, circumventing the witches from that time to this.

In teen-age fiction, the fairy tale pattern persists in modern dress: adolescent girls rein in their spirit, compete for fairest-of-them-all, pray for a boy to "notice" them, and put their brains to sleep hoping to be claimed and kissed.[77] Teenage boys are still trying to be king—now known as *Fullback Fury* or *Saturday's Hero*[78]—only their exploits are no longer geared to female conquest. Modern boys inherit the kingdom by taking themselves seriously, rising above romance, and pursuing personal success.

What to do? First, read enough critiques to sensitize yourself to sexism in children's literature.[79] Read three or four of the worst and best books so you'll understand the potential for negativism and the possibilities for betterment. Form a book review/action group (like your network of neighborhood film critics); share news of books to enjoy or avoid; exchange and borrow; discuss and write protest letters; petition publishers, book stores, and libraries to make more nonsexist books available. Over twenty-five hundred children's books are published every year and precious few are sex role-resistant. Too often "tokenism has been masquerading as progress."[80]

To see sexism in black and white in the library's card catalogue or in the reference work *Books in Print,* look up books intended especially for one sex or the other. (*Boy's Book of Tools . . . of Outdoor Discovery . . . of Model Railroading . . . of Hiking,* etc., etc., etc.) Organize a boycott (or girlcott) to bring attention to the problem.

Order the pamphlet *10 Quick Ways to Analyze Children's Books for Racism and Sexism,* and choose books appropriate to your children's age level from one of the bibliographies of nonsexist books.[81]

Provide nonsexist books for your son as well as your daughter. Read aloud to your children. Learning to read is one thing, learning to imagine is equally important. Be there to help their imaginings stay open-ended and free.

These activities will start things moving:

• *Balancing the bookshelf.* Pull six books at random from your son's bookshelf. Visit a friend who has a daughter of the same age and borrow six of *her* books. Compare the subject matter, illustrations, characters, and what happens to them. Fill in the blanks in your son's book collection and vice versa.

• *Screen for sexism and racism simultaneously.* If blacks or Italians were consistently portrayed as females are portrayed in fairy tales, would blacks or Italians read them to their children? Similarly, if Pippi Longstocking, Mary Poppins, or Nancy Drew is a strong female character but functions in a racist context, how can we applaud her?

• *Make a "Quote Card" collection.* On 3×5 cards children can note book excerpts that gave them "the shock of recognition."[82] For example, from *Little Women:*

> Jo immediately sat up, put her hands in her pockets and began to whistle.
> "Don't Jo; it's so boyish!"
> "That's why I do it."

• *Go stereotype-hunting in each literary genre.* Not just in fairy tales and Dick and Jane stories, but in *nursery rhymes* (note Contrary Mary, Lazy Mary, squeamish Bo-Peep, Jill tumbling *after*); in *fables and fantasies* (Wendy returns to Never-Never Land once a year to do Peter Pan's spring cleaning; and in *Winnie the Pooh,* the only female is Kanga, a mother); in *picture books* (where animals and vehicles are almost always "he" and where you'll find those notorious lines "Boys invent things" and "Girls use what boys invent"[83]); in young readers' *science fiction* (where, with all that freedom to imagine, authors seem unable "to imagine a

Book to send for

two-sexed egalitarian society"[84]); in *biographies, historical fiction, diaries, poetry,* and *letters*—where the truth of the writer's experience makes the sexism all the more telling; and in your *dictionary* whose entries under "woman," "man," "mother," "father," "ambition," "sweet," and "strong," will give away the game.

• *Be a creative revisionist.* Do not censor the classics or ban sexist books; use them as examples of what's wrong, hurtful, and ridiculous. In one of the Bobbsey Twins books, the cat gets stuck on a newly varnished floor and Mother Bobbsey calls Father Bobbsey home from the office to deal with it. Robin and I stopped reading, laughed, and talked about how *we* would have solved the problem (With turpentine, walking on a board, and revarnishing the spots. As we read on, of course, that was how Father Bobbsey did it.) More revisionist ideas:
- Have children write new endings.
- Change the sexes of the characters and see if the story suffers.
- Act out beloved stories and let children take any part regardless of gender.
- Challenge girls' and mothers' *roles,* not girls and mothers.
- Change the "he's" to "she's" when reading aloud to a young child. Read the dialogue spoken by a brave character or a scary animal in a woman's tone of voice instead of a deep male timbre.
- Stop for some "what ifs": What if the Queen didn't want a child, or the King lost his kingdom—could they still be happy? What if they had a son who refused to slay dragons or a daughter who was plain but pleased with herself? What if . . .

• *Ask children to draw four pictures*—of a plumber, a teacher, a doctor, and a parent reading to a child. If pictures 1 and 3 are males and 2 and 4 are females, introduce your child to books that show women and men in nontraditional occupations and shared parenting activities.

• *Look for evidence in life* to refute literary stereotypes: the man who bakes all the bread for his family, the mommy who is also a cop.

• *Look for literary refutations* that speak for themselves. A perfect example is the book *Womenfolk and Fairytales,* [85] folklore chosen because each tale has a capable or courageous girl or woman as its "moving force"—clever females who use their wits to escape danger or rescue others.

• *Let children write their own stories,* or tape them so they can be re-heard and embellished. When one gifted novelist was asked how he drew women so well he said that "he wrote the stories first and chose up sexes afterward."[86] Try it.

• *Help children "get into" a difficult or heavily descriptive book.* Start them off. Explain obscure references, help them visualize beautiful things and places, suggest parallels in their life to help them empathize with a character's feelings. Don't give up on the grounds that "boys need more action," or "boys don't have patience for lyrical writing." Nonsense.

• *Adopt a great person.* To interest children in biography, diaries, history, suggest some detective work (particularly for "lost women"). Choose a life that might inspire. Read the person's autobiography, letters, poetry, newspaper accounts of her activities. Visit places she lived, worked, or left a legacy. Robin adopted Susan B. Anthony and John Stuart Mill when she was twelve, and produced a broadsheet called "The Women's Advocate" full of made-up news stories set in the year Mill died (Robin wrote his obituary) and Anthony was tried for the crime of voting (Robin "covered" the trial). In seventh grade, Abigail became an expert on George Sand. David got hooked on the Statue of Liberty, not exactly a person, but a symbol and a powerful female image. He read about the sculptor, the woman who modeled her, the campaign to raise money for her pedestal, and the woman whose poetry is carved on her base. When David visited the statue and Ellis Island, the immigrant experience was his.

• *Have children choose a library book that is "the opposite of their usual selection."*[87] Usually, girls do this willingly, but boys mutter obscenities while browsing through student nurse books and dollhouse pictures. Talk about their different reactions and examine the differences in their choices.

Authors and publishers have justified the preponderance of more exciting and varied books for and about boys because of boys' slower reading proficiency and the importance of motivating Johnny to read.[88] It doesn't hurt profits either. Only girls will read about girls, but both sexes will read and buy boys' stories.[89]

"Don't be fooled," says one critic, who denies that authors need to put down girls in order to motivate boys. Eventually, boys learn to read, but what anti-female lessons have they learned in the process—and what self-deprecating by-products have girls had to swallow for boys' sake?[90]

It makes sense that "boys wouldn't read about dull children —male or female"[91]—after getting used to books that have adventure, action, heroism, open access to life, and funloving boys. But what an irony that girls suffer twice:

> Boys are the dominant figures in the nonfiction section of the library because they are thought to be *more* able than girls in such fields as math, science and statesmanship. Then they are the dominant figures in beginning-to-read books for just the opposite reason. They are thought to be *less* able than girls in language arts.[92]

Don't let your daughter get caught in that double bind. Don't let your son grow up all action and no poetry.

Comics, Magazines, and Newspapers

Add sexist advertisements to stories and pictures, and you enlarge the problem of in-print gender prejudice by about 50 percent. In *Plastic Man* comic books, for example, children are enticed by promises of instant macho: "Kung fu and Karate By Mail!" "Build Mighty Muscles," "Stand Taller Fast," and for twenty-five cents, a pamphlet entitled "Masculinity and Virility Versus Frailty and Impotence!"

Seventeen and *Teen* magazine have admirable features for the adolescent girl about sex, health, colleges, and careers, but the ads still sell "tight jeans that guys will love!"

Boys' Life discontinued gun ads after the Kennedy assassination but a few years ago the gun lobby won out over the magazine's social conscience and now the advertising message is:

"Discover what a great friend a gun can be."[93]

Appealing to Boy Scouts (and Cub Scouts as young as eight), *Boys' Life* also bows to the almighty dollar with ads for bullets, rifles, uniforms, bayonets, Nazi helmets, a "widow-maker" drag car, a knife described as a "powerful brute," and "One heckuva fine pump shotgun . . . clean, businesslike . . . rugged and dependable."

Except in early childhood, kids do not limit themselves to media they're *supposed* to read. They thumb through our magazines and newspapers[94] where they see such "gender advertisements"[95] as these:

• Birds-Eye will do almost anything to get your husband's attention.

• Tame. The perfect answer for tangle-haired tomboys and their ex-tomboy mothers.

• The Ideal Playhouse! It's a log cabin playhouse for the girls, or a log cabin hut for the boys.

• Daddy's best girls all pampered in pink.
All angels and innocence. All Christian Dior.

• The Colesta Sportshirt. It's silky.
But it's no sissy.

• For mom and the girls: lavish interiors.
For dad and the boys: a Rocket 350 V-8.

In a new burst of high fashion decadence, some clothing ads show women posed as killers and victims with whips and chains, one squatting with a horse saddle strapped to her back, another in a raincoat being shot with water from a fire hose, a little girl selling a nightgown in a pornographic posture.[96]

No sense ignoring such ads if children have seen them. Explain the merchandising psychology behind the sexual sell, point out the most blatant examples of sex role coercion, but then, as with television advertising, accentuate the positive.

On the bright side, make a collection of *Ads We Adore.* These are in my folder:

• The Omega watch ad picturing a young father holding a child in his arms, with the headline: "You can tell a lot about a person by the time he keeps."

• "Could your child grow up to be President of the United States? Sure she could." (Condé Nast publications)

• "Kanon Cologne. Conceived in the country where men are so sure of themselves, some of them stay home and take care of the children."

• Tampax ads showing women involved in strenuous athletics on "those" days.

• "Right now she wants to be a doctor and maybe she will be. Only you can make it happen." (Emigrant Savings Bank ad with an illustration of a girl bandaging a cat.)

• The Wamsutta sheets ad showing a daddy reading in bed to three pajamaed little girls.

When you clip an ad for your folder, don't forget to drop a note of commendation to the product manufacturer, too.

Editorial copy surrounding these ads can be S.O.S.—Same Old Stereotypes. Comic books and Sunday comic strips (with the notable exception of *Doonesbury, Peanuts* and the new *Koky*) still feature nuclear families with stay-home women (in aprons 25 percent of the time[97]) who are never shown reading or having fun[98] but are often shown being dominant/aggressive (because what little power women have at home isn't really important). There are the same old henpecked husbands who are competent in the world but well-meaning idiots in their families (where it doesn't matter because the *father* role isn't crucial for "masculinity.")[99]

There are some new lifestyle love comics with old lifestyle endings. And svelte female superheroes whose exploits are either male-imitative or sexually titillating. And old male superheroes who continue to glorify violence in the name of morality, to punish "bad" men without establishing that it is bad to treat women as sex objects or to be hostile to the point of rape (which is mercifully forbidden by the comics "Code").[100]

Watch for the surprisingly awful children's stories tucked within such tepid comics as *Sad Sack* and *Little Lotta*. This one, called "Growing Pains," tells of a girl who desperately talked her way onto the boys' baseball team, played fabulously, and then realized the effect of her excellence on her beau:

> Like a flash, it hit her. In Billy's eyes now, she was "one of the boys" instead of the pretty girl he'd first admired! Mary Ellen swallowed hard and made the biggest decision of her

yuck

life. She stepped up to the plate and one . . . two . . . three
. . . *she deliberately struck out.*
    His delighted smile and the quick, warm way he
squeezed her hand told her she'd done the right thing . . . and
taken a long step down the path of growing up.

Learn to lose gracefully, and on purpose, is advice given
frequently to growing girls in magazines addressed especially to
them. To the girl who has been weight-lifting and feeling terrific:
"Just remember not to challenge him to an Indian arm wrestling
match. But if you do—be smart. Remember to lose." And to a girl
who is a much better player than her boyfriend: "Play as best you
can, but when you leave the court, allow him to carry your
racket."[101] More advice:

Be a reporter for your school paper . . .
Better yet, start a gossip column.

Dazzle your boyfriend. Become a Sports Buff.

Teen magazines, like conventional women's magazines, tend
to be *"for* females but *about* males."[102] If children should wander
into such publications as *McCall's, Ladies' Home Journal,* or *New
Woman,* they will find a greater awareness of changing roles and
the strains that go with them. But the "new woman" remains
preoccupied with how her looks, career success, housekeeping,
and cooking will affect *the man* in her life.[103]
    General interest magazines still treat women as sex objects
("the curvy gymnast"), appendages of men[104] or a category separate from mainstream affairs. (Highlights of the Year: Foreign.
Domestic. The Economy. Women.) Pay attention to these magazines if your children are junior high school age or older; about
10 percent of *Newsweek* and *Time* readers are between twelve and
nineteen.[105]
    Men's magazines, found lying around the barber shop if
not in the back of the garage, are basic primers for the objec-
tification and victimization of the female. If a father can't live
without such "entertainment," he ought to take himself off to
a therapist before his children find out that he gets his kicks
from an airbrushed centerfold. There is no way such maga-

zines are useful, even to illustrate what's wrong with gender relationships in our culture.

As for the daily newspaper, if yours doesn't report about the Equal Rights Amendment and breast cancer on the Style pages right next to hemline news and recipes for banana bread, put me on its subscription list.

Children who flip through the paper on their way to the TV listings or comics can't help but notice the preponderance of men in the news and sports pages (but no pictures of bridegrooms-to-be); captions that identify the female in the picture as a satellite of a man ("Dr. William J. Ronan's wife"[106]); stories that describe a man by his current act or occupation but a woman by her age or looks ("the pert grandmother"); advice columns, astrological forecasts, and personality profiles that assume everyone lives according to sex roles; and obituaries so focused on a man's accomplishments that it's hard to tell it was his wife who died.

This time your sample folder should contain clippings of both the best and the worst, because the worst are so bad they're radicalizing. *Sample:* The headline said "Seven Women Quit State Police School," but the story reported that among those who found the training too rigorous there were *forty-eight* male quitters.[107] *Sample of the best:* a front page picture of Dr. David Baltimore, winner of the Nobel Prize, photographed with his baby in his arms because he was home caring for her the day he found out he'd won.[108]

Most children learn what society expects them to like in a book, comic, magazine, or newspaper, *even before they learn to read.*[109] Don't let gender-blinders narrow your children's view. Help them ignore the label "For Boys" or "For Girls," and read for themselves—freely, widely and well.

THEATER ARTS

Out there somewhere is a lingering belief that dance is for artsy women and homosexual men, and theater is too expensive and too sophisticated for children. Anyone who subscribes to such generalizations deserves a seat behind a post in the last row of the balcony.

Theater of All Kinds for All Ages

Children, like adults, need the magic of theater, spiritually, intellectually, and for sex role catharsis. I don't mean children need *children*'s theater. With four exceptions that I know of (Paper Bag Players, Bill Baird's Marionnettes, Merri Mini Players, and Performing Arts Repertory Theatre), the words "children's theater" make me think of Saturday afternoons in a grimy loft; radiators steaming, actors in safety-pinned costumes condescending to squirming children, and an absurd Fairy Godmother vamping the daddies in the first row.

I mean *real* theater, avant-garde or Shakespeare, where something happens to someone a child can care about. I mean a well-crafted mystery that children as young as five or six can understand on their own level while we glean the psychological subtext. I mean cutting-edge drama and urbane comedy that can be understood by a seven-year-old if an adult provides the bare bones of the plot in advance and whispers a translation now and then during the confusing scenes. And I mean musicals that make something gala, growth-producing.

It shouldn't be Broadway or nothing; it should be good shows or nothing. And good shows may be found in church basements (and occasionally, I suppose, grimy lofts), in college gyms, summer stock and little theaters, and school productions that are worth seeing even if your kids aren't in them.

Stars and polish can come later. For now, the play's the thing. The idea is to orient your children toward imagined lives smaller, larger, and far different than their own; to feel and see sexism before they have to live it; to meet characters on stage that they might never know in life; to look at female and male experience not through the eyes of their parents and friends, but through those of George Bernard Shaw and Elizabeth Swados, Lillian Hellman and Henrik Ibsen.

Of course, you'll be seeking plays with strong women, sensitive male characters, and nonstereotypical power relationships. But not every play need be *A Doll's House.* You can talk with your children about women's and men's roles just as meaningfully after you see a Greek tragedy, Restoration Comedy, black protest drama or a Neil Simon comedy. Do not protect children from conventionally dramatized gender relationships, whether set in Scarsdale or Sherwood Forest. Use the plays of the Angry Young Men of the 1950s to illuminate the plays of the angry young women writing today.

Use the status quo the way the oyster uses sand, as the irritant that produces pearls of wisdom. Ask your children:

- Which character in the play would you have liked to be?

- From whose point of view were the events on the stage portrayed?

- How might the play have differed if it had been written by a woman (man)?

- What if a woman (man) had been the leading character?

Dance

If your children have never seen a live dance performance, start with something short and dazzling, with exciting music, costumes, and sets. Expose kids to dancers executing high-energy choreography (Twyla Tharp rather than Martha Graham, Edward Villela before Merce Cunningham), a strong children's story-line *(Nutcracker Suite* or *Peter and the Wolf),* or a program balanced between solos and ensembles, romance, drama, and jazz.

Before the performance, tell your children the story of the ballet. Play the music for several days so it becomes familiar. Give them some background on the dancers (he once had polio, she never thought she'd be successful because she's so tall). Have them try some pirouettes and high leg extensions to sense in their bodies the difficulty and the wonder of what dancers do.

Obviously, ballet is for both sexes. However, in particular we want to enhance the art of movement for our sons, to make dance a positive, unambivalent art and means of self-expression. Because we know that in most peer groups a boy's interest in ballet is perceived as a renunciation of manhood, the parental finger points at strong male dancers as if to say "See, it's okay. Doesn't he look masculine!"

Efforts to "virile-up" the image of ballet make me uncomfortable. An art form should not have to be cleansed of its homosexual tinges to be appealing. Moreover, I've never quite accepted ballet as "effete" in the first place. The training is more rigorous than that for most sports, the muscles developed in a male dancer are more impressive than Bruce Jenner's, and frankly, the sex roles in classical ballet couldn't be more traditional and "straight": she's all fluttery and tippy-toe and he's all power, leaping, lifting, supporting, and leading her around the stage.

It would be a supreme irony if ballet became right for boys for all the wrong reasons. Make it right for its own sake:

- Encourage both boys and girls to move to music. Get up and sway, rock, and glide with them—you too, Father—until movement becomes as comfortable as tapping your finger to the beat.

- See if your son can imitate the dance styles of Fred Astaire (a cane and top hat would help), Alvin Ailey, John Travolta, Rudi Nureyev, a Russian cossack.

- Ask children to choreograph a dance to a favorite classical composition, then a jazz number, then a rock song. Suggest they work up a routine with a group of friends.

- Ask local dance teachers, schools, or YMCA's to actively promote ballet and modern dance for boys. Perhaps they can offer the first few lessons free as an introductory offer; or import a professional male dancer to give a master class. (Jacques d'Amboise, lead dancer with the New York City Ballet for nearly thirty years, gave start-up classes in dozens of public and private schools.[110] That effort plus the media hype of Nureyev and Baryshnikov, made ballet *the* hot after-school activity for hundreds of city boys, my son among them.)

- Make it fun to dance and prestigious to be a dancer. At parties have boys and girls leap over a progressively raised rope, do high kicks, splits, and leaps as competitively as they try for an ace in tennis or a double play in baseball. Have half the group do fifteen minutes of ballet warm-ups and half do fifteen minutes of football exercises, then compare charley-horses. The idea is not to make ballet a macho contest, but to recognize the *athletic* skills involved.

• Follow favorite dancers' careers. We've clipped stories on Jacques d'Amboise since David's acquaintance with him[111]; we know about his teenage son, Chris (who once stepped into his father's role when he was taken ill), and about his twin daughters, who are a year older than Robin and Abigail. We also have many friends who paper their walls with pictures of Baryshnikov, "the first male classical dancer to become a national pinup."[112]

• Introduce interested boys to such books as *Max* (a picture book) and *A Special Gift* (a novel for ages eight to twelve),[113] which make ballet a valid and admirable activity. (They also establish that the boy heroes are good at "normal" stuff—basketball and baseball—but that sort of defensiveness should disappear as more boys take dance more casually.)

Theatrical Activities

• Children can write their own "Playbills," costume themselves from dress-up clothes, put up a blanket for a curtain, charge admission, and invite the neighborhood to a home-made play.

• They can use theater more personally. Act out events that have made them angry (someone teased your son for his long hair. Let him play all the parts: the tease, the onlookers, the punishing agent, himself.)

• Do imitations: parents at breakfast, the coach after a losing game, the way a friend sings.

• Improvise from a given situation: a girl enrolling in auto mechanics, a boy telling his friends he's taking needlepoint.

• "Be" someone you admire, talk like her, act like her, get into her head. Try being someone of the other sex to see what it feels like.

• Play characters at extremes of humanity: an active baby girl, an old man in a nursing home; a woman marathon runner, a blind woman; a man being fired, a man getting married.

If top-flight theater and dance are out of reach financially or geographically, do-it-yourself projects can create the culture of possibility in your own house and hometown. A theater workshop for girls and boys under twelve, or a teen jazz-ballet company, an improvisation group, or a self-selected cast rehearsing a play everyone believes in can flex the aesthetic muscles while establishing that the performing arts belong to girls and boys alike.

Art. Film. Music. Print. Theater and dance. The more entertainment encompasses, the more it can be enjoyed. So, raise consciousness without censorship, discover the perils and pleasures of feminist revisionism, short-circuit sexist images and filter them through a layer of ridicule. Children who can make fun of stereotypes are better able to resist them.

VII
Community and Society

22

Other People, Other Places . . . And Similar Problems of Everyday Life

What happens when you open the door to let the world in, or the children out? Are your nonsexist principles irrevocably subverted? Must you bow to "other people's" values? Not if you and your children learn to react to sexism constructively.

Let me give you a few hundred examples.

AT HOME

The corruptive world can enter the house in the person of friends, relatives—and repair men. The man who came to fix our dishwasher was watched in rapt fascination by our three children, then six, six, and three. Just as he finished, he handed the wrench to three-year-old David. "Here, big boy," he chuckled. "You can have the last turn."

We had to intervene to get Abigail and Robin a chance with the tool.

This year, when we finally bought a new dishwasher, Robin started to fill out the warrantee form. A minute later, she asked, "Who do I put down for 'Head of Household'?"

"We're a two-headed monster," I joked, and wrote *Letty and Bert Pogrebin, co-heads.*

I find it hard to believe, but people tell me they know contractors who will only discuss remodeling with "the Mister,"[1] painters who will only sign a contract with "the man of the house," and door-to-door salespeople who prefer to come back when "the little lady" is home because their product line is for housework.

If you've just moved in, some well-meaning friendship wagon representative may come to the door asking for Mother, not Father, in order to present her with a basket of cleaning products, discount coupons and a Harlequin paperback:

Harlequins help me to escape from housework into a world of romance, adventure and travel.[2]

VISITING FRIENDS AND RELATIVES

The nicest people can be burdensome big mouths in the presence of one's children.

I remember one of Bert's law partners complaining about the firm's being shorthanded. "We could use a couple of extra secretaries, girls, how 'bout it?" he said with a smile. "And Davey can be his daddy's junior partner."

Bert stopped the man in his tracks. "There are already two places reserved for Robin and Abigail in the class of 1990 at Harvard Law," he said. "And David wants to be a farmer."

A friend told me about the time her son returned from school shouting proudly, "Ma, I won second place in the essay contest. Miriam was first."

"How could my nephew be beaten by a mere girl!" said the boy's uncle, who was visiting.

The mother squirmed in her chair, but her son replied matter-of-factly, "Girls are not as mere as they used to be, Uncle Sidney."

Three families were sharing a potluck Sunday dinner. After dessert, the children went upstairs to play and a while later summoned the parents to admire their block construction.

"Okay," called one of the women. "The mommies will come up and if it's interesting we'll call the daddies."

One of the daddies, to his everlasting credit, refused the implication that the fathers' attention was too important to squander on their children's handiworks.

"We *all* want to see what you've made," he said, and the other men followed.

Some nonsexist parents hold their tongues politely, then let off steam to the family after the visitor departs. Others, myself included, gently but firmly challenge sexist comments on the spot and permit their children to do the same.

Like the time a woman visitor got up from the table apologizing, "I'd love to stay for another cup of coffee, but I have to go home and feed Harry."

"Is Harry your baby?" asked the four-year-old of the house.

"No, Harry's my husband," laughed the woman.

"Then how come he can't feed himself?" asked the child.

Or the time the twelve-year-old was showing her grand-mother her new quilt.

"You're so lucky to have such a wonderful quilt," said Grandma. "When you grow up I hope you'll be lucky enough to marry a man who can afford to buy you such beautiful things."

"When I grow up, I'll make the money to buy the beautiful things myself, Grandma," said the girl.

Another friend always remembered the exchange that took place a few years ago when she was babysitting . . . and before her consciousness was raised:

> The little boy cried bitterly when he fell and bumped his head on the corner of a table. I tried comforting him but when his tears increased, I said, "Come on, it wasn't *that* bad. A big boy like you shouldn't be such a crybaby." Witnessing this, the boy's older brother, who couldn't have been more than eight, took the little boy in his arms and said, "In this family, people cry when they're hurt and they stop crying when the pain goes away."

Just as my friend never forgot that sentence, before long, people you know become so sensitive to your values that they start to see and hear things as you do.

For example, we were congratulating a visiting neighbor whose son had hit a grand slam home run the day before.

"What did Greg have for breakfast yesterday?" we teased.

"Whatever it was, I'm going to ask his mother to get *me* some," laughed the proud father; then, reddening, he quickly added, "Or I'll have to get me some myself."

CONVERSATIONAL POLITICS

As if it weren't enough to hear sex stereotypes expressed overtly, children also pick up patriarchal messages from tone of voice, speaking styles, and body language.

Even when they don't know they're listening, they *hear* fe-male powerlessness. Typically, they hear a woman use excessively polite speech and formal grammar (perhaps trying to upgrade her status via "fancy" talk), empty adjectives (such as "divine"), intensifiers ("*really* terrific"), and qualifiers ("sort of," "I guess"). Children know, for instance, which sentence—"That's an adorable movie" or "Damn it, the set broke"—is more likely to be said by a man and which by a woman.[3]

A woman reveals tentativeness and lack of authority by apologizing for and disparaging her own statements ("This is probably silly, but . . ."). She often ends sentences with a tag question ("It's really cold, isn't it?) or turns simple commands into questions ("Could you close the door?").[4] In general conversation, contrary to stereotype, men speak more than women.[5] A woman tends to ask three times as many questions as a man (a bid for attention), is more likely to lose the floor to a man, and is simply not listened to as carefully as a man, even if she makes the same statement.[6]

Children also learn that noise is associated with power. In particular, a strong, deep, and resonant voice is so associated with the male role that young boys speak with a much lower pitch than would be expected from their vocal anatomy prior to their voice change.[7] So, even when they don't know they're listening, children hear sex roles in sound.

By the same token, even when they don't know they're watching, children *see* sexual politics in nonverbal communication—the patronizing pat on the back, the hand on the shoulder, as well as the sexual squeeze. Between any two people, when touching isn't mutual, it's an assertion of power. That's why bosses feel more entitled to touch subordinates than vice versa, whites to touch blacks, adults to touch children, and most often, men to touch women.[8]

Children also see women taking up little space in the world: ankles crossed demurely, limbs held close, hands folded—while men spread out, sprawl, and use grand gestures. They see people keep less distance when talking to a woman than a man (either because males seem to demand space around them or females seem to permit proximity);[9] they see men shepherd, guide, and lead while women follow;[10] and through it all they see women smiling.[11] The smile is the "nice" girl's equivalent of the shuffle.

How much of this do children really *notice?*

Everything. Consciously or unconsciously, they draw profiles of caste and status from our sex-differentiated uses of not just money and things but invisible entities—in this case, sound and space.

HUMOR AND HUMILIATION

Other people's sexism often comes wrapped in a joke. If you don't laugh, you might be accused of lacking a sense of humor, of "going too far" with this movement stuff.[12] If you do laugh, your children may ask you what's so funny, and you might have to explain such lines as "When your Aunt Ethel turns fifty I'm going to turn her in for two twenty-fives." Which might make you think seriously about humor and sexism.

Actually, jokes account for one in five laughs,[13] but the average person laughs about fifteen times a day.[14] That means two parents laugh ten thousand times a year, which gives kids plenty of clues to the comical and the absurd. Among other things, they learn that male chauvinism is funny especially in a sexual joke:

"Is this the Salvation Army?"
"Yes."
"Do you save bad women?"
"Yes."
"Well save me three for Saturday night."[15]

The predominant, almost exclusive, sources and tellers of jokes are men, not women—a pattern that emerges in childhood: "Boys repeat more jokes and riddles than girls as early as age six when formal joking first appears."[16]

We can speculate that males try harder to be funny because joketelling is a skill they want to add to their list of capabilities, or because "humor is based on a sense of superiority"[17]—with which males are inculcated from well before age six—or, along Freudian lines, because "humor is a way of expressing sexual as well as aggressive impulses,"[18] impulses that boys and men acquire as part and parcel of their sex role.

Girls, on the other hand, understand that being funny isn't

"feminine" (Joan Rivers and Phyllis Diller are anything but sex symbols), and that too many jokes are amusing at their own expense.[19] That includes the riddles and "dirty jokes" of childhood, of which the following is but a soupçon:

What are the three quickest ways to spread the news?
Telephone, telegraph, and tell a girl.

In what month do girls talk the least?
February, because it's the shortest month.

What's the difference between a girl and an umbrella?
You can shut up the umbrella.

In this soliloquy, Mr. Goodbar gets all the moves:

After breaking up with Peppermint Patty, Mr. Goodbar went out with Mary Jane. They hid behind the Powerhouse and he felt her Mounds and said they were pure Almond Joy. Then he stuck his Butterfinger up her Milky Way and that's how they got Baby Ruth.

Although women don't laugh at sex jokes as readily as men, all too often women "laugh at events or jokes they really don't find very funny simply to present a 'charming' personality in public."[20] It is vitally important to children of both sexes that women stop laughing at jokes that degrade them, and that boys and men stop telling such jokes or making girls feel that they have to laugh to be loved.

A DAY IN TOWN

Your family is off on some errands. As you drive into town, a yellow road sign warns *Flagman Ahead.* Shortly after, another proclaims, *Men Working.* Ignore it? No, at least not the first time, or such formalized masculinisms will begin to seem "natural." Look for *women* working and you can prove the signs inaccurate on the spot. If there happen to be none at that particular site (admittedly they're still rare), you might remark upon how foolish it is for the State Highways Department to print up single-gender signs when more and more women are taking construction jobs.

As you drive along, notice the advertising billboards. *"Men's*

Liberation. Honda." "Women's Liberation. Kentucky Fried Chicken." Those two billboards recently faced each other across a Cincinnati street.[21] I'd have pointed them out to my children and asked them what they thought about those two kinds of "liberation."

Continuing along, look at the National Safety Council sign picturing a busty woman driver passing a truck on a curve: *Curves Can Be Dangerous,* it warns. Turning into the shopping center, your car is stopped by people handing out promotional bumper stickers—*Nice People Support Boy's Baseball* (Casey's Sporting Goods Outlet)—and printed litterbags from Smith's Hardware:

The Amsterdam Little Giants
"Today I made the best investment of my life . . . I invested in a boy."

and free pin-up calendars from the plumbing supply store. Take the names of the sponsors of these giveaways so you can write protest letters, and if they don't discontinue their sexist promotions, put them on your boycott/girlcott list.

When you go to open a checking account and the children hear the bank officer offer Father checks imprinted with a hunting scene, and Mother a floral print with perfumed paper, say you prefer the usual undecorated style.

"We'll both be using these checks," you might add. "And neither of us thinks of hunting or flowers when we spend our money."

Father stops at the stationery store for a telephone message pad. He refuses to buy the one that says

WHILE YOU WERE OUT

Mr. _____

Telephoned _____   Please call him _____

Called to see you _____   Will call again _____

"How can I be sure every caller is going to be a man?" Dad explains to the storekeeper.

Mom takes a broken chair to the carpentry shop.

"Couldn't your husband fix this, lady?" the carpenter teases.

"No," says Mother. "Carpentry skills didn't come in with my husband's whiskers, but *I'm* pretty handy so if you don't want the job, I'll make time to do it myself."

In the supermarket, the family laughs when the store public address system calls, "Attention, Mothers: Don't miss the Pampers on sale today in aisle four" just as *Father* is reaching for a box of diapers. You pick up and put back the box of cereal with the premium on the back offering a *Workshop Book for Boys* and *The Beginner Cookbook for Girls,* and the cereal box with a coupon enticing *Men—the pocket knife that does it all!* But you do take the free *Handi-Wipes Coloring Book* so that you can send it back to "the friendly folks at Colgate-Palmolive" who are responsible for its pictures of Mom and Sis cleaning everything in sight, while Dad and Junior use Handi-Wipes to make a kite, boat sail, pirate blindfold, and bullfight sheet.

Next stop, the laundry and dry cleaners, where you notice that each of Mother's cotton shirts is banded with a paper strip saying "Good morning, Sir!" You also discover that, like half of the dry cleaners surveyed in one California town, your dry cleaner charges more for women's clothes than men's[22] even though virtually every item in question has less fabric in the female version. You take your business away and let your children hear you tell the dry cleaner why.

Leaving the shopping center, you turn toward central city until traffic is stopped by a Founder's Day Parade, which includes in its procession a float sponsored by a local automobile dealer. On it, a girl wearing a bikini—in *December*—is lying under the front wheels of a car festooned in bunting and banners. A placard says, *I'd die for a guy in a Chevy from Cartown.* Don't just honk your disapproval—tell the City Council that you don't want municipal thoroughfares clogged up for such tripe.

There's no avoiding the "bad" blocks as you work your way across town, past the newsstands with obscene magazines hanging from clothespins like dirty laundry, past the record shops displaying album covers that picture bound and beaten women ("I'm black and blue from the Rolling Stones"), past the topless bars, sex shops, "adult" bookstores, and X-rated live shows and massage parlors with their tawdry snapshots and illustrated flyers.

You can let the kids think *Blow Job and the Seven Dwarfs* is a misprint but the rest of the scene bears explaining. Somehow, despite growing evidence to the contrary, we must teach our children that violence against women is not a normal way of life.

You relax after the car is parked and you're all walking along the "good" blocks where there are respectable stores—Montgomery Ward, Charles A. Stevens Company. But when *their* windows display nude and semi-dressed mannikins in torture scenes, it cannot be explained away. You must do what an ad hoc protest group did in Chicago: badger the Chamber of Commerce, or in their case the State Street Merchants Council, to prohibit scenes of violence in all retail window displays.[23]

You find a department store with humane displays and go in to buy Mother and Father the clothes they need for winter. When Father buys a suit, the alterations are free. In Mother's suit department, even a hem is extra. Is this because women are expected to sew their own? One woman got mad enough to file a sex discrimination complaint against Bloomingdales.[24] Short of that, you might complain to the buyer and if the alterations policy is firm, refuse to buy the suit or cancel your charge account.

When Father goes on ahead to the children's department, he is ignored until he pointedly asks for assistance. "Sorry," says the saleswoman. "Men hardly ever shop here alone, so I thought you were just waiting for your wife."

Father's search for jeans for the kids unearths the fact that the same style is priced two dollars higher in the girls' department. Gender-neutral socks, sweaters, sweatshirts, T-shirts, and ski jackets—also identical to those in the boys' department—cost more on the girls' side of the store where they're labeled with girls' sizes. Father cannot believe that blue jeans with the name Gloria Vanderbilt on the back pocket cost twenty-nine dollars in girls' sizes 4 to 6X. He notes that for twenty-nine dollars in the boys' aisles, you can buy two pair of Health-tex overalls, one pair of no-name jeans, two long-sleeve shirts, and two pair of socks, and still have three dollars left over.[25] He also notices that boys' apparel is better-made than girls', with reinforced knees and sturdier fabric—presumably in the belief that "boys wear clothes harder."

Father resolves to shop for both sexes in the boys' department and to write a letter to the editor of the newspaper in order to embarrass the store and alert other parents to save money by ignoring gender labels.

Why put children's clothes on two sides of a barrier? Why have to button a boy's shirt left to right and a girl's right to left? One analyst likens the fear that males and females will look indistinguishable, to the anger some whites feel when blacks "pass" in white society. The despairing "How can you tell them apart?" is really asking, *"How can a man know which to treat as an equal and which to treat as a woman?"*[26]

The cult of sex differences knows no bounds. One male psychologist worries that undifferentiated diapers are "only the beginning" of the end of "masculinity" and "femininity."

> A diaper folded in front conveyed masculinity and one folded in back connoted femininity because of differences in the direction of the child's urination . . . this difference has almost vanished as a result of the disposable diaper and the "ready fold."[27]

Whenever you have to put one of those unisex doomsayers in their place, you should have at your fingertips a few trenchant truths about the history of clothing and gender.[28]

First, through the ages, skirts have always been worn by men: the loin cloth, Egyptian apron, Turkish caftan, Greek chiton, Roman toga, Japanese kimono, Polynesian sarong, medieval tunic, and today's Arab jalaba, Scottish kilt, and priestly robes come immediately to mind. In various periods, a man's man also wore lace, ruffles, silks, brocades, earrings, girdles, high heels, perfume, cosmetics, and elaborate hairdos. He brought attention to his genitals with padded codpieces and tight breeches as revealing as any décolleté bosom. In Elizabethan times, men's tunics were so daring that a fine of twenty shillings was imposed on any knight whose gown "is not long enough when he stands upright to cover his privities and his buttocks."[29]

In the mid-eighteenth century, men began to favor trousers and skirts were phased out. Fashion assigned men the frockcoat, waistcoat and eventually the jacket during the course of the nineteenth century, although little boys continued wearing dresses into the early twentieth century—and to this day men sometimes wear a vestigial male skirt: formal tails.

The point is, it was not until the Victorian period, after all of human history, that female and male clothing styles diverged sharply, and it is no accident that this divergence coincided with sexual Victorianism and "the vast separation in male and female roles that came in with the Industrial Revolution."[30]

The second trenchant truth about clothes and fashion is that they are often used to impose a sex role from the outside in. For instance, tight lacing and whalebone stays kept women fashionably wasp-wasted, but also sick with internal injuries, weak, and immobile.[31] Bloomers, favored by nineteenth-century feminists, were jeered at precisely because they freed women from such constraints,[32] and allowed them a more physically active role in society.

In Old China, bound feet in tiny slippers were the ultimate in "femininity." To achieve them, at age three or four, a girl's toes were broken, turned in against the sole of the foot and bound tightly, however ulcerated or gangrenous, to force a curled-under three-inch "Golden Lotus." The result, if she didn't die of infection, was a girl who could not walk and certainly couldn't work or survive on her own—the ideal passive wife, proof of a rich man's ability to support idleness and assure fidelity.[33]

Sometimes I think of the Golden Lotus women when I see seven-year-old girls hobbling on fashionable clogs or teenagers teetering on this year's drop-dead spike heels. Fashion's decree—in feet or "femininity"—is almost always the enemy of female freedom. If your daughter can't climb a fence, kick a ball, or run away from a rapist in what "all the little girls are wearing this year"—don't buy it.

Third trenchant truth: Males become dependent on females for their clothing decisions because parents don't train boys to take responsibility for their clothes as girls are expected to do.[34] The stereotype of the guy who puts on any old thing, who mixes plaids and stripes, who needs a mother, wife, or salesperson to "assemble" his wardrobe, is very often real. It is the outcome of raising boys according to stereotyped views: that aesthetics, color, texture, and coordination or style are "girls' stuff," that taking care of a boys' wardrobe is a mother's job, and that men have more important things to worry about than clothes.

The outcome: Little boys never learn to put themselves together or choose their own clothes or maintain them properly.

It is easy enough, as you look through stores' children's clothing racks and bins, to help your son make his own choices, appraise the fabrics and construction of a garment, and guess what might go best with what. With both sexes, Father *and* Mother should take responsibility for wardrobe oversight: don't teach them rules, teach them judgment.

With purchases in hand, you make a brief detour to the toy department where Santa on a plaster throne is taking children's wishes under advisement. (I know better than to ask the heretical question—"If Santa is 'the spirit of Christmas,' why does the spirit always have to be a man, and a white man at that?"—outside of a parenthesis.)

When your toddler sits on Santa's lap and whispers his heart's desires in Santa's ear, and Santa's bushy eyebrows knit in dismay, you know your son has just asked for a Tiny Tears doll and a pot holder set.

Your older daughter wants to stop at the hobby department to check out new additions to her stamp collection, even though she always feels a bit odd at the stamp counter where she is usually the only girl. Nearly 90 percent of American philatelists (stamp collectors) are males, largely because school stamp clubs have traditionally been male-dominated and the Boy Scouts have promoted philately more actively than the Girl Scouts have.[35]

It is possible your daughter would feel at home with her hobby nonetheless, if there were more postage stamps honoring women. To make up for this, she might sign up for the National Organization for Women's First Day Covers, featuring Women of Achievement.[36] And wherever possible, for daily postal use, you might choose stamps with a woman's likeness so kids will see or subliminally absorb female images representing government officialdom. Unfortunately, unlike the 15 cent stamps picturing Steinbeck, Einstein or Endangered Flora, the denominations assigned to Lucy Stone (50¢), Harriet Tubman (13¢), and Sybil Ludington (8¢) are not used every day.[37]

You should also pester the Citizen's Stamp Advisory Committee, which recommends stamp subjects to the U.S. Postal Service, to issue more stamps honoring great women—and to do so more frequently than one every three years.[38]

Taking on the Post Office isn't that different from other successful drives for sex equality in national symbology. For years, I was hard-pressed to explain to my kids why hurricanes, those deadly temper tantrums of nature, were named exclusively for women. Letters and protests from women's groups and individuals persuaded the Commerce Department and the World Meteorological Organization to change that practice and in 1979, hurricanes Anna, Claudette, and Elena were alternated with hurricanes Bob, David, and Frederick.[39] What's fair is fair, even in foul weather.

Similarly, until 1979, American coins and currency pictured real birds, real buffalo, U.S. Presidents, and Benjamin Franklin, but never a real woman. Then, when Congress authorized a dollar coin, the female originally designed for its face was the mythical winged liberty. In the end, Susan B. Anthony got the honor, a dubious one since the dollar coin, readily confused with the quarter, is unpopular with the public. Thus far no one is blaming Anthony, or women, for the U.S. Mint's folly—and children still get to see a woman as a symbol of value.[40]

Last stop of your productive day: the doctor's office. Because a doctor is the quintessential competence-authority figure, having a woman as your physician would be a giant step for equality. If your family uses a male physician who employs a female nurse and subscribes to the usual formalities, the children could catch a dose of sex-rolitis: She's Carol, he's Doctor Jones; she sits at a small desk in the waiting room, he has a private office. Often, they seem like a traditional husband and wife.

If it's a pediatrician you are consulting about a child's "behavior problem," think about the doctor's biases before accepting his (or her) referral to a psychiatrist. As noted in Chapter 4, studies have found that

> the child exhibiting the behavior inappropriate to his/her sex was seen as more severely disturbed, as more in need of treat-

ment, . . . than the child exhibiting sex-role appropriate behaviors.[41]

When a parent is the patient, be aware that doctors tend to take a man's complaints more seriously than those of a woman who describes the same symptoms.[42] Although your children aren't present in the examining room, they may pick up this attitudinal difference in the reception area during the doctor-patient greetings, small-talk, and farewells. One easy route to equity: if your doctor calls you by *your* first name, call him by his.

EAT, DRINK, AND BE MANLY

After a busy day, everyone's hungry for dinner.

Choose a Chinese restaurant and the message in your fortune cookie might insult mother: *"Man can beat rug, egg and woman, but not time."* Go to McDonald's and your paper placemat might ignore father: "MOTHERS. Have your child's next birthday party at McDonald's." At Kentucky Fried Chicken, the blurb printed on the bucket promotes chicken "For Family Dinner. Guests. Picnics. Mom's Day Off." (So *that's* what the billboard meant by "Women's Liberation.")

If you splurge on a high class restaurant, the wine list and the check will be presented to Father (only he is presumed to know enough and earn enough), unless Mother requests them, which she should do frequently. She should also give the dinner order to the waiter as often as Father does. One woman I know always says "I'm the wine expert here" to increase the sensitivity of waiters and wine stewards wherever she dines. Another wonderful troublemaker leaves this printed card along with the tip: *"Your gratuity would have been double had you not automatically assumed that the man would pay the bill."*

Should Mother enter the restaurant with children and no man, the group might be seated behind a potted palm (women and children don't class up the atmosphere). Women are reputed to be low tippers although it seems more to the point that when not dining with a man, a woman gets inferior service[43] and is often patronized ("Are you aware, Madam, that escargot are snails?").

Then too Mother might be leched by the man at the next table, because

a. a woman alone is fair game;[44]
b. a woman with children is as good as alone since children are nonpersons;
c. a single mother is assumed to be desperate for male attention.

If you smile and take it, that expensive meal will be digested with a lot of bile. Resolve to get up and leave if you are mistreated. It's your money, your meal, and your children who are watching.

Obviously this day on the town is a composite. But every bout with sexism has happened to me or parents I know, not once but many times. The same is true for events in the next section.

AROUND THE COMMUNITY

In pursuit of good fun, many communities unwittingly hurt children's feelings and freedoms.

Take The Little Miss North Woodmere Pageant, a bathing beauty contest for three-to-seven-year-old girls:[45] "I had so much fun fixing her hair this morning," said the mother of one little contestant.

A father claimed he entered his shy little girl

Just so she can learn to get the butterflies out of her stomach. So that when she walks down the aisle at her wedding fifteen, sixteen years from now, she'll remember this experience and she'll be more at ease.

"At ease" is not what newspaper reports saw eighty little girls being. After the winner was crowned,

. . . the little girls stood in a row dumbfounded, unable to comprehend why they were rejected. Then Bari Swedlow let out a help, "I'm never coming back to this park again," she sobbed.

The parks director who organized the event thought it an unqualified success. Next year? The boys. "We could have a Mr. Muscle contest for three-to-five-year-olds," said he.

More routine community events can hit you with sexism when you least expect it: On Sunday morning, everyone turns out for the pancake breakfast at the firehouse. The fireman are flipping flapjacks. Their wives are cleaning up. Every kid gets to try on firehats, climb on the equipment, and take home a free comic book in which Sparky, the fire dog, says of fire engines: *"It takes real men to man them,"* making every woman volunteer firefighter a mirage or a misfit. Hey! Sound the sirens, look at that blaze. *"She's through the roof already!"* says Sparky.[46]

Well, at least the fire is female.

Sex stereotypes are one community hazard. Exclusion another. The exclusion of wives' names from the telephone book, for instance. Submerged in their husband's identities, women you're looking for may as well be dead. What does this have to do with children?

Many times, when we've wanted to arrange visits for our kids with one of their friends, all we have had to go on is the child's last name and the first name of the child's mother (which our child has learned because only the mother was home when our child went *there* to visit). If the phone book has several entries under the child's last name (*i.e.,* Smith or Goldberg, in the Manhattan directory), then finding the number is a lost cause. Mothers' names are not listed; only male first names appear, or an occasional set of initials behind which usually lurks a single woman who's afraid listing her name will bring obscene phone calls. Due to women's protests, you can now get dual listings free—*Smith, Mary and John*—but you have to make a special request of the telephone business office.

Despite legislation prohibiting sex discrimination in school programs, President Gerald Ford and the Congress gave approval to one loophole: father-son/mother-daughter events, the "family custom" that unites the men of the family at ball games and banquets, and the women of the family at teas and bake sales.[47] The perpetuation of this community "custom" excludes the cross-sex parent from joining in some of a child's most exciting activities. It overlooks the child with a single parent whose gender doesn't fit the line-up—the boy with no father to take him to father-son volleyball, for instance. It ignores the parent or child whose skills and interests don't fit the activity prescribed; the boy a few chapters back who couldn't hit a baseball or the mother who burns TV dinners and can't do her daughter proud at the bake-off. What, pray tell, would be un-American about a *parent-child* bake-off or ball game?

In Rapatee, Illinois, the mothers of the high school athletes, who cart their sons to practices and games all season, asked to be "allowed" to attend the father-son awards banquet. They've always been asked to cook the dinner for the banquet—

> but not once in 20 years have they been invited to it . . . [This year] the school board said the mothers might be able to get in after the table is cleared.[48]

In Hannibal, Missouri, the "Tom Sawyer Days Fence Painting Contest" is only for boys, because, said the president of the Jaycees who sponsor the contest,

> No other literary character so typifies and makes vivid the wonderfulness of boyhood as Tom Sawyer. No literary character better exemplifies the charm, frailty and mysteries of feminine youth as Becky Thatcher. We believe none of the characteristics of either Tom or Becky should be blurred.[49]

(Such a reaction is in keeping with the National Jaycees' continued refusal to admit adult women members, thus excluding women from the financial and social benefits of the Old Boys network.[50])

Communities practice sex discrimination in many other ways: For example, men's league softball games are scheduled on weekends when all fathers can participate and the whole family can watch and cheer. Women's softball is played Monday afternoons when wage-earning women can't join in, and husbands and kids are involved in their weekday lives.

Similarly, some tennis clubs reserve weekend court time for men on a priority basis. This assumes every woman in town could play during the week if she wanted to. It makes women and children competitors for weekday play time, and co-pariahs on weekends. And it prevents women, children, and men from playing *together,* the only time families can coordinate their schedules, because a men's doubles group can always exercise their priority privilege.

If you doubt that sexism underpins such policies, listen to golfer Jack Nicklaus differentiate between "players" and "ladies" as he blames the decrease in men's standings on the influx of females on the golf courses. "There's nothing wrong with the ladies, God bless them; let them play. But what they're doing is eliminating much of the available time when young players can get on the course."[51]

Some community pools require bathing caps for girls but not for boys, regardless of who has the long hair. My daughters and I would rather not swim than encase our heads in a rubber cloche that impairs the hearing, tears the hair going on and off, and always lets water seep in. But if hair fall-out is a problem for the pool's drainage system, we would learn to tolerate a bathing cap rule that was enforced according to hair length, not gender.

If I were appraising how egalitarian a society is on another planet, I'd go straight to its playgrounds. On weekdays, at every playground in Central Park, for instance, one might get the impression that the world is made up of children and mothers, female housekeepers, female babysitters, and big sisters. That's who line the benches watching the children play.

When I see a fair proportion of men in playgrounds, I'll know that we've succeeded in radically altering the patterns of child-rearing and child caring: Less Mom and more Dad, day in and day out, is the answer. Those Saturday morning Pops-and-Tots mudpie contests are a sop. Which doesn't mean they shouldn't happen, or that the Moms-and-Tots gym class held weekday mornings couldn't be renamed Parents-and-Tots to include fathers who have charge of preschoolers during the day. Admit, though, that society does not make it easy for fathers to practice parity parenthood, especially fathers of girls. When one man "went to his daughter's Brownie fly-up, he felt like an idiot standing in line to let her pin a gardenia corsage on him. Nobody expected a father to be there . . ."[52]

Part of a community's collective personality shows in its YMCA and YWCA, Girls Club and Boys Club, Girl Scouts and Boy Scouts, Brownies and Cubs, Campfire Girls and Boys Brotherhood. Some single-sex organizations have become coed as a result of lawsuits and membership plebescites,[53] but many groups prefer to remain sex segregated. The Girl Scouts voted down male membership on the grounds the boys would dominate, which strikes me as a head-in-the-sand solution to female passivity, especially since about sixty thousand adult men continue as Girl Scout troup leaders and board members,[54] leaving males in authority from the top down.

As long as girls and boys are sharing the world, separatism seems a foolhardy reaction to sexual inequality. It's terrific that the Girl Scouts have gone so far beyond selling cookies and baby-sitting and now offer competence-building activities, sex education workshops (which lost some troups church sponsorship),[55] and projects supporting the Equal Rights Amendment.[56] And it's marvelous that the Girls Clubs of America are in the vanguard of girls' career counseling, role-model programs, and efforts to combat teen pregnancy.[57] But it would be doubly heartening if boys were inside partners in such efforts.

Without separatism, perhaps girls' programs would not be suffering from outrageously unequal funding patterns. In one year, for example, the Tampa, Florida, Boys Club had only twice the membership of the Girls Club but got nine times the support from United Fund.[58] Nationwide, the United Way allocated almost twice as much money to boys' organizations as to their female counterparts.[59] Even the foundations that derive their assets from sales of cosmetics to women (Avon, Revlon, Lauder) give the lion's share of their children's grants to boys' groups.[60]

In addition to sex segregation, these clubs still practice sex stereotyping. The YMCA, for instance, has "groups for fathers and sons (Y-Indian Guides), fathers and daughters (Y-Indian Princesses), and mothers and daughters (Y-Indian Maidens)."[61] There seems to be no group for sons and mothers (would they call it Y-Braves and Squaws, God forbid?).

In one inner-city YWCA, classes are held for girls in Afro-Ballet, Sewing, and Charm, and for boys in Congo Drum and Maracas.[62]

The 4-H Club advises a camp counselor confronted with a homesick boy to

Suggest that he take charge of pulling the flag to the pole's top because the girls aren't strong enough to do it. This gives him a sense of importance.[63]

In Cub Scout terminology, a mother volunteer used to be called a Den Mother; a father volunteer, a Den Leader.[64] Now both are called Den Leaders. However only a man can be "Scoutmaster" for ten- to eighteen-year-old Scouts, because, as a BSA spokesperson put it, "boys that age need a man to look up to."[65]

Why a competent *person* to look up to isn't good enough becomes clear if you look back at the Boy Scouts' original statement of purpose, which was to give boys a testing ground for manhood that would replace the lost frontier and provide an escape from the feminizing influence of his home—

The REAL Boy Scout is not a "sissy." He is not a hothouse plant, like little Lord Fauntleroy. There is nothing "milk and water" about him; he is not afraid of the dark. . . . He is not hitched to his mother's apronstrings.[66]

Likewise, the founders of Scouting wanted to offer adult men "a sphere of masculine validation," an opportunity for the new white-collar class "to be men as traditionally defined." The kind of men sought as Scoutmasters were

REAL, live men—red-blooded and right-hearted men—BIG men . . . No Miss Nancy need apply.[67]

Girl Scouts can justify looking up to male troup leaders because it's a man's world. But Boy Scouts can't have female leaders because Boys Are Better, and Girls Are Meant to Be Mothers— and mothers are what REAL men are supposed to leave behind.

ON VACATION

Maybe you're looking into summer camps for your child. Don't just inquire about the food, ·bunks, and bathrooms; stay tuned for sexism. If a camp's brochures tantalize you, their directors usually will come to your house with a slide show and enticing sales pitch about the camp's philosophy and facilities.

After one of these presentations, we asked David how he liked the camp described. "It's nice," he said. "But it's sexist."

"Funny, we didn't notice anything," Bert replied. "Boys and girls seem able to do the same things."

"Yes," agreed David. "But the director said they have 'a manmade lake.'"

(We assured him that was an expression, not an admission of sex bias, but David still turned the camp down.)

Make sure it's a coed camp or brother-sister camp with over-lapping sports, arts and social programs. (Single-sex camps tend to be too competitive[68] or escapist.) Whether it's a sleepaway, day, Bible, sports, or scout camp, find out if all its activities are available to both sexes. The camp's clothing list is often your best clue. A California camp listed backpacking clothes on the boys' side of the sheet only. When a girl applicant asked to be allowed in the hiking program, the camp returned her deposit with a curt note.[69] A camp in Florida advertised bodysurfing for boys and water ballet for girls.

Camp Watitoh in the Berkshires said girls get a special trip to nearby Jacob's Pillow Dance Festival. When we objected that it seemed unfair to exclude boys, the directors, to their credit, agreed. Admitting it had been an unthinking practice for years, they changed the description to "A trip to Jacob's Pillow for any interested camper."

TRIPS AND TOURS

Instead of camp, suppose you opt for a vacation trip *en famille*. In the airport, the shoeshine stand is in the men's bathroom, the baby nursery is in the ladies' room. A father with a baby to change or a mother with scuffed shoes is out of luck.

On the plane, the flight attendant once gave pilot's wings to my son and stewardess pins to my daughters. That's no longer done, but since the captain, co-captain, and flight engineer are undoubtedly all men, and the flight attendants are more than likely women, you'll still have a tough time convincing your kids that girls can be pilots.

If your destination takes you out of the country, the customs officer gives a declaration form to the "Head of household."

Just as you've calmed your temper, the clerk at the rent-a-car office makes a remark about women drivers, with a conspiratorial wink at the children. Take a few seconds to disabuse him, and anyone else listening, of the myth of women's driving inadequacy. According to the AMA, insurance and highway statistics, and car rental surveys, a woman behind the wheel has fewer accidents, superior vision and hearing, and is less impulsive, less ego-invested, and less *emotional* than a man.[70]

Your vacation itself consists of day after fascinating day of sightseeing: Grant's Tomb, the Lincoln Memorial, famous battle-grounds where men fought and died, the birthplace of this general and that president, the trails male explorers blazed, the scene of Billy the Kid's last gunfight, the Baseball Hall of Fame, old ceme-teries with weather-worn gravestones:

Here Lies John Spenser,

printer, a righteous and godly man,
who lived in proud bondage to temperence
and died in certainty of deliverance

Also, Prudence, wife of the above

Your tour will literally be a tour of *his*toric places unless you "Remember the Ladies," as Abigail Adams begged her husband to do when forming our American government in the first place.[71] Before leaving home, be sure your itinerary includes such places as Seneca Falls, site of the First Women's Convention (1848); the home of Louisa May Alcott; the battleground where Deborah Sampson, disguised as a man, fought in the Revolutionary War; the road that Sybil Ludington traveled when she raced forty miles on horseback rallying the militia. A broad familiarity with women's history or a feminist travel guide[72] will help you mark a route that covers landmarks for both sexes wherever you go.

Finally, consider a vacation close to nature: a family camping trip where everyone pitches the tent and pitches in with cooking and camptending; a family hosteling trip, or skiing, canoeing, biking, hiking, horseback riding, or sailing[73]—as long as everyone is in it together, unified by physical adventure and love of the outdoors.

CELEBRATIONS

Adult Rituals

A quick quiz: Is your child witnessing quaint sexist customs at your adult dinner parties? Do all the guests come in matched sets, like Noah's Ark, or do you invite odd numbers of single women or men without pairing them? As a couple, have you ever entertained guests, a majority of whom were of the female persuasion?[74]

Does Mother cook and serve solo? Does Father, and no one but Father, dispense the wine or cocktails? Which guests get up to clear the table and who remains seated down to the last man? At a buffet, how many of the women prepare plates for their husbands? Does even one man do the same for his wife?

Does conversation split along sex lines? Do the men dominate and interrupt the women when conversation *is* integrated? (Men interrupt women five times as often as women interrupt men —and according to conversational politics, interrupting is a power play.[75]) After dinner, do the women retire to one end of the living room and the men to another? If anyone would be inconsiderate enough to turn on the TV after dinner to catch the end of the Big Game, what might be the gender of that person?

If you were a child imagining yourself a grownup at such a party, which sex would you rather be?

Birthday Parties

In traditional families, birthday parties seem to celebrate a child's sex role rather than her or his birth. Between ages four and ten, there are apt to be ballerina candles for her, and paper pirate hats for him, and for the guests, sex-typed party favors on the order of water pistols and plastic mirrors.

To turn eleven or twelve is to want something more grown up, something like taking a few select friends to a pro basketball game (him) or the Ice Capades (her). At thirteen, a Jewish male gets a

simple Bar Mitzvah—a catered affair with flowers shaped like
footballs and an uncle zooming into the hall on a motorcycle for the
birthday boy[76]—or an extravaganza on the field of the Orange Bowl
with waitresses costumed as cheerleaders, waiters as referees, the
hundred-member Hialeah High School Band playing dance music,
and the scoreboard flashing *Happy Birthday, Harvey.* [77]

A girl's Bat Mitzvah is less lavish since there is still the Sweet
Sixteen (and the wedding) ahead.

By sixteen, a boy is supposed to be too cool for birthday
parties (though he'll warmly accept a new car, stereo, or hard
cash). But for girls, the Sweet Sixteen "is the coming out party of
the middle class."[78] In training for her sex role as bride-in-waiting
and hostess-to-be, the sixteen-year-old birthday girl wears a corsage of sugar cubes and greets 120 friends at a disco party, or has
50 intimates for chili and tacos.[79]

If my daughters had been among the "lucky" 25 girls at Gail
Negbauer's Sweet Sixteen, I would have severely resented their presumptuous "surprise" of the day: After lunch at the Hotel Pierre
(shrimp-stuffed tomatoes and chicken crepes), Gail and friends
were "treated" to . . . a magician? No. A string quartet? No. The
treat was—"A couple of makeup professionals from the Glemby
company would do each girl over with all the glamor tricks!"[80]

If you're like me, you don't send your child off to birthday
parties to be taught such "tricks" or to receive the news that she
needs to be made over.

However, unless you are willing to embarrass your children
and gain the reputation of town eccentric, you can't do much
about their exposure to such rituals. It's best to view them with
the bemused fascination of a cultural anthropologist; let your kids
know your feelings and limit your activism to giving the birthday
child a nonsexist present. Give gifts that are mind-enlarging and
life-expanding: a subscription to *Art News* or the *Sierra Club
Bulletin,* a kite-building kit, a tour behind the scenes at the Opera
or local TV station, a sculpture class or a trial lesson from a
professional magician, an antique toy with a special history, membership in The Academy of Model Aeronautics[81] or a short wave
radio.

For your children's birthday celebrations, choose a party

theme and activities that fit the individual child's interests. Children can help plan everything with you. As soon as they could write, I gave my kids a big yellow pad and they filled in Date, Time, Main Event of Party, Theme of Party Decorations, Menu, Prizes, Games, Guest List.

Choose a time for the party when both parents can be there to set up, serve and keep things popping.

Be original and open-minded about decorations. Don't limit yourself to children's party supplies—check out the adult paper goods; use 4th of July plates for a party with an American history theme, or silver party stuff intended for a silver wedding anniversary for a very elegant kids' party (take out your silver candlesticks for this one). We've done France as a party theme by decorating with French Line posters, speaking in simple French phrases and Gallic accents, eating French bread and cheese, giving each child a tricolor flag to take home. (age nine) Another party theme was Springtime, where everything at the party had to be green, including the guests' clothes, the food (pistachio ice cream, for example), and the table decor—and the guests' party favors were green plants. (age twelve) At our Winnie the Pooh party, we offered Pooh's favorite, honey, and provided props mentioned in Milne's story so that party guests could play pin-the-tail on Eeyore, and enact various adventures of Piglet and gang (regardless of sex); the party prizes were Pooh placemats. (age six)

We've also had baseball parties in Central Park, dividing the group into teams called Abigail's Angels *vs.* Robin's Robins. Bert and I took turns pitching and catching for seven exciting innings, and to top it off, we had an All-American picnic on the grass. (age eleven)

Try slumber parties (you can have a mixed guestlist but boys' dorm/girls' dorm sleeping arrangements), or beach parties for summer birthdays with sand castle contests, a peanut hunt, swimming, and a picnic lunch for each child packed in a pail that becomes the party favor. The idea is to love the idea, and sex-suitability be damned.

One of the best parties I know about is the one Blake Morgan Pitchford gave himself when he was nine:

Since my birthday is in the summer when my classmates are all away, I wanted to give a party during the school year and I decided to celebrate my ninth birthday last year on Susan B. Anthony's birthday: February 15th. My parents helped me plan it. We decorated the house with streamers and balloons in green, white, and purple—the colors of the suffrage movement. The party favors included Susan B. Anthony posters, and the cake candles were in the shape of the numbers one, five, and eight. (Ms. Anthony would have been 158 years old.)[82]

The activities included S.B.A. biographical charades, crosswords, and hit-the-unratified states (a map marked with those States that had not yet ratified the Equal Rights Amendment).

Holidays

Speaking of Blake, it was his mother, Robin Morgan, who raised my consciousness about patriarchal holidays. She asked me how I could give a children's Halloween Party with commercialized symbols and witches in ugly masks and pointed hats, when nine *million* real women were tortured and burned at the stake in the Middle Ages.

I learned that women of the time were condemned as "witches" basically because they defied acceptable norms of "feminine" passivity: they practiced folk medicine, befriended Jewish Cabbalists, and refused Christianity in favor of an ancient goddess–worshipping religion. The pagan, meaning peasant, Wiccean, meaning "wise women," religion of the witches acknowledged the solstices and equinoxes, the changing seasons that affected people's lives in an agrarian society.

Halloween, properly called Samhain, is the Wiccean New Year. It marks the late harvest, the death of the old year and the birth of the new. On this night, modern Wicceans or sympathizers decorate the house with gourds, dried corn, pumpkins and wheat. They wear black (for the peace of the winter night) with touches of red (for the blood of the newborn), and kindle black and red candles.

Friends arrive to the traditional witches' greeting, "Merry

Meet," and wrists are anointed with crushed hyacinth and perfumed oil. The Sabbat ceremony—toasts, blessings, stories, meditation, chants, incense, bells, and prayer—is followed by a vegetarian feast, crescent cakes made from a thousand-year-old recipe, and mulled wine and cider for the children. Handmade gifts are exchanged, medieval music is played, and there are number games, Tarot readings, and finally the Wiccean farewell, "Merry part."

To those lucky enough to be invited to such a Samhain celebration, trick or treating will never again suffice. (You can create alternate rituals with the help of a few library sources.[83])

Anti-sexist radicals like Robin Morgan can run through the calendar with hackles rising: virtually every holiday reeks of patriarchy, *patr*iotism (rooted in the idea of fatherland and hypernationalism); each betrays ethnocentric and androcentric (male-centered) definitions of "greatness."

There are, for instance, official days for Lincoln, but not Harriet Tubman; for Washington, father of this country, but not Susan B. Anthony, mother of women's right to vote in this country; for the birth of Martin Luther King, Jr., but not Rosa Parks, whose refusal to move (to the back of the bus) gave birth to a movement.

Why celebrate Flag Day instead of Betsy Ross Day? How can children believe Veteran's Day honors the war dead but celebrates peace when the parades are full of xenophobic veterans and show-off weaponry? Why expiate our guilt and ambivalence toward our mothers (as did the founder of Mother's Day[84]) by making a woman queen for a day—one day—especially when that day has been co-opted by reactionaries to fight everything from women's suffrage to equal job rights?[85]

Why congratulate ourselves for sharing our corn with the Indians when it was *their* corn, *their* cultivation secrets, and *everyone's* earth that invading Europeans appropriated with their ideas of "private ownership" and their puritan self-righteousness. If Thanksgiving is not a racist holiday, why don't we see today's Native Americans sitting around the old turkey platter?

And while we're asking, how dare we celebrate Columbus' "discovery" of America, when the native population had been living here for millennia? From that perspective, calling the white man's intrusion a "discovery" is surely the height of arrogance and scant inspiration for a national holiday.

My understanding of these matters came late, and I'm slightly embarrassed to confess that our family still celebrates just about *everything* (except for Christmas and Easter; Jews who adopt Christian symbols practice more religio-ethnic assimilation than I find comfortable). But we celebrate in our own quirky, personal way.

I suppose we like holidays, American and Jewish, because we like ceremony; we welcome excuses to make a fuss. Just last year we celebrated several goings away and comings home, Bert's ascension to adjunct professor at NYU Law School, my finishing this book, each child's separate theatrical triumph, David's and Robin's move to new schools, our housekeeper's birthday, Valentine's Day, and every Sabbath Eve that finds us all together at dinnertime (a phenomenon that's increasingly infrequent with each year of adolescence).

We decorate the doorway with flowers, ribbons, and hand-painted signs, make a special dinner, and set a "fancy" table on which the children arrange the "good" dishes, placecards, and unexpected centerpieces—all of their own invention. Candles are lit, appropriate songs sung, poems or stories read, meaningful food is consumed, the children drink their juice from wine goblets, and it makes for a festive, intimate family time conducive to leisurely conversation in the midst of five busy lives.

On each of our birthdays and on our anniversary, Bert and I have always taken *A Day* to ourselves, a day for exploring unfamiliar parts of New York City, ambling through museums and galleries, eating lavishly at lunch *and* dinner, splurging on plays, movies, symphonies, ballets, and generally indulging our whims. Recently, we extended the treat to the children and now each has *A Day* a year to fill with "heart's desire" activities.

For as long as we've had children, I've been awakened on Mother's Day with a gift of flowering plants. At first Bert brought the plants to my bedside with cards "from" the babies composed and forged by him. Then, as Robin and Abigail grew older and David joined them, it became a real activity and is now a cherished tradition. They awaken me with the rustle of leaves and the smell of flowers, tell me of their adventures in the wholesale flower market early in the morning, how they chose those particular plants, and how they managed this year to sneak out and back without waking me. The plants themselves acknowledge my love of spring, and the start of my new season of gardening. Breakfast in bed may come with the plants, but that's no big deal; I get that whenever I stay put for it. And certainly, there's no drudgery to relieve me of that isn't already shared. So why not celebrate Mother's Day, I say to myself, and if you have a ritual that feels authentic to you, don't give it up.

Make no mistake: our homemade nonsexist holiday celebrations aren't radical or even revisionist. They glean, winnow, and embellish; they do not challenge the underpinnings of holidays one can agree are objectionable. I so admire the scholarship that produces alternate celebrations out of the treasure of myth, mysticism, or forgotten history. But I don't get around to researching and creating them.

For me, and perhaps for you, things to avoid in celebrations are challenge enough:

• Avoid role-oriented gestures of generosity: children shouldn't get off with one day of watering the lawn or doing the dishes on Mother's or Father's Day.

• Avoid celebrations that put unequal stress on one family member: a July 4 cookout is no party if Dad spends all day tending the charcoal fire.

• Avoid grab-bag presents that don't suit both sexes. Why toss in a card of hair barrettes when a boy might pluck it out?

• Avoid sexist adult gifts, too: on Mother's Day give the story of Mother Jones, labor activist; on July 4, a book about the *black* revolution; on Thanksgiving, *Bury My Heart at Wounded Knee.*

• Avoid Halloween costumes that trade on sex or race stereotypes: no Indian chiefs in feathers, no Aunt Jemimas, no witches. Try Hollywood for your inspiration: David was once a great Harpo Marx with horn, blond curly wig, and baggy pants; or literature: Abigail was Rebecca of Sunnybrook Farm; or period dress: Robin was a 1920s flapper.

• Avoid sex stereotypes on greeting cards. Don't send the Father's Day card with the picture of the sports car, shotgun, coat of arms, chess set, or pipe and slippers. Spare your girl graduate the leering message "You have a lot going for you under that cap . . . to say nothing of what's under your gown." On Valentine's Day avoid the 445 sexist love messages out of 587 checked out in a NOW survey.[86] And the birthday cards that show Suzy with her dolly and Tommy with his computer.

Why let a card company put words in your mouth when you and your children can enjoy making greetings of your own? Believe me, a few couplets and a crayon creation on a plain piece of paper show you care enough to *make* the very best.

If you feel homemade cards are tacky, order a catalog from one of the feminist card companies,[87] whose printed messages might read:

And we heard him exclaim, as he drove out of sight,
Merry Christmas to all, and to all equal rights.
Or send the now classic greeting,

PEACE ON EARTH, GOOD WILL TO PEOPLE

Send it to people in your community who make your children's world not sexist, not stifling, but celebratory.

23

Dear Old Sexist School Days: The Fourth "R" Is Role-playing

You can change family relationships and children's play experiences, turn off the TV, help kids choose good toys and good friends, and avoid sexism in public places. But what can you do about the six hours a day when your children are captives of the classroom?

"I had to give the wrong answer to be right," said our son David about this problem in his workbook:[1]

> Ruth had favors for her party.
> Each boy got a toy gun and each girl got:
>   a. a football
>   b. toy dishes
>   c. toy airplane
>   d. a baseball

When David was younger, he might not have known which choice to check. According to his upbringing, Ruth could have given the girls any toy on the list. But as a calloused veteran of "the hidden curriculum" of sex role learning,[2] David told the book what it wanted to hear.

Sexism in school is not unlike sexism outside. There is a patriarchal hierarchy—99 percent of school superintendents and 97 percent of high school principals are male, while 84 percent of elementary school teachers are female[3] (men rule women and women rule children). And schools, as much as any patriarchal institution, reward sex role conformity, and socialize girls for reproduction[4] and boys for wage-earning and leadership.

Yes sexism in school is not unlike sexism outside, it's just a lot more infuriating because it's subsidized by our tax dollars—even though there's a law against it.

Title IX of the Education Amendments of 1972 (effective July 21, 1975) says:

No person in the United States shall,
on the basis of sex,
be excluded from participation in,
be denied the benefits of,
or be subjected to discrimination under
any education program or activity
receiving federal financial assistance . . .

Simple words. No discrimination in *any* education program or activity. That means calculus, calisthenics, and career guidance. Simple justice. Yet Title IX has been and still is being watered down.[5] Despite mountains of evidence that girl children get a second-class education in America, the two issues that were addressed as soon as Title IX passed didn't help girls one iota: one affirmed the legality of separate father/son, mother/daughter events and the other affirmed the right of a Connecticut school to keep girls out of its all-boy choir.[6] As one educator put it, "the fight for sex equality seems plagued with frivolity."[7]

Distorted priorities aside, Congress intended Title IX to correct gross nationwide inequities and the new Department of Education (formerly part of HEW) is supposed to require that schools comply or else lose their federal funds. A few clearly written pamphlets[8] explain how easy it is to file a Title IX complaint or a lawsuit.[9] To find out if—or rather how much—sexism pervades your school is a little bit harder.

There are three potential sore spots: textbooks, curricula, and teacher attitudes.

TEXTBOOKS

Problems arise when instructional materials have sexism as their subtext, when they omit women's past achievements, misrepresent present options for both sexes, and when they call sex stereotypes "right" answers. A sampling:

History text: beginning in 1492, not one woman is mentioned for the first 150 years of American history.[10]

A music book for primary grades contains these sex-specific ditties:

> Boys' March
> *I am a boy, marching along*
> *When I grow up, I will be strong*
> *I'll be a man for the world to see*
> *building a home, for my family.*
> *I'm a boy. I'm a boy, a fine boy*
>
> Girls' Ballet
> *Girls like to dance a waltz, a ballet,*
> *Girls like to skip or gracefully sway.*
> *Girls like to play dress up and pretend.*
> *Girls like a party and girls like a friend.*
> *Because I'm a girl, I whirl and whirl.* [11]

Kindergarten reading readiness text shows a boy saying "I can cut," "I can dig," and a girl saying "I can dust," "I can mop." [12]

Advice in a secretarial manual supposedly for use by both sexes: "Wear fresh lingerie always." [13]

Mental health text: "A boy who does not have much athletic ability compensates by developing his hobby of photography. A girl who worries about being awkward joins a Y class in modern dance so that she will become more graceful." [14]

World history: in 877 pages of a book called, appropriately, *Men and Nations,* five pages are devoted to Napoleon III, described as a "mediocrity" (not to be confused with Napoleon I), while Queen Elizabeth I, called "one of the greatest of English rulers," gets one paragraph. [15]

Ecology book: Rachel Carson, the only woman in the book, is described as "bright and pretty" and "modest and gracious" when she takes on the chemical industry. [16]

Vocational interest inventory: Boys: would you like to "travel to outer space" or "explore the bottom of the ocean?" Girls: would you rather "marry a rancher" or "marry a corporation president?" [17]

Government text, high school: the index lists 246 men and 9 women. One of the 9, "Mrs. Ulysses S. Grant," is represented on page 243 by a picture of her inaugural gown.[18]

Third-grade math:[19]
    Mary's way: $2+2+2+2+2+2 = 12$
    Jack's way: $2 \times 6 = 12$

Some of the bias is gratuitous. Math problems have boys computing large sums, distances, and speed while girls (when they are not doing math the dumb way) are measuring dress fabric, adding the grocery bill, and learning fractions via pie slices. Whatever the educational intent, the problems add up to boys make rockets, girls make dessert; his eye is on the stars, hers is on the oven.

Some textbooks push sex roles flagrantly: "home economics" speaks to the housewife-mother, "family life" portrays the life of the (usually white, usually middle-class) nuclear family, "health and sex education" assumes an aggressive male and a passive female, and "career" materials seem years behind occupational realities.

And some textbooks—especially in science and history—commit the sin of omission, neglecting female contributions almost to the vanishing point. Other than Eleanor Roosevelt, Harriet Beecher Stowe, Betsy Ross, and Helen Keller, if ten great women and their achievements can be found in a sixth-grade history book, it's a bonanza.

One searches in vain for a book that gives full credit to Marie Curie without giving equal or more credit to her husband, Pierre;[20] or for an accurate portrayal of Maria Mitchell and other women astronomers or inventors; for a high school text that pays serious attention to the suffrage movement and the long parallels between racism and sexism in this country; or the courageous battle for the right to contraception and reproductive freedom (which has revolutionized modern life); or the changing roles of women and men in families, business and government.

Title IX does not prohibit the publication or use of biased textbooks, for fear of tampering with publishers' First Amendment rights. So it's up to us to identify objectionable materials, bring them to the attention of teachers and administrators, and pressure publishers to produce texts that are nonsexist, nonracist, creative, and accurate.

Wanted: New Words, New Pictures

Changing textbooks isn't easy. Once publishers succeed in getting a series accepted by curriculum specialists and adopted by many school systems, they resist making revisions for as long as possible. New editions of outdated texts cost a fortune and altogether new texts take publishers years to develop, test, and market. But they have learned that sexism can be even more expensive. One house invested five million dollars in a math series so laden with sex stereotypes that it was unacceptable to the centralized textbook adoption committees in Texas and California. Several more millions were required to clean up the sexism.[21]

In response to feminist criticism, some publishers have issued guidelines on the treatment of women and minorities.[22] Authors, illustrators, and editors are thus sensitized to such text components as occupational titles (letter carriers, not mailmen), image (not every woman is shorter than every man), and content. One fifth-grade math text replaced marginal references to Mozart and Bach with Phillis Wheatley, a black poet, and Molly Pitcher, the Revolutionary War heroine—without in the least bit affecting the math unit.[23] Which proves how extraneous sexism is in the first place.

If you have any doubt that feminist consciousness, historical accuracy and an inviting style can coexist between book covers, take a look at my favorite text, *America: In Space and Time,* a social studies overview that effortlessly includes females and people of color in the continuum of human events.[24]

CURRICULUM

A school's curriculum, meaning course content and recreational programs, can make equality either an imperative or an impossibility, depending on what information and skills are taught to which students in what facilities and with how many resources.

Most public schools are coeducational. (Title IX and a Supreme Court decision permit sex-segregated schools as long as the education they provide is "separate but equal,"[25] but most previously single-sex schools have voluntarily integrated their enrollment.[26]) "Coeducational" does not, however, seem to mean equal-educational. In 1977, the government found nearly two-thirds of the nation's schools had "failed to meet legal requirements for banning sex discrimination in classes and activities."[27] And a 1979 report ranking schools in all fifty states still found "galloping apathy toward the needs of today's girls."[28]

Consider a few past complaints:

• Five- and six-year-olds were placed in sex-segregated classes in a coed school on the theory that girls' presence may be detrimental to boys.

• Elementary school boys could choose from nine different sports, girls from only four—among them, "slimnastics."

• Three junior high school girls were refused admission to the school's carpentry class.

• While all the boys' teams were outfitted to the letter, the thirty-six-member girls' field hockey team had to share eleven pairs of shoes and twelve warm-up suits.

• An assignment in the girls' home economics curriculum: washing the boys' football uniforms.[29]

While these inequities are dramatic and concrete, others take the form of subtle tracking and gender type-casting.

The Making of Math Phobia

Studies show that more boys than girls have been math-encouraged at home, yet in elementary school, girls do about as well in math as boys. Until eighth grade or so. Then, when math begins to be typecast as "masculine" and math talent marks a girl as "unfeminine," math participation and performance dip precipitously. By high school graduation, only 8 percent of girls have four years of math to their credit, compared to 57 percent of boys.[30]

A curriculum that does not take this socioemotional phenomenon into account, and compensate for it, is by inaction teaching girls "math anxiety." This is not a cute deficiency but rather a severe handicap. High school math is the "critical filter"[31] for many satisfying careers. For instance, the four-year high school math sequence is required for admission to courses that in turn "are required for majoring in every field at the University of California except the traditional female (and hence lower-paying) fields."[32] Math proficiency adds 36 percent to a girl's future income.[33]

Teachers seem to recognize this when it comes to counseling boys to take advanced math "because they'll probably need it." But sex stereotypes clog the critical filter and advisors tend to coddle girls with, "Oh well, you're probably not going to be a physicist, so why ruin your grade average?"[34]

I myself was a sweaty-palm victim of math anxiety. I took a "Mind Over Math" course[35] when I was in my thirties, and discovered, some twenty years too late, to trust my "math intuition," to check my findings against the "reasonableness test," and to give up two beliefs drummed into me as a girl: "If it's not difficult, it's not math," and "Girls have no head for figures."

Until the curriculum gets rid of these beliefs and gives every girl the psychic and academic keys to math confidence,[36] too few will discover that numbers can be as agreeable as words—and up to twice as profitable.

Science, Too

Much that can be said of math may be said of science, too. Several have said it, *and* done something about it, adding women's scientific accomplishments to the male-focus of the curriculum, and sponsoring conferences and counseling to dispel myths about women in scientific and technical careers.[37] The National Science Foundation, for example, brings women chemists, physicists, and biologists into tenth-grade classrooms to motivate girls, help them pinpoint their interests, and to serve as role models for the "normalcy" of the scientific female.[38]

Humanities for the Other Half of Humanity

If female deprivation centers on the math-science curriculum, boys are most likely missing out in the humanities. Under the flag of sexism, many have picked up the impression that English courses and foreign languages are "feminine," that accents (especially French) are fey, and that literature is for "ladies," not for life.[39]

Because it is well known that boys do poorly on tasks they believe to be "girlish"[40] (since the "opposite" sex should do "opposite" things), the responsive curriculum will use radical methods to attract boys to poetry,[41] and expose them to writers of both sexes, to literary careers, work opportunities for the bi-lingual, and the superior pleasures of foreign travel when one speaks the native tongue.

Social Relations: Teaching "to Live" As Well As "to Know"

Sex education and family life courses are the curriculum areas where sex role training can be most pernicious. Common complaints:

• Experts from fifteen countries recommend sex education be designed for "the enhancement of life and personal relationships" and not just for dealing with "procreation or sexually transmitted diseases." They also agree that the cult of male dominance "makes it difficult to introduce the idea of sexual enjoyment for both partners."[42]

• "Despite the fact that most students are single and non-engaged, the present focus of most family/sex education courses at this age is not on dating but on marriage."[43]

• Student: "I'm tired of watching that ovum come bouncing down the fallopian tube; I want to know how girls feel about petting."[44]

• Kids get "the miracle of new life," love, monogamy, marriage, intercourse for procreation, and pollination of flowers. What kids need is masturbation, the clitoris, venereal disease, homosexuality, contraception, and a clear connection between penis-in-vagina and teenage pregnancy.[45]

• Student: "I already know all about girls. I want to know about boys and what they think about us. Why can't boys and girls have sex ed. together so we can ask each other questions?"

At best, sex education is given once a week for 45 minutes. When we realize that human sexuality plays a far larger part in a person's life than basketball or British dynasties—and when we remember the data on parental silence and children's ignorance (see Chapter 14)—the low priority of sex education becomes a shameful failure of the school system. We need more sex ed. and better sex ed. What is taught now in many classes makes the information kids pick up in the streets seem sage by comparison. Courses present sex as pathology, biology, or mythology; the male urge is the female's responsibility; V.D. is something girls carry and boys get; the girl does not "do," she is "done to."[46]

Family life courses offer a prudish, moralizing view of marriage. Child care remains women's work and the parent role is seen as a biological inevitability, not an option and not an aptitude.[47] Many still portray "the family" as Mommy-Daddy-baby; the props are an apron for her and a briefcase for him; everyone goes to church; and divorce is an unfortunate thing that happens to "other people."

Real-Life Relationships

Instead of inaccuracy and sex role propaganda, let's imagine a new curriculum mode, perhaps under the broad rubric "Relationships." Just as English and history are presented with added complexity layer by layer at each grade level, human relations can be taught first as a unit on parents-and-children, then as a study of "taking care of babies," then as "elementary psychology" in the elementary school grades. In junior high, it can become more "relevant" with study units on peer relationships, sexuality, and dating, moving into a high school curriculum that includes the art and effort of parenting for both sexes, patterns of child abuse, varieties of emotional and sexual relationships, making commitments, responsibilities of adult life, and alternate lifestyles—all explored in a nonjudgmental manner.

Your children might never need drugs and mystical religions

if their schools address the Self as Subject. We know what children think and worry about: how to feel good about themselves and get along with others; how to find an "identity," some pleasures of the flesh and spirit, and a way of life that "fits" without harming or exploiting others. Why not be honest about their needs instead of yoking them to our fantasy of their innocence?

There are many excellent approaches to sex education that take into account rights, responsibilities, children's health, and religious perspectives.[48] But ask a young adolescent her or his greatest fear and I'd take bets the answer won't have anything to do with physical sex. Most kids I know say their greatest fear is "not being liked" or "not knowing what to say" when they're alone with someone of the other sex. That's why a wider focus on relationships—on hetero*social* behavior, not just heterosexual sex —makes more sense.

We should have a curriculum that improves their self-concept, lowers their anxiety about rejection, and asks whether sex role etiquette is necessary or comfortable. They need to explore who should take the initiative, what decisions can be shared, how to overcome shyness, and how to communicate what they want or need from someone else.

For example, the aim of sex education for girls has been to build "decision-making skills that enable her to say 'no' and still feel good about herself,"[49] when in the case of a high school senior for example it should also enable her to say "yes" and feel good about herself.

If children learn to balance gratification with consideration in adolescence, we won't have to teach them formal rules for some mysterious future existence called "marriage and family living." Their respecting, honest heterosocial relationships will have become a habit and a model for harmonious adult coupling, with or without heterosexual sex.

Parenthood Education for Children

Due to the patriarchy's demand for sex only within marriage, schools have not helped young people learn heterosexual intimacy. And due to its need to establish mythic trust in the "maternal instinct" (see Chapter 8), young people do not *learn* to be parents; they stumble into the most important job in the world full of ignorance or unrealistic expectations:

• A young man spanks his seven-month-old baby for pulling the nipple off his bottle. "He's been asking for this all day!" says the father.[50]

• A teenage mother says of her baby: "If he does not go on the potty by the time he's a year and a half, he shouldn't eat."[51]

• More than half the teenagers in one study felt it was all right to spank a one-year-old for dropping and throwing things. And fewer than one-third (21 percent of the boys) knew that lack of love and affection during the first year of life is psychologically damaging.[52]

Our "Relationships" curriculum should give children hands-on experience with younger children to develop nurturing competence—bathing, changing, feeding, empathy, discipline-without-abuse—just as we build math and reading competence. Furthermore, students should study the economics of childrearing from birth to age eighteen. They can visit hospital nurseries and child care centers and help out in nursery or kindergarten classes in school. Older groups might conduct speak-outs on battered children, adoption, divorce, living with a single parent, custody arrangements, and foster care.

Several organized programs for parenthood education already exist[53] or teachers can develop an original curriculum combining parenting, sex education, and contemporary living, as did a teacher in an Iowa high school. In two semesters, one on single life and one on marriage, her students practiced how to get a job, buy insurance, apply for a loan or mortgage, make a household budget, pay taxes, buy a car, decide among birth control methods, and at least think through tough problems like being fired, unwanted pregnancy, living with a disability, alcoholism, and death. For each project they used the resources of the community—banks, courts, clergy, employers, and their own parents.

In the "married semester," they studied the logistics and economics of a wedding and spent a morning in divorce court, and analyzed common disputes about division of labor among two working parents and typical conflicts about childrearing.

"Each student couple had a hypothetical baby (really a raw egg) to carry around with them for a week," says the teacher. "This symbol made them aware of the fragility and constant responsibility a child can be. The couple had to have it with one or the other of them constantly. The results were a true eye-opener, even though the egg was far less demanding than a child would be. Child abuse court cases were drawn up and hearings held for those couples who abused (broke) their child (egg)."[54]

Another teacher says of the Oregon seniors who take his contemporary living class, "Many decide that for now, they are more interested in cars and fun than babies and buying furniture."[55] The lucky ones discover this *before* they marry and have babies.

Human Ecology

The life maintenance courses—cooking, nutrition, sewing, home economics, building, repairing—finally are becoming sex-integrated after years of sex-typing.

Margaret Mead once suggested lumping such subjects into one curriculum called Human Ecology;[56] I couldn't agree more.

Everyone needs survival skills. To be well fed, clothed, and housed, to build and to fix what breaks, are the most basic requirements of self-sufficiency. Your child should be able to maintain herself or himself without waiting for the sex that's "supposed" to make the meal, fix the flat, change the fuse, or build the fire.

We all know how hard it is to acquire such skills in later life; we have no time, we get set in our ways or convinced of our irreversible ineptitudes. The time for basic learning is youth, the place is school, and the image must be genderless.

A course entitled "Powderpuff Mechanics" might lure girls, but patronizing white-glove projects won't help them. Calling a Home Ec elective "Bachelor Living" and appealing to boys because "men make the best chefs" bows too low in the direction of the male ego and suggests that unless a man is a bachelor he need not learn to cook.[57]

Human ecology studies should start early. Girls and boys introduced to carpentry in kindergarten, with the right tools and teaching guides,[58] can be proficient cabinetmakers by eighth grade. Sewing classes that make vests or decorated blue jeans (instead of aprons or pot holders) will appeal to over-eight-year-olds of both sexes. The metal shop needn't label jewelry-making for girls, nor should woodworking mandate a salad bowl for her and a go-cart for him. In these classes, only the support system should differ according to which sex needs more emotional reinforcement for which nontraditional activity.

Similarly, automotive courses should phase in female students with some sensitivity, perhaps putting four girls to work fixing a car together instead of sending one girl under the hydraulic lift with three hostile boys.

In his senior year, James Foley was six-foot-four, weighed 200 pounds, was the second best rebounder on his basketball team, put the shot and threw the javelin on the track team, was a member of the school's curriculum committee and the chess club, was as handsome as Alan Bates—and was enrolled in an elective called, "Gourmet Cooking."[59] If *he* got heckled for cooking, imagine how much buttressing ordinary kids need when they choose the unconventional course.

It's not enough to teach a boy to fix crepes or a girl to fix carburetors. Children need to see many female mechanics at work and many men (not necessarily professional chefs) who enjoy cooking and in fact admire a boy like James Foley for his ratatouille more than for his rebounding.

Vocational and Educational Guidance

When a seventh grade girl wanted to sign up for *World of Construction* (formerly shop) instead of *Designs for Living* (formerly home ec), a counselor told her not to take it because all the rest of the students would be boys.[60]

A high school counselor discouraged a senior girl from pursuing a career in veterinary medicine on the grounds that her interest was nothing more than "the maternal instinct."[61]

"Counselors of both sexes react most favorably to students who hold occupational goals traditional to their sex."[62]

Actually, school counselors' sex role rigidities have relaxed considerably since the beginning of the seventies,[63] and with Title IX and other laws directed against vocational and counseling bias,[64] girls are less likely to be steered into, say, teaching elementary school science while boys of similar scholastic interests are directed into medicine.

As Ghandi said, "There go my people, and I must run and catch up with them for I am their leader," guidance counselors—and the curriculum materials on which they rely—are often several steps behind occupational trends even when they are miles ahead of their prior prejudices.

More than 60 percent of teenage girls in one poll "feel they are not receiving adequate counseling about jobs, schools and opportunities available to them."[65] Girls constitute half of the total enrollment in vocational education programs but only one-quarter of the enrollment in courses leading to paid work (rather than consumer and homemaking programs).[66] Although 9 out of 10 women will be employed during their lives, almost half of the sixteen-year-old girls polled in 1978 do not think they'll hold jobs in their futures.[67]

Clearly, there is an information gap here that the guidance programs have failed to close. Two educational consultants[68] suggest parents might step into the breech: look at the enrollment pattern in vocational education courses. Ask to see copies of texts:

Sample: "If you are by nature a helper—reliable, painstaking, accurate—as a laboratory assistant or technician, you could lend a hand to the professional scientist, freeing him for more difficult original work."[69]

Interview the guidance and counseling staff about their attitude toward girls and women in traditionally male occupations and inform school administrators and the Board of Education about the availability of federal funds for model programs.[70]

Parents can help motivate their children but it is counselors who should channel the motivation into suitable work or school options suitable for that particular child, not for an abstract gender class.

Physical Education

We've seen how important sports are in child development and peer group relations (see Chapters 17 and 18), yet many girls are deprived of a sporting chance in school. Typical complaints:

• Boys got new equipment, uniforms, first aid supplies, an athletic director, trainer, team room with showers, training room with whirlpool bath, special lockers, a room for the visiting team, free transportation to "away" games with paid meals and lodging for overnights, five-dollar varsity patches, fancy trophies, and a steak banquet.

For the girls, there were bake sales, car washes, and candy stands to pay for their own uniforms, transportation, meals, and lodging; equipment so old it was finally outlawed; use of the tax-paid swimming pool only before 8 A.M. and after 6 P.M. (when the boys didn't use it), no trainer; and for league winners, a paper certificate and a potluck dinner.[71]

• "We play softball on the outfield of the boys' baseball field," complains another girl. "The infield is watered every day and kept in excellent condition. Our outfield is never watered and is a mess of stones and dirt.

"Our volleyball team was first in our division, our gymnastics team was second in New York City and our girls' tennis team was first in the whole city for the second time in a row . . . (yet) In the school paper, each victory got an inch of space while the boys had three-fourths of the same page under the headline *Boys' Basketball Finishes Worst Season Ever.*"[72]

In virtually every sport, girls have been living on leftovers. But thanks to Title IX, things are changing. One Virginia school official delights in the oft-heard sentence, "This year for the first time, the girls are _____." Whether the sentence is completed with the words, "using the main gym," "playing their games at night so parents can attend," or "trying out for coed teams,"[73] it is being repeated all over the country.

In 1972, only two hundred thousand high school girls participated in interscholastic sports; by 1979, the figure was 2.5

million.[74] In 1975, only sixty colleges gave athletic scholarships to girls; three years later the figure was up to five hundred.[75]

Still, the news is not all good. Nationally, girls are half of the student body but only a third of the school athletes, and it seems to me the lag can be blamed on two provisions in the law:

1. *Schools must maintain "overall equal opportunity" for both sexes but not identical athletic programs or identical versions of the same sport.* For example, half-court "girls' rules" basketball—which once inspired a sociologist to remark that "girls play a form of basketball, as do paraplegics in wheel chairs"[76]—is required for girls in a few states. Although Title IX allows this, girls from these states are disadvantaged when competing for college scholarships against players experienced in the standard full-court game.

2. *Schools must have sex-integrated physical education classes and teams—but are allowed two exemptions: a. "contact" sports may be sex-segregated; and b. teams and classes may be single-sex if they turn out that way as a result of "ability grouping."* These two exceptions—which, remember, are allowed but not *required* —cause a pack of problems.

Some states do it by age,[77] while others do it by sport, and still others prohibit all mixed competition in the six "contact" sports —football, basketball, ice hockey, rugby, boxing, and wrestling. (Baseball, softball, and soccer are not classified as "contact sports" though why basketball *is* and soccer isn't, I don't know—and how sports that consider "contact" illegal—that is, fouls—can be called "contact" sports seems entirely perverse.)

At any rate, suppose a school has separate teams for girls' and boys' basketball. An outstanding girl who is overqualified for the girls' team, and better than most of the boys besides, would still have to play on the girls' team. Another school that has only a boys' team could also keep the girl from trying out on the grounds that basketball is a "contact" sport. As long as the school has something comparable—a girls' field hockey team or volleyball team—it can claim "overall equal opportunity" in the phys ed program as a whole, and the girl basketball whiz would be out of luck. And if she's benched in junior high, "it makes no difference if there's a team in college. She will already have dropped out."[78]

One often hears the argument that schools cannot afford to

develop female athletics to the level of "revenue-producing" sports like football and basketball. Many claim these sports support the female programs in high school and college. Senate hearings found, on the contrary, that more than 90 percent of so-called "revenue-producing sports" run at huge deficits and actually "depend heavily on mandatory student fees," half contributed by female students.[79]

Even if schools did show a profit on male-only policies, since when is making money an excuse to discriminate? Since when is the glory of a few elite athletes and the entertainment demands of alumni worth sacrificing the potential of all our children's healthy bodies, or depriving even one child who wants it of the joy of sport?

To fight foul plays in your child's school sports programs, consult one of the resources developed for your use.[80]

TEACHER ATTITUDES

The teachers' sex role ideology is the third potential sore spot in the hidden curriculum. Most teachers perceive girls and boys as "significantly different" before any particular girl or boy takes a seat in the classroom.[81] As a result, not surprisingly, studies also show that "boys and girls do not necessarily have similar experiences in the same classroom."[82]

Like most of us, teachers who are not conscious of the damaging effects of sex stereotypes tend to act on them. But unlike most of us, in the course of a career, a teacher influences hundreds or even thousands of children.

Ask a third-grade teacher, say, to picture a normal child[83] who is disruptive . . . loves to read . . . likes to help Mommy . . . would make a good audio-visual assistant . . . and the images that come to mind will very likely be sex-specific in each case. Teachers often make class jobs gender-linked and segregate girls and boys in line-ups, spelling bees, and study projects, giving official sanction to the destructive us-them dichotomy that we saw in the peer group.

Classroom events pay sex role dividends in maturity. Being placed on the "girls' line" becomes a mortifying punishment for a boy, and in later life a man finding himself in a female group, no matter how elite the women, feels a diminution of his status. Similarly, being excluded from audio-visual or other "boys' jobs" trains girls to accept discriminatory hiring as women's lot.

What the teacher does or says is not trivial. It is authoritative and *educational.* Everything matters. Everything sinks in. Yet, just as school cafeteria workers didn't realize "that they were automatically serving the boys bigger portions,"[84] until they were observed, teachers do not realize all the ways they treat the sexes differently.

• *Math teacher:* "Girls, you'll never be able to follow a recipe if you don't learn fractions."

• *Fifth-grade teacher* (ignoring that several girls tower over boys in the class): "May I have two strong boys to carry the chairs."

• *Industrial arts:* "After I show everyone how to do this, the boys will help the girls get it right."

• *Girl in a chemistry class:* "When my experiment exploded, my teacher said, 'Isn't that just like a girl.' But I know for a fact that last semester all the explosions were caused by boys."

• *On a class field trip,* passing a car junkyard, a male teacher quipped: "There's women's greatest contribution to the world."

• *Letter from principal to parents:* "The girls are permitted to wear slacks under a dress for our physical education program *only.* I'm all for equality, but I think girls should look like girls —and if that means skirts or dresses, so be it." (Incidentally, discriminatory dress codes are illegal under Title IX.)

• *When a high school history teacher* suggested a Women's Studies course be introduced into the curriculum, her (male) department chairman protested, "But when will the students get *real* history?"[85]

Observers in many classrooms have found more subtle but even more damaging forms of sex bias than these teachers verbalize. Remember the reasoning (described in Chapter 2) that gives rise to the cult of sex differences: *the two sexes are different*

. . . the two sexes are opposites . . . one sex is better than the other. Since teachers have been found to subscribe to the first two tenets, inevitably they subscribe to the third. However, they split up their perception of "better": they think girls are better behaved, but boys have better brains, bodies, and value in society.[86]

This means that although girls seem to be teachers' pets, preferred by predominantly women teachers in the supposedly "feminizing" environment of the school,[87] it is actually boys who are favored because of teachers' more deeply held beliefs about male worth.[88] Conventional sex role ideology may make them think of a boy as "the student who gives teachers trouble," but it also makes them give a boy more attention, more help, and more *teaching.* One educator explains:

> Because girls are considered to be neater, better-behaved, and harder-working, teachers assume that they are already doing the best they can. Because boys are considered to be sloppier and less diligent by nature, teachers tend to tell them, "You can do better. You're just not trying hard enough." The boys believe it. They do try harder, and do better.[89]

Studies have shown that from nursery school on, teachers (most, not all of course) shape children's learning styles and dependence behaviors differently according to sex.[90] They talk to boys more than girls[91] and interact more with boys, whether "asking questions, criticizing, accepting or rejecting ideas, giving approval and disapproval," or listening to them. Girls volunteer answers more often than boys but are called on less often.[92]

Teachers do a task for a girl, but give boys *eight* times as much detailed instruction in how to solve problems for themselves.[93]

Teachers interact with boys wherever they may be in the classroom, which lets boys move about independently without risking neglect, but teachers respond to girls mainly when they are nearby, which inspires clingy, help-seeking dependency.[94]

Teachers have clearer perceptions of boys' characteristics and abilities than of girls'.[95] They spend more time with boys than girls, including in cooking and sewing classes.[96] They have different expectations of the two sexes in line with gender stereotypes.[97]

In a shop class, for instance, girls started the term full of confidence but ended up turned off—"not because girls couldn't learn to enjoy working with their hands, but because, by and large, the teachers treated them as *though* they couldn't."[98] Teacher preconceptions become student profiles.

> Teachers generally prefer males to females, and they like children who fit sex stereotypes better than those who do not. In one survey, teachers said they like male students because they were more outspoken, active, willing to exchange ideas, honest and easy to talk to. The only characteristic that endeared female students to them was their lower frequency of disciplinary problems.[99]

Most male teachers show the same patterns and attitudes as female teachers except that they also give boys more leadership positions than girls.[100] In any case, whether the differentiated attention is outright favoritism or comes in the form of "control messages" given to boys in "harsh and angry tones," it is still more attention. It results in an "increase in independent, autonomous behavior by boys."[101]

With all this research data in mind, let's put a few ironies in the fire. Most of the national concern among educators seems focused on boys' being discriminated against, not girls'.[102] The big worry is about boys' stultified physical activity and boys' reading problems in the early grades, not girls' total educational swindle and lifelong math and science handicap. The cures proposed range from paying men more money to attract them to early childhood teaching where they are in short supply (with no concomitant proposal to attract women to college teaching where *they* are under-represented), to single-sex classes in the early grades.[103]

Although nurturant males in early childhood education could provide wonderful male role models,[104] that cure begs the question. If women teachers "feminize" (*i.e.,* weaken, make dependent, squelch the spirit of) boys, aren't they also visiting that harm on girls? If it's not good for boys, why is it all right for girls? And if it is the result of female socialization, why not change the socialization rather than the sex of the teacher?

The answer is to stop "feminizing" anyone (because "feminizing" has come to mean weakness and dependency.) And that cannot happen with the second prescription, single-sex classrooms. Besides rigidifying the old us-them division, you get all-girl classes whose teachers like to "orient" instruction to the supposed interests of the girls. As one teacher proudly illustrated the point: "The other day, they counted by tens up to a hundred by shaking up an instant pudding mix."[105]

With all the talk about boys' needs, the fact is that one item on patriarchy's hidden agenda is to teach boys better. That's why, by junior high, boys manage to catch up and surpass girls.

• *Item:* In math, social studies, and science, both sexes are equally proficient at age nine. By thirteen, the girls drop back.[106]

• *Item:* In reading and literature, girls outscore boys until age seventeen, then fall behind.[107]

• *Item:* More girls than boys take the College Boards, but more boys than girls go to college. Girls' high school grade average is higher than boys', but boys score higher on the scholastic aptitude test. (Boys learn to aspire, strive, compete; girls learn to give up.)[108]

• *Item:* Girls most often plan to study education, nursing, and social sciences; boys decide to study biology, business, and engineering.[109] (Do these occupational choices just *happen* to parallel teachers' sex stereotypes and schools' sex-typed courses?)

The only areas in which females continue to outperform males throughout life are writing ability and music.[110]

It is the function of a sex role stereotype to create self-fulfilling prophecies. (Chapter 3) We've seen that school subjects are gender-linked,[111] and we know that children concentrate on subjects that are gender-appropriate rather than risk sex role conflict. Since sex role *standards* are known long before the age at which sex differences in *performance* appear,[112] the sad truth is that *standards influence performance.* Sixth graders think spatial relations performance is "masculine," but the difference in male and female aptitudes doesn't show up until ninth grade[113]—the *stereotype* of male superiority preceded the *fact* of male superiority by three years!

Sex-of-the-Mind as Excuse for the Status Quo

It has become fashionable to skip over all the environmental influences on intellectual development and go straight to the "source" of intellect: the brain. The split-brain theorists propose that girls and boys have different aptitudes because the two sexes "think differently."[114]

In simple terms, the claim is that at birth everyone's two cerebral hemispheres are "of approximately equal dominance,"[115] but sex hormones differentially determine boys' and girls' brain circuitry—that is, how each hemisphere processes various kinds of information in order for the mind "to know."

Assuming that a child is right-handed, they say a girl's left temporal lobe, the site of language function, develops more precociously than a boy's. That's why girls are more verbal and better readers while boys are slow to learn to read and have a higher incidence of dyslexia.

Boys, on the other hand, are said to have a right hemisphere advantage. The right lobe is the site of nonverbal tasks and spatial reasoning, hence boys' superior math aptitude.

The split-brain theory (with variations[116]) is gaining steam though not scientific unanimity.[117] It has won no converts among egalitarians because the idea of a male brain and female brain is used, as most sociobiological theories are used, to justify the status quo. Were it instead an analytical stepping stone to methods that might *reduce* dichotomies of cognition and feeling—to overcome boys' reading retardation by teaching them with right hemisphere–oriented sound and space techniques, and to help girls remediate their math through "left-lobish" linguistic presentations of numerical concepts—then I might feel more comfortable about this line of inquiry.

But even if sex differences in brain functions are proven indisputable, the existence of gifted female mathematicians and scientists provides counterproof that culture (math training, encouragement from parents and teachers, and personal motivation) can overtake biology.

And even if the brain is "split," the biology-environment interaction must be confronted. Why else are females—the natural

• The New York primary school kids who built a sculpture garden, mini-park, camping shelter, and award-winning playground, with the guidance of a wife-and-husband architect team.[128]

• The kindergarten teacher who divides her class into smaller groups according to shoe size, hair length, shirt color, birthdates (summer, winter, spring, fall), or who had an egg for breakfast—never boys here, girls there.

• "Should boys wash dishes?" "Should women be trained for combat?" "Should men stay home to care for their children?" "Should women use Miss and Mrs. or just Ms.?" With such questions teachers have sparked animated class discussions from Florida to Oregon, while teaching children the skills of debate, the sociology of roles, and the tough issues raised by challenges to tradition.

• Diary of the integration of a playyard that had been monopolized by boys playing punchball:
1. Teacher orders territorial rights on alternating days: girls, boys, girls, boys.
2. On their days, girls stand on playyard, talking.
3. Boys protest waste of space. Boys stage incursion.
4. Girls refuse to return to sidelines. Girls defend their use of the grounds.
5. Teacher facilitates discussion of merits of both positions.
6. To solve impasse, teacher orders coed teams.
7. Boys' first reaction: annoyance and anger.
8. Girls' first reaction: helpless "feminine" ineptness.
9. Boys' second reaction: teach girls punchball.
10. Girls' second reaction: great effort to improve skills.
11. Boys give up their superior posture, begin to differentiate among the girls when choosing sides, instead of seeing them as all alike.
12. Girls give up playing helpless in favor of playing good punchball.

Ultimately, the teacher is the key. A nonsexist teacher can transform conflict into growth. A sensitive, imaginative teacher can take a sexist text book and make it a primer for human liberation. An innovative teacher can create a life-enhancing curriculum out of an accidental event, a chance sentence, or a bad joke. If you are that teacher, you can make miracles happen between September and June. If you are a parent who wants your children to have such a teacher, you'll need to take action.

ACTION ON ALL FRONTS

In order to persuade educators to make changes for the better you may first have to convince them, with the aid of examples and exhibits, that something is wrong. For a few weeks, pay special attention to your children's homework. Spend an evening or two thumbing through their notebooks and texts. Listen to their daily anecdotes. Ask them about class discussions, how groups are divided, how tasks are assigned.

On Open School Day, notice the room layout, browse through the books on the shelves, study the pictures on the walls and the class charts. Compare notes with other parents and consider joining forces. Study the strategies, experiences and mistakes of activist groups elsewhere.[129]

Give your school system a quick once-over with the questionnaire prepared by a Michigan group.[130] Your children get an annual health check-up, why not give them a *"BACK-TO-SCHOOL STUDENT'S RIGHTS CHECK-UP."*

During parent-teacher conferences, express your concerns. Offer the teacher consciousness-raising articles and research studies.[131] Collect the resources listed in footnotes 131 & 132 and make a packet of course models, teachers' guides, and curriculum catalogues suitable for the particular grade level.[132]

Since teachers generally assume parents lack pedagogical sophistication (for good reason), assure them that *educational* objectives, not political preconceptions, have inspired your efforts and explain that most of the materials you've gathered were developed by their professional teaching colleagues.

Ask to meet also with department heads, school administrators, and coaches. Discuss your findings in a spirit of helpfulness, not accusation. Establish your respect for their expertise; you are not attacking their methods but merely adding a new layer of awareness, saving them the drudgework of accumulating teaching materials you believe they'll be glad to have. Be patient. Explain "sexism" and "sex stereotypes" from square one if you must. Be sensitive to the teacher stereotypes that teachers resent[133] as much as we resent sex stereotypes, and remember that anyone can get defensive when being observed and evaluated.

Put your name and the names of interested teachers, principals, the school superintendent, and school board members on the mailing lists of the major national organizations that monitor Title IX enforcement and nonsexist educational issues.[134]

Offer to round up parents and community people to host a student tour of their work places, or to visit classes and talk about what they do.[135]

Organize extra special extracurricular projects: a skiing or camping trip could utilize outdoorsy mothers as role models and helpers; young fathers might bring their babies to class and answer questions about parenting; other parents could help teachers set up a women's culture week, highlighting women artists, poets, musicians, and performers;[136] a sexism-racism workshop; a "Nontraditional Careers Day"; a conference on sexual assault with a self-defense demonstration;[137] a workshop on "the male role in flux."

To tackle the textbook problem, if you live in a state with a centralized adoption procedure, find out when its public hearings are held and prepare yourself to testify against objectionable texts and for the positive ones.[138]

In other localities, ask your school to take the initiative to review its own curriculum materials for sex and race bias.

A poll of school administrators in fifty states indicates that those who seek, find. About as many systems as checked their texts for stereotypes found plenty of them. But 84 percent of the administrators (some of whom called sexism "Hogwash!" and ". . . a figment of some feminist's frustrated imagination") denied there was a problem and never bothered to look. However, of these, 70 percent claimed they *would* stop using biased books, finances permitting, if presented with convincing examples and arguments.[139]

That's your cue to mark and annotate like mad. Give teachers and curriculum planners critiques analyzing textbook sexism,[140] lists of nonsexist books and supplementary materials,[141] and a sample or two of the sort of good book you mean.

For your sample case you might choose *Macmillan Mathematics: Series M,* nine volumes of comfortable, casual equality in math problems, such as, "Working alone, a mechanic can do a job in 6 hours, but her helper needs 15 hours . . ."[142] Or the *Discovery* series,[143] in which women like Elizabeth Blackwell, the first woman to become a doctor, and Mary McLeod Bethune, the great black educator, are given their overdue due.

As always, group action gets the best results. In response to protests from N.O.W., one publisher, at a cost of a hundred thousand dollars, revised its highly successful reading program, ALPHA ONE, to make the girl vowels wise and witty instead of weak and in need of protection by the boy consonants.[144]

Be prepared for cries of censorship to greet your protests against sex and race bias.[145] Don't be cowed. Make yourself "perfectly clear": you do not want homemakers excised from books, you want female electricians added. You are not asking for book banning as dictators do to protect those in power. What you want is balance and fairness toward those who are powerless. When administrators, librarians, or teachers insist they will not be "pressured into spouting the feminist or any other party line," point out that "any author who presents one-sided depictions of females is . . . a party hack for the status quo."[146]

And to anyone who underestimates the impact of the printed word, recommend that they eavesdrop, as I did, on a couple of six-year-olds.

BOY: Do you want to be a clown when you grow up?
GIRL: No, I'm going to be a farmer.
BOY: *You* can't be a farmer. Farmers are men.
GIRL: Oh, yes I can. Here's a book about a farmer who raises sheep and she's a woman.[147]
BOY: Hmmm. . . . (looking through the book). Maybe I could shave the wool off the sheep on your farm. I could still be a clown on weekends.

24
Everything Else

Some things have to change on a grand scale: the law, for one. Sex-typed jobs. The design of our communities. Religion. And the very language we speak.

If that sounds like *everything,* it's because gender prejudice is built into "the system." Each of those vast social institutions is founded on the belief that *Men Are Better* and *Women Are Meant to Be Mothers.* And in one way or another, each of those institutions touches every person's life.

It is beyond the scope of this book to explore long-term political solutions to "institutionalized sexism." For the nonsexist parent raising children in the here and now, the idea is to find an alternative to paranoia and paralysis, and to bring a heightened consciousness into one's dealings with "the system."

RELIGION

The Bible and the Church have been the greatest stumbling blocks in the way of women's emancipation.
— ELIZABETH CADY STANTON, 1896

The male chauvinism of our churches and synagogues is perhaps even more entrenched than most of our other establishment institutions.

— DAVID HYATT, President
National Conference of
Christians and Jews, 1978

Religion transmits culture. It is considered "very important" by 4 youngsters out of 10.[1] It socializes our children with imagery, awe, and the immense authority of divine will—and it proselytizes the sex roles in apocalyptic terms.

God the Father. Ultimate patriarch. King of the Universe. Ruler, Master, Lord. God the Father which art in heaven. Man the father which art on earth—created in God's image to be the rightful patriarch of the human family.

Thus does religion imbue male domination with ethical logic and provide the template for all man's earthly hierarchies, from "King of his country" to "master of his house."

Many have proposed that God is man's cosmic overreaction to woman's transcendent power, the power to give birth to life itself. To save himself from insignificance, man has given birth to God and God makes woman's biology insignificant. He creates not one life, like a woman, but The World and All Life. He creates the human male—first—and then from Adam's body brings forth Eve, woman, the rib, a second thought. Thus is human creation turned upside down.[2]

> For a man . . . is the image and glory of God; but the woman is the glory of the man. For the man is not of the woman, but the woman of the man. Neither was the man created for the woman, but the woman for the man.
> —I CORINTHIANS 11:7–9

Imagine children reading or hearing this for the first time. And then think of all the incarnations of the female served up to them by the world's great religions. Woman, created by a He God *from* man and *for* man, is forever defined by her relationship *to* man. Virgin. Temptress. Evil Eve, the "universal scapegoat."[3] Submissive wife. Meant to Be a Mother.

> If a woman grows weary and at last dies from childbearing, it matters not. Let her only die from bearing, she is there to do it.
> —MARTIN LUTHER

Ideally, woman is the mother of sons. Nurse and nourisher to the body but unfit to minister to the spirit. In Judaism, often "unclean" and unseen, always supportive and subordinate. In Christianity, she is most revered in a condition no human female can hope to match:

Virgin Mother of the Son . . . Spouse of The Holy Spirit
. . . The handmaid of humanity . . . Queen of the Apostles
without herself being inserted into the hierarchical constitution of the Church.

—POPE JOHN PAUL II
October 1979[4]

For many of us, patriarchal religions are too sexist to be
saved. For others, usually as a result of childhood resonances, our
own religion is too meaningful to renounce.[5] We do the best we
can with it, largely for our children's sake, struggling over where
to compromise and what to keep. Or we cling to our faith, observing basic traditions perhaps or maintaining membership in a "regular" church or temple, but also seeking such new forms of expressions as:

• *Services* conducted by a woman rabbi, priest, or minister,
that might utilize prayer books and liturgies free of sexist terminology.[6] Is it so hard, we ask, to change "mankind" to "humanity," or "forefathers" to "ancestors"? Can't we remove the word
"men" from the Eucharistic formula and stop addressing congregations full of girls and women as "brothers" or "sons" of God?[7]

• *Symposia* that will help older children think about issues
such as "equal rites" for women;[8] about the "problem" of the
deity's "masculine" gender ("Dear God: Are boys better than
girls? I know you are one, but try to be fair. Love, Sylvia."[9]); and
the prevalence of male supernal symbology and imagery.[10] If your
children are too young to follow such debates in person, bring the
issues home translated into terms they understand. Start by asking
a small child to "describe God"—and take it from there.

• *Religious alternatives*—I don't mean signing on with the
Moonies, Muslims, or Hari Krishna, but taking an historical interest in religions of pre-*his*tory;[11] the recently found early Christian
(gnostic) gospels that describe God as both father and mother and
regard women as men's spiritual equals;[12] the "original" version
of Genesis in which God creates man, Adam, and woman, *Lilith,*
simultaneously;[13] and the Cabbalistic concept of the Shechinah,
the female presence of The Holy One.[14] Give children the freedom

to speculate and encourage them to study all forms of spiritual faith, especially those that honored female creativity and power before such beliefs were branded pagan heresy.

• *Congregations* offering full participation to both sexes: a church that allows your daughter to serve as altar girl, or a synagogue where she may be called to the Holy Ark, to hold the Torah, and to read from it if she is able.

• *Religious schools* that eradicate sexism from their programs; this Sunday School prayer for example:

For Boys	*For Girls*
Lord Jesus, I can't decide what to be when I'm grownup. Sometimes I think it must be neat to be an astronaut or a mechanic, or a football player. What do you think, Lord?[15]	Lord, I get tired of washing dishes and cleaning my room . . . Remind me when I feel this way, that these jobs are even more endless for my mom.[16]

And, for another example, the Hebrew school essay contest on "What's a Jewish Mother?" Although "nobody ever asks kids to write essays about Jewish fathers. (because) An essay on the Jewish father would be synonymous with an essay on the Jew."[17]

• *Reading* materials and guidelines for nonsexist worship, provocative commentaries, and fresh interpretations of the Scriptures, a glossary of gender-fair terminology, and Elizabeth Cady Stanton's amazing Woman's Bible.[18]

• *Revisionist rituals* to add meaning and fill in the blanks: a ceremony for the birth of a daughter,[19] a celebration of a girl's first menstruation, a wedding poetically and politically altered to equalize the vows, or a feminist seder, such as the one created by Esther Broner and Phyllis Chesler, in which my daughters and I have participated for the past several Passovers.[20]

Some twenty to twenty-five women of all ages sit in a circle on pillows. The floor of an artist's loft is our Seder table. We introduce ourselves: "I am Letty, daughter of Cyral, daughter of Jenny, daughter of a woman unknown." We read in the Woman's Haggaddah[21] of the legacy of Miriam, sister of Moses; and of

Beruriah, the only female Talmudic sage;[22] and of all the women, wise and strong, forgotten and never known, silenced and killed.

We honor our mothers and grandmothers. We honor the women who only cooked and served at seders through the centuries and in our own lives. We ask four questions about female destiny and deliverance and recite the ten plagues of women's oppression. We drink four cups of wine, toasting our own redemption and our daughters' bright futures.

Holding hands around the circle, we pray for peace. And then we pray for women all over the world. Just for women, for a change, as few spiritual gatherings ever have. And I think my daughters and I stand taller on that night of Passover than at any other time in the calendar of Judaism. Abraham, Isaac, Jacob, Samson, Samuel, Solomon, David, Jonathan, Jonah, and Joshua recede into the shadows of our self-made sanctuary along with all the fathers who begat sons who begat sons who begat sons. It is an ebullient thrill to speak women's names, honor women's heroism, and feel a link in the chain of one's heritage.

Because my own observant Jewish upbringing has been stripmined by the personal experience of exclusion from male-only rituals, I am ambivalent about how much substantive Judaism to pass to my children. My compromise—considered a sellout by some feminists and a travesty by many Jews—is to belong to the culture of Judaism but not to its institutionalized structures.

However you may choose to resolve the contradictions between patriarchal religion and the ethics of equality, belief in male supremacy must not be permitted to be the badge of the faithful.

COMMUNITY PLANNING

One summer a white suburban family was host to a black fourteen-year-old from the Bronx, despite their fear that the experience would be psychologically damaging to the child because he would "see how happy we are here and won't be able to face living any other way." But at the end of the summer the black child said he felt very sorry for the two white suburban boys who lived too far to walk to visit their friends and who had to depend on their mother to drive them everywhere.[23]

In more ways than one, *where* you live determines how you live, how your raise your children, and whether you can achieve parity parenthood and a nonsexist family life.

For instance, contemplate the suburbs: Communities organized around the assumption that the sex role division of labor operates in every household. The man commutes to his job in "the city" and the housewife is very nearly married to her house. She is expected to spend her day cleaning it, watching children in it, cooking in it, buying things for it, and preparing it for the husband's return to it.

When she is not in her house, the suburban housewife is in her car. The two-car family is "normal" as the two-income family is not. But the woman behind the wheel on suburban roads is rarely cruising along alone; invariably the back seat is full of groceries and children.

Suburban sprawl imposes full-time parenthood on one adult. Women in cars are their children's only link to club meetings, sports, medical care, and friends who live beyond the immediate cul-de-sac. If there is no second car, the housewife *and* children can be stranded in that cul-de-sac.

Trains are scheduled according to the rush hour needs of the commuter. Once the men are on their way, midday trains are infrequent and inter-community connections via other public transportation are nearly nil. (The stay-home population is assumed to have limited interests,[24] nothing that the local shopping center cannot fulfill.) So it becomes a major maneuver for a woman to get to the theater, a college course, or museum, to visit friends or take a part-time job when her children are in school. It's just too much of a hassle.

No wonder researchers find that housewives go to shopping centers when they don't need to buy anything.[25] They go because they *do* need stores for arousal, for stimulation, to escape the boredom and isolation of their houses and quiet streets.

Children eventually perceive their mothers primarily as shoppers, chauffeurs, and servicers of the household. It cannot be helped; the woman's role is built into the design of the community. Grocery shopping requires a car trip even if she only runs out of milk, and the weekly marketing takes several hours and the super-markets do not deliver, and housecleaning help is hard to find (because the poverty areas, from whence most domestic workers come, are quite far from the suburbs and household workers prefer not to travel), and job sites are too distant to justify part-time working hours, and there is no child care facility anyway, and older children who might babysit are too young to drive, and many school systems insist that children go home for lunch, mean-ing someone has to be there at noontime[26]—so, I repeat, the role of the conventional full-time housewife is built into the design of the community.

Father's estrangement from his family also comes with the territory. His long hours and frazzling commuter routine make him a weekend daddy at best. On a daily basis, his absence, oddly enough, adds to his importance: Mother dramatizes it ("Wait till your father gets home"); she primps the house and family mem-bers for his return (which gives men an idealized, sanitized view of what a day at home with the kids really looks like), and she times everything—her activities, meals, and the children's activi-ties—to his arrival. "Daddy's schedule is the schedule with which all other time schedules must mesh."[27] No one has to *teach* male supremacy to a suburban child raised in this fathercentric atmo-sphere.

The city has different drawbacks. Although the proximity of residence and workplace allows city parents to divide employment and child care between them more easily, those families in which the mother remains the primary stay-home caretaker are beset by the indignities of urban planning.

Isolation is based on depersonalization rather than geogra-phy. Households that might share child care or borrow eggs have barely a nodding acquaintance. Licensed child care facilities for kids under two or three are hard to find. Parents either must earn almost nothing to qualify for a public day-care center (assuming it offers quality care to begin with), or earn enough to afford a private nursery school.

High-rise housing has its pluses and minuses: a good chance

of nearby babysitters, for example, and a poor chance of a playground that can be watched from one's apartment window.[28]

With a baby carriage or a stroller, a parent is forever struggling with elevators, escalators, stairways, narrow doorways, and crowded sidewalks—or else is refused admission to restaurants, museums, buses, subways, and taxis.

The threat of crime inspires excessive caution and constant adult supervision of city children. Many are watched over by mothers sitting in playgrounds or on tenement "stoops," or in one another's apartments during "play dates." One woman admits to choosing her child's playmates according to which mother she wants to have coffee with.[29]

A glance around many urban neighborhoods reveals that daytime street and social life is for mothers-and-children, and male "losers": the drug dealer or addict, the pimp, the perpetually unemployed, and the men who drink from liquor bottles hidden in brown paper bags. The occasional daytime father stands out like a reproach. I remember specifically when one young man pushing his baby in a swing was the subject of two women's park bench conversation:

"That poor guy's been spending every morning in the playground," said one mother sympathetically.

"Must have lost his job in the cutbacks," offered the other. "Or maybe his wife ran off and left him with the baby."

To make involved fathers less of an oddity, and parity parenthood more feasible, and communities more livable, we need

• people serving on community planning boards who understand the daily life of a town or neighborhood—not absentee "Town Fathers" who make policies they rarely live with.

• transportation planning boards that do not force the homemaker to become "an unpaid provider of transportation services"; boards that take into account the "trip generating needs" of small children and their caregivers.[30]

• communities that provide services for *all* the people; for instance,

• *24-hour child care centers* staffed by trained personnel, (because no child should be unattended and no parent should be unable to do paid work because of one-on-one child care responsibilities).

- *shopper services and house-cleaning teams* to communalize tedious housework and marketing for several families at once.

- *community cafeterias* built into housing complexes and large office buildings that would relieve the cooking-and-clean-up burden for working parents, while also integrating the worlds of business and children to the benefit of both.

- *tot lots (playrooms)* in stores, markets, and offices.

- *school hot lunch programs* to keep children well-fed and assure that none must return to an empty house at midday.

- *mini-buses* with an intra-community route offering free transportation to give small children mobility in the suburbs and to eliminate use of gas-eating automobiles for trips to medical care, recreation, friends, and so on.

- *outdoor gathering places* in the suburbs (whether central squares, bandstands, bocce courts, pony rides, roller skating areas in parking lots or sandboxes and oversized fountain sprinklers); *indoor community lounges* equipped with a lending library, Ping-Pong table and the like.

- *a community bulletin board* listing local job openings, dates of club meetings, a "skills trading post" (will trade four loaves homemade bread for babysitting services), a used-toy or baby equipment exchange (will exchange playpen for size 12½ ice skates), etc.

- *organized integration of child, youth, and senior citizens programs* so that teens might shop for old people, and old people might tell stories to children, and each group might help the other feel needed while providing very necessary services.

- *a network of households* that would display an official "open house" sticker to designate a safe harbor for latch-key children, homes where anyone's child is welcome to stop for a glass of milk, to make a phone call, use the bathroom, or just get a kind word or two.

These may be pie-eyed ideas or they may be possible and perfectible. The question is, where are the city planners' ideas when it comes to humanizing the environment so that we can be less role-restricted and more genuinely devoted to our children?

THE LAW

Let me briefly state my case: Justice is not, as it should be, blind to gender. As long as in the mind's eye there are sex stereotypes, there is bound to be sex bias in the hearts of the men (and sometimes women) who make, interpret, and enforce the law. To wit:

• *Afterschool jobs.* In a few states your daughter, but not your son, may be prohibited from working at certain jobs or during certain hours, even if she wants to and you approve.

She is "protected" from dangerous (read "unladylike") work and late hours because she is assumed to be a "nice girl" (read "virgin"). She is "protected" from collecting a paycheck "for her own good."

Although sex discrimination in hiring is illegal at any age, such practices are rarely challenged when applied to the young because the notion of protecting the vulnerable, virginal girl is central to institutionalized sexism. (In a moment, we'll see how quickly this chivalrous concern disappears when the girl involved is a known non-virgin, for what really is being protected is not the girl herself, but her virginity.)

• *Minimum age for marriage.* In some states, girls are permitted to marry at a younger age than boys.[31] While this discrepancy is unfair to boys, it does not mean to favor girls or to acknowledge their superior maturity. It is based on sex role stereotypes according to which girls merely move from one dependent condition to another, from father to husband, but boys are expected to assume full economic responsibility in the marriage and hence must be protected from the rash impetuosity of youth.

• *The laws against statutory rape.* Also seemingly "protective," these laws make it a crime for a male of a certain age to have sex with a female minor (usually sixteen or under).[32] In very few states do laws similarly protect the innocence and purity of a young boy. A boy is considered *capable* of informed sexual consent (or entitled to sexual desire); a girl is not. A teenage girl does not own her sexuality; a teenage boy controls his own body. If two sixteen-year-olds *choose* to have sex together, the girl is automatically assumed to be the passive victim (unless she has an "unchaste reputation"). The boy is guilty by reason of sex role stereotypes: "feminine" purity, and "masculine" aggressiveness condemn him under the law, regardless of the facts.

The "crime" of statutory rape is an archaic reminder of the patriarchal objective to keep a daughter's virginity intact until it can be "given away" by father in marriage. Statutory rape is a "crime" against fathers and prospective husbands. That is why the daughter's consent, granted or not, doesn't count. And that is why the law does not "protect" the sons whose bodies belong neither to their mothers nor their prospective wives.

There should be laws against abuse of any child by any adult. If our concern is age disparity between sexual partners, then we must show gender-neutral consideration for all *children's* psychic and physical vulnerability.

And if any person forces himself (or herself, for that matter) on another person, he is guilty of rape, real rape, forcible rape, which is legally defined as "sexual intercourse without one person's consent."[33] Age is as irrelevant to that definition as gender.

The state has no business in anyone's private sex life except to protect everyone, male and female, from sexual harassment and involuntary sexual intercourse. If society really cares about girls, it must be tough on all forms of molestation, not just penetration; and if society really cares about children, it must care about boys as well.

• *Crime and punishment.* National statistics tell the story:

> . . . girls serve longer sentences on the average than do boys, even though girls are sentenced for less serious matters.[34]

Boys commit many of the same acts as girls, but girls are more than twice as likely to be arrested for them.[35]

Because girls are expected to behave, when they misbehave authorities are more shocked and the punishment meted out is more severe than that given to boys. Girls who end up in juvenile court, in jail, in grisly "reform" schools, are usually being punished for acts that are not crimes when anyone but a girl does them: things such as cursing, coming in late, keeping "bad company," talking back, "incorrigibility," running away from home (often from a violent home and abusive parents[36]), and most of all "promiscuity."

"Promiscuity" as a criminal concept does not exist for boys, but it fills the arrest records of girls.[37] In many places, girls picked up for any reason can be strip-searched and then charged with sexual delinquency.

> Just the suspicion of sexual intercourse is often all juvenile authorities need to arrest and ultimately convict an unmarried girl, as if she were guilty of shoplifting, assault or robbery. . . . Parents are willing to see their daughters in jail to punish them for real or suspect sexual activity.[38]

Even the courts, the American Bar Association admits, try to act as a "legal chastity belt."[39]

Patriarchal society wants girls to suffer for not being "nice." The legal system (and some parents) would rather treat a girl like a criminal than let her be sexually autonomous like a boy. What merits a smile and a wink when a boy does it puts a girl behind bars. Says a juvenile court judge:

> I have yet to see a boy brought to court because he is "promiscuous" or simply because he fornicates.

And a probation officer adds,

> I've never had a situation where the mother or father complained about the son's going out with an older woman or the hours he keeps.[40]

Same laws. Sexist justice.

And boys? Boys commit many of the same offenses as girls but for them those offenses—cursing, coming in late, acting out—are close enough to the "normal" male role to be ignored. For a boy to be arrested he has to commit assault, burn crosses, steal cars, mug, rape, and kill. A boy's crimes must wreak property damage and leave human victims before they are noticed; a girls' crimes are violations of her sex role and if there is damage done, it is only to herself.

Boys will be boys. The trouble is some boys don't know when to stop. They "overconform" to the "masculine" ideal,[41] they resort to criminal acts to get Big Man money and power; maybe they use violence as a hyper-"masculine" defense against "femininity,"[42] or to prove their toughness to their peer group,[43] or just in imitation of some Western or TV hero.[44] In any case, it all boils down to "their sex role made them do it." Societies that do not idealize aggressive "masculinity" also do not reap the whirlwind of male violence.[45]

This too must be said: In recent years,

Young female arrests for all offenses have increased more than twice those for young males—69 percent, compared to 30 percent.[46]

Whether that statistic represents a real increase or just more efficient FBI record-keeping, the point is that people are alarmed. Books, tabloids, and pop sociology blame the rising crime rate on increased female opportunity.[47] The conventional wisdom is, when roles blur, girls' crimes resemble boys' crimes.[48] The fear is that girls will start destroying people and property instead of just themselves.

Narcotics arrests rose 635 percent for females under eighteen,[49] yet we are warned about rising female violence, not a rising generation of drug-dependent girls. In truth, adolescent girls (as well as adult women) have not increased their involvement in crimes of violence, but in crimes of financial aggrandizement.[50] And while "women's lib" and "equality" have been blamed for antisocial trends, it is doubtful that anyone seriously believes the girls mugging senior citizens or robbing Johns in cheap hotel rooms are feminists.

The choice of being a "nice girl," a passive sexual delinquent, or a male-imitative criminal is not good enough for our daughters. They must have the option of being human under the law—of being more than simply virgin or nonvirgin, good girl or slut.

• *Sexist human rights.* Simone de Beauvoir writes that today's young girl is free to go out alone, but

> ... how hostile the street is to her, with eyes and hands lying in wait everywhere; if she wanders carelessly, her mind drifting ... if she goes alone to the movies, a disagreeable incident is soon bound to happen. She must inspire respect by her costume and manner. But this preoccupation rivets her to the ground and to herself.[51]

The thing a nontotalitarian society cherishes most, the basic right on which other rights depend, is the right to move about freely.[52] Because he is not seen as sexual prey, a boy is free to adventure by foot or vehicle and therefore "in the intoxication of liberty and discovery," as de Beauvoir puts it, he "learns to regard the entire earth as his territory."[53]

While female citizens are granted freedom of movement by law, they are not guaranteed it in reality in those circumstances when it is not believed to be *deserved*.

If your daughter happens to wear a short skirt, take a walk after dark, hitchhike, or ride a bicycle on deserted roads, she seems to forfeit the full sympathy and shelter of the law. Nowhere is it written, but in a felt sense she loses the presumption of innocence when she ventures into the world as an independent person. A girl's innocence is sexual before it is criminological. If she leaves the house (Woman's Place) at certain hours, if she goes to certain places using public space as if it belonged to her, if she "provokes" by walking proudly in the body she was born with, or "incites" by failing to tiptoe around on her pedestal, your daughter compromises her own innocence. Or as one newspaper wrote:

> These girls know the score. Some get raped, a few are murdered; generally speaking they asked for it.[54]

By this magical mindset, a girl who steps out of her role can't be a victim, she can only be a perpetrator. "She asked for it ... she should have known better ... we warned her ... she made him do it ... it was her fault ... what's a nice girl like you doing in a place like this? ... she had only herself to blame ..." Echoes of the law that lies, that makes excuses when human rights for females are a hollow promise.

Law or no law, we are dealing with entrenched patriarchal beliefs:

- A girl unattached to a male protector (father, brother, boyfriend) is fair game to all males.

- The way to control male sexual passion is to restrict female freedom, *i.e.,* "If there is an epidemic of rapes, keep the girls off the streets."

- Because males find the female body highly provocative, females wearing certain clothes are responsible if the male sex urge is aroused to violent action—which is tantamount to saying that a person wearing a gold watch is responsible if a thief steals it.

These entrenched patriarchal beliefs account for wildly distorted interpretations of laws guaranteeing female safety. For example, the California judge who found a rapist not guilty because female hitchhikers "should anticipate sexual advances";[55] and the judge in Hawaii who decided that the victim who had been run down with a car and then sodomized wasn't really raped because she hadn't fought back;[56] or, conversely, the London judge who concluded that the victim caused her own broken ribs, internal injuries, and temporary paralysis by fighting back *too* much, as though "refusing to be raped is a kind of contributory negligence."[57]

The most notorious instance of sexist justice in recent years involved the Wisconsin judge (subsequently driven out of office by feminist protests) who let off a fifteen-year-old boy, who raped a sixteen-year-old girl, on the grounds that revealing female fashions and general social permissiveness made rape a "normal reaction" for a high school boy.[58]

In Moslem countries there are external prohibitions to regulate female sexuality: either concealment (the veil) or confinement (to female sections of the building).[59] The social control of Western women is accomplished by *internalized* sexual prohibitions.

Between ages seven and eleven, girls more than boys are "anxious about what might happen when they go outside."[60] Eventually your daughter is imprisoned by her own fear. The "nice girl" role is her veil and the need for male protection is her confinement.[61] Unless she learns karate:

An 11-year-old girl successfully fought off two would-be child molesters. As she was walking home from school, a car with two men stopped, and the passenger opened his door and grabbed her by the arm. She flipped him onto his back on the sidewalk, chopped him in the neck with the edge of her hand, and jabbed him in the eyes with her fingers . . . both men were apprehended. The girl . . . was unharmed.[62]

It made my children's eyes glisten, that swashbuckling true story, but self-defense classes are not the answer. Neither is teaching our daughters to beware of strangers, to avoid bad neighborhoods, to run or fight back or call for help or name her attacker in a police lineup. Those are skimpy Band-Aids on a mortal wound. They're not enough.

For the law to guarantee both sexes their human rights, the word "female" must mean "human," and not have just a sexual connotation. For women and girls to be safe, we must give up the comforts of chaperonage and the myth of chivalry, understand that the gestures of chivalry demand female passivity;[63] that chivalry makes equal unequal, and that the flip side of chivalry is rape.

If you have hope for our legal institutions, you must act to make them work for your children. Protest sexist law enforcement. Keep informed. Write letters to lawmakers. One U.S. Congressman confessed to me that he gets far more mail about mistreatment and oppression of the porpoise than about the American child.

JOBS AND DREAMS

Interview: What does your mother want you to be when you grow up?
Joanna (age five): Be a mother. But I think I want to be a basketball player.
I: Can't you be both?
J: No.
I: Describe what you'll do on a typical day 20 years from now.
J: I'll sleep late, wake up, have breakfast, get dressed, take my child to school, come back home, and watch TV.[64]

when kindergarten is typed female and physics labs are typed male?

For one thing, sexism is good for business. All-female fields historically have been easier to exploit. Women workers cost less and demand little. When men entered teaching to avoid the draft, teaching became a militant profession with a tough union. Men in beauty shops and restaurants "class up" the establishment (because service from a female is expected but from a male it's special), but also jack up the wage rates.

For another thing male workers do not tolerate women's working conditions and employers have no excuse to treat men the way sexism lets them treat women. And finally, when men "slum" in the occupations of their inferiors, the prestige of the privileged caste is pulled down a peg or two.

What can and can't a parent do to counter occupational barriers?

• You cannot guarantee your daughter and son the same professional success. But you can raise them to understand that job training and career commitment are equally important and necessary for both of them.

• You cannot mislead children to believe that females and males are well distributed and accepted in all occupations. But you can give them the widest career perspective and the deepest confidence to pursue their own goals. That means tracking down vocational information on any field that piques their interest or parallels their talent; and exposing children to admirable role models in books and in life, since kids set higher goals when informed of outstanding occupational achievements of others of their sex.[81] As a wise father once said: "A girl can't want to be something she's never heard of."[82]

• You cannot (and should not) raise a child to fit *your* aspirations. But you can make your own life an example. Studies find "that girls with higher self-perceptions of their competence have received both support for and modeling of such self-images from their mothers."[83] Sex-typed occupations can even be turned inside-out within a family. I'm thinking of four-year-old Val, who loves to paint and care for her plants. Her mother, who is a doctor, asked what Val wants to be when she grows up, suggesting, "Perhaps you'd like to be a gardener or an artist?"

"Oh no, Mommy," Val replied with complete certainty. "I just want to be a *plain* doctor like you!"[84]

LANGUAGE

A 10-year-old Newark boy was charged Monday with stabbing to death an 8-year-old who called him a "sissy."

THE NEW YORK TIMES
November 21, 1979

Names *can* harm you. Language is power. Words are symbols.

Nonsexist parents must listen hard because what we say and how we say it lets all the secrets of the patriarchy out of the bag.

I have saved language for last because it is first, last, and all ways. Sexist reality begins with The Word. Leave language untouched in your child's life, and nothing else can truly change. Change language and *everything else* will never be the same. Language speaks for *the cult of sex differences.*

If the word "sissy" can incite a child to murder, it is because we as a culture have allowed sex differences to become as important as life itself. We've made the sex difference the First Self. Especially for the male child. The word "sissy" denies that critical "Self"-defining difference between the boy and the nonboy.

"Manhood" has been made a word to live up to and a word worth dying for—which makes words that challenge manhood worth killing for.

In this devotedly differentiated society, when young children engage in name-calling, the great joke is to call a girl a boy, or a boy a girl, or to call a boy by a girl's name. But the victim, especially if it's a male, is rarely amused. Verbal sex reassignment conjures up the infantile terror that "to change the name would mean to change the thing."[85] The terror, deeply rooted at an early age, is becoming one's "opposite."

What's in a name or a word—besides the *power to deny* a

coveted gender difference? Four more "d's": the *power to define,* to *devalue,* to *defame,* and to make *disappear.*

1. The Power to Define

"Woman" is defined most often by the euphemisms *girl* and *lady* . An old, gray-haired woman is a "girl" to her "girlfriends," as is a secretary of any age ("Did your girl call my girl?"). Lady, is used most when compensating for a woman's low status (". . . one of the Slavic ladies who clean the offices of Manhattan late at night"),[86] or when imposing propriety out of context—"a real lady" as opposed to "a real woman."

The word "woman" is avoided because it is too "trait-free," meaning simply "female person," or because it connotes aggressive sexuality.[87] "Girl" infantilizes; "girls" don't run for Congress. "Lady" sanitizes, doesn't make sexual demands, and minimizes. A "lady scientist" is less threatening to her colleagues than an equal.

In contrast, "gentlemen" is most often found on bathroom doors in public places. An anachronism (as "lady" has not been allowed to be), the word "gentleman" is rarely heard spoken outside of opening remarks at meetings—as in "Good evening, gentlemen." And, although some women find flattery in "girl," the word "boy" is an insult to men across the board. Except when "our boys" go to war. Then sentimentalizing soldiers' youthfulness helps the home-front propaganda effort while "over there," we're told, our "boys" fight like men.

2. The Power to Devalue

The so-called female courtesy titles devalue the individual woman by laying stress on her either/or status relative to a man. They advertise either sexual availability ("Miss") or another man's prior claims ("Mrs."). Those conventional honorifics do the patriarchy's detective work, but "Ms." only says "woman" the way "Mr." only says "man."

As a class, women are either over-familiarized—by public nicknames such as "honey" or "baby," and cutesy first names such as "Cher" and "Dinah"—or are over-formalized: "Koch and Miss Bellamy win in NYC."[88] Miss Bellamy or Dinah. Again, it's a choice between the lady or the girl.

3. The Power to Defame

"Cookie," "doll," "tomato," "broad," "chick," "cunt." There are few male equivalents of female names that objectify and defame: studies show that college males know twice as many slang expressions for women as women do, and almost all of them are sexual. Other surveys found 220 slang words for the sexually active female and only 22 for the sexually active male.[89]

Slang—expletives in particular—gives us cultural misogyny at its unguarded worst. A nasty woman is a "bitch," but a nasty man isn't nasty in his own right: he's a "*son* of a bitch" or a "bastard," both words reflecting badly on his mother.

"Son of a bitch" and "bastard" connote general offensiveness without male sex role implications, whereas "bitch" and its cruder sister, "ball-breaker," are meant to discredit the female for being a role rebel, a woman who adopts the "male prerogative of being goal-directed, blunt, direct and arrogant."[90] To hurt a woman's gender dignity, the language objectifies her sexuality or defames her "femininity." To wound male gender dignity, the expletive must explicitly suggest homosexuality. (Among homosexuals— since outcasts need scapegoats, too—slang is also sexist: *i.e.,* "butch" is better than "femme" to lesbians and gay men alike.[91])

In "polite circles," profanity is taboo to females. "Not in front of the children" means "not in front of little girls," and "not in mixed company," means "not for a lady's ear." Eventually, boys are initiated by their fathers or other boys who learn the words girls are not supposed to say or hear. Writes Shulamith Firestone:

A man is allowed to blaspheme the world because it belongs to him to damn—but the same curse out of the mouth of a woman or a minor, i.e., an incomplete "man" to whom the world does not belong, is considered presumptuous.[92]

That profanity is a linguistic totem of the patriarchy is made plain by Haim Ginott in a section of *Between Parent and Child,* called "Dirty Words":

> Father can say, "Not around ladies, George. That's man-to-man talk."
> Mother can say, "I don't like them at all but I know boys use them. I prefer not to hear them. Spare them for the locker room."[93]

If by now you are not suspicious of any rule that "protects" the female, you should be. Usually it protects the male from exposure, in this case exposure of the savagery behind his "respect" for the "ladies." Firestone explains:

> . . . to overhear a bull session is traumatic to a woman: all this time she has been considered only "ass," "meat," "twat," or "stuff," to be gotten a "piece of . . ."[94]

So potent is the right to blaspheme women that Jonathan, an eleven-year-old whose "masculinity" was under peer attack because he was unathletic, asked his mother to let him curse at her in front of his pals to "score" points with the fifth-grade boys.[95]

One weeps at the quid pro quo: defame mother and become a man. But one also sees in Jonathan's experience the importance of letting girls curse if we are going to let boys curse. Although I do not favor conversation riddled with profanity, to defuse "dirty words" and to inactivate them as defamers of the female, we must give them to our daughters to use when they must. Words are weapons and girls have been unarmed too long.

Just as boys must have the right to utter such forbidden words as "I'm sorry," "Help me," "I'm unhappy," "I was wrong,"[96] so that hurt can find words, we must give girls the power to profane so that words cannot hurt. Then we can get rid of the words themselves.

4. The Power to Make Someone Disappear

Rather than take the slave name Toby, Kunte Kinte almost died to keep his own name. He refused to disappear. His name contained his past. He wanted it to be his connection to the future. His master knew that to take the name Toby, Kunte Kinte would have to let another man tell him who he was. Kunte was the *person,* Toby was the slave. Pressing the metaphor, female human beings hug their chains. We let marriage erase our own names, subsume the identity we each accumulate in the nineteen or twenty-three or thirty-five years before we marry—all in return for the status "wife." We become "Mrs. Man,"[97] "Mrs. Him"; "The Walter Bacons Die in Car Accident" says the headline.[98] Were there two Walter Bacons, or did an invisible woman die that day, too?

If your daughter grows up thinking well of herself and living fully, she may choose to keep her birth name (not "maiden" name) rather than disappear on her wedding day.

Just as names encode the cult of sex differences, so do certain adjectives, similes, and homonyms (words that sound the same but mean different things). For example:

• The "man in the street" is Mr. Average. The "woman of the street" is a prostitute.

• A man who's down-and-out is a "bum." A woman who's a "bum" is a slut.

• If a man says, "I am married to a big baby," he means his wife is fearful or can't take responsibility for her own life. If a woman says it, she means her husband makes as many emotional and caretaking demands as her children.

• The unmarried man is a "bachelor," a "swinger," a "free agent." The unmarried woman is a "spinster," an "old maid," a sexual "reject."

• "I now pronounce you man and wife" keeps him intact as a person but makes her a role.

• "Like a man" (as in "You think like a man") is synonymous with "better than most women." But "like a woman" ("You drive like a woman") is an insult to a man *or* a woman. It simply means "inferior."

(When a friend told me a man he knew acted "like an old woman," I asked him *which* old woman: Golda Meir, Lillian Carter, or Georgia O'Keeffe?)

To advance the asymmetrical relationship of the sexes, people use different adjectives to describe identical behavior:

If a Person Is . . .	A Male Is Called . . .	A Female Is Called . . .
forceful	charismatic	domineering
aggressive	ambitious	castrating
angry	outraged	hysterical
talkative	articulate	gabby
curious	inquisitive	nosy
forgetful	absent-minded	scatterbrained
thinking idio-syncratically	brilliant	using women's logic
efficient	competent	compulsive
a strategist	shrewd	scheming
argumentative	persistent	strident
being sociable	chatting	gossiping
courageous	brave	brazen
plain-looking	average	homely

LANGUAGE TELLS CHILDREN "GIRLS ARE MEANT TO BE MOTHERS"

It does this by indicating in subtle, slippery ways that women are not meant to be very much else, and are peculiar if they are other than mothers.

To connote out-of-role behavior, we have such expressions as "career girl," "working mother," "woman lawyer." Similar modifiers—"career boy," "working father," "man lawyer"— would be ludicrous.

The universal salutations "Dear Sir" and "Gentlemen" on a business letter proclaim that people in responsible positions are *expected* to be males. (The informal "Dear Friend" and the inclusive "Dear Madam or Sir" are effortless alternatives.)

Job titles are supposed to be genderless designations for certain types of work. But language *usage* announces who is expected to occupy each job. James Reston writes:

Every U.S. Ambassador in capitals that have political problems with the United States has to be concerned about his safety and the security of his wife and children.[99]

Here's a riddle for you: The professor is a brother to the jockey but the jockey is not a brother to the professor. How can this be?

Answer: The professor is a man. The jockey is a woman. The jockey is a sister to the professor.

Riddle: Why don't we think of a female when we see nouns like jockey and professor?

Answer: Because the language never accustoms us to the sound of female authority or the names and titles that would inspire free associations between the word "woman" and something other than "mother."

LANGUAGE TELLS CHILDREN "BOYS ARE BETTER"

But first it establishes "the linguistic feeling that people are male until proven female."[100]

Children (and many of the rest of us) are totally literal about the spoken and written word. It takes years for a child to understand that Man is the name of the whole human race, not just that person with hair on his face, and that "he" is a generic pronoun meaning "he and she" some of the time.

When they hear "Man's Fight Against Cancer" or read "Man's Conquest of Space," children imagine male doctors and scientists.[101] "Every child should brush his teeth after meals" conjures a boy at the sink. Many people never do learn to include girls and women in such phrases as "the best man for the job," "the man of the hour," or "the champion of the working man."

Linguists insist that "Man" is understood to mean male and female, but little girls know better. They "have the task of making sense of the fact that they are both 'man' and 'not man' at the same time."[102]

Here's proof that the patriarchy is deceiving us:

- A few textbook statements tell who Man really is:
  - "Man's vital interests are life, food, and access to females."

- ". . . his back aches, he ruptures easily, his women have difficulty in childbirth."[103]

- "Man is the only primate that commits rape."[104]

- "All men are mortal" means to say we're all going to die. In a famous syllogism, that phrase introduces the paradigm test of philosophical validity:

All men are mortal. Socrates is a man. Therefore Socrates is mortal.

Substitute a woman's name for "Socrates" and there goes philosophy.[105]

Slogan: "Give a kid a job and help mold a man." (The Job Corps would have a job convincing me they mean a girl kid.) *Slogan:* "When your Heart Fund volunteer calls, give her a generous contribution." (Whatever became of the generic "he"?)
    In a patriarchal society the paid jobs "mold a man," and the volunteer jobs go to women.

- When researchers asked children to draw pictures illustrating "Social Man," "Industrial Man," and "Political Man," or "Society," "Industrial Life," and "Political Behavior," they all drew pictures of men for the first references, but the neutral references evoked both female and male images.[106]

- If "he" is really all-inclusive, why do vocational catalogues use "he" when referring to most subjects, but switch to "she" when describing secretarial and nursing courses?[107]

- If precision and accuracy are the bedrock of language, isn't there something absurd about saying: "Man, being a mammal, breastfeeds his young."[108] Or crying "Man Overboard" when a woman is swept off a ship. Or charging a driver with "Manslaughter" when the accident victim is a woman. Or writing, with a straight face, "Menstrual pain accounts for an enormous loss of man hours."[109]

- If "he" is simply the all-purpose *human* pronoun, why is nearly every *nonhuman* organism also referred to in English as "he"—with the exception of the pussycats, black widow spider and Miss Piggy? Is language saying that life itself is male?

- And if "he" is so multifunctional, why does "she" suddenly show up in the language as the generic pronoun to personify ships ("She's listing"), weather ("She's a twister, all right"), oceans, countries, cities, cars, and machines?[110]

Unconsciously our children take in that whatever is irrational or in need of man's control is a "she": a country, a ship, a thing, or a woman.

Who's kidding whom? Language functions to establish that it's a man's world and to equate man, the male person, with the condition of being human. Then man's needs become *human* needs. And many of women's needs are lost. For instance, when we say "the juvenile runaway, he . . ." or "the diabetic, he . . ." or "the senior citizen, he . . . ," we hide the fact that *most* individuals in those categories are female.[111]

Not important. What is important is the message that "he" is the main Man and "she" is the Other. He is the norm and she is either "like" or "unlike" him. He is the standard. This is communicated partly by exposure, by the hundreds of "he's" for every "she" in books, conversation, advertising, entertainment, schools, everywhere. In classrooms presided over mostly by women, it is mostly "man" and the names of specific men that children hear and see.[112]

In phonetic alphabets, long-distance telephone operators, police, air traffic controllers, and ham radio operators use male referents, ("C" as in "Charlie") for 9 out of 10 sex-linked words in seven alphabets studied.[113] Everywhere, "he," "him," "his," "man," "men" and the names of men.

Repetition gives boys a linguistic reality wherever they turn. The infrequency of "she" makes female reality unfamiliar and obscure. When "she" appears as a counterpart to "he," it is in a separate category—the ladies' auxiliary of the man's language.

The clues leak from the "feminine" suffixes, which add letters but deplete status. Man is an "actor," one who acts; woman is an "actress," a *female* who acts. These are just male and female titles of the same craft, you say? Then take it further. A "priest" is a religious leader; a "priestess" suggests "mumbo jumbo and pagan goings on."[114] A governess is hardly the equal of a governor, nor a major the same as a majorette.

Just as leather is to leatherette so is man's title to woman's title—as real is to imitation.

Now, about prefixes. Put a female-specifying word in front of a noun and you designate a subspecies (doctor/woman doctor; the gym/the girls' gym; golf/ladies' golf). Or an annex: "the women's page" as opposed to the whole newspaper, which is for men, and of course "Woman's Place," as opposed to every place else.

Again, who's kidding whom? Why does your daughter have to learn to count herself *in* when she hears "All men are brothers," but keep out when she sees "Men Only"?[115]

Even if he was desperate for a job, would your son apply for a "waitress" opening? Studies show the answer is *No* whatever the sex-linked job.[116]

What man or boy would feel significantly connected to history if he read "The pioneers moved West taking their husbands and children with them." What man would feel included in "All women are sisters," or "The child is mother to the woman"?

Language is not trivial when you are part of the group left out. Those who have been hearing "me" and "I" in "Man" and "he" may not immediately understand that visibility starts with The Word. Even a pronoun can be an image-maker. College women exposed to the generic "she" in a research experiment reported gaining "feelings of pride, importance, superiority, freedom and power."[117] Let boys and men who think words "trivial" try to live for just one week with reverse linguistics: say "Every child should brush her teeth." Shout "Woman Overboard" next time a boy falls out of your rowboat. Ask a local merchant to "Give a kid a job and help mold a woman," and remember that Woman is the name of the human race. How does it feel?

Business men should understand. When a brand name is used for a generic product—Kleenex instead of tissues, or Xerox instead of photocopy—other tissue and photocopier manufacturers feel angry and left out.[118] Well, Man is a brand name for male human. Use it and female humans feel left out.

After you finish with the "trivia" objectors, get ready for the purists. Nonsexist language is awkward, ugly, cumbersome, they claim. "He or she" is not graceful. "What do you want, *person-*

holes?" (No, "streetholes" or "workholes" will do.) Ask the purists,

> What is clear or graceful about referring to women as men? What is fine or beautiful in perpetuating a usage that makes nonpersons out of 53 percent of the population?[119]

If we can tolerate hundreds of words of three or more syllables and such leaden expressions as "finalize" or "personal flotation device," surely we can handle "he or she" and "her and him." (The sequence of pronouns matters, too). "She or he," even more than the plural "solution," to sexist pronouns ("children should brush their teeth"), reminds listeners that "she" belongs in every context.

There are endless "solutions," most of them entirely graceful and reasonable—"synthetic," "handmade," or "machine-made" instead of that "manmade" lake David objected to—and if they don't come readily to mind, you can get a few booklets to start you thinking of nonsexist alternatives for every form of speech.[120]

People who cared enough to consciously change their speaking habits were found to be at ease with the new speech style within months.[121] (How long did it take you to learn to say black instead of Negro?) Parents of young children should be among those most motivated to change, for it is the words of their mother and father that echo in children's heads forever.

With consciousness and those few principles of nonsexist language usage comes the compulsion to unlearn. Believe me, once your mind "knows," old words will not form in your mouth. You will not be content to answer without answering back. You will see differently because you hear the language as if for the first time. And along with your new sensitivity to words will come awareness of actions and reactions, gestures, attitudes, and patterns of behavior—your own, your children's, and everyone else's—until you become, almost without trying, proudly and irresistibly antisexist and prochild.

You'll change a thousand no's to yeses, and open up your children's half-lives to the world. And that's when your children will start growing up free.

Notes

2 • Girls and Boys: What's the Difference?, page 8

1. The physical, biological, and behavioral differences described in this chapter were culled from a variety of sources:
—L. M. Terman and L. Tyler, "Psychological Sex Differences," in L. Carmichael, ed. *Manual of Child Psychology,* John Wiley and Sons (New York: 1954) 1080–1100.
—J. E. Garai and A. Scheinfeld, "Sex Differences in Mental and Behavioral Traits," *Genetic Psychology Monographs,* 1968, 77, 169–299.
—M. S. Teitelbaum, ed. *Sex Differences: Social and Biological Perspectives,* Anchor Books (New York: 1976).
—E. Tobach and B. Rosoff, eds. *Genes and Gender,* Gordian Press (New York: 1978).
—J. Money and A. A. Ehrhardt, *Man and Woman, Boy and Girl,* Johns Hopkins University Press (Baltimore: 1972).
—J. Money and P. Tucker, *Sexual Signatures: On Being a Man or a Woman,* Little, Brown (Boston: 1975).
—B. Birns, "The Emergence and Socialization of Sex Differences in the Earliest Years," *Merrill-Palmer Quarterly,* 1976, 22, 3, 229–253.
—E. E. Maccoby, ed. *The Development of Sex Differences,* Stanford University Press (Stanford, Calif.: 1966).
—E. E. Maccoby and C. N. Jacklin, *The Psychology of Sex Differences,* Stanford University Press (Stanford: 1974).
2. J. Money and P. Tucker, *op. cit.* (note 1) 47.
3. M. B. Parlee, "The Rhythm in Men's Lives," *Psychology Today,* April 1978, 82.
4. R. Edwards, *Sexual Behavior,* January 1972, 16.
5. M. Miller, Boston, Mass., letter to the editors, *Ms.* magazine, September 1977, 4.
6. Gazette, *Ms.* magazine, June 1978, 22.
7. J. K. Meuli, "In Brief," *National NOW Times,* December 1977, 2.
8. S. Edmiston, "Some Women Are Equal and Others Are More Equal," *Your Place,* April 1978, 60.
9. J. Ullyot, "Are Women Stronger than Men?" *Harpers Bazaar,* May 1977, 46.
10. S. Edmiston, *op. cit.* (note 8) 63.
11. "Who Says Athletes Can't Be Pregnant," *Ms.* magazine, July 1978, 47–51.
12. J. E. Garai and A. Scheinfeld, *op. cit.* (note 1).
13. E. E. Maccoby and C. N. Jacklin, *op. cit.* (note 1).
14. J. H. Block, "Issues, Problems and Pitfalls in Assessing Sex Differences," *Merrill-Palmer Quarterly,* 1976, 22, 4, 283–307.
15. L. W. Hoffman, "Changes in Family Roles, Socialization and Sex Differences," *American Psychologist,* August 1977, 32, 8, 644–657.
16. E. H. Erickson, "Sex Differences in the Play Configurations of Preadolescents," *American Journal of Orthopsychiatry,* 1951, 21, 667.
17. This drawing is adapted from Figure 1, illustrating overlap in height, as it appears in J. Trebilcot, "Sex Roles: the Argument from Nature," in M. B. Mahowald, ed. *Philosophy of Woman,* Hackett Photography (Indianapolis: 1978) 290.
18. G. T. Hirsch, "Non-Sexist Childrearing: Demythifying Normative Data," *The Family Coordinator,* April 1974, 166.
19. *Ibid.*
20. S. G. Kennedy, "In a Study of Newborns, the Boys Seem More Active," *The New York Times,* March 31, 1978.

21. G. Mitchell, W. K. Redican and J. Gomber, "Lesson from a Primate: Males Can Raise Babies," *Psychology Today,* April 1974, 63–68.
22. I. K. Broverman, D. M. Broverman, F. E. Clarkson, P. S. Rosenkrantz and S. R. Vogel, "Sex-Role Stereotypes and Clinical Judgements of Mental Health," *Journal of Consulting and Clinical Psychology,* 1970, 34, 1, 1–7.
23. R. Rosenthal and L. Jacobson, *Pygmalion in the Classroom: Teacher Expectation and Pupil's Intellectual Development,* Holt, Rinehart and Winston (New York: 1968).
24. L. S. Radloff, "Sex Differences in Helplessness—with Implications for Depression," in L. S. Hansen and R. S. Rapoza, eds. *Career Development and Counseling of Women,* Charles Thomas, publishers (Springfield, Ill.: 1978) 199–221.
25. K. Millett, *Sexual Politics,* Avon Books (New York: 1971) 221.
26. D. W. Tresemer, "Assumptions Made about Gender Roles," in M. Millman and R. M. Kanter, eds. *Another Voice,* Anchor Books (New York: 1975) 313.
27. E. E. Maccoby & C. N. Jacklin, *op. cit.* (note 1) 227, 352.
28. E. W. Goodenough, "Interest in Persons as an Aspect of Sex Differences in the Early Years," *Genetic Psychology Monographs,* 1957, 55, 302.
29. P. Sexton, *The Feminized Male,* Random House (New York: 1969) 127.
30. C. Loo and C. Wenar, "Activity Level and Motor Inhibition," *Child Development,* 1961, 42, 967–971.
31. E. W. Goodenough, *op. cit.* (note 28) 302.
32. E. E. Maccoby and C. N. Jacklin, *op. cit.* (note 1) 327–329.
33. R. G. D'Andrade, "Sex Differences and Cultural Institutions," in E. E. Maccoby, (1966) *op. cit.* (note 1) 191–194.
—C. Pope and B. Whiting, "A Cross-cultural Analysis,of Sex Differences in the Behavior of Children Aged Three to Eleven," *Journal of Social Psychology,* 1973, 91, 171.
—H. A. Barry, M. K. Bacon and I. L. Child, "A Cross-Cultural Survey of Some Sex Differences in Socialization," *Journal of Abnormal and Social Psychology,* 1957, 55, 327–332.
—R. P. Rohner, "Sex Differences in Aggression: Phylogenic and Enculturation Perspectives," *Ethos,* Spring 1976, 4, 1, 57–72.
34. R. P. Rohner, *ibid.,* 61–62.
35. H. Barry III, 1975, personal communication cited in R. P. Rohner, *ibid.,* 63–64.
36. *Ibid.,* 70.
37. The study was originally reported in J. Money and A. A. Ehrhardt, 1972, *op. cit.* (note 1) 95–103. A popularized, nonacademic version appears in J. Money and P. Tucker, (1975) *op. cit.* (note 1) 63–72.
38. J. Money and A. A. Ehrhardt, *ibid.,* 99.
39. J. Money and P. Tucker, *ibid.,* 70.
40. J. Money and A. Ehrhardt, *op. cit.* 99.
41. J. Money and P. Tucker, *op. cit.* 70.
42. *Webster's Collegiate Dictionary,* Fifth Edition.
43. G. Steinem, "Women's Liberation Aims to Free Men, Too," *Washington Post,* June 7, 1970.
44. For this insight and for many of the critical concepts in the following sections, I am indebted to E. Reed, *Sexism in Science,* Pathfinder Press (New York: 1978).
45. T. P. Hanaway and G. M. Burghardt, "Girls, Boys and Books," *Psychology Today,* August 1976, 67.
46. K. Lorenz, *On Aggression,* Harcourt, Brace & World (New York: 1966) 29.
47. E. Reed, *op. cit.* (note 44) 75.
48. *Ibid.,* 80.
49. L. Tiger, *Men in Groups,* Vintage (New York: 1970) 241.
50. "Why You Do What You Do—Sociobiology: A New Theory of Behavior," *Time,* August 1, 1977, 57.
51. E. O. Wilson, *Sociobiology: The New Synthesis,* Belknap Press (Cambridge, Mass.: 1975); E. O. Wilson, *On Human Nature,* Harvard (Cambridge: 1978).
52. "Sociobiology and Sex," *Time,* August 1, 1977, 63.
53. R. Ardrey, *The Territorial Imperative,* Dell (New York: 1966) 45–51, quoted in M. Crawford, "Evolution Made Me Do It: Women, Men and Animal Behavior," *International Journal of Women's Studies,* 1978, 1, 534. The reasoning in this section is based on Crawford's arguments.
54. M. Crawford, *ibid.* For a taste of the controversy aroused by sociobiology, see A. L. Caplan, ed. *The Sociology Debate,* Harper and Row (New York: 1978); C. Geertz, "Socio-sexology," *The New York Review of Books,* January 24, 1980, 3–4.

552

55. S. L. Washburn and D. A. Hamburg, "Aggressive Behavior in Old World Monkeys and Apes," quoted in Reed, *op. cit.* (note 44) 9.
56. G. G. Simpson, referred to in E. Reed, *ibid.,* 13.
57. C. L. Carpenter, "Societies of Monkeys and Apes," quoted in Reed, *ibid.,* 29.
58. E. Friedl, "Society and Sex Roles," *Human Nature,* April 1978, 71.
59. L. Tiger and R. Fox, *The Imperial Animal,* Holt, Rinehart and Winston (New York: 1971) 211.
60. A. Snider, "Female Governments Called Key to Survival," *New York Post,* (date unknown); H. Block, *Psychic War in Men and Women,* New York University Press (New York: 1976) xiii.
61. P. Sexton, *op. cit.* (note 29) 112.
62. *Statistical Abstracts,* 1977, 65.
63. E. E. Maccoby and C. N. Jacklin, *op. cit.* (note 1) 239; L. Holliday, *The Violent Sex: Male Psychobiology and the Evolution of Consciousness,* Bluestocking Books (Guerneville, Calif.: 1978), 95–103; and H. D. Williams, "A Survey of Predelinquent Children in Ten Middle Western Cities," *Journal of Juvenile Research,* 1933, 17, 163.

3 • *The Politics of Sex Roles, page 30*

1. D. A. Hamburg and D. T. Lunde, "Sex Hormones in the Development of Sex Differences in Human Behavior," in E. E. Maccoby, *The Development of Sex Differences,* Stanford University Press (Stanford, Calif.: 1966) 16. and R. J. Stoller, *Sex and Gender,* Science House (New York: 1968) 39. Also J. A. Kleeman, "Establishment of Core Gender Identity in Normal Girls," *Archives of Sexual Behavior* 1971, 1, 2, 103–129.
2. R. G. Slaby and K. S. Frey, "Development of Gender Constancy and Selective Attention to Same-Sex Models," *Child Development,* 1975, 46, 849–856.
3. S. K. Thompson, "Gender Labels and Early Sex Role Development," *Child Development,* 1975, 46, 339–347. Also, M. Rabban, "Sex Role Identification in Young Children in Two Diverse Social Groups," *Genetic Psychological Monographs,* 1950, 42, 81–158; D. G. Brown, "Sex Role Development in a Changing Culture," *Psychological Bulletin,* 1958, 55, 232–242; J. Kagan, *Understanding Children: Behavior Motives and Thought,* Harcourt Brace Jovanovich, (New York: 1971); L. Kohlberg, "A Cognitive-Developmental Analysis of Children's Sex-Role Concepts and Attitudes," in E. Maccoby, (1966) *op. cit.* (note 1) 94.
4. L. Kohlberg, *ibid.,* 95–96.
5. *Ibid.,* p. 104. Also L. Kohlberg and D. Z. Ullian, "Stages in the Development of Psychosexual Concepts and Attitudes," in R. C. Friedman, R. Richart and R. L. Vande Wiele, *Sex Differences in Behavior,* John Wiley and Sons (New York: 1975).
6. H. Gershman, "The Myth of Masculinity: A Panel," *American Journal of Psychoanalysis,* 1973, 33, 1, 63–64.
7. J. Money, J. Hampson and J. Hampson, "Imprinting and the Establishment of Gender Role," *Archives of Neurological Psychiatry,* 1957, 77, 333–336.
8. C. C. Naffziger and K. Naffziger, "Development of Sex Role Stereotypes," *The Family Coordinator,* July 1974, 251–252.
9. *Ibid.*
10. B. Roszak and T. Roszak, "Forward," in *Masculine/Feminine: Readings in Sexual Mythology and the Liberation of Women,* Harper Colophon Books (New York: 1969) vii.
11. A. Vener and C. Snyder, "The Preschool Child's Awareness and Anticipation of Adult Sex Roles," *Sociometry,* 1966, 29. Also S. K. Thompson, *op. cit.* (note 3); M. Rabban, *op. cit.* (note 3) 106–118; L. Kohlberg, *op. cit.* (note 3) 117.
12. E. E. Maccoby and C. N. Jacklin, *The Psychology of Sex Differences,* Stanford University Press (Stanford, Calif.: 1974) 284.
13. B. I. Fagot, "Consequences of Moderate Cross-Gender Behavior in Preschool Children," *Child Development,* 1977, 48, 902–907.
14. A. Bandura, D. Ross and S. A. Ross, "A Comparative Test of the Status Envy, Social Power and Secondary Reinforcement Theories of Identificatory Learning," *Journal of Abnormal Social Psychology,* 1963, 67, 6, 527–534.
15. D. E. Papalia and S. S. Tennent, "Vocational Aspirations in Preschoolers: A Manifestation of Early Sex Role Stereotyping," *Sex Roles,* 1975, 1, 2, 197–199.
16. A. Beuf, "Doctor, Lawyer, Household Drudge," *Journal of Communications,* Spring 1974, 142–145.

17. G. Woodruff, "The Sex Role Concepts of the Kindergarten, First and Second Grade Child as a Function of Their Home Environment," thesis submitted for the Ph.D. in Education, Graduate College of Boston College, 1974, 55.

18. J. E. Williams, S. M. Bennett and D. L. Best, "Awareness and Expression of Sex Stereotypes in Young Children," *Developmental Psychology,* 1975, 11, 5, 635–642.

19. L. Kohlberg, *op. cit.* (note 3) 99–101.

20. R. E. Hartley, "Sex-Role Pressures and the Socialization of the Male Child," *Psychological Reports,* 1959, 5, 457–458.

21. R. E. Hartley and A. Klein, "Sex-Role Concepts among Elementary-School-Age Girls," *Marriage and Family Living,* February 1959, 59–64.

22. P. Sexton, *The Feminized Male,* Random House (New York: 1969) 119.

23. P. Minuchin, "Sex Differences in Children," *National Elementary Principal,* November 1966, 46, 2, 47.

24. A. H. Stein and J. Smithells, "Age and Sex Differences in Children's Sex Role Standards about Achievement," *Developmental Psychology,* 1969, 1, 252–259.

25. J. Kagan, "The Child's Sex-Role Classification of School Objects," *Child Development,* 1965, 34, 1051–1056.

26. F. Wesley and C. Wesley, *Sex-Role Psychology,* Human Sciences Press (New York: 1977) 63.

27. L. Terman and C. Miles, *Sex and Personality,* McGraw-Hill (New York: 1936).

28. L. F. Bernhagen, "Sexuality, Personality and Stereotyping," *School Health Review,* November–December 1974, 5, 23–26.

29. *Ibid.*

30. J. Kagan, *op. cit.* (note 25).

31. A. H. Stein and J. Smithells, *op. cit.* (note 24) 258.

32. "30 Percent of Youths Say Women Belong Home," *The New York Times,* June 13, 1977.

33. P. Rosenkrantz, S. Vogel, H. Bee, I. Broverman and D. Broverman, "Sex-Role Stereotypes and Self-Concepts in College Students," *Journal of Consulting and Clinical Psychology,* 1968, 32, 3, 287–293.

34. J. E. Williams and S. Bennett, "The Definition of Sex Stereotypes via the Adjective Check List," *Sex Roles,* 1975, 1, 4, 327–337.

35. Salzman-Webb quoted in M. H. Garskof, *Roles Women Play,* Brooks/Cole (Calif.:1971).

36. B. Yorburg and I. Arafat, "Current Sex-Role Conceptions and Conflict," *Sex Roles,* 1975, 1, 2, 137.

37. B. I. Fagot, "Sex Related Stereotyping of Toddlers' Behaviors," *Developmental Psychology,* 1973, 9, 3, 429; also K. J. Zucker, "Sex-Typing of Children's Toys by College Students and Fourth Graders," *Catalog of Selected Documents in Psychology,* February 1977, 7, 6–7.

38. C. V. Kiser, ed. *Research in Family Planning,* Princeton University Press (Princeton, N. J.: 1962); D. Grass, *Population and Population Policies in Europe;* K. Davis and J. Blake, "Social Structure and Fertility: An Analytic Framework," *Economic Development and Cultural Change,* 1956, 4, 211–214; Dr. C. Titze, Population Council, New York City; J. Dornberg, "Eastern Europe: Programming the Population," *Ms.* magazine, November 1974, 128–130.

39. S. de Beauvoir, *The Second Sex,* Bantam (New York: 1961) 58–59.

40. L. Kohlberg, *op. cit.* (note 3) 100.

41. G. T. Hirsch, "Nonsexist Childrearing: Demythifying Normative Data," *Family Coordinator,* April 1974, 168.

42. S. Sontag, lecture presented at the National Women's Political Caucus luncheon, New York City, June 22, 1978.

43. L. Kohlberg, *op. cit.* (note 3) 101–102.

44. *Ibid.*

45. D. L. Gillespie, "Who Had the Power? The Marital Struggle," *Journal of Marriage and the Family,* 1971, 33, 445–458.

46. J. W. Thibaut and H. H. Kelley, *The Social Psychology of Groups,* John Wiley and Sons (New York: 1959) and D. M. Wolfe, "Power and Authority in the Family," in D. Cartwright, ed. *Studies in Social Power,* University of Michigan (Ann Arbor: 1959), 99–117.

47. J. Bernard, *The Future of Marriage,* Bantam (New York: 1973).

48. L. Kohlberg, *op. cit.* (note 3) 116.

554

49. *Ibid.,* 100.
50. "Men, Women, What's the Difference?" National Educational Television poll, taken on the program *Woman Alive!* Results dated January 14, 1977.
51. R. E. Hartley, *op. cit.* (note 20) 463–464.
52. *Ibid.,* 464.
53. M. Mead, *Male and Female,* William Morrow (New York: 1975) 315.
54. B. Yorburg and I. Arafat, *op. cit.* (note 36).
55. D. G. Brown, "Sex-Role Development in a Changing Culture," *Psychological Bulletin,* 1958, 55, 4, 232–242.
56. National Educational Television poll, *op. cit.* (note 50).
57. *The New York Times,* July 29, 1978, 1. Then see "Christina Onassis Kin Say She Plans Divorce," *The New York Times,* December 9, 1979.
58. J. P. McKee and A. C. Sherriffs, "The Differential Evaluation of Males and Females," *Journal of Personality,* 1957, 25, 356–371; D. G. Brown, *op. cit.* (note 55); J. D. Osofsky and H. J. Osofsky, "Androgyny as a Life Style," *The Family Coordinator,* October 1972, 21, 4, 415; S. C. Nash, "The Relationship Among Sex-Role Stereotyping, Sex-Role Preference and the Sex Difference in Spatial Visualization," *Sex Roles,* 1975, 1, 1, 27–29.
59. A. Battle-Sister, "Conjectures on the Female Culture Question," *Journal of Marriage and the Family,* August 1971, 411–420.
60. D. G. Brown, *op. cit.* (note 55) 235.
61. A. Beuf, *op. cit.* (note 16) 144.
62. S. Smith, "Age and Sex Differences in Children's Opinions concerning Sex Differences," *Journal of Genetic Psychology,* 1939, 54, 18.
63. B. Certner, *Sex Roles and Mental Health: A Proposal for the Development of the Sex Roles Institute,* 1976, The Psychiatric Institute Foundation, Washington, D.C., 11–21.
64. M. Rabban, *op. cit.* (note 3).
65. B. Rice, "The Power of a Frilly Apron: Coming of Age in Sodom and New Milford," *Psychology Today,* September 1975, 64.
66. T. Simpson, in *Texas High School Coaches Association Magazine,* May 1973, quoted in *The New York Times,* May 22, 1973.
67. M. Mead, *op. cit.* (note 53) 318.
68. D. G. Brown, "Sex Role Preference in Young Children," *Psychological Monographs,* 1956, 70, 14, 10.
69. R. E. Hartley, *op. cit.* (note 20) 460.
70. D. B. Lynn, "Sex Differences in Masculine and Feminine Identification," *Psychological Review,* 1959, 66, 2, 128–129.
71. K. Millett, *Sexual Politics,* Doubleday (New York: 1970).
72. N. K. Schlossberg and J. Goodman, "A Woman's Place: Children's Sex Stereotyping of Occupations," *Vocational Guidance Quarterly,* 1972, 20, 266–270.
73. K. Deaux and T. Emswiller, "Explanations of Successful Performances on Sex-Linked Tasks," *Journal of Personality and Social Psychology,* 1974, 29, 1, 80–85.
74. L. Bennetts, "More Women Become Surgeons, Even Though Barriers Fall Slowly," *The New York Times,* July 18, 1978, C2.
75. R. E. Hartley and A. Klein, *op. cit.* (note 21) 63.
76. A. Beuf, *op. cit.* (note 16) 144.
77. I. Broverman, S. R. Vogel, D. M. Browerman, F. Clarkson and P. Rosenkrantz, "Sex-Role Stereotypes: A Current Appraisal," *Journal of Social Issues,* 1972, 28, 2, 72–75. Also R. E. Hartley and A. Klein, *op. cit.* (note 21) 61.

4 • Everything to Gain. . . , page 55

1. E. E. Maccoby, "Sex Differences in Intellectual Functioning," in E. E. Maccoby, ed. *The Development of Sex Differences,* Stanford University Press (Stanford, Calif.: 1966) 31–32; J. H. Pleck, "Masculinity-Femininity: Current and Alternative Paradigms," *Sex Roles,* 1975, 1, 2, 167.
2. H. B. Biller, *Paternal Deprivation: Family School, Sexuality and Society,* Lexington Books/D. C. Heath (Lexington, Mass.: 1974) 145–149. Also P. Sexton, *The Feminized Male,* Random House (New York: 1969), 61; P. Minuchin, "Sex Differences in Children: Research Findings in an Educational Context," *National Elementary Principal,* November 1966, 46, 2, 47.

3. A. B. Heilbrun, Jr., "Sex-Role Identity and Achievement Motivation," *Psychological Reports*, 1963, 12, 483–490; V. O'Leary, "Some Attitudinal Barriers to Occupational Aspirations in Women," *Psychological Bulletin*, 1974, 81, 809–826; A. P. Webb, "Sex-Role Preferences and Adjustment in Early Adolescence," *Child Development*, 1963, 34, 609–618; J. Joesting, "Comparison of Women's Liberation Members with Their Non-member Peers," *Psychological Reports*, 1971, 29, 1291–1294; B. A. Putnam and J. C. Hansen, "Relationship of Self-Concept and Feminine Role Concept to Vocational Maturity in Young Women," *Journal of Counseling Psychology*, 1972, 19, 436–440; L. J. Neiman, "The Influence of Peer Groups upon Attitudes toward the Feminine Role," *Social Problems*, 1954, 2, 104–111.
4. Z. Ponzo, "A Study to Determine Relations in Role Identity, Scholastic Aptitude, Achievement and Non-academic Factors among Male and Female Students," Office of Education, (1967) Department of Health, Education and Welfare, Bureau of Research, Washington, D.C.; H. B. Biller, *op. cit.* (note 2) 143–144.
5. E. E. Maccoby, *op. cit.* (note 1).
6. M. Whiteside, "Age and Sex Differences in Self-Perception as Related to Ideal Trait Selections," *Adolescence*, 1976, II, 44, 589.
7. P. Sexton, *op. cit.* (note 2) 59–71, 86, 220.
8. A. P. Webb, *op. cit.* (note 3) 616–617.
9. E. E. Maccoby, *op. cit.* (note 1) 27; P. Sexton, *op. cit.* (note 2) 106–110. Also see findings of *National Assessment of Educational Progress*, Denver, Colorado, 1974.
10. C. Dweck, University of Illinois experiment reported in A. Rosenfield, "Learning to Give Up," *Saturday Review*, September 3, 1977, 37.
11. J. O. Robertson, "Sugar 'n Spice 'n Male Chauvinism," *The New York Times*, July 17, 1974.
12. J. S. Coleman, *The Adolescent Society*, The Free Press (Glencoe, Ill.: 1961).
13. Z. Ponzo, *op. cit.* (note 4) 112.
14. J. Frymier, et al., "A Longitudinal Study of Academic Motivation," *Journal of Educational Research*, 1975, 69, 63–66; J. Lipman-Blumen, "How Ideology Shapes Women's Lives," *Scientific American*, January 1972, 226, 1.
15. P. Minuchin, "Sex-Role Concepts and Sex-Typing in Childhood as a Function of School and Home Environment," *Child Development*, 1965, 36, 1033–1048.
16. W. Mischel, "A Social-Learning View of Sex Differences in Behavior," in E. E. Maccoby, ed. *op. cit.* (note 1) 71; J. W. Seaver, "The Sex Differentiated Interaction of Environmental and Hereditary Determinants of Intelligence," unpublished paper, Pennsylvania State University, *ERIC #ED 131946PS008977*.
17. V. J. Crandall, et al., "Motivational and Ability Determinants of Young Children's Intellectual Achievement Behaviors," *Child Development*, 1962, 33, 643–661.
18. V. J. Crandall and A. Rabson, "Children's Repetition Choices in an Intellectual Achievement Situation Following Success and Failure," *Journal of Genetic Psychology*, 1960, 97, 161–168; B. S. Wallston, "The Effects of Sex-Role Ideology, Self-Esteem and Expected Future Interactions with an Audience on Male Help-seeking," *Sex Roles*, 1976, 4, 353–365.
19. "He's Smart, She Tries," *Psychology Today*, September 1978, 78; "College Women and Self-Esteem," *The New York Times*, December 10, 1978.
20. K. Deaux and T. Emswiller, "Explanations of Successful Performance on Sex-linked Tasks: What Is Skill for the Male Is Luck for the Female," *Journal of Personality and Social Psychology*, 1974, 29, 1, 80–85; K. Deaux, "Ah She Was Just Lucky," *Psychology Today*, December 1976, 70, 75; N. T. Feather and J. G. Simon, "Reactions to Male and Female Success and Failure in Sex-Linked Occupations," *Journal of Personality and Social Psychology*, 1975, 31, 20–31; H. Teglasi, "Sex-Role Orientation, Achievement Motivation, and Causal Attributions of College Females," *Sex Roles*, 1978, 5, 3, 381–397.
21. R. Levine, et al., "Fear of Failure in Males: A More Salient Factor Than Fear of Success," *Sex Roles*, 1976, 2, 4, 389–398.
22. E. E. Maccoby and C. N. Jacklin, *The Psychology of Sex Differences*, Stanford University Press (Stanford, Calif.: 1974) 133; J. Kagan and H. A. Moss, *From Birth to Maturity*, John Wiley and Sons (New York: 1962); R. B. Kundsin, ed. *Women and Success: The Anatomy of Achievement*, William Morrow (New York: 1974); J. Arbuthnot, "Sex, Sex-Role Identity and Cognitive Style," *Perceptual and Motor Skills*, 1975, 41, 435–440; S. C. Nash, "The Relationship between Sex-Role Stereotyping, Sex-Role Preference and the Sex Difference in Spatial Visualization," *Sex Roles*, 1975, 11, 15–32.

23. L. Kohlberg, "A Cognitive-Developmental Analysis of Children's Sex-Role Concepts and Attitudes," in E. E. Maccoby, *op. cit.* (note 1) 121.

24. D. C. McClelland, et al., *The Achievement Motive,* Appleton Century Crofts (New York: 1953); S. L. Sutherland, "The Unambitious Female: Low Professional Aspirations," *Signs,* 1978, 3, 4, 791.

25. L. Kohlberg, *op. cit.* (note 23).

26. M. H. Kingston, "Hers," *The New York Times,* July 13, 1978, C2. Also see, V. Murphy-Berman, "Effects of Success and Failure on Perceptions of Gender Identity," *Sex Roles,* 1976, 2, 4, 373.

27. M. Mead, *Male and Female* (1949), Morrow Paperback (New York: 1975) 321.

28. Erwin N. Griswold, Dean 1946–1967, Harvard Law School.

29. M. Mead, *op. cit.* (note 27) 322.

30. M. S. Horner, "Sex Differences in Achievement Motivation and Performance in Competitive and Non-competitive Situations," Ph.D. dissertation, University of Michigan, 1968, 157.

31. M. S. Horner, "Fail: Bright Women," *Psychology Today,* November 1969, 36. Also see the following revisions and refinements of the concept: N. Romer, "Sex-related Differences in the Development of the Motive to Avoid Success, Sex-Role Identification and Performance in Competitive and Non-competitive Conditions," *Psychology of Women Quarterly,* Spring 1977, 1, 3, 261; V. O'Leary and B. Hammack, "Sex-Role Orientation and Achievement Context as Determinants of the Motive to Avoid Success," *Sex Roles,* 1975, 1, 3, 225–234; G. K. Baruch, "Sex-Role Stereotypes, the Motive to Avoid Success and Parental Identification: A Comparison of Preadolescent and Adolescent Girls," *Sex Roles,* 1975, 1, 303–309; special issue on "Fear of Success" published by *Sex Roles,* 1976, 2, 3; D. W. Tresemer, *Fear of Success,* Plenum (New York: 1977).

32. M. S. Horner, *op. cit.* (note 31) 37.

33. N. Romer, *op. cit.* (note 31) 265.

34. B. Kimball and R. L. Leahy, "Fear of Success in Males and Females," *Sex Roles,* 1976 2, 3, 280; B. Mausner and B. Colles, "Avoidance of Success Among Women," *International Journal of Women's Studies,* 1, 1, 47.

35. J. S. Coleman, *op. cit.* (note 12).

36. A. Symonds, "The Myth of Femininity: A Panel," *American Journal of Psychoanalysis,* 1973, 33, 1, 43; S. L. Sutherland, *op. cit.* (note 24) 783–784; M. S. Horner, "Toward an Understanding of Achievement-Related Conflict in Women," in J. Stacey, S. Bereaud and J. Daniels, eds. *And Jill Came Tumbling After,* Dell (New York: 1974) 53.

37. D. M. Kipnis, "Inner Direction, Other Direction and Achievement Motivation," *Human Development,* 1974, 17, 333; J. T. Spence, "The TAT and Attitudes toward Achievement in Women: A New Look at the Motive to Avoid Success and a New Method of Achievement," *Journal of Consulting and Clinical Psychology,* 1974, 42, 427–437; L. Monahan, et al., "Intrapsychic versus Cultural Explanations of the 'Fear of Success' Motive," *Journal of Personality and Social Psychology,* 1974, 29, 60–64.

38. M. E. Lockheed, "Female Motives to Avoid Success," *Sex Roles,* 1975, 1, 1, 46.

39. L. W. Hoffman, "Early Childhood Experiences and Women's Achievement Motives," *Journal of Social Issues,* 1972, 28, 129–155; B. Kimball and R. L. Leahy, *op. cit.* (note 34) 279; S. W. Morgan and B. Mausner, "Behavioral and Fantasied Indicators of Avoidance of Success in Men and Women," *Journal of Personality,* 1973, 41, 457–470; D. W. Tresemer, "Fear of Success: Popular but Unproven," *Psychology Today,* July 1974, 7, 82–83.

40. J. M. Jellison, et al., "Achievement Behavior: A Situational Interpretation," *Sex Roles,* 1975, 1, 4, 369–384; L. M. Argote, et al., "Competitiveness in Males and Females: Situational Determinants of Fear of Success Behavior," *Sex Roles,* 1974, 2, 3, 295–303; R. Winchel, et al., "Impact of Co-education on 'Fear of Success' Imagery Expressed by Male and Female High School Students," *Journal of Educational Psychology,* 1974, 66, 726–730; L. Shapiro, "Did Fear of Success Fail?" *Ms.* magazine, July 1977, 19; P. Shaver, "Questions concerning Fear of Success and Its Conceptual Relatives," *Sex Roles,* 1976, 2, 3, 305–320.

41. From the Collected Poetical Works of John Greenleaf Whittier, cited in M. Mead, *op. cit.* (note 27) 317.

42. L. Shapiro, *op. cit.* (note 40).

43. S. Polykoff, *Does She or Doesn't She?,* Doubleday (Garden City, New York: 1975) printers' galleys, 64.

44. National Educational Television Poll on Masculinity and Femininity, "Men, Women,

What's the Difference?" taken for the program *Woman Alive!* Results dated January 14, 1977. Also see M. Mead, *op. cit.* (note 27) 315.

45. R. Wahrman and M. D. Pugh, "Sex, Non-conformity and Influence," *Sociometry,* 1974, 37, 137–147; N. T. Feather and J. G. Simon, *op. cit.* (note 20); N. Costrich, et al., "When Stereotypes Hurt: Three Studies of Penalties for Sex-Role Reversals," *Journal of Experimental Social Psychology,* 1975, 11, 520–530; R. P. Hawkins and S. Pingree, "A Developmental Exploration of the Fear of Success Phenomenon as a Cultural Stereotype," *Sex Roles,* 1978, 4, 4, 539–547.

46. W. Mischel, *op. cit.* (note 16) 70; A. S. Epstein and N. Radin, "Motivational Components Related to Father Behavior and Cognitive Functioning in Pre-schoolers," *Child Development,* 1975, 46, 831–839; H. Biller, *op. cit.* (note 2) 147; R. K. Unger, "Status, Power and Gender: An Examination of Parallelisms," paper presented at the conference, New Directions for Research on Women, Madison, Wisconsin, 1975.

47. M. Mead, *op. cit.* (note 27) 310–311.

48. J. Nuttal, "Sex Differences in Patterns of Emotion," National Institute of Education, Department of Health, Education and Welfare, ERIC #ED131365CG010913; J. Money and P. Tucker, *Sexual Signatures,* Little, Brown (Boston: 1975) 199.

49. A. H. Stein and M. M. Bailey, "The Socialization of Achievement Motivation in Females," in M. T. S. Mednick, S. S. Tangri and L. W. Hoffman, eds. *Women and Achievement,* John Wiley and Sons (New York: 1975); R. Jackaway and R. Teevan, "Fear of Failure and Fear of Success: Two Dimensions of the Same Motive," *Sex Roles,* 1976, 2, 3, 283–293.

50. E. Goodman, "Great (Male) Expectations," *Washington Post,* September 3, 1977.

51. R. Jackaway and R. Teevan, *op. cit.* (note 49) 291.

52. B. Linner, "What Does Equality Imply?" *American Journal of Orthopsychiatry,* October 1971, 41, 5, 750; J. Harrison, "Warning: The Male Sex Role May Be Dangerous to Your Health," *Journal of Social Issues,* 1978, 34, 1, 65–86; "Urban Life Found Harder on Males," *The New York Times,* July 11, 1976, 22; "Life Expectancy Up to 72.4 Years in U.S.," UPI story in *The New York Times,* July 11, 1976.

53. B. Certner, "Sex Roles and Mental Health: A Proposal for the Development of the Sex Roles Institute," 1976, The Psychiatric Institute Foundation, Washington, D.C., quoting Dr. Rene Gonzalez, Chief, Division of Mental Health, World Health Organization, 2, 51.

54. See my chapter 2.

55. R. Sokolov, "In Short, I've Had It," *Psychology Today,* April 1978, 104–105.

56. "Survey Finds that Most Children Are Happy at Home But Fear World," *The New York Times,* March 2, 1977, A12.

57. M. Chad, "The Incredible Shrinking Woman," *Ms.* magazine, October 1974, 19; V. Packard, *The People Shapers,* Little, Brown (Boston: 1977).

58. L. Bennets, "At 7 Foot 7, They Make the Best of a Burden," *The New York Times,* August 7, 1978, D9.

59. A. B. McBride, "Cooking," in *A Married Feminist,* Harper and Row (New York: 1976) 126–140; *Ms.* magazine special issue on Food, February 1980.

60. V. H. Orbach, "Food Junkie," *New Directions for Women,* Summer 1978, 9; S. Orbach, *Fat Is a Feminist Issue,* Paddington Press (New York: 1978). For more information: *Fat Underground,* P. O. Box 5621, Santa Monica, Calif. 90405.

61. R. Lindner, *The Fifty-Minute Hour,* Bantam (New York: 1976).

62. J. Thurman, "Never Too Thin to Feel Fat," *Ms.* magazine, September 1977, 48.

63. L. C. Pogrebin, "Barbara Cook: Fat Can Set You Free," *Ms.* magazine, September 1977, 51.

64. J. Thurman, *op. cit.* (note 62).

65. R. Morgan, "The Politics of Body Image," *Ms.* magazine, September 1977, 48.

66. S. Reiss, "Each Hunger Pain Delighted Me," *Ms.* magazine, August 1976, 108.

67. *Ibid.,* 109.

68. J. Ramsey, "Anorexia Nervosa: Dying of Thinness," *Ms.* magazine, August 1976, 103–110.

69. V. Cosstick, "Anorexia Nervosa," *New Directions for Women,* Summer 1978, 9; H. Bruch, *The Golden Cage: The Enigma of Anorexia Nervosa,* Harvard University Press (Cambridge, Mass.: 1978). For more information: *Anorexia Nervosa and Associated Disorders,* Suite 2020, 550 Frontage Rd. Northfield, Ill. 60093, (312) 831–3438.

70. M. Selvini-Palazzoli, *Self-Starvation: From Individual to Family Therapy in the Treatment of Anorexia Nervosa,* Jason Aronson publishers (New York: 1978).

558

71. M. Boskind-Lodahl, "Cinderella's Stepsisters: A Feminist Perspective on Anorexia Nervosa and Bulimia," *Signs: A Journal of Women in Culture and Society,* 1976, 2, 2, 342–356.

72. H. Bruch, *Eating Disorders,* Basic Books (New York: 1973). Also, see the novelized presentation of an anorexic family, S. Levenkron, *The Best Little Girl in the World,* Contemporary Books (Chicago: 1978); S. Minuchin, et al., *Psychosomatic Families: Anorexia Nervosa in Context,* Harvard University Press, (Cambridge, Mass.: 1974).

73. J. Ramsey, *op. cit.* (note 68) 103.

74. M. Boskind-Lodahl, *op. cit.* (note 71) 346–347.

75. *Ibid.*

76. *Ibid.*

77. J. Ramsey, *op. cit.* (note 68) 103.

78. B. Elena Dujovne, "Relationship of Self to Body and to Mind: An Exploratory Study," *Dissertation Abstracts,* 34, 3-B, 1256.

79. E. E. Maccoby, *op. cit.* (note 1) 36.

80. M. W. Osmond and P. Y. Martin, "Sex and Sexism: A Comparison of Male and Female Sex Role Attitudes," *Journal of Marriage and the Family,* November 1975, 744–758; M. P. Zanna and S. I. Pack, "On the Self-Fulfilling Nature of Apparent Sex Differences in Behavior," *Journal of Experimental Social Psychology,* 1975, 11, 583–591.

81. S. E. Asch, "Studies of Independence and Conformity: A Minority of One Against a Unanimous Majority," *Psychological Monographs,* 1956, 70, 9, cited in J. Freeman, "The Building of the Guilded Cage," in *Notes from the Third Year: Women's Liberation 1971.* K. Brehony, et al., "Psychological Androgyny and Social Conformity," paper presented to American Psychological Association, San Francisco, August 1977.

82. J. Hassett, "How Women Cope with Stress: Contrasting Styles," *Psychology Today,* June 1978, 116; W. W. Tryon, et al., "Smoking Behavior as a Function of Social Cues and Sex: A Naturalistic Study," *Sex Roles,* 1977, 3, 4, 337–344.

83. M. I. Oberlander, et al., "Sex Role Development and Creative Functioning in Preadolescent and Adolescent Students," paper presented to the Society for Research in Child Development, Denver, April 1975.

84. D. W. MacKinnon, "The Nature and Nurture of Creative Talent," *American Psychologist,* 1962, 17, 488. Also see F. Barron, "Originality in Relation to Personality and Intellect," *Journal of Personality,* 1957, 25, 737; E. P. Torrance, *Guiding Creative Talent,* Prentice Hall (Englewood Cliffs, N. J.: 1962).

85. J. Joesting and R. Joesting, "Equalitarianism and Creativity: A Tentative Relationship," *Psychological Reports,* 1973, 32, 1125–1126; M. Mannes, "The Problems of Creative Women" and E. E. Maccoby, "Women's Intellect," both in S. M. Farber and R. H. L. Wilson, eds. *The Potential of Women,* McGraw-Hill (New York: 1963) 37, 116–130.

86. J. H. Block, et al., "Sex-Role Typing and Instrumental Behavior," paper presented to Society for Research in Child Development, Denver, April 1975.

87. R. O. Manley, "The Relationship between the Parental Warmth-Hostility Dimension and the Development of Achievement Orientation in Males and Females," paper presented to American Educational Research Association, Washington, D. C., April 1975.

88. A. Anastasi and C. E. Shaefer, "Biographical Correlates of Artistic and Literary Creativity in Adolescent Girls," *Journal of Applied Psychology,* 1969, 53, 267–273; R. Helson, "Women Mathematicians and the Creative Personality," *Journal of Consulting Clinical Psychology,* 1971, 36, 210–220.

89. P. S. Weisberg and K. J. Spring, "Environment Factors in Creative Function: A Study of Gifted Children," *Archives of General Psychiatry,* 1961, 5, 554–564; L. E. Datta and M. B. Parlott, "Parent-Child Relationships and Early Scientific Creativity," *Proceedings of the 75th Annual Convention of the American Psychological Association,* 1967, 149–150.

90. H. J. Cross, "The Relation of Parental Training Conditions to Conceptual Level in Adolescent Boys," *Journal of Personality,* 1966, 34, 348–365.

91. D. W. MacKinnon, *op. cit.* (note 84) 493.

92. F. S. Perls, *Gestalt Therapy Verbatim,* Real People Press (Lafayette, Calif.: 1969).

93. I. K. Broverman, et al., "Sex Role Stereotypes: A Current Appraisal," *Journal of Social Issues,* 1972, 28, 2, 60.

94. M. Mead, *Sex and Temperament,* (1935) Morrow Paperback, (New York: 1963) 293. Also H. B. Lewis, *Psychic War in Men and Women,* New York University Press (New York: 1976).

95. P. Mussen, "Some Antecedents and Consequents of Masculine Sex-typing in Adolescent Boys," *Psychological Monographs,* 1961, 77 (whole 506), 2, 19.

96. J. Pleck, "My Male Sex Role—And Ours," in D. S. David and R. Brannon, eds. *The Forty-Nine Percent Majority: The Male Sex Role,* Addison-Wesley (Reading, Mass.: 1976) 261–262.

97. J. Lester, "Being a Boy," *Ms.* magazine, July 1973, 112.

98. W. J. Goode, "A Theory of Role Strain," *American Journal of Sociology,* August 1960, 25, 483–490. Also T. M. Kando, "Role Strain: A Comparison of Males, Females and Transsexuals," *Journal of Marriage and the Family,* August 1972, 459–464; M. Komarovsky, "Some Problems in Role Analysis," *American Sociological Review,* 1974, 38, 649–662.

99. M. Brenton, *The American Male,* Fawcett (New York: 1966) 186–208. Also W. E. Knox and H. J. Kupferer, "A Discontinuity in the Socialization of Males in the United States," *Merrill-Palmer Quarterly,* 17, 251–261; D. T. Hall, "A Model for Coping With Role Conflict," *Administrative Science Quarterly,* 1972, 17, 471–486; N. Chodorow, "Being and Doing: A Cross-Cultural Examination of the Socialization of Males and Females," in V. Gornick and B. K. Moran, eds. *Woman in Sexist Society,* Basic (New York: 1971) 173–197.

100. T. M. Kando, *op. cit.* (note 98); C. Vincent, "Implication of Changes in Male-Female Role Expectations for Interpreting M-F Scores," *Journal of Marriage and the Family,* 1966, 28, 196–199.

101. L. A. Bernknopf, "A Comparison of the Responses of Behavior of Disordered and Normal Adolescents on a Masculinity-Femininity Scale and on a Stereotyping Questionnaire," paper presented at the Annual International Convention of the Council for Exceptional Children, Chicago, Ill., April 4–6, 1976. Also J. Glidewell and C. Swallow, "The Prevalence of Maladjustment in Elementary Schools," University of Chicago Press 1968, cited by H. F. Clarizio and G. F. McCoy, *Behavior Disorders in School Aged Children,* Changler (Scranton, Pa.: 1970).

102. P. Sexton, *op. cit.* (note 2) 6. Also see E. Yachnes, "The Myth of Masculinity: A Panel," *American Journal of Psychoanalysis,"* 1973, 33, 1, 56; D. G. Brown, "Sex Role Development in a Changing Culture," *Psychological Bulletin,* 1958, 55, 4, 232–242; S. W. Gray, "Masculinity and Femininity in Relation to Anxiety and Social Acceptance," *Child Development,* June 1957, 28, 2, 203–214; R. E. Hartley, "Sex-Role Pressures and the Socialization of the Male Child," *Psychological Reports,* 1959, 5.

103. Dr. David Foulkes, University of Wyoming psychologist quoted in R. Flaste, "In the Nursery, Some Nightmares and a Lot of Ordinary Dreaming," *The New York Times,* October 29, 1976, B4.

104. J. S. Bohan, "Age and Sex Differences in Self-Concept," *Adolescence,* 1973, 8, 379–384. Also J. Hollander, "Sex Differences in Sources of Social Self-Esteem," *Journal of Consulting and Clinical Psychology* 1972, 38, 343–347; N. Albert and A. Beck, "Incidence of Depression in Early Adolescence: A Preliminary Study," *Journal of Youth and Adolescence,* 1976; B. Putnam and J. C. Hansen, "Relationship of Self-Concept and Feminine Role Concept to Vocational Maturity in Young Women," *Journal of Counseling Psychology,* 1972, 19, 436–440; S. M. Tiedt, "Realistic Counseling for High School Girls," *The School Counselor,* 1972, 19, 354–356; L. Serbin, "Sex Role Socialization and Psychopathology: Current Directions for Research," paper presented at a symposium, Current Research on Sex Role Socialization, American Psychological Association, September, 1974.

105. P. Chesler, "Women as Psychiatric and Psychotherapeutic Patients," *Journal of Marriage and Family,* November 1971, 750 (cites five studies related to this point). Also, M. Mazer, "People in Predicament: A Study in Psychiatric and Psychosocial Epidemiology," *Social Psychiatry,* 1974, 85, 85–90.

106. B. Bayh, Introduction, A. Kosof, *Runaways,* Franklin Watts (New York: 1977) 2.

107. J. Whiting, et al., "The Function of Male Initiation Ceremonies at Puberty," in E. E. Maccoby, R. M. Newcomb and E. L. Hartley, eds. *Readings in Social Psychology,* 3rd ed., Holt, Rinehart and Winston (New York: 1958) 359–370; P. Sexton, *op. cit.* (note 2) 114; J. J. Teevan, "Reference Groups and Premarital Sexual Behavior," *Journal of Marriage and Family,* 1972, 24, 283–291; L. Komisar, "Violence and the Masculine Mystique," *Washington Monthly,* July 1970.

108. S. Lipshitz, "Women and Psychiatry," in J. Chetwynd and O. Hartnett, *The Sex Role System,* Routledge & Kegan Paul (London: 1978) 96–97.

109. J. J. Teevan, *op. cit.* (note 107).

110. D. Katz, "Why Children Attempt Suicide," *Detroit Free Press,* February 3, 1974, 1A.

111. *Suicide among Youths* (1970), U. S. Government Printing Office.

560

112. H. E. Kaye, *Male Survival: Masculinity without Myth,* Grosset and Dunlap (New York: 1974) 160.
113. M. Brenton, *op. cit.* (note 99) 65; H. C. Harford, C. H. Willis and H. L. Deabler, "Personality Correlates of Masculinity and Femininity," *Psychological Reports,* 1967, 21, 881–884.
114. M. Guttentag and S. Salasin, "Women, Men and Mental Health," in L. A. Cater, A. F. Scott and W. Martyna, eds. *Women and Men: Changing Roles, Relationships and Perceptions,* Aspen Institute for Humanistic Studies (New York: 1976) 153–180; "Early Clues Reported" (on problem drinkers), *The New York Times,* August 2, 1972.
115. J. H. Pleck, (1975) *op. cit.* (note 1) 168. Also C. J. Burchardt and L. A. Serbin, "Psychological Androgyny and Personality Adjustment in College and Psychiatric Populations," paper presented to the Eastern Psychological Association, April 1977, Boston, Mass.; R. M. Inselberg and L. Burke, "Social and Psychological Correlates of Masculinity in Young Boys," *Merrill-Palmer Quarterly,* April 1973, 17, 2, 41–47.
116. P. Mussen, *op. cit.* (note 95) 435, 440.
117. M. Mead, (1949) *op. cit.* (note 27) 300.
118. M. E. P. Seligman, "Depression and Learned Helplessness," in R. T. Friedman and M. M. Katz, eds. *The Psychology of Depression: Contemporary Theory and Research,* V. H. Winston (Washington, D. C.: 1974); L. S. Radloff, "Sex Differences in Helplessness with Implications for Depression," in L. S. Hansen and R. S. Rapoza, eds. *Career Development and Counseling of Women,* Charles Thomas publishers (Springfield, Ill.: 1978) 199–221; M. E. P. Seligman, *Helplessness: On Depression Development and Death,* W. H. Freeman (San Francisco: 1975); G. K. Litman, "Clinical Aspects of Sex-Role Stereotyping," in J. Chetwynd and O. Hartnett, eds. *The Sex Role System,* Routledge & Kegan Paul (London: 1978) 115; C. Wolman and H. Frank, "The Solo Woman in a Professional Peer Group," *American Journal of Orthopsychiatry,* 1975, 45, 164–171.
119. M. Guttentag and S. Salasin, *op. cit.* (note 114) 162; E. Stengel, *Suicide and Attempted Suicide,* Penguin Books (Middlesex, England: 1964); M. M. Weissman, "The Epidemiology of Suicide Attempts," *Archives of General Psychiatry,* 1974, 30, 737–746; M. M. Weissman, E. S. Paykel and N. French, et al., "Suicide Attempts in an Urban Community," *Social Psychiatry,* 1973, 8, 82–91.
120. F. E. Gordon and D. T. Hall, "Self-Image and Stereotypes of Femininity: Their Relationships to Women's Role-Conflicts and Coping," *Journal of Applied Psychology,* 1974, 59, 241–243; S. L. Bem, *Psychology Today,* September 1975, 59; J. B. Miller, *Toward a New Psychology of Women,* Beacon Press (Boston: 1976); G. K. Baruch, "Feminine Self-Esteem, Self-Ratings of Competence and Maternal Career Commitment," *Journal of Counseling Psychology,* 1973, 20, 487–488.
121. A. R. Hochschild, "The Sociology of Feeling and Emotion: Selected Possibilities," in M. Millman and R. M. Kanter, eds. *Another Voice,* Doubleday Anchor Press (Garden City, N. Y.: 1975) 291–294; D. Bugental, L. Love and R. Gianetto, "Perfidious Feminine Faces," *Journal of Personality and Social Psychology,* 1971, 17, 314–318; P. B. Johnson and J. Goodchilds, "How Women Get Their Way", *Psychology Today,* October 1976, 69–70.
122. S. W. Gray, *op. cit.* (note 103). Also Dr. Gertrude M. Hengerer cited in M. Brenton, *op. cit.* (note 99) 65; A. P. Webb, *op. cit.,* (note 3) 609–618; T. C. Harford, C. H. Willis and H. L. Deabler, *op. cit.* (note 113).
123. G. Winokur and P. Clayton, "Family History Studies II: Sex Differences in Alcoholism in Primary Affective Illness," *British Journal of Psychiatry,* 1967, 113, 973–979; E. S. Gomberg, "Women and Alcoholism," in V. Franks and V. Burtle, eds. *Women in Therapy,* Brunner/Mazel (New York: 1974) 169–190; U. Hannerz, "What Ghetto Males Are Like," in D. David and R. Brannon, *op. cit.* (note 96) 250; M. Guttentag and S. Salasin, *op. cit.* (note 114) 158; M. Mazer, *op. cit.* (note 105); H. J. Parry, et al., "National Patterns of Psychotherapeutic Drug Use," *Archives of General Psychology,* 1973, 28, 769–783.
124. K. Clancy and W. Gove, "Sex Differences in Mental Illness," *American Journal of Sociology,* 1974, 80, 205–216. Also S. Jourard, *The Transparent Self,* Van Nostrand Company (New York: 1971) 34–41; P. Chesler, *Women and Madness,* Doubleday (Garden City, N.Y.: 1972); L. S. Radloff and D. S. Rae, "Susceptibility and Precipitating Factors in Depression: Sex Differences and Similarities," based on a paper presented at the American Statistical Association Meeting, Chicago, Ill., August 16, 1977; M. M. Weissman and G. L. Klerman, "Sex Differences and the Epidemiology of Depression," *Archives of General Psychiatry,* January 1977, 34, 98–111; M. Guttentag and S. Salasin, *op. cit.* (note 114); L. Phillips, "A Social View of Psychopathology," in P. London and D. Rosenham, eds.

19. R. A. Bradley, *Husband-Coached Childbirth,* Harper & Row (New York: 1965); D. Tanzer and J. Block, *op. cit.* (note 17); D. Sutherland, "Childbirth Is Not for Mothers Only," *Ms.* magazine, May 1974, 47–51.

20. M. Gunther, *Infant Feeding,* Henry Regnery (Chicago: 1971); M. S. Eiger and S. W. Olds, *The Complete Book of Breastfeeding,* Workman (New York: 1973); also contact La Leche League (in your local telephone directory), whose manual is available from their national office, 9616 Minneapolis Avenue, Franklin Park, Ill. 60131. (Bear in mind that La Leche is *very* pro-breast.) For an up-to-date review of the pros *and* cons, including concern for contamination of breast milk, see *Birthright Denied: The Risks and Benefits of Breastfeeding,* Environmental Defense Fund, 1525 18th St. N.W., Washington, D.C. 20036. ($1.50).

21. A. Rich, *op. cit.* (note 16) 182.

22. S. H. Anderson, "A Plea for Gentleness to the Newborn," *The New York Times,* January 15, 1978, 48.

23. M. H. Klaus and J. H. Kennell, *Maternal-Infant Bonding,* C. V. Mosby (St. Louis, Mo.: 1976).

24. R. Grobstein of Stanford University Medical Center quoted in "Babies: Early Separation—It's a Problem," *Psychology Today,* April 1977, 30; J. Gray, et al., "Prediction and Prevention of Child Abuse and Neglect," *Child Abuse and Neglect: The International Journal,* 1977, 1, 45; C. Spezzano and J. Waterman, "The First Day of Life," *Psychology Today,* December 1977, 110–116; C. H. Kempe, J. Gray, C. A. Cutler and J. G. Dean, "Child Abuse Detectives: Early Warnings in the Maternity Ward," *Human Behavior,* May 1978, 67.

25. W. Jarvis, "Some Effects of Pregnancy and Childbirth on Men," *Journal of American Psychoanalytic Association,* 1962, 10, 689–699.

26. V. Pollard, *op. cit.* (note 5) 10. Also comb through the 28-page bibliography, *The Social Aspects of Pregnancy* (1974) available from Dr. Ruth Seiden Miller, Rhode Island College, Providence, R.I. or from The Sex Roles Section of the American Sociology Assoc.

27. M. Greenberg and N. Morris, "Engrossment: The Newborn's Impact upon the Father," *American Journal of Orthopsychiatry,* 1974, 44, 520–531; also see my chapter 8, notes 45–47, page 568.

28. C. Spezzano and J. Waterman, *op. cit.* (note 24) 116.

29. R. Flaste, "Closeness in the First Minutes of Life May Have a Lasting Effect," *The New York Times,* August 16, 1977, 30.

30. L. Chandler and M. D. Roe, "Behavioral and Neurological Comparisons of Neonates Born to Mothers of Different Social Environments," *Child Psychiatry and Human Development,* 1977, 8, 1, 25–30.

31. C. Spezzano and J. Waterman, *op. cit.* (note 24) 110, 113.

32. D. Dinnerstein, *The Mermaid and The Minotaur: Sexual Arrangements and Human Malaise,* Harper & Row (New York: 1976).

33. J. DeFrain, "Sexism in Parenting Manuals," *The Family Coordinator,* July 1977, 245–251.

34. B. Spock, *Raising Your Child in a Difficult Time,* Pocket Books (New York: 1976); and J. Church, *Understanding Your Child from Birth to Three,* Random House (New York: 1973).

35. H. Ginott, *Between Parent and Child,* Avon (New York: 1965) 201.

36. A. Janov, *The Feeling Child,* Simon & Schuster (New York: 1973) 207.

37. F. Dodson, *How to Parent,* NAL (New York: 1970) 179.

38. Council on Interracial Books, 1841 Broadway, New York, N.Y. 10023. ($3).

39. Pocket Books (New York: 1976).

40. P. Hagan, "Dr. Spock Tells Why He No Longer Sings in Praise of Hims," *The New York Times,* October 13, 1973, 30. Also see, J. Martin, "Sexism and Dr. Spock: Women's Lib—War and Peace," *Washington Post,* September 24, 1971, B1; P. Slater, "Spocklash: Age, Sex, Revolution," *Washington Monthly,* February 1970; "Male Chauvinist Spock Recants—Well Almost," *The New York Times Magazine,* September 12, 1971, 98ff.

41. B. Spock, *Baby and Child Care,* Meredith Press (New York: 1968) 30–31.

42. B. Spock, *Baby and Child Care,* Pocket Books (New York: 1976) 47.

43. B. Spock, (1968) *op. cit.* (note 41) 321.

44. B. Spock, (1976) *op. cit.* (note 42) 357.

45. Random House (New York: 1978).

46. Houghton Mifflin (Boston: 1978).

47. Beacon Press (Boston: 1977).

48. M. G. Marcus, "The Power of a Name," *Psychology Today,* October 1976, 76; also see, W. Ames, ed. *What Shall We Name The Baby?* Pocket Books (New York: 1974).
49. D. Adelson, "Attitudes Toward First Names," *International Journal of Social Psychiatry,* 1964, 1, Sec. A, 81–86; W. F. Murphy, "A Note on the Significance of Names," *Psychoanalytic Quarterly,* 1957, 26, 91–106.
50. M. G. Marcus, *op. cit.* (note 48).
51. *Ibid.,* 75, 108. Also, C. P. Andersen, *The Name Game,* Simon & Schuster (New York: 1977).
52. A. W. Turner, *Rituals of Birth,* McKay (New York: 1978) 7; "About Indian Names," *The Weewish Tree,* September 1979, 7, 4, 15.
53. M. G. Marcus, *op. cit.* (note 48) 75.
54. B. M. Savage and F. L. Wells, "A Note on Singularity in Given Names," *Journal of Social Psychology,* 1948, 27, 271–272; A. Ellis and R. M. Beechley, "Emotional Disturbance in Children with Peculiar Given Names," *Journal of Genetic Psychology,* 1954, 85 337–339.
55. M. G. Marcus, *op. cit.* (note 48) 76. For a discussion of sex differences in preference for nicknames see, P. Horn, "A Rose Is a Rose Is a Rosie," *Psychology Today,* February 1975, 22–24.
56. E. L. Hoover, "Plain Janes and Uncommon Miltons—a Look at Stereotypes in the Name Game," *Human Behavior,* January 1979, 16–17.
57. See studies by J. McDavid and H. Harari and by S. Gray Garwood, cited in M. G. Marcus, *op. cit.* (note 48).
58. R. Zweigenhaft, "The Other Side of Unusual First Names," *Journal of Social Psychology,* 1977, 103, 291–302.

7 • *Nonsexist Infancy, page 116*

1. R. R. Sears, E. E. Maccoby and H. Levin, *Patterns of Childrearing,* Row, Peterson (Evanston, Ill.: 1957) 400.
2. J. D. Grambs, and W. W. Waetjen, *Sex: Does It Make A Difference?* Duxbury Press (North Scituate, Mass.: 1975) 91.
3. A. W. Turner, *Rituals of Birth,* McKay (New York: 1978) 102.
4. E. G. Belotti, *What Are Little Girls Made Of? The Roots of Feminine Stereotypes,* Schocken Books (New York: 1976) 43.
5. A. Macfarlane, *The Psychology of Childbirth,* Harvard University Press (Cambridge, Mass.: 1977) 61–63.
6. E. G. Belotti, *op. cit.* (note 4) 29.
7. *Pandora* (Seattle, Wash.) October 5, 1971, 7.
8. L. Gould, *Baby X,* Daughters, Inc. (New York: 1978).
9. E. Mintz, "The Prejudice of Parents," paper presented to the American Psychological Association, September 1972, 5.
10. Personal communication, Robert L. Trivers, Harvard, July 1973.
11. Rust Craft 75 AC 8802–2, written by Alan Beck.
12. Ibid., #75 AC 8804–2.
13. For example, see Hallmark 50 G-579-2 or 100G 577-2.
14. Hallmark 300HE80-6, written by Marjorie F. Ames.
15. Hallmark 300HE80-7, same author.
16. Norcross 35J 275-2 (Incidentally, the baby pictured is a black child).
17. Carlson Crafts catalog, quoted in *Ms.* magazine, April 1976, 105.
18. San Francisco *Examiner,* quoted in *Ms.* magazine, *ibid.*
19. *Whig-Standard,* Kingston, Ont., quoted in *Ms.* magazine, *ibid.*
20. J. Z. Rubin, J. J. Provenzano, Z. Luria, "The Eye of the Beholder: Parents' Views on Sex of Newborns," *American Journal of Orthopsychiatry,* 1974, 44, 512–519.
21. *Ibid.,* 519.
22. M. Mead, *Sex and Temperament,* Morrow Paperback (New York: 1963) 171–172.
23. C. A. Seavey, P. A. Katz and S. R. Zalk, "Baby X: The Effect of Gender Labels on Adult Responses to Infants," *Sex Roles,* 1975, 1, 2, 103–109.
24. J. A. Will, P. A. Self, N. Datan, "Maternal Behavior and Perceived Sex of Infant," *American Journal of Orthopsychiatry,* 1976, 46, 1.
25. *Ibid.*
26. T. Murry, H. Hollien and E. Muller, "Perceptual Responses to Infant Crying: Mater-

nal Recognition and Sex Judgements," *Journal of Child Language,* November 1975, 2, 2, 199–204.

27. J. Condry and S. Condry, "The Development of Sex Differences: A Study of the Eye of the Beholder," unpublished manuscript, Cornell University, 1974, cited in B. Birns, "The Emergence and Socialization of Sex Differences in the Earliest Years," *Merrill-Palmer Quarterly,* 1976, 22, 3, 244.

28. J. Church, *Understanding Your Child From Birth to Three,* Random House (New York: 1973) 156.

29. See for example, B. Birns, *op. cit.* (note 35); S. Goldberg and M. Lewis, "Play Behavior in the Year-old Infant: Early Sex Differences," *Child Development,* 1969, 40, 21–31; M. Lewis, "State as an Infant-Environment Interaction: An Analysis of Mother-Infant Interaction as a Function of Sex," *Merrill-Palmer Quarterly,* 1972, 18, 2, 95–121; H. B. Gallas and M. Lewis, "Gender Differences in the Relationship Between Mother-Infant Interaction and the Infant's Cognitive Development," paper presented to the Eastern Psychological Association, Boston, Mass., April 1977; C. M. BelCastro et al., "The Effects of Increased Maternal Visual Regard of Neonate Upon the Neonate-Mother Interaction," paper presented to Eastern Psychological Association, New York, April 1976; H. Moss, "Sex, Age, and State as Determinants of Mother-Infant Interaction," *Merrill-Palmer Quarterly,* 1967, 13, 19–36; E. Thoman, P. Leiderman and J. Olson, "Neonate-Mother Interaction During Breastfeeding," *Developmental Psychology,* 1972, 6, 110–118; L. Cherry and M. Lewis, "Mothers and Two-Year-Olds: A Study of Sex-Differentiated Aspects of Verbal Interaction," *Developmental Psychology,* 1976, 12, 4, 281.

30. M. Lewis, "Parents and Children: Sex-Role Development," *School Review,* February 1972, 229–240.

31. H. Moss, *op. cit.* (note 29) 30.

32. M. Lewis, (1972) *op. cit.* (note 29) 105, 110.

33. R. Parke, S. E. O'Leary and S. West, "Mother-Father-Newborn Interaction in the Newborn Period: Some Findings, Some Observations and Some Unresolved Issues," cited in B. Birns, *op. cit.* (note 27) 244–245.

34. M. E. Lamb, "Development and Function of Parent-Infant Relationships in the First Two Years of Life," paper presented to the Society for Research in Child Development, New Orleans, La., March 1977, 4–5.

35. H. Biller and D. Meredith, *Father Power,* Anchor (New York: 1975) 52.

36. E. Pohlman, *Psychology of Birth Planning,* Schenkman (New York: 1969) 209.

37. B. S. Jacobs and H. A. Moss, "Birth Order and Sex of Sibling as Determinants of Mother-Infant Interaction," *Child Development,* 1976, 47, 317.

38. E. G. Belotti, *op. cit.* (note 4) 32–33.

39. *Ibid.,* 33. Also see S. Brun-Gulbrandsen, "Sex Roles and The Socialization Process," in E. Dahlstron, ed. *The Changing Roles of Men and Women,* Beacon Press (Boston: 1971) 65.

40. E. G. Belotti, *op. cit.* (note 4) 38–39.

41. For example, B. Spock, *Baby and Child Care,* Pocket Books (New York: 1976) 286–290.

42. E. G. Belotti, *op. cit.* (note 4) 41.

43. *Ibid.,* 42.

44. J. Segal, ed. *Mental Health Program Reports,* No. 5, Department of Health, Education and Welfare, Public Health Service: Publication Number (HSM) 72-9042, (Rockville, Md.: 1971) 69, 79.

45. J. B. Gleason, "Code Switching in Children's Language," paper presented to the *Linguists Institute,* Buffalo, N.Y., August 1971.

46. *The Atlantic,* March 1963, 90.

47. J. Kagan, "Psychology of Sex Differences," in F. Beach, ed. *Human Sexuality,* McGraw-Hill (New York: 1972).

48. *Ibid.,* and personal communication, July 1973.

8 • *Parity Parenthood, page 131*

1. *Human Nature,* June 1978 reports of First International Conference on Infant Studies, Brown University, Providence, R. I., March 1978.

2. T. Berry Brazelton, quoted in "Conference on Infants Studies the First Experiences of Life," *The New York Times,* March 14, 1978.

3. M. E. Lamb, "Infants, Fathers and Mothers: Interaction at Eight Months of Age in the

568

Home and in the Laboratory," paper presented to the Eastern Psychological Association, New York, April 1975.

4. M. E. Lamb, "Effects of Stress and Cohort on Mother and Father-Infant Interaction," *Developmental Psychology,* 1976, 12, 435–443; M. E. Lamb, "Twelve Month Olds and Their Parents: Interaction In a Laboratory Playroom," *Developmental Psychology,* 1976, 12, 237–244.

5. M. E. Lamb, "Development and Function of Parent-Infant Relationships in the First Two Years of Life," paper presented to the Society for Research in Child Development, New Orleans, La., March 1977, 3.

6. R. D. Parke and D. B. Sawin, "Fathering: It's a Major Role," *Psychology Today,* November 1977, 111; I. Rendina and J. D. Dickerschand, "Father Involvement with First-Born Infants," *Family Coordinator,* October 1976, 25, 4, 373–378.

7. L. D. Droppelman and E. S. Schaefer, "Boys and Girls Reports of Maternal and Paternal Behavior," *Journal of Abnormal and Social Psychology,* 1963, 67, 6, 653.

8. R. D. Parke and D. B. Sawin, *op. cit.* (note 6).

9. M. E. Lamb, (1977) *op. cit.* (note 5) 3–5.

10. *American College Dictionary,* Random House (New York, 1963) 881.

11. J. M. Bardwick, *In Transition,* Holt, Rinehart and Winston (New York: 1979) is among those who misinterpret the call for domestic equality as a self-serving "liberation" of women from housework. For a more trenchant analysis of domestic change as an analogue of political and social change, see M. Z. Rosaldo, "Woman, Culture and Society: A Theoretical Overview," in M. Z. Rosaldo and L. Lamphere, eds. *Woman, Culture & Society,* Stanford University Press (Stanford, Calif.: 1974) 17–42.

12. G. Dullea, "The Increasing Single Parent Families," *The New York Times,* December 3, 1974, 46.

13. R. D. Gasser and C. M. Tayl, "Role Adjustment of Single Parent Fathers with Dependent Children," *Family Coordinator,* October 1976, 25, 4, 397–401.

14. For example, R. Reed, "Changing Conceptions of the Maternal Instinct," *Journal of Abnormal Psychology and Social Psychology,* 1923, 18, 78–87; J. Bernard, *The Future of Motherhood,* Dial Press, (New York: 1974); B. L. Forisha, *Sex Roles and Personal Awareness,* General Learning Press (Morristown, N.J.: 1978).

15. E. Pohlman, *The Psychology of Birth Planning,* Schenckman (New York: 1969) 248–255; M. A. Parlee, "Psychological Aspects of Menstruation, Childbirth and Menopause," presented to the Conference on New Directions for Resources on Women," Madison, Wis., June 1975.

16. E. Peck and J. Senderowitz, eds. *Pronatalism: The Myth of Mom and Apple Pie,* Crowell (New York: 1974).

17. F. X. Clines, "About New York: Where Mothers Learn Mothering," *The New York Times,* June 10, 1978. Also, E. O. Goodman, "Modeling: A Method of Parent Education," *The Family Coordinator,* January 1975, 7–11.

18. A. B. McBride, *The Growth and Development of Mothers,* Harper & Row (New York: 1973) 37–53. Also, J. Bernard, *op. cit.* (note 14) 259.

19. A. Rich, *Of Woman Born,* Norton (New York: 1976) 250ff.

20. G. B. Shaw, *The Quintessence of Ibsenism* (1891).

21. L. Rainwater, *And the Poor Get Children,* Quadrangle (New York: 1960) 83.

22. R. A. Fein, "Research on Fathering: Social Policy and an Emergent Perspective," *Journal of Social Issues,* 1978, 34, 1, 128.

23. J. W. Torrey, "Psychoanalysis: A Feminist Revision," paper presented at a conference on Problems and Solutions: The Women's Liberation Movement, University of Bridgeport, Conn., March 27, 1971.

24. *American College Dictionary,* Random House (New York: 1963) 326.

25. *Ibid.,* 4.

26. For this insight, I credit A. Rossi, "Equality Between the Sexes: An Immodest Proposal," in R. J. Lifton, *The Woman in America,* Beacon Press (Boston: 1965) 108.

27. M. Millman, "Observations on Sex Role Research," *Journal of Marriage and the Family,* November 1971, 774.

28. D. Moynihan, "A Family Policy for the Nation," in L. Rainwater and W. Yancey, eds. *The Moynihan Report and the Politics of Controversy,* MIT Press (Cambridge, Mass.: 1967).

29. S. L. Bem and D. J. Bem, "Training the Woman to Know Her Place: The Power of a Nonconscious Ideology," in D. J. Bem, *Beliefs, Attitudes and Human Affairs,* Wadsworth (Monterey, Calif.: 1970).

30. E. Newton and P. Webster, "Matriarchy and Power," *Quest,* Summer 1975, 2, 1, 69.
31. R. and H. Exley, eds. *To Mom,* Houghton Mifflin (Boston: 1978).
32. *Ibid.*
33. L. P. McGrath and J. Scobey, *What Is a Father,* publisher unknown.
34. From the Mead-Johnson booklet, "Useful Facts for the Father-To-Be," reprinted in *No Comment, Ms.* magazine, December 1974 and May 1979, 95.
35. R. LaRossa, *Conflict and Power in Marriage,* vol. 50, Sage Library of Social Research, (Beverly Hills, Calif.: 1977).
36. R. and H. Exley, *op. cit.* (note 31).
37. L. P. McGrath and J. Scobey, *op. cit.* (note 33).
38. A. S. Rossi, "A Biosocial Perspective on Parenting," *Daedalus,* 1977, 106, 1–31.
39. I. M. Josselyn, "Cultural Forces, Motherliness, and Fatherliness," *American Journal of Orthopsychiatry,* 1956, 26, 264–271. Also, J. O. Wisdom, "The Role of the Father in the Mind of Parents in Psychoanalytic Theory and in the Life of the Infant," *International Review of Psychoanalysis,* 1976, 3, 2, 233–234.
40. D. Kavanaugh, ed. *Listen to Us! The Children's Express Report,* Workman (New York: 1978) 31–33.
41. J. Bowlby quoted in M. E. Lamb, "Fathers: The Forgotten Contributors to Child Development," *Human Development,* 1975, 18, 247.
42. S. Fraiberg, *Every Child's Birthright: In Defense of Mothering,* Basic Books (New York: 1978). Also, L. A. Sroufe, "Attachment and the Roots of Competence," *Human Nature,* October 1978, 50–57.
43. J. Kagan, "The Baby's Elastic Mind," *Human Nature,* Preview 1977, 58–66. Also, A. Schaffer, *Mothering,* Harvard University Press (Cambridge, Mass.: 1978).
44. H. Parens, "Research in Normal Growth and Development," paper presented to the International Association for Child Psychiatry and Allied Professions, Philadelphia, July 31, 1974. Also, J. Dunn, *Distress and Comfort,* Harvard University Press (Cambridge: 1977); J. Bowlby, *Attachment and Loss,* vols. I (1969) and II (1973), Basic (New York); M. Ainsworth and S. M. Bell, "Attachment, Exploration and Separation: Illustrated by the Behavior of One-Year-Olds in a Strange Situation," *Child Development,* 1970, 41, 49–67.
45. M. E. Lamb and J. E. Lamb, "The Nature and Importance of the Father Infant Relationship," *The Family Coordinator,* October 1976, 25, 4, 380.
46. A small sampling of those studies follows: M. Greenberg and N. Morris, "Engrossment: The Newborn's Impact upon the Father," *American Journal of Orthopsychiatry,* 1974, 44, 520–531; R. D. Parke and S. O'Leary, "Father-Mother-Infant Interaction in the Newborn Period: Some Findings, Some Observations and Some Unresolved Issues," in K. F. Riegel and J. Meachan, eds. *The Developing Individual in a Changing World, vol. 2, Social and Environmental Issues,* Mouton (The Hague: 1976); M. Kotelchuck, "The Infant's Relationship to the Father," and other relevant studies may be found in M. E. Lamb, ed. *The Role of the Father in Child Development,* Wiley (New York: 1976); E. Williemsen, et al., "Attachment Behavior of One-Year-Olds as a Function of Mother vs. Father, Sex of Child, Session and Toys," *Genetic Psychology Monographs,* 1974, 90, 305–324; S. S. Feldman and M. E. Ingham, "Attachment Behavior: A Validation Study in Two Age Groups," *Child Development,* 1975, 46, 319–330; M. E. Lamb, "Development of Mother and Father-Infant Attachment in the Second Year of Life," *Developmental Psychology,* 1977, 13; also by Lamb, "Father-Infant and Mother-Infant Interaction in the First Year of Life," *Child Development,* 1977, 48; B. Coates, et al., "Interrelation in the Attachment Behavior of Human Infants," *Developmental Psychology,* 1972, 6, 231–237; F. A. Pederson, "Mother, Father and Infant as an Interactive System," paper presented to the American Psychological Association, Chicago, September 1975; J. A. Manion, "A Study of Fathers and Infant Caretaking," *Birth and the Family Journal,* 1977, 4, 174–179.
47. R. D. Parke and D. B. Sawin, "The Father's Role in Infancy: A Re-evaluation," *The Family Coordinator,* October 1976, 368; D. B. Sawin and R. D. Parke, "Fathers' Affectionate Stimulation and Caregiving Behaviors with Newborn Infants," *The Family Coordinator,* October 1979, 509–513.
48. This discussion relies upon U. Stannard, "Adam's Rib or the Woman Within," *Trans-Action,* November/December 1970, 24–45; P. Chesler, *About Men,* Simon & Schuster (New York: 1978); C. B. Rypma, "Biological Bases of the Paternal Response," *The Family Coordinator,* October 1976, 335–339; and N. Chodorow, "Being and Doing: A Cross-Cultural Examination of the Socialization of Males and Females," in V. Gornick and B. K. Moran, *Woman in Sexist Society,* Basic Books (New York: 1971) 173–197. Also see, J. Leonard, "The Fathering Instinct," *Ms.* magazine, May 1974, 52.

570

49. G. D. Mitchell, W. K. Redican and J. Gomber, "Males Can Raise Babies," *Psychology Today,* 1974, 7, 63–67; G. D. Mitchell, "Paternalistic Behavior in Primates," *Psychological Bulletin,* 1969, 71, 399–417; J. G. Howells, "Fathering," in J. G. Howells, ed. *Modern Perspectives in Child Psychiatry,* Bruner-Mazel (New York: 1971) 128–30; N. Tinbergen, "The Curious Behavior of the Stickleback," *Scientific American,* December 1952; J. A. Thompson, *The Biology of Birds,* Macmillan (New York: 1923); W. Etkin, *Social Behavior and Organization Among Vertebrates,* University of Chicago Press (Chicago: 1964); S. Itani, "Paternal Care in the Wild Japanese Monkey," in S. H. Southwick, *Primate Social Behavior,* Van Nostrand (Princeton, N.J.: 1963).
50. C. B. Rympa, *op. cit.* (note 48) 335.
51. H. B. Biller and D. L. Meredith, *Father Power,* Anchor (New York: 1975); D. B. Lynn, *The Father: His Role in Child Development,* Brooks/Cole (Monterey, Calif.: 1974).
52. N. Chodorow, *op. cit.* (note 48) 187.
53. P. Berman, "Sex Differences in Young Children's Responses to an Infant," study presented at Biennial Southeastern Conference on Human Development, Nashville, Tenn., April 15, 1976.
54. H. Barry, III, M. Bacon and I. L. Child, "Cross-Cultural Survey of Some Sex Differences in Socialization," *Journal of Abnormal Social Psychology,* 1957, 55, 327. Also, P. Berman, et al., "Sex Differences in Attraction to Infants: When Do They Occur?" *Sex Roles,* 1975, 1, 311–318; P. Berman, "Social Context as a Determinant of Sex Differences in Adults' Attraction to Infants," *Developmental Psychology,* 1976, 12, 365–366; P. Berman, "Comment," *Signs,* Winter 1977, 515–516; W. G. Krieger, "Infant Influences and the Parent Sex-Child Sex Interaction in the Socialization Process," *Catalog of Selected Documents in Psychology,* May 1976, 6, 36–37, 19.
55. K. Horney, "Distrust Between the Sexes," in B. Roszak and T. Roszak, *Masculine/Feminine,* Harper Colophon (New York: 1969) 197–118; K. Horney, "The Flight From Womanhood," *International Journal of Psychoanalysis,* 1926, 7, 324–339.
56. J. W. Torrey, *op. cit.* (note 23).
57. U. Stannard, *op. cit.* (note 48) 32.
58. B. Bettleheim, *Symbolic Wounds,* The Free Press (Glencoe, Ill.: 1954).
59. E. Erikson, "Inner and Outer Space: Reflections on Womanhood," in R. J. Lifton, *The Woman in America,* Houghton Mifflin (New York: 1965).
60. U. Stannard, *op. cit.* (note 48).
61. N. F. Russon, "The Motherhood Mandate," *Journal of Social Issues,* 1976, 32, 3, 143–153.
62. A. Rich, *op. cit.* (note 19); A. B. McBride, *op. cit.* (note 18). Also see, N. Friday, *My Mother/My Self,* Delacorte (New York: 1978); S. Spinner, ed. *Motherlove,* Dell (New York: 1978); L. DelliQuadri and K. Breckenridge, *Mother Care: Helping Yourself Through the Physical and Emotional Transitions of New Motherhood,* J. P. Tarcher (Los Angeles, Calif.: 1978); J. Lazarre, *The Mother Knot,* McGraw-Hill (New York: 1976).
63. R. Rebelsky and C. Hanks, "Fathers' Verbal Interaction with Infants in the First Three Months of Life," in F. Rebelsky and L. Dorman, *Child Development and Behavior,* Knopf (New York: 1974) 145–148.
64. R. D. Parke and D. B. Sawin, *op. cit.* (note 6) 111.
65. P. L. Ban and M. Lewis, "Mothers and Fathers, Girls and Boys: Attachment Behavior in the One-Year-Old," *Merrill-Palmer Quarterly,* July 1974, 20, 3, 202.
66. Dr. Jung Bay Ra's study reported by A. Zullo, "Nearly 50% of Young Children Prefer TV to Their Fathers," *National Enquirer,* October 12, 1976, 3.
67. *Foundation for Child Development,* National Survey of Children, March 1977.
68. N. Broznan, "For Children Who May Be Parents Someday," *The New York Times,* March 30, 1973.
69. D. Knox and R. C. Gilman, "The First Year of Fatherhood," paper presented at the National Council on Family Relations, St. Louis, Mo., October 1974.
70. R. Wetzsteon, "The Feminist Man," *Mother Jones,* November 1977, 58.
71. S. Bear, M. Berger, L. Wright, "Even Cowboys Sing the Blues: Difficulties Experienced by Men Trying to Adopt Nontraditional Sex Roles and How Clinicians Can Be Helpful to Them," *Sex Roles,* 1979, 5, 2.
72. J. Leonard, "The Fathering Instinct," *Ms.* magazine, May 1974, 52.
73. P. G. Filene, *Him Her Self: Sex Roles in Modern America,* Harcourt Brace Jovanovich (New York: 1975) 238.
74. K. M. Rosenthal and H. F. Keshet, "The Impact of Child Care Responsibilities on Part-time or Single Fathers," *Alternate Lifestyles,* November 1978, 1, 4, 467.
75. *Ibid.,* 470.

76. G. Jonas, "Jonas and Daughters," *Ms.* magazine, May 1974, 112.

77. "How Men are Changing," *Newsweek,* January 16, 1978.

78. D. L. Anderson, "Parenting and Perceived Sex Role of Rural Iowa Fathers," paper presented to Adult Education Research Conference, Minneapolis, Minn., April 1977. Also, C. Tavris, "Masculinity," *Psychology Today,* January 1977, 35, 82.

79. R. A. Fein, "Men's Entrance to Parenthood," *The Family Coordinator,* October 1976, 25, 4, 344–346; J. Money and P. Tucker, *Sexual Signatures,* Little, Brown (Boston: 1975) 204–205.

80. K. M. Rosenthal and H. F. Keshet, *op. cit.* (note 74) 470.

81. H. F. Keshet and K. M. Rosenthal, "Fathering After Marital Separation," *Social Work,* January 1978, 23, 11–18. Previewed in Brandeis University Bulletin, December 1977, 4.

82. G. Dullea, "Divorced Fathers: Who Are Happiest?" *The New York Times,* February 4, 1978.

83. *Ibid.*

84. E. Pohlman, *The Psychology of Birth Planning,* Schenkman (New York: 1969) 117.

85. R. S. Paffenberger and L. H. McCabe, "The Effect of Obstetric and Perinatal Events on Risk of Mental Illness in Women of Childrearing Age," *American Journal of Public Health,* 1966, 56, 400–407.

86. S. Lipshitz, "Women and Psychiatry," in J. Chetwynd and O. Hartnett, eds. *The Sex Role System,* Routledge & Kegan Paul (London: 1978) 97; W. R. Gove, "The Relationship Between Sex Roles, Marital Status and Mental Illness," in A. G. Kaplan and J. P. Bean, eds. *Beyond Sex-Role Stereotypes,* Little, Brown (Boston: 1976) 282–292.

87. D. Onstad, "Post-partum Depression," *American Baby,* October 1973, 41.

88. R. G. Ryder, "Longitudinal Data Relating Marriage Satisfaction and Having a Child," *Journal of Marriage and the Family,* November 1973, 606.

89. For example, K. S. Power, "Maternal Employment in Relation to Family Life," *Marriage and Family Living,* 1961, 23, 4, 350–355.

90. Clairol ad, inside front cover, *Ladies Home Journal,* January 1975.

91. E. Pohlman, *op. cit.* (note 84) 153.

92. See for instance, B. K. Schwartz, "Easing the Adaptation to Parenthood," *Journal of Family Counseling,* Fall 1974, 2, 2, 32–9; D. G. Brown, et al., "Social Class and Psychiatric Disturbance Among Women in an Urban Population," *Sociology,* 1975, 9, 225–254; M. Guttentag and S. Salasin, "Women, Men and Mental Health," in L. A. Cater, A. F. Scott, W. Martyna, eds. *Women and Men: Changing Roles,* Aspen Institute for Humanistic Studies (New York: 1976) 153–179.

93. Celeste Sexauer, personal communication, February 13, 1979.

94. Sandra Thompson, *Mom as Pariah,* unpublished manuscript, 1979, 5.

95. C. Ehrlich, "The Male Sociologist's Burden: The Place of Women in Marriage and Family Texts," *Journal of Marriage and Family,* August 1971, 429–430; M. M. Parlee, "The Confused American Housewife," *Psychology Today,* September 1976, 80.

96. M. Mannes, quoted by M. Horner, *Psychology Today,* November 1969, 3, 6.

97. A. S. Rossi, "Equality Between the Sexes: An Immodest Proposal," *Daedalus,* Spring 1964.

98. N. Kelton, "A New Mother's Confessions of Ambivalence," *The New York Times,* April 26, 1978.

99. B. Rollin, "Motherhood: Need or Myth?" *Look* magazine, September 22, 1970.

100. A. B. Blackwell, "On Marriage and Work," (1875) quoted in D. Uris, *Say It Again,* E. P. Dutton (New York: 1979) 157.

101. "What's New? Ten-year-old fashions," *Life* magazine, March 3, 1972, 51.

102. A. Quindlen, "Relationships: Independence vs. Intimacy," *The New York Times,* November 28, 1977, 36.

103. P. Bart, "Portnoy's Mother's Complaint," *Trans-action,* November/December 1970, 69–74. Also, D. Spence and T. Lonner, "The 'Empty Nest': A Transition Within Motherhood," *The Family Coordinator,* October 1971, 369–375.

104. "Motherhood: When the Last Chicken Flies the Coop," *Working Woman,* July 1979, 23. Also, N. Glenn, "Analyses of Six National Surveys of Parent Satisfaction," *Journal of Marriage and the Family,* 37, 1; B. C. Rollins and H. Feldman, "Marital Satisfaction Over the Family Life Cycle," *Journal of Marriage and the Family,* 1970, 32, 20–28.

105. J. Money and P. Tucker, *op. cit.* (note 79) 195. Also, J. Ridley, "Number of Children Expected in Relation to Nonfamilial Activities of the Wife," *Milbank Memorial Fund Quarterly,* 1959, 37, 277–296; I. K. Broverman, et al., "Sex Role Stereotypes: A Current Appraisal," *Journal of Social Issues,* 1972, 28, 2, 59–78; J. Farley, "Graduate Women: Career Aspirations and Desired Family Size," *American Psychologist,* 1970, 25, 1099–1100.

106. B. E. Lott, "Who Wants Children," *American Psychologist,* July 1973.

107. *Ibid.*

108. J. Long Laws, "A Feminist Review of Marital Adjustment Literature: The Rape of the Locke," *Journal of Marriage and the Family,* August 1971, 495.

109. J. Maynard, "Hers," *The New York Times,* March 22, 1979, C2.

110. *Ibid.*

111. R. O. Blood and D. M. Wolfe, *Husbands and Wives: The Dynamics of Married Living,* The Free Press (Glencoe, Ill.: 1960). Also, M. H. Meyerowitz, "Satisfaction During Pregnancy," *Journal of Marriage and the Family,* 1970, 32, 38–42; L. Fosburgh, "Study of New Parents Looks at Impact of Baby's Arrival on the Marriage," *The New York Times,* January 7, 1978, 10.

112. R. G. Ryder, *op. cit.* (note 88) 604–606. And E. E. LeMasters, "Parenthood as Crisis," *Marriage and Family Living,* 1957, 19, 4, 352–355; H. Feldman and M. Feldman, study cited in "Parenting Can Harm a Marriage," *Human Behavior,* January 1979, 59–60.

113. E. Pohlman, *op. cit.* (note 84) 92.

114. M. J. Bienvenu, *Talking it Over Before Marriage,* Public Affairs Pamphlet 512 (New York: 1974) 4.

115. E. Pohlman, *op. cit.* (note 84) 90–91.

116. R. J. Estes and H. L. Wilensky, "Life Cycle Squeeze and the Morale Curve," *Social Problems,* 1977, 25, 3, 277–292.

117. A. Campbell, "The American Way of Mating: Marriage Si, Children Only Maybe," *Psychology Today,* May 1975, 39.

118. A. S. Rossi, "Sex Equality: The Beginning of Ideology," *The Humanist,* September-/October 1969, 29, 5, 3–6, 16.

119. B. Yorburg, *Sexual Identity,* Wiley (New York: 1974) 170–171.

120. J. D. Grambs and W. B. Waetjen, *Sex: Does it Make a Difference?* Duxbury Press (North Scituate, Mass.: 1975) 87.

121. S. B. Coley and B. E. James, "Delivery: A Trauma for Fathers?" *The Family Coordinator,* October 1976, 25, 4, 359–363.

122. D. Knox and R. C. Gilman, *op. cit.* (note 69).

123. R. Gilman and D. Knox, "Coping with Fatherhood: The First Year," *Child Psychiatry and Human Development,* 1976, 6, 3, 135.

124. P. Bart, *op. cit.* (note 103).

125. H. Z. Lopata, "The Secondary Features of a Primary Relationship," *Human Organization,* 1965, 24, 116–123.

126. A. S. Wente and S. B. Crochenberg, "Transition to Fatherhood: Lamaze Preparation, Adjustment Difficulty and the Husband-Wife Relationship," *The Family Coordinator,* October 1976, 25, 4, 351–357.

127. I. Deutscher, "Socialization for Post-Parental Life," in A. M. Rose, ed. *Human Behavior and Social Progress,* Houghton Mifflin (Boston: 1962).

128. S. R. Orden and N. M. Bradburn, "Working Wives and Marriage Happiness," *American Journal of Sociology,* 1968, 24, 392–407; R. Rapoport and R. N. Rapoport, *Dual Career Families,* Penguin (New York: 1971).

129. N. Kelton, *op. cit.* (note 98).

130. L. Pratt, "Conjugal Organization and Health," *Journal of Marriage and the Family,* February 1972, 85–95.

131. "Stale Marriages: When a Lovely Flame Dies," *Human Behavior,* February 1979, 25.

132. J. Long Laws, *op. cit.* (note 108) 508.

133. D. K. Lewis, "The Black Family: Socialization and Sex Roles," *Phylon,* Fall 1975, 36, 3, 221–237. Also, "The War Between the Sexes: Is It Manufactured or Real?" *Ebony,* June 1979.

9 • *Advice for Adults, page 154*

1. V. Cadden, "Women's Lib? I've Seen It on TV," *Redbook,* February 1972, 93.

2. Dr. Marvin S. Eiger, personal communication (p.c.).

3. Kathleen Graham, (p.c.).

4. Theresa S. Church, (p.c.).

5. Patricia Bowen, (p.c.).

6. R. Hartley and A. Klein, "Sex Role Concepts among Elementary School-Age Girls," *Marriage and Family Living,* February 1959, 64.

7. *Ibid.,* 63.

8. A. S. Rossi, "Why Seek Equality Between the Sexes: An Immodest Proposal," *Daedalus,* Spring 1964.

9. J. Bardwick, *In Transition,* Holt, Rinehart and Winston (New York: 1979) 76.

10. M. M. Ferree, "Working-Class Jobs: Housework and Paid Work as Sources of Satisfaction," *Social Problems,* April 1976, 23, 431–441.

11. Robert Sears, Stanford University, March 12, 1979; L. S. Radloff, "Sex Differences in Helplessness with Implications for Depression," in L. S. Hansen and R. S. Rapoza, *Career Development and Counseling of Women,* Charles Thomas (Springfield, Ill.: 1978).

12. R. Barnett and G. K. Baruch, *The Competent Woman,* Irvington (New York: 1978); R. B. Kundsen, ed. *Women and Success: The Anatomy of Achievement,* William Morrow (New York: 1974).

13. R. M. Kelly and M. A. Boutelier, "Mothers, Daughters and the Socialization of Political Women," *Sex Roles,* 1978, 4, 3, 415–443; L. W. Hoffman, "Changes in Family Roles, Socialization and Sex Differences," *American Psychologist,* August 1977, 654; I. K. Broverman, et al., "Sex Role Stereotypes: A Current Appraisal," *Journal of Social Issues,* 1972, 28, 2, 74.

14. S. Vogel, et al., "Maternal Employment and Perception of Sex Role Among College Students," *Journal of Developmental Psychology,* 1970, 3, 384–391; E. E. Maccoby, "Children's Concepts of Male and Female Roles," *Merrill-Palmer Quarterly,* 1960, 6, 84–91.

15. E. Douvan, "Employment and the Adolescent," in F. I. Nye and L. W. Hoffman, eds. *The Employed Mother in America,* Rand-McNally (Chicago: 1963).

16. H. S. Astin, "Women and Work," paper presented at the conference New Directions for Research on Women, Madison, Wis., 1975.

17. J. A. Kelly and L. Worell, "Parent Behaviors Related to Masculine, Feminine and Androgynous Sex Role Orientations," *Journal of Consulting and Clinical Psychology,* 1976, 44, 5, 844.

18. L. W. Hoffman, *op. cit.* (note 13).

19. L. W. Hoffman, "Effects of Maternal Employment on the Child—A Review of the Research," *Developmental Psychology,* 1974, 10, 2, 204–228.

20. S. D. Kamerman, *Parenting in an Unresponsive Society,* Columbia University School of Social Work, April 1979.

21. S. Trotter, "Day Care Given a Clean Bill of Health," *American Psychological Association Monitor,* April 1976, 4.

22. J. Kagan, et al., "The Effects of Infant Day Care on Psychological Development," presented at a symposium on "The Effect of Early Experience on Child Development," *American Association for the Advancement of Science,* February 19, 1976, Boston, Mass. Also see *Who Cares For America's Children? An interview with Urie Bronfenbrenner,* Science Interface (Dayton, N.J.: 1977).

23. The Harris Poll, *Playboy Report on American Men,* January 1979. Also, *Psychology Today* poll, Carol Tavris report, 1973; Public Broadcasting Service/Louis Harris poll for the program "Men, Women: What's the Difference," reported January 14, 1977.

24. M. McGrady, *The Kitchen Sink Papers,* Doubleday (New York: 1975).

25. H. Biller and D. Meredith, *Father Power,* Anchor (New York: 1975) 68–69.

26. R. E. Gould, "Nonsexist Childrearing," *New Woman,* August 1971, 20.

27. R. D. Parke and D. B. Sawin, "The Father's Role in Infancy: A Re-evaluation," *The Family Coordinator,* October 1976, 25, 4, 369.

28. R. Flaste, "Looking at the Role of Father—What It Has Been and Might Be," *The New York Times,* June 13, 1975, 43.

29. J. Leonard, "The Fathering Instinct," *Ms.* magazine, May 1974, 112.

30. See especially, E. A. Daley, *Father Feelings,* William Morrow (New York: 1978); D. S. David and R. Brannon, eds. *The Forty-Nine Percent Majority: The Male Sex Role,* Addison-Wesley (Reading, Mass.: 1976); J. Snodgrass, ed. *For Men Against Sexism,* Times Change Press (Albion, Calif.: 1977); J. H. Pleck and J. Sawyer, eds. *Men and Masculinity,* Prentice-Hall (Englewood Cliffs, N.J.: 1974); J. H. Pleck and R. Brannon, eds. "Male Roles and the Male Experience," a special issue of *Journal of Social Issues,* 1978, 34, 1; M. F. Fasteau, *The Male Machine,* McGraw-Hill (New York: 1974); J. Levine, *Who Will Raise the Children,* Lippincott (Philadelphia: 1976); W. Farrell, *The Liberated Man,* Random House (New York: 1975).

31. J. Maynard, "Do Fathers Make Good Mothers?" *Ladies Home Journal,* March 1979, 152.

574

32. R. Flaste, *op. cit.* (note 28).

33. *Ibid.*

34. R. Flaste, "Fathers and Infants: Getting Close," *The New York Times,* December 5, 1975, 45.

35. J. Leonard, *op. cit.* (note 29) 53.

36. K. Pitchford, "Poem Desperate in Naptime," in K. Pitchford, *Color Photos of the Atrocities,* Atlantic Monthly Press (Boston: 1973).

37. B. Spock, *Baby and Child Care,* Pocket Books (New York: 1976) 47.

38. A few examples of such argumentation may be found in: M. L. Hamilton, *Fathers Influence on Children,* Nelson Hall (Chicago: 1977); M. L. Hoffman, "Father Absence and Conscience Development," *Developmental Psychology,* 1971, 4, 3, 400–406; H. Biller, *Father Child and Sex Role: Paternal Determinants of Personality Development,* Heath (Lexington, Mass.: 1971); M. E. Lamb and J. E. Lamb, "The Nature and Importance of the Father-Infant Relationship," *The Family Coordinator,* October 1976, 25, 4, 379–385; W. Churchill, *Homosexual Behavior Among Males,* Prentice-Hall (Englewood Cliffs, N.J.: 1967) 160–161; L. Bartemeier, "The Contribution of the Father to the Mental Health of the Family," *American Journal of Psychiatry,* 1953, 110, 277–280; W. A. Westley and N. B. Epstein, "Parental Interaction as Related to the Emotional Health of Children," *Social Problems,* 1960, 8, 87–92; K. M. Tooley, "Johnny I Hardly Knew Ye: Toward a Revision of the Theory of Male Psychosexual Development," *American Journal of Orthopsychiatry,* April 1977, 47, 2, 194–195; J. W. Santrock, "Effects of Father Absence on Sex-Typed Behaviors in Male Children," *Journal of Genetic Psychology,* 1977, 130, 9; R. G. D'Andrade, "Father Absence, Identification and Identity, *Ethos,* Winter 1973, 1, 4, 440–455; L. K. Frank, "The Father's Role in Child Nurturance," *Child Study Journal,* March 1939, 16, 135.

39. "A Father's Love: It Strengthens the Mother-Child Bond," *Human Behavior,* October 1978, 59 (citing study by R. K. Barrett of California State University).

40. K. M. Rosenthal and H. F. Keshet, "The Impact of Child Care Responsibilities on Part Time or Single Fathers," *Alternate Lifestyles,* November 1978, 1, 4, 466. Also see F. A. Pederson, "Does Research on Children Reared in Father-Absent Families Yield Information on Father Influences?" *The Family Coordinator,* October 1976, 25, 4, 459–463; C. Harrington, *Errors in Sex Role Behavior in Teen Age Boys,* Teachers College Press (New York: 1970) 73; R. H. Rubin, "Matricentric Family Structure and Self-Attitudes of Negro Children," R. and E. Research Associates (San Francisco, Calif.: 1976).

41. J. S. Mill, *The Subjection of Women* (1869) quoted in A. S. Rossi, "Sentiment and Intellect: The Story of John Stuart Mill and Harriet Taylor Mill," *Midway,* Spring 1970, 10, 4, 47.

42. E. W. Burgess, "Companionship Marriage in the United States," *Studies of the Family* 69–87, cited in J. Long Laws, "A Feminist Review of Marital Adjustment Literature: The Rape of the Locke," *Journal of Marriage and the Family,* August 1971, 489.

43. S. L. Bem and D. J. Bem, "Training The Woman to Know Her Place: The Power of a Nonconscious Ideology," in D. J. Bem, *Beliefs, Attitudes, and Human Affairs,* Brooks/-Cole (Belmont, Calif.: 1970).

44. C. Ehrlich, "The Male Sociologist's Burden: The Place of Women in Marriage and Family Texts," *Journal of Marriage and the Family,* August 1971, 426.

45. S. L. Bem and D. J. Bem, *op. cit.* (note 43).

46. G. Z. Gass, "Equitable Marriage," *The Family Coordinator,* October 1974, 369.

47. K. A. Clarke-Stewart, "Interactions Between Mothers and Their Young Children," *Monographs of the Society for Research in Child Development,* 1973, 38, 153.

48. B. Raphael, "Mothers and Daughters," *Ladies Home Journal,* September 1978, 107.

49. L. Benson, *Fatherhood: A Sociological Perspective,* Random House (New York: 1968) 67.

50. S. deBeauvoir, *The Second Sex,* Knopf (New York: 1968) xvi, xviii.

51. J. Kellerman, "Sex Role Stereotypes and Attitudes Toward Parental Blame for the Psychological Problems of Children," *Journal of Consulting and Clinical Psychology,* 1974, 42, 153–55. Also, L. C. Pogrebin, "Do Women Make Men Violent," *Ms.* magazine, November 1974, 49ff.

52. J. L. Turk and N. W. Bell, "Measuring Power in Families," *Journal of Marriage and the Family,* May 1972, 34, 2.

53. To compare your answers with public response on many of these questions, see results and discussion in B. Yorburg and I. Arafat, "Current Sex Role Conceptions and Conflict," *Sex Roles,* 1975, 1, 2, 135–146; C. Safilios-Rothschild, "Family Sociology or Wives' Family Sociology? A Cross-Cultural Examination of Decision-Making," *Journal of Marriage and* *the Family,* 1969, 31, 2, 290–301; H. P. Dreitzel, ed. *Family, Marriage and the Struggle of the Sexes,* Macmillan (New York: 1972).

54. This is a dense and controversial area of inquiry in which the following sources are especially lucid: W. J. Goode, "World Revolution and Family Patterns," in A. S. Skolnick and J. H. Skolnick, eds. *Family in Transition,* Little, Brown (Boston: 1977 revised) 47–58; D. M. Heer, "Dominance and the Working Wife," in F. I. Nye and L. W. Hoffman, *op. cit.* (note 15); R. O. Blood and D. M. Wolfe, *Husbands and Wives: The Dynamics of Married Living,* The Free Press (Glencoe, Ill.: 1960); D. L. Gillespie, "Who Has the Power? The Marital Struggle," *Journal of Marriage and the Family,* August 1971, 445–458.

55. J. Long Laws, *op. cit.* (note 42) 493.

56. B. Certner, "Sex Roles and Mental Health: A Proposal for the Development of the Sex Roles Institute," *Psychiatric Institute Foundation,* Washington, D.C., 1976, II-27.

57. For further development of this position see: M. M. Poloma and T. N. Garland, "The Married Professional Woman: A Study in the Tolerance of Domestication," *Journal of Marriage and the Family,* August 1971, 531–540; J. R. Chapman and M. Gates, *Women Into Wives: The Legal and Economic Impact of Marriage,* Sage (Beverly Hills, Calif.: 1977); J. Long Laws, *op. cit.* (note 42) 492–493; G. R. Hawkes and M. Taylor, "Power Structure in Mexican and Mexican-American Farm Labor Families," *Journal of Marriage and the Family,* November 1975, 807–811; J. Scanzoni, "Sex Roles, Economic Factors and Marital Solidarity in Black and White Marriages," *Journal of Marriage and the Family,* February 1975, 130–144; R. O. Blood and R. L. Hamblin, "The Effect of the Wife's Employment on the Family Power Structure," *Social Forces,* 1958, 36, 347–352. (For a telling critique, Long Laws should be read *after* the other books and articles.).

58. L. E. Walker, *The Battered Woman,* Harper & Row (New York: 1979).

59. B. Certner, *op. cit.* (note 56) VI-37.

60. S. J. Bahr and B. C. Rollins, "Crisis and Conjugal Power," *Journal of Marriage and the Family,* May 1971, 366; also D. Kiernan and I. Tallmans, "Spousal Adaptability: An Assessment of Marital Competence," *Journal of Marriage and the Family,* May 1972, 247–255.

61. D. B. Lynn, *The Father: His Role in Child Development,* Brooks/Cole (Monterey, Calif.: 1974) 281. (Lynn defines the situation but overlooks the problem).

62. B. L. Forisha, *Sex Roles and Personal Awareness,* Scott, Foresman and Co./General Learning Press (Morristown, N.J.: 1978) 339.

10 • Working Together, page 177

1. K. Gough, "The Origin of the Family," *Journal of Marriage and the Family,* November 1971, 76–770; P. Aries, *Centuries of Childhood,* Knopf (New York: 1962); J. B. Victor and J. Sander, *The Family: The Evolution of Our Oldest Human Institution,* Bobbs-Merrill (Indianapolis: 1978); L. Benson, *The Family Bond,* Random House (New York: 1971) 321–345; E. Shorter, *The Making of the Modern Family,* Basic Books (New York: 1975); C. C. Zimmerman, "The Future of the Family in America," *Journal of Marriage and the Family,* May 1972, 323–333; R. Winch, *The Modern Family,* Holt, Rinehart and Winston (New York: 1971); D. A. Schultz, *The Changing Family: Its Function and Future* (2nd ed.), Prentice-Hall (Englewood Cliffs, N.J.: 1976).

2. J. K. Galbraith, "The Housewife: How the Economy Hangs on Her Apron Strings," *Ms.* magazine, May 1974, 74 ff; S. Firestone, *The Dialectic of Sex,* William Morrow (New York: 1970) 97–103; I. V. Sawhill, "Economic Perspectives on the Family," *Daedalus,* Spring 1977, 106, 2, 115–125; J. Z. Giele, "Changes in the Modern Family: Their Impact on Sex Roles," *American Journal of Orthopsychiatry,* October 1971, 41, 5; H. Kahne, "Economic Research on Women and Families," *Signs,* 1978, 3, 3, 652–665; E. Fisher, *Woman's Creation,* Anchor/Doubleday (New York: 1979); H. P. Dreitzel, ed. *Family, Marriage, and the Struggle of the Sexes,* Macmillan (New York: 1972); L. K. Howe, ed., *The Future of the Family,* Simon & Schuster (New York: 1972); E. Zaretsky, *Capitalism, The Family and Personal Life,* Harper/Colophon (New York: 1973); T. W. Schultz, ed. *Economics of the Family,* University of Chicago Press (Chicago: 1975) 397–526.

3. C. F. Etheridge, "Equality in the Family: Comparative Analysis and Theoretical Model," *International Journal of Women's Studies,* (undated) 1, 1, 50–63; G. Gibson, "Kin Family Network: Overheralded Structure in Past Conceptualizations of Family Functioning," *Journal of Marriage and the Family,* February 1972, 13–23; C. Lasch, *Haven in a Heartless World,* Basic Books (New York: 1977); G. Zuk, "Strengths and Weaknesses of the Jewish Family," cited in *Psychology Today,* February 1977, 146; R. Staples, ed. *The Black Family,* Wadsworth (New York: 1971); H. A. Barry, M. K. Bacon and I. L. Child, "A Cross-Cultural Survey of Some Sex Differences in Socialization," *Journal of Abnormal and Social Psychology,* 1957, 55, 327–332; A. S. Skolnick and J. H. Skolnick, eds. *Family in Transition* (2nd ed.) Little, Brown (Boston: 1977); J. Lorber, "Beyond Equality of the Sexes: The Question of the Children," *The Family Coordinator,* October 1975, 465–472; R. M. Kanter, et al., "Coupling, Parenting and the Presence of Others: Intimate Relationships in Communal Households," *The Family Coordinator,* October 1973, 433–452; T. S. Weisner and J. C. Martin, "Learning Environments for Infants: Communes and Conventionally Married Families in California," *Alternate Lifestyles,* May 1979, 2, 2, 201–242; M. Gerson, *Family, Women and Socialization in the Kibbutz,* Lexington Books (Lexington, Mass.: 1978); R. B. Hill, *Strengths of Black Families,* National Urban League (Washington, D.C.: 1971).

4. G. Lish, "Parents and Children and the Debts of Love," *The New York Times,* November 22, 1978, C6.

5. For some provocative exploration of family diversity see, J. Howard, *Families,* Simon & Schuster (New York: 1978).

6. U.S. Statistical Abstract 1977; V. George and P. Wilding, *Motherless Families,* Routledge & Kegan Paul (London: 1972).

7. E. Einstein, "Stepfamily Lives," *Human Behavior,* April 1979, 63.

8. Population Reference Bureau chart in J. Nordheimer, "The Family in Transition," *The New York Times,* November 27, 1977.

9. S. V. Roberts, "The Family Fascinates a Host of Students," *The New York Times,* April 28, 1978; "Home Is A Crucial Factor," *The New York Times,* May 17, 1973.

10. G. Dullea, "The Stepfamilies: New Guides to Live By," *The New York Times,* January 4, 1979, C1; E. B. Visher and J. S. Visher, *Stepfamilies,* Brunner/Mazel (New York: 1979); P. Bohannan and R. Erickson, "Stepping In," *Psychology Today,* January 1978, 53–54; K. L. Wilson, et al., "Stepfathers and Stepchildren: An Exploratory Analysis from Two National Surveys," *Journal of Marriage and the Family,* August 1975, 526–536.

11. C. E. Sudia, *The Family Coordinator,* January 1972, 136; C. J. Lehr, *Psychology Today,* May 1979, 12; E. Ogg, *One-Parent Families,* Public Affairs Pamphlets no. 543 (New York: 1976); R. A. Gardner, *The Boys and Girls Book About One-Parent Families,* G. P. Putnam's (New York: 1978).

12. A. Crittendon, "Nearly Half of All Fatherless Families Said to Live in Poverty," *The New York Times,* April 18, 1977, 26.

13. U. S. Department of Labor, 1975.

14. U. Bronfenbrenner, quoted in A. G. Kaplan and J. P. Bean, eds. *Beyond Sex Role Stereotypes: Readings Toward a Psychology of Androgyny,* Little, Brown (Boston: 1976).

15. "The Women's Work Is Not Yet Done," *The New York Times,* November 23, 1977.

16. N. Glazer-Malbin, "Housework," *Signs,* 1976, 1, 4, 905–922; A. Oakley, *Woman's Work,* Pantheon (New York: 1974); A. Oakley, *The Sociology of Housework,* Pantheon (New York: 1977); H. Z. Lopata, *Occupation: Housewife,* Oxford (New York: 1971).

17. P. Mainardi, "The Politics of Housework," in N. Glazer-Malbin and H. Y. Waehrer, eds. *Woman in a Man-made World,* Rand-McNally (Chicago: 1972) 289–292.

18. S. Porter, "What's a Wife Worth," *The New York Post Magazine,* July 13, 1966, 2; also A. C. Scott, "The Value of Housework: For Love or Money," *Ms.* magazine, July 1972, 56–59.

19. J. K. Galbraith, *Economics and the Public Purpose,* Houghton Mifflin (Boston: 1973).

20. B. Berch, "The Development of Housework," *International Journal of Women's Studies,* (undated) 1, 4, 336–348; *Scientific American,* April 1976.

21. P. Felig, "Confessions of a Surrogate Housewife," *The New York Times,* February 11, 1978, 21. Also see, Mel Scult, "Letters to the Editor," *Ms.* magazine, December 1974, 4; S. M. Miller, "Confusions of a Middle-Class Husband," in L. K. Howe, *op. cit.* (note 2).

22. L. B. Franke, "Hers," *The New York Times,* October 13, 1977, C2.

23. Much of this data comes from K. Walker and M. Woods, "Time Use: A Measure of Household Production of Family Goods and Services," *American Home Economics Association,* Washington, D.C., 1976; J. Robinson, *How Americans Use Time: A Social Psychological Analysis,* Praeger (New York: 1977); *Redbook* magazine survey reported August 1972, 127; K. E. Walker and W. H. Ganger, *The Dollar Value of Household Work,* Cornell University Press (Ithaca, N.Y.: 1973); J. Vanek, "Time Spent in Housework," *Scientific American,* November 1974, 116–120; C. W. Berheide, S. F. Berk and R. A. Berk, "Household Work in the Suburbs: The Job and Its Participants," *Pacific Sociological Review,*

October 1976, 19, 4, 491–518; M. Heins, "Women Physicians," *Radcliffe Quarterly,* June 1979, 13; R. Stafford, et al., "The Division of Labor Among Cohabiting and Married Couples," *Journal of Marriage and the Family,* February 1977, 39, 1, 43–57; J. N. Hedges and J. K. Barnett, "Working Women and the Division of Household Tasks," *The Monthly Labor Review,* April 1972, 9–14.

24. C. Tavris, "Men and Women Report Their Views on Masculinity," *Psychology Today,* January 1977, 82.

25. J. H. Pleck, "Men's Family Work: Three Perspectives and some New Data," *The Family Coordinator,* October 1979, 481–488.

26. J. Long Laws, "A Feminist Review of Marital Adjustment Literature: The Rape of the Locke," *Journal of Marriage and the Family,* August 1971, 490–492.

27. S. F. Berk, R. A. Berk and C. W. Berheide, "The Nondivision of Household Labor," paper presented to the American Association for the Advancement of Science, Chicago, February 1976.

28. J. Long Laws, *op. cit.* (note 26) 490–491.

29. R. Stafford, et al., *op. cit.* (note 23) 54.

30. A. M. Propper, "The Relationship of Maternal Employment to Adolescent Roles, Activities and Parental Relationships," *Journal of Marriage and the Family,* August 1972, 417; J. N. Hedges and J. K. Barnett, *op. cit.* (note 24) 11.

31. R. M. Kanter, et al., *op. cit.* (note 3) 448.

32. R. R. Sears, E. E. Maccoby and H. Levin, *Patterns of Child Rearing,* Row, Peterson (Evanston, Ill.: 1957); D. Duncan, H. Schuman and B. Duncan, *Social Change in a Metropolitan Community,* Russell Sage (New York: 1973).

33. G. Puffer, "Sexual Concepts of Kindergarten, First and Second Grade Children as a Function of Their Home Environments," paper presented to the American Educational Research Association, San Francisco, Calif., April 1976; J. M. Baldigo, "An Exploration of Elementary School Children's Conceptions of Family Roles," *Dissertation Abstracts International,* June 1976, Sec. A, 3611, 7672-A; J. and E. Newson, D. Richardson and J. Scaife, "Perspectives in Sex-Role Stereotyping," in J. Chetwynd and O. Hartnett, eds. *The Sex Role System,* Routledge & Kegan Paul (London: 1978) 37.

34. *Life* magazine, undated issue in 1973.

35. S. Edmiston, "How to Write Your Own Marriage Contract," *Ms.* magazine, Spring 1972, 66–67; also see A. Shulman, "A Challenge to Every Marriage," in A. Arkoff, ed. *Psychology and Personal Growth,* Allyn and Bacon (Boston: 1975).

36. Unless otherwise specified all quotes are from personal communications or interviews.

37. M. McGrady, *The Kitchen Sink Papers,* Doubleday (New York: 1975) 182–185.

38. B. Yorburg and J. Arafat, "Current Sex Role Conceptions and Conflict," *Sex Roles,* 1975, 1, 2, 142.

39. *Ibid.,* 143.

40. "Raising Children in a Changing Society," *The General Mills American Family Report,* 1976–77, 90.

41. J. R. Kellerman and E. R. Katz, "Attitudes Toward the Division of Child-Rearing Responsibilities," *Sex Roles,* 1978, 4, 4, 505–511.

42. J. D. DeFrain, "New Meaning for Parenthood," paper presented at Banff International Conference on Behavior Modification, Banff, Alberta, Canada, March 1974.

43. K. Keniston and the Carnegie Council on Children, *All Our Children: The American Family in Trouble,* Harcourt Brace Jovanovich (New York: 1977).

44. J. K. Meuli, "In Brief," *National Now Times,* March 1979, 2.

45. J. Reston, "Back to Basics," *The New York Times,* October 7, 1977, A31.

46. R. B. Semple, Jr., "Seven Months With New Baby: Parent Leave Is Hit in Sweden," *The New York Times,* December 7, 1976, 55.

47. B. Rosen, T. Jerdee and T. Prestwich, "Dual Career Marital Adjustment: Potential Effects of Discriminatory Managerial Attitudes," *Journal of Marriage and the Family,* 1975, 37, 3, 565–572.

48. C. Greenwald, "Part-Time Work: When Less is More," *Ms.* magazine, May 1976, 41–42.

49. A. Pifer, *Women Working: Toward a New Society,* annual report of the president of the Carnegie Corporation, 1976. Also see J. Z. Giele, *Women and the Future: Changing Sex Roles in America,* The Free Press (New York: 1978) 188–235.

50. R. A. Fein, "Research on Fathering: Social Policy and an Emergent Perspective," *Journal of Social Issues,* 1978, 34, 1.

578

11 • Living Together, page 195

1. "Pink" poster copyright 1974 by Sheila Levrant deBretteville.
2. O. Hammerstein, "Soliloquy," *Carousel,* copyright 1949.
3. P. Goldberger, "Design Notebook," *The New York Times,* May 25, 1978, C10.
4. D. E. Smith, "Household Space and Family Organization," *Pacific Sociological Review,* January 1971.
5. J. C. Belcher and P. B. Vazquez-Calcerrada, "A Cross-Cultural Approach to the Social Function of Housing," *Journal of Marriage and the Family,* November 1972, 760.
6. N. P. Birkby and L. K. Weisman, "A Woman-Built Environment: Constructive Fantasies," *Quest,* Summer 1975, 2, 1, 7–18.
7. C. Graff, "Making a House a Home," *Journal of Home Economics,* May 1977, 11–12.
8. N. P. Birkby and L. K. Weisman, *op. cit.* (note 6) 9.
9. L. Hazleton, *Israeli Women,* Touchstone (New York: 1977).
10. D. Hayden and G. Wright, "Architecture and Urban Planning," *Signs,* 1976, 1, 4, 923–933. Also Belcher and Vazquez-Calcerrada, *op. cit.* (note 5).
11. D. Hayden, "Two Utopian Feminists and Their Campaigns for Kitchenless Homes," *Signs,* 1978, 4, 2, 274–290. Also, D. Hayden, "Redesigning the Domestic Workplace," *Chrysalis,* 1977, 1, 19–29; and B. Bettleheim, *Children of the Dream,* Macmillan (New York: 1969) 82, 331.
12. D. E. Smith, *op. cit.* (note 4) 66.
13. N. P. Birkby and L. K. Weisman, *op. cit.* (note 6) 9.
14. D. E. Smith, *op. cit.* (note 4) 57.
15. J. C. Belcher and P. B. Vazquez-Calcerrada, *op. cit.* (note 5) 759.
16. Irene Hanson Frieze, University of Pittsburg, interviewed by J. N. Shurking, "Psychologist Strikes Blow for Sex Role Stereotypes," *Boston Sunday Globe,* May 5, 1974, A19.
17. D. E. Smith, *op. cit.* (note 4) 70.
18. *Ibid.,* 72.
19. Supposedly, most women consider the bedroom their favorite room: J. Klemesrud, "Purchasing a House: A Matriarchal Move," *The New York Times,* September 5, 1967.
20. R. D. Parke and D. B. Sawin, "Children's Privacy in the Home: Developmental, Ecological and Child-Rearing Determinants," paper presented to the Society for Research in Child Development, Denver, April 1975.
21. D. E. Smith, *op. cit.* 69.
22. N. P. Birkby and L. K. Weisman, *op. cit.* (note 6) 8.
23. M. Cohen, "Self-Defense in a Man-Made World," *Ladies Home Journal,* October 1978, 12.
24. "Tools for a Woman's Trade," *Human Behavior,* October 1977, 72.
25. A. Mehrabian, *Public Places and Private Spaces,* Basic (New York: 1976).
26. J. Lester, *Two Love Stories,* Dial Press (New York: 1972).
27. H. L. Rheingold and K. V. Cook, "The Contents of Boys' and Girls' Rooms as an Index of Parents' Behavior," *Child Development,* 1975, 46, 459–463.
28. J. C. Barden, "Children and Thrift: Taking the Magic Out of Money," *The New York Times,* January 10, 1980, C1.
29. Gallup Youth Survey, published October 5, 1977.
30. M. Fricke, "Fathers Rethink Views on Raising Daughters," *New Directions for Women,* Winter 1977–78, 4.
31. *Raising Children in a Changing Society,* General Mills American Family Report, 1976–77, 88, 112.
32. *Ibid.,* 89.
33. C. Claiborne, *The New York Times,* February 12, 1979, B13.
34. E. Mavis Hetherington, et al., "Beyond Father Absence: Conceptualization of Effects of Divorce," Society for Research in Child Development, Denver, April 1975.
35. M. L. Wald, "Saving Youth from Demon Rum—A Futile Exercise?" *The New York Times,* July 29, 1979, 6E. Also, *Kids and Alcohol: The Deadliest Drug,* Lothrop, Lee and Shepard (New York: 1975).
36. Abigail Van Buren, quoted in "Hot Flashes," *Majority Report,* date unknown.
37. T. J. Cottle, C. N. Edwards and J. Pleck, "The Relationship of Sex Role Identity and Social and Political Attitudes," *Journal of Personality,* 1970, 38, 435–452.
38. General Mills American Family Report, *op. cit.* (note 31) 96–97.
39. J. Dunn, *Distress and Comfort,* Harvard University Press (Cambridge, Mass.: 1977) 39.

40. E. Weisberger, *Your Young Child and You,* E. P. Dutton (New York: 1979) 55.
41. W. G. Krieger, "Infant Influences and the Parent Sex–Child Sex Interaction in the Socialization Process," *Catalog of Selected Documents in Psychology,* May 1976, 6, 36.
42. B. Spock, *Baby and Child Care,* Pocket Books (New York: 1976) 557–560; also see T. B. Brazelton, *Doctor and Child,* Delta (New York: 1978) 140.

12 • Family Feelings, page 213

1. "My Parents," in M. Bradley, et al., *Unbecoming Men,* Times Change Press (New York: 1971).
2. D. Kavanaugh, ed. *Listen to Us! Children's Express Report,* Workman (New York: 1978) 206.
3. *Ibid.,* 36.
4. J. A. Doster and B. R. Strickland, "Perceived Childrearing Practices and Self-Disclosure Patterns," *Journal of Consulting and Clinical Psychology,* 1969, 33, 3, 382.
5. D. Kavanaugh, *op. cit.* (note 2) 52.
6. E. E. Maccoby and C. N. Jacklin, *The Psychology of Sex Differences,* Stanford University Press (Stanford, Calif.: 1974) 183.
7. D. Bugental et al., "Perfidious Feminine Faces," *Journal of Personality and Social Psychology,* 1971, 17, 314–318.
8. P. B. Johnson and J. Goodchild, "How Women Get Their Way," *Psychology Today,* October 1976, 69–70.
9. E. Yachnes, "The Myth of Masculinity," *American Journal of Psychoanalysis,* 1973, 33, 1, 58.
10. A. R. Hochschild, "The Sociology of Feelings and Emotion," W. M. Millman and R. M. Kanter, eds. *Another Voice,* Anchor Press (Garden City, N.Y.: 1975) 296.
11. A. Ginott, "How To Drive Your Child Sane," *Ladies Home Journal,* August 1977, 108.
12. J. Howard, *Families,* Simon & Schuster (New York: 1978).
13. R. M. Weist and B. Kruppe, "Parent and Sibling Comprehension of Children's Speech," *Psycholinguistic Research,* January 1977, 6, 1, 49–58.
14. B. McLaughlin, "The Mother Tongue," *Human Nature,* December 1978, 89.
15. *Ibid.*
16. A. Ginott, *op. cit.* (note 11).
17. "Fathers and Sons: Earmarks of Understanding," *Human Behavior,* December 1978, 61.
18. L. Van Gelder, "Paul Dooley, a Household Theatrical Face, Gets Used to Being a Name, Too." *The New York Times,* July 23, 1979, C13.
19. M. L. Papanek, "Authority and Sex Roles in the Family," *Journal of Marriage and the Family,* February 1969, 94.
20. J. Horn, "Love Is the Most Important Ingredient in Happiness," *Psychology Today,* July 1976.
21. B. C. Rosen and R. D'Andrade, "The Psychosocial Origins of Achievement Motivation," *Sociometry,* 1959, 22, 185–218.
22. L. F. Cervantes, "Family Background, Primary Relationships, and High School Dropout," *Journal of Marriage and the Family,* 1965, 27, 218–223; P. H. Mussen et al., "The Influence of Father-Son Relationships on Adolescent Personality and Attitudes," *Journal of Child Psychology and Psychiatry,* 1963, 4, 3–16.
23. Mark Reuter and Henry Biller cited in J. Money and P. Tucker, *Sexual Signatures,* Little, Brown (Boston: 1975) 204–205.
24. Susan, Steven and Mitzi are case histories discussed in J. A. Levine, "Real Kids vs. 'The Average' Family," *Psychology Today,* June 1978.
25. J. D. Grambs and W. B. Waetjen, *Sex: Does It Make a Difference?* Duxbury (North Scituate, Mass.: 1975) 94.
26. N. St. John, "The Validity of Children's Reports on Their Parents' Educational Level: A Methodological Note," *Sociology of Education,* Summer 1970, 43, 255–269.
27. E. K. Beller and J. L. B. Turner, "Personality Correlates of Children's Perception of Human Size," *Child Development,* 1964, 35, 441–449.
28. J. Walters and N. Stinnett, "Parent-Child Relationships: A Decade Review of Research," *Journal of Marriage and the Family,* February 1971, 96.
29. "What They're Doing Together," *The New York Times Magazine,* March 11, 1979, 64.

580

30. F. Caplan, ed. *Parents' Yellow Pages,* Anchor (New York: 1978) 449.
31. R. Flaste, "In Families That Have Two Children, Rearing Isn't Done By Parents Alone," *The New York Times,* December 26, 1976.
32. C. Harrington, *Errors in Sex Role Behavior in Teen-Age Boys,* Teachers' College Press (New York: 1970) 75–76.
33. M. Mead, *Male and Female,* Morrow Paperback (New York: 1975) 313.
34. G. R. Bach and P. Wyden, "The Art of Family Fighting," in K. C. W. Kammeyer, ed. *Confronting the Issues,* Allyn and Bacon (Boston: 1975) 314.
35. M. A. Straus, "Leveling, Civility and Violence in the Family," *Journal of Marriage and the Family,* February 1974, 36.
36. *Ibid.,* 323; W. I. Goode, "Force and Violence in the Family," *Journal of Marriage and the Family,* November 1971, 630; M. Straus, R. Gelles, and S. Steinmetz, *Behind Closed Doors: Violence in the American Family,* Anchor Press (New York: 1979).
37. R. R. Sears, E. E. Maccoby and H. Levin, *Patterns of Childrearing,* Row, Peterson (Evanston, Ill.: 1957).
38. M. E. Lamb, "Observational Analysis of Sibling Relationships in Infancy," paper presented at the International Conference on Infant Studies, Providence, R. I., March 1978, 3.
39. B. G. Gilmartin, "The Case Against Spanking," *Human Behavior,* February 1979, 22.
40. Adapted from V. Moberg, "Consciousness Razors," *National Education Association,* Washington, D.C.
41. *Ibid.*
42. D. Kavanaugh, *op. cit.* (note 2) 55.
43. R. J. Gelles, "The Myth of Battered Husbands and New Facts about Family Violence," *Ms.* magazine, October 1979, 72.
44. S. Hawke and D. Knox, *The Family Coordinator,* 27, 3, cited in "Advantages of the One-Child Family," *Human Behavior,* February 1979, 24.
45. D. Lynn, *Parental and Sex Role Identification: A Theoretical Formulation,* McCutchen (Berkeley: 1969); L. M. Lansky, "The Family Structure Also Affects the Model: Sex Role Attitudes in Parents of Preschool Children," *Merrill-Palmer Quarterly,* 1967, 13, 2, 139–150.
46. Irving Harris, Illinois State Psychiatric Institute, source unknown.
47. L. K. Forer and H. Still, *The Birth Order Factor,* Pocket Books (New York: 1977).
48. M. Hennig, "Family Dynamics and the Successful Woman Executive," in R. B. Kundsin, ed. *Women & Success,* Morrow (New York: 1974) 88–93.
49. V. G. Cicirelli, "Siblings Helping Siblings," in V. Allen, ed. *Inter-age Interaction in Childhood,* Academic (New York: 1976).
50. R. M. Kelly and M. A. Boutilier, "Mothers, Daughters and The Socialization of Political Women," *Sex Roles,* 1978, 4, 3, 440.

13 • *Managing Freedom, page 228*

1. R. Flaste, "The Frustrating Battle Against Sex Stereotyping," *The New York Times,* November 1976.
2. M. M. Rodgon, C. Gralewski and J. Hetzel, "Maternal Attitudes Toward Sex Roles Related to Children's Attitudes Toward Maternal Roles in Second and Sixth Grade Children," University of Chicago, ERIC #ED 136935 PS 009180.
3. L. P. Lipsitt and C. Spikes, "Cross Sex Effect of Child and Adult," *Advances in Child Development and Behavior,* Academic Press, (New York: 1965) 101–103.
4. H. W. Stevenson, et al., "Determinants of Children's Preferences for Adults," *Child Development,* 1967, 38, 1–14.
5. E. Fisher, "If Only You'd Been a Boy," *Aphra,* Winter 1972–1973, 4, 5–6.
6. K. Bruno, "Sexism and the Family Tree," *The Spirit of '48 Women's Paper,* Stockton State College, Pomona, New Jersey, date unknown.
7. *Ibid.;* also see D. M. Young, et al., "Quality of Life and Communication of Family Skills: Who Gets the Goodies?" paper presented to the Western Psychological Association, Los Angeles, April 1976.
8. P. Adams, et al., *Children's Rights,* Praeger (New York: 1971) 56.
9. E. E. Maccoby and C. N. Jacklin, *The Psychology of Sex Differences,* Stanford University Press (Stanford: Calif.: 1974) 309–311. Also see, S. Saegert, "The Development of Environmental Competence in Girls and Boys," in P. Burnett, ed. *Women in Society,* Maaroufa Press (Chicago, Ill.: 1976); W. G. Krieger, "Infant Influences and the Parent

Sex Child Sex Interaction in the Socialization Process," *Catalog of Selected Documents in Psychology,* May 1976, 6, 36; F. A. Pederson and K. S. Robson, "Father Participation in Infancy," *American Journal of Orthopsychiatry,* 1969, 39, 466–472.

10. C. M. Minton, J. Kagan and J. A. Levine, "Mother-Child Interaction in 27-months-old Children," unpublished manuscript 1970. Also, C. Minton, J. Kagan and J. A. Levine, "Maternal Control and Obedience in the Two-Year-Old," *Child Development,* 1971, 42, 1873–1874.

11. B. I. Fagot, "Sex Differences in Toddlers' Behavior and Parental Reaction," *Developmental Psychology,* 1974, 10, 4, 558.

12. R. Hart, "The Child's Landscape in a New England Town," Department of Geography, Clark University, Worcester, Mass. Ph.D. dissertation 1975. Also S. Saegert, *op. cit.* (note 9) 5.

13. M. L. Papanek, "Authority and Sex Roles in the Family," *Journal of Marriage and the Family,* February 1969, 94.

14. J. Newson and E. Newson, *Seven Years Old in the Home Environment,* Allen & Unwin (London: 1976); J. Newson and E. Newson, et al., "Perspectives in Sex Role Stereotyping," in J. Chetwynd and O. Hartnett, *The Sex Role System,* Routledge & Kegan Paul (London: 1978) 34.

15. D. G. Gil, "Violence Against Children," *Journal of Marriage and the Family,* November 1971, 639.

16. H. A. Witkin, et al., *Psychological Differentiation,* Wiley (New York: 1962).

17. T. D. Kemper and M. L. Reichler, *Journal of Genetic Psychology,* 1976, 129, 207, referring to the findings of E. E. Maccoby, "The Choice of Variables in the Study of Socialization," *Sociometry,* 1961, 24, 357–371.

18. B. G. Gilmartin, "The Case Against Spanking," *Human Behavior,* February 1979, 18.

19. J. Kagan, "The Psychology of Sex Differences," unpublished 1974, 17; A. S. Hampson, "A Study of Parent Perception of the Motivations of Their Children," *Character Potential,* 1965, 3, 1–2, 120–128.

20. E. E. Maccoby and C. N. Jacklin, op. cit. (note 9) 343–344.

21. For example, B. I. Fagot, "Sex Determined Parental Reinforcing Contingencies in Toddler Children," presented to the Society for Research in Child Development, Biennial Meeting, New Orleans, La., March 1977; E. W. Goodenough, "Interest in Persons as an Aspect of Sex Differences in the Early Years," *Genetic Psychology Monographs,* 1957, 55, 287–323; *General Mills American Family Report,* 1976–1977, 89; I. K. Broverman, et al., "Sex Role Stereotypes: A Current Appraisal, *Journal of Social Issues,* 1972, 28, 59–78; J. H. Block, "Another Look at Sex Differentiation in the Socialization Behaviors of Mothers and Fathers," *New Directions for Research on Women,* Madison, Wis., 1975; J. H. Block, "Assessing Sex Differences: Issues, Problems and Pitfalls," *Merrill-Palmer Quarterly,* 1976, 22.

22. M. K. Rothbart and E. E. Maccoby, "Parents' Differentiated Reactions to Sons and Daughters," *Journal of Personality and Social Psychology,* 1966, 4, 238–243; S. B. Gurwitz and K. A. Dodge, "Adult Evaluations of a Child as a Function of Sex of Adult and Sex of Child," *Journal of Personality and Social Psychology,* 1975, 32, 5, 822–828; K. K. Dion, "Children's Physical Attractiveness and Sex as Determinants of Adult Punitiveness," *Developmental Psychology,* 1974, 10, 5, 772–778.

23. L. M. Terman and L. E. Tyler, "Psychological Sex Differences," in L. Carmichael, ed. *Manual of Child Psychology,* Wiley (New York: 1954).

24. J. Walters and N. Stinnett, "Parent-Child Relationships: A Decade Review of the Research," *Journal of Marriage and the Family,* February 1971, 96.

25. J. H. Block, 1975 and 1976 op. cit. (note 21); M. L. Papanek, *op. cit.* (note 13); B. Birns, "The Emergence and Socialization of Sex Differences in the Earliest Years," *Merrill-Palmer Quarterly,* 1976, 22, 3, 246; G. Margolin and G. R. Patterson, "Differential Consequences Provided by Mothers and Fathers for Their Sons and Daughters," *Developmental Psychology,* 1975, 11, 4, 537–538; E. E. Maccoby and C. N. Jacklin, *op. cit.* (note 9) 328–329.

26. R. D. Hess, et al., "The Cognitive Environments of Urban Preschool Children," *Report to the Graduate School of Education,* University of Chicago, 1968–1969; E. E. Maccoby and J. Masters, "Attachment and Dependency" in P. Mussen, *Carmichael's Manual of Child Psychology,* vol. 2, Wiley (New York: 1970) 73–157; also in same volume, W. Mishel, "Sex Typing and Socialization," 3–72; J. H. Block, "Conceptions of Sex Role: Some Cross-Cultural and Longitudinal Perspectives," *American Psychology,* 1973, 28, 512–526.

582

27. B. I. Fagot, (1977) *op. cit.* (note 21); L. M. Lansky, "The Family Structure Also Affects the Model: Sex Role Attitudes in Parents of Preschool Children," *Merrill-Palmer Quarterly,* 1967, 13, 2, 148.

28. M. K. Rothbart and M. Rothbart, "Birth Order, Sex of Child and Maternal Help-Giving," *Sex Roles,* 1976, 2, 1, 39–45.

29. B. I. Fagot, (1977) *op. cit.* (note 21).

30. L. F. Droppleman and E. S. Schaefer, "Boys' and Girls' Reports of Maternal and Paternal Behavior," *Journal of Abnormal and Social Psychology,* 1963, 67, 6, 648–654.

31. L. G. Domash, "Selected Maternal Attitudes As Related to Sex, Sex-Role Preference and Level of Psychological Differentiation of the Five-Year-Old Child," *Dissertation Abstracts,* December 1973, 34, (6-B), 2925-B; J. M. Bardwick and E. Douvan, "Ambivalence: The Socialization of Women," in V. Gornick and B. K. Moran, eds. *Woman in Sexist Society,* Basic Books (New York: 1971) 147.

32. W. Mishel, "A Social-Learning View of Sex Differences in Behavior," in E. E. Maccoby, ed. *The Development of Sex Differences,* Stanford University Press (Stanford, Calif.: 1966) 56–81.

33. J. C. Savitsky and T. G. Hess, "A Child's Emotions and Adult Authoritarianism as Determinants of Punishment," *Journal of Genetic Psychology,* 1975, 127, 249.

34. For a small sample, see: D. G. McKinley, *Social Class and Family Life,* Free Press (New York: 1964); V. Gecas and F. I. Nye, "Sex and Class Differences in Parent-Child Interaction," *Journal of Marriage and the Family,* November 1974, 36, 4, 742–749; L. C. Rubin, *Worlds of Pain: Life in the Working Class Family,* Basic (New York: 1977); S. K. Steinmetz, "Occupation and Physical Punishment," *Journal of Marriage and the Family,* 1971, 33, 664–666; W. J. Goode, "Force and Violence in the Family," *Journal of Marriage and the Family,* November 1971, 624–636; D. Kemper and M. L. Reichler, "Marital Satisfaction and Conjugal Power as Determinants of Intensity and Frequency of Rewards and Punishments Administered by Parents," *Journal of Genetic Psychology,* 1976, 129, 221–234; M. E. Durrett, et al., "Childrearing Reports of White, Black and Mexican-American Families," *Developmental Psychology,* November 1975, 11, 6, 871.

35. "Raising Children in a Changing Society," *General Mills America Family Report,* 1976–1977, 86, 87.

36. E. E. Maccoby and C. N. Jacklin, *op. cit.* (note 9) 348.

37. *Ibid.,* 331, 332.

38. M. Mead, *Sex and Temperament,* Morrow Paperback (New York: 1963) 296–297.

39. J. U. Zussman, "Demographic Factors in Influencing Parental Discipline Techniques," paper presented at the American Psychological Association, Chicago, Ill., August 1975.

40. E. M. Hetherington, et al., "Beyond Father Absence: Conceptualization on Effects of Divorce," paper presented to Society for Research in Child Development, Denver, April 1975, 11.

41. J. U. Zussman, *op. cit.* (note 39) 8.

42. T. D. Meddock, et al., "Effects of an Adult's Presence and Praise on Young Children's Performance," in F. Rebelsky and L. Dorman, eds. *Child Development and Behavior,* Knopf (New York: 1973) 240–249.

43. "Raising Children in a Changing Society," *op. cit.* (note 35) 105.

44. D. L. Johnson, Georgia University, "Child Abuse: Some Findings From the Analysis of 1172 Reported Cases," paper Presented to the Southern Association of Agricultural Scientists, New Orleans, La., February 1975; D. G. Gil, *op. cit.* (note 15) 639; J. E. Brody, "Child Abuse Held a Leading Killer," *The New York Times,* June 27, 1973.

45. M. A. Straus, "Some Social Antecedents of Physical Punishment: A Linkage Theory Interpretation," *Journal of Marriage and the Family,* November 1971, 658–663.

46. E. E. Maccoby and C. N. Jacklin, *op. cit.* (note 9) 331–332.

47. G. Steinem, "Erotica and Pornography: A Clear and Present Difference," *Ms.* magazine, November 1978, 53–54.

48. M. A. Straus, *op. cit.* (note 45) 660.

49. B. I. Fagot, (1974) *op. cit.* (note 11).

50. S. L. Sutherland, "The Unambitious Female," *Signs,* 1978, 3, 4.

51. S. D. Britain and M. Abad, Union College, "Field Independence: A Function of Sex and Socialization in Cuban and American Adolescents," unpublished manuscript, 3.

52. J. C. La Voie, "The Effect of an Aversive Stimulus, a Rationale, and Sex of Child on Punishment Effectiveness and Generalization," *Child Development,* 1973, 44, 3, 505–510.

53. B. G. Gilmartin, "The Case Against Spanking," *Human Behavior,* February 1979, 20.

54. W. J. Goode, *op. cit.* (note 34) 629.
55. M. L. Hoffman, "Power Assertion by the Parent and Its Impact on the Child," *Child Development,* 1960, 31, 129–143; also M. L. Hoffman, "Parent Practices and Moral Development: Generalizations From Empirical Research," *Child Development,* 1963, 34, 295–318; M. L. Hoffman and D. Saltzstein, "Parental Discipline and Child's Moral Development," *Journal of Personality and Social Psychology,* 1967, 5, 45–57; S. Feshbach and N. D. Feshbach, "Children's Rights and Parental Punishment Practices," paper presented to the American Psychological Association, Chicago, Ill., August 30–September 2, 1975.
56. E. E. Maccoby, ed. *The Development of Sex Differences,* Stanford University Press (Stanford, Calif.: 1966) 347; M. L. Hoffman, "Sex Differences in Moral Internalization and Values," *Journal of Personality and Social Psychology,* 1975, 32, 4, 720.
57. B. G. Gilmartin, *op. cit.* (note 53) 18; W. J. Goode, *op. cit.* (note 34) 630; S. Feshbach, "Aggression," in P. H. Mussen, ed. *Carmichael's Manual of Child Psychology,* 3rd ed., Wiley (New York: 1970) chapter 22.
58. D. J. Bearison, "Sex-Linked Patterns of Socialization," *Sex Roles,* 1970, 5, 1.
59. R. Loeb, Lehigh University, "Family Interaction Patterns Associated with Self-Esteem in Preadolescent Girls and Boys," unpublished 1979.
60. R. O. Manley, "Parental Warmth and Hostility as Related to Sex Differences in Children's Achievement Orientation," *Psychology of Women Quarterly,* Spring 1977, 1, 3, 229–246; N. Bayley and E. S. Schaefer, "Correlations of Maternal and Child Behaviors with the Development of Mental Abilities," Berkeley Growth Study, *Monographs of the Society for Research in Child Development,* 1964, 29, 63–79; J. Kagan and H. A. Moss, *Birth to Maturity,* Wiley (New York: 1962).
61. N. Radin and A. Epstein, "Observed Paternal Behavior and the Intellectual Functioning of Preschool Boys and Girls," paper presented at the Society for Research in Child Development, Denver, April 1975; V. J. Crandall, et al., "Parents' Attitudes and Behaviors and Grade-School Children's Academic Achievements," *Journal of Genetic Psychology,* 1964, 104, 53–66; H. A. Moss and J. Kagan, "Maternal Influences on Early I.Q. Scores," *Psychological Reports,* 1958, 4, 655–661.
62. A. S. Epstein and N. Radin, "Motivational Components Related to Father Behavior and Cognitive Functioning in Preschoolers," *Child Development,* 1975, 46, 831–839; N. Bayley, "Research in Child Development: A Longitudinal Perspective, *Merrill-Palmer Quarterly,* 1965, 11, 183–208.
63. J. A. Kelley and L. Worell, "Parent Behaviors Related to Masculine, Feminine and Androgynous Sex-Role Orientations," *Journal of Consulting and Clinical Psychology,* 1976, 44, 5, 843–851; J. A. Kelley and L. Worell, "The Joint and Differential Perceived Contribution of Parents to Adolescent Cognitive Functioning," *Developmental Psychology,* 1973, 3, 282–283; J. W. McDavid, "Imitative Behavior in Preschool Children," *Psychological Monographs,* 1959, 73, 16, 20–23.
64. U. Bronfenbrenner, "Toward a Theoretical Model for the Analysis of Parent-Child Relations in a Social Context," in J. Glidewell, ed. *Parental Attitudes and Child Behavior,* Conference on Community Mental Health Research, Washington University, St. Louis, 1961, 90–109.
65. R. Sears, et al., *Identification and Child Rearing,* Stanford University Press (Stanford, Calif.: 1965).
66. E. M. Hetherington, et al., "Divorced Fathers," *Psychology Today,* April 1977, 45.
67. E. L. Phillips, "Children's Reactions to Separation and Divorce," presented to American Association of Psychiatric Services for Children, November 1976, 6.
68. P. Bohannan and R. Erickson, "Stepping In," *Psychology Today,* January 1978, 59.

14 • Nonsexist Sexuality, page 247

1. W. Simon and J. H. Gagnon, "On Psychosexual Development," from D. Goslin, *Handbook of Socialization Theory and Research,* Rand-McNally (Chicago: 1969) chapter 16.
2. M. S. Calderone, "Eroticism as a Norm," *The Family Coordinator,* October 1974, 338–339; A. C. Kinsey, et al., *Sexual Behavior in the Human Male* (1948) and *Sexual Behavior in the Human Female* (1953) Saunders (Philadelphia).
3. W. Masters and V. Johnson, *Human Sexual Response,* Little, Brown (Boston: 1966); M. J. Sherfey, *The Nature and Evolution of Female Sexuality,* Random House (New York: 1972); S. Fisher, *The Female Orgasm,* Basic (New York: 1971); S. Lydon, "Understanding Orgasm," in B. Roszak and T. Roszak, *Masculine/Feminine,* Harper Colophon (New

York: 1969); J. Money and P. Tucker, *Sexual Signatures,* Little, Brown (Boston: 1975) 135–136; W. J. Gadpaille, *The Cycles of Sex,* Scribner's (New York: 1975) 95.

4. P. S. Faunce and S. Phipps-Yonas, "Women's Liberation and Human Sexual Relations," *International Journal of Women's Studies,* 1, 83–85.

5. E. J. Roberts, et al., *Family Life and Sexual Learning: A Study of the Role of Parents in the Sexual Learning of Children, "* Project on Human Sexual Development, Population Education, Inc. (New York: 1978) 43.

6. For example, S. Sarnoff and I. Sarnoff, *Sexual Excitement, Sexual Peace,* M. Evans (New York: 1979); A. Hass, *Teenage Sexuality,* Macmillan (New York: 1979) chapter 6; A. Yates, *Sex Without Shame: Encouraging the Child's Healthy Sexual Development,* Morrow (New York: 1978); B. Seaman, *Free and Female,* Coward McCann and Geoghegan (New York: 1972) 100–103.

7. M. Mead, *Coming of Age in Samoa,* Morrow Paperback (New York: 1973) 136.

8. S. Fisher, *Understanding the Female Orgasm,* Bantam (New York: 1973) 125; G. Kline-Graber and B. Graber, *Woman's Orgasm,* Popular Library (New York: 1976) 102–108; S. Hite, *The Hite Report,* Macmillan (New York: 1976) 5–54; B. Zilbergeld, *Male Sexuality,* Bantam (New York: 1978) 160–176; A. Pietropinto and J. Simenauer, *Beyond the Male Myth,* Times Books (New York: 1977) 312.

9. M. S. Calderone, *op. cit.* (note 2) 340.

10. E. J. Roberts, *op. cit.* (note 5) 43.

11. R. R. Sears, E. E. Maccoby and H. Levin, *Patterns of Child Rearing,* Row Peterson (Evanston, Ill.: 1957).

12. E. J. Roberts, *op. cit.* (note 5) 45.

13. S. Fisher and R. L. Fisher, *What We Really Know About Child Rearing,* Basic Books (New York: 1976) 96.

14. *Ibid.,* R. R. Sears, "Sex-Typing, Object Choice and Child Rearing," in H. A. Katchadourian, ed. *Human Sexuality: A Comparative and Developmental Perspective,* University of California Press (Berkeley, Calif.: 1979) 217–219.

15. Boston Women's Health Collective, *Our Bodies, Ourselves,* Simon & Schuster (New York: 1973) 14.

16. W. Simon and H. Gagnon, "Psychosexual Development," in J. Heiss, ed. *Family Roles and Interaction,* Rand McNally (Chicago: 1976) 315; also, E. J. Roberts, *op. cit.* (note 5) 80.

17. J. Gagnon and W. Simon, *Sexual Conduct: The Social Sources of Human Sexuality,* Aldine (Chicago: 1973); H. J. Gagnon, "The Interaction of Gender Roles and Sexual Conduct," in H. A. Katchadourian, ed. *op. cit.* (note 14) 233–235; J. Gagnon, "The Creation of the Sexual in Early Adolescence," in J. Kagan and R. Coles, eds. *12 to 16 Early Adolescence,* Norton (New York: 1972) 231–257.

18. W. Simon and J. Gagnon, *op. cit.* (note 1) 743.

19. P. S. Faunce and S. Phipps-Yonas, *op. cit.* (note 4) 83.

20. R. Wetzsteon, "Woody Allen: Schlemiel as Sex Maniac," *Ms.* magazine, November 1977, 14; also, A. M. Barclay, "Sex and Personal Development in the College Years," in A. Arkoff, ed. *Psychology and Personal Growth,* Allyn and Bacon (Boston: 1975) 160–174.

21. P. S. Faunce and S. Phipps-Yonas, *op. cit.* (note 4) 84.

22. J. K. Meuli, "In Brief," *NOW Times,* August 1979, 2.

23. Roberts, et al., *op. cit.* (note 5) 58.

24. K. E. Money, "Physical Damage Caused by Sexual Deprivation in Young Females," *International Journal of Women's Studies,* 3, 5, 431–437.

25. R. M. Vaughter, "Psychology," *Signs,* 1976, 2, 1, 131.

26. A. C. Kinsey, (1953) *op. cit.* (note 2) chapter 1; also, K. S. Rook and C. L. Hammen, "A Cognitive Perspective on the Experience of Sexual Arousal," *Journal of Social Issues,* 1977, 33, 2, 14.

27. L. Rubin, *Worlds of Pain: Life in the Working Class,* Basic (New York: 1976).

28. W. Pomeroy and P. Arnow, "A Conversation," *Resource Guide,* Multi-Media Resource Center (San Francisco: Fall 1977).

29. H. Colton, *How to Talk Sex with Our Children,* Family Forum, 1539 N. Courtney, Los Angeles, Calif. 90046 (60¢). Also *Our Bodies, Ourselves, op. cit.* (note 15) 27.

30. Despite a few shortcomings, the books I like best for very young children are: M. Sheffield, *Where Do Babies Come From: A Book for Children and Their Parents,* Knopf (New York: 1973); S. Gordon, *Girls Are Girls and Boys Are Boys—So What's the Difference?* Ed-U Press (Fayettsville, N.Y.: 1979); S. Waxman, *What Is a Girl? What Is a Boy?* Peace Press (San Francisco, 1976). For school-age children: J. J. Aho and J. W. Petras,

585

Learning About Sex: A Guide for Children and Their Parents, Holt, Rinehart and Winston (New York: 1978); L. Nilsson, *How Was I Born? A Photographic Story of Reproduction and Birth for Children,* Delacorte Press (New York: 1975); C. B. Johnson and E. W. Johnson, *Love and Sex and Growing Up,* Bantam (New York: 1979); A. Comfort and J. Comfort, *The Facts of Love,* Crown (New York: 1979). For adolescents: R. Mintz and L. M. Mintz, *Threshold: Straightforward Answers to Teenagers' Questions About Sex,* Walker (New York: 1978); P. Mayle, *Will I Like It?* Corwin Books (New York: 1977); S. Gordon, *You,* Times Books (New York: 1978); D. Carlson, *Loving Sex for Both Sexes,* Franklin Watts (New York: 1979); G. F. Kelly, *Learning About Sex,* Barrons (Woodbury, N.Y.: 1976); *A Part of Our Lives: A Discussion of Sexuality and Birth Control By Young Women for Young Women;* also, *What's Now?! Under 18 and Pregnant.* Both from Origins, Inc., 169 Boyton St., Salem Mass. 01970. For parents, I recommend three vital mind openers: J. L. Hymes, *How to Tell Your Child About Sex,* Public Affairs Pamphlet #147 (New York: 1977); A. Yates, *Sex Without Shame: Encouraging the Child's Healthy Sexual Development,* Morrow (New York: 1978); and A. Haas, *Teenage Sexuality,* Macmillan (New York: 1978).
31. M. S. Calderone, paper presented to Girls Club of America, National Seminar, Racine, Wis., June 1978.
32. H. D. Thornburg, "Educating the Preadolescent about Sex," *The Family Coordinator,* January 1974, 37.
33. E. J. Roberts, *op. cit.* (note 5) 57, 66.
34. J. L. Hymes, *op. cit.* (note 30).
35. E. Galenson and H. Roiphe, "Some Suggested Revisions Concerning Early Female Sexual Development," *Journal of American Psychoanalytic Association,* 1976, 24, 29–58. Additional news of these studies of infants and toddlers were reported in G. Carro, "What Parents Need to Know About a Child's Sexuality," *Ladies Home Journal,* August 1979, 30.
36. J. L. Hymes, *op. cit.* (note 30) 6.
37. E. J. Roberts, *op. cit.* (note 5) 47. And N. Gartrell and D. Mosbacher, "Sex Differences in the Naming of Children's Genitalia," in progress, 1979 (Gartrell, Beth Israel Hospital, 330 Brookline Ave., Boston, Mass. 02215).
38. H. E. Lerner, "And What Do Little Girls Have . . . Some Thoughts on Female Sexuality," *Behold the Woman,* Topeka, Kans., September 1975, 5–6. Also, H. E. Lerner, "Parental Mislabeling of Female Genitals as a Determinant of Penis Envy and Learning Inhibitions in Women," *Journal of the American Psychoanalytic Association,* 1976, 24, 5, 269–283; W. Simon and J. Gagnon, *op. cit.* (note 1) 744.
39. E. J. Roberts, *op. cit.* (note 5) 46.
40. E. G. Belotti, *What Are Little Girls Made Of?* Schocken (New York: 1976) 43.
41. E. J. Roberts, *op. cit.* (note 5) 26.
42. V. Herndon, "Some Surprises About Male Nudity," *Ms.* magazine, March 1978, 12.
43. E. J. Roberts, *op. cit.* (note 5) 46.
44. *Ibid.,* 47, 67.
45. A. C. Kinsey, (1948) *op. cit.* (note 2) 365–367.
46. For example, B. Spock, *Baby and Child Care,* Pocket Books (New York: 1976) 420–421; J. S. Fass, *How to Raise an Emotionally Healthy Child,* Pocket Books (New York: 1969) 61; F. Dodson, *How to Father,* Nash (Los Angeles: 1974) 118.
47. J. G. Selzer, *When Children Ask About Sex,* Beacon (Boston: 1974) 9.
48. E. Weissberger, *Your Young Child and You,* E. P. Dutton (New York: 1979) 79, 96ff. Also, L. Salk, *What Every Child Wants His Parents to Know,* McKay (New York: 1972) 105; F. Coplan, ed. *Parents' Yellow Pages,* Anchor (New York: 1978) 441, contains three views on nudity.
49. J. G. Selzer, *op. cit.* (note 47) 9.
50. A. Yates, *op. cit.* (note 6) 30.
51. G. Murdock, *Social Structure,* Macmillan (New York: 1960).
52. R. Flaste, "Parental Nudity: Bad for Youngsters?" *The New York Times,* September 17, 1976; "Is It Harmful for Children to See Parents in the Nude?" *Medical Aspects of Human Sexuality,* April 1971, 35–41.
53. Personal communication.
54. Personal communication.
55. W. J. Gadpaille, *op. cit.* (note 3) 101–102.
56. D. Dinnerstein, *The Mermaid and the Minotaur,* Harper & Row (New York: 1976) 93.

586

57. Among the experts who recommend this approach are: J. Chutch, *Understanding Your Child from Birth to Three,* Random House (New York: 1973) 171–172; W. Pomeroy, *Your Child and Sex,* Delacorte (New York: 1974); A. S. Neill, *Summerhill: A Radical Approach to Child Rearing,* Hart (New York: 1960) 205–230.
58. R. Flaste, *op. cit.* (note 52).
59. *Our Bodies, Ourselves, op. cit.* (note 15) 85–86; A. S. Neill, *op. cit.* (note 57) 229–230.
60. K. A. Hildebrandt and H. E. Fitzgerald, "Adults' Perceptions of Infant Sex and Cuteness," *Sex Roles,* 1979, 5, 4, 471.
61. M. B. Rosenbaum, "The Changing Body Image of the Adolescent Girl," in M. Sugar, ed. *Female Adolescent Development,* Brunner/Mazel (New York: 1979) 239.
62. K. A. Hildebrandt and H. E. Fitzgerald, *op. cit.* (note 60) 480.
63. S. Firestone, *The Dialectic of Sex,* Morrow (New York: 1970) 178, 167; also see U. Stannard, "The Mask of Beauty" in V. Gornick and B. K. Moran, eds. *Woman in Sexist Society,* Basic Books (New York: 1972) 118–132.
64. See my chapter 4; also, T. I. Rubin, "How Teenagers Can Survive," *Ladies Home Journal,* July 1978, 64.
65. L. C. Pogrebin, "Competing Among Women," *Ms.* magazine, July 1972.
66. M. B. Rosenbaum, *op. cit.* (note 61) 240.
67. *Ibid.,* 242. Also A. Frazier and L. Lisonbee, "Adolescent Concerns with the Physique," *School Review,* 1950, 58, 397–405; S. Harrison, "The Body Experience of Prepubescent, Pubescent and Post-pubescent Girls and Boys," *Dissertation Abstracts International,* February 1976, 36, 8-B, 4132-B; *Common Focus: An Exchange of Information About Early Adolescence,* February 1979, 1, 2, University of North Carolina, Chapel Hill.
68. M. B. Rosenbaum, *op. cit.* (note 61) 241.
69. *Ibid.*
70. *Ibid.,* 243.
71. R. A. Latorre, "Body Parts Satisfaction and Sexual Preferences," *Psychological Reports,* 1975, 36, 2, 430. Also, J. LoPiccolo and J. Heiman, "Cultural Values and the Therapeutic Definition of Sexual Function and Dysfunction," *Journal of Social Issues,* 1977, 33, 2, 180.
72. E. Jerome, "A Physician's View of the Adolescent Woman," Girls Club National Seminar, Racine, Wis., June 1978.
73. A. Frazier and L. Lisonbee, *op. cit.* (note 67); J. Dwyer and J. Mayer, "Psychological Effects of Variations in Physical Appearance During Adolescence," 1968–1969, 3, 353–360; P. Mussen and M. C. Jones, "The Behavior-Inferred Motivations of Late and Early Maturing Boys," *Child Development,* 1958, 29, 61–67.
74. C. Safilios-Rothschild, *Women and Social Policy,* Prentice-Hall (Englewood Cliffs, N.J.: 1974) 92; also, "A Female View of the Male Physique," *Psychology Today,* October 1975, 65.
75. E. J. Roberts, *op. cit.* (note 5) 50. Also *Human Behavior,* February 1979, 32.
76. *Ibid.,* 67, 79.
77. *Ibid.,* 51, 60.
78. *Ibid.,* 63.
79. L. White, "A Sexual Revolution? It's Just a Myth, Harvard Report Says," *Boston Herald-American,* December 17, 1978.
80. E. J. Roberts, *op. cit.* (note 5) 27–30.
81. *Ibid.,* 28.
82. J. Elias and P. Gebhard, "Sexuality and Sexual Learning in Childhood," Phi Delta Kappan 1969, 50, 401–406; S. Gordon and I. R. Dickman, "Sex Education: The Parents' Role," Public Affairs Pamphlet 549, 1977, 4; J. R. Hopkins, "Sexual Behavior in Adolescence," *Journal of Social Issues,* 1977, 33,2, 81.
83. P. H. Mussen and M. C. Jones, "Self-Conceptions, Motivations and Interpersonal Attitudes of Late and Early Maturing Boys," *Child Development,* 1957, 28, 243–256; P. H. Landis, "Coming of Age: Problems of Teenagers," Public Affairs Pamphlet 234, 14; A. M. Nicholi, Jr., "The Adolescent," in *The Harvard Guide to Modern Psychiatry,* Belknap Press (Cambridge, Mass., 1978) 523–524.
84. P. A. Katz, "The Development of Female Identity," *Sex Roles,* 1979, 5, 2, 168–169.
85. L. Zacharias, W. Rand and R. Wurtman, in *Obstetrical and Gynecological Survey,* April 1976, 31, 4; A. C. Peterson, "Puberty," *Psychology Today,* February 1979, 48.
86. E. J. Roberts, *op. cit.* (note 5) 48.
87. "Moms Are Still Mum About Sex," *Human Behavior,* February 1979, 58.
88. V. L. Ernster, "American Menstrual Expressions," *Sex Roles,* 1975, 1, 1, 3–13.

89. L. F. Snow and S. M. Johnson, "Myths About Menstruation: Victims of our Own Folklore," *International Journal of Women's Studies,* 1, 1, 64–72.; also, *Ms.* Gazette, March 1979, 18.

90. M. B. Parlee, "The Declining Taboo Against Menstrual Sex," *Psychology Today,* December 1978, 50–51; K. E. Paige, "Sexual Pollution: Reproductive Sex Taboos in American Society," *Journal of Social Issues,* 1977, 33, 144–163.

91. S. Weitz, *Sex Roles: Biological, Psychological and Social Foundations,* Oxford University Press (New York: 1977) 161–163.

92. L. V. Ernster, *op. cit.* (note 88) 5.

93. D. Ruble, *Science,* 197, 4300.

94. I. Douvan and J. Adelson, *The Adolescent Experience,* Wiley (New York: 1966) 239n.

95. J. Brody, "Personal Health: Menstruation," *The New York Times,* May 24, 1978, C10.

96. K. Dalton, *The Menstrual Cycle,* Pantheon (New York: 1969).

97. Dr. Charles Debrovner, personal communication.

98. J. Gomez, *A Dictionary of Symptoms,* Bartan (New York: 1972) 370–373.

99. L. F. Snow and S. M. Johnson, *op. cit.* (note 89) 64; V. L. Larsen, "Psychological Study of Colloquial Menstrual Expressions," *Northwest Medicine,* 1963, 62, 877.

100. M. Eichler, "Power and Sexual Fear in Primitive Societies," *Journal of Marriage and the Family,* November 1975, 922.

101. J. Bardwick, *The Psychology of Women,* Harper & Row (New York: 1971) 49.

102. J. Gallatin, *Adolescence and Individuality,* Harper and Row (New York: 1975) 260.

103. R. Long, "Premarital Sexual Behavior in the Sixties," *Journal of Marriage and the Family,* February 1971, 44.

104. E. J. Roberts, *op. cit.* (note 5) 59.

105. *Ibid.,* 57.

106. W. J. Gadpaille, "Adolescent Sexuality—A Challenge to Psychiatrists," *Journal of American Academy of Psychoanalysis,* April 1975, 3, 2, 168. Also, R. Reinhold, "Birth Rate Among Girls 15–17 Rises in Puzzling 10-Year Trend," *The New York Times,* September 21, 1977, 1; and *The Spokeswoman,* October 15, 1977.

107. "Study Asks Earlier Education About Sex," *The New York Times,* August 28, 1979, C11.

108. *Ibid.;* also, *11 Million Teenagers,* a report of the Alan Gutmacher Institute, Planned Parenthood, 1976; G. Sackman-Reed, "Who Pays The Price?" *National NOW Times,* September/October 1979, 1.

109. J. E. Brody, "Teenagers' Use of Contraception Found By Survey to be Effective," *The New York Times,* June 7, 1978.

110. E. J. Roberts, *op. cit.* (note 5) 55.

111. F. S. Jaffe, "Teenage Pregnancies: A Need for Education," Report to Girls' Clubs of America National Seminar, Racine, Wis., June 1978, 23.

112. L. Fosburgh, "The Make-Believe World of Teenage Maternity," *The New York Times Magazine,* August 7, 1977; also, see references in note 108.

113. M. S. Calderone, "Nothing Less Than the Truth Will Do . . ." Girls Clubs of America National Seminar, Racine, Wis., June 1978, 30.

114. E. J. Haeberle, *The Sex Atlas,* Seabury Press (New York: 1978) 172.

115. S. Gordon and C. Snyder, "Tomorrow's Family," *Journal of Current Social Issues,* April 1978, 32.

116. A. M. Vener and C. W. Stewart, "The Sexual Behavior of Adolescents in Middle America," *Journal of Marriage and the Family,* November 1972, 699; "Teen Sex Ed Advisors," *Human Behavior,* August 1977, 62; J. Klemesrud, "Parents Encounter Teen Age Sex," *The New York Times,* June 6, 1978, C1; P. Y. Miller and W. Simon, "Adolescent Sexual Behavior: Content and Change," *Social Problems,* October 1974, 58–76; R. L. Currier, "Debunking the Doublethink on Juvenile Sexuality," *Human Behavior,* September 1977, 16; C. Tavris, "Good News About Sex," *New York* magazine, December 6, 1976, 57.

117. L. Fosburgh, *op. cit.* (note 112) 32.

118. L. A. Kirkendall, "Why Boys Lose Respect," in I. Rubin and L. Kirkendall, eds. *Sex in the Childhood Years,* Association Press (New York: 1970).

119. M. S. Calderone, *op. cit.* (note 113) 28.

120. S. Gordon and C. Snyder, *op. cit.* (note 115) 33.

121. *Sexual Encounters Between Adults and Children,* SIECUS Study Guide No. 11, ($1.25), Human Sciences Press, 72 Fifth Ave, N.Y. 10011; also see, "Being Molested" in D. Kavanaugh, ed. *Listen To Us! The Children's Express Report,* Workman (New York:

1978) 156–159; M. I. Levine and J. H. Seligmann, *The Parents' Encyclopedia,* Crowell (New York: 1973) 429–430; S. Gordon and I. R. Dickman, *Sex Education: The Parents' Role,* Public Affairs Pamphlet 549 (New York: 1977) 19–22.
122. E. Weber, "Sexual Abuse Begins at Home," *Ms.* magazine, April 1977 and follow-up Letters to the Editor; "Incest: Personal Testimonies," *Ms.* magazine, September 1977; I. Thomas, "Daddy's Little Girls: Growing Up with Love and Sex," *The Village Voice,* October 17, 1977, 27–28; J. Herman and L. Hirschman, "Father-Daughter Incest," *Signs,* 1977, 2, 4, 735–756; V. DeFrancis, ed. *Sexual Abuse of Children,* American Humane Association (Denver: 1967); I. K. Weinberg, *Incest Behavior,* Citadel Press (New York: 1955); K. Brady, *Father's Days,* Seaview Books (New York: 1979); A. O. Sulzberger, Jr., "Conferees Hear a Controversial View of Incest," *The New York Times,* December 3, 1979, D9; F. Rush, *The Best Kept Secret,* Prentice-Hall (Englewood Cliffs, N.J.: 1980).
123. H. Dudar, "America Discovers Child Pornography," *Ms.* magazine, August 1977, 45ff; G. Dullea, "Child Prostitution: Causes Are Sought," *The New York Times,* September 14, 1979, C11; D.E.H. Russell and S. Griffin, "On Pornography," *Chrysalis,* 4, 11–17; also see the special issue, "Erotica and Pornography: Do You Know the Difference?" *Ms.* magazine, November 1978; N. M. Malamuth, et al., "Sexual Arousal and Aggression," *Journal of Social Issues,* 1977, 33, 2, 126–128.
124. F. Rush, "The Freudian Cover-Up," *Chrysalis,* 1, 31ff.
125. F. Rush, "The Sexual Abuse of Children," in N. Connell and C. Wilson, eds. *Rape: The First Sourcebook for Women,* NAL (New York: 1974); S. Firestone, *op. cit.* (note 63); G. Steinem, "Child Pornography," *Ms.* magazine, August 1977; S. A. McConahay and J.B. McConahay, "Sexual Permissiveness, Sex Role Rigidity and Violence Across Cultures," *Journal of Social Issues,* 1977, 33, 2, 134–143.

15 • Homosexuality, Hysteria, and Children, page 274

1. R. E. Gould, personal communication, 1971. This initial interview provided much of the inspiration, impetus and scope of my first *Ms.* article on nonsexist childrearing. Dr. Gould's experience and authoritative support has continued to give me confidence in my position on homosexuality and other issues throughout this book.
2. W. Churchill, *Homosexual Behavior Among Males,* Prentice-Hall (Englewood Cliffs, N.J.: 1971) 278; J.L. Mathis, "Homosexuality," in *Clear Thinking About Sexual Deviations,* Nelson-Hall (Chicago: 1972) 18.
3. G.K. Lehne, "Homophobia among Men," in D. S. David and R. Brannon, eds. *The Forty-nine Percent Majority: The Male Sex Role,* Addison-Wesley (Reading, Mass.: 1976) 68; M. Hoffman, *The Gay World,* Basic Books (New York: 1968); R. A. L. Humphreys, *Tearoom Trade,* Aldine Press (Chicago: 1970).
4. D. Kopay and P. D. Young, *The David Kopay Story,* Bantam, (New York: 1977) back cover.
5. L. Rosellini, "Why Gay Athletes Have Everything to Lose: Homosexuals in Sports," *Washington Star,* December 9, 1975, 1, D4.
6. L. Rosellini, "That Lesbian Images Haunts Women Athletes," *Washington Star,* December 10, 1975, E1, E6.
7. For example, see V. Bullough and B. Bullough, "Lesbianism in the 1920's and 1930's: A Newfound Study," *Signs: Journal of Women in Culture and Society,* 1977, 2, 4, 895–904.
8. L. Rosellini, *op. cit.* (note 6) E6.
9. Admissions to this effect may be found in these sources among others: E. Ogg, *Homosexuality in Our Society,* Public Affairs Pamphlet 484, 3; and E. Ogg, *Changing Views of Homosexuality,* Public Affairs Pamphlet 563; R. Flaste, "The Question of Homosexuality: Are Families the Reason?" *The New York Times,* October 15, 1976, A16; C. W. Socarides, "The Literature of Homosexuality," in *The Overt Homosexual,* Grune & Stratton (New York: 1968) 9; E. Hooker, *Homosexuality,* National Institute of Mental Health Task Force on Homosexuality. Final Report and Background Papers, DHEW Publication # HMS 72-9116, 14; R. E. Gould, "What We Don't Know About Homosexuality," *The New York Times Magazine,* February 24, 1974, 13, 63; P. J. Fink, M.D. "Homosexuality—Illness or Life-Style?" *Journal of Sex and Marital Therapy,* Spring 1975, 1, 3, 227 10. S. J. Gould, *Ever Since Darwin: Reflections in Natural History,* W. W. Norton & Co. (New York: 1977) 266–267, commenting on E. O. Wilson, *N. Y. Times Magazine,* October 12, 1975, 38.
11. R. C. Friedman, et al., "Reassessment of Homosexuality and Transsexualism," *Annual Review of Medicine,* 1976, 27, 59.
12. F. J. Kallman, "Psychogenetic Studies of Twins," in S. Koch, ed. *Psychology: A Study*

of a Science, McGraw-Hill (New York: 1959) 328–329; J. Marmor and R. Green, "Homosexual Behavior," in J. Money and H. Musaph, *Handbook of Sexology,* Elsevier/North Holland Biomedical Press, 1977, 1053.

13. For example, R. Kolodny, et al., "Depression of Plasma Testosterone Levels after Chronic Intensive Marihuana Use," *New England Journal of Medicine,* 290, 872–874; H. K. Brodie, et al., "Plasma Testosterone Levels in Heterosexual and Homosexual Men," *American Journal of Psychiatry,* 1974, 131, 82–83; T. Garfield, et al., "Hormonal Relationships in Homosexual Men," *American Journal of Psychiatry,* 1975, 132, 3, 288–290; R. C. Friedman, et al., "Hormones and Sexual Orientation in Men," *American Journal of Psychiatry,* 1977, 134, 5, 571–572; P. Doerr et al., "Further Studies on Sex Hormones in Male Homosexuals," *Archives of General Psychiatry,* May 1976, 33, 611–614.

14. N. Gartrell, et al., "Homosexual Women Have a Hormonal Difference," *American Journal of Psychiatry,* 134, 10; M. Scarf, *Body, Mind, Behavior,* New Republic Book Company (Washington, D.C.: 1976) 29.

15. M. S. Teitelbaum, ed. *Sex Differences: Social and Biological Perspectives,* Anchor Press (New York: 1976) 95.

16. W. Churchill, *op. cit.* (note 2) 98.

17. L. J. Hatterer, M.D. *Changing Homosexuality in the Male,* Delta (New York: 1970) 186–187.

18. W. Churchill, *op. cit.* (note 2) 107.

19. M. Hoffman, "Homosexual," *Psychology Today,* July 1969, 45.

20. S. Freud, *Three Essays on the Theory of Sexuality* (1905), translated and edited by J. Strachey, Avon (New York: 1965) 21–45. Other psychiatrists take the position that heterosexuality is innate and homosexuality is pathological—for instance: I. Bieber, et al., *Homosexuality: A Psychoanalytic Study,* Basic Books (New York, 1962); C. Socarides, "Homosexuality and Medicine," *Journal of the American Medical Association,* 1970, 212, 1199–1202; J. J. Rue and L. Shanahan, *Daddy's Girl, Mama's Boy,* Bobbs Merrill (New York: 1978) 82–101.

21. P. J. Fink, Professor and Chairman of the Department of Psychiatry and Human Behavior, Jefferson Medical College, and Physician-in-Chief, Department of Psychiatry, Thomas Jefferson University Hospital. Dr. Fink was the Seminar Leader at a two-day conference, Understanding Homosexuality & Other Gender Problems, June 19–20, 1978, New York City. All quotes hereinafter attributed to Dr. Fink originated at this Seminar unless otherwise noted.

22. S. Freud, *An Outline of Psychoanalysis,* W. W. Norton (New York: 1936) chapter 7.

23. W. W. Meissner, "Theories of Personality," in A. M. Nicholi, Jr., ed. *The Harvard Guide to Modern Psychiatry,* Belknap Press of Harvard University Press (Cambridge, Mass.: 1978) 119.

24. S. Freud, *The Question of Lay Analysis,* W. W. Norton (New York: 1949) chapter 4.

25. S. Freud, *op. cit.* (note 22); S. Freud, "The Passing of the Oedipus-Complex," (1924) in S. Freud, *Sexuality and the Psychology of Love,* Collier Books (New York: 1966) 176–182.

26. S. Freud, *New Introductory Lectures on Psychoanalysis,* W. W. Norton (New York: 1933) chapter 5.

27. S. Freud, *ibid.*

28. S. Freud, "On the Psychogenesis of a Case of Female Homosexuality," *International Journal of Psychoanalysis,* 1920, 1, 125–149. Also H. Deutsch, *The Psychology of Women* (1944), Bantam Books (New York: 1973) 332–361.

29. S. Freud, *op. cit.* (note 26).

30. D. Tennov, *Psychotherapy: The Hazardous Cure,* Anchor Press (New York: 1976) 239.

31. P. J. Fink.

32. S. Freud, *op. cit.* (note 20) 72.

33. P. J. Fink.

34. *American Psychiatric Glossary,* 48.

35. J. Money and P. Tucker, *Sexual Signatures,* Little, Brown (Boston: 1975) 166; J. Money and A. A. Ehrhardt, *Man & Woman, Boy & Girl,* Johns Hopkins University Press (Baltimore: 1972) 22.

36. A. Kinsey, et. al., *Sexual Behavior in the Human Male,* Saunders (Philadelphia: 1948); R. C. Sorenson, *Adolescent Sexuality in Contemporary America,* World Publishing Company (New York: 1973) 285–286; A. Kinsey, et al., *Sexual Behavior in the Human Female,* Saunders (Philadelphia: 1953); J. Williams, *Psychology of Women: Behavior in a Biosocial Context,* W. W. Norton (New York: 1977) 234.

37. For stimulating critiques of the religious positions on homosexuality see J. Matt, "Sin, Crime, Sickness or Alternative Life Style?: A Jewish Approach to Homosexuality," *Judaism,* Winter 1978, 105, 27, 1, 13–24; Gearhart and W. R. Johnson, *Loving Women/Loving Men: Gay Liberation and the Church,* Glide Publications (San Francisco: 1974).
38. P. Greenberg and S. Fisher, "Testing Dr. Freud," *Human Behavior,* September 1978, 28; S. Fisher and R. P. Greenberg, *The Scientific Credibility of Freud's Theories and Therapy,* Basic (New York: 1977).
39. M. T. Saghir and E. Robins, *Male and Female Homosexuality: A Comprehensive Investigation,* Williams & Wilkins Company (Baltimore: 1973) 318–319; C. A. Tripp, *The Homosexual Matrix* McGraw-Hill (New York: 1975) 251; J. Bancroft, *Deviant Sexual Behavior,* Oxford University Press (London: 1974).
40. W. Churchill, *op. cit.* (note 2) 102; M. Brenton, *The American Male,* Fawcett Publications (Greenwich, Conn.: 1970) 132. For an interesting ancillary thesis see R. Seidenberg, "Oedipus and Male Supremacy", *The Radical Therapist*, January, 1971, 1, 9.
41. R. J. Stoller, "The Sense of Maleness," *Psychoanalytic Quarterly,* 1965, 34, 207–218.
42. B. F. Reiss, et al., "Psychological Test Data on Female Homosexuality: A Review of the Literature," *Journal of Homosexuality,* 1974, 1, 1, 77.
43. P. Slater, *Footholds: Understanding the Shifting Sexual and Family Tensions in Our Culture,* E. P. Dutton (New York: 1977) 25.
44. W. Masters and V. Johnson, *Human Sexual Response,* Little, Brown (Boston: 1966).
45. F. Wesley and C. Wesley, *Sex-Role Psychology,* Human Science Press (New York: 1977) 135.
46. R. E. Gould, *op. cit.* (note 9).
47. T. I. Rubin, "Psychiatrist's Notebook," *Ladies Home Journal,* October 1977, 36, 40.
48. E. Levitt and A. Klassen, "Public Attitudes Toward Sexual Behavior," paper presented to the American Ortho-Psychiatric Association, 1973.
49. M. S. Teitelbaum, *op. cit.,* (note 15) 93; "Extensive Homosexuality Is Found Among Seagulls Off Coast of California," *The New York Times,* November 23, 1977; "Newsline," *Psychology Today,* March 1977, 30; C. S. Ford and F. A. Beach, *Patterns of Sexual Behavior,* Harper (New York: 1951) 143.
50. C. S. Ford and F. A. Beach, *ibid.;* J. Marmor and R. Green, *op. cit.* (note 12) 1051; J. Money and P. Tucker, *op. cit.* (note 35) 22–23; L. J. Hatterer, *op. cit.* (note 17) 121–154.
51. J. Marmor and R. Green, *op. cit.* (note 12) 1051.
52. M. Brenton, *op. cit.* (note 40) 32.
53. E. M. Almquist, et al., *Sociology: Men, Women and Society,* West Publishing Co. (St. Paul, Minn.: 1978) 452.
54. M. S. Teitelbaum, *op. cit.* (note 15) 95.
55. S. Freud, "Letter to An American Mother," *American Journal of Psychiatry,* 1951, 107, 786–787.
56. R. D. Lyons, "Psychiatrists, in a Shift, Declare Homosexuality No Mental Illness," *The New York Times,* December 16, 1973, 1.
57. R. E. Hooberman, *Dissertation Abstracts International,* April 1976, 36, 10A, 6554-A.
58. A. K. Oberstone and H. Sukoneck, "Homosexuality: Lesbians Life Adjustment—The Same As Straights," paper presented to the American Psychological Association, Chicago, 1975.
59. B. F. Riess, et al., *op. cit.* (note 42) 71–85.
60. *Ibid.*
61. M. G. Fleener, "The Lesbian Lifestyle," paper presented to the Western Social Sciences Association, Denver, April 1977.
62. A. P. Bell and M. S. Weinberg, *Homosexualities: A Study of Diversity Among Men & Women,* Simon & Schuster (New York: 1978); W. Masters and V. Johnson, *Homosexuality in Perspective,* Little, Brown (Boston: 1979).
63. J. L. Simmons, "Public Stereotypes of Deviants," *Social Problems,* Fall 1965, 13, 223–232.
64. S. F. Morin, et al., "Gay Is Beautiful at a Distance," paper presented to the American Psychological Association, Chicago, August 1975; M. E. Okum, "Personal Space as a Reaction to the Threat of an Interaction with a Homosexual," *Dissertation Abstracts International,* October 1975, 36, 4B, 1973-B.
65. H. J. Sobel, "Adolescent Attitudes Toward Homosexuality in Relation to Self-Concept and Body Satisfaction," *Adolescence,* Fall 1976, 11, 43, 447–448.
66. Source: *Demystifying Homosexuality Project,* Human Rights Foundation, San Francisco, Calif., August 1978.

67. A. P. MacDonald, Jr., "Homophobia: Its Roots and Meanings," *Homosexual Counseling Journal,* January 1976, 3, 1, 27. Also see L. VanGelder, "Anita Bryant on the March: The Lessons of Dade County," *Ms.* magazine, September 1977, 78.
68. "Not Guilty Verdict Finds Killer Insane," *The New York Times,* April 27, 1978.
69. L. Rosellini, "Tough Credo of Macho Coaches," *Washington Post,* December 12, 1978, E1.
70. Letters to the Editor, *Ms.* magazine, July 1973, 8.
71. A. P. MacDonald, Jr., *op. cit.* (note 67) 30–33; F. A. Minnigerade, "Attitudes Toward Homosexuality: Feminist Attitudes and Sexual Conservation," *Sex Roles,* 1976, 2, 4, 347–352; J. Snodgrass, ed., *For Men Against Sexism,* Times Change Press (Albion, Calif.: 1977) 160–169; A. P. MacDonald, Jr., "The Importance of Sex Role to Gay Liberation," *Homosexuality Counseling Journal,* October 1974, 169–180.
72. S. F. Morin and E. M. Garfinkle, "Male Homophobia," *Journal of Social Issues,* 1978, 34, 1, 31–32.
73. D. I. Gottlieb, *The Gay Tapes,* Stein and Day (New York: 1977) 176–177.
74. D. S. David and R. Brannon, *op. cit.* (note 3) 18.
75. A. K. Offit, *The Sexual Self,* Ballantine (New York: 1977) 104.
76. G. K. Lehne, *op. cit.* (note 3) 77–78.
77. S. F. Morin and E. M. Garfinkle, *op. cit.* (note 72) 39; D. Beyer, "Interview: Gloria Steinem," *Christopher Street,* August 1977, 10; M. Schofield, *Sociological Aspects of Homosexuality,* Longmans Green (London: 1965); D. S. David and R. Brannon, *op. cit.* (note 3) 18, 80.
78. Personal communications with several homosexual women and men corroborate this political analysis.
79. J. L. Mathis, *op. cit.* (note 2) 17.
80. E. E. Maccoby and C. N. Jacklin, *The Psychology of Sex Differences,* Stanford University Press (Stanford, Calif.: 1974) 339.
81. S. Abbott and B. Love, "Is Women's Liberation A Lesbian Plot?" in V. Gornick and B. K. Moran, *Woman in Sexist Society,* Basic Books (New York: 1971) 438.
82. S. deBeauvoir, *The Second Sex,* Alfred A. Knopf (New York: 1968) 408–409.
83. R. C. Friedman, et al., "Reassessment of Homosexuality and Transsexualism," *Annual Review of Medicine,* 1976, 27, 59.
84. D. Kopay and P. D. Young, *op. cit.* (note 4) 59.
85. P. J. Fink.
86. W. Churchill, *op. cit.* (note 2) 159.
87. S. F. Morin and E. M. Garfinkle, *op. cit.* (note 72) 43.
88. W. Simon and J. H. Gagnon, "Psychosexual Development," in J. Heiss, ed. *Family Roles and Interaction,* Rand McNally (Chicago: 1976) 312.
89. E. B. Bremer and T. T. Wiggers, "Homosexuality, Counseling and the Adolescent Male," *Personnel and Guidance Journal,* October 1975, 54, 2, 96.
90. H. Marano, "Homosexuality 'Inborn': O.R. For Deviates," *Medical Tribune,* March 2, 1977, 8, 9, 1 and 12.
91. P. Werner, "The Role of Physical Education in Gender Education," *Physical Educator,* 1972, 20, 27–28.
92. J. Marmor and R. Green, *op. cit.* (note 12) 1062.
93. "Girlish Boys," *Time* magazine, November 26, 1973, 134.
94. J. Marmor and R. Green, *op. cit.* (note 12) 1063–1064. In contrast, see the sensitive nonsexist treatment of four "gender incongruity" patients, described in E. Higham, "Case Management of the Gender Incongruity Syndrome in Childhood and Adolescence," *Journal of Homosexuality,* Fall 1976, 2, 1, 49–57; G. A. Rekers, et al., "Assessment of Childhood Gender Behavior Change," *Journal of Child Psychology and Psychiatry,* 1977, 18, 63.
95. P. J. Fink.
96. J. Money and P. Tucker, *op. cit.* (note 35) 165–165; W. Churchill, *op. cit.* (note 2) 107–109; M. Calderone quote in E. Goodman, "Hysteria and Homosexuality," *New York Post,* June 24, 1977.
97. G. K. Lehne, *op. cit.* (note 3) 74.
98. *Ibid.,* 70; R. Sorensen, *Adolescent Sexuality in Contemporary America,* World (New York: 1973).
99. A. P. Bell and M. S. Weinberg, *op. cit.* (note 62) 230.
100. R. Green, M.D. "Sexual Identity of 37 Children Raised by Homosexual or Transsexual Parents," *American Journal of Psychiatry,* June 1978, 135, 6, 695; R. B. Weeks, et al., "Two Cases of Children of Homosexuals," *Child Psychiatry and Human Development,* Fall

592

1975, 6, 1, 26–32; J. S. Greenberg, "A Study of Personality Change Associated with the Conducting of a High School Unit on Homosexuality," *Journal of School Health,* September 1975, 45, 1, 398.

101. E. Pohlman, *The Psychology of Birth Planning,* Schenkman (New York: 1969) 186.

102. C. B. Broderick, "The Importance of Being Ernest—or Evelyn," in Abe Arkoff, ed. *Psychology and Personal Growth,* Allyn and Bacon (Boston: 1975) 80; L. Ovesey, *Homosexuality and Pseudohomosexuality,* Science House (New York: 1969) 72–80. Also see K. A. Adler, "Life Style, Gender Role and the Symptoms of Homosexuality," *Journal of Individual Psychology,* 1967, 25, 1, 70–71.

103. P. Sexton, *The Feminized Male,* Random House (New York: 1969) 186; T. I. Rubin, "Psychiatrist's Notebook," *Ladies Home Journal,* August 1977, 28; M. Martino, *Emergence: A Transsexual Autobiography,* Crown (New York: 1977).

104. S. Rourke, "On Being a Man," in N. Larrick and E. Merriam, eds. *Male & Female Under 18,* Avon Books (New York: 1973) 59.

105. "Lesbian Lifestyles," *Human Behavior,* November 1977, 51; D. Belote and J. Joesting, "Demographic and Self-Report Characteristics of Lesbians," *Psychological Reports,* 1976, 39, 621.

106. W. Churchill, *op. cit.* (note 2) 93.

107. A. T. Fleming, "The Private World of Truman Capote," *The New York Times Magazine,* July 9, 1978, 23.

108. Personal communication (p.c.) anonymous.

109. A. Ebert, *The Homosexuals,* Macmillan (New York: 1977) 23.

110. J. Marmor, "Homosexuality—Mental Illness or Moral Dilemma," *International Journal of Psychiatry,* 1972, 10, 1, 115; "Is Homosexuality Normal or Not?" *Life,* December 31, 1971, 72; L. M. Kanthack, "Left or Right Handed . . . Which Will Your Baby Be?" *Baby Talk,* May 1979, 27; B. Spock, *Baby and Child Care,* Pocket Books (New York: 1976) 269.

111. P. Donohue with H. LaBarre, *Ladies Home Journal,* September 1978, 70, 78.

112. D. Kopay, *op. cit.* (note 4) 38–40, 53.

113. Dr. Lee Salk, personal communication.

114. K. Poole, "The Etiology of Gender Identity and the Lesbian," *The Journal of Social Psychology,* 1972, 87, 56; Dr. June Singer, quoted in R. Flaste, "The Question of Homosexuality; Are Families the Reason?" *The New York Times,* October 15, 1976, A16.

115. J. Money and P. Tucker, *op. cit.* (note 35) 215–216.

116. D. I. Gottlieb, *op. cit.* (note 73) 19–20.

117. A. Ebert, *op. cit.* (note 109) 22.

118. J. Larkin, "Three Women on Lesbians and Fathers," *Christopher Street,* April 1977, 24–25.

119. P.C. anonymous.

120. J. Kelly, "Sister Love: An Exploration of the Need for Homosexual Experience," *The Family Coordinator,* October 1972, 21, 473–474.

121. P. Chesler, "Sons and Fathers," *The New York Times,* April 13, 1978, op-ed page.

122. D. Clark, "Homosexual Encounter in All-Male Groups," in J. Pleck and J. Sawyer, eds. *Men and Masculinity,* Spectrum/Prentice-Hall (Englewood Cliffs, N.J.: 1974) 91.

123. J. Mathis, "Homosexuality," *op. cit.* (note 2), 23.

124. A. Yates, M.D. *Sex Without Shame: Encouraging the Child's Healthy Sexual Development,* Morrow (New York: 1978) 219; T. Mintz, M.D. and L.M. Mintz, *Threshold: Straightforward Answers to Teenagers' Questions About Sex,* Walker (New York: 1978) 100–102.

125. *Answers to a Parent's Questions about Homosexuality,* National Gay Task Force, 80 Fifth Ave., New York, N.Y. 10011 (15¢); C. Silverstein, *A Family Matter: A Parent's Guide to Homosexuality,* McGraw-Hill (New York: 1977); E. Ogg, *Changing Views of Homosexuality,* Public Affairs Pamphlets, 381 Park Ave. South, New York, N.Y. 10016 (50¢); *Growing Up Gay,* Youth Liberation Press, 2007 Washtenaw Ave., Ann Arbor, Mich. 48104 ($1.75); S. F. Morin, *Annotated Bibliography of Research on Lesbianism and Male Homosexuality* (1967–1974), Journal Supplement Abstract Service, 1200-17th St. N.W., Washington, D.C. 20036 ($6).

126. For example, R. J. Stoller, *Sex and Gender,* Science House (New York: 1968); D. H. Feinbloom, *Transvestites and Transsexuals,* Delta Books (New York: 1977); R. Green and J. Money, eds. *Transsexualism and Sex Reassignment,* Johns Hopkins University Press (Baltimore: 1969); R. Green, *Sexual Identity Conflict in Children and Adults,* Penguin Books (New York: 1975); D. K. Montague, M.D., "Transsexualism," *Urology,* July 1973,

2, 1, 1–12; R. J. Stoller, "The Male Transsexual as Experiment," *International Journal of Psychoanalysis,* 1973, 54, 2, 215–225; and V. Siomopoulos, "Transsexualism: Disorder of Gender Identity, Thought Disorder or Both?" *Journal of the American Academy of Psychoanalysis,* 1974, 2, 3, 201–213.
127. V. Siomopoulos, *ibid.,* 208–209.
128. P. J. Fink.
129. M. Martino, *op. cit.* (note 103) 36.
130. *Ibid.,* 254–254.
131. R. M. Restak, "The Sex-Change Conspiracy," *Psychology Today,* December 1979, 20–25; J. E. Brody, "Benefits of Transsexual Surgery Disputed as Leading Hospital Halts the Procedure," *The New York Times,* October 2, 1979, C1.
132. G. Steinem, "If the Shoe Doesn't Fit, Change the Foot," *Ms.* magazine, February 1977, 76.
133. J. Raymond, *The Transsexual Empire,* Beacon (Boston: 1979); J. Raymond, "Transsexualism: The Ultimate Homage to Sex Role Power," *Chrysalis,* 1977, 3, 11–23.
134. L. Rosellini, *op. cit.* (note 69).

16 • My Sex Role/My Self, page 302

1. With help from R. H. Block, "Untangling the Roots of Modern Sex Roles: A Survey of Four Centuries of Change," *Signs,* 1978, 4, 237–252; and A. Skolnick, "The Limits of Childhood: Conceptions of Child Development and Social Context," *Law and Contemporary Problems,* Summer 1976, 39, 3.
2. Main sources for this distillation are: C. C. Beels, "Whatever Happened to Father," *The New York Times Magazine,* August 25, 1974, 10ff; R. A. Elder, "Traditional and Developmental Concepts of Fatherhood," *Marriage and Family Living,* 1949, 11, 98–106. For a provocative parallel, see L. J. Rupp, "Mother of the Volk: The Image of Women in Nazi Ideology," *Signs,* 1977, 3, 2, 362–379.
3. Main sources for this précis are: U. Bronfenbrenner, "Freudian Theories of Identification and Their Derivatives," *Child Development,* 1960, 31, 15–40; J. Bowlby, *Maternal Care and Mental Health,* World Health Organization (Geneva: 1951); S. Freud, *Group Psychology and the Analysis of the Ego,* Hogarth (London: 1948); S. Freud, *New Introductory Lectures on Psychoanalysis,* Norton (New York: 1933); S. Freud, "The Passing of the Oedipus Complex," in *Collected Papers Vol. II,* Hogarth Press (London: 1924) 269–282; O. H. Mowrer, *Psychotherapy: Theory and Research,* Ronald Press (New York: 1953); N. Sanford, "The Dynamics of Identification," *Psychological Review,* 1955, 62, 106–117; E. Fromm, *Man for Himself,* Rinehart (New York: 1947). The quote at the end of II. is from A. Skolnick, *op. cit.* (note 1).
4. T. Parsons, R. F. Bales and E. A. Shils, *Working Papers in the Theory of Action,* Free Press (Glencoe, Ill.: 1953) 21–22.
5. Main sources: *Ibid.;* T. Parsons and R. F. Bales, *Family, Socialization and Interaction Process,* Free Press (Glencoe, Ill.: 1955); especially M. Zelditch, "Role Differentiation in the Nuclear Family: A Comparative Study," in T. Parsons and R. F. Bales, 307–351.
6. D. Bakan, *The Duality of Human Existence,* Rand McNally (Chicago: 1966).
7. Main sources: L. Kohlberg, "A Cognitive-Developmental Analysis of Children's Sex-Role Concepts and Attitudes," in E. E. Maccoby, ed. *The Development of Sex Differences,* Stanford University Press (Stanford, Calif.: 1966) 82–172; L. Kohlberg and D. Z. Ullian, "Stages in the Development of Psychosexual Concepts and Attitudes," in R. C. Friedman, et al., eds. *Sex Differences in Behavior,* Wiley (New York: 1974); J. Piaget, *The Construction of Reality in the Child,* Basic Books (New York: 1954); N. Isaacs, *A Brief Introduction to Piaget,* Agathon Press (New York: 1973); J. Bruner, *On The Will to Learn,* in A. Skolnick and J. Skolnick, eds. *Family in Transition,* 1st ed. Little, Brown (New York: 1970) 310–317.
8. A. Bandura, et al., "A Comparative Test of the Status Envy, Social Power and Secondary Reinforcement Theories of Identificatory Learning," *Journal of Abnormal and Social Psychology,* 1963, 67, 6, 527–534.
9. Main sources for this distillation are: W. Mischel, "A Social Learning View of Sex Differences," in E. E. Maccoby, *op. cit.* (see note 7) 56–81; W. Mischel, "Sex-Typing and Socialization," in P. Mussen, ed. *Carmichael's Manual of Child Psychology,* 3rd ed., Wiley (New York: 1970) 3–72; R. R. Sears, et al., *Identification and Child Rearing,* Stanford University Press (Stanford, Calif.: 1965); A. Bandura, *Psychological Modeling: Conflicting Theories,* Aldine-Atherton (Chicago: 1971); A. Bandura, "Social Learning Through Imita-

tion," in M. R. Jones, ed. *Nebraska Symposium on Motivation,* University of Nebraska Press (Lincoln, Neb.: 1962) 211–269; A. Steinmann and D. J. Fox, "Male-Female Perceptions of the Female Role in the United States," *Journal of Psychology,* 1966, 64, 265–276; A. Bandura and R. H. Walters, *Social Learning and Personality Development,* Holt, Rinehart and Winston (New York: 1963).

10. I am indebted to Dr. Judith Minton and the late Dr. Marcia Guttentag, for personal communications clarifying these competing viewpoints.

11. J. Aldous, "Children's Perceptions of Adult Role Assignment, Father-Absence, Class, Role and Sex Influences," *Journal of Marriage and the Family,* February 1972, 55–65; F. I. Nye, "Child Adjustment in Broken and in Unhappy Unbroken Homes," *Marriage and Family Living,* 1957, 19, 356–361; A. J. Crain and C. S. Stamn, "Intermittent Absence of Fathers and Children's Perceptions of Parents," *Journal of Marriage and the Family,* 1965, 27, 344–347; H. Biller, "Father-absence, Maternal Encouragement and Sex Role Development in Kindergarten Age Boys," *Child Development,* 1969, 40, 539–49; E. Herzoz and C. Sudia, "Children in Fatherless Families," in E. M. Hetherington and P. Ricciuti, eds., *Review of Child Development Research,* Vol. 3, University of Chicago (Chicago: 1974).

12. J. Aldous, *ibid.,* 64.

13. R. Hartley, "Children's Concepts of Male and Female Roles," *Merrill-Palmer Quarterly,* 1959–1960, 6, 153–154.

14. M. Morgan, *Total Woman,* Fleming Revell (Old Tappan, N.J.: 1973).

15. M. Millman, "Observations on Sex Role Research," *Journal of Marriage and the Family,* November 1971, 776.

16. L. W. Hoffman, "Changes in Family Roles, Socialization and Sex Differences," *American Psychologist,* August 1977, 644–657.

17. M. Rabban, "Sex Role Identification in Young Children in Two Diverse Social Groups," *Genetic Psychology Monographs,* 1950, 43, 150–151.

18. A. B. Heilbrun, Jr., "Parent Identification and Filial Sex Role Behavior: The Importance of Biological Context," *Nebraska Symposium on Motivation,* University of Nebraska Press (Lincoln, Neb.: 1974), 131.

19. S. Fisher and R. P. Greenberg, *The Scientific Credibility of Freud's Theories and Therapy,* Basic Books (New York: 1977), 219–224.

20. J. Money and E. Ehrehardt, *Man & Woman, Boy & Girl,* Johns Hopkins University Press (Baltimore: 1972); also see my chapter 3.

21. L. Kohlberg, (1966) *op. cit.* (note 7) 159; D. E. Payne and P. H. Mussen, "Parent-Child Relations and Father Identification Among Adolescent Boys," *Journal of Abnormal Social Psychology,* 1956, 52, 358–362; P. H. Mussen, "Some Antecedents and Consequents of Masculine Sex-typing in Adolescent Boys," *Psychology Monographs,* 75, 506; P. H. Mussen and L. Distler, "Masculinity, Identification and Father-Son Relationships," *Journal of Abnormal Social Psychology,* 1959, 59, 350–356; P. H. Mussen and E. Rutherford, "Parent-Child Relations and Parental Personality in Relation to Young Children's Sex Role Preferences," *Child Development,* 1963, 34, 389–407.

22. E. Erikson, *Childhood and Society,* Norton (New York: 1950).

23. J. Bernard, *The Future of Marriage,* Bantam, (New York: 1973).

24. T. Parsons and R. F. Bales, (1955) *op. cit.* (note 5).

25. P. E. Slater, "Parental Role Differentiation," *American Journal of Sociology,* 1961, 67, 296–308.

26. *Ibid.,* 298.

27. *Ibid.,* 307.

28. R. Rapp, "Anthropology," *Signs,* 1979, 4, 3, 508.

29. R. B. DuPlessis, "The Feminist Apologues of Lessing, Piercy and Russ," *Frontiers,* 1979, 4, 1, 1.

30. This discussion leans heavily on S. B. Ortner, "Is Female to Male as Nature Is to Culture?" in M. Z. Rosaldo and L. Lamphere, eds. *Woman, Culture and Society,* Stanford University Press (Stanford, Calif.: 1974) 67–88.

31. R. Rapp, *op. cit.* (note 28).

32. *Ibid.,* 511; M. Fuller, "Sex-Role Stereotyping and Social Science," in J. Chetwynd and O. Hartnett, *The Sex Role System,* Routledge & Kegan Paul (London: 1978) 151–157.

33. N. E. Waxler and E. G. Mishler, "Experimental Studies of Families," in L. Berkowitz, ed. *Advances in Experimental Social Psychology,* Academic Press (New York: 1970) 249–304.

34. E. Almquist, et al., *Sociology: Women, Men and Society,* West Publishing (St. Paul, Minn.: 1978) 351.
35. A. Skolnick, *op. cit.* (note 1).
36. Report on the findings of Andrew N. Meltzoff and M. Keith Moore, University of Washington, Seattle, in "Putting a New Face on Baby," *The New York Times,* October 9, 1977; and *Science* magazine, October 7, 1977.
37. L. Festinger, *A Theory of Cognitive Dissonance,* Row, Peterson (New York: 1957).
38. L. Kohlberg, *op. cit.* (note 7) 101.
39. A. Constantinople, "Sex Role Acquisition: In Search of the Elephant," *Sex Roles,* 1979, 5, 2, 121.
40. P. A. Katz, "The Development of Female Identity," *Sex Roles,* 1979, 5, 2.
41. M. M. Johnson, "Sex Role Learning in the Nuclear Family," *Child Development,* 1963, 34, 320; A. B. Heilbrun, *op. cit.* (note 18).
42. Many of these trailblazers are anthologized in A. G. Kaplan and J. P. Bean, eds. *Beyond Sex-Role Stereotypes,* Little, Brown (Boston: 1976), especially pages 49–62, 63–78, and 89–98. Also see J. T. Spence and R. L. Helmreich, *Masculinity and Femininity,* University of Texas Press (Austin, Tex.: 1978); J. B. Harrison, "Men's Roles and Men's Lives," *Signs,* 1978, 4, 2, 324–336. Although some socialization theorists embrace the concept of androgyny (defined differently by each), I have purposely avoided that paradigm. I consider "femininity" and "masculinity" inseparable from their stereotypes. Androgyny-theorists accept them as a valid, discernable set of human characteristics from which to posit a healthy "blend." I see "femininity" as an expression of survival behavior under patriarchy, not a distillation of the Universal Female; I consider "masculinity" an expression of ruling class behavior. Put women in positions of power and put men in oppressive situations and the trait repertoires of "femininity" and "masculinity" become so skewed that the androgyny model is rendered meaningless. Nevertheless, androgyny literature is worth our consideration from various viewpoints: J. Raymond, "The Illusion of Androgyny," *Quest,* Summer 1975, 2, 1, 57–66; J. English, "Philosophy," *Signs,* 1978, 3, 4, 827–828; J. A. Kelly and J. Worell, "New Formulations of Sex Role and Androgyny: A Critical Review," *Journal of Consulting and Clinical Psychology,* 1977, 45, 1101–1115; "Special Issue: Androgyny," *Sex Roles,* December 1979, 5, 6.
43. J. Pleck, "Masculinity-Femininity: Current and Alternative Paradigms," *Sex Roles,* 1975, 1, 2, 161–178.
44. *Ibid.,* 176.
45. *Ibid.,* 172.
46. *Ibid.,* 174.
47. *Ibid.*
48. *Ibid.,* 173.
49. *Ibid.*
50. M. Lewis and M. Weinraub, "Origins of Early Sex Role Development," *Sex Roles,* 1979, 5, 2, 144.
51. J. Pleck, *op. cit.* 173.
52. *Ibid.*

17 • *Liking and Loving, page 321*

1. Willard W. Hartup, University of Minnesota Institute of Child Development, in M. Brenton, *Playmates: The Importance of Childhood Friendships,* Public Affairs Pamphlet 525, 2.
2. J. H. Gagnon and W. Simon, *The Sexual Scene,* Transaction Books (New Brunswick, N. J.: 1970).
3. J. S. Chafetz, *Masculine/Feminine or Human?* F. E. Peacock (Itasca, Ill.: 1974) 164.
4. W. W. Hartup, "Peer Interaction and Social Organization," in P. Mussen, ed. *Carmichael's Manual of Child Psychology,* vol. 2, Wiley (New York: 1970); J. H. Langlois, et al., "The Influence of Sex of Peer on the Social Behavior of Preschool Children," *Developmental Psychology,* 1973, 8, 1, 93–98.
5. S. W. Gray, "Masculinity-Femininity in Relation to Anxiety and Social Acceptance," *Child Development,* 1957, 28, 2, 204.
6. S.W. Gray, "Perceived Similarity to Parents and Adjustment," *Child Development,* 1959, 30, 1, 91–107.
7. S. W. Gray, *op. cit.* (note 5) 213.
8. L. Kohlberg, "A Cognitive-Developmental Analysis of Children's Sex-Role Concepts

and Attitudes," in E. E. Maccoby, ed. *The Development of Sex Differences,* Stanford University Press (Stanford, Calif.: 1966) 119–121.
9. E. Donelson and J. E. Gullahorn, *Women: A Psychological Perspective,* Wiley (New York: 1977) 158; also Dr. Jan Duker, Adjunct Professor Columbia University, Lecture, New Lincoln School, November 16, 1978.
10. S. B. Damico, "Sex Differences in the Responses of Elementary Pupils to Their Classroom," *Psychology in the Schools,* 1975, 12, 4, 462–466.
11. J. and E. Newson, et al., "Perspectives in Sex-Role Stereotyping," in J. Chetwynd and O. Hartnett, *The Sex Role System,* Routledge & Kegan Paul (London: 1978) 35.
12. *Child Time Study,* University of California (Berkeley: 1979).
13. J. Henry, *Culture Against Man,* Vintage (New York: 1963) 150.
14. J. Bardwick, "Some Aspects of Women's Relationship With Women," *American Psychological Association,* San Francisco, August 1977, 2; also see, E. E. Maccoby and C. N. Jacklin, *The Psychology of Sex Differences,* Stanford University Press (Stanford, Calif.: 1974) 326, 353.
15. L. M. Terman and L. E. Tyler, "Psychological Sex Differences," in L. Carmichael, ed. *Manual of Child Psychology,* Wiley (New York: 1954); R. Inselberg and L. Burke, "Social and Psychological Correlates of Masculinity in Young Boys," *Merrill-Palmer Quarterly,* 1973, 19, 2, 45–46.
16. P. Sexton, *The Feminized Male,* Random House (New York: 1969) 129.
17. J. Leonard, "Introduction," in B. P. Wolff, *Friends and Friends of Friends,* E. P. Dutton (New York: 1978) xii.
18. M. Sherif and C. Sherif, *Reference Group,* Harper & Row (New York: 1964); J. Toby, "Violence and the Masculine Ideal," cited in J. D. Grambs and W. B. Waetjen, *Sex: Does It Make a Difference?* Duxbury Press (North Scituate, Mass.: 1975) 107.
19. E. Douvan and J. Adelson, *The Adolescent Experience,* Wiley (New York: 1966) 188.
20. C. Harrington, *Errors in Sex Role Behavior in Teenage Boys,* Teachers College Press (New York: 1970) 76–77.
21. J. Wallace, "A Promise to the Oriole," *Human Behavior,* August 1978.
22. L. M. Terman and L. E. Tyler, *op. cit.* (note 15).
23. P. Theroux, "A 7-Year-Old Groom Gets Cold Feet," *The New York Times,* March 29, 1979, C1.
24. J. and E. Newson, et al., *op. cit.* (note 11) 30–31.
25. B. Certner, *A Proposal for the Sex Roles Institute,* 1976, The Psychiatric Institute Foundation, Washington, D.C., II-61.
26. *Unbecoming Men,* Times Change Press (New York: 1971).
27. L. Tiger, *Men in Groups,* Random House (New York: 1969) 145–149.
28. C. Tavris, "Men and Women Report Their Views on Masculinity," *Psychology Today,* January 1977, 38; "Early Clues Reported," *The New York Times,* August 2, 1972.
29. U. Hannerz, "What Ghetto Males Are Like," in D. David and R. Brannon, *The Forty-Nine Percent Majority: The Male Sex Role,* Addison-Wesley (Reading, Mass.: 1976) 249.
30. J. Pleck, "My Male Sex Role—And Ours," *WIN,* April 11, 1974.
31. E. P. Kerchner and S. I. Vondracek, "Perceived Sources of Esteem in Early Childhood," *Journal of Genetic Psychology* 1975, 126, 169–176.
32. See these fine examples: C. Smith-Rosenberg, "The Female World of Love and Ritual: Relations Between Women in Nineteenth Century America," *Signs,* 1975, 1, 1, 10–26; B. W. Cook, "Female Support Networks and Political Activism: Lillian Wald, Crystal Eastman, Emma Goldman," *Chrysalis,* 1977–1978, 3; N. Auerbach, *Communities of Women: An Idea in Fiction,* Harvard University Press (Cambridge, Mass.: 1978); E. Showalter, ed. Introduction to *These Modern Women,* The Feminist Press (Old Westbury, N.Y.: 1978).
33. L. C. Pogrebin, "Competing With Women," *Ms.* magazine, July 1972.
34. A. Pogrebin and R. Pogrebin, "Friend Problems," *Getting There,* Washington, D.C., March/April 1979; S. Chess and J. Whitbread, *Daughters: From Infancy to Independence,* Doubleday (New York: 1978) 98–101.
35. M. F. Waldrop and C. F. Halverson, Jr. "Intensive and Extensive Peer Behavior," *Child Development,* 1975, 46, 19–26.
36. J. Lever, "Sex Differences in the Games Children Play," *Social Problems,* 1976, 23, 478–487.
37. J. M. Bardwick and E. Douvan, "Ambivalence: The Socialization of Women," in V. Gornick and B. K. Moran, *Woman in Sexist Society,* Basic Books (New York: 1971) 151.

38. I. Opie and P. Opie, *The Lore and Language of Schoolchildren,* Oxford (London: 1959) 323, 324.
39. N. Brozan, "Teen-Age Peer Pressure: Often a Positive Influence," *The New York Times,* November 17, 1978.
40. A. Gesell, F. L. Ilg and L. B. Ames, *Youth: The Years from Ten to Sixteen,* Harper & Brothers (New York: 1956) 198.
41. J. Bardwick, *op. cit.* (note 14); E. E. Maccoby and C. N. Jacklin, *op. cit.* (note 14) 229, 234.
42. J. Bardwick, *ibid.*
43. J. Henry, *op. cit.* (note 13) 158.
44. J. Bardwick, *op. cit.* (note 14).
45. F. R. Rosenberg and R. G. Simmons, "Sex Differences in the Self-Concept in Adolescence," *Sex Roles,* 1975, 1, 2, 147.
46. Simone de Beauvoir, *The Second Sex,* Bantam (New York: 1968) 321.
47. S. O'Neil, et al., "Sex Differences in Preadolescent Self-Disclosure," *Sex Roles,* 1976, 21, 1, 85–88; R. Carlson, "Identification and Personality Structure in Preadolescents," *Journal of Abnormal and Social Psychology,* 1963, 67, 566–573.
48. J. B. Miller, *Toward a Psychology of Women,* Beacon (Boston: 1976).
49. C. Farmer, "Words and Feelings: A Developmental Study of the Language of Emotion in Children," 1967, Columbia University Ph.D. dissertation, *ERIC # ED 029031.*
50. R. L. Selman and A. P. Selman, "Children's Ideas About Friendship: A New Theory," *Psychology Today,* October 1979, 80.
51. S. R. Tulkin, et al., "Need for Approval and Popularity: Sex Differences in Elementary School Students," *Journal of Consulting and Clinical Psychology,* 1969, 33, 1, 38.
52. J. O. Balswick and C. W. Peek, "The Inexpressive Male: A Tragedy of American Society," *The Family Coordinator,* October 1971.
53. These four points are adapted from, R. A. Lewis, "Emotional Intimacy Among Men," *Journal of Social Issues,* 1978, 34, 1, 108–119.
54. I. Opie and P. Opie, *op. cit.* (note 38).
55. J. Henry, *op. cit.* (note 13) 187.
56. M. F. Fasteau, *The Male Machine,* McGraw-Hill (New York: 1974) 8.
57. J. Leonard, op. cit. (note 17) x, xiii.
58. J. Henry, *op. cit.* (note 13) 193.
59. K. Lorenz, "The Enmity Between Generations," in M. W. Piers, ed. *Play and Development,* Norton (New York: 1972) 80.
60. K. C. Garrison, "A Study of the Aspirations and Concerns of 9th Grade Pupils From the Public Schools of Georgia," *Journal of Social Psychology,* 1966, 69, 245–252. Also see C. B. Broderick, "Social Heterosexual Development Among Urban Negroes and Whites," *Journal of Marriage and Family,* 1965, 27, 200–203. Black male adolescents are also enthusiastic about marriage.
61. A. Gesell, et al., *op. cit.* (note 40) 436.
62. E. Douvan and J. Adelson, *op. cit.* (note 19) 44.
63. J. Henry, *op. cit.* (note 13) 169.
64. K. McCoy, "Love, Who Needs It?" *Teen,* February 1975, 34.
65. W. Kephart, "Some Correlates of Romantic Love," *Journal of Marriage and the Family,* 1967, 29, 470–474.
66. J. Henry, *op. cit.* (note 13) 168–169, 176–179.
67. C. Safilios-Rothschild, *Love, Sex and Sex Roles,* Prentice-Hall (Englewood Cliffs, N.J.: 1977).
68. S. Firestone, *The Dialectic of Sex,* William Morrow (New York: 1970) 148.
69. T. Atkinson, "Radical Feminism and Love," position paper, *October 17th Movement,* New York City, April 12, 1969.
70. E. Donelson and J. E. Gullahorn, *op. cit.* (note 9) 161; C. Safilios-Rothschild, *op. cit.* (note 67); J. and E. Newson, et al., *op. cit.* (note 11) 40.
71. N. B. McCormick, "Power Strategies in Sexual Encounters," paper presented to The American Psychological Association, San Francisco, August 1977; L. A. Peplau, et al., "Sexual Intimacy in Dating Relationships," *Journal of Social Issues,* 1977, 33, 2, 82–109.
72. J. A. Kulik and J. Harackiewitz, "Opposite-Sex Interpersonal Attraction as a Function of the Sex Roles of the Perceiver and the Perceived," *Sex Roles,* 1979, 5, 4, 443–452; J. T. Spence, R. Helmreich, et al., "Likability, Sex-Role Congruence of Interest and Competence," *Journal of Applied Social Psychology,* 1975, 5, 2, 93–109; L. A. Gilbert, et al.,

"Femininity and Masculinity Dimensions of the Typical Desirable and Ideal Woman and Man," *Sex Roles,* 1978, 4, 5, 767–768; M. S. Lattin and R. E. Ackerman, "Sex Typing—A Factor in Adolescent Attitude Stability?" *Child Study Journal,* 1975, 5, 3, 143–150; M. Komarovsky, *Dilemmas of Masculinity,* Norton (New York: 1976); M. Wallace, *Black Macho and the Myth of the Superwoman,* Dial (New York: 1978).
73. J. S. Chafetz, *op. cit.* (note 3) 95; E. Douvan and J. Adelson, *op. cit.* (note 19) 191.
74. J. H. Pleck and J. Sawyer, *Men and Masculinity,* Prentice-Hall (Englewood Cliffs, N.J.: 1974) 3.
75. W. E. Knox and H. J. Kupferer, "A Discontinuity in the Socialization of Males in the United States," *Merrill-Palmer Quarterly,* 1971, 17, 251–261.
76. G. Brown, et al., "Social Class and Psychiatric Disturbance Among Women in an Urban Population," *Sociology,* 1975, 9, 225–254; M. M. Weissman and E. S. Paykel, *The Depressed Woman,* University of Chicago Press (Chicago, Ill.: 1974).
77. E. Yachnes, "The Myth of Masculinity: A Panel," *American Journal of Psychoanalysis,* 1973, 33, 1, 58; B. Yorburg and I. Arafat, "Current Sex Role Conceptions and Conflict," *Sex Roles,* 1975, 1, 2.
78. H. Goldberg, "The Psychological Pressures on the American Male," in K. C. W. Kammeyer, *Confronting the Issues: Sex Roles, Marriage and the Family,* Allyn & Bacon (Boston: 1975) 434.
79. C. Rivers, et al., *Beyond Sugar and Spice,* G. P. Putnam's (New York: 1979) 135.
80. *The Word is Out,* National Public Broadcasting Service, October 14, 1978.
81. R. Heinlein, *Stranger in a Strange Land,* G. P. Putnam's (New York: 1961) 345.
82. J. S. Chafetz, *op. cit.* (note 3) 164–165.
83. A. Rich, *Of Woman Born,* Norton (New York: 1976) 207.
84. J. Church, *Understanding Your Child From Birth to Three,* Random House (New York: 1973) 159–160.

18 • Sports and Child's Play, page 341

1. J. Huizinga, *Homo Ludens: A Study of the Play Element in Culture,* Beacon (Boston: 1955) 1.
2. E. E. Snyder and J. E. Kivlin, "Perceptions of Sex Role Among Female Athletes and Nonathletes," *Adolescence,* Spring 1977, 12, 45, 23–29; E. Wughalter, "Ruffles and Flounces: The Apologetic in Women's Sports," *Frontiers,* 1978, 3, 1, 11; F. and T. Caplan, *The Power of Play,* Doubleday (New York: 1973) 22–23; A. M. Myers and H. M. Lips, "Participation in Competitive Amateur Sports as a Function of Psychological Androgyny," *Sex Roles,* 1978, 4, 4, 578; P. Sexton, *The Feminized Male,* Random House (New York: 1969) 69, 86–87.
3. E. Spreitzer, et al., "A Summary of Some Research Studies Concerning The Female Athlete," *Frontiers,* 1978, 3, 1, 15.
4. "Why Girls Fall in Love—With Horses," *The New York Times,* February 22, 1978, 68.
5. *Ibid.*
6. "Advance Notice," *US,* June 26, 1979, 4.
7. R. Rief, "The Women of Chess—So Far It Hasn't Been Their Move," *The New York Times,* August 16, 1972, 44.
8. "For a Freckled Brooklyn Girl, Pool Is No Game," *The New York Times,* August 5, 1973.
9. UPI clipping, The Dalles, Oregon, date and origin unknown.
10. "Utah Girl Boxer, 11, Found a Friend in Gilmore," *The New York Times,* January 20, 1977.
11. G. Potter, *Daily Record* (Morris County, N.J.) March 5, 1976, 15.
12. "Barefoot Girl, 12, Wins 1500," *The New York Times,* June 21, 1979, D16.
13. AP wire story, *The New York Times,* August 4, 1976.
14. J. B. Treaster, "Little League Baseball Yields to Social Climate and Accepts Girls," *The New York Times,* June 13, 1974, 2; L. C. Pogrebin, "Baseball Diamonds Are a Girl's Best Friend," *Ms.* magazine, September 1974, 79–82.
15. "No Girls, No Goalie," *The New York Times,* January 23, 1978.
16. UPI wire story, "Soap Box Derby Open to Girls," *The New York Times,* April 9, 1971.
17. "Nancy Lopez Is a Winner," *Civil Liberties,* July 1978, 2.
18. C. Lavin, "Girl Hooks Boys' Sports Trophy," *Ms.* magazine, October 1978, 18.
19. J. Michener, *Sports in America,* Random House (New York: 1976); M. F. Fasteau, *The Male Machine,* McGraw-Hill (New York: 1974) 103–104.

20. M. Novak, *The Joy of Sport,* Basic (New York: 1976).
21. P. J. Stein and S. Hoffman, "Sports and Male Role Strain," *Journal of Social Issues,* 1978, 34, 1, 136–150.
22. J. S. Coleman, "Athletics in High School," in D. S. David and R. Brannon, eds. *The Forty-Nine Percent Majority: The Male Sex Role,* Addison-Wesley (Reading, Mass.: 1976) 264.
23. P. J. Stein and S. Hoffman, *op. cit.* (note 21) 139.
24. J. S. Coleman, *op. cit.* (note 22) 267.
25. P. J. Stein and S. Hoffman, *op. cit.* (note 21) 142, 148.
26. C. Candell, "When I Was About Fourteen . . ." in J. H. Pleck and J. Sawyer, eds. *Men and Masculinity,* Prentice-Hall (Englewood Cliffs, N.J.: 1974) 3.
27. J. Pleck, "My Male Sex Role—And Ours," *WIN,* April 11, 1974, 8.
28. J. H. Gagnon, "Physical Strength, Once of Significance," in D. S. David and R. Brannon, eds. *op. cit.* (note 22) 173.
29. L. Komisar, "Violence and the Masculine Mystique," *The Washington Monthly,* July 1970.
30. K. Bednark, *The Male in Crisis,* Knopf (New York: 1970) 34; F. Baron, "Violence in Athletics: An International Blight," *The New York Times,* March 30, 1975.
31. W. Farrell, "Super Bowl Ritual: Mix Masculinity With Patriotism," *The New York Times,* January 15, 1978, 2; W. Farrell, *The Liberated Man,* Random House (New York: 1975) chapter 5, "Super Bowl."
32. R. Smith, "Good Old Boy Woody Hayes," *The New York Times,* January 3, 1979, B7.
33. "Suit Filed for Schoolboy," *The New York Times,* December 31, 1977.
34. "A Player's Death Is Investigated," *The New York Times,* December 31, 1977, 11; R. C. Yeager, *Seasons of Shame,* McGraw-Hill (New York: 1980).
35. J. Baskin, "Football's Painful Pageant," *Human Behavior,* October 1978.
36. J. M. Connor and L. A. Serbin, "Behaviorally-Based Masculine and Feminine-Activity Preference Scales for Preschoolers," *Child Development,* 1977, 48, 1411; B. G. Rosenberg and B. Sutton-Smith, "The Measurement of Masculinity and Femininity in Children," *Journal of Genetic Psychology,* 1964, 104, 259–263; L. A. DeLucia, "The Toy Preference Test: A Measurement of Sex Role Identification," *Child Development,* 1963, 34, 107–117; W. W. Hartup and E. A. Zook, "Sex-Role Preference in 3 and 4-Year-Old Children," *Journal of Consulting Psychology,* 1960, 24, 420–426.
37. B. I. Fagot, "Sex Differences in Toddlers' Behavior and Parental Reaction," *Developmental Psychology,* 1974, 10, 4, 554–558.
38. L. V. Harper and K. M. Sanders, "Preschool Children's Use of Space: Sex Differences in Outdoor Play," *Developmental Psychology,* 1975, 11, 1, 119; D. R. Omark, et al., "Dominance Hierarchies," *Instructional Science,* 1976, 5, 407; E. Maccoby and C. Jacklin, *The Psychology of Sex Differences,* Stanford University Press (Stanford, Calif.: 1974) 205; N. W. Gottfried and B. Seavy, "Early Social Behavior," *Journal of Genetic Psychology,* 1974, 125, 1, 61–69; N. L. Cohen and L. Faust-Cohen, "The Role of Gender in Determining the Influence of Mothers and Peers on Toddler Play," paper presented to the Southeastern Conference on Human Development, Atlanta, Ga., April 1978.
39. B. I. Fagot and I. Littman, "Stability of Sex Role and Play Interests from Preschool to Elementary School," *The Journal of Psychology,* 1975, 89, 285–292.
40. J. Lever, "Games Children Play: Sex Differences and the Development of Role Skills," *Dissertation Abstracts International,* July 1975, 36 (1-A), 553–554; J. Lever, "Child's Play: What Every Parent Needs to Know," *Ms.* magazine, February 1977, 22.
41. B. I. Fagot, "Consequences of Moderate Cross-Gender Behavior in Preschool Children," *Child Development,* 1977, 48, 902–907; F. P. Noe and K. W. Elifson, "The Pleasures of Youth: Parent and Peer Compliance Toward Discretionary Time," *Journal of Youth and Adolescence,* 1976, 5, 1, 37–58; C. A. Downs and J. H. Langlois, "Mother and Peer Influences on Children's Sex-Role Play Behaviors," paper presented to the Midwestern Psychological Association, Chicago, Ill., May 1977.
42. E. T. Peterson, "The Adolescent Male and Parental Relationships," paper presented to the National Council of Family Relations, New Orleans, La., October 1968.
43. M. Lewis, "Parents, Children, Sex Role Development," *School Review,* 1972, 80, 229–240.
44. Basic sources for this section: G.L. Rarick, "Competitive Sports for Girls: Effects on Growth, Development and General Health," in D. V. Harris, ed. *DCWS Research Reports: Women in Sports,* AAHPER (Washington, D. C.: 1971) 48–51; K.R. Church, "Children's Exercise: Facts and Fiction," *Elementary School Journal,* November 1976, 77, 2, 111–115; P. J. Hirsch, "Sporting Chance," *New Directions for Women,* Autumn 1979, 22; *Sprint*

600

Myth/Fact Sheet, January 1978, Women's Equity Action League, Washington, D.C.; E. Spreitzer, et al., *op. cit.* (note 3) 16.
45. K. R. Church, *ibid.*
46. G. L. Rarick, *op. cit.* (note 44).
47. J. K. Meuli, "In Brief," *National NOW Times,* December 1978, 2.
48. J. Gerston, "In Dallas, They Learn the Womanly Art of Self-Defense," *The New York Times,* September 30, 1973; Morehouse and Rasch, *The Sexual Basis of Athletic Training,* quoted in J. S. Weis, "Second Inning in Little League Suit," *Majority Report,* October 1973.
49. *Sprint Myth/Fact Sheet, op. cit.* (note 44).
50. J. K. Meuli, *op. cit.* (note 47).
51. "A Medical Puzzle in Women's Sports," *The New York Times,* April 23, 1978.
52. N. Brozan, "Training Linked to Disruption of Female Reproductive Cycle," *The New York Times,* April 17, 1978, C1; D. Larned-Romano and J. Leavy, "Athletics and Fertility," *Ms.* magazine, October 1979, 38–41.
53. M. Shangold, "Female Runners Advised to Follow Common Sense," *The New York Times,* May 14, 1978.
54. N. Brozan, *op. cit.* (note 52).
55. L. A. Serbin, et al., "Effects of Peer Presence on Sex-Typing of Children's Play Behavior," paper presented to the Society for Research in Child Development, New Orleans, La., March 1977; also see citations in note 41; B. Fagot, "The Consequences of Same-sex, Cross-sex and Androgynous Preferences in Early Childhood," paper presented to the Western Psychological Association, San Francisco, April 1978.
56. M. W. Evans, "Play Is Life Itself," *Theory Into Practice,* October 1974, 13, 4, 267.
57. F. and T. Caplan, *op. cit.* (note 2); R. E. Harley, et al., *Understanding Children's Play,* Columbia University Press (New York: 1952).
58. J. S. Bruner, "Play Is Serious Business," *Psychology Today,* January 1975, 81.
59. L. Liepmann, *Your Child's Sensory World,* Penguin (New York: 1974); J. Piaget, *Play, Dreams and Imitation in Childhood,* Norton (New York: 1962); L. B. Murphy, "Infants Play and Cognitive Development," and E. H. Erikson, "Play and Actuality," both in M. W. Piers, ed. *Play and Development,* Norton (New York: 1972); S. Miller, *The Psychology of Play,* Pelican (London: 1968, 1972); S. Smilansky, *The Effects of Sociodramatic Play on Disadvantaged Preschool Children,* Wiley (New York: 1968); C. Garvey, *Play,* Harvard University Press (Cambridge, Mass.: 1977); D. W. Winnicott, *Playing and Reality,* Basic (New York: 1972); "The Value of Play for Learning," *Theory into Practice,* October 1974, 13, 239–323.
60. J. A. Sherman, "Problems of Sex Difference in Space Perception and Aspects of Psychological Function," *Psychological Review,* 1967, 74, 290–299; L. A. Serbin and J. M. Connor, "Sex Typing of Children's Play Preferences and Patterns of Cognitive Performance," unpublished manuscript 1978 (contact Serbin, Concordia College, Quebec, Canada).
61. S. Saegart and R. Hart, "The Development of Environmental Competence in Girls and Boys," in P. Burnett, ed. *Women in Society,* Maaroufa Press (Chicago, Ill.: 1976).
62. J. Piaget, *Moral Judgement of the Child,* Free Press (Glencoe, Ill.: 1932).
63. M. Pines, "Invisible Playmates," *Psychology Today,* September 1978, 38ff; M. A. Pulaski, "The Rich Rewards of Make Believe," *Psychology Today,* January 1974, 68–74.
64. M. A. Pulaski, *ibid.*
65. "Comes the Revolution," *Time* magazine, June 26, 1978, 55; G. I. Maeroff, "Games Aid Integration and Foster Teamwork," *The New York Times,* May 1, 1979, C5.
66. G. Eskenazi, "In the Stands, Many Cheers Have a Higher Pitch," *The New York Times,* June 6, 1977, 34; D. Shaw, "The Roots of Rooting," *Psychology Today,* February 1978, 48ff.
67. "Title IX and Sports," *WEAL Washington Report,* October 1978, 7, 5; M. Hennig and A. Jardim, *The Managerial Woman,* Doubleday (New York: 1977).
68. K. F. Clarenbach, "Human Status for Women," paper presented to the Midwest Association for Physical Education of College Women, October 16, 1970; "What Are Little Girls Made Of? Puppy Dogs Tails Too," *Psychology Today,* August 1974, 43; J. K. Meuli, "In Brief," *National NOW Times,* September 1977, 2; M. Hennig and A. Jardim, *op. cit.* (note 67).
69. E. Spreitzer, *op. cit.* (note 3) 19.
70. J. English, "Sex Equality in Sports," *Philosophy and Public Affairs,* Spring 1978, 7, 270.
71. T. Field, "Infant-Peer Interactions in the Absence of Mother," paper presented to the International Conference on Infant Studies, Providence, R. I., March 1978.

72. E. B. Fiske, "Toys Can Hone Preschool Skills," *The New York Times,* February 20, 1979, C1.

73. "Male and Female: The Difference Between Them," *The New York Times,* March 20, 1972, 44; E. Maccoby and C. Jacklin, *op. cit.* (note 38).

74. S. de Beauvoir, *The Second Sex,* Knopf (New York: 1968) 333.

75. R. Montemayor, "Children's Performance in a Game and Their Attraction to It as a Function of Sex-Stereotyped Labels," *Child Development,* 1974, 45, 152–156.

76. L. A. Serbin, et al., "Sex Stereotyped and Non-Stereotyped Introduction of New Toys in the Preschool Classroom," *Psychology of Women Quarterly,* read in manuscript.

77. "Time Out: The Secret Lives of Sports Stars," *SMASH,* 1975, 1, 5, 26.

78. W. S. Mathews, "Sex Role Perception, Portrayal and Preference in the Fantasy Play of Young Children," paper presented to the Society for Research on Child Development, New Orleans, La., March 1977.

79. *Ibid.;* also, V. Paley, "Is the Doll Corner a Sexist Institution?" *School Review,* August 1973, 81, 4, 569–576.

80. I. Klackenberg, "Small Boys Worse Off," *Hertha* (Stockholm, Sweden, February 1975) 42.

81. P. Sexton, *op. cit.* (note 2) 101.

82. I. Klackenberg, *op. cit.* (note 80) 41.

83. T. Wolf, "Effects of Life Modeled Sex-Inappropriate Play Behavior in a Naturalistic Setting," *Developmental Psychology,* 1973, 9, 120–123; B. J. Zimmerman and R. Koussa, "Sex Factors in Children's Observational Learning of Value Judgements of Toys," *Sex Roles,* 1975 1, 2; T. Wolf, "Response Consequences to Televised Modeled Sex-Inappropriate Play Behavior," *The Journal of Genetic Psychology,* 1975, 127, 35.

84. M. K. Brady, "This Little Lady's Gonna Boogaloo: Elements of Socialization in the Play of Black Girls," in *Black Girls at Play,* Southwest Educational Development Laboratory (Austin, Tex.: 1975).

85. B. I. Fagot, "Sex Determined Parental Reinforcing Contingencies in Toddler Children," paper presented to the Society for Research in Child Development, New Orleans, La., March 1977; S. Fling and M. Manosevitz, "Sex Typing in Nursery School Children's Play Interests," *Developmental Psychology,* 1972, 7, 2, 146–152.

86. F. L. Whitam, "Childhood Indicators of Male Homosexuality," *Archives of Sexual Behavior,* 1977, 6, 2, 89–95.

87. Dr. Sirgay Sanger, personal communication.

88. D. B. Lynn and A. R. Cross, "Parent Preference of Preschool Children," *Journal of Marriage and the Family,* August 1974, 36, 3, 555–559.

89. M. Ellis, "Youth and Sports: Beware of Underage Chauvinists," *The New York Times,* September 11, 1977, 2.

90. W. Weil, "Daughters and Mothers," *Ms.* magazine, June 1975, 78.

91. R. Smith, "Mother Was a Third Baseperson," *The New York Times,* March 20, 1973.

92. S. A. Friedman, *How Was School Today Dear? Fine, What's For Dinner,* Readers Digest Press (New York: 1977).

93. M. Tyson, "Mouths of Babes," *Womensports,* September 1977, 58.

94. A. Harvin, "Rugby: Women Join in Traditions," *The New York Times,* April 17, 1978.

95. "U. S. Men Skaters Liberated," *The New York Times,* February 5, 1979.

96. C. Rivers, et al., *Beyond Sugar and Spice,* G. P. Putnam's (New York: 1979) 123, 131–132.

97. J. Rohrs, "Is There Too Much Sex on the Sidelines? PRO," *Daily News,* November 12, 1978.

98. R. Morgan, "Is There Too Much Sex on the Sidelines? CON," *Ibid.*

99. L. Bernikow, "Confessions of an Ex-cheerleader," *Ms.* magazine, October 1973, 64–67.

100. E. Maccoby and C. Jacklin, *op. cit.* (note 38) 327.

101. J. Horn, "Parent Egos Take the Fun Out of Little League," *Psychology Today,* September 1977; S. Hotchkiss, "Parents and Kids' Sport," *Human Behavior,* March 1978, 35.

102. R. E. Pigott, "Youth and Sports: Beware of Child Abuse," *The New York Times,* September 11, 1977, 2.

103. *Ibid.;* also E. Kranepool, "Youth and Sports: Beware of Pressures to be a Star and the Obsession to Win," *The New York Times,* September 11, 1977; C. Berman, "The Pressure to Win, The Pain of Losing," *The New York Times,* August 6, 1976.

104. M. Niehoff, "The Psychology of Sport: Competition or Self-Fulfillment?" *Frontiers,* 1978, 3, 1, 26–27.

105. J. and E. Newson, *Toys and Playthings,* Pantheon (New York: 1978); J. and D. Singer, *Partners in Play,* Harper & Row (New York: 1977); E. L. Scharlatt and C. Cerf, *Kids: Day In and Day Out,* Simon & Schuster (New York: 1979); A. Stallibrass, *The Self-Respecting Child: How to Use the Joy of Play to Start Your Child on the Path to Lifelong Self-Confidence,* Warner (New York: 1979); T. Orlick, *The Cooperative Sports and Games Book: Challenge Without Competition,* Pantheon (New York: 1978); *Equal Play: A Resource Magazine for Adults Who Are Guiding Young Children Beyond Stereotypes,* $10 for four issues, from Women's Action Alliance, 370 Lexington Avenue, New York, N.Y. 10017. To motivate girls in sports: K. F. Jacobs, *Girlsports,* Bantam (New York: 1978); S. L. Twin, *Out of the Bleachers: Writings on Women and Sport,* Feminist Press (Old Westbury, N.Y.: 1979); C. A. Oglesby, *Women and Sport from Myth to Reality,* Lea and Febiger (Philadelphia: 1979); J. Kaplan, *Women in Sports,* Viking (New York: 1979); L. D. O'Neill, *The Women's Book of World Records and Achievements,* Doubleday (New York: 1979); *Resource Roundup: Girls and Women in Sports,* (annotated bibliography), WEECN, Far West Laboratory, 1855 Folsom St., San Francisco, Calif. 94103 (15¢); A. Siegel and M. McLoone, *It's a Girl's Game Too,* Holt, Rinehart and Winston (New York: 1980).
106. R. Lipsyte, "Sports: Sexism's Last Stand," *New Directions for Women,* Spring 1978, 10.
107. L. A. Serbin, et al., "Shaping Cooperative Cross-Sex Play," *Child Development,* December 1977, 48, 3, 924–929; J. B. Rohrbaugh, "Femininity on the Line," *Psychology Today,* August 1979, 42.
108. "Raising Children in a Changing Society," *The American Family Report,* General Mills, 1976–1977, 130; R. Selby and J. H. Lewko, "Children's Attitudes Toward Females in Sports: Their Relationship with Sex, Grade, and Sports Participation," *American Association for Health, Physical Education and Recreation Research Quarterly,* October 1976, 47, 3, 453–463.
109. M. Fasteau, *op. cit.* (note 19) 103.
110. C. Rivers, et al., *op. cit.* (note 96) 65.
111. R. Graves, "Real Women," in B. and T. Roszak, eds. *Masculine/Feminine,* Harper (New York: 1969) 36; E. Maccoby and C. Jacklin, *op. cit.* (note 38) 254; M. C. Madsen and A. Shapira, "Cooperative and Competitive Behavior of Urban Afro-American, Anglo-American and Mexican American and Mexican Village Children," *Developmental Psychology,* 1970, 3, 16–20; L. Larwood and B. Moely, "Sex Role and Developmental Evaluations in the Just World," *Sex Roles,* 1979, 5, 19–28; B. E. Moely, et al., "Sex Differences in Competition-Cooperation Behavior of Children at Two Age Levels," *Sex Roles,* 1979, 5, 3,; H. H. Solomons, "It's Not How She Plays the Game—It's How She Loses," *Ms.* magazine, May 1978, 20; I. Galejs, "Social Interaction of Preschool Children," *Dissertation Abstracts,* November 1973, 34 (5-B), 2282; M. G. Wiley, "Sex Roles in Games," *Sociometry,* December 1973, 36, 526–541.
112. S. B. Greenberg and L. F. Peck, "A Study of Preschooler's Spontaneous Social Interaction Patterns in Three Settings; All Female, All Male and Coed," paper presented to AERA Convention, Chicago, 1974.
113. W. Farrell, "The Resocialization of Men's Attitudes Toward Women's Role in Society," paper presented to the American Political Science Association, Los Angeles, September 1970, 15.
114. M. Lockheed and K. P. Hall, "Conceptualizing Sex as a Status Characteristic: Applications to Leadership Training Strategies," *Journal of Social Issues,* 1976, 32, 3, 111–124.

19 • *Toys Are Us, page 365*

1. Renee Taylor, p. c.
2. B. Sutton-Smith, *A Psychiatrist's Journal: Questions and Answers About Toys and Play,* Harshe Rotman and Druck (New York: 1976) 11.
3. Lionel commercial, 1973.
4. Lionel spokesman, at company's press conference, November 1973, Four Seasons, New York City.
5. L. C. Pogrebin, "Gifts for Free Children," *Ms.* magazine, December 1976, 56. See December issues of *Ms.* every year since 1972 for additional guidelines and gift lists of nonsexist toys, games and books.
6. National Organization for Women, Toy Survey, Washington, D.C.
7. F. Denmark quoted in F. Bruning, "Separating the Sexes in Toyland," *Newsday,* (Garden City, N.Y.) November 27, 1973.

8. "A Report on Children's Toys," *Ms.* magazine, December 1972, 57. Reports on the study conducted by L. Wolf Goodman and J. Lever; N. G. Kutner and R. M. Levinson, "The Toy Salesperson: A Voice for Change in Sex-Role Stereotypes," *Sex Roles,* 1978, 4, 1, 1–7.
9. N. Lyon, "More Than Child's Play," *Ms.* magazine, December 1972, 55.
10. S. Millar, *The Psychology of Play,* Penguin (Middlesex, England: 1968) 220–222.
11. B. Spock, quoted in *The New York Times,* November 18, 1971.
12. B. Spock, quoted in *London Daily Mail,* June 12, 1974.
13. *Ibid.,*
14. L. Hammel, interview with Betty Friedan, November 1971, exact date unknown, *The New York Times.*
15. *The New York Times,* February 18, 1974, 20.
16. G. Savastano and W. Daily, Jr., p. c.
17. National Organization for Women, press release, November 15, 1971.
18. "Nabisco Picketed Over Monster Toys," *The New York Times,* November 16, 1971.
19. V. H. Reiss, "Taming a Toymaker," *Harpers,* March 1974.
20. S. C. Soman, "A Gun Is No Fun," *Ms.* magazine, June 1975, 65; "Guns and People," *The New York Times,* August 10, 1976, Editorial; for more information contact National Coalition to Ban Handguns, 100 Maryland Avenue, N.E., Washington, D.C. 20002.
21. Flyer issued by Parents for Responsibility in the Toy Industry, 799 Broadway, New York, N. Y. 10003.
22. J. Klemesrud, "And the War Toys Are Rolling Along," *The New York Times,* December 22, 1974.
23. "Peace Dividend," *The Wall Street Journal,* December 7, 1972, 1; "Guns, Guns, Guns, Guns," *Fortune Society News,* December 1975 (29 East 22 St., New York, N.Y. 10010).
24. Quoted in "Guidelines For Choosing Toys," *Public Action Coalition on Toys,* 11.
25. *Ibid.*
26. B. Sutton-Smith, *op. cit.* (note 2). 19.
27. Dr. E. Tanay, p. c.
28. H. L. Rheingold and K. V. Cook, "The Contents of Boys' and Girls' Rooms as an Index of Parents' Behavior," *Child Development,* 1975, 46, 459–463.
29. B. Sutton-Smith, *op. cit.* (note 2).
30. *Ibid.*
31. "Notes on People," *The New York Times,* December 3, 1977, 21; N. Broznan, "Using Toys to Free Children From The Roles Society Dictates," *The New York Times,* May 12, 1971, 38.
32. U. S. Consumer Product Safety Commission, Washington, D. C. 20207; complain about deceptive packaging to the Federal Trade Commission, Washington, D. C. 20580.
33. Toy Manufacturers of America, 200 Fifth Avenue, New York, N. Y. 10010.
34. Public Action Coalition on Toys, 38 West 9 Street, New York, N. Y. 10011 ($1); Catalog of Nonsexist Multiracial Toys from The Women's Action Alliance, 370 Lexington Avenue, New York, N. Y. 10017; "The Natural Child," Guide to Nonsexist Toys, 591 Rockport Drive, Sunnyvale, Calif. 94087 ($2.50).

20 • *Television Is Sexistvision, page 393*

1. "Excerpts from Carnegie Commission's Study on Future of Public Broadcasting," *The New York Times,* January 31, 1979, C20.
2. H. Himmelwait, et al., "Communications for Social Needs," A White House Study, 1958, cited in *Down Sesame Street,* The Network Project, Columbia University.
3. W. Schramm, et al., *Television in the Lives of Our Children,* Stanford University Press (Stanford, Calif.: 1961).
4. G. L. Looney, "The Ecology of Childhood," *Action for Children's Television,* Avon Books (New York: 1971) 55–56.
5. *Ibid.*
6. *Ibid.*
7. J. B. Ra, quoted in *National Enquirer,* October 12, 1976, 3; *The New York Council on Children's Television,* Funding Proposal, December 1976; H. Kupferberg, "What *You* Think of Children's TV," *Parade,* March 4, 1973.
8. W. Schramm, *op. cit.* (note 3); S. H. Sternglanz and L. A. Serbin, "Sex-Role Stereotyping in Children's Television Programs," *Developmental Psychology,* 1974, 10, 5, 710–715.
9. L. J. Busby, *University of Michigan News,* April 9, 1975; H. W. Streicher, "The Girls in the Cartoons," *Journal of Communications,* Spring 1974, 125–129.

10. C. Isber and M. Cantor, *The Report of the Task Force on Women in Public Broadcasting,* Corporation for Public Broadcasting, Washington, D.C., quoted in *Media Report to Women,* January 1, 1976.

11. *Ibid.;* also see C. Cathey-Calvert, "Sexism on Sesame Street," KNOW, Inc., Box 86031, Pittsburgh, Pa. 15221.

12. R. K. Goldsen, "Throwaway Husbands, Wives and Lovers," *Human Behavior,* December 1975; "Report on Daytime Network Television 1977," B.B.D.&O., 383 Madison Avenue, New York, N.Y. 10017.

13. *National Organization for Women,* Washington, D.C.

14. K. Lindsey, "The Lure of Soap Operas," *Sojourner,* December 1979.

15. E. Peck, " 'I Have 7 Children' She Said to Wild Applause," *The New York Times,* August 13, 1972, 13.

16. J. Lyle and H. R. Hoffman, "Children's Use of Television and Other Media," in E. A. Rubenstein, et al., eds. *Television and Social Behavior,* Reports and Papers Vol. IV: Television in Day-to-Day Life: Patterns of Use. Washington, D. C., U.S. Government Printing Office, 1972; J. J. McIntire and J. Teevan, "Television Violence and Deviant Behavior," in *Television and Social Behavior,* Reports and Papers, Vol. III: Television and Adolescent Aggression. Washington, D.C., U.S. Government Printing Office, 1973.

17. *Channeling Children: Sex Stereotyping on Prime Time TV,* Women on Words and Images (Princeton, N.J.: 1975); *Window Dressing on the Set: Women and Minorities in Television,* a report of the U.S. Commission on Civil Rights, August 1977; and update of the report, January 1979; N. S. Tedesco, "Patterns in Prime Time," *Journal of Communications,* Spring 1974, 119–124; G. Gerbner and N. Signorelli, *Ten Year Study of Prime-Time TV,* Screen Actor's Guild (Hollywood, Calif.: 1979).

18. R. Pareja, "Children Learn Whether or Not We Teach Them," masters thesis, Cornell University, 1974.

19. J. Hennessee and J. Nicholson, "Now Says: TV Commercials Insult Women," *The New York Times Magazine,* May 28, 1972; L. Z. McArthur and B. G. Resko, "The Portrayal of Men and Women in American TV Commercials," *Journal of Social Psychology,* 1975, 97, 209–220; A. E. Courtney and T. W. Whipple, "Women in TV Commercials," *Journal of Communications,* Spring 1974, 110–118.

20. Sacramento AAUW, "The Images of Women in Television," in *Media Report to Women,* September 1, 1974.

21. L. C. Pogrebin, "Ten Cogent Reasons Why TV News Fails Women," *TV Guide,* October 4–10, 1975.

22. *Pandora,* Seattle, Washington, July 1972.

23. L. C. Pogrebin, "The Working Women," *Ladies Home Journal,* October 1974.

24. Lin Bolen, Vice President, Daytime Programming, NBC, in A. Unger, "Daytime Television: The Lucrative Wasteland," *Christian Science Monitor,* March 20, 1975, 5.

25. *Ibid.*

26. "A Nation of Videots: David Sohn Interviews Jerzy Kosinski," *Media and Methods,* April 1975, 25.

27. A. Bandura and R. H. Walters, *Social Learning and Personality Development,* Holt, Rinehart and Winston (New York: 1963).

28. R. M. Liebert, et al., *The Early Window: Effects of Television on Children and Youth,* Pergamon Press (New York: 1973) 162.

29. T. Freuh and P. E. McGhee, "Traditional Sex Role Development and the Amount of Time Spent Watching Television," *Child Development,* January 1975; A. Beuf, "Doctor, Lawyer, Household Drudge," *Journal of Communication,* Spring 1964; L. Z. McArthur and S. V. Eisen, "Television and Sex Role Stereotyping," *Journal of Applied Social Psychology,* 1976, 6, 4, 329–351.

30. M. M. Miller and B. Reeves, "Dramatic TV Content and Children's Sex Role Stereotypes," *Journal of Broadcasting,* Winter 1976, 20, 1, 35–49.

31. C. K. Atkin and M. M. Miller, "Experimental Effects of Television Advertising on Children," paper presented to the International Communications Association, Chicago, April 1975; "Boys and Girls Alike," *Human Behavior,* January 1978, 62.

32. T. P. Meyer, "The Impact of 'All In the Family' on Children," *Journal of Broadcasting,* Winter 1976, 20, 1, 23–33; L. Zebrowitz and S. V. Eisen, *op. cit.* (note 29).

33. W. Darrow, Jr., *I'm Glad I'm a Boy, I'm Glad I'm a Girl,* Simon & Schuster (New York: 1970).

34. B. Friedan, *The Feminine Mystique,* Norton (New York: 1963) 208.

35. M. Margolis, "In Hartford, Hannibal, and (New) Hampshire, Heloise Is Hardly Helpful," *Ms.* magazine, June 1976, 28.

36. Report on Curtis Conference on Advertising for Children, L. C. Clapp, "The TV Child as a Consumer," *Toy Review,* December 1972.

37. J. D. Culley, et al., "The Experts Look at Children's Television," *Journal of Broadcasting,* Winter 1976, 20, 1, 4; J. Condry, "Broadcasting and the Needs of Children," *Action for Children's Television,* Avon Books (New York: 1971) 70–71.

38. M. Mayer, *About Television,* Harper & Row (New York: 1972), quoted in R. Liebert, et al., *op. cit.* (note 28) 122; T. J. Jacobs, "Advertising and Children: Investigations by Nader's Raiders," *Action for Children's Television, op. cit.* (note 37) 106; E. McDowell, "Storm Ahead on TV Ads for Children," *The New York Times,* August 7, 1978, D1; "Sugar in the Morning . . . ," *Newsweek,* January 30, 1978, 75.

39. R. B. Choate and N. M. Debevoise, "Battling the Electronic Babysitter," *Ms.* magazine, April 1975, 92.

40. G. Thain, "The Federal Trade Commission and Advertising Directed to Children," *Action for Children's Television, op. cit.* (note 37) 113.

41. J. Morgenstern, "Children's Hour," *Newsweek,* August 16, 1971; R. Liebert, et al., *op. cit.* (note 28) 130; M. L. Smith and T. G. Bever, in P. H. Dougherty, "Commercials' Impact on Children," *The New York Times,* October 29, 1975; T. Robertson and J. Rossiter, study cited in *Psychology Today,* June 1977, 90–92.

42. D. Cater and S. Strickland, *TV Violence and The Child: The Evolution and Fate of the Surgeon General's Report,* Russell Sage Foundation (New York: 1975) 62.

43. F. E. Barcus, *Commercial Children's Television on Weekends and Weekdays,* Action for Children's Television, June 1978; *Media Report to Women,* Washington, D.C. 1972.

44. Dr. M. B. Rothenberg writing in the *Journal of the American Medical Association,* December 8, 1975, quoted in J. E. Brody, "TV Violence Cited as Bad Influence," *The New York Times,* December 17, 1975; also see, R. K. Goldsen, *The Show and Tell Machine,* Dial (New York: 1977); F. E. Barcus, *Weekend Commercial Television,* and *Television in the Afterschool Hours,* Action for Children's Television, October 1975.

45. D. Cater and S. Strickland, *op. cit.* (note 42) 13.

46. *Television and Growing Up: The Impact of Televised Violence,* The Surgeon General's Scientific Advisory Committee on Television and Social Behavior, U. S. Government Printing Office (Washington, D.C.: 1972).

47. Action for Children's Television (ACT), 46 Austin Street, Newtonville, Mass., 02160; Washington Association for Television and Children (WATCH), 4418 MacArthur Blvd. N.W. #202, Washington, D.C. 20007; The National Citizens Committee for Broadcasting, 1028 Connecticut Ave. N.W., Washington, D.C. 20036; Citizen Communications Center, 1812 N. Street, N.W., Washington, D.C. 20036; Council on Children, Media and Merchandising, 1346 Connecticut Ave. N.W., Washington, D.C. 20036; National Association for Better Broadcasting, Box 43640, Los Angeles, Calif. 90043; *Parents' Television Guide* (1979), The Quaker Oats Company, Box 4504, Chicago, Ill. 60677; National Parent-Teacher Association TV Action Center, 700 N. Rush Street, Chicago, Ill. 60611.

48. *Violence on Television,* A Report of the House Subcommittee on Communications Hearings, July 1977. Also see J. J. O'Connor, "Who to Blame for TV Violence? Everybody, Said the Panel," *The New York Times,* November 6, 1977, 35; N. Sheppard, Jr., "National PTA Rates Television Programs," *The New York Times,* February 16, 1978; *Television's Action Arsenal: Weapon Use in Prime Time,* U.S. Conference of Mayors, Washington, D.C.

49. J. J. O'Connor, "TV Is Getting Tough on Violence and Loose with Sex," *The New York Times,* September 11, 1977, II-1; "Sex and TV," *Newsweek,* February 20, 1978, 54ff; B. Greenberg, "Substance Use and Sexual Intimacy on Commercial Television," Michigan State University, March 1978; D. E. Kreeland, "TV Violence Down, Health Study Says," *The New York Times,* April 3, 1978, C22.

50. *Parade,* March 4, 1973; Louis Harris Poll reported in R. K. Baker and S. J. Ball, *Mass Media and Violence,* National Commission on the Causes and Prevention of Violence, Vol. 9, Government Printing Office, (Washington, D.C.), November 1969, 332.

51. D. Cater and S. Strickland, *op. cit.* (note 42) 39.

52. T. B. Brazelton, M.D., "How to Tame the TV Monster: A Pediatrician's Advice," *Redbook,* April 1972.

53. I. Ziferstein, M.D., in *Childhood,* Blue Cross Association (New York: 1976).

54. S. H. Fraiberg, *The Magic Years,* Scribners (New York: 1959) 270ff; J. E. Schowalter, in *Who Is Talking to Our Children: Third National Symposium on Children and Television,* Action for Children's Television, 1972, 10–12.

55. J. Condrey, "Broadcasting and the Needs of Children," *Action for Children's Television,* Avon Books (New York: 1971) 67; G. Comstock and M. Fisher, *Television and*

Human Behavior: A Guide to the Pertinent Scientific Literature, Rand (Santa Monica, Calif.: 1975).
56. D. Cater and S. Strickland, *op. cit.* (note 42) 29–56; *Television and Growing Up, op. cit.* (note 46); American Broadcasting Company, "Anti-Social and Pro-Social Effects of Television on Children," (New York: 1976); M. Kaplan, "Queens Youth Accused of Trying to Extort $700 from Father with Fake Kidnapping," *The New York Times,* January 31, 1978, 54; J. Footlick, "The Trials of TV," *Newsweek,* October 10, 1977, 70; B. D. Ayres, Jr., "TV Is on Trial and at Trial, in Miami," *The New York Times,* October 7, 1977, A18; "Despite Conviction of Youth, Debate over TV Violence Continues," October 8, 1977; L. Greenhouse, " 'Incitement' Is Held Issue in NBC Trial," *The New York Times,* August 3, 1978; R. M. Liebert, *op. cit.* (note 28) 1–3.
57. "Study Finds Children's TV More Violent," *The New York Times,* April 23, 1979, C19.
58. D. Cater and S. Strickland, *op. cit.* (note 42) 50; J. R. Milarsky, et al., "Exposure to TV Violence and Aggressive Behavior in Boys," paper presented to the American Sociological Association, 1972; "Is Violence Popular," *Human Nature,* June 1978, 16; W. A. Belsen, *Television Violence and the Adolescent Boy,* Lexington (Lexington, Mass.: 1979).
59. G. Gerbner, "Violence in Television Drama: Trends and Symbolic Functions," in G. A. Comstock and E. A. Rubinstein, eds. *Television and Social Behavior,* Vol. 1: Media Content and Control, U. S. Government Printing Office (Washington, D. C.: 1972).
60. M. DeFleur, "Occupational Roles as Portrayed on Television," *Public Opinion Quarterly,* 1964, 28, 57–74; D. Cater and S. Strickland, *op. cit.* (note 42) 127–128.
61. T. F. Baldwin and C. Lewis, "Violence in Television: The Industry Looks at Itself," in G. A. Comstock and E. A. Rubinstein, *op. cit.* (note 59) 295.
62. M. Winn, *The Plug-In Drug,* Viking Press (New York: 1977) 11.
63. M. P. Winick and C. Winick, *Television: What Children and Adults See,* National Association of Broadcasters' Television Code Review Board, May 1977, 2; P. C. Rosenblatt and M. C. Cunningham, "Television Watching and Family Tensions," *Journal of Marriage and the Family,* February 1976, 105–111; E. Maccoby, "Why Do Children Watch Television?" *Public Opinion Quarterly,* Fall 1954, 239–244.
64. T. B. Brazelton, *op. cit.* (note 52).
65. R. Blake, Advertising Manager, General Mills, Inc., August 9, 1977, p.c.
66. M. Jeary, Wheaties Account Supervisor, Dancer, Fitzgerald and Sample Agency, August 9, 1977, p.c.
67. Dr. Percy Tannenbaum, in D. Cater and S. Strickland, *op. cit.* (note 42) 137.
68. To focus your complaint to the correct responsible parties, consult one of the activist organizations listed in note 47 above.
69. "Listerine Must Now Come Clean," *The New York Times,* April 9, 1978, 20E.
70. P. H. Dougherty, "Schlitz 'Concerned' about TV Violence," *The New York Times,* February 8, 1977; N. Sheppard, Jr., "P.T.A. Meets TV Advertisers," *The New York Times,* May 31, 1978; E. McDowell, "TV Sex Upsetting Sponsors," *The New York Times,* May 30, 1978, D1.
71. "Television, The Great Debate," *The Washington Spectator,* January 15, 1979, 5, 1; Federal Communications Commission, Washington, D.C. 20554; M. Wexler and G. Levy, "Women on Television: Fairness and the 'Fair Sex,' " *Yale Review of Law and Social Action,* 1971, 2, 59–68.
72. Kathy Bonk, p.c.; also see *Media Report to Women,* June 1, 1977 (Washington, D.C.) for coverage of a Model Settlement; or contact WATCH (note 47) for guidance in monitoring and license challenge procedures.
73. L. S. Hanford, *New York,* July 25, 1977, 5.
74. J. Sandrich, quoted in B. O'Hallaren, "Nobody (in TV) Loves You When You're Old and Gray," *The New York Times,* July 24, 1977, 21.
75. G. and F. M. Hechinger, "There Are No Sexists on Sesame Street," *The New York Times,* January 30, 1972, 19–20.
76. *The New York Times,* September 4, 1977, editorial page.
77. D. W. Rintels, "How Much Truth Does 'The FBI' Tell About the FBI?" *The New York Times,* March 5, 1972, 2, 1, 17.
78. *Ibid.*
79. N. Johnson, *How to Talk Back to Your Television Set,* Little, Brown (Boston: 1967).
80. C. Winfrey, "Week Without Television Tunes Several Families Into Different Channels," *The New York Times,* April 27, 1977, B1.
81. F. Mankiewitcz and J. Swerdlow, *Remote Control,* Times Books (New York: 1978);

J. Mander, *Four Arguments for the Elimination of Television,* Morrow (New York: 1978).
82. R. K. Goldsen, *op. cit.* (note 44).
83. M. Winn, *op. cit.* (note 62) 41.
84. *Ibid.,* 42–43.
85. *Ibid.,* 35–37; H. Lesser, *Television and the Preschool Child,* Academic Press (New York: 1977).
86. M. Winn, *op. cit.* (note 62) 71.
87. *Ibid.,* 76–86.
88. *Ibid.,* 147.
89. D. Cohen in *Who Is Talking to Our Children? op. cit.* (note 54) 17–18.
90. N. Larrick, "Schools Get Tough on TV Addicts," *The New York Times,* November 13, 1977.
91. M. Winn, *op. cit.* (note 62) 197–199.
92. R. M. Liebert, *op. cit.* (note 28) 162.

21 • *That's Entertainment?*, page 426

1. C. R. Stimpson, "Sex, Gender and American Culture," in L.A. Cater, et al., *Women and Men: Changing Roles, Relationships and Perceptions,* Aspen Institute (New York: 1976) 207.
2. S. G. Feinburg, "Children Play at War," *Learning* magazine, January 1975, 10–16; E. G. Belotti, *What Are Little Girls Made Of?* Schocken (New York: 1976) 143–147; P. Sexton, *The Feminized Male,* Random House (New York: 1968) 232.
3. D. Archer, et al., "Face-ism," *Psychology Today,* September 1978, 65–66.
4. G. Vaughan-Jackson, *Drawing for Boys,* Grosset & Dunlap (New York: 1956).
5. G. Vaughan-Jackson, *Drawing for Girls,* Grosset & Dunlap (New York: 1977 ed).
6. C. R. Stimpson, *op. cit.* (note 1) 215; also, H. Kramer, "Does Feminism Conflict with Artistic Standards?" *The New York Times,* January 27, 1980, 1.
7. G. F. Orenstein, "Women Artists," *Signs,* 1975, 1, 2, 507.
8. J. Russell, "Art: 500 Years of Women at the Met," *The New York Times,* July 14, 1978.
9. L. Lippard, "Women in Art," *Chrysalis,* 1977, 2, 33.
10. F. D. Gray, "Women Writing About Women's Art," *Helicon Nine,* Fall 1979, 1, 11.
11. K. Larson, "Anonymous Was A Woman," *Village Voice,* October 17, 1977, 81.
12. G. F. Orenstein, *op. cit.* (note 7).
13. A. Flack, "The Haunting Images of Luisa Roldan," *Helicon Nine,* Fall 1979, 1, 70–79.
14. G. F. Orenstein, *op. cit.* (note 7) 509.
15. The book, H. W. Janson's *History of Art;* the reference, G. Glueck, "The Woman as Artist," *New York Times Magazine,* September 25, 1977, 50.
16. C. Nemser, *Conversation with Twelve Women Artists,* Scribners (New York: 1975); A. S. Harris and L. Nochlin, *Women Artists: 1550–1950,* Knopf (New York: 1977); G. Greer, *The Obstacle Race: The Fortunes of Women Painters and Their Work,* Farrar, Straus & Giroux (New York: 1979); L. Nochlin, "Why Have There Been No Great Women Artists?" in V. Gornick and B. K. Moran, *Woman in Sexist Society,* Basic (New York: 1971); E. Munro, *Originals: American Women Artists,* Simon & Schuster (New York: 1979).
17. A. S. Harris and L. Nochlin, *op. cit.* (note 16).
18. G. Glueck, *op. cit.* (note 15) 54–56.
19. F. D. Gray, *op. cit.* (note 10) 11.
20. *Ibid.* and K. Larson, *op. cit.* (note 11) 81.
21. M. Walters, *The Nude Male: A New Perspective,* Paddington Press (New York: 1978) 7.
22. *Ibid.,* 13; A. Hollander, *Seeing Through Clothes,* Viking (New York: 1978).
23. G. Thornton, "From the Ideal to the Erotic," *The New York Times,* June 18, 1978, D27; G. Thornton, "They're Making Sex Objects Out of Men," *The New York Times,* March 18, 1973, 34; H. Smith, "Ruckus Aroused: The Male Nude Taboo," *The Village Voice,* October 8, 1979, 21.
24. G. F. Orenstein, *op. cit.* (note 7) 517–521; A. Pagnozzi, "Onward from Mary Cassatt," *The New York Post,* July 7, 1979, 16.
25. L. Lippard, *op. cit.* (note 9) 37–46.
26. M. H. Mitchell, "Sexist Art Criticism: Georgia O'Keefe, a Case Study," *Signs,* 1978, 3, 3, 681.
27. Capsule descriptions of films, videotape, slide shows, listed alphabetically and indexed by subject in:

608

—*Positive Images: A Guide to Nonsexist Films for Young People,* by L. Artel and S. Weingraf, Booklegger Press (1976) 555 29 Street, San Francisco, Calif. 94131.
—*Films Kids Like* (1973) and *More Films Kids Like* (1977) ed. by S. Rice, The American Library Association, 50 E. Huron Street, Chicago, Ill. 60611.
—*Kids Flicks: Move Over Donald Duck,* compiled by J. Sternburg, *Ms.* magazine, 370 Lexington Avenue, New York, N.Y. 10017 ($1.00).
—*Young Viewers,* ed. by Maureen Gaffney, Media Center for Children, 3 West 29 Street, New York, N.Y. 10011 ($15 for 4 issues).
—*Parents' Choice: A Review of Children's Media,* Box 185, Waban, Mass. 02168 ($7 for 6 issues).
—*A Multimedia Approach to Children's Literature: A Selective List of Films, Filmstrips and Recordings Based on Children's Books,* ed. by E. Greene and M. Schoenfeld, American Library Association (see above).
28. E. Goldstein, "Letters to Editor," *Ms.* magazine, May 1979, 4.
29. C. P. Kottak, "Social Science Fiction," *Psychology Today,* February 1978.
30. B. Wagner, "The Masculine Image: A Film-Centered Approach," *Media and Methods,* September 1976, 50–52; M. Malone, *Heroes of Eros; Male Sexuality in the Movies,* E. P. Dutton (New York: 1979); D. J. Leab, *From Sambo to Superspace: The Black Experience in Motion Pictures,* Houghton Mifflin (Boston: 1976); D. Bogle; *Toms, Coons, Mulattoes, Mammies and Bucks: An Interpretive History of Blacks in American Film,* Viking (New York: 1973).
31. M. Haskell, *From Reverence to Rape: The Treatment of Women in the Movies,* Holt, Rinehart and Winston (New York: 1974) 265.
32. *Ibid.,* 140.
33. R. Patrick and W. Haislip, "Thank Heaven for Little Girls: An Examination of the Male Chauvinist Musical," *Cineaste* magazine, 1973, 1, 23–25.
34. N. Sayre, "Did Cooper and Stewart Have to Be So Stupid?" *The New York Times,* August 7, 1977.
35. R. Patrick and W. Haislip, *op. cit.* (note 33).
36. M. Haskell, *op. cit.* (note 31) 328–329; M. Rosen, *Popcorn Venus: Women, Movies and the American Dream,* Avon (New York: 1974); K. Weibel, "Images of Women in Movies," *Mirror, Mirror,* Anchor Press (New York: 1977) 91–134.
37. K. Weibel, *ibid.,* 91.
38. *Gallup Poll,* August 31, 1977, 32.
39. *Newspage,* Women Against Violence in Pornography & Media, November 1977.
40. *Ibid.;* "Pornography: The Ideology of Cultural Sadism," *Newspage,* November/-December 1979.
41. *Ibid.;* to order WAVPM literature write P. O. Box 14614, San Francisco, Calif. 94114.
42. H. Movshovitz, "The Delusion of Hollywood's 'Women's Films,' " *Frontiers,* 1979, 4, 1, 9–13; J. Mellen, "Hollywood Rediscovers the American Woman," *The New York Times,* April 23, 1978; "Hollywood's New Heroines," *Newsweek,* October 10, 1977, 78ff.
43. M. Malone, "Will America's Sweetheart Grow Up?" *Human Behavior,* December 1977, 67–71; M. Haskell, "Tatum O'Neal and Jodie Foster: Their Combined Age Is 27— What Is Hollywood Trying to Tell Us?" *Ms.* magazine, April 1977, 49–51.
44. M. Beller, "Hollywood's Kids Are Becoming Cherubs Again," *The New York Times,* October 14, 1979, II-1.
45. D. Turner, p.c.
46. Simon Sargon, composer-conductor, p.c.
47. Going Out Guide, *The New York Times,* September 5, 1979.
48. H. C. Schonberg, "How Sex Plays a Role at the Piano," *The New York Times,* May 27, 1979, D1.
49. J. Rockwell, "Why Are The New Stars of Disco Mostly Women," *The New York Times,* March 4, 1979, 23.
50. J. Dew, *The Women of Country Music: Singers & Sweethearts,* Doubleday (New York: 1977); T. Palmer, *All You Need Is Love: The Story of Popular Music,* Penguin (New York: 1977).
51. A. Copland, "Copland Salutes Boulanger," and V. Perlis, "Boulanger—20th Century Music Was Born in Her Classroom," both in *The New York Times,* September 11, 1977, II.
52. Charles Mingus, p.c.
53. There are few sources, none specifically written for children, so interested parents will have to distill the history from: J. G. Pool, *Women in Music History: A Research Guide,*

Box 436, Ansonia Station, New York, N.Y. 10023; J. M. Bowers, "Teaching About the History of Women in Western Music," *Women's Studies Newsletter,* Old Westbury, N.Y., Summer 1977, 11–16; K. Hoover, "Women in the Arts: Fanny and Lili Who?" *New Directions for Women,* Winter 1978–1979, 6; D. Hixon and D. Hennessee, *Women in Music: A Bio-Bibliography,* Scarecrows Press (Metuchen, N.J.: 1975); J. Rosen and G. Rubin-Rabson, "Why Haven't Women Become Great Composers?" *High Fidelity and Musical America,* February 1973, 23, 2, 46–52; J. Tick, "Why Have There Been No Great Women Composers," *The International Musician,* July 1975, 74, 1, 6.

54. J. Norell, "Elizabeth Jacquet de La Guerre," *Helicon Nine,* Fall 1979, 1, 1, 64–69.

55. C. Lawson, "In Soho, Review of Songs by Women Tunesmiths," *The New York Times,* April 28, 1978; C. Johnson, "The Silenced Songbirds," *Neworld,* 1978, 1, 19–22.

56. *Women in Jazz: All Women Groups* (#111) *Pianists* (#112) *Swingtime to Modern* (#113), three discs from Stash Records, Box 390, Brooklyn, N.Y.

57. J. S. Wilson, "Jazzwomen Jam First Festival," *The New York Times,* March 20, 1978; J. S. Wilson, "Women in Jazz Past and Present," *The New York Times,* June 11, 1978.

58. P. Freudiger and E. M. Almquist, "Male and Female Roles in the Lyrics of Three Genres of Contemporary Music," *Sex Roles,* 1978, 4, 1, 53.

59. *Media Decisions,* October 1976, 77–78.

60. *Ms.* magazines Arts section is your best bet for current releases; also *New Directions for Women; Off Our Backs; Sisterhood Bookstore,* 1351 Westwood Blvd., Los Angeles, Calif. 90024; *TABS,* 744 Carroll Street 2A, Brooklyn, N.Y. 11215; *Women's Book and Record Mail-Order Catalog,* Djuna Books, 154 W. 10th St., New York, N.Y. 10014.

61. Olivia Records, Box 70237, Los Angeles, Calif. 90070.

62. *Redwood Records,* P. O. Box 40400, San Francisco, Calif. 94140.

63. M. S. Smith, "Career vs. Family—Most Women Make a Choice," *Harvard Today,* Summer 1976.

64. At this writing, three Cryer and Ford albums are available: *Cryer & Ford,* RCA #APL 1-1235 (1975); *You Know My Music,* RCA #APL 1-2146 (1977); *I'm Getting My Act Together and Taking It on the Road,* Collector's Series, CBS Records (1979).

65. "Miss America," lyrics by Gretchen Cryer, copyright 1978 Fiddleback Music Publishing Co., Inc., from *I'm Getting My Act Together . . . , ibid.*

66. "Big Bill Murphy," lyrics by Gretchen Cryer and Nancy Ford, Copyright 1976 Fiddleback Music Publishing Co., Inc., from *You Know My Music, op. cit.* (note 64).

67. Elizabeth Rider Montgomery, quoted in *Women Today,* July 25, 1977, 96.

68. See excerpts from nonsexist kids books published each month in "Stories for Free Children," feature, *Ms.* magazine, 370 Lexington Avenue, New York, N.Y. 10017.

69. B. Bettleheim, *The Uses of Enchantment: The Meaning and Importance of Fairy Tales,* Knopf (New York: 1976).

70. *Ibid.,* 187.

71. *Ibid.,* 291.

72. *Ibid.,* 6.

73. *Ibid.,* 5.

74. E. G. Belotti, *op. cit.* (note 2) 103.

75. The most keen-witted feminist analyses are: M. R. Lieberman, "Some Day My Prince Will Come," in D. Gersoni-Stavn, ed. *Sexism and Youth,* R. R. Bowker (New York: 1974) 228–243; A. Dworkin, "The Fairy Tales," Part I, in *Woman Hating,* E. P. Dutton (New York: 1974); C. H. Stapen, "Women-Portent: Disenchanting The Fairy Tale," *Sibyl-Child: A Women's Arts and Culture Journal,* Aphra-Behn Press (Baltimore, Md.) Winter 1975; a somewhat more idiosyncratic interpretation is delivered by A. Lurie, "Witches and Fairies: Fitzgerald to Updike," *New York Review of Books,* December 21, 1971.

76. C. Heilbrun, *Reinventing Womanhood,* Norton (New York: 1979) 146.

77. C. Jaffee, "More Pain Than Pleasure: Teen Romances," *School Library Journal,* January 1979, 30; "Advice to Girls Then and Now," *The New York Times,* May, 23, 1979, C1.

78. Intext Press, 1973.

79. The best critiques: L. J. Weitzman, et al., "Sex Role Socialization in Picture Books for Preschool Children," *American Journal of Sociology,* 1972, 77, 6, 1125–1148; D. Gersoni-Staven, ed. "Books: Propaganda and the Sins of Omission," *Sexism and Youth,* Part III, contains 21 essays by various authors, 163–384; A. Graham, "The Making of a Nonsexist Dictionary," *Ms.* magazine, December 1973, 12–16; B. A. Mason, *The Girl Sleuth: A Feminist Guide to Nancy Drew and Her Sisters,* The Feminist Press, (Old Westbury, N.Y.: 1974); J. S. Hillman, "An Analysis of Male and Female Roles in Two Periods of Children's

Literature," *Journal of Educational Research,* 1974, 68, 2, 84–88; S. M. Czaplinski, "Sexism in Award-Winning Picture Books," *KNOW,* Box 86031, Pittsburgh, Pa. 15221.
80. "Kids Books: Independence Is 'Just a Stage,' " *Ms.* magazine, July 1978, 22.
81. Pamphlet and special interest bibliographies on children's books relating to ageism, racism and sexism from Interracial Books for Children, 1841 Broadway, New York, N.Y. 10023; children's booklists published periodically and nonsexist children's stories published in each issue of *Ms.* magazine, 370 Lexington Avenue, New York, N.Y. 10017 (reprints of back issues available); *Parents' Choice; A Review of Children's Media,* Box 185, Waban, Mass. 02168 ($7 for 6 issues, not impeccable feminist consciousness, but responsible choices for the most part); J. Fassler, *Helping Children Cope,* The Free Press (New York: 1978) includes recommended books on divorce, hospitalization, separation from parent, adoption, new baby, etc. for ages 4–8; E. David, ed. *The Liberty Cap: A Catalogue of Non-Sexist Materials For Children,* Academy Press (Chicago: 1977); J. Adell and H. D. Klein, *A Guide to Nonsexist Children's Books,* Academy Press (Chicago: 1976); *Little Miss Muffet Fights Back: A Bibliography of Recommended Non-Sexist Books About Girls for Young Readers,* compiled by Feminists on Children's Media, 1974 revised, from Feminist Book Mart, 162–11 Ninth Ave, Whitestone, N.Y. 11357; *The Acorn Groweth: Resource Materials on Sexism in Library Materials for Children and Young Adults,* ed. by R. Kort and N. Parikh, 48 Sunset Ave, Venice, Calif. 90291; "Checklist for Evaluating Sexism in Children's Books," Women on Words and Images, Box 2163, Princeton, N.J. 08540. Feminist publishers of children's books: The Feminist Press, Box 334, Old Westbury, N.Y. 11568; Lollipop Power, Box 1171, Chapel Hill, N.C.; The Joyful World Press, 468 Belvedere St., San Francisco, Calif.; Peoplebooks, 8504 N. Germantown Ave., Philadelphia, Pa. 19118; Daughters Publishing Co., M. S. 590, Box 42999, Houston, Tex. 77042.
82. S. G. Lanes, *Down The Rabbit Hole: Adventures and Misadventures in the Realm of Children's Literature,* Atheneum (New York: 1971) 129.
83. W. Darrow, Jr., *I'm Glad I'm a Boy, I'm Glad I'm a Girl,* Simon & Schuster (New York: 1970).
84. M. Hacker, "Science Fiction and Feminism: The Work of Joanna Russ," *Chrysalis,* 1977–1978, 4, 75; J. Russ, "Reflections on Science Fiction: An Interview," *Quest,* Summer 1975, 2.
85. R. Minard, ed. *Womenfolk and Fairytales,* Houghton Mifflin (Boston: 1975).
86. W. Sheed, *The Good Word,* Henry Robbins/Dutton (New York: 1978).
87. J. K. Floyd, *Classroom Practices in Teaching English 1976–77: Responses to Sexism,* 1976, National Council of Teachers of English.
88. "Equal Reading Opportunity," *Publishers' Weekly,* July 13, 1970, 76.
89. A. P. Nilsen, "Women in Children's Literature," *College English,* May 1971, 72.
90. N. F. Russo, "Kids Learn Their Lessons Early and Learn Them Well," in K.C.W. Kammeyer, ed. *Confronting the Issues,* Allyn and Bacon (Boston: 1975) 384.
91. A. P. Nilsen, *op. cit.* (note 89) 80.
92. *Ibid.,* 79.
93. *Boys' Life,* July 1976.
94. *Media Decisions,* October 1976, 78.
95. E. Goffman, *Gender Advertisements,* Harvard University Press (Cambridge, Mass.: 1979), Introduction by Vivian Gornick. Other good analyses of print advertising: K. Weibel, *op. cit.* (note 36) 135–174; D. Stemple and J. E. Tyler, "Sexism in Advertising," *The American Journal of Psychoanalysis,* 1974, 34, 271–273; A. Courtney and S. W. Lockeretz, "A Women's Place: An Analysis of the Roles Portrayed by Women in Magazine Advertisements," *Journal of Market Research,* February 1971, 8, 92–95.
96. Just two examples out of too many: "Come Clean," John Thawley raincoat ad, *Ms.* magazine, "No Comment," November 1978; L. Morrow, "The Fascination of Decadence," *Time,* September 10, 1979, 85–86.
97. "Quiz," *Mother Jones,* November 1977, 34.
98. S. Brabant, "Sex Role Stereotypes in the Sunday Comics," *Sex Roles,* 1976, 2, 4, 331–337.
99. J. S. Chafetz, *Masculine, Feminine or Human?,* Peacock (Itasca, Ill.: 1974) commenting on M. Brenton theory, 43.
100. D. K. Shah, "Superwomen Fight Back," *Newsweek,* March 20, 1978, 75; J. Klemesrud, "Female Superheroes Get Star Roles in the Comics," *The New York Times,* January 4, 1980, A14.
101. S. Greenberg, *Right From the Start,* Houghton Mifflin (Boston: 1978) 197.
102. J. S. Chafetz, *op. cit.* (note 99) 48.

103. Good critiques of women's magazines: K. Kaiser, "The New Women's Magazines: It's the Same Old Story," *Frontiers,* 1979, 4, 1, 14–17; L.A. Geise, "The Female Role in Middle Class Women's Magazines from 1955–1976: A Content Analysis of Nonfiction," *Sex Roles,* 1979, 5, 1, 51–62; H. H. Franzwa, "Working Women in Fact and Fiction," *Journal of Communication,* Spring 1974, 104–108; C. B. Flora, "The Passive Female: Her Comparative Image by Class and Culture in Women's Magazine Fiction," *Journal of Marriage and the Family,* August 1971, 435–444; G. Tuchman, A. K. Daniels and J. Benet, eds. *Hearth and Home: Images of Women in the Mass Media,* see Part II, "Women's Magazines," and Part III, "Newspapers Women's Pages," Oxford University Press (New York: 1978) 91–221.

104. J. S. Chafetz, *op. cit.* (note 99) 47.

105. *Media Decisions,* November 1976, 96.

106. *The New York Times,* November 19, 1974.

107. Item about a story in *The New York Times* appeared in *The Village Voice,* December 4, 1978.

108. *The New York Times,* October 17, 1975, 1.

109. G. Hanna and M. McAllister, *Books, Young People and Reading Guidance,* Harper & Row (New York: 1960) 46; M. Ross, "Are Story Preferences Sex-Linked for 2 and 3-Year-Olds and for 4 and 5-Year-Olds?" 1976, *ERIC* # ED 134324 PS 009052; J. M. Connor and L. A. Serbin, "Children's Responses to Stories with Male and Female Characters," *Sex Roles,* 1978, 4, 5, 637–645; S. L. Tibbetts, "Sex Differences in Children's Reading Preferences," *The Reading Teacher,* December 1974, 279–281.

110. J. Dunning, "D'Amboise Crusades to Drive 'Sissy' Stigma from Ballet," *The New York Times,* December 1, 1976, C16.

111. W. Terry, "A Father-and-Son Team at City Ballet," *The New York Times,* July 9, 1978, 10.

112. M. Haskell, "Sex Symbols," *Ladies Home Journal,* January 1979, 56.

22 • Other People, Other Places . . . , page 461

1. K. Widmer, "Reflections of a Male Housewife," *Village Voice,* June 10, 1971.

2. P. D. Kelly, "Letters to the Editor," *Ms.* magazine, September 1978.

3. For a thorough analysis of language and sex, see: C. Miller and K. Swift, *Words and Women,* Anchor/Doubleday (New York: 1976); C. Edelsky, "Recognizing Sex-Linked Language," *Language Arts,* October 1976, 53, 7, 746–752; R. Lakoff, *Language and Woman's Place,* Harper/Colophon (New York: 1975); B. Thorn and N. Henley, *Language and Sex: Difference and Dominance,* Newbury House (Rowley, Mass.: 1975).

4. J. R. McMillan, et al., "Women's Language," Illinois State University, thesis 1977; G. C. Gleser, et al., "The Relationship of Sex and Intelligence to Choice of Words: A Normative Study of Verbal Behavior," *Journal of Clinical Psychology,* 1959, 15, 182–191.

5. N. Henley and B. Thorne, "Womanspeak and Manspeak: Sex Differences and Sexism in Communication, Verbal and Nonverbal," in A. G. Sargent, *Beyond Sex Roles,* West (St. Paul: 1977) 201–218; M. Octigan and S. Niederman, "Male Dominance in Conversations," *Frontiers,* 1979, 4, 1, 50–54.

6. J. Bernard, *The Sex Game,* Atheneum (New York: 1972); K. J. Gruber and J. Gaebelein, "Sex Differences in Listening Comprehension," *Sex Roles,* 1979, 5, 3, 299–309; M. B. Parlee, "Conversational Politics," *Psychology Today,* May 1979, 48–56.

7. J. Sachs, et al., "Anatomical and Cultural Determinants of Male and Female Speech," paper presented at Georgetown Roundtable, Georgetown University, March 1972; A. Mehrabian, *Public Places, Private Spaces,* 319; A. Meditch, "The Development of Sex Specific Speech Patterns in Young Children," *Anthropological Linguistics,* December 1975, 17, 9.

8. N. M. Henley, *Body Politics: Power, Sex and Nonverbal Communication,* Prentice-Hall (Englewood Cliffs, N.J.: 1977); B. W. Eakins and R. G. Eakins, *Sex Differences in Human Communication,* Houghton Mifflin (Boston: 1978); S. Weitz, "Sex Differences in Nonverbal Communication," *Sex Roles,* 1976, 2, 12; D. L. Summerhayes and R. W. Suchner, "Power Implications of Touch in Male-Female Relationships," *Sex Roles,* 1978, 4, 1; C. Silverthorne, et al., "Attribution of Personal Characteristics as a Function of the Degree of Touch on Initial Contact and Sex," *Sex Roles,* 1976, 2, 2, 185–193.

9. N. M. Henley, *ibid.;* G. H. Tennis and J. M. Dabbs, Jr., "Sex, Setting and Personal Space: First Grade Through College," *Sociometry,* 1975, 38, 2, 385–394; M. A. Wittig and P. Skolnick, "Status Versus Warmth as Determinants of Sex Differences in Per-

sonal Space," *Sex Roles,* 1978, 4, 493–503; S. M. Jourard, "An Exploratory Study of Body-Accessibility," *British Journal of Social Clinical Psychology,* 1966, 5, 221–231.
10. E. Morgan, "The Erotization of Male Dominance-Female Submission," *KNOW* (Pittsburgh: 1975) 30; R. J. Border and G. M. Homleid, "Handedness and Lateral Positioning in Heterosexual Couples: Are Men Still Strong-Arming Women?" *Sex Roles,* 1978, 4, 1, 72.
11. D. Cohen, "Smiling—It's a Worrier's Game," *Psychology Today,* March 1977, 90; S. Firestone, *The Dialectic of Sex,* William Morrow (New York: 1970) 101; A. R. Hochschild, "The Sociology of Feeling and Emotion: Selected Possibilities," in M. Millman and R. M. Kanter, eds. *Another Voice,* Anchor/Doubleday (New York: 1975).
12. R. Morgan, *Going Too Far,* Random House (New York: 1977).
13. J. Hassett and J. Houlihan, "Different Jokes for Different Folks," *Psychology Today,* January 1979.
14. "What's So Funny?" *Psychology Today,* June 1978, 101.
15. *Ibid.*
16. J. Hassett and J. Houlihan, *op. cit.* (note 13) 70.
17. V. Adams, "The Anatomy of a Joke—Studies Take a Serious Look," *The New York Times,* August 28, 1979, C1.
18. *Ibid.,* C3.
19. A. Chapman and N. J. Gadfield, "Is Sexual Humor Sexist?" *Journal of Communications,* 1976, 26, 3.
20. J. Hassett and J. Houlihan, *op. cit.* (note 13) 70.
21. "No Comment," *Ms.* magazine, March 1975, 105.
22. D. L. Bristol, "Letters to the Editor," *Ms.* magazine, August 1979.
23. "Store Window Clean-Up," *Off Our Backs,* March 1978, 9.
24. "Bloomingdale's Customer Charges Sex Bias," *The New York Times,* December 8, 1977.
25. R. Alexander, "Now It's Name Jeans for the Under-10 Set," *The New York Times,* October 9, 1979, B10.
26. J. D. Grambs and W. B. Waetjen, *Sex: Does It Make a Difference?* Duxbury Press (North Scituate, Mass.: 1975) 259.
27. C. Winnick, *The New People: Desexualization in American Life,* Pegasus (New York: 1968) 217–221.
28. Virtually all of the following historical information comes from U. Stannard, "Clothing and Sexuality," *Sexual Behavior,* May 1971.
29. *Ibid.*
30. K. Weibel, "Images of the Fashionable Woman," *Mirror Mirror,* Anchor Press (New York: 1977) 176.
31. H. E. Roberts, "The Exquisite Slave: The Role of Clothes in the Making of the Victorian Woman," *Signs,* 1977, 2, 3, 554–569.
32. J. Parrent and S. Rennie, "The Tyranny of Women's Clothes," *Chrysalis,* 1977, 2, 91–97.
33. S. Greenhalgh, "Bound Feet, Hobbled Lives: Women in Old China," *Frontiers,* 1978.
34. N. Beach, "You Are What You Wear," *The New York Times Magazine,* August 26, 1979, 187.
35. J. Kaplan, "Women in Philately," *S.P.A. Journal,* May 1977, 571–572.
36. NOW-NY, 47 East 19 Street, New York, N.Y. 10003.
37. "Women on U.S. Stamps," 1975, U.S. Government Printing Office, Pamphlet 652–757; *U.S. Postage Service News,* Washington, D.C. 20260; "Stamp Order," Philatelic Sales Unit, Washington, D.C. 20036; *Stamps and Stories,* U.S. Postal Service, Washington, D.C. 20260.
38. J. K. Meuli, "In Brief," *National NOW Times,* December 78/January 79, 2.
39. R. D. Lyons, "Another Sexist Bastion Falls: Hurricanes Renamed," *The New York Times,* May 13, 1978.
40. *The New York Times,* May 24, 1978 and July 26, 1978 and September 1, 1978; J. K. Meuli, "In Brief," *National NOW Times,* September 1978, 2; "The Susan B. Edsel," *The New York Times,* January 20, 1980, F21.
41. J. A. Feinblatt, A. R. Gold, "Sex Roles and the Psychiatric Referral Process," *Sex Roles,* 1976, 2, 2, 109; A. C. Israel, et al., "Gender and Sex-Role Appropriateness: Bias in the Judgment of Disturbed Behavior," *Sex Roles,* 1978, 4, 3, 399–413; *Psychiatric Viewpoints,* Report XIII, Hoffman-LaRoche, Nutley, N.J. (1974).
42. H. M. Schmeck, Jr., "Study Backs Charge of Sexism in Medicine," *The New York Times,* June 5, 1979, C1.

43. "The Entertaining Woman," Gallup Survey conducted for the Magic Pan Restaurants, Fall 1979; "Career Travel Tipping Survey (1979)" and "National Restaurant Association Survey 1976" from P.O.B. 125, Westminster, Pa. 19874.
44. S. Jacoby, "Hers," *The New York Times,* February 23, 1978, C2; also for related indignities, see B. Rice, "Sex and the Single Check," *Psychology Today,* May 1979, 45; C. Mauro, "It Serves Them Right," *Ms.* magazine, November 1977, 22; F. J. Prial, "Wine: Even Now It's Still a Man's World," *The New York Times,* July 8, 1973; A. Gruen, "So What If My Escort Is 2½ Feet Tall," *Majority Report,* October 16–29, 1976, 7; S. Thompson, "Children Welcome," *Ms.* magazine, November 1979.
45. L. Haney, "A Day of Small Smiles and Tears," *The New York Times,* July 15, 1973.
46. *Sparky* comic, a publication of National Fire Protection Association, Boston, Mass.
47. "President Saves a Family Custom," *The New York Times,* July 8, 1976; *Woman Today,* September 13, 1976, 123.
48. "Mothers Want to Attend Awards Banquet," *Newsday,* March 25, 1976.
49. *Christian Science Monitor,* 1975. Date unknown.
50. "Jaycees See 'Positive' Side to Suits on Male Rule," *The New York Times,* September 16, 1979.
51. *Ms.* magazine, "Gazette," December 1978, 22.
52. C. Rivers, et al., *Beyond Sugar and Spice,* Putnams (New York: 1979) 53.
53. "Girls Can Be in Boys' Club: Michigan Court Rules," *The New York Times,* July 17, 1977.
54. "Proposal to Admit Boys Is Voted Down by the Girl Scouts," *The New York Times,* October 29, 1975.
55. *The Spokeswoman,* April 15, 1975.
56. "Facts About Girl Scouts of the U.S.A." November 1977, GSA, 830 Third Avenue, New York, N.Y. 10022; A. Finkelstein, "What's It All About," *Girl Scout Leader,* January/February 1973.
57. "Patterns of Growth," and "Today's Girl/Tomorrow's Women," Girls Clubs of America, 205 Lexington Avenue, New York, N.Y. 10016.
58. "No Comment," *Ms.* magazine, February 1979, 92.
59. *Women's Agenda* (1978), 370 Lexington Avenue, New York, N.Y. 10017.
60. "Survey of Six Foundations," *Women and Foundations,* Corporate Philanthropy Report (April 1978) 35 S. Main St., Hanover, N.H. 03755.
61. J. Kujoth, *The Boys' and Girls' Book of Clubs and Organizations,* Prentice-Hall (Englewood Cliffs, N.J.: 1975) 36.
62. *Ibid.,* 40.
63. "No Comment," *Ms.* magazine March 1975.
64. J. Kujoth, *op. cit.* (note 61) 8.
65. Source, BSA, New Jersey Regional Office: 201-821-6500.
66. J. P. Hantover, "The Boy Scouts and the Validation of Masculinity," *Journal of Social Issues,* 1978, 34, 1, 191.
67. *Ibid.*
68. F. Caplan, ed., *Parents Yellow Pages,* Doubleday (New York: 1978) 464.
69. K. Storms, "Letters to the Editor," *Ms.* magazine, December 1974, 5.
70. "Accident Prone Personalities: Who Does Best Behind the Wheel?" *Human Behavior,* February 1979, 49; "Daddy The Rowdy," *Time,* May 1, 1972; "Ajax Rent a Car Says Women Are Safer Drivers," *Women Today,* December 11, 1978, 142; L. Menefee, "Women's Lib Pro and Con: The Compleat Argument," *The Greensburg Accent,* reprint from KNOW, Inc. Pittsburgh, Pa; "Higher Car Insurance for Young Women Feared," *The New York Times,* June 4, 1979.
71. Abigail Adams to John Adams, March 31, 1776 in A. S. Rossi, ed. *The Feminist Papers: From Adams to deBeauvoir,* Columbia University Press (New York: 1973) 10.
72. L. G. DePauw, "Where to Find Our Foremothers," *Ms.* magazine, July 1974, 100–102; L. Sherr and J. Kazickas, *The American Woman's Gazetteer,* Bantam (New York: 1976); R. Eby, "Ride on Sibyl Ludington," *Ms.* magazine, July 1975, 55–58; C. Hymowitz and M. Weisman, *A History of Women in America,* Bantam (New York: 1978); C. R. and L. W. Ingraham, *An Album of Women in American History,* Franklin Watts (New York: 1972); A. McGovern, "The Secret Soldier," *Ms.* magazine, July 1976, 73–76.
73. *American Youth Hostels Family Program,* 20 W. 17th St., New York, N.Y. 10011.
74. T. D. Allman, "Panic Before a Dinner Party: All the Men Sent Regrets," *The New York Times,* May 23, 1979, C3.
75. M. B. Parlee, *op. cit.* (note 6).

76. G. Eskenazi, "To Life, to Life! To Young Womanhood," *The New York Times*, L. I. Section, June 18, 1978, 2.

77. "Orange Bowl Is Site of Bar Mitzvah Party," *The New York Times*, May 14, 1978; "So What's New Under the Sun? A Bowl-Mitzvah," *Variety*, May 10, 1978.

78. L. Ames, "Sweet Sixteen: A Rite That Persists," *The New York Times*, January 4, 1978.

79. *Ibid.*

80. A. Taylor, "Sweet 16: Makeup Lesson Was the Surprise," *The New York Times*, March 13, 1978.

81. The Academy of Model Aeronautics, 806–15th St. N.W., Washington, D.C. 20005.

82. B.A.M. Pitchford, "Give Yourself a Susan B. Anthony Birthday Party—I DID!" *Ms.* magazine, February 1979, 67–68.

83. P. Washbourn, *Becoming Woman,* and *Seasons of Woman,* both Harper & Row (San Francisco: 1979); M. Stone, *Ancient Mirrors of Womanhood,* New Sibylline Books (New York: 1980); Starhawk, *The Spiral Dance,* Harper & Row (San Francisco: 1979); R. Graves, *The White Goddess,* Farrar, Straus & Giroux (New York: 1974); M. Stone, *When God Was a Woman,* Dial (New York: 1976).

84. J. P. Johnson, "How Mother Got Her Day," *American Heritage,* April-May 1979, 14–21.

85. *Ibid.*

86. C. Gilbert-Neiss, "NOW Knocks Sexist Greeting Cards," *New Directions for Women,* Winter 1975–1976.

87. Ms. Christmas Cards, 370 Lexington Avenue, New York, N.Y. 10017; The Notables, 6019 Kenwood, Kansas City, Mo. 64110; Equality Products, 1554 T T Bardstown Rd., Louisville, Ky. 40205; Feminist History Series, Sappho Graphics, 503 E. 78th St., New York, N.Y. 10021; Lenore and Daughters, 8601 Falkstone Lane, Alexandria, Va. 22309; WEAL Holiday Cards, Mary Stanley, 604 E. Olive, Fresno, Calif. 93728.

23 • *Dear Old Sexist School Days, page 491*

1. *Reading for Understanding,* Science Research Association, 1963, 3, 9.

2. N. Frazier and M. Sadker, *Sexism in School and Society,* Harper & Row paperback (New York: 1973).

3. *Fact Sheets on Institutional Sexism,* The Racism/Sexism Resource Center (New York: 1976).

4. N. F. Russo, "Sex Role Stereotypes, Schools and the Socialization for Reproduction," *Equilibrium,* January 1974.

5. T. Pasquale and M. Dunkle, "An Upset Victory for Women," *Women's Agenda,* June 1976.

6. D. Henry, "H.E.W Rules Wethersfield All-Boy Choir Can Resume if Girls Can Have Their Own," *The New York Times,* April 15, 1977.

7. "Laughing at All The Wrong Places," *Learning* magazine, April 1977.

8. *Title IX Resources:* from Project on Equal Education Rights, (PEER) 1112 13 Street, N.W., Washington, D.C. 20005:

- "Cracking The Glass Slipper: PEER's Guide to Ending Sex Bias in Your Schools"
- "Anyone's Guide to Filing a Title IX Complaint" from U.S. Government Printing Office, Washington, D.C. 20402:
- "A Student Guide to Title IX" (#017-080-01710-5)
- "Identifying Discrimination" (#017-080-01671-1)

FOR MORE DETAILED EXPLANATION OF TITLE IX COVERAGE AND IMPLEMENTATION:

Title IX: How It Affects Elementary and Secondary Education, from
Education Commission of the States,
1860 Lincoln,
Denver, Colo. 80203

Guidelines and Self-Evaluation Kit for Title IX, from
Women's Equity Action League (WEAL),
377 National Press Building,
Washington, D.C. 20045

Combating Discrimination in the Schools: Legal Remedies & Guidelines, from

National Education Association,
1201 16 Street, N.W.,
Washington, D.C. 20036

Important Title IX Resources, from
Project on the Status and Education of Women,
Association of American Colleges,
1818 R. St. N.W.,
Washington, D.C. 20009

Complying With Title IX: Implementing Institutional Self-Evaluation
Resource Center on Sex Roles in Education
Foundation for the Improvement of Education
1201 16 Street, N.W.
Washington, D. C. 20036

Also: "An Analysis of H.E.W. Regulations Concerning Sex Discrimination in Education," *Women's Rights Law Reporter,* 1976, 3, 68–77.

FOR INDIVIDUAL ASSISTANCE:
Title IX Assistance Center
University of Michigan
Ann Arbor, Mich. 48104

9. "Supreme Court Votes Yes On Title IX Suits," *PEER Perspective,* September 1979, 2.
10. *The Land of the Free,* Amereon (location unknown).
11. *Sing Trouble Away,* Teachers Library (New York).
12. *To Read, Write and Listen,* J. B. Lippincott (Philadelphia).
13. *Applied Secretarial Procedures,* McGraw-Hill (New York).
14. *Health and Growth,* Scott Foresman and Co. (Glenview, Ill.).
15. *Men and Nations,* Harcourt Brace Jovanovich (New York).
16. *Guardians of Tomorrow: Pioneers in Ecology,* Viking Press.
17. "Sex Bias and the Strong Vocational Interest Test," from WEAL, (see footnote 8).
18. *Our American Government,* J. B. Lippincott (Philadelphia).
19. *Elementary Mathematics Three,* Harcourt Brace Jovanovich (New York).
20. J. S. Chafetz, *Masculine/Feminine or Human?,* F. E. Peacock (Itasca, Ill.: 1974) 85.
21. J. E. Collins, "Publishers Depict Women in New Ways," *The New York Times,* April 30, 1978, 19.
22. *Guidelines for Equal Treatment of the Sexes in McGraw-Hill Books,* McGraw-Hill, 1221 Ave. of Americas, New York, N.Y. 10020; *Guidelines for Improving the Image of Women in Textbooks,* Scott Foresman and Co., 1900 E. Lake Avenue, Glenview, Ill. 60025; *Guidelines for Multiethnic/Nonsexist Survey,* Random House Education Division, 201 East 50th Street, New York, N.Y. 10022; *The Treatment of Sex Roles: Guidelines for the Development of Elementary and Secondary Instructional Materials,* Holt, Rinehart and Winston, 383 Madison Avenue, New York, N.Y. 10036.
23. J. E. Collins, *op. cit.* (note 22).
24. *America: In Space and Time,* Addison-Wesley (Cambridge, Mass.: 1976).
25. A. Novick and D. Griffiths, "Sex Segregated Public Schools: Vorcheimer v. School District of Philadelphia and The Judicial Definition of an Equal Education for Women," *Women's Rights Law Reporter,* 1978, 4, 2, 79–96.
26. "Girls Admitted By Boston Latin," *The New York Times,* September 10, 1972; "Boys High Adding 'Girls' To Its Name After Blissful Year of Co-education," *The New York Times,* June 16, 1975.
27. "Schools Found to Lag in Banning Sex Bias," *The New York Times,* March 16, 1977.
28. *Back To School Line-Up: Where Girls and Women Stand in Education Today,* Project on Equal Education Rights, (PEER) Washington D.C., 1979; "Survey Charges Schools Remain Male Strongholds," *The New York Times,* September 5, 1979.
29. "What Are They Complaining About?" *PEER Perspective,* November 1976.
30. J. Ernest, *Mathematics and Sex,* University of California at Santa Barbara, 1976. (Available from the Ford Foundation, 320 E. 43 Street, New York, N.Y. 10017.)
31. L. W. Sells, "High School Math as the Critical Filter in The Job Market," University of California at Berkeley (available from Wesleyan University Math Clinic).
32. *Ibid.*
33. "Math Misery: Why Jane Can't Do Calculus," *Human Behavior,* January 1979, 67.
34. "Women Suffer from Lack of Math Skills," *Student Press Service,* 1015 20 Street, N.W. Washington, D.C. 20036. November 1978.

616

35. The course is now a book: S. Kogelman and J. Warren, *Mind Over Math,* McGraw-Hill (New York: 1979).

36. S. Tobias and B. Donady, "Counseling the Math Anxious," presented at Girls Clubs of America, Wingspread Seminar, June 1978; G. M. Burton, "Regardless of Sex," *Mathematics Teacher,* April 1979, 261–270; E. B. Fiske, "Does Math Fear Have a Solution?" *The New York Times,* October 3, 1979, 9; S. Tobias, *Overcoming Math Anxiety,* Norton (New York: 1978).

37. N. Kreinberg, *Public Affairs Report,* December 1976, Institute of Governmental Studies, University of California at Berkeley.

38. "New Programs Highlight Science Options for Women," *PEER Perspective,* February 1978; "I'm Madly in Love With Electricity and Other Comments About Their Work by Women in Science and Engineering," *Careers,* Lawrence Hall of Science, University of California at Berkeley; and *A Selected Annotated Bibliography,* Human Sciences Press (New York: 1977).

39. T. I. Rubin, *Ladies Home Journal,* date unknown.

40. D. Gold and C. Berger, "Problem-Solving Performance of Young Boys and Girls as a Function of Task Appropriateness and Sex Identity," *Sex Roles,* 1978, 4, 2, 183–193.

41. K. Koch, *Wishes, Lies and Dreams: Teaching Children to Write Poetry,* Vintage (New York: 1971).

42. "W.H.O. Panel Urges Widening The Scope of Sex Education," *The New York Times,* January 11, 1976.

43. J. Springer, et al., "An Approach to Teaching a Course on Dating Behavior," *The Family Coordinator,* January 1975, 13.

44. This and other quotes from young people, recorded at the conference, Sex Role Myths We Teach, April 7, 1973, Fordham University, high school students workshop.

45. L. Maslinoff, "Sex Education Films: A Content Analysis," *The Family Coordinator,* October 1973, 405–412.

46. J. Tebbel, "Sex Education: Yesterday, Today and Tomorrow," *Today's Education,* January-February 1976, 70–72.

47. A. Steinmann and A. P. Jurick, "The Effects of a Sex Education Course on the Sex Role Perceptions of Junior High School Students," *The Family Coordinator,* January 1975, 27.

48. "Adolescent Sexuality," a complete, special issue of the *Journal of Clinical Child Psychology,* Fall-Winter 1974, 3, 3.

49. Report on Ford Foundation grant to NYC Family Living and Sex Education Peer Information Service, *The New York Times,* September 22, 1973.

50. E. Ogg, *Preparing Tomorrow's Parents,* Public Affairs Pamphlet 520.

51. *Ibid.*

52. "A New Teenage Course: Learning to be Parents," *Psychology Today,* March 1975, 79–80.

53. Parenthood Education Program, 1196 Prospect Avenue, Westbury, N.Y. 11590; Education for Parenthood Project, BESE, Office of Education, Washington, D.C. 20202; "Parenthood Questionaire," Behavior Associates, 330 East 13 St., Tucson, Ariz. 85701.

54. Jacqueline Schlemmer, Van Meter Community School, Van Meter, Iowa, p.c. Also see *Family Circle,* July 1975.

55. A. H. Malcolm, "For Students, a Course on Marriage Reality," *The New York Times,* November 16, 1975.

56. M. Mead, "Speaking to the Issues: Men's Work, Women's Work?" *Rockefeller Foundation Illustrated,* August 1975, 2, 3.

57. L. Stone, "Why Johnny Can't Cook," *Majority Report,* March 1974.

58. "The House That Jack and Jill Built: Curriculum Manual for Kindergarten through Grade 3," Berkeley Unified School District, from *Advocates for Women,* San Francisco, 1976.

59. "Male Basketball Star Is School's Best Cook," *The New York Times,* February 5, 1973, 21.

60. A. Huston-Stein and R. L. Welch, "Sex Role Development and the Adolescent," in J. Adams, ed. *Understanding Adolescence,* Allyn and Bacon (Rockleigh, N.J.: 1976).

61. *Carnegie Quarterly,* Summer 1978, 26, 3, 2.

62. A. Huston-Stein and R. L. Welch, *op. cit.* (note 60).

63. C. S. Petro and B. A. Putnam, "Sex Role Stereotypes: Issues of Attitudinal Changes," *Sex Roles,* 1979, 5, 1, 29–39. Also see, A. H. Thomas and N. R. Stewart, "Counselor

Response to Female Clients With Deviate and Conforming Career Goals," *Journal of Counseling Psychology,* 1971, 18, 352–357.

64. *Summary of the Final Regulation Implementing the Vocational Education Amendments of 1976: Provisions Relating to Sex Bias and Sex Stereotyping,* National Advisory Council on Women's Educational Programs, Suite 821, 1832 M St. N.W. Washington, D.C. 20036.

65. Helen Southard, director, National YWCA Resource Center, New York City.

66. E. B. Fiske, "U.S. Acts to End Alleged Sexism in Vocational Education," *The New York Times,* October 20, 1976.

67. "Young Women Don't Expect to Hold Jobs," *Student Press Service,* (note 34), February 1979, quoting statistics from the National Assessment of Educational Progress.

68. J. M. Steiger and R. Sherman, "When Your Daughter Wants To Be a Plumber—What Kind of Counseling Will She Get?" *Women's Agenda,* September 1976, 5,12.

69. A. Huston-Stein and R. L. Welch, *op. cit.* (note 60).

70. *Career Education Incentive Act of December 1977;* contact PEER (note 8) for details.

71. Judith Shallenberger, p.c.

72. C. Dovzak, p.c.

73. N. Brozan, "Girls on the Athletic Field: Small Gains, Long Way to the Goal," *The New York Times,* January 12, 1976.

74. *Back to School Line-Up, op. cit.* (note 28).

75. *Sprint Fact Sheet,* January 1978, WEAL, (note 8).

76. A. Hochschild, "The American Woman: Another Idol of Social Science," *Trans-Action,* November-December 1970, 14.

77. For clarification of Title IX, I thank Grace Mastalli at Project on the Status and Education of Women (note 8); also see "H.E.W. Title IX Policy Interpretation," *Federal Register,* December 11, 1979, 44, 239, 71413–71423.

78. Holly Knox of PEER quoted in N. Brozan, *op. cit.* (note 73).

79. WEAL Washington Report, October 1978, 6.

80. RESOURCES FOR ACTION AGAINST DISCRIMINATION IN SPORTS:

Sports Kit—How To File Complaints under Title IX
Sprint: The National Clearinghouse on Information on Sex Equity in Sports
In the Running (quarterly bulletin), all from WEAL, Suite 822, 805 15 St. N.W., Washington, D.C. 20005 Toll-free: 800-424-5162.

Sex Discrimination in Athletics and Physical Education (awareness, legal and organizing materials), from Women's Rights Project, ACLU, 22 E. 40 St, New York, N.Y. 10016.

Title IX and Physical Education: A Compliance Overview
Competitive Athletics: In Search of Equal Opportunity, both from
U.S. Government Printing Office
Washington, D.C. 20402

Subject: Elimination of Sex Discrimination in Athletic Programs, Memorandum, U.S. Department of Health, Education and Welfare

Girls Sports: On the Right Track (17-minute film summarizes recent progress in school sports programs), from Phoenix Films, 470 Park Avenue South, New York, N.Y. 10016.

81. G. W. Wise, "The Relationship of Sex-Role Perception and Levels of Self-Actualization in Public School Teachers," *Sex Roles,* 1978, 4, 4, 605–617.

82. B. I. Fagot, "Teacher Reinforcement of Feminine-Preferred Behavior—Revisited," paper presented to The Society for Research in Child Development, Denver, April 1975.

83. Retarded children seem to be exempt from sex role standards; see, A. P. Copeland and C. S. Weissbrod, "Differences in Attitudes Toward Sex-Typed Behavior of Non-retarded and Retarded Children," *American Journal of Mental Deficiency,* 1976, 81, 3, 280–288.

84. L. P. Simpson, "From Title IX to Project IX," *TABS,* Spring 1978.

85. A. Martin-Leff, "Women's History," *New Directions for Women,* Winter 1978–1979, 4.

86. A. Huston-Stein and R. L. Welch, *op. cit.* (note 60).

87. P. Sexton, *The Feminized Male,* Random House (New York: 1969).

88. J. E. Brophy and T. L. Good, "Teacher-Student Relationships: Causes and Consequences," reported in *Learning,* April 1974, 83.

89. A. Rosenfeld, "Learning to Give Up," *Saturday Review,* September 4, 1977, 37, reporting on studies by Carol Dweck.

90. L. A. Serbin, J. M. Connor and C. C. Citron, "Environmental Control of Independent

618

and Dependent Behaviors in Preschool Girls and Boys: A Model for Early Independence Training," *Sex Roles,* 1978, 1, 6, 867–875; L. A. Serbin, "Sex Role Socialization and Psychopathology," paper presented at symposium on Current Research on Sex Role Socialization, American Psychological Association, September 1974.

91. L. Cherry, "Preschool Teacher-Child Dyad: Sex Differences in Verbal Interaction," *Child Development,* 1975, 46, 532–537.

92. L. A. Serbin and K. D. O'Leary, "How Nursery Schools Teach Girls to Shut Up," *Psychology Today,* December 1975, 57ff.

93. L. A. Serbin, quoted in *Instructor* magazine, April 1977, 23.

94. L. A. Serbin, et al., "A Comparison of Teacher Response to the Preacademic and Problem Behavior of Boys and Girls," *Child Development,* 1975, 46, 532–537.

95. P. W. Jackson and H. M. Lahadern, "Inequalities of Teacher-Pupil Contacts," *Psychology in Schools,* 1967, 4, 204–211.

96. J. Wirtenberg, U.S. Commission on Civil Rights, reported in "Sexism in Shop Class: It Hammers Female Egos," *Human Behavior,* April 1979, 57.

97. T. E. Levitan and J. C. Chananie, "Responses of Female Primary School Teachers to Sex-Typed Behaviors in Male and Female Children," *Child Development,* 1972, 43, 1309–1316.

98. J. Wirtenberg, *op. cit.* (note 96).

99. A. Huston-Stein and R. L. Welch, *op. cit.* (note 60).

100. B. I. Fagot, "Preschool Sex Stereotyping: Effect of Sex of Teacher vs. Training of Teacher," paper presented to Society for Research in Child Development, New Orleans, La., March 1977.

101. P.S. Sears and D. H. Feldman, "Teacher Interactions with Boys and With Girls," *The National Elementary Principal,* 1966, 46, 2.

102. D. McGuinness, "How Schools Discriminate Against Boys," *Human Nature,* February 1979, 82–88.

103. E. Kernkamp and E. Price, "Coeducation May Be a No-No for the Six-Year-Old Boy," *Phi Delta Kappan,* June 1972, 662–663; J. Brock, "All Male, Female, Kindergarten Classes First in Orange District," *The Register,* March 18, 1974, D-1.

104. S. Johnson, "A Nursery School Has Men to Look Up To," *The New York Times,* February 28, 1977, 32; "New Hands in Finger Paint," *Newsweek,* February 9, 1976, 45; "Who's That Man in Room 7?" *Life* magazine, October 20, 1972, 43–47; U. Vils, "New Male Image: a Gender Blender in the Nursery," *L.A. Times,* October 1, 1975, 1.

105. *Santa Ana* (Calif.) *Register;* "No Comment," *Ms.* magazine, December 1974.

106. National Assessment of Educational Progress, Denver, Colo., 1975; H. S. Astin, "Sex Differences in Mathematical and Scientific Precocity," *Journal of Special Education,* Spring 1975, 9, 1.

107. National Assessment, *ibid.*

108. *College Board Summary Reports,* High School Seniors Composite.

109. *Ibid.*

110. National Assessment, *op. cit.* (note 106).

111. J. E. Garai and A. Scheinfeld, "Sex Differences in Mental and Behavioral Traits," *Genetic Psychology Monographs,* 1968, 77, 207; E. E. Maccoby and C. N. Jacklin, *The Psychology of Sex Differences,* Stanford University Press (Stanford, Calif.: 1974) 351.

112. B. I. Fagot and I. Littman, "Relation of Preschool Sex-Typing to Intellectual Performance in Elementary School," *Psychological Reports,* 1976, 39, 699–704; J. Lockman, et al., "Development of Mental Representations of Spatial Layouts," paper presented at American Psychological Association, Washington, D.C., September 1976; L. M. Connor, et al., "Sex-related Differences in Response to Practice on a Visual-Spatial Test and Generalization to a Related Test," *Child Development,* 1978, 49, 24–29.

113. A. Huston-Stein and J. Smithells, "Age and Sex Differences in Children's Sex Role Standards About Achievement," *Developmental Psychology,* 1969, 1.

114. L. Landsmann, "The Brain's Division of Labor," *The New York Times,* April 30, 1978; R. Ornstein, "The Split and the Whole Brain," *Human Nature,* May 1978, 76–83; D. A. Goodman, "Learning from Lobotomy," *Human Behavior,* January 1978, 44–49; D. Kimura, "The Asymmetry of the Human Brain," *Scientific American,* March 1973; R. Restack, *The Brain: The Last Frontier,* Doubleday (New York: 1979).

115. J. Kagan, "The Emergence of Sex Differences," *School Review,* February 1972, 221–222.

116. S. F. Witelson, "Sex and the Single Hemisphere: Specialization of the Right Hemisphere for Spatial Processing," *Science,* July 30, 1976, 425–427; P. H. Wolff, "Maturational

Factors in Behavioral Development," in M. F. McMillan, ed. *Child Psychiatry,* Brunner/-Mazel (New York: 1977).

117. Research by J. McGlone, University Hospital, London, Ontario, Canada, reported in "Women's Brains Don't Neatly Fit the Split Theory," *Psychology Today,* October 1978, 29–31; research by E. Zaidel and R. Sperry, California Institute of Technology, reported in "The Right Hemisphere Has Something to Say After All," *Psychology Today,* December 1975, 121; F. Salzman, "Are Sex Roles Biologically Determined?" *The Jane and Dick Reader,* Portland, Oreg., November 1977; *Effects of Biological Factors on Sex-Related Differences in Mathematics Achievement,* National Institute of Education, Education and Work Group (Washington, D.C.: 1977); D. B. Lynn, "Determinants of Intellectual Growth in Women," *School Review,* February 1972, 241–260.

118. P. Orvis, "Illiteracy IS Growing Global Problem," *The New York Times,* April 30, 1978.

119. H. B. Biller, *Paternal Deprivation,* Lexington Books (Lexington, Mass.: 1974) 144.

120. J. N. Polardy, "What Teachers Believe, What Children Achieve," *Elementary School Journal,* 1969, 69, 370–374.

121. P. P. Minuchin, "Sex Differences in Children," *National Elementary School Principal,* November 1966, 46, 2, 45–48.

122. L. A. Serbin, "Sex Stereotyped Play Behavior in the Preschool Classroom: Effects of Teacher Presence and Modeling," presented to The Society for Research in Child Development, New Orleans, La., March 1977.

123. E. M. Byrne, "Inequality in Educational-Discriminal Resource Allocation in Schools?" *Educational Review,* 1975, 27, 3, 179–191. Also see, E. P. Torrance, *Guiding Creative Talent,* Prentice-Hall (Englewood Cliffs, N.J.: 1962) for discussion of how teacher intervention and help can increase technical creativity in girls.

124. N. F. Russo, *op. cit.* (note 4).

125. A. M. Juhasz, "The Teacher and Sex Role Stereotyping," *School Health Review,* November/December 1974, 5, 20.

126. G. W. Wise, *op. cit.* (note 81).

127. For example, *Changing Learning: A Nonsexist Approach to Teaching,* four-sessions developed by The Feminist Press, Box 334, Old Westbury, N.Y. 11568.

128. "Small Architects, Big Plans," *The New York Times,* April 5, 1979.

129. BENEFIT FROM OTHER PARENTS' STRATEGIES AND EXPERIENCES: P. Boring, "Getting Rid of Sexism in School: A Step-by-Step Strategy," *Ms.* magazine, June 1974.

We Can Change It! by S. Shangel and I. Kane—Ideas for eliminating sex and race stereotypes in preschool and elementary school. Change for Children, 2588 Mission St., San Francisco, Calif. 94110.

Liberating Young Children from Sex Roles: Experiences in Day Care Centers, Play Groups and Free Schools, by P. T. Greenleaf, New England Free Press, 60 Union Square, Somerville, Mass. 02143.

Sexism in Schools—A Handbook for Action, from N. Rothchild, 14 Hickory Street, Mahtomedi, Minn. 55115.

Unlearning the Lie: Sexism in School, by B. G. Harrison, Liveright Publishers (New York: 1973).

Stop Sex Stereotypes in Elementary Education: A Handbook for Parents and Teachers, by M. Cohen, from Public Interest Research Group, Box 1571, Hartford, Conn. 01601.

"Let Them Aspire!: A Plea and Proposal for Equality of Opportunity for Males and Females in the Ann Arbor Public Schools," by M. Federbush, in D. Gersoni-Stavn, *Sexism and Youth,* R. R. Bowker (New York: 1974) 127.

How to Deal With Sex Role Stereotyping: At a School Board Meeting, in a Workshop, in the Classroom, by N. Bostick, P. Kaspar and N. Sallan, Resource Center for Women, 445 Sherman Ave., Palo Alto, Calif. 94306 ($2.25).

Eliminating Sexism from the Public Schools, from G. Kunkel, 3409, S. W. Trenton St., Seattle, Wash. 98126 ($1.50).

Committee to Study Sex Discrimination in the Kalamazoo Public Schools, various publications available from Instructional Media Department, 1220 Howard Street, Kalamazoo, Mich. 49008 (Free order form).

130. *Back-to-School-Student's Rights Check-up,* Michigan PEER, 508 N. Main St., Milford, Mich. 48042.

131. CONSCIOUSNESS-RAISING BOOKS AND ARTICLES ON SCHOOL SEXISM:

D. Gersoni-Staven, ed. *Sexism and Youth,* R. R. Bowker (New York: 1974).

N. Frazier and M. Sadker, *Sexism in School and Society,* Harper & Row paperback (New York: 1973).

J. Stacey, S. Bereaud and J. Daniels, *And Jill Came Tumbling After: Sexism in American Education,* Dell paperback (New York: 1974).

B. Levy, "The School's Role in the Sex-Stereotyping of Girls," *Feminist Studies,* Summer 1972, 1, 1.

"Sex Discrimination," special issue of *Inequality in Education,* October 1974, 18. Center for Law and Education, Harvard University.

Bibliography on Essential Readings in Sex Role Stereotyping and Sexism in the Schools, Cornelia Wheadon Task Force on the Socialization of Children, Women's Center, 2214 Ridge Ave., Evanston, Ill. 60202.

Taking Sexism Out of Education, U.S. Government Printing Office, Washington, D.C. 20402 (#017-080-01794-6) $3.30.

P.H. Gillespie and A. H. Fink, "The Influence of Sexism on the Education of Handicapped Children," *Exceptional Children,* November 1974.

"Sexism and Racism: Feminist Perspectives," *Civil Rights Digest,* Spring 1974.

Sexism in the Elementary School, KNOW, Box 86031, Pittsburgh, Pa. 15221.

Sex Discrimination in Guidance and Counseling, WEEA, 55 Chapel St., Newton, Mass. 02160, (toll free 800-225-3088).

"Sex Bias in Educational Testing," in *Women and Educational Testing: A Selective Review of the Research Literature and Testing Practices,* Educational Testing Service, Princeton, N.J. 1975.

Self-Study Guide to Sexism in Schools, Pennsylvania Department of Education, Box 911, Harrisburg, Pa. 17126.

J. Pottker and A. Fishel, eds. *Sex Bias in the Schools: The Research Evidence,* Farleigh Dickinson University Press (Cranbury, N.J.: 1977).

132. CURRICULUM MATERIALS, TEACHERS' GUIDES FOR NONSEXIST EDUCATION

Child care and early childhood classrooms:

Equal Play magazine; *Nonsexist Education for Young Children: A Practical Guide,* B. Sprung; *Perspectives on Nonsexist Early Childhood Education,* B. Sprung, ed.; Filmstrip: *A Nonsexist Curriculum for Early Childhood*; Training project: *Training Resources for Educational Equity.* Other learning materials. All from
    The Women's Action Alliance
    370 Lexington Avenue
    New York, N.Y. 10017

Catalog of publications and curriculum planning guides from
    Day Care and Child Development Council
    1401 K. St. N.W. Washington, D.C. 20005

Choosing Child Care: A Guide by S. Auerbach and L. Freeman
    Parents and Child Care Resources
    1855 Folsom Street, San Francisco, Calif. 94103

Elementary and secondary school classrooms:

Feminist Resources for Schools and Colleges: A Guide to Curricular Materials
    Nonsexist Curricular Materials for Elementary Schools
    High School Feminist Studies, all from
    The Feminist Press
    Box 334, Old Westbury, N.Y. 11568

PEER Resources for Ending Sex Bias in the Schools
    PEER
    1112 13 St N.W. Washington, D.C. 20005

Sexism: A Handbook of Teacher Intervention
    Confluent Education Development Center
    Box 30128, Santa Barbara, Calif. 93105

Today's Changing Roles: An Approach to Nonsexist Teaching ($4) *A Resource List for Nonsexist Education Sex Role Stereotyping: Helping Teachers Teach Edu-Pack*—posters, cassettes, books, etc.

The Resource Center on Sex Roles in Education
1201 16 Street N.W. Washington, D. C. 20036

Being a Man: A Unit of Instructional Activities on Male Role Stereotyping, D. Sadker—
64-page manual for junior high
U.S. Government Printing Office
Washington, D.C. 20402

identity: FEMALE—multi-media cross-discipline course grades 9–12.
Dun-Donnelley Publishing
666 Fifth Avenue, New York, N.Y. 10019

Images of Women—228 instructional resources, teaching aids
Informedia
Box 1020, Pearl River, N.Y. 10965

Sex Role Stereotypes: Teachers Guide
L. Lansberry
49 Parker Street, Watertown, Mass. 02172

"41 Ways to Teach About Sex Role Stereotyping", P. B. Gough
Learning magazine, January 1977, 72–80

Teaching Kits on Work, Schools, Family, Sexism in Language
Men and Women Unlimited
712 33 St N.W.
Calgary, Alberta, Canada T2N2W6

Changing Sex Roles in a Changing Society—40 lesson plans; 11th grade.
Dissemination Unit, D.E.P.S.
Board of Education, 131 Livingston St.
Brooklyn, N.Y. 11201

Growing Free: Ways to Help Children Overcome Sex Role Stereotypes
Association for Childhood Education
3615 Wisconsin Ave N.W.
Washington, D.C. 20016

Re-evaluating Basic Premises: Curricula Free of Sexism, H. K. Cuffaro
Young Children, September 1975, 469–478

Positive Images: A Guide to Nonsexist Films for Young People
Booklegger Press
555 29 Street, San Francisco, Calif. 94131

Changing Sexist Practices in the Classroom, M. Stern
American Federation of Teachers
1012 14 St N.W. Washington, D.C. 20005

TABS (Aids for Ending Sexism in School)—a quarterly idea bulletin
TABS, 744 Carroll St., Brooklyn, N.Y. 11215

Undoing Sex Stereotypes, M. Guttentag and H. Bray—lesson plans, case studies, work
sheets, activities, resources, teacher-training.
McGraw-Hill, 1221 Ave. of Americas, New York, N.Y. 10020

Catalog of nonsexist curriculum materials—developed under the Women's Educational
Equity Act (WEEA)
WEEA Dissemination
Educational Development Center, 55 Chapel St.
Newton, Mass. 02160 (toll free 800-255-3088)

Again At The Looking Glass—language arts curriculum to combat sex role stereotypes in
100 class activities
Feminists Northwest, 7347 20th Ave N.E.
Seattle, Wash. 98115

*200 Plus: A Framework for Non-Stereotyped Human Roles in Elementary Media Center
Materials* or in *Secondary Media Center Materials*—both from
Media Services, Kalamazoo Public Schools
1220 Harvard Street, Kalamazoo, Mich. 49008

Fair Play: A Bibliography of Non-Stereotyped Materials
Training Institute for Sex Desegregation

622

Federation Hall, Douglass College
Rutgers University, New Brunswick, N.J. 08903

"Sugar 'n Spice in The Classroom", M.E. Calabrese
  Media and Methods, September 1974, 42ff

"Sexism in the Fourth Grade—Being an Account of How I Tried To Make Fourth-Graders Aware of Sex Roles, Stereotypes", etc., K. Karkau.
  KNOW, Box 86031, Pittsburgh, Pa. 15221

"Sexist Teaching: What You Can Do", H. T. Fillmer,
  Teacher, January 1974

"The Molding of a Nonsexist Teacher"—special issue
  Journal of Teacher Education, Winter 1975, 96

Vocational/career guidance materials:

UNIACT—Sex-balanced Vocational Interest 9th grade up
  ACT Publications, 2201 N. Dodge St.
  Box 168, Iowa City, Iowa 52240

Women at Work: A Counselor's Sourcebook
  Human Interaction Research Institute
  Los Angeles, Calif.

Sex Fairness in Career Guidance: a Learning Kit
  Abt Associates, 55 Wheeler Street
  Cambridge, Mass. 02138

Counseling aids, documents, studies, from
  ERIC Clearinghouse in Career Education
  204 Gabel Hall, Northern Illinois University
  DeKalb, Ill. 60115

Curriculum guides, resource materials, technical assistance, from
  Sex Equality in Guidance Opportunities
  APGA, 1607 New Hampshire Avenue
  Washington, D.C. 20009

Money, Jobs and Women—nontraditional careers project
  Project Four, Box 123
  Syracuse, N.Y. 13215

"Counseling: Superbomb Against Sexism", M. Verheyden-Hilliard,
  American Education, April 1977, 12–15

Career Exploration for High School Women, J. Birk and M. Tanney
  NEA, 1201 16 St. N.W. Washington, D.C. 20036

Children's Dictionary of Occupations (intermediate grades)
  CFI, 2100 Locust Street
  Philadelphia, Pa. 19103

All About Eve—film on girls in skilled trades
  Center for Human Resources
  University of Houston, Houston, Tex. 77004

133. S. L. Lightfoot, "Family-School Interaction: The Cultural Image of Mothers and Teachers," *Signs,* 1977, 3, 2, 395–408.

134. MAJOR NATIONAL ORGANIZATIONS: NONSEXIST EDUCATION:

WEECN Network, 1855 Folsom St., San Francisco, Calif. 94103

Women's Action Alliance, 370 Lexington, New York, N.Y. 10017

Project on Equal Education Rights (PEER)
  1112 13 St. N.W., Washington, D.C. 20005

Project on the Status and Education of Women
  AAC, 1818 R St. N.W., Washington, D.C. 20009

Resource Center on Sex Roles in Education
  1201 16 St. N.W., Washington, D.C. 20036

Education Task Force of the National Organization for Women, 425 13 St. N.W., Washington, D. C. 20004

KNOW, Box 86031, Pittsburgh, Pa. 15221

TABS, 744 Carroll St., Brooklyn, N.Y. 11215

American Federation of Teachers, Women's Rights Committee, 1012 14 St. N.W., Washington, D.C. 20005

135. L. Hammel, "When I Grow Up I'm Going to Be . . . an Old Game, New Ideas," *The New York Times,* June 12, 1975; G. Dullea, "For Forward-Looking Kindergartners, Career Education," *The New York Times,* October 29, 1974.

136. G. Vecsey, "Schools Subject for the Day was Consciousness-Raising," *The New York Times,* March 1, 1975, 18; "How to Run a Susan B. Anthony Day in Your School," *TABS,* February 1978

137. "Teaching the Truth About Sexual Assault," *TABS,* Spring 1979.

138. "Guidelines For Evaluation of Instructional Materials," California State Department of Education, Sacramento, Calif.

139. "Schoolbook Sex Bias: Seek and Ye Shall Find," *Nation's Schools* (date unknown).

140. ANALYSES OF TEXTBOOK SEXISM AND STEREOTYPING

Stereotypes, Distortions and Omissions in U.S. History Textbooks, Council on Interracial Books for Children, 1841 Broadway, New York, N.Y. 10023.

Sex Equality in Educational Materials: Stereotyping in Textbooks and How To Get Rid of It, American Association of School Administrators, 1801 N. Moore St., Arlington, Va. 22209

Sexism in Foreign Language Texts, Women on Words and Images, Box 2163, Princeton, N.J. 08540

Putting Women in Their Place: Report on American History High School Textbooks, Lexington NOW, Box 651, Lexington, Mass. 02173

"The Image of Women in Textbooks", M.B. U'Ren, in V. Gornick and B. K. Moran, eds. *Woman in Sexist Society,* Basic Books (New York: 1971)

"Sex Stereotyping in Elementary School Health Education Texts", *Journal of School Health,* September 1975, 519–523

"Sexism in Science Books? Absolutely!", P.R. Giller, *Appraisal,* Fall 1976, Harvard Graduate School of Education

Issues of Sex Bias and Sex Fairness in Career Interest Measurement, Career Education Program, National Institute of Education, Washington, D.C. 20238

Help Wanted: Sexism in Career Education Materials: How to Detect It and How to Counteract Its Effects, Women in Words and Images, Box 2163, Princeton, N.J. 08540

"The Sexual Bias of Textbook Literature", S. L. Wilk, *English Journal,* February 1973

You Won't Do: What Textbooks on U.S. Government Teach High School Girls, J. Macleod and S. T. Silverman, KNOW, Inc.

Biased Textbooks, Resource Center on Sex Roles in Education, 1201 16 St., N.W., Washington, D.C. 20036 ($1).

141. BIBLIOGRAPHIES OF NONSEXIST BOOKS AND SUPPLEMENTARY MATERIALS:

Books for Today's Children: An Annotated Bibliography of Non-Stereotyped Picture Books, Feminist Press, Box 334, Old Westbury, N.Y. 11568

On Equal Terms: A Thesaurus for Nonsexist Indexing and Cataloging, ABC-Clio Press, Riviera Campus, 2040 A.P.S., Box 4397, Santa Barbara, Calif. 93103

Math Equals: Biographies of Women Mathematicians and related activities, T. Perl., Addison-Wesley (Reading, Mass.: 1978)

Images of Women: A Bibliography of Feminist Resources for Pennsylvania Schools, Penna. Dept. of Education, Box 911, Harrisburg, Pa. 17126

Bibliography in the History of American Women, G. Lerner, Women's Studies, Sarah Lawrence College, Bronxville, N.Y. 10708.

Also see bibliographies listed in chapter 21, footnote 81.

142. T. Thoburn, et al., *Macmillan Mathematics: Series M,* Macmillan (New York: 1976 and 1977).

143. Garrard Publishing, Champaign, Ill.

144. Arista Corporation, 2440 Estard Way, P.O.B. 6146, Concord, Calif. 94524.

145. "Book Censorship Increasing in Schools," *The New York Times,* January 2, 1979, C12; R. Flaste, "Banning 'Bad' Books in a 'Good' Cause," *The New York Times,* July 10, 1977; "Librarians Adopt Proposal on Sexism, Racism," *Women's Studies Newsletter,* Fall 1976, 4, 4, 1.

146. D. Gersoni-Stavn, "Feminist Criticism: An Overview," *School Library Journal,* January 1974, 12.
147. C. Goodyear, *The Sheep Book,* Lollipop Power Publishers (Chapel Hill, N.C.).

24 • *Everything Else, page 519*

1. *Gallup Poll,* November 2, 1977, 58.
2. M. Daly, *Beyond God the Father,* Beacon (Boston: 1973); M Daly, *The Church and the Second Sex, with a New Feminist Post-Christian Introduction by the Author,* Harper & Row (New York: 1975); J.G. Raymond, "An Ethical Analysis of Patriarchy," *The Holy Cross Quarterly,* Fall 1971, 4, 4.
3. M. Griffin, "Founding Mothers," *Listening: A Journal of Religion and Culture,* Spring 1978, 13, 2, 128.
4. Remarks made at The Sanctuary of the Immaculate Conception, Washington, D.C., quoted in *The New York Times,* October 8, 1979.
5. A. B. Driver, "Religion," *Signs,* 1976, 2, 2, 434–442.
6. S. N. Emswiler and T. N. Emswiler, *Women and Worship,* Harper & Row (New York: 1974); *Passover Haggadah,* Rabbinical Assembly (New York: 1979); N. Janowitz and M. Wenig, "Selections from a Prayerbook Where God's Image Is Female," *Lilith,* Fall/Winter 1978, 27–29.
7. P. McCormack, "Nun Attacks Sexist Language in Church," *San Juan Star,* February 14, 1978; Letter to the Bishop's Commission on the Liturgy From The National Coalition of American Nuns, in J. K. Meuli, "In Brief," *The National NOW Times,* February 1979, 2; K.A. Briggs, "Women and Catholic Church: American Bishops' Decision to Keep Word 'Men' in Liturgy Appears To Have Worsened Relations," *The New York Times,* November 16, 1979, A13.
8. G. Vecsey, "Quest for Equality in Church Dividing Catholic Women," *The New York Times,* October 2, 1979, A12; R. B. Kaiser, "Pope Sides With St. Paul in Debate on Priesthood," *The New York Times,* October 14, 1979, E9; R. Ruether and E. McLaughlin, *Women Of Spirit,* Simon & Schuster (New York: 1979); Rabbi S. Priesand, *Judaism And The New Woman,* Behrman House (New York: 1975); G. Fink, *Great Jewish Women,* Bloch (New York: 1978); B.C. Smith, *Breakthrough: Women in Religion,* Walker & Co. (New York: 1978); "Church Women and the Women's Movement," special issue of *Church Woman,* November 1978; A. C. Zuckoff, *Bibliography on the Jewish Woman,* Jewish Feminist Organization, c/o Network, 36 West 37 Street, New York, N.Y. 10018.
9. S. Hample and E. Marshall, *Children's Letters to God,* Pocket (New York: 1975) I. Shenker, "Is God a Woman Is Debated Here," *The New York Times,* February 10, 1974, 35; J. Litman, Bay Area Jewish Women's Conference, *Lilith,* 1978, 5, 7; C. Ozick, "Notes Toward Finding the Right Question: A Vindication of the Rights of Jewish Women," *Lilith,* 1979, 6, 19.
10. C. Ozick, *ibid.;* N. Goldenberg, "Women and The Image of God: A Psychological Perspective on the Feminist Movement in Religion," *International Journal of Women's Studies,* 1, 5, 468–474.
11. M. Stone, *When God Was a Woman,* Dial (New York: 1977).
12. E. Pagels, *The Gnostic Gospels,* Random House (New York: 1979); J. Morris, *The Lady Was a Bishop,* Macmillan (New York: 1973).
13. L. Rivlin, "Lilith," *Ms.* magazine, December 1972, 92ff.
14. M. Mirsky, *My Search for the Messiah,* Macmillan (New York: 1977) 8.
15. C. Jones, *Lord, I Want to Tell You Something,* Augsburg (Minneapolis: no date).
16. L. Johnson, *Just a Minute, Lord,* Augsburg (Minneapolis: no date).
17. "From Dallas, Children's Essays: What's a Jewish Mother," *Lilith,* Fall/Winter 1977–1978, 18. For more on Sunday school sexism see, A. Daum, "Summary of 1976 Conference on Alternatives in Jewish Education," N. Y. Federation of Reform Synagogues, 838 Fifth Avenue, New York, N.Y. 10021; M. Crist and T. Norberg, "Sex Role Stereotyping in the United Methodist Nursery Curriculum," New York Conference Task Force on the Status of Women in the Church, 1970.
18. E. C. Stanton and the Revising Committee, *The Woman's Bible,* Seattle Task Force on Women and Religion, 4759 15 Avenue, N.E. Seattle, Wash. 98105; L.M. Russell, ed. *The Liberating Word,* Westminster Press (National Council of Churches, 475 Riverside Drive, New York, N.Y. 10027); R. Wahlberg, *The Gospel According to a Woman,* Paulist Press (New York: 1975); M.I. Lee, "Religion and the Socialization of Women: A Working Bibliography," *Listening: Journal of Religion and Culture,* Spring 1978, 13, 2, 176–181; "Menorah: Sparks of Jewish Renewal," Project on Jewish Institutions Public Resource

Center, 1747 Connecticut Avenue, N.W., Washington, D.C. 20009; also request nonsexist guides from The Task Force on Equality, New York Federation of Reform Synagogues (see note 17).

19. D. I. Leifer and M. Leifer, "On the Birth of a Daughter," in E. Koltun, ed. *The Jewish Woman,* Schocken (New York: 1976).

20. E. M. Broner and N. Nimrod, "A Woman's Passover Haggadah and Other Revisionist Rituals," *Ms.* magazine, April 1977, 53; *New Union Haggadah,* Union of American Hebrew Congregations, 838 Fifth Avenue, New York, N.Y. 10021;

21. *Ibid.;* R.S. Friedman, "How Was This Passover Different From All Other Passovers?" *Lilith,* Spring/Summer 1977.

22. L. Swidler, "Beruriah: Her Word Became Law," *Lilith,* Spring/Summer 1977, 9–12.

23. L. Greenhouse, "These Wives Found Cure to Some of the Ills of Suburban Life," *The New York Times,* October 1, 1971, 46.

24. K. Hapgood and J. Getzels, *Planning, Women and Change,* Report No. 301, April 1974, Planning Advisory Service, American Society of Planning Officials, 1313 E. 60 Street, Chicago, Ill. 60637.

25. A. Mehrabian, *Public Places and Private Spaces,* Basic (New York: 1976) 289–293; J. Davison, *The Fall of A Doll's House,* Holt, Rinehart and Winston (New York: 1980).

26. G. Dullea, "A Town Where Bringing Lunch to School Is a Punishable Offense," *The New York Times,* September 22, 1973, 16; W.K. Stevens, "School Closings in Ohio Vex Working Mothers," *The New York Times,* February 1, 1977; *Lakewood, Ohio Task Force Report,* from A. P. Johnson, 1261 West Clifton Blvd., Lakewood, Ohio 44107 ($1).

27. S. Greenberg, *Right From The Start,* Houghton Mifflin (Boston: 1978) 95.

28. A. R. Gillis, "High Rise Housing and Psychological Strain," *Journal of Health and Social Behavior,* December 1977, 18, 4, 418–431; R. E. Mitchell, "Misconceptions About Man-Made Space: In Partial Defense of High Density Housing," *Family Coordinator,* January 1974, 51; G. B. Spanier and C. P. Fishel, "The Housing Project and Family Functions: Consequences for Low-Income Urban Families," *The Family Coordinator,* 1973, 22, 235–240.

29. R. Flaste, "To Raise a Family in the City or in the Suburbs? The Total Dilemma," *The New York Times,* April 2, 1976.

30. G. Malakoff, *Transportation Policy and the Homemaker,* Fact Sheet #7, April 1976; Clearinghouse on Women's Issues, 1346 Connecticut Avenue, N.W., Washington, D.C. 20036.

31. A. Sussman, *The Rights of Young People,* Avon (New York: 1977) 229.

32. "The Strange World of Statutory Rape," *Children's Rights Report,* March 1978, ACLU II, 6.

33. *Ibid.*

34. S. D. Ross, *The Rights of Women,* Avon (New York: 1973) 168; *Little Sisters and the Law* (1977) LEAA, Office of Juvenile Justice and Delinquency-Prevention, U.S. Department of Justice; R. Flaste, "Is Juvenile Justice Tougher on Girls Than on Boys?" *The New York Times,* September 6, 1977.

35. C. Wilson and H. Harris, "Making Sex a Crime," *Human Behavior,* February 1979, 43.

36. A. Kosof, *Runaways,* Franklin Watts (New York: 1977).

37. F. Rush, "The Myth of Sexual Delinquency," *Rough Times,* 1972, 2, 7.

38. C. Wilson and H. Harris, *op. cit.* (note 35).

39. *Survey of the Female Offender Resource Center,* affiliate of the American Bar Association, 1977.

40. C. Wilson and H. Harris, *op. cit.* (note 35).

41. D. Russell, "Rape and the Masculine Mystique," paper presented to the American Sociological Association, New York City, August 1973.

42. J. Toby, "Violence and the Masculine Mystique: Some Qualitative Data," *The Annals,* 1966, 36, 4, 19–27.

43. W. B. Miller, "Violent Crimes and City Gangs," in T. Dye, *Politics in the Metropolis,* Charles E. Merrill (Columbus, Ohio: 1967).

44. S. Brownmiller, *Against Our Will,* Simon & Schuster (New York: 1975) 181.

45. J. D. Grambs and W. B. Waetjen, *Sex: Does It Make A Difference?* Duxbury (North Scituate, Mass.: 1975) 111; J. Paddock, "Studies on Anti-Violent and 'Normal' Communities," *Aggressive Behavior,* 1975, 1, 217–233.

46. J. M. Rector, LEAA Administrator, "Justice for Young Women," paper presented to

National Conference on Juvenile Justice for Young Women, Kissimonee, Fla., December 1977.

47. F. Adler, *Sisters in Crime: The Rise of the New Female Criminal,* McGraw-Hill (New York: 1975); R. J. Simon, *Women and Crime,* Lexington Books (Lexington, Mass.: 1975); G. Sheehy, "The New Breed," *New York,* July 26, 1971; N. Hill, *The Violent Women,* Popular Library (New York: 1971).

48. N. Shorer and S. Norland, "Sex Roles and Criminality: Science or Conventional Wisdom," *Sex Roles,* 1978, 4, 1, 111–125.

49. J. M. Rector, *op. cit.* (note 46).

50. F. Adler, *op. cit.* (note 47).

51. S. de Beauvoir, *The Second Sex,* Bantam (New York: 1961) 670.

52. N. Brozan, "The Curfew: It's At The Center Of A National Controversy," *The New York Times,* January 6, 1978, B4.

53. S. de Beauvoir, *op. cit.* (note 51).

54. *Toronto Star,* in "No Comment," *Ms.* magazine, October 1974, 112.

55. "300 Women Protest Rape Case Acquittal," *The New York Times,* July 31, 1977, 24.

56. "News," *Off Our Backs,* Washington, D.C., April 1978, 3.

57. "Gazette," *Ms.* magazine, November 1977, 20.

58. "Ousted Judge in Rape Case Says Feminists Will 'Stoop' To Any Low," *The New York Times,* January 4, 1978; "Judge in Wisconsin Calls Rape By Boy a 'Normal Reaction,' " *The New York Times,* May 27, 1977, A9.

59. F. Mernisi, *Beyond The Veil,* Schenkman (New York: 1975).

60. "National Survey of Children," Foundation for Child Development (New York: 1977).

61. G. L. Fox, " 'Nice Girl' Social Control of Women Through a Value Construct," *Signs,* 1977, 2, 4, 805–817.

62. "Child's Play," *Off Our Backs,* Washington, D. C., January 1978.

63. D. Densmore, "Chivalry: The Iron Hand in the Velvet Glove," KNOW (Pittsburgh: 1969); L. C. Pogrebin, "Do Women Make Men Violent?" *Ms.* magazine, November 1974, 49ff; S. Chess and J. Whitbread, *Daughters: From Infancy to Independence,* Doubleday (New York: 1978) 82.

64. Feminist Press interview, *Colloquy Magazine,* November 1973.

65. A. Rich, *Of Woman Born,* W. W. Norton (New York: 1976) 248.

66. K. R. Thornburg and M. O. Weeks, "Vocational Role Expectations of 5-Year-Old Children and Their Parents," *Sex Roles,* 1975, 1, 4; G. R. Adams and J. C. LaVoie, "Parental Expectations of Educational and Social Performance and Childrearing Patterns as a Function of Attractiveness, Sex and Conduct of the Child," *Child Study Journal,* 1975, 5, 3, 140–141; S. E. Estler, "Women in Education", *Signs,* Winter 1975, 1, 2.

67. M. Mead, *Male and Female,* Morrow paperback (New York: 1975) 306.

68. L. H. Janda, et al., "Fear of Success in Males and Females in Sex-Linked Occupations," *Sex Roles,* 1978, 4, 1, 43–50; L. S. Fidell, "Empirical Verifications of Sex Discrimination in Hiring Practices in Psychology," *American Psychologist,* 1976, 25, 1094–1098.

69. A. Kadushin, "Men In a Women's Profession," *Social Work,* 1976, 21, 6, 440–447.

70. J. D. Grambs and W. B. Waetjen, *op. cit.* (note 45) 217.

71. *Ibid.,* 226; T. Tobias, "It's Becoming O.K. in America for Boys to Dance," *The New York Times,* January 9, 1977, 6.

72. *New York Student Babysitting Directory,* 500½ East 84 Street, New York City, N.Y. 10028; E. Ames, "Would You Hire a Boy as Your Child's Sitter?" *Sunday News,* June 6, 1976, 96.

73. F. Cherry and K. Deaux, "Fear of Success Versus Fear of Gender-Inappropriate Behavior," *Sex Roles,* 1978, 4, 1, 97–101; G. Puffer, "Sexual Concepts of Kindergarten, First and Second Grade Children as a Function of Their Home Environments," paper presented to the American Educational Research Association, San Francisco, April 1976; N. K. Schlossberg and J. Goodman, "A Woman's Place: Children's Sex Stereotyping of Occupations," *Vocational Guidance Quarterly,* 1972, 20, 266–270.

74. "Young Women and Employment: What We Know and Need to Know About The School-To-Work Transition," The Women's Bureau, Department of Labor, Washington, D.C., 1978.

75. S. L. Beedle, et al., "Sex Role Orientations of High School and College Students," *Sex Roles,* 1979, 5, 3, 363–364; F. L. Denmark and H. M. Goodfield, "A Second Look at Adolescence Theories," *Sex Roles,* 1978, 4, 3, 375–379.

76. A. C. Hernandez, "Sister and Brother: Getting Ahead Together," *Contact,* Fall 1972, 81.

77. G. K. Baruch, "Sex Role Attitudes of Fifth Grade Girls," in J. Stacey, et al., eds. *And Jill Came Tumbling After: Sexism in American Education,* Dell (New York: 1974) 199; I. Karre, "Self-Concept and Sex Role Stereotype: An Empirical Study," *Dissertation Abstracts,* February 1976, 36, 8A, 4850; S. L. Bem and D. J. Bem, "On Liberating the Female Student," *School Psychology Digest,* 1973, 2, 3, 11; K. R. Thornburg and M. O. Weeks, *op. cit.* (note 66).

78. *Gallup Poll,* May 29, 1977, 62; P. Sexton, *The Feminized Male,* Random House (New York: 1969) 90.

79. L. M. Terman and M. H. Oden, *Genetic Studies of Genius, V. The Gifted Group at Mid-Life: Thirty-Five Years Follow-Up of the Superior Child,* Stanford University Press (Stanford, Calif.: 1959); E. Maccoby, *The Development of Sex Differences,* Stanford University Press (Stanford, Calif.: 1966) 27, 31; M. M. Marini, "Sex Differences in the Determination of Adolescent Aspirations: A Review of the Research," *Sex Roles,* 1978, 4, 5, 723–753.

80. R. Yalow, "Thank You But No Thank You," *The New York Times,* June 12, 1978; L. Johnston, "A Bronx Public School Product: Rosalyn Sussman Yalow," *The New York Times,* October 14, 1977.

81. J. E. Stake, "The Effect of Information Regarding Sex Group Performance Norms on Goal-Setting in Males and Females," *Sex Roles,* 1976, 2, 1, 23–28; L. Barclay, "The Emergence of Vocational Expectations in Preschool Children," *Journal of Vocational Behavior,* 1974, 4, 1–14.

82. Alexis Herman, Director of the Women's Bureau, quoting her father, January 14, 1980.

83. G. K. Baruch, "Girls Who Perceive Themselves as Competent: Some Antecedents and Correlates," *Psychology of Women Quarterly,* Fall 1976, 38–49; S. M. Shoffner and R. H. Klemer, "Parent Education for the Parental Role in Children's Vocational Choices," *The Family Coordinator,* October 1973, 419–427; J. G. Goodale and D. T. Hall, *On Inheriting a Career: The Influence of Sex, Values and Parents,* Ford Foundation (New York: 1973); E. M. Almquist, "Sex Stereotyping in Occupational Choice: The Case for College Women," *Journal of Vocational Behavior,* 1974, 5, 1, 13–21.

84. G. M. Landau and M. W. Piers, *A Guide to Fun and Learning in the Romper Room Years: The Wonderful World of Play,* Hasbro Industries (Pawtucket, R.I.); "Plain doctors" are happily becoming more common among women, i.e., "Medical College Rolls at Record: Percentage of Women Is On Rise," *The New York Times,* December 2, 1979, 2.

85. M. Wolfenstein, *Children's Humor,* Indiana University Press (Bloomington, Ind.: 1978) 77.

86. M. T. Kaufman, "The World of Mother Teresa," *The New York Times Magazine,* December 9, 1979, 45.

87. H. Lerner, "Girls, Ladies . . . Or Women? The Unconscious Dynamics of Language Choice," *Comprehensive Psychiatry,* 1976, 17, 2, 295.

88. "Victories of Koch and Miss Bellamy . . ." *The New York Times,* September 21, 1977, 1.

89. C. Kramer, et al., "Perspectives on Language and Communication," *Signs,* 1978, 3, 3, 643; N. G. Kutner and D. Brogan, "An Investigation of Sex-Related Slang Vocabulary and Sex Role Orientation Among Male and Female University Students," *Journal of Marriage and the Family,* August 1974, 474–484.

90. J. C. Coyne, et al., "Expletives and Women's Place," *Sex Roles,* 1978, 4, 6, 827–837.

91. J. P. Stanley, "When We Say 'Out of The Closets!' " *College English,* 1974, 36, 3, 387.

92. S. Firestone, *The Dialectic of Sex,* Morrow (New York: 1970) 98–99.

93. H. Ginott, *Between Parent and Child,* Avon (New York: 1970) 195–196.

94. S. Firestone, *op. cit.* (note 92) 170; "Naming Genitals: Men and Women Are Worlds Apart," *Psychology Today,* November 1979, 28.

95. M. Schwartzfarb, "How Jonathan Scored," *Ms.* magazine, October 1976, 16–18.

96. J. Russ, "Dear Colleague: I Am Not an Honorary Male," *Colloquy,* April 1974, 7, 4, 42.

97. U. Stannard, *Mrs. Man,* Germain Books (San Francisco: 1977).

98. J. Barbanel, "The Walter Bacons Die in Car Accident," *The New York Times,* December 23, 1979, obituary page.

99. J. Reston, "The Meaning of Tragedy," *The New York Times,* April 19, 1978.

100. C. Miller and K. Swift, *Words and Women: New Language in New Times,* Doubleday (New York: 1975).

101. *Ibid.;* V. One, "Manglish," *Everywoman,* Venice, Calif., 1971; O. M. Y. Eberhart, "Elementary Students' Understanding of Certain Masculine and Neutral Generic Nouns,"

628

Ph.D. dissertation, Kansas State University, 1976; A. M. Schmid, "Why I Won't Celebrate Brotherhood Week," in D. Gersoni-Stavn, *Sexism and Youth,* R. R. Bowker, (New York: 1974) 3–5; A. P. Nilsen, "Grammatical Gender and Its Relationship to the Equal Treatment of Males and Females in Children's Books, Ph.D. thesis, *University of Iowa,* 1973.

102. B. A. Bate, "Genetic Man, Invisible Woman: Language, Thought and Social Change," *University of Michigan, Papers in Women's Studies,* 1975, 1, 2–13.

103. A. Graham, "The Making of a Nonsexist Dictionary," *Ms.* magazine, December 1973, 12–16.

104. C. Miller and K. Swift, *op. cit.* (note 100) 25.

105. C. Pierce, "Philosophy," *Signs,* 1975, 1, 2, 493–494.

106. J. Schneider and S. Hacker, "Sex Role Imagery and Use of the Generic *Man* in Introductory Texts," *American Sociologist,* February 1973, 12–18.

107. *WEAL Washington Report,* February 1975, 4, 1, 1.

108. A. Graham, *op. cit.* (note 103).

109. E. Wright, *Painless Menstrual Periods,* Hart (New York: 1968).

110. M. S. Blaubergs, "The Nurse Was a Doctor," presented to the Southeastern Conference on Linguistics, Women and Language meeting, Nashville, Tenn., March 1975, 5.

111. E. Burr and S. Dun, "He Is Not She," Westside Women's Committee, Los Angeles, December 1972.

112. N. Barron and M. Marlin, "Sex of the Speaker and the Grammatical Case and Gender of Referenced Persons," University of Missouri, Columbia, February 24, 1972.

113. G. S. Felton and L. S. Felton, cited in *Human Behavior,* October 1977, 55.

114. Carter Heyward quoted in *New York State NOW Newsletter,* date unknown, 5.

115. C. Miller and K. Swift, *op. cit.* (note 100) 28.

116. C. Kramer, *op. cit.* (note 89) 645.

117. *Ibid.*

118. C. Pierce, *op. cit.* (note 105).

119. Association for Women in Psychology, "Help Stamp Out Sexism: Change the Language!" *APA Monitor,* November 1975, 6, 11, 16.

120. Send for language-changing guidelines as follows: Publication Manual Change Sheet 2, *Guidelines for Nonsexist Language,* American Psychological Association, 1200 17th Street, N.W., Washington, D.C. 20036; *Guidelines for Nonsexist Use of Language,* National Council of Teachers of English, 111 Kenyon Road, Urbana, Ill. 61801. Also see M. R. Key, *Male/Female Language,* Scarecrow Press, Metuchen, N.J.: 1975).

121. C. Kramer, *op. cit.* (note 89) 650.

Index

About the Author

Letty Cottin Pogrebin is one of the developers and editors of *Free to Be... You and Me* (McGraw-Hill). She is a founder, editor, and writer for *Ms.* Magazine and contributes the "Working Woman" column to *The Ladies' Home Journal*. She is the author of *Getting Yours: How to Make the System Work for the Working Woman,* and *How to Make It in a Man's World*. She lives in New York City with her husband, two daughters, and son.